The ETS Test Collection Catalog

The ETS Test Collection Catalog

Volume 4: Cognitive Aptitude and Intelligence Tests

Compiled by Test Collection,
Educational Testing Service

Table of Contents

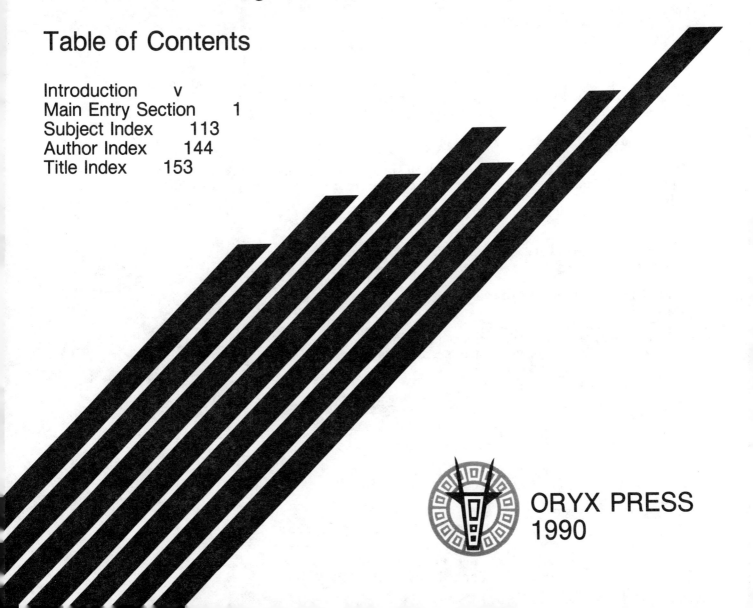

ORYX PRESS
1990

The rare Arabian Oryx is believed to have inspired the myth of the unicorn. This desert antelope became virtually extinct in the early 1960s. At that time several groups of international conservationists arranged to have 9 animals sent to the Phoenix Zoo to be the nucleus of a captive breeding herd. Today the Oryx population is nearly 800, and over 400 have been returned to reserves in the Middle East.

Library of Congress Cataloging-in-Publication Data
(Revised for vol. 4)

The ETS Test Collection catalog.

  Includes indexes.
  Contents: v. 1. Achievement tests and measurement devices — v. 2. Vocational tests and measurement devices —   —v. 4. Cognitive aptitude and intelligence tests.
  1. Educational tests and measurements—United States —Catalogs.   2. Achievement tests—United States— Catalogs.   3. Occupational aptitude tests—United States —Catalogs.   4. Educational Testing Service—Catalogs.

I. Educational Testing Service. Test Collection.
LB3051.E79   1986   016.3712'6   86-678
ISBN 0-89774-248-6 (pbk. : v. 1)
ISBN 0-89774-558-2 (pbk. : v. 4)

INTRODUCTION

The Test Collection, Educational Testing Service, is an extensive library of approximately 16,250 tests and other measurement devices. It was established to provide information on tests and assessment materials to those in research, advisory services, education, and related activities. As part of its function, the Test Collection acquires and disseminates information on hard-to-locate research instruments as well as on commercially available, standardized tests. Because the Test Collection deals only with tests and evaluation tools, it has been able to provide a reasonable amount of bibliographic control over what has historically been a scattering of information among many and diverse sources.

This volume, the fourth of The ETS Test Collection Catalog Series, describes approximately 1,300 tests in the general areas of cognitive abilities, aptitude, and intelligence. Other volumes in the series include *Volume 1: Achievement Tests and Measurement Devices, Volume 2: Vocational Tests and Measurement Devices,* and *Volume 3: Tests for Special Populations.* The information is drawn from the Test Collection's computer-retrievable database. The tests described cover all age and grade levels from preschool children through adults. Some of the instruments can be used with special populations and some have been adapted or translated for Spanish-speaking populations. There are also several nonverbal measures of intelligence and cognitive ability.

Examples of the skills and abilities assessed by the tests described in this volume include language aptitude, general intelligence, art and music aptitude, academic aptitude, creativity, abstract reasoning, critical thinking, logical thinking, ability to visualize, spatial ability, verbal and quantitative aptitudes, ability to apply knowledge, concept formation, the ability to recall, perceptual speed, and various vocational aptitudes. Also included are descriptions of tests to access Guilford's Structure of Intellect and a series of instruments, the Kit of Factor-Referenced Cognitive Tests, that are used as markers for 23 aptitude factors.

For each entry in the main entry section of the directory, the following information is always present: test title, author, descriptors and/or identifiers (subject indexing terms), availability source, age or grade level, and an abstract. Other information, which is provided when available, includes publication or copyright date, subtests, number of test items, and the time required for an individual to complete the test. The test descriptions are arranged sequentially by the Test Collection's identification number in the Main Entry section.

There are three indexes that provide access to the Main Entry section: Subject, Author, and Test Title. The Subject Index uses ERIC descriptors from the *Thesaurus of ERIC Descriptors,* 11th edition. Each test title and its unique identification number is listed under the major descriptors assigned to it, so that there are several subject access points. In addition, some tests may be indexed under major identifiers, which are additional subject indexing terms not found in the *Thesaurus of ERIC Descriptors* but which help in describing the content of the test. In the Author Index, tests and their corresponding identification numbers are listed under the author's name. The Title Index is an alphabetical list of all tests included in the directory and their identification numbers.

At the time the test catalog was compiled, all the tests included were still available from the test distributors indicated in the availability source. However, distribution of certain tests may be discontinued by test publishers and new tests developed and published.

The staff of the Test Collection will be happy to answer any questions about this catalog or other products and services. Inquiries may be addressed to Test Collection, Educational Testing Service, Princeton, NJ 08541.

Sample Entry

ACCESSION NO.

INSTITUTIONAL AND/OR PERSONAL AUTHOR

TITLE

MAJOR DESCRIPTORS
(Indexed)

IDENTIFIERS

AVAILABILITY

GRADE LEVEL AND/OR AGE LEVEL
(Target Audience)

1661
Culture Fair Intelligence Test, Scale 3   Cattell, Raymond B.; Cattell, A.K.S. 1963
Subtests: Series; Classifications; Matrices; Conditions (Topology)
Descriptors: *Adults; *College Students; *Culture Fair Tests; Higher Education; High Schools; *High School Students; Individual Testing; *Intelligence; *Intelligence Tests; *Non English Speaking, Nonverbal Tests, *Spatial Ability; Timed Tests
Identifiers: Cattell Culture Fair Intelligence Test; CFIT
Availability: Institute for Personality and Ability Testing; P.O. Box 188, Champaign, IL 61820
Grade Level: 15–64
Notes: Time, 13 approx.; Items, 50
Designed to measure individual intelligence in a manner designed to reduce the influence of verbal fluency, cultural climate, and educational level. May be administered to groups or individuals. Scale consists of 4 subtests, involving different perceptual tasks. Forms A and B are available. Scale 3 is more difficult than Scales 1 or 2 and obtains a greater refinement in the higher intelligence ranges. Useful with high school and college students and adults of superior intelligence.

PUBN. DATE

SUBTESTS

MINOR DESCRIPTORS

NOTES (Time to Take Test;
No. of Items in Test)

ABSTRACT

MAIN ENTRY SECTION

88
Picture Story Language Test. Myklebust, Helmer R. 1965
Subtests: Productivity Scale; Syntax Scale; Abstract-Concrete Scale
Descriptors: Adolescents; Children; Diagnostic Tests; *Elementary School Students; Elementary Secondary Education; *Language Acquisition; *Language Tests; Mental Retardation; Neurological Impairments; *Secondary School Students; *Sensory Integration; *Writing Skills; *Written Language
Availability: Grune and Stratton; 111 Fifth Ave., New York, NY 10003
Grade Level: 2-12
Target Audience: 7-17
Notes: Time, 20 approx.

Consists of a picture about which a story is written. Measures one's facility with the written word. The instrument studies language developmentally and diagnostically. Valuable in the appraisal and classification of nonhandicapped and handicapped children. The Picture Story Language Test is contained in: Myklebust, Helmer. Development and Disorders of Written Language. Vol. I. New York: Grune and Stratton, 1965.

152
Pimsleur Language Aptitude Battery. Pimsleur, Paul 1966
Subtests: Grade Point Average in Major Subjects; Interest; Vocabulary; Language Analysis; Sound Discrimination; Sound-Symbol Association
Descriptors: Aptitude; *Aptitude Tests; Audiotape Recordings; *Grade 6; *Modern Languages; Screening Tests; Secondary Education; *Secondary School Students; *Second Language Learning
Identifiers: Test Batteries
Availability: The Psychological Corp.; 555 Academic Ct., San Antonio, TX 78204-0952
Grade Level: 6-12
Notes: Time, 60 approx.

Designed for use in screening potential modern foreign language students and grouping them for instruction. Used for predicting student success in foreign language learning and diagnosing language learning difficulties. May be used with students from end of grade 6 through grade 12.

195
Bruce Vocabulary Inventory. Bruce, Martin M. 1974
Descriptors: Adults; *Aptitude Tests; *Definitions; *Employees; *Intelligence; Multiple Choice Tests; *Verbal Ability; Verbal Tests; *Vocabulary Development
Availability: Martin M. Bruce, Publishers; 50 Larchmont Rd., P.O. Box 248, Larchmont, NY 10538
Target Audience: Adults
Notes: Time, 20 approx.; Items, 100

Measures the verbal comprehension and usage of employed populations via use of vocabulary words which have been standardized on industrial and business populations instead of the usual educational and academic groups. It is a self-administering test, under supervision, with no time limit. Most individuals with a high school education will complete the test in about 15 or 20 minutes. The author designed this test as an indication of one's intelligence since verbal comprehension and usage are highly correlated with intelligence. However, he warns that the test results should be considered as suggestive NOT as definitely diagnostic.

210
Horn Art Aptitude Inventory. Horn, Charles C. 1951
Subtests: Scribble and Doodle Exercise; Imagery
Descriptors: Adults; *Aptitude Tests; Art; *College Freshmen; Counseling Techniques; *Creativity; Creativity Tests; Higher Education; High Schools; *High School Students; Imagery; Imagination
Availability: Stoelting Co.; 620 Wheat Ln., Wood Dale, IL 60191
Grade Level: 9-16
Target Audience: Adults
Notes: Time, 40 approx.; Items, 32

Designed to assess originality and compositional sense, as well as the scope of interests, fertility of imagination, and picture mindedness of the individual. Has been useful for individual counseling as well as counseling for groups of students.

227
Seashore Measures of Musical Talents. Seashore, Carl E.; And Others 1960
Subtests: Pitch; Loudness; Rhythm; Time; Timbre; Tonal Memory
Descriptors: *Adults; *Aptitude Tests; *Audiodisks; Audiotape Recordings; *Auditory Discrimination; *College Students; *Elementary School Students; Higher Education; Intermediate Grades; *Music; Secondary Education; *Secondary School Students; Talent
Identifiers: *Music Ability; Pitch (Music); Rhythm; Test Batteries
Availability: The Psychological Corp.; 555 Academic Ct., San Antonio, TX 78204-0952
Grade Level: 4-16
Target Audience: 10-64
Notes: Time, 60 approx.; Items, 230

Designed to assess musical aptitude of subjects from fourth grade level through adulthood. Test is administered to groups or individuals using a 33-1/3 rpm long playing record or reel-to-reel tape recording. Fundamental capacities of musical aptitude are assessed. These include pitch, loudness, rhythm, time, timbre and tonal memory.

228
Musical Aptitude Profile. Gordon, Edwin E. 1965
Subtests: Melody; Harmony; Tempo; Meter; Phrasing; Balance; Style
Descriptors: Adolescents; *Aptitude Tests; Audiotape Recordings; Auditory Discrimination; Children; *Elementary School Students; Intermediate Grades; *Music; Secondary Education; *Secondary School Students; Talent
Identifiers: Cumulative Record Folder; *Music Ability; Rhythm; Test Batteries
Availability: Riverside Publishing Co.; 8420 Bryn Mawr Ave., Chicago, IL 60631
Grade Level: 4-12
Notes: Time, 110 approx.

Designed to assess musical aptitude, rather than achievement. Measures basic factors of musical expression, aural perception, and kinesthetic musical feeling. Profile is an objective measure designed for use in combination with the music teacher's judgment of a student's musical aptitude.

259
Modern Language Aptitude Test. Carroll, John B.; Sapon, Stanley M. 1959
Subtests: Number Learning; Phonetic Script; Spelling Clues; Words in Sentences; Paired Associates
Descriptors: *Adults; *Aptitude Tests; *Audiotape Recorders; Audiotape Recordings; Classical Languages; *College Students; Higher Education; High Schools; *High School Students; *Language Aptitude; Modern Languages; Predictive Measurement; *Second Language Learning
Identifiers: MLAT
Availability: The Psychological Corp.; 555 Academic Ct., San Antonio, TX 78204-0952
Grade Level: 9-16
Target Audience: 18-64
Notes: Time, 70 approx.; Items, 164

Designed to provide an indication of an individual's probable degree of success in learning a modern or classical foreign language. May be used to predict success in speaking, understanding, reading, writing and translation. The complete test requires use of a pre-recorded audiotape. A short form consisting of spelling clues, words in sentences, and paired associates may be used when time is limited or playback equipment is unavailable. Short form requires approximately 30 minutes to complete.

404
Wonderlic Personnel Test. Wonderlic, E.F. 1942
Descriptors: Abstract Reasoning; Adults; *Cognitive Ability; Cognitive Tests; *Employees; French; *Job Applicants; Large Type Materials; Mathematical Concepts; Occupational Tests; Spanish
Availability: E.F. Wonderlic and Associates, Inc.; 820 Frontage Rd., Northfield, IL 60093
Target Audience: 18-64
Notes: Time, 12; Items, 50

Designed as objective measure of applicant potential for job success. Critical scores are established for each occupation by test administrator or corporation. Equivalent forms are available. Employers use forms A, B, I, II, IV, V, T-11 and T-21. Employment agencies use forms EM,

APT, BPT, and CPT. Forms A and B are available in French and Spanish editions. A large print version for use with elderly or economically handicapped persons with uncorrected vision impairments is now available.

405
Wesman Personnel Classification Test. Wesman, Alexander G. 1965
Subtests: Verbal; Numerical
Descriptors: Adults; Arithmetic; Employees; *Job Applicants; *Mathematical Concepts; *Occupational Tests; *Personnel Selection; *Verbal Ability
Identifiers: CAST; Controlled Administration of Standardized Tests; WPCT
Availability: The Psychological Corp.; 555 Academic Ct., San Antonio, TX 78204-0952
Target Audience: 18-64
Notes: Time, 28 approx.; Items, 60

Designed to measure general mental ability for use in selection of employees for clerical, sales, supervisory, and managerial positions. Emphasizes power rather than speed. WPCT has wide applicability from recent school graduates to older applicants. Three forms A, B, and C are available. Form C-Verbal is more difficult than Forms A and B-Verbal. Tapes for administering WPCT in a "CAST" system are available.

413
Wechsler Adult Intelligence Scale. Wechsler, David 1955
Subtests: Information; Comprehension; Arithmetic; Similarities; Digit Span; Vocabulary; Digit Symbol; Picture Completion; Block Design; Picture Arrangement; Object Assembly
Descriptors: *Adults; Individual Testing; *Intelligence; *Intelligence Quotient; *Intelligence Tests; Nonverbal Ability; *Older Adults; Performance Tests; Verbal Ability
Identifiers: WAIS
Availability: The Psychological Corp.; 555 Academic Ct., San Antonio, TX 78204-0952
Target Audience: 16-75
Notes: Time, 60 approx.

Designed to measure verbal and performance intelligence levels of subjects above 16 years of age. Sets, replacement parts, and printed forms remain available for users of this edition. This form was revised in 1981 to create the Wechsler Adult Intelligence Scale—Revised (WAIS-R) (TC011190).

414
Wechsler Intelligence Scale for Children. Wechsler, David 1949
Subtests: General Information; General Comprehension; Arithmetic; Similarities; Vocabulary; Picture Completion; Picture Arrangement; Block Design; Object Assembly; Coding or Mazes
Descriptors: Adolescents; Children; *Elementary School Students; Elementary Secondary Education; Individual Testing; *Intelligence; *Intelligence Quotient; *Intelligence Tests; Performance Tests; *Secondary School Students; Verbal Ability
Identifiers: Test Batteries; WISC
Availability: The Psychological Corp.; 555 Academic Ct., San Antonio, TX 78204-0952
Target Audience: 5-15
Notes: Time, 60 approx.

Designed to measure intelligence of children ages 5 to 15. Scale overlaps Wechsler-Bellevue Scales as both may be used for adolescents. Verbal and Performance scales are subdivided into five areas each. Superseded by Wechsler Intelligence Scale for Children—Revised (TC007461) published in 1974. However, sets, replacement parts, and printed forms remain available for users who prefer this 1949 edition. Yields Verbal and Performance IQ's as well as Full Scale IQ.

415
Escala de Inteligencia Wechsler para Ninos. Wechsler, David 1967
Subtests: Verbal; Performance
Descriptors: *Elementary School Students; Elementary Secondary Education; Individual Testing; *Intelligence; Intelligence Quotient; *Intelligence Tests; *Secondary School Students; *Spanish; *Spanish Speaking
Identifiers: *Puerto Rico; *Wechsler Intelligence Scale for Children
Availability: The Psychological Corp.; 555 Academic Ct., San Antonio, TX 78204-0952

Target Audience: 5-15
Notes: Time, 60 approx.

Spanish-American translation and adaptation of the WISC (1949), developed in Puerto Rico. Uses same set of materials for Performance Scale. Spanish language manual and verbal items.

496
Infant Intelligence Scale. Cattell, Psyche 1960
Descriptors: *Cognitive Ability; *Individual Testing; *Infants; *Intelligence Quotient; *Intelligence Tests; Mental Age; *Performance Tests; *Young Children
Identifiers: Cattell Infant Intelligence Scale; CIIS; IIS
Availability: The Psychological Corp.; 555 Academic Ct., San Antonio, TX 78204-0952
Target Audience: 0-3
Notes: Time, 30 approx.

Individually administered intelligence instrument. Many parts involve administrator's observation of the child's performance. Requires various objects, pictures, etc. Number of items varies with child's age.

497
Analysis of Relationships. Ghiselli, Edwin E. 1960
Descriptors: *Adults; *College Students; *High School Students; Intelligence Tests; *Problem Solving
Identifiers: *Inferential Reasoning
Availability: Consulting Psychologists Press; 577 College Ave., Palo Alto, CA 94306
Target Audience: 18-64
Notes: Time, 30 approx.; Items, 40

Measures general intellectual abilities with slightly more emphasis on verbal facility, reasoning, and problem solving. Specifically designed to yield finer discriminations at the higher levels of ability without introduction of a speed factor.

712
Western Personnel Test. Gunn, Robert L.; Manson, Morse P. 1962
Descriptors: Adults; Aptitude Tests; *Cognitive Ability; Cognitive Tests; Computation; Employment Qualifications; *Intelligence; *Learning; *Mathematical Applications; Mathematical Concepts; Multiple Choice Tests; Timed Tests; *Verbal Ability; Vocational Aptitude
Identifiers: WPT
Availability: Western Psychological Services; Order Dept., 12031 Wilshire Blvd., Los Angeles, CA 90025
Target Audience: Adults
Notes: Time, 5; Items, 24

A quickly administered instrument used to evaluate general mental ability and learning ability. Includes both verbal and mathematical abilities. Items require a brief answer based upon one's mathematical calculations or are multiple choice. Used with the general population, professional, college, clerical, skilled, and unskilled populations to evaluate general ability and for screening by personnel departments. Scores are given in terms of percentiles. Available in Forms A, B, C, and D. Also available in Spanish (Western Personnel Test: Spanish, TC004192).

715
Oregon Academic Ranking Test. Derthick, Charles H. 1965
Subtests: Making Sentences; Making Comparisons; Numbers; Secret Words; Working Problems; Reasoning; Completing Sentences; Sayings
Descriptors: *Ability Identification; Abstract Reasoning; Academic Ability; *Academically Gifted; Aptitude Tests; Creativity; Elementary Education; *Elementary School Students; Individual Testing; Screening Tests; Special Education
Identifiers: OART
Availability: Western Psychological Services; 12031 Wilshire Blvd., Los Angeles, CA 90025
Grade Level: 3-7
Notes: Time, 30 approx.

Designed to identify exceptionally bright children. Measures creativity and abstract thinking as indices of brightness. May be used as individual or group test. Useful for selection and placement of students into enriched programs and identification of highly creative youngsters.

794
The Denny-Ives Creativity Test. Denny, David A.; Ives, Sammie 1964
Subtests: Fluency and Redefinition; Originality and Sensitivity
Descriptors: Children; Creativity; *Creativity Tests; *Dramatics; *Elementary School Students; *Grade 6; Intermediate Grades
Identifiers: TIM(B)
Availability: Tests in Microfiche; Test Collection, Educational Testing Service, Princeton, NJ 08541

Grade Level: 6
Notes: Time, 45 approx.; Items, 4

Research device designed to assess creativity in the dramatic arts, is in two parts. Scores for fluency and redefinition are derived from Part I, while Part II yields scores for originality and sensitivity. Audiotapes and slides are required to administer the test and may be purchased from author.

811
School and College Ability Tests—Series II, Level 1. Educational Testing Service, Princeton, NJ 1966
Subtests: Verbal; Quantitative
Descriptors: *Academic Aptitude; *Aptitude Tests; Higher Education; *Mathematics; Nonverbal Ability; *Predictive Measurement; *Undergraduate Students; *Verbal Ability
Identifiers: SCAT Series II
Availability: Publishers Test Service; 2500 Garden Rd., Monterey, CA 93940
Grade Level: 13-14
Notes: Time, 45 approx.; Items, 100

Designed to provide estimates of basic verbal and mathematical ability for students in first two years of college. Three parallel forms are available.

841
Arthur Point Scale of Performance, Form I. Arthur, Grace 1943
Subtests: Mare-Foal Formboard; Sequin-Goddard Formboard; Pintner-Paterson 2 Figure Formboard; Casuist Formboard; Pintner Manikin Test; Knox-Kempf Feature Profile Test; Knox Cube Imitation Test; Healy Pictorial Completion Test; Kohs Block and Design Cards; and Porteus Mazes
Descriptors: *Adults; Deafness; Disabilities; *Elementary School Students; Elementary Secondary Education; Emotional Disturbances; Individual Testing; *Intelligence; *Intelligence Tests; Nonverbal Tests; Performance Tests; *Preschool Children; *Secondary School Students
Identifiers: Arthur Point Scale of Performance Tests
Availability: Stoelting Co.; 620 Wheat Ln., Wood Dale, IL 60191
Target Audience: 4-64

Nonverbal measure of intelligence designed to supplement Binet tests. Useful for subjects with speech defects, language difficulties, or emotional problems.

842
Arthur Point Scale of Performance Tests, Revised Form II. Arthur, Grace 1947
Subtests: Knox Cube Test (Arthur Revision); Sequin Form Board (Arthur Revision); Arthur Stencil Design Test I; Porteus Maze Test (Arthur Revision); Healy Picture Completion Test II
Descriptors: *Adolescents; *Children; Deafness; *Individual Testing; *Intelligence Tests; Non English Speaking; *Nonverbal Tests; Reading Difficulties; Speech Handicaps
Identifiers: Test Batteries
Availability: Stoelting Co.; 620 Wheat Ln., Wood Dale, IL 60191
Target Audience: 4-17
Notes: Time, 90 approx.

Designed to furnish an Intelligence Quotient comparable to that obtained with the Binet Scales. Subtests include: Knox Cube Test, Sequin Form Board, Arthur Stencil Design Test I, Porteus Maze Text, and the Healy Picture Completion Test II. Tests afford a means of measuring adequately the ability of deaf children, those suffering from reading disabilities, those with delayed or defective speech, and non-English speaking students.

858
Inter-American Series: Test of General Ability, Level 1, Primary. Manuel, Herschel T. 1962
Subtests: Oral Vocabulary; Number; Association; Classification
Descriptors: *Academic Aptitude; Aptitude Tests; Cognitive Ability; *Elementary School Students; *Grade 1; *Kindergarten Children; Language Acquisition; Number Concepts; Primary Education; *School Readiness; *School Readiness Tests; *Spanish; Spatial Ability
Identifiers: GA1CE; HG1CEs; Test Batteries
Availability: Guidance Testing Associates; P.O. Box 28096, San Antonio, TX 78228
Grade Level: K-1
Target Audience: 6
Notes: Time, 60 approx.; Items, 80

Designed to provide an estimate of the ability to do academic work. Two forms are available in English and Spanish parallel editions. Subtests in oral vocabulary and number yield a Verbal-Numerical score. Subtests of association and classification yield a nonverbal score. Tests may

be administered in 2 sessions. Level One tests are designed for use as a readiness test for 6-year olds at the end of kindergarten and beginning of grade one.

859
Inter-American Series: Test of General Ability, Level 2, Primary. Manuel, Herschel T. 1965
Subtests: Oral Vocabulary; Number; Classification; Analogies
Descriptors: *Academic Aptitude; *Aptitude Tests; *Cognitive Ability; Computation; *Elementary School Students; *Grade 2; *Grade 3; Language Acquisition; Number Concepts; Primary Education; *Spanish; Spatial Ability
Identifiers: GA2CE; HG2CEs; Test Batteries
Availability: Guidance Testing Associates; P.O. Box 28096, San Antonio, TX 78228
Grade Level: 2-3
Target Audience: 7-8
Notes: Time, 50 approx.; Items, 100

Subtests in oral vocabulary and number yield a verbal-numerical score. Subtests of Classification and Analogies yield a nonverbal score. There are 60 verbal-numerical items and 40 nonverbal items. Designed to provide an estimate of the ability to do academic work. Two forms are available in English and Spanish parallel editions.

860
Inter-American Series: Test of General Ability, Level 3, Elementary. Manuel, Herschel T. 1962
Subtests: Sentence Completion; Analogies; Computation; Word Relations; Classification; Number Series
Descriptors: *Academic Aptitude; *Aptitude Tests; *Cognitive Ability; Cognitive Tests; Computation; *Elementary School Students; Intermediate Grades; Number Concepts; Mathematics Tests; *Spanish; Spatial Ability; Timed Tests; Verbal Ability
Identifiers: GA3CE; HG3CEs; Test Batteries
Availability: Guidance Testing Associates; P.O. Box 28096, San Antonio, TX 78228
Grade Level: 4-6
Target Audience: 9-11
Notes: Time, 52 approx.; Items, 150

Six subtests yield 3 subscores in verbal, numerical, and nonverbal areas. There are 50 verbal items, 50 numerical items, and 50 nonverbal items. Designed to provide an estimate of the student's ability to do academic work. Two forms are available in English and Spanish parallel editions.

861
Inter-American Series: Test of General Ability, Level 4, Intermediate. Manuel, Herschel T. 1962
Subtests: Sentence Completion; Analogies; Computation; Word Relations; Classification; Number Series
Descriptors: *Academic Aptitude; *Aptitude Tests; *Cognitive Ability; Cognitive Tests; Computation; Junior High Schools; *Junior High School Students; Number Concepts; Mathematics Tests; *Spanish; Spatial Ability; Timed Tests; Verbal Ability
Identifiers: GA4CE; HG4CEs; Test Batteries
Availability: Guidance Testing Associates; P.O. Box 28096, San Antonio, TX 78228
Grade Level: 7-9
Target Audience: 12-14
Notes: Time, 52 approx.; Items, 150

Six subtests yield 3 subscores: Verbal, Numerical, and Non-Verbal. There are 50 verbal items, 50 numerical items, and 50 nonverbal items. Designed to provide an estimate of the students' ability to perform academic work. Two forms are available in English and Spanish parallel editions.

862
Inter-American Series: Test of General Ability, Level 5, Advanced. Manuel, Herschel T. 1962
Subtests: Sentence Completion; Analogies; Computation; Word Relations; Classification; Number Series
Descriptors: *Academic Aptitude; *Aptitude Tests; *Cognitive Ability; Cognitive Tests; Computation; High Schools; *High School Students; Number Concepts; Mathematics Tests; *Spanish; Spatial Ability; Timed Tests; Verbal Ability
Identifiers: GA5CE; HG5CEs; Test Batteries
Availability: Guidance Testing Associates; P.O. Box 28096, San Antonio, TX 78228
Grade Level: 10-12
Target Audience: 15-18
Notes: Time, 52 approx.; Items, 150

Six subtests yield 3 subscores: Verbal, Numerical, and Non-Verbal. There are 50 verbal items, 50 numerical items, and 50 nonverbal items. Designed to provide an estimate of the student's ability to perform academic work. Two forms are available in English and Spanish parallel editions.

886
Secondary School Admission Test. Secondary School Admission Test Board, Inc., Princeton, NJ 1981
Subtests: Verbal; Quantitative; Reading Comprehension
Descriptors: *Academic Aptitude; *Admission (School); *Aptitude Tests; Elementary Secondary Education; Mathematics Tests; Reading Comprehension; Verbal Ability
Identifiers: SSAT
Availability: Educational Testing Service; Secondary School Admission Test, P.O. Box 922-R, Princeton, NJ 08541
Grade Level: 5-10
Designed for use as a uniform measure of scholastic ability for students applying for admission to grades 6-11. Administered at testing centers. Registration for the test is through ETS, which administers it for the Secondary School Admissions Test Board, Inc. Test is updated periodically.

890
Scholastic Aptitude Test. College Board, New York, NY 1982
Subtests: Verbal; Quantitative
Descriptors: *Academic Aptitude; *Aptitude Tests; Braille; *College Bound Students; *College Entrance Examinations; High Schools; *High School Students; Large Type Materials; *Mathematics Tests; *Verbal Ability
Availability: College Board Admissions Testing Program; P.O. Box 592, Princeton, NJ 08541
Grade Level: 11-12
Notes: Time, 180; Items, 145
A multiple choice test designed to assist colleges and universities in evaluating applications for admission. Measures verbal and mathematical reasoning skills. Administered at testing centers nationwide. Braille and large print editions are available (see also TC001003). Updated and revised regularly.

999
Scott Company Mental Alertness Test. Scott Co. 1923
Descriptors: Adults; *Cognitive Ability; *Cognitive Tests; *Job Applicants; *Personnel Selection
Availability: Stoelting Co.; 620 Wheat Ln., Wood Dale, IL 60191
Target Audience: Adults
Notes: Time, 15 approx.
A test of mental alertness which may be administered individually or to groups. Used to assess job applicants. Test involves arithmetical reasoning, quickness and accuracy of judgment, clearness of perception, degree of comprehension, and ability to follow instructions.

1001
The Immediate Test. Corsini, Raymond J. 1951
Descriptors: Adolescents; Adults; Children; Individual Testing; *Intelligence; *Intelligence Quotient; *Intelligence Tests; *Mental Age; *Verbal Ability; Verbal Tests
Identifiers: IT; Quick Verbal Intelligence Test
Availability: Sheridan Psychological Services, Inc.; P.O. Box 6101, Orange, CA 92667
Target Audience: 10-64
Notes: Time, 5 approx.
Basically designed to be used as an emergency clinical test which provides a quick estimate of mental age and IQ. The 66 words have been chosen both for their relative freedom of cultural and emotional effects and for their interest. Especially adaptive to those adults who can not be easily motivated to take the usual, longer intelligence tests. Individually administered.

1003
Scholastic Aptitude Test: Braille Edition and Large Print Edition. College Board, New York, NY 1982
Subtests: Verbal; Quantitative
Descriptors: *Academic Aptitude; *Aptitude Tests; *Braille; *College Bound Students; *College Entrance Examinations; High Schools; *High School Students; Large Type Materials; *Mathematics Tests; *Verbal Ability
Availability: College Board Admissions Testing Program; P.O. Box 592 Princeton, NJ 08541
Grade Level: 11-12
Notes: Time, 180; Items, 145
A multiple choice test designed to assist colleges and universities in evaluating applications for admission. Measures verbal and mathematical reasoning abilities. Administered at testing centers nationwide. Registration is made through ETS. Updated and revised regularly.

1015
Curtis Verbal-Clerical Skills Tests. Curtis, James W. 1965
Subtests: Capacity Test; Computation Test; Checking Test; Comprehension Test

Descriptors: *Achievement Tests; Adults; *Clerical Workers; Computation; *Job Applicants; Logical Thinking; *Personnel Selection; Reading Comprehension; Timed Tests
Identifiers: Accuracy; Clerical Checking; Clerical Skills; Speededness (Tests)
Availability: Psychometric Affiliates; P.O. Box 807, Murfreesboro, TN 37133
Target Audience: 16-61
Notes: Time, 8; Items, 100
Designed to provide estimates of individual competence in basic areas of verbal skill usually associated with office and clerical work, as well as with potential for training at advanced or college level. May be administered to individuals or groups. Examinee may be given any 1 or all 4 subtests. Tests are independent of one another.

1201
Stanford Multi-Modality Imagery Test. Dauterman, William L. 1972
Descriptors: Adolescents; Adults; *Blindness; Geometric Constructions; *Imagination; Individual Testing; Rehabilitation; *Spatial Ability; *Visual Impairments
Identifiers: SMIT
Availability: American Foundation for the Blind; 15 W. 16th St., New York, NY 10011
Target Audience: 16-64
Designed to measure ability of blind and visually handicapped subjects to imagine geometric patterns. This aptitude is believed to be related to success in rehabilitation.

1208
Computer Programmer Aptitude Battery. Palormo, Jean Maier 1964
Subtests: Verbal Meaning; Reasoning; Letter Series; Number Ability; Diagramming
Descriptors: Adults; *Aptitude Tests; Data Processing Occupations; *Job Placement; *Personnel Selection; Predictive Measurement; *Programers; Programing; Systems Analysis
Identifiers: CPAB
Availability: Science Research Associates; 155 N. Wacker Dr., Chicago, IL 60606
Target Audience: 18-64
Notes: Time, 75; Items, 123
Designed to measure skills and aptitudes related to success in fields of computer programing and systems analysis. May be used for selection and placement of personnel.

1214
Meier Art Tests: Meier Art Judgment Test. Meier, Norman Charles 1940
Descriptors: Adolescents; *Adults; *Aesthetic Values; *Aptitude Tests; Art; *Art Appreciation; Forced Choice Technique; Secondary Education; *Secondary School Students; *Value Judgment
Identifiers: Self Administered Tests
Availability: Stoelting Co.; 620 Wheat Ln., Wood Dale, IL 60191
Target Audience: 13-64
Notes: Time, 45 approx.; Items, 100
Designed to measure art aptitude. Student examines 2 versions of reconstructed works of art. Aesthetic judgment is assumed to be one of the most important factors in artistic competence. May be administered as a single test or in combination with Meier Aesthetic Perception Test (TC001215).

1316
Goodenough-Harris Drawing Test. Goodenough, Florence L.; Harris, Dale B. 1963
Descriptors: Adolescents; Children; *Cognitive Ability; Cognitive Tests; *Elementary School Students; Elementary Secondary Education; Individual Testing; Learning Problems; *Nonverbal Tests; *Preschool Children; Preschool Education; *Secondary School Students
Identifiers: *Drawing
Availability: The Psychological Corp.; 555 Academic Ct., San Antonio, TX 78204-0952
Target Audience: 3-15
Notes: Time, 15 approx.
A nonverbal test of mental ability, this instrument may be administered to groups or individuals. Student is asked to draw 3 pictures—man, woman, and self. Drawings are scored according to details included as described in the manual.

1318
Bender-Gestalt Test. Bender, Lauretta 1951

Descriptors: Adolescents; Adults; Aptitude Tests; Children; Clinical Diagnosis; Cognitive Development; Individual Development; Individual Testing; Intelligence; *Maturity (Individuals); Maturity Tests; Medical Evaluation; Mental Retardation; Motor Development; *Neurological Impairments; Patients; Perceptual Development; Perceptual Motor Coordination; *Perceptual Motor Learning; *Performance Tests; Personality Measures; *Personality Traits; *Prognostic Tests; Psychological Characteristics; *Psychological Evaluation; *Psychomotor Objectives; Visual Measures; Visual Perception; Visual Stimuli
Identifiers: The Bender
Availability: Pascal, Gerald R.; Suttell, Barbara J. The Bender-Gestalt Test. New York: Grune and Stratton, 1951.
Target Audience: 5-64
Notes: Time, 10 approx.; Items, 9
Untimed, individually administered instrument with many uses. Has been used to estimate maturation, intelligence in children but not adults, psychological disturbances, effects of injury to the cortex; as a repetitive visuo-motor test; and to follow the effects of convulsive therapy. The instrument consists of 9 designs which the subject is asked to copy on a sheet of paper; the designs were originally used by Wertheimer (1921) in his studies of visual perception. According to the authors, one may think of the performance as a work sample, which involves certainly the cortical capacity to perceive the designs as presented and the psychomotor capacity to reproduce them; but it also involves (especially with subjects of normal intelligence) a factor that seems to be best described as an attitude toward reality. Requires the use of a set of cards with the designs depicted thereon. Used with patients and nonpatients. The 9 designs adapted from the Wertheimer version were simplified and adapted to accentuate a particular Gestalt feature. The original version required only a verbal description of figures.

1343
School Readiness Test Kit. Ilg, F.L.; And Others 1965
Subtests: Interview; Pencil and Paper Tests; Copy Forms Test; Incomplete Man Test; Right and Left Tests; Form Tests-Monroe Visual 1 and 3; Animals and Interests; Examination of Teeth
Descriptors: Behavior Development; *Maturity Tests; Performance; Primary Education; *School Readiness Tests
Identifiers: Behavior Analysis; Gesell Developmental Tests; Test Batteries
Availability: Programs for Education; 1200 Broadway, New York, NY 10001
Target Audience: 5-6
A battery of behavior tests to determine a child's readiness for school.

1402
Stanford-Binet Intelligence Scale: Form L-M. Terman, Lewis M.; Merrill, Maud A. 1973
Descriptors: Abstract Reasoning; *Academic Aptitude; *Adolescents; *Adults; *Children; Elementary School Students; Elementary Secondary Education; Individual Testing; *Intelligence; *Intelligence Quotient; *Intelligence Tests; Preschool Children; Preschool Education; Secondary School Students
Identifiers: Test Batteries
Availability: The Riverside Publishing Co.; 8420 Bryn Mawr Ave., Chicago, IL 60631
Target Audience: 2-64
Designed to measure intelligence of children and adults from 2 years of age. Assesses general cognitive functioning and mental abilities necessary for abstract reasoning. Form L-M is the third revision of the Stanford-Binet Scale.

1422
General Aptitude Test Battery. United States Employment Service, Div. of Testing, Salem, OR 1967
Subtests: Name Comparison; Computation; 3-Dimensional Space; Vocabulary; Tool Matching; Arithmetic Reason; Form Matching; Mark Making; Place; Turn; Assemble; Disassemble
Descriptors: Adults; *Aptitude Tests; Career Guidance; High School Students; Job Placement; *Occupational Tests; Perceptual Motor Coordination; Personnel Evaluation; *Personnel Selection; Professional Occupations; Semiskilled Occupations; Skilled Occupations; Spatial Ability; Unskilled Occupations; Verbal Ability; Vocational Aptitude
Identifiers: *Clerical Aptitude; Finger Dexterity; GATB; *Manual Dexterity; Mathematical Aptitude
Availability: State Employment Service Offices only
Target Audience: 13-64

Notes: Time, 150

Designed for use in vocational guidance and employment selection of literate individuals. Twelve tests measure 9 vocational aptitudes: general learning ability; verbal aptitude; numerical aptitude; spatial aptitude; form perception; clerical perception; motor coordination; finger dexterity; manual dexterity. Research and development on this test is continuous. A Spanish version is available (TC010648) as is a non-reading measure of the same aptitudes (TC012014) and a special edition for deaf persons. Validated to predict performance in over 400 professional, skilled, semi- and unskilled occupations. See Specific Aptitude Test Batteries (TC001012) for examples. Not available to the general public. For information, contact a state employment service agency, which is responsible for the operational use of the GATB.

1424

Wechsler Preschool and Primary Scale of Intelligence. Wechsler, David 1967
Subtests: Information; Vocabulary; Arithmetic; Similarities; Comprehension; Animal House; Picture Completion; Mazes; Geometric Design; Block Design; Sentences
Descriptors: Elementary School Students; *Grade 1; Individual Testing; *Intelligence; *Intelligence Quotient; *Intelligence Tests; *Kindergarten Children; Performance Tests; *Preschool Children; Preschool Education; Primary Education; Verbal Ability
Identifiers: Test Batteries; WPPSI
Availability: The Psychological Corp.; 555 Academic Ct., San Antonio, TX 78204-0952
Target Audience: 4-6
Notes: Time, 60 approx.

Designed to measure intelligence of children aged 4 to 6 1/2 years. Scale overlaps Wechsler Intelligence Scale for Children (TC000414) and WISC-R (TC007461). Verbal and Performance Intelligence Quotients as well as Full Scale Intelligence Quotients may be derived. Downward extension of WISC and a separate scale designed to cope more effectively with problems of testing young children.

1438

Flanagan Aptitude Classification Tests. Flanagan, John C. 1953
Subtests: Inspection; Coding; Memory; Precision; Assembly; Scales; Coordination; Judgment and Comprehension; Arithmetic; Patterns; Components; Tables; Mechanics; Expression; Reasoning; Ingenuity
Descriptors: Adolescents; *Adults; *Aptitude Tests; Career Counseling; High Schools; *High School Students; Job Placement; *Job Skills; Occupational Tests; *Predictive Measurement
Identifiers: FACT; Test Batteries
Availability: Science Research Associates; 155 N. Wacker Dr., Chicago, IL 60606
Target Audience: 14-64

Developed to measure 16 important on-the-job skills. Each skill is assessed in a separate test booklet which may require 5 to 40 minutes to complete. May be used in vocational counseling for high school students. May also be used in selection, placement, and reclassification of employees. All tests are timed except "Judgment and Comprehension" and "Expression."

1479

Full Range Picture Vocabulary Test. Ammons, R.B.; Ammons, H.S. 1948
Descriptors: Adolescents; Adults; *Children; *Comprehension; *Disabilities; Individual Testing; Intelligence; *Intelligence Tests; *Nonverbal Tests; Pictorial Stimuli; Screening Tests; *Young Children
Identifiers: FRPV
Availability: Psychological Test Specialists; P.O. Box 9229, Missoula, MT 59807
Target Audience: 2-34
Notes: Time, 10 approx.; Items, 16

Designed to measure intelligence based on verbal comprehension. Useful for age levels from 2 through adulthood. No reading or writing is required of examinee. Subject points to picture which corresponds to word given by examiner. Words were organized in approximate order of difficulty. May be used with physically handicapped subjects and those with speech defects. Forms A and B are available.

1519

Experimental Comparative Prediction Battery. Educational Testing Service, Princeton, NJ 1964
Subtests: Induction (50); Following Directions (15); Paper Folding Test (35); Year 2000 (20); Induction (50); Spatial Rotation Test (10); Paper Folding Test (40); Artificial Language (15); Sentence Completion (70); Similar Figures (48); Arithmetic Speed Test (125); Interest Index (192)

Descriptors: *Abstract Reasoning; *Academic Aptitude; Aptitude Tests; Higher Education; High Schools; *High School Students; *Interest Inventories; Predictive Measurement; *Undergraduate Students
Identifiers: TIM(B)
Availability: Tests in Microfiche; Test Collection, Educational Testing Service, Princeton, NJ 08541
Grade Level: 9-16
Notes: Time, 165; Items, 675

Battery measures 6 aptitudes including induction integration, visualization, meaningful memory, number facility and spatial orientation. Book A1 has 125 items and is suitable for high school students; Book A2 with 115 items is suitable for college students. Books B and C may be used at either level. Book B has 243 items and book C has 192 items. Because no available statistical data apply to tests in their present form, the batteries are considered experimental and should not be used in making educational decisions.

1521

Logical Reasoning. Hertzka, Alfred F.; Guilford, J.P. 1955
Descriptors: Adolescents; *Adults; *Cognitive Tests; *Critical Thinking; *Students; Timed Tests; Verbal Tests
Identifiers: Evaluation of Semantic Implications; LR; *Reasoning Ability; Structure of Intellect
Availability: Consulting Psychologists Press; 577 College Ave., Palo Alto, CA 94306
Target Audience: 14-64
Notes: Time, 20

Measures the factor known as evaluation of semantic implications, which is defined as the ability to judge the logical soundness of meaningful conclusions. It is commonly known as critical-thinking ability.

1533

Alternate Uses. Christensen, Paul R.; And Others 1960
Descriptors: Adolescents; *Adults; Children; *Cognitive Style; *Cognitive Tests; *Divergent Thinking; *Students; Timed Tests; Verbal Tests
Identifiers: Christensen Guilford Fluency Tests; Divergent Production of Semantic Classes
Availability: Consulting Psychologists Press; 577 College Ave., Palo Alto, CA 94306
Target Audience: 11-64
Notes: Time, 12; Items, 9

Designed to measure spontaneous flexibility, that is, the ability to think of a variety of class ideas in relationship to or in connection with an object or other unit of thought. Has 3 parts; each part is timed for 4 minutes.

1557

SRA Pictorial Reasoning Test. McMurry, Robert N.; Arnold, Phyllis D. 1966
Descriptors: *Abstract Reasoning; Adults; Aptitude Tests; *Blacks; Concept Formation; *Culture Fair Tests; Entry Workers; High Schools; *High School Students; *Hispanic Americans; Screening Tests; *Vocational Aptitude; *Whites
Identifiers: PRT; Self Administered Tests; Self Scoring Tests
Availability: Science Research Associates, Inc.; 155 N. Wacker Dr., Chicago, IL 60606
Grade Level: 9-12
Target Audience: 14-64
Notes: Time, 15; Items, 80

Designed as a test of general ability to measure learning potential of individuals from diverse backgrounds with reading difficulties. Instrument is culturally fair and predictive of job success. Most useful as a screening test for entry level jobs. Directions have been written at a sixth grade reading level to facilitate understanding.

1596

Anton Brenner Development Gestalt of School Readiness. Brenner, Anton 1964
Subtests: Number Producing; Number Recognition; Ten Dot Gestalt; Sentence Gestalt; Draw-A-Man
Descriptors: *Concept Formation; Disadvantaged; Non English Speaking; *Perceptual Development; *Preschool Children; Preschool Education; *School Readiness; *School Readiness Tests
Identifiers: BGT; Gestalt Psychology
Availability: Western Psychological Services; 12031 Wilshire Blvd., Los Angeles, CA 90025
Target Audience: 5-6
Notes: Time, 10 approx.; Items, 40

Predicts success in kindergarten and first grade. Almost culture free; can be used with culturally deprived and non-English speaking children. Provides quantitative and qualitative evaluation of child's perceptual and conceptual development. Uses Gestalt and developmental principles, and can be used to identify early maturing and/or gifted;

slowly maturing and/or retarded; and emotionally disturbed children. The child's performance is then interpreted through readiness rating scales.

1608

Short Employment Tests. Bennett, George K.; Gelink, Marjorie 1972
Subtests: Verbal; Numerical; Clerical Aptitude
Descriptors: Adults; *Aptitude Tests; *Clerical Workers; *Computation; *Job Applicants; Occupational Tests; *Predictive Measurement; Mathematics Tests; *Semantics
Identifiers: CAST; Controlled Administration of Standardized Tests; SET; Test Batteries
Availability: The Psychological Corp.; 555 Academic Ct., San Antonio, TX 78204-0952
Target Audience: 18-64
Notes: Time, 15 approx.; Items, 200

A series of 3 aptitude tests designed to meet needs of employers of office help. Three separate booklets test vocabulary as an indicator of intelligence; computational ability and speed; and speed and accuracy in completion of a clerical task. Each test requires 5 minutes to administer. Tests are restricted and sold only to personnel departments of business and industrial firms. Not sold to schools or employment agencies. Equivalent forms 1-4 are available. Form 1 is sold only to member banks of ABA. Tapes for administering SET in a "CAST" system are available.

1614

Revised Minnesota Paper Form Board Test. Likert, Rensis; Quasha, William H. 1934
Descriptors: Adults; Career Counseling; Employees; Mechanical Design Technicians; Occupational Tests; Perception Tests; *Spatial Ability; *Trainees
Availability: The Psychological Corp.; 555 Academic Ct., San Antonio, TX 78204-0952
Target Audience: 18-64
Notes: Time, 20; Items, 64

Designed to measure mechanical or artistic ability by measuring ability to visualize and manipulate objects in space. Four equivalent forms are available, forms AA and BB for hand scoring and forms MA and MB for machine scoring. A French-Canadian edition is available from Institut de Recherches Psychologiques, 34 ouest, rue Fleury, Montreal, Quebec H3L 1S9 Canada.

1656

Ship Destination Test. Christensen, Paul R.; Guilford, J.P. 1956
Descriptors: Adolescents; *Adults; *Aptitude Tests; Cognitive Ability; *Problem Solving; *Students; Timed Tests
Identifiers: Cognition of Semantic Systems; *Reasoning; *Reasoning Ability; SD; Structure of Intellect
Availability: Consulting Psychologists Press; 577 College Ave., Palo Alto, CA 94306
Target Audience: 14-64
Notes: Time, 15; Items, 48

Measures the factor known as general reasoning or cognition of semantic systems. The publisher refers to this test as a well-disguised arithmetic-reasoning test, which measures an ability important in the type of problem-solving which involves seeing interrelationships of variable or elements.

1659

Culture Fair Intelligence Test, Scale 1. Cattell, Raymond B.; Cattell, A.K.S.
Subtests: Substitution; Classification; Mazes; Selecting Named Objects; Following Directions; Wrong Pictures; Riddles; Similarities
Descriptors: Adolescents; *Adults; Children; Culture Fair Tests; *Elementary School Students; *Individual Testing; *Institutionalized Persons; *Intelligence; *Intelligence Tests; *Mental Retardation; Spatial Ability; Timed Tests
Identifiers: Cattell Culture Fair Intelligence Test; CFIT
Availability: Institute for Personality and Ability Testing; P.O. Box 188, Champaign, IL 61820
Target Audience: 4-64
Notes: Time, 22 approx.; Items, 96

Designed to measure individual intelligence. Only 4 of 8 subtests are culture fair. These include Substitution; Classification; Mazes; and Similarities. Scale 1 is to be used with children 4 to 8 years of age and retarded adults who are institutionalized.

1660

Culture Fair Intelligence Test, Scale 2. Cattell, Raymond B.; Cattell, A.K.S. 1961
Subtests: Series; Classifications; Matrices; Conditions; Topology

Descriptors: *Adults; *Culture Fair Tests; *Elementary School Students; Elementary Secondary Education; Individual Testing; *Intelligence; *Intelligence Tests; *Junior High School Students; *Non English Speaking; *Nonverbal Tests; *Spatial Ability; Timed Tests
Identifiers: Cattell Culture Fair Intelligence Test; CFIT
Availability: Institute for Personality and Ability Testing; P.O. Box 188, Champaign, IL 61820
Target Audience: 8-64
Notes: Time, 13 approx.; Items, 46

Designed to measure individual intelligence in a manner designed to reduce the influence of verbal fluency, cultural climate, and educational level. May be administered to groups or individuals. Scale consists of 4 subtests, involving different perceptual tasks. Forms A and B are available. May be used with children ages 8-14 and adults in average intelligence range. Scale 2 is appropriate for majority of subjects.

1661
Culture Fair Intelligence Test, Scale 3. Cattell, Raymond B.; Cattell, A.K.S. 1963
Subtests: Series; Classifications; Matrices; Conditions (Topology)
Descriptors: *Adults; *College Students; *Culture Fair Tests; Higher Education; High Schools; *High School Students; Individual Testing; *Intelligence; *Intelligence Tests; *Non English Speaking; Nonverbal Tests; *Spatial Ability; Timed Tests
Identifiers: Cattell Culture Fair Intelligence Test; CFIT
Availability: Institute for Personality and Ability Testing; P.O. Box 188, Champaign, IL 61820
Target Audience: 15-64
Notes: Time, 13 approx.; Items, 50

Designed to measure individual intelligence in a manner designed to reduce the influence of verbal fluency, cultural climate, and educational level. May be administered to groups or individuals. Scale consists of 4 subtests, involving different perceptual tasks. Forms A and B are available. Scale 3 is more difficult than Scales 1 or 2 and obtains a greater refinement in the higher intelligence ranges. Useful with high school and college students and adults of superior intelligence.

1668
Memory-for-Designs Test. Graham, Frances K.; Kendall, Barbara S. 1960
Descriptors: Adolescents; Adults; Children; Diagnostic Tests; *Neurological Impairments; *Perceptual Motor Coordination; *Screening Tests; *Short Term Memory
Identifiers: MFD
Availability: Psychological Test Specialists; P.O. Box 9229, Missoula, MT 59807
Target Audience: 8-60
Notes: Time, 10 approx.; Items, 15

Drawing test of perceptual motor coordination, which depends on immediate memory. Differentiates between groups of patients with brain disorders including those with focal and diffuse lesions. Useful as a screening device to identify patients with functionally based behavior disorders from those associated with brain injury. Subject is shown a series of 15 designs which he/she reproduces immediately from memory.

1676
Word Fluency. Christensen, Paul R.; Guilford, J.P. 1959
Descriptors: Adolescents; *Adults; *Cognitive Ability; *Cognitive Tests; Constructed Response; *Divergent Thinking; *Students; Timed Tests; *Verbal Ability; Verbal Tests
Identifiers: Christensen Guilford Fluency Tests; Divergent Production of Symbolic Units; Structure of Intellect; WF
Availability: Consulting Psychologists Press; 577 College Ave., Palo Alto, CA 94306
Target Audience: 12-64
Notes: Time, 4

Measures the factor known as divergent production of symbolic units. In this test the respondent is to produce as rapidly as possible words which fulfill specified symbolic (letter) properties. In other words, the test requires a rapid selection and production of words through an associational process based upon the structure of the words rather than upon their meanings.

1677
Ideational Fluency. Christensen, Paul R.; Guilford, J.P. 1957
Descriptors: Adolescents; *Adults; *Cognitive Ability; *Cognitive Tests; Constructed Response; *Divergent Thinking; *Students; Timed Tests; Verbal Ability; Verbal Tests
Identifiers: Christensen Guilford Fluency Tests; Divergent Production of Semantic Units; IF; *Reasoning Ability; Structure of Intellect

Availability: Consulting Psychologists Press; 577 College Ave., Palo Alto, CA 94306
Target Audience: 14-64
Notes: Time, 12

Measures the factor known as divergent production of semantic units, which is defined as the ability to produce with efficiency many ideas which fulfill meaningful specifications. One is to write down as quickly as possible ideas about a given topic; the emphasis is upon quantity rather than quality of the ideas expressed.

1678
Associational Fluency I. Christensen, Paul R.; Guilford, J.P. 1957
Descriptors: Adolescents; *Adults; Children; *Cognitive Style; *Cognitive Tests; *Divergent Thinking; *Semantics; *Students; Timed Tests; *Verbal Ability; Verbal Tests
Identifiers: Christensen Guilford Fluency Tests; Divergent Production of Semantic Relations
Availability: Consulting Psychologists Press; 577 College Ave., Palo Alto, CA 94306
Target Audience: 11-64
Notes: Time, 4; Items, 4

Designed to measure one factor of divergent production of semantic relations, which is defined as the ability to produce efficiently ideas bearing prescribed relations to other ideas or to produce alternative relations. The respondent is given a word and asked to list as many words as possible which are similar in meaning to the given word. Form A uses adjectives and Form B uses verbs.

1679
Expressional Fluency. Christensen, Paul R.; Guilford, J.P. 1958
Descriptors: Adolescents; *Adults; *Cognitive Ability; *Cognitive Tests; *Divergent Thinking; *Students; Timed Tests; Verbal Ability; Verbal Tests
Identifiers: Divergent Production of Semantic Systems; EF; Structure of Intellect
Availability: Consulting Psychologists Press; 577 College Ave., Palo Alto, CA 94306
Target Audience: 12-64
Notes: Time, 8; Items, 64

Measures the factor known as divergent production of semantic systems. The factor is defined as the ability to produce with efficiency appropriate verbal expressions of organized thought. The respondent is to write as many 4-word sentences as he or she can by using words which begin with the letters given in the test.

1680
Consequences. Christensen, Paul R.; And Others 1958
Subtests: Ideational Fluency; Originality
Descriptors: Adolescents; *Adults; *Cognitive Ability; *Cognitive Tests; *Creative Thinking; *Creativity Tests; *Students; Timed Tests; Verbal Ability; Verbal Tests
Identifiers: Divergent Production of Semantic Transformations; Divergent Production of Semantic Units; Structure of Intellect
Availability: Consulting Psychologists Press; 577 College Ave., Palo Alto, CA 94306
Target Audience: 12-64
Notes: Time, 10

Measures 2 factors: ideational fluency (divergent production of semantic units) and originality (divergent production of semantic transformations). Ideational fluency is defined as the ability to produce with efficiency many ideas which fulfill meaningful specifications. Originality is defined as the ability to give remotely associated ideas which are likely to demand the revisions of other ideas.

1681
Possible Jobs. Gershon, Arthur; Guilford, J.P. 1963
Descriptors: *Abstract Reasoning; Adolescents; *Adults; *Cognitive Ability; *Cognitive Tests; *Divergent Thinking; *Students; Timed Tests; Verbal Ability; Verbal Tests
Identifiers: Divergent Production of Semantic Implications; Structure of Intellect
Availability: Sheridan Psychological Services, Inc.; P.O. Box 6101, Orange, CA 92667
Target Audience: 12-64
Notes: Time, 10

Measures the factor known as divergent production of semantic implications, which means the ability to expand upon given information or to recommend alternative deductions or extensions.

1682
Making Objects. Gardner, Sheldon; And Others 1963
Descriptors: Adolescents; *Adults; *Cognitive Style; Constructed Response; Creative Thinking; *Creativity Tests; Nonverbal Tests; *Spatial Ability; *Students; Timed Tests; *Visual Measures; Visual Stimuli

Identifiers: Divergent Production of Figural Systems; MO
Availability: Sheridan Psychological Services, Inc.; P.O. Box 6101, Orange, CA 92667
Target Audience: 12-64
Notes: Time, 6

Measures the factor known as divergent production of figural systems, which might be called figural expressional fluency, or visual-figural expressional fluency. This test parallels those which measure expressional fluency in the verbal, i.e., semantic category. The respondent is given a group of very simple figural elements and instructed to construct specified objects by joining the figural elements together.

1683
Match Problems. Berger, Raymond M.; Guilford, J.P. 1963
Descriptors: Adolescents; *Adults; Cognitive Processes; *Creativity Tests; *Divergent Thinking; Nonverbal Tests; *Spatial Ability; *Students; Timed Tests; Visual Measures; *Visual Stimuli
Identifiers: Divergent Production of Figural Transformations; MP
Availability: Sheridan Psychological Services, Inc.; P.O. Box 6101, Orange, CA 92667
Target Audience: 12-64
Notes: Time, 14

Measures the factor known as divergent production of figural transformations; this factor was formerly known as adaptive flexibility, and represents the ability to revise conceptions of figures.

1684
Decorations. Gardner, Sheldon; And Others 1963
Descriptors: Adolescents; *Adults; Constructed Response; *Creativity; *Creativity Tests; *Divergent Thinking; Nonverbal Tests; *Pictorial Stimuli; *Students; Timed Tests; *Visual Measures
Identifiers: Divergent Production of Figural Implications
Availability: Sheridan Psychological Services, Inc.; P.O. Box 6101, Orange, CA 92667
Target Audience: 14-64
Notes: Time, 12

Measures the factor known as divergent production of figural implications which means the ability to add meaningful details to information given. The respondent is given outlines of well-known articles of furnishings and told to add decorative lines. The authors point out that artistic quality is not important, but figural ideas are important.

1719
Paragraph Completion Test. Schroder, Harold M. 1967
Descriptors: Adults; Cognitive Measurement; *Cognitive Style; *Concept Formation; *Projective Measures; Verbal Tests
Identifiers: Complex Behavioral Performance; TIM(A)
Availability: Tests in Microfiche; Test Collection, Educational Testing Service, Princeton, NJ 08541
Target Audience: Adults
Notes: Time, 15 approx.; Items, 7

Semi-projective device designed to provide a measure of the integrative component of conceptual complexity in adults. For less verbal populations, longer periods of time should be established or the test should be administered orally.

1722
The Lester Point Score Method for the Shaw Blocks Test. Lester, David 1965
Descriptors: Adolescents; Adults; Children; *Creativity; Culture Fair Tests; *Deafness; Elementary Secondary Education; *Illiteracy; *Individual Testing; *Intelligence; Intelligence Tests; Nonverbal Tests; *Performance Tests
Identifiers: Oral Testing; TIM(D)
Availability: Tests in Microfiche; Test Collection, Educational Testing Service, Princeton, NJ 08541
Target Audience: 8-65
Notes: Time, 12

A method for scoring the Shaw Block Test, a nonverbal measure of intelligence requiring the manipulation of blocks. The respondent (ages 8 and older) is told to arrange the blocks and to give a reason for placing them in that order. Respondent is to complete as many arrangements as possible in 12 minutes. Responses are divided into 5 classes: unique and objective, based on observation; unique and objective, based on guesswork; subjective series; groupings, nonsense sequences, analogies; and incoherent groupings.

1752
Decision-Style Inventory. Roskin, Rick 1975
Descriptors: *Administrators; Adults; *Decision Making Skills; Problem Solving; Rating Scales

Availability: University Associates; 8517 Production Ave., P.O. Box 26240, San Diego, CA 92126
Target Audience: Adults
Notes: Items, 10

Developed to increase manager's awareness of importance of flexibility in decision style. Decision making focuses on quality, as in mathematical models, or acceptance, as in behavioral models. This instrument is used to illustrate that focus of decision should be influenced by the nature of the problem. It is included in the 1975 Annual Handbook for Group Facilitators.

1759
PMA Readiness Level. Thurstone, Thelma Gwinn 1974
Subtests: Auditory Discrimination; Verbal Meaning; Perceptual Speed; Number Facility; Spatial Relations
Descriptors: *Academic Aptitude; *Grade 1; *Kindergarten Children; Learning Readiness; Primary Education; *School Readiness; School Readiness Tests
Identifiers: Test Batteries
Availability: Science Research Associates; 155 N. Wacker Dr., Chicago, IL 60606
Grade Level: K-1
Notes: Time, 60 approx.

Designed to assess mental factors associated with learning readiness. May be used to determine degree of maturity of ability in areas of auditory discrimination, verbal meaning, perceptual speed, number facility, and spatial relations which are indicators of child's readiness for academic instruction. Individual test booklets examine child's verbal facility, perceptual speed, number facility, and ability to perceive spatial relations.

1760
Computer Operator Aptitude Battery. Holloway, A. Joanne 1973
Subtests: Sequence Recognition; Format Checking; Logical Thinking
Descriptors: Adults; *Aptitude Tests; *Computers; Job Applicants; *Logical Thinking; *Occupational Tests; *Personnel Evaluation; Predictive Measurement; Programing
Identifiers: COAB; *Computer Operators
Availability: Science Research Associates; Business Programs Div., 155 N. Wacker Dr., Chicago, IL 60606
Target Audience: 18-64
Notes: Time, 45; Items, 37

Designed to measure aptitudes important to success in performing the computer operator job. Useful in evaluation of applicants. Also used to assess potential for learning computer programing.

1793
DIAL. Mardell-Czudnowski, Carol D.; Goldenberg, Dorothea S. 1975
Subtests: Gross Motor Skills; Fine Motor Skills; Concepts; Communication Skills
Descriptors: *Ability Identification; Concept Formation; Individual Testing; Language Skills; *Learning Disabilities; Observation; Performance Tests; *Preschool Children; Preschool Education; Psychomotor Skills; *Screening Tests; Special Education
Identifiers: Development Indicators for Assessment of Learning
Availability: Childcraft Education Corp.; 20 Kilmer Rd., Edison, NJ 08818
Target Audience: 2-5
Notes: Time, 30 approx.; Items, 28

A team-administered, individual observation for screening preschool children's gross motor, fine motor, concepts, and communication skills. The team should consist of a coordinator and 4 operators. Used to identify child who should be referred for diagnosis of special educational needs.

1810
School Readiness Test. Anderhalter, Oliver F. 1974
Subtests: Word Recognition; Identifying Letters; Visual Discrimination; Auditory Discrimination; Comprehension and Interpretation; Handwriting Readiness; Number Readiness
Descriptors: *Academic Ability; *Grade 1; *Kindergarten Children; *Learning Readiness; Primary Education; *School Readiness; *School Readiness Tests; Student Placement
Identifiers: Oral Testing; SRT
Availability: Scholastic Testing Service, Inc.; 480 Meyer Rd., P.O. Box 1056, Bensenville, IL 60106
Grade Level: K-1
Notes: Time, 60 approx.

Designed to measure learning readiness of students in late kindergarten or before the full third week of first grade. A Spanish manual of directions which translates all teacher's oral statements and directions to children into Spanish is available.

1814
American College Testing Program. American College Testing Program, Iowa City, IA, Research and Development Div. 1979
Subtests: English Usage; Mathematics Usage; Social Studies Reading; Natural Sciences Reading
Descriptors: *Academic Achievement; *Aptitude Tests; *College Bound Students; College Freshmen; Higher Education; High Schools; Predictive Measurement; Student Placement
Identifiers: ACT Assessment
Availability: ACT Publications; P.O. Box 168, Iowa City, IA 52240
Grade Level: 11-13
Notes: Time, 160 approx.; Items, 219

ACT Assessment Program includes student profile section plus a battery of tests of educational development. Predictor of academic success in college.

1824
Dental Admission Testing Program. American Dental Association, Chicago, IL
Subtests: Survey of Natural Sciences; Perceptual Ability; Reading Comprehension; Quantitative Reasoning
Descriptors: *Academic Ability; Academic Achievement; *Achievement Tests; Adults; *College Admission; *College Applicants; *College Entrance Examinations; *Dental Schools; Multiple Choice Tests; Occupational Tests; Timed Tests
Identifiers: American Association of Dental Schools; DAT; Dental Aptitude Testing Program
Availability: American Dental Association; Div. of Educational Measurements, 211 E. Chicago Ave., Chicago, IL 60611
Target Audience: Adults
Notes: Time, 240

A selection tool for dental school candidates which measures general academic ability, comprehension of scientific information and perceptual ability. Under continuous revision, thus the number of items and the exact testing time varies. Not distributed to individuals; given only at designated testing sites within the U.S. and Puerto Rico. Restricted.

1825
Dental Hygiene Aptitude Testing Program. American Dental Hygienists Association, Chicago, IL
Subtests: Numerical Ability; Science; Verbal; Study-Reading
Descriptors: Admission Criteria; Adults; *Aptitude Tests; *College Entrance Examinations; *Dental Hygienists; Higher Education; High Schools; *High School Seniors; Undergraduate Students
Availability: American Dental Hygienists Association; 444 N. Michigan Ave., Chicago, IL 60611
Grade Level: 12-14
Target Audience: Adults
Notes: Time, 330 approx.

Used as an admission test for many dental hygiene programs and is one factor considered by schools in evaluating candidates' qualifications. The test covers 4 basic areas: numerical ability, science, verbal, and study-reading.

1841
STS High School Placement Test. Scholastic Testing Service, Bensenville, IL 1963
Subtests: Verbal; Quantitative; Reading; Mathematics; Language
Descriptors: Academic Ability; Academic Achievement; Achievement Rating; *Achievement Tests; *Admission (School); Cognitive Ability; *Cognitive Tests; *Grouping (Instructional Purposes); Intelligence Quotient; Junior High Schools; *Junior High School Students; Mental Age; Student Evaluation; *Student Placement
Identifiers: *Academic Aptitude; HSPT; Proficiency Tests; STS Closed High School Placement Test; STS HSPT; STS Open High School Placement Test
Availability: Scholastic Testing Service; 480 Meyer Rd., Bensenville, IL 60106
Grade Level: 8-9
Notes: Time, 150; Items, 298

A testing program designed to aid in the selection and/or placement of high school students. May be used as a proficiency test or as part of a placement program. Comes in two forms: The Closed form (new each year) measures those ability and skills basic to the high school curriculum. The Open form is a reprint of the recent Closed form. Optional tests—Mechanical Aptitude, Science, and Catho-

lic Religion—are also available and take about 20 minutes each. Includes both cognitive skills (verbal and quantitative) and achievement in reading, math and language arts.

1946
Simile Interpretations. Christensen, Paul R.; And Others 1963
Descriptors: Adolescents; *Adults; *Cognitive Ability; *Cognitive Tests; *Divergent Thinking; *Students; Timed Tests; Verbal Ability; Verbal Tests
Identifiers: Divergent Production of Semantic Systems; *Similes; Structure of Intellect
Availability: Sheridan Psychological Services, Inc.; P.O. Box 6101, Orange, CA 92667
Target Audience: 14-64
Notes: Time, 6

Measures the factor known as divergent production of semantic systems; this factor is defined as the ability to produce with efficiency appropriate verbal expressions of organized thought. Incomplete sentences are given. The respondent is to complete each sentence by giving (for each simile) as many as possible different explanations.

1972
Plot Titles. Berger, Raymond M.; Guilford, J.P. 1963
Subtests: Ideational Fluency; Originality
Descriptors: Adolescents; *Adults; *Cognitive Ability; *Cognitive Tests; *Creative Thinking; *Creativity Tests; *Students; Timed Tests; Verbal Ability; Verbal Tests
Identifiers: Divergent Production of Semantic Transformations; Divergent Production of Semantic Units; Structure of Intellect
Availability: Sheridan Psychological Services, Inc.; P.O. Box 6101, Orange, CA 92667
Target Audience: 14-64
Notes: Time, 6

Measures 2 factors: ideational fluency (divergent production of semantic units) and originality (divergent production of semantic transformations). Ideational fluency is defined as the ability to produce with efficiency many ideas which fulfill meaningful specifications. In this test originality is determined by ability to produce with efficiency ideas of high quality with respect to the criterion of cleverness.

1988
Seeing Problems. Merrifield, Philip R.; Guilford, J.P. 1969
Descriptors: Adolescents; *Adults; *Cognitive Processes; *Cognitive Tests; *Predictive Measurement; *Students; Timed Tests
Identifiers: Cognition of Semantic Implications; Reasoning; *Reasoning Ability; SP; *Structure of Interest
Availability: Sheridan Psychological Services, Inc.; P.O. Box 6101, Orange, CA 92667
Target Audience: 12-64
Notes: Time, 4

Measures the factor known as cognition of semantic implications. This factor is defined as the ability to see implications of a meaningful type, which are used when having anticipations, being aware of consequences, and making predictions.

2001
Match Problems V. Merrifield, Philip R.; Guilford, J.P. 1963
Descriptors: Adolescents; *Adults; Cognitive Processes; Cognitive Tests; *Creativity Tests; *Divergent Thinking; Nonverbal Tests; *Spatial Ability; *Students; Timed Tests; Visual Measures; *Visual Stimuli
Identifiers: Divergent Production of Figural Transformations; MPV; Structure of Intellect
Availability: Sheridan Psychological Services, Inc.; P.O. Box 6101, Orange, CA 92667
Target Audience: 12-64
Notes: Time, 10

An alternative and shorter version of Match Problems (TC001683). Measures the factor known as divergent production of figural transformations, this factor formerly known as adaptive flexibility. This factor represents the ability to revise conceptions of figures. Measures the same factor but at a lower level of task complexity.

2035
Quick Word Test: Level I. Borgatta, Edgar F.; Corsini, Richard J. 1967
Descriptors: Adolescents; *Adults; *Cognitive Ability; Intelligence Tests; Screening Tests; Secondary Education; *Secondary School Students; *Verbal Ability
Identifiers: QWT
Availability: F.E. Research Publishers, Inc.; 115 N. Prospect Ave., Itasca, IL 60143
Grade Level: 7-12
Target Audience: 13-64
Notes: Time, 15 approx.; Items, 100

Designed for use as a rapid screening or assessment of general mental ability. May be used with students of secondary school age as well as adults of average intelligence. Four parallel forms are available. Rationale for instrument is the theory that word knowledge is one of best single indicators of mental ability.

2041
Quick Screening Scale of Mental Development. Banham, Katharine M. 1963
Subtests: Bodily Coordination; Manual Performance; Speech and Language; Listening Attention and Number; Play Interests
Descriptors: Behavior Rating Scales; *Children; *Cognitive Ability; Individual Testing; Infant Behavior; *Infants; *Intelligence; *Intelligence Tests; *Special Education
Identifiers: QSS
Availability: Psychometric Affiliates; P.O. Box 807, Murfreesboro, TN 37133
Target Audience: 0-10
Notes: Time, 30 approx.
Designed to provide a preliminary estimate of a child's level of mental development. Used for children ages 6 months to 10 years in clinics, hospitals, and special schools.

2047
Proverbs Test: Forms I, II, and III. Gorham, Donald R. 1956
Descriptors: *Abstract Reasoning; Adolescents; *Adults; *Cognitive Tests; Emotional Disturbances; Essay Tests; Higher Education; High Schools; *High School Students; Individual Testing; *Patients; Proverbs; Psychiatric Hospitals; Schizophrenia
Identifiers: Schizophrenic Patients; Verbal Reasoning
Availability: Psychological Test Specialists; P.O. Box 9229, Missoula, MT 59807
Target Audience: 16-64
Notes: Time, 30 approx.; Items, 12
Designed to measure verbal comprehension and abstract reasoning by requiring subjects to explain the meaning of several proverbs. May be used with hospitalized mental patients as well as nonhandicapped populations. Instrument is sensitive to temporary intellectual impairment associated with severe emotional disturbance or schizophrenic disorganization. Forms I, II, and III are equivalent and each is scaled for difficulty.

2048
Proverbs Test: Best Answer Form. Gorham, Donald R. 1956
Subtests: Abstract; Concrete
Descriptors: *Abstract Reasoning; *Adolescents; *Adults; *Children; *Cognitive Tests; *Elementary School Students; Emotional Disturbances; Higher Education; Intermediate Grades; Multiple Choice Tests; Proverbs; Schizophrenia; Secondary Education; Secondary School Students; Undergraduate Students
Identifiers: Schizophrenic Patients; Verbal Reasoning
Availability: Psychological Test Specialists; P.O. Box 9229, Missoula, MT 59807
Grade Level: 5-16
Target Audience: 10-64
Notes: Time, 40 approx.; Items, 40
Designed to measure verbal comprehension and abstract reasoning, or intelligence. Useful in clinical research and evaluation, screening and survey. Subject must select response which indicates meaning of given proverb. May be used with hospitalized mental patients, as well as non-handicapped populations.

2049
Subsumed Abilities Test—A Measure of Learning Efficiency. Sanders, Joseph R. 1963
Subtests: Demonstrated Abilities Score (DAS); Potential Abilities Score (PAS)
Descriptors: *Adults; Cognitive Ability; *Cognitive Processes; *Cognitive Tests; Nonverbal Tests; Secondary Education; *Secondary School Students; *Spatial Ability
Identifiers: SAT
Availability: Martin M. Bruce, Publishers; 50 Larchmont Rd., P.O. Box 248, Larchmont, NY 10538
Target Audience: 10-64
Notes: Time, 30 approx.; Items, 30
Designed to determine ability and willingness to learn or use previously learned visual symbol system. Measures ability to learn and use skills important in most learning processes. Valuable in academic, rehabilitation, and business assessment and selection. Success requires three hierarchical perceptual skills: recognition, abstraction, and conceptualization.

2065
Whisler Strategy Test. Whisler, Laurence 1959

Subtests: General Information; Drawings and Sketches; Checking and Proofreading; Specialized Information; Paths
Descriptors: *Administrators; Adults; *Competence; *Decision Making Skills; Managerial Occupations; *Occupational Tests; Problem Solving
Availability: Psychometric Affiliates; P.O. Box 807, Murfreesboro, TN 37133
Target Audience: 18-64
Notes: Time, 25; Items, 126
Designed to measure intelligent action in a business setting. Used to identify individuals as "risk-avoiders" or "plungers." Strategic ability is measured. Subject must demonstrate effectiveness in drawing on abilities and knowledge to demonstrate general competence.

2066
Pertinent Questions. Berger, Raymond M.; Guilford, J.P. 1960
Descriptors: Adolescents; *Adults; *Cognitive Processes; Cognitive Tests; *Predictive Measurement; *Students; Timed Tests
Identifiers: Cognition of Semantic Implications; PQ; Reasoning; *Reasoning Ability; *Structure of Intellect
Availability: Sheridan Psychological Services, Inc.; P.O. Box 6101, Orange, CA 92667
Target Audience: 14-64
Notes: Time, 12
Measures the factor known as cognition of semantic implications, or conceptual foresight. This factor is defined as the ability to see implications of a meaningful type, which are used when having anticipations, being aware of consequences, and making predictions.

2067
Gesell Developmental Schedules. Gesell, Arnold
Descriptors: *Adjustment (to Environment); Cognitive Tests; *Infant Behavior; *Infants; *Language Acquisition; *Motor Development; *Preschool Children; Social Behavior; Young Children
Availability: Programs for Education; 82 Park Ave., Flemington, NJ 08822
Target Audience: 0-6
Designed as a clinical measure of young child's mental growth. Assesses pre-school children from 4 weeks to 6 years of age.

2069
Closure Flexibility (Concealed Figures). Thurstone, L.L.; Jeffrey, T.E. 1965
Descriptors: Adults; *Cognitive Style; Personality Traits; Problem Solving; *Spatial Ability; Timed Tests; *Visual Measures
Identifiers: Mechanical Aptitude; Test Batteries; Thurstone Closure Flexibility Scale; Thurstone Primary Mental Abilities Schema
Availability: London House Management Consultants; 1550 Northwest Hwy., Park Ridge, IL 60068
Target Audience: 18-64
Notes: Time, 10; Items, 49
Designed to measure Thurstone's "second closure factor," ability to hold a configuration in mind despite distraction. Capacity to see a given configuration which is embedded in a larger more complex figure. May also be a measure of temperament and shows potential for differentiating among occupational groups in industry. Scores are positively related to measures of mechanical interest and experience and to measures of analytic reasoning.

2070
School Readiness Survey. Jordan, F.L.; Massey, James 1969
Subtests: Number Concepts; Discrimination of Form; Color Naming; Symbol Matching; Speaking Vocabulary; Listening Vocabulary; General Information; General Readiness Checklist
Descriptors: Individual Testing; *Parent Participation; *Preschool Children; Preschool Education; *School Readiness; *School Readiness Tests
Identifiers: SRS
Availability: Consulting Psychologists Press; 577 College Ave., Palo Alto, CA 94306
Target Audience: 4-6
Notes: Items, 96
Designed to assess child's readiness for kindergarten. May be administered by parent to furnish information about child's readiness for school. Should be given about 6 months prior to kindergarten entrance to permit parent to assist child in developing necessary skills. Parent's booklet includes suggestions for aiding growth in skill areas by constructive play at home.

2071
Closure Speed (Gestalt Completion). Thurstone, L.L.; Jeffrey, T.E. 1966

Descriptors: *Adults; *Cognitive Style; Personality Traits; *Spatial Ability; Timed Tests; *Visual Measures
Identifiers: *Gestalt Completion; Test Batteries; *Thurstone Primary Mental Abilities Schema
Availability: London House Management Consultants; 1550 Northwest Hwy., Park Ridge, IL 60068
Target Audience: 18-64
Notes: Time, 3; Items, 24
Designed to measure Thurstone's "first closure factor," the ability to perceive an apparently disorganized or unrelated group of parts as a meaningful whole. Basic perceptual capacity may manifest itself at a more general level as the conceptual ability to grasp and unify a complex situation. Performance on this test is associated with certain temperament characteristics. May be used with subjects of all ages; however, present usage is predominantly in industry and government organizations.

2072
Perceptual Speed (Identical Forms). Thurstone, L.L.; Jeffrey, J.E. 1959
Descriptors: Adults; *Cognitive Style; *Spatial Ability; Timed Tests; *Visual Measures
Identifiers: *Perceptual Speed; Test Batteries; Thurstone Primary Mental Abilities Schema
Availability: London House Management Consultants; 1550 Northwest Hwy., Park Ridge, IL 60068
Target Audience: 18-65
Notes: Time, 5; Items, 140
Designed to test perceptual speed, the ability to compare visual configurations and identify 2 figures as similar or identical. May be used with subjects of all ages from childhood through adult years. Present norms were based on industrial employees.

2073
Space Thinking (Flags). Thurstone, L.L.; Jeffrey, T.E. 1959
Descriptors: Adolescents; *Adults; Children; Cognitive Ability; *Cognitive Tests; *Secondary School Students; *Spatial Ability; *Visual Measures
Identifiers: Personnel Classification Series; Test Batteries
Availability: London House Management Consultants; 1550 Northwest Hwy., Park Ridge, IL 60068
Target Audience: 18-64
Notes: Time, 5; Items, 21
Designed to measure ability to visualize a rigid configuration when it is moved into different positions, or mechanical aptitude. Useful for identifying subjects with high mechanical interest and aptitude.

2077
Doppelt Mathematical Reasoning Test. Psychological Corp., San Antonio, TX
Descriptors: *College Entrance Examinations; *Graduate Study; Higher Education; Logical Thinking; *Mathematical Concepts
Identifiers: DMRT
Availability: The Psychological Corp.; 555 Academic Ct., San Antonio, TX 78204-0952
Grade Level: 16-20
Notes: Items, 50
Designed primarily as an aid in selecting students for admissions to graduate study. May also be used in selecting applicants for positions in business and industry that require mathematical reasoning. Test measures ability to perceive mathematical relationships. Substantive content of items is derived from secondary school mathematics content.

2078
Miller Analogies Test. Miller, W.S. 1981
Descriptors: *Academic Aptitude; Admission Criteria; *Adults; *Aptitude Tests; *College Graduates; *Graduate Students; Graduate Study; Higher Education; Personnel Selection
Identifiers: *Analogies; MAT
Availability: The Psychological Corp.; 555 Academic Ct., San Antonio, TX 78204-0952
Grade Level: 16-20
Notes: Time, 50; Items, 100
Designed to measure scholastic aptitude at graduate school level. May be used in business and government for selection of high level personnel. Analogy items are used to assess knowledge in vocabulary, literature, social sciences, chemistry, biology, physics, mathematics and general information. May be administered to groups or individuals. Instrument is restricted for distribution only to authorized personnel. Test is not administered in New York State.

2079
Minnesota Engineering Analogies Test. Dunnette, Marvin D. 1955

Descriptors: *Abstract Reasoning; Academic Achievement; *Achievement Tests; Adults; Cognitive Tests; College Seniors; *Engineering; Engineering Education; *Engineers; *Graduate Students; *Job Applicants; Job Placement; Logical Thinking; Multiple Choice Tests; Occupational Tests
Identifiers: *Analogies; MEAT
Availability: The Psychological Corp.; 555 Academic Ct., San Antonio, TX 78204-0952
Target Audience: Adults
Notes: Time, 45 approx.; Items, 50

A restricted test designed for the selection of graduate engineering students in universities and for placement of engineers in business, industry, and government. Measures achievement in the engineering field as well as mathematical reasoning ability. Given at designated testing centers, not distributed to individuals. Untimed.

2081
Thurstone Test of Mental Alertness. Thurstone, Thelma Gwinn; Thurstone, L.L. 1952
Subtests: Linguistic; Quantitative; Total
Descriptors: *Academic Achievement; *Adults; *Aptitude Tests; *Cognitive Ability; High Schools; *High School Students; Job Placement; Language Tests; *Personnel Evaluation; Predictive Measurement; Mathematics Tests
Identifiers: TMA
Availability: Science Research Associates; Business Programs Div., 155 N. Wacker Dr., Chicago, IL 60606
Grade Level: 9-12
Target Audience: Adults
Notes: Time, 20; Items, 126

Measures general mental ability. Aids in determining if an applicant has the capacity for learning the requirements of one job, if a person's ability to understand meets the requirements of one job better than another, and if a present employee can change easily to another job and learn it quickly. Recommended for use in selection, placement, and evaluation. Was also found to be predictive of scholastic success for high school students.

2082
Porteus Mazes: Vineland Revision. Porteus, Stanley D. 1959
Descriptors: *Adolescents; *Adults; Aptitude Tests; *Children; *Cognitive Ability; *Language Handicaps; *Nonverbal Tests; Psychological Evaluation; Spatial Ability
Identifiers: *Mazes; Porteus Maze Test (Original)
Availability: The Psychological Corp.; 555 Academic Ct., San Antonio, TX 78204-0952
Target Audience: 3-12; 14; 18-64
Notes: Time, 15 approx.; Items, 12

A nonlanguage test of mental ability used with verbally handicapped subjects in anthropological studies and in research on the effects of drugs and psychosurgery. Basic tests consisting of 12 mazes used in routine clinical examinations.

2083
Porteus Mazes: Extension. Porteus, Stanley D. 1965
Descriptors: *Adolescents; *Adults; Aptitude Tests; *Children; *Cognitive Ability; *Language Handicaps; *Nonverbal Tests; Psychological Evaluation; Spatial Ability
Identifiers: *Mazes; Porteus Maze Test; *Retesting
Availability: The Psychological Corp.; 555 Academic Ct., San Antonio, TX 78204-0952
Target Audience: 7-12; 14; 18-64
Notes: Time, 25 approx.; Items, 8

A nonlanguage test of mental ability used with verbally handicapped subjects in anthropological studies and in research on the effects of drugs and psychosurgery. Developed to provide for retesting a series of 8 mazes, each slightly more difficult than the 1 for matching year in the Vineland series. Should not be used as an initial test.

2084
Porteus Mazes: Supplement. Porteus, Stanley D. 1965
Descriptors: *Adolescents; *Adults; Aptitude Tests; *Children; *Cognitive Ability; *Language Handicaps; *Nonverbal Tests; Psychological Evaluation; Spatial Ability
Identifiers: *Mazes; Porteus Maze Test; *Retesting
Availability: The Psychological Corp.; 555 Academic Ct., San Antonio, TX 78204-0952
Target Audience: 7-12; 14; 18-64
Notes: Time, 25 approx.

A nonlanguage test of mental ability used with verbally handicapped subjects in anthropological studies and in research on the effects of drugs and psychosurgery. Developed to meet need for a third testing in certain clinical and research situations. For use with subjects who have previously been tested with both the Vineland Revision and the Extension. Mazes are slightly more difficult than those in extension series.

2090
Employee Aptitude Survey: Test 1—Verbal Comprehension. Grimsley, G.; And Others 1956
Descriptors: Adults; *Aptitude Tests; Career Choice; Career Counseling; College Students; Employees; Employment Potential; *High School Seniors; *Intelligence; *Job Applicants; Job Placement; Job Skills; Multiple Choice Tests; *Occupational Tests; Timed Tests; *Verbal Ability; Verbal Tests; Vocabulary Skills; Vocational Aptitude; Vocational Education
Identifiers: EAS; *Synonyms
Availability: Psychological Services; 3450 Wilshire Blvd. Ste. 1200, Los Angeles, CA 90010
Target Audience: 17-65
Notes: Time, 5; Items, 30

Used to measure the ability to use words in communications, thinking, and planning. The authors feel that 1) verbal ability is the most important single aspect of general intelligence; and 2) verbal comprehension is a basic element for executives, administrators, accountants, secretaries, stenographers, professional personnel, and the higher levels of office workers. Each item consists of 1 word in capital letters followed by 4 words in small letters. The respondent is to choose the word in small letters that means about the same as the word in capital letters. Scoring is the number right minus 1/3 the number wrong. Comes in 2 forms, A and B.

2091
Employee Aptitude Survey: Test 2—Numerical Ability. Grimsley, G.; And Others 1956
Subtests: Integers; Decimals; Fractions
Descriptors: Adults; *Aptitude Tests; Career Choice; Career Counseling; College Students; Computation; Employees; Employment Potential; *High School Seniors; *Job Applicants; Job Placement; Job Skills; Mathematics; *Mathematics Tests; Multiple Choice Tests; *Occupational Tests; Timed Tests; Vocational Aptitude; Vocational Education
Identifiers: EAS; *Mathematical Aptitude; Number Operations; Numerical Ability (Grimsley)
Availability: Psychological Services, Inc.; 3450 Wilshire Blvd., Ste. 1200, Los Angeles, CA 90010
Target Audience: 17-65
Notes: Time, 10; Items, 75

A battery of 3 tests: integers, decimal fractions, and common fractions; each is timed separately. Designed to measure skill in the 4 basic operations of addition, subtraction, multiplication, and division. Also measures the ability to work easily with numbers, and to do basic arithmetic fast and accurately. Executives, supervisory, engineering, accounting, sales, and many types of clerical jobs require good ability in this area. Comes in 2 forms: Form A (copyrighted 1952) and Form B (copyrighted 1956). Scoring is the number right minus 1/4 the wrong answers. Also available in Spanish.

2094
Employee Aptitude Survey: Test 5—Space Visualization. Grimsley, G.; And Others 1957
Descriptors: Adults; *Aptitude Tests; Career Choice; Career Counseling; Cognitive Ability; Cognitive Tests; College Students; Employees; Employment Potential; *High School Seniors; *Job Applicants; Job Placement; Job Skills; *Occupational Tests; *Spatial Ability; Timed Tests; Visual Measures; *Visual Perception; Vocational Aptitude; Vocational Education
Availability: Psychological Services, Inc.; 3450 Wilshire Blvd., Ste. 1200, Los Angeles, CA, 90010
Target Audience: 17-65
Notes: Time, 5; Items, 50

Designed to measure the ability to visualize forms in space and to manipulate these forms or objects mentally. The test taker is shown a group of numbered, piled blocks and must determine, for a specifically numbered block, how many other blocks touch it. The authors feel that this test is a requirement for drafting engineers, and personnel in technical positions. They refer to space personnel visualization as a strong component of mechanical aptitude. Comes in both English (Forms A and B) and in Spanish.

2095
Employee Aptitude Survey: Test 6—Numerical Reasoning. Grimsley, G.; And Others 1957
Descriptors: Adults; *Aptitude Tests; Career Choice; Career Counseling; Cognitive Ability; Cognitive Tests; College Students; Employees; Employment Potential; *High School Seniors; *Induction; Intelligence; *Job Applicants; Job Placement; Job Skills; *Occupational Tests; Mathematics Tests; *Serial Ordering; Timed Tests; Vocational Aptitude; Vocational Education
Identifiers: EAS; *Reasoning Ability
Availability: Psychological Services, Inc.; 3450 Wilshire Blvd., Ste. 1200, Los Angeles, CA 90010
Target Audience: 17-65
Notes: Time, 5; Items, 20

Designed to measure the ability to analyze logical relationships and to see the underlying principles of such relationships. This is also known as the process of inductive reasoning—making generalizations from specific instances. The authors feel that this ability is an important part of general intelligence and is a valuable ability in technical, supervisory, and executive positions. The test taker is given a series of numbers and determines what the next number will be. Scoring is the number right minus 1/4 the number wrong. Comes in 2 English forms (A and B) and in Spanish.

2096
Employee Aptitude Survey: Test 7—Verbal Reasoning (Revised). Grimsley, G.; And Others 1957
Descriptors: Adults; *Aptitude Tests; Career Choice; Career Counseling; Cognitive Ability; Cognitive Tests; College Students; *Decision Making Skills; Employees; Employment Potential; *High School Seniors; *Job Applicants; Job Placement; Job Skills; *Logical Thinking; *Occupational Tests; Timed Tests; Verbal Tests; Vocational Aptitude; Vocational Education
Identifiers: EAS; Reasoning; *Reasoning Ability
Availability: Psychological Services, Inc.; 3450 Wilshire Blvd., Ste. 1200, Los Angeles, CA 90010
Target Audience: 17-65
Notes: Time, 5; Items, 30

Designed to measure the ability to analyze verbally stated facts and to make valid judgments on the basis of the logical implications of such facts; and thus, the ability to analyze available information in order to make practical decisions. An important feature of this test is the measurement of the ability to determine whether the available facts provide sufficient information to draw a definite conclusion. The authors recommend this ability for executive, administrative, supervisory, scientific, accounting, and technical maintenance personnel. Scoring is the number of right answers minus 1/2 the wrong answers. Comes in 2 English forms (A and B) and in Spanish.

2097
Employee Aptitude Survey: Test 8—Word Fluency. Psychological Services, Inc., Los Angeles, CA 1953
Descriptors: Adults; *Aptitude Tests; Career Choice; Career Counseling; *Cognitive Ability; Cognitive Tests; College Students; Constructed Response; *Divergent Thinking; Employees; Employment Potential; *High School Seniors; *Job Applicants; Job Placement; Job Skills; *Occupational Tests; Timed Tests; *Verbal Ability; Verbal Tests; Vocational Aptitude; Vocational Education
Identifiers: EAS; SRA Primary Mental Abilities Test
Availability: Psychological Services, Inc.; 3450 Wilshire Blvd., Ste. 1200, Los Angeles, CA 90010
Target Audience: 17-65
Notes: Time, 5

Designed to measure the ability to express oneself rapidly, easily and with flexibility. Word fluency involves the speed and freedom of word usage as opposed to understanding verbal meanings. People who measure high in this ability are particularly good at expressing themselves and in finding the right word at the right time. The authors recommend this test for such professions as salespersons, journalists, field representatives, technical writers, receptionists, personal secretaries, and executives. The test taker is given a letter of the alphabet and asked to write as many words as possible that begin with that letter. An adaptation of the subtest with the same name is the SRA Primary Mental Abilities (Thurstone, 1947).

2099
Employee Aptitude Survey: Test 10—Symbolic Reasoning. Ruch, F.L.; Ford, J.S. 1957
Descriptors: *Abstract Reasoning; Adults; *Aptitude Tests; Career Choice; Career Counseling; Cognitive Ability; Cognitive Tests; College Students; Employees; Employment Potential; *High School Seniors; *Job Applicants; Job Placement; Job Skills; *Logical Thinking; *Occupational Tests; Timed Tests; Vocational Aptitude; Vocational Education
Identifiers: EAS; Reasoning Ability
Availability: Psychological Services, Inc.; 3450 Wilshire Blvd., Ste. 1200, Los Angeles, CA 90010
Target Audience: 17-65
Notes: Time, 5; Items, 30

Designed to measure the ability to think and reason abstractly, using symbols rather than words or numbers; to manipulate abstract symbols mentally; and to make judgments and decisions which are logical and valid. Each problem contains a statement and a conclusion and uses certain symbols such as the equal sign and mathematical symbols for greater than and smaller than, etc. The test taker determines whether the conclusion is definitely true, definitely false, or impossible to determine on the basis of the statement. Scoring is the number of right answers minus 1/2 the wrong answers. Comes in 2 English language forms, Forms A and B, and in Spanish.

2100
Ohio Penal Classification Test. Sell, DeWitt E. 1954
Subtests: Block Counting; Digit Symbol; Number Series; Memory Span for Objects
Descriptors: *Adult Literacy; Adults; Correctional Institutions; *Culture Fair Tests; Disadvantaged; *Illiteracy; Intelligence Quotient; *Intelligence Tests; Mental Age; *Nonverbal Ability; Nonverbal Tests; *Prisoners; Semiskilled Workers; Timed Tests; Unskilled Workers; Visual Stimuli
Identifiers: OPCT; Power Tests
Availability: Psychometric Affiliates; P.O. Box 807, Murfreesboro, TN 37133
Target Audience: Adults
Notes: Time, 15; Items, 230
A culture fair, timed instrument designed to measure the mental ability of inmates in penal institutions. Measures the spatial, perceptual, numerical, memory, and reasoning aspects of intellectual functioning. Though timed for 14.5 minutes, it is considered a power rather than speed test. Standardized on penal inmates and ninth grade males; considered applicable in industrial and other nonacademic situations. Available as Form F.

2101
Ohio Classification Test. Sell, DeWitt E.; And Others 1957
Subtests: Block Counting; Digit Symbol; Number Series; Memory Span
Descriptors: *Adult Literacy; Adults; *Culture Fair Tests; Disadvantaged; *Illiteracy; Intelligence Quotient; *Intelligence Tests; *Job Applicants; Mental Age; *Nonverbal Ability; Nonverbal Tests; Personnel; *Semiskilled Workers; Timed Tests; *Unskilled Workers; Visual Stimuli
Identifiers: OCT; Power Tests
Availability: Psychometric Affiliates; P.O. Box 807, Murfreesboro, TN 37133
Target Audience: Adults
Notes: Time, 15; Items, 230
A timed, culture fair, group administered adult intelligence test for the general adult population which minimizes verbal factors and which emphasizes power rather than speed. Basically the same test as the Ohio Penal Classification Test (TC002100); this slightly changed version includes industrial norms as well as some specific validation evidence from industry. Used for factory workers, sales and managerial applicants, middle management personnel, graduate engineers, scientific students, and technical students; the authors feel that it may be administered to near-illiterates or non-English language applicants.

2124
Portland Prognostic Test for Mathematics-Grades 8 and 9. Hayes, Ernest 1960
Subtests: Number Series; Arithmetic Comprehension
Descriptors: *Academically Gifted; Junior High Schools; *Junior High School Students; Predictive Measurement; Prognostic Tests; *Mathematics Tests; *Screening Tests; *Secondary School Mathematics; *Student Placement
Identifiers: *Reasoning Ability
Availability: Hayes Educational Test Laboratory; 7040 N. Portsmouth Ave., Portland, OR 97203
Grade Level: 8-9
Notes: Time, 35 approx.
Designed to discriminate between students ranging from average to high aptitude in mathematics. Placement instrument for junior high students from late grade 7 through grade 9. Used to identify students who can profit by taking college preparatory courses in mathematics. There are two forms, A and B, of the test for each grade level 8 and 9. Calculations were kept as simple as possible so as to maximize measurement of reasoning.

2128
Pictorial Test of Intelligence. French, Joseph L. 1964
Subtests: Picture Vocabulary; Form Discrimination; Information and Comprehension; Similarities; Size and Number; Immediate Recall
Descriptors: *Disabilities; Individual Testing; *Intelligence; *Intelligence Tests; *Pictorial Stimuli; Preschool Children; Preschool Education; Primary Education; Recall (Psychology); *Young Children
Identifiers: PTI
Availability: Riverside Publishing Co.; 8420 Bryn Mawr Ave., Chicago, IL 60631
Target Audience: 3-8
Notes: Time, 45 approx.; Items, 137

Designed to assess general intellectual level of nonhandicapped and handicapped children, ages 3 to 8. A shorter form is available for 3 and 4 year olds which reduces administration time by about 15 minutes.

2177
American Numerical Test. McCarty, John J. 1962
Descriptors: Adults; *Aptitude Tests; *Arithmetic; *Business Skills; Computation; Employees; Industrial Education; Mathematics Tests; *Students; Timed Tests; *Vocational Aptitude; Vocational Education
Identifiers: *Clerical Skills; Number Operations; *Numerical Ability
Availability: Psychometric Affiliates; P.O. Box 807, Murfreesboro, TN 37133
Target Audience: Adults
Notes: Time, 4; Items, 60
Designed to measure numerical alertness and adaptability. The author's theory is that quantification of aspects of reality requires not only a readiness to count but also a flexibility in shifting from one type of arithmetical operation to another. He feels that this type of continuous numerical adaptation and flexibility presents the formation of a static mechanical set. The test contains 60 addition, subtraction, multiplication, and division problems; each problem requires a different numerical operation from the preceding and succeeding problem.

2183
Veterinary Aptitude Test. Psychological Corp., San Antonio, TX
Subtests: Reading Comprehension; Quantitative Ability; Biology; Chemistry; Study Reading
Descriptors: Academic Ability; *Academic Aptitude; *Achievement Tests; Adults; Aptitude Tests; College Admission; *College Applicants; *College Entrance Examinations; Computation; Multiple Choice Tests; *Natural Sciences; Timed Tests; *Veterinary Medical Education
Identifiers: American Veterinary Medical Association; VAT
Availability: The Psychological Corp.; 555 Academic Ct., San Antonio, TX 78204-0952
Target Audience: Adults
Notes: Time, 240
Group administered entrance exam. Measures the scholastic aptitude and achievement of those candidates seeking admission to a college of veterinary medicine. Instrument revised as needed. Restricted distribution. Test given only at specifically designated testing centers throughout the U.S. Under constant revision; thus, the number of items and time varies (from 3-1/2 to 4 hours).

2199
Medical College Admission Test. Association of American Medical Colleges, Washington, DC 1977
Subtests: Chemistry; Science Problems; Skills Analysis; Reading; Skills Analysis; Quantitative; Biology; Physics
Descriptors: Achievement Tests; *Admission Criteria; *Biology; *Chemistry; *College Applicants; *College Entrance Examinations; *College Seniors; Higher Education; Knowledge Level; *Medical Schools; *Physics; *Problem Solving; Mathematics Tests; *Reading Comprehension; Science Tests; Undergraduate Students
Identifiers: MCAT
Availability: American College Testing Program; P.O. Box 414, Iowa City, IA 52243
Grade Level: 16
Notes: Time, 390; Items, 327
Designed to assess medical college applicant's knowledge of sciences, problem solving ability, and ability to comprehend, evaluate and utilize information presented in a narrative or numerical format. Examination is given in the spring and fall of each year at established test centers. It consists of 4 subtests which yield 6 scores. The subtests are science knowledge, science problems, skills analysis: reading, and skills analysis: quantitative. Items are updated periodically.

2201
PTI Verbal Test. Wesman, Alexander G. 1969
Descriptors: Adults; Apprenticeships; *Industrial Personnel; *Occupational Tests; Predictive Measurement; *Trainees; *Verbal Ability; Vocabulary
Identifiers: CAST; Controlled Administration of Standardized Tests; Personnel Tests for Industry
Availability: The Psychological Corp.; 555 Academic Ct., San Antonio, TX 78204-0952
Target Audience: 18-64
Notes: Time, 5; Items, 50
Designed to measure verbal competence, the ability to understand and use essential information in the performance of industrial jobs. May be used to estimate learning ability. Four equivalent forms are available. Tapes for administering the PTI in a "CAST" system are available. PTI verbal may be used in conjunction with PTI-Numerical (TC002202).

2202
PTI Numerical Test. Doppelt, Jerome E. 1969
Descriptors: Adults; Apprenticeships; *Industrial Personnel; *Mathematics Achievement; *Occupational Tests; Predictive Measurement; Mathematics Tests; *Trainees
Identifiers: CAST; Controlled Administration of Standardized Tests; Personnel Tests for Industry
Availability: The Psychological Corp.; 555 Academic Ct., San Antonio, TX 78204-0952
Target Audience: 18-64
Notes: Time, 20; Items, 30
Designed to measure numerical competence, ability to reason and apply numerical skills to practical computing and measuring problems encountered in shops and plants. Four equivalent forms are available. PTI-Numerical may be used in conjunction with PTI Verbal (TC002201). Tapes for administering the PTI in a "CAST" system are available.

2219
Academic Aptitude Tests (Verbal Intelligence). Kobal, Andrew; And Others 1943
Subtests: General Information: Academic and General Science; Mental Alertness: Comprehension; Mental Alertness: Judgment; Mental Alertness: Arithmetic Reasoning; Comprehension of Relations: Logical Selection; Comprehension of Relations: Analogies; Comprehension of Relations: Classification
Descriptors: *Abstract Reasoning; *Academic Aptitude; Adolescents; Adults; *Aptitude Tests; Career Counseling; Predictive Measurement; Students; Timed Tests; Verbal Tests
Identifiers: Acorn National Aptitude Tests
Availability: Psychometric Affiliates; P.O. Box 807, Murfreesboro, TN 37133
Target Audience: 12-64
Notes: Time, 40; Items, 140
To measure those mental aptitudes which are considered, according to the authors, to be the essential basics for academic and professional work, such as law, medicine, teaching, etc. May be used in secondary schools, colleges, and industry, though the emphasis is upon secondary school and first year college.

2267
Domino Test, D48 Form. Anstey, E.; And Others 1962
Descriptors: Adolescents; Adult Literacy; Adults; Children; *Culture Fair Tests; *Illiteracy; Intelligence Quotient; *Intelligence Tests; Mental Age; *Nonverbal Ability; Nonverbal Tests; Timed Tests; *Visual Stimuli
Identifiers: British Army Dominoes Test; D48 Test; Dominoes Test; Group Test 100
Availability: Consulting Psychologists Press; 577 College Ave., Palo Alto, CA 94306
Target Audience: 10-64
Notes: Time, 25; Items, 44
Timed, group administered, nonverbal, cross-cultural instrument that measures the "g" or general factor in intelligence. Based upon the British Army Dominoes Test and Group 100. Each item contains a number of dominoes with a black domino. The subject is to determine the number of dots appropriate for each half of the blank domino. Each item (group of dominoes) depicts a principle of progression. First developed in 1943 by Anstey and Illing for the British War Office; later, various revisions were developed. French and Italian adaptations were prepared in the 1940s and this American version was first published in the U.S. in 1962. The Manual for the U.S. edition prepared by John D. Black. Experimental and research edition.

2308
Survey of Object Visualization. Miller, Daniel R. 1970
Descriptors: Adults; Aptitude Tests; *Perception Tests; *Spatial Ability; *Technical Occupations
Identifiers: SOV
Availability: Psychological Services; 3450 Wilshire Blvd., Ste. 1200, Los Angeles, CA 90010
Target Audience: 18-64
Notes: Time, 25; Items, 44
Designed to measure aptitude for solving problems in perceptual recognition of an object's appearance in altered position or shape. Ability to perceive spatial relationships is usually required in technically oriented positions.

2322
Bayley Scales of Infant Development. Bayley, Nancy 1969
Subtests: Mental Scale; Motor Scale
Descriptors: *Behavior Rating Scales; *Cognitive Ability; Infants; *Psychomotor Skills
Identifiers: BSID
Availability: The Psychological Corp.; 555 Academic Ct., San Antonio, TX 78204-0952
Target Audience: 0-2
Notes: Time, 45 approx.

Mental and motor scales for the assessment of early mental and psychomotor development of babies and young children up to 2.5 years of age. The Infant Behavior Record provides for ratings of qualitative aspects of infant behavior and for overall evaluation.

2376
Shipley Institute of Living Scale for Measuring Intellectual Impairment. Shipley, W.C. 1940
Subtests: Vocabulary Test; Abstraction Test
Descriptors: *Abstract Reasoning; *Adults;
  *Cognitive Ability; *Cognitive Tests;
  *Elementary School Students; Elementary Secondary Education; Higher Education;
  *Neurological Impairments; *Patients;
  *Psychiatric Hospitals; *Secondary School Students; *Undergraduate Students; Vocabulary
Identifiers: Psychiatric Patients
Availability: Western Psychological Services;
  12031 Wilshire Blvd., Los Angeles, CA 90025
Grade Level: 4-16
Target Audience: 9-64
Notes: Time, 20 approx.

Designed to measure intellectual ability and impairment. Useful in detecting mild degrees of intellectual impairment in individuals of normal original intelligence. May be administered to individuals or groups. Impairment is determined by the extent to which the individual's abstract thinking falls short of his or her vocabulary. This deficit is expressed in the Conceptual Quotient (C.Q.).

2399
Leiter International Performance Scale. Leiter, Russell Graydon 1966
Descriptors: *Adolescents; *Adults; *Children; Culture Fair Tests; Disabilities; Disadvantaged;
  Hearing Impairments; Individual Testing;
  *Intelligence; *Intelligence Tests; Neurological Impairments; *Nonverbal Tests; Preschool Children; Spatial Ability
Identifiers: LIPS
Availability: Stoelting Co.; 620 Wheat Ln., Wood Dale, IL 60191
Target Audience: 2-64

Nonverbal intelligence test designed for ages 2 through adult. Does not require speech by examiner or subject. Suitable for use with mentally retarded through intellectually gifted subjects. Binet-type year scale has 4 tests at each year-level from Year II through Year XVI, and 6 tests at Year XVIII. Examination is begun with the first test in the year level which is 2 year levels below that of the subject's estimated mental age.

2403
Wilson Driver Selection Test. Wilson, Clark L. 1971
Subtests: Visual Attention; Depth Visualization;
  Recognition of Simple Detail; Recognition of Complex Detail; Eye-Hand Coordination;
  Steadiness; Biographical Information
Descriptors: Adults; Aptitude Tests; Eye Hand Coordination; *Job Applicants; *Occupational Tests; *Personnel Selection; *Spatial Ability; Visual Perception
Identifiers: *Driver Performance; *Drivers
Availability: Martin M. Bruce, Publishers; 50 Larchmont Rd., P.O. Box 248, Larchmont, NY 10538
Target Audience: 18-64
Notes: Time, 30 approx.; Items, 420

Designed to screen driver applicants with the aim of reducing accidents. Measures certain aspects of basic aptitudes which, if present to an adequate degree in a vehicle operator, reduce the risk of operator-caused accidents.

2425
Kit of Selected Distraction Tests. Cognitive Tests, Brooklyn, N.Y. 1962
Subtests: Distracting Contexts Test (16);
  Arithmetic Operations Test C (24); Distracting Contexts Test 2A (13); Distracting Context Test 2B (13); Cancellation Test C (2)
Descriptors: Adults; *Cognitive Measurement;
  Higher Education
Identifiers: *Distraction; *Distraction Tests;
  TIM(A)
Availability: Tests in Microfiche; Test Collection, Educational Testing Service, Princeton, NJ 08541
Grade Level: 13-16
Target Audience: Adults
Notes: Items, 68

Contains a series of 6 cognitive tests developed for an experimental study of distraction. Each of the distraction situations involves the location or manipulation of visual objects (figures, letters, or numbers) which are in some manner surrounded or obscured by a background of irrelevant objects. Some scores are based on time needed to complete the item.

2428
Quick Test. Ammons, R.B.; Ammons, C.H. 1958
Descriptors: Adolescents; Adults; Children;
  *Disabilities; Individual Testing; *Intelligence;
  *Intelligence Tests; Mental Retardation; Preschool Children; *Screening Tests
Identifiers: QT
Availability: Psychological Test Specialists; P.O. Box 9229, Missoula, MT 59807
Target Audience: 2-64
Notes: Time, 10 approx.; Items, 50

Designed to estimate general level of intellectual ability in a brief time. Words are defined nonverbally as examinee selects appropriate drawings. Assesses intelligence levels from 2 years to superior adult. May be used with any subject able to see the drawings, hear or read word items, and indicate yes-no. Requires no reading, writing or speaking. Useful with severely handicapped individuals and as screening procedure with mentally retarded subjects.

2451
Kasanin-Hanfmann Concept Formation Test.
Kasanin, Jacob; Hanfmann, Eugenia
Descriptors: *Abstract Reasoning; *Adolescents;
  *Adults; *Children; Classification; Cognitive Tests; *Concept Formation; *Educationally Disadvantaged; Patients; *Performance Tests;
  *Psychosis
Identifiers: Blocks; Vigotsky Test
Availability: Stoelting Co.; 620 Wheat Ln., Wood Dale, IL 60191
Target Audience: 3-64
Notes: Items, 22

Designed to measure ability to think in abstract concepts. Subject must find common factor in a set of 22 blocks of different colors, shapes, and sizes. Useful with children, disadvantaged adults and special populations.

2503
Group Diagnostic Reading Aptitude and Achievement Tests, Intermediate Form. Monroe, Marion; Sherman, Eva Edith 1966
Subtests: Paragraph Understanding; Speed; Word Discrimination; Arithmetic Computation; Spelling; Letter Memory; Form Memory; Discrimination and Orientation; Copying Text; Crossing Out Letters; Vocabulary
Descriptors: *Academic Aptitude; *Achievement Tests; *Aptitude Tests; *Computation; Elementary Education; *Elementary School Students;
  Junior High Schools; *Junior High School Students; *Reading Achievement; Spelling
Availability: C.H. Nevins Printing Co.; 311 Bryn Mawr Island, Bayshore Gardens, Bradenton, FL 33505
Grade Level: 3-9
Notes: Items, 390

Designed to measure achievement and aptitude of students in grades 3 through 9. Yields educational, word discrimination, and aptitude data percentile scores.

2523
Purdue Creativity Test. Lawshe, C.H.; Harris, Douglas H. 1957
Descriptors: Ability Identification; Adults;
  *Aptitude Tests; *College Students; *Creative Thinking; *Creativity; Creativity Tests; Employment Qualifications; *Engineering; Engineering Education; *Engineers; Occupational Tests; Talent Identification; Timed Tests; Verbal Tests;
  Vocational Aptitude
Identifiers: Purdue Personnel Tests
Availability: University Book Store; 360 State St., W. Lafayette, IN 47906
Target Audience: 20-64
Notes: Time, 40; Items, 20

Designed to measure flexibility and fluency in the creative thinking of engineers and engineering students, e.g., identification of design engineers who demonstrate creative ability in the designs they produce, and in the identification of research and development engineers whose abilities include the production of new ideas. The subject is shown 1 or 2 figures and asked to list possible uses. Available in Forms G and H. Sale of test is restricted to industrial personnel departments and psychologists using tests for instruction or vocational guidance.

2585
Otis-Lennon Mental Ability Test, Level I, Primary. Otis, Arthur S.; Lennon, Roger T. 1967
Descriptors: *Abstract Reasoning; *Academic Aptitude; Aptitude Tests; *Cognitive Ability; Cognitive Measurement; *Intelligence Tests; Kindergarten; *Kindergarten Children; Large Type Materials; Pictorial Stimuli; Primary Education; Visual Impairments
Identifiers: OLMAT; Oral Testing; *Reasoning Ability; Verbal Comprehension; Verbal Reasoning

Availability: The Psychological Corp.; 555 Academic Ct., San Antonio, TX 78204-0952
Grade Level: K
Notes: Time, 30 approx.; Items, 55

Designed to provide assessment of general mental ability, or scholastic aptitude. Parallel Forms J and K are available at each level. Two parts of test should be administered in separate sittings. No reading is required by examinee. Level I is designed for use with pupils in the last half of kindergarten. Each test item is presented orally by the examiner. Samples mental processes of classification, following directions, quantitative reasoning, and comprehension of verbal concepts. Available in large-type print for visually impaired subjects from American Printing House for the Blind, 1839 Frankfort Ave., Louisville, KY 40206.

2586
Otis-Lennon Mental Ability Test, Level II, Primary. Otis, Arthur S.; Lennon, Roger T. 1967
Descriptors: Abstract Reasoning; *Academic Aptitude; Aptitude Tests; *Cognitive Ability; Cognitive Measurement; Elementary School Students; *Grade 1; *Intelligence Tests; Large Type Materials; Pictorial Stimuli; Primary Education; Visual Impairments
Identifiers: OLMAT; Oral Testing; *Reasoning Ability; Verbal Comprehension; Verbal Reasoning
Availability: The Psychological Corp.; 555 Academic Ct., San Antonio, TX 78204-0952
Grade Level: 1
Notes: Time, 35 approx.; Items, 55

Designed to provide assessment of general mental ability, or scholastic aptitude. Parallel Forms J and K are available at each level. Two parts of test should be administered in 2 sittings separated by a brief rest period. Each test item is presented orally by the examiner and requires no reading by the examinee. Primary Level II is designed for students in the first half of grade 1. The content is identical to Primary Level I (TC002585), only the method of hand-scoring differs. Instrument samples mental processes of classification, following directions, quantitative reasoning, and comprehension of verbal concepts. Available in large-type print for visually impaired subjects from American Printing House for the Blind, 1839 Frankfort Ave., Louisville, KY 40206.

2587
Otis-Lennon Mental Ability Test, Level I, Elementary. Otis, Arthur S.; Lennon, Roger T. 1967
Descriptors: Abstract Reasoning; *Academic Aptitude; Aptitude Tests; *Cognitive Ability; Cognitive Measurement; *Elementary School Students; Grade 1; Grade 2; Grade 3; *Intelligence Tests; Large Type Materials; Pictorial Stimuli; Primary Education; Visual Impairments
Identifiers: Analogical Reasoning; OLMAT; Oral Testing; *Reasoning Ability; Verbal Comprehension; Verbal Reasoning
Availability: The Psychological Corp.; 555 Academic Ct., San Antonio, TX 78204-0952
Grade Level: 1-3
Notes: Time, 60 approx.; Items, 80

Designed to provide assessment of general mental ability, or scholastic aptitude. Parallel Forms J and K are available. This 3-part test should be administered in 2 separate sittings. Elementary Level I is designed for students in the last half of first grade through the end of grade 3. May be used in early grade 4 with pupils who are experiencing reading difficulties. Pictorial items sample the mental processes of classification, following directions, quantitative reasoning, comprehension of verbal concepts, and reasoning by analogy. No reading is required by examinee. Available in large-type print for visually impaired subjects from American Printing House for the Blind, 1839 Frankfort Ave., Louisville, KY 40206.

2588
Otis-Lennon Mental Ability Test, Level II, Elementary. Otis, Arthur S.; Lennon, Roger T. 1967
Descriptors: *Abstract Reasoning; *Academic Aptitude; Aptitude Tests; *Cognitive Ability; Cognitive Measurement; Cognitive Processes;
  *Elementary School Students; Grade 4; Grade 5;
  Grade 6; *Intelligence Tests; Intermediate Grades; Large Type Materials; Visual Impairments
Identifiers: Analogical Reasoning; OLMAT;
  *Reasoning Ability; Verbal Comprehension;
  Verbal Reasoning
Availability: The Psychological Corp.; 555 Academic Ct., San Antonio, TX 78204-0952
Grade Level: 4-6
Notes: Time, 50 approx.; Items, 80

Designed to provide assessment of general mental ability, or scholastic aptitude. Parallel Forms J and K are available at each level. Elementary Level II is designed for use with students in grades 4 through 6. Items are verbal and nonverbal in nature and are arranged in spiral omnibus form. Available in large-type print for visually impaired subjects from American Printing House for the Blind, 1839 Frankfort Ave., Louisville, KY 40206.

2589
Otis-Lennon Mental Ability Test, Intermediate Level. Otis, Arthur S.; Lennon, Roger T. 1967
Descriptors: *Abstract Reasoning; *Academic Aptitude; Aptitude Tests; *Cognitive Ability; Cognitive Measurement; Cognitive Processes; *Intelligence Tests; Junior High Schools; *Junior High School Students; Large Type Materials; Visual Impairments
Identifiers: Analogical Reasoning; OLMAT; *Reasoning Ability; Verbal Comprehension; Verbal Reasoning
Availability: The Psychological Corp.; 555 Academic Ct., San Antonio, TX 78204-0952
Grade Level: 7-9
Notes: Time, 50 approx.; Items, 80
Designed to provide assessment of general mental ability, or scholastic aptitude. Parallel Forms J and K are available at each level. Intermediate Level is recommended for use with students in grades 7 through 9. Items are verbal and nonverbal in nature and are arranged in spiral omnibus form. Available in large-type print for visually impaired subjects from American Printing House for the Blind, 1839 Frankfort Ave., Louisville, KY 40206.

2590
Otis-Lennon Mental Ability Test, Advanced Level. Otis, Arthur S.; Lennon, Roger T. 1967
Descriptors: *Abstract Reasoning; *Academic Aptitude; Aptitude Tests; *Cognitive Ability; Cognitive Measurement; Cognitive Processes; High Schools; *High School Students; *Intelligence Tests; Large Type Materials; Visual Impairments
Identifiers: Analogical Reasoning; OLMAT; *Reasoning Ability; Verbal Comprehension; Verbal Reasoning
Availability: The Psychological Corp.; 555 Academic Ct., San Antonio, TX 78204-0952
Grade Level: 10-12
Notes: Time, 50 approx.; Items, 80
Designed to provide assessment of general mental ability, or scholastic aptitude. Parallel Forms J and K are available at each level. Advanced Level is recommended for use with students in grades 10 through 12. Items are verbal and nonverbal in nature and are arranged in spiral omnibus form. Available in large-type print for visually impaired subjects from American Printing House for the Blind, 1839 Frankfort Ave., Louisville, KY 40206.

2621
Embedded Figures Test. Witkin, Herman A. 1950
Descriptors: *Adolescents; *Adults; *Children; *Cognitive Measurement; *Cognitive Style; Individual Testing; *Perception Tests; Field Dependence Independence
Identifiers: EFT; *Figure Ground; Gestalt Psychology
Availability: Consulting Psychologists Press; 577 College Ave., Palo Alto, CA 94036
Target Audience: 10-64
Notes: Items, 24
An individually administered, perceptual test in which the subject locates a previously seen simple figure within a larger complex figure which has been organized to obscure or embed the simple figure. In addition to serving as indicator of cognitive functioning and cognitive style, tests have been used in assessment studies relating to analytic ability in other tasks, social behavior, body concept, preferred defense mechanisms, and other processes.

2632
An Abstraction Test for Use with Cerebral Palsied Children. Irwin, Orvis C.; Hammill, Donald D. 1964
Descriptors: *Abstract Reasoning; Adolescents; *Cerebral Palsy; Children; Cognitive Tests; *Disabilities; *Elementary School Students; Elementary Secondary Education; Individual Testing; Neurological Impairments; Secondary School Students
Availability: Cerebral Palsy Review; v25 n4, Jul-Aug 1964
Target Audience: 6-17
Notes: Items, 25
Designed to assess ability of cerebral palsied children. Measures levels of abstraction and categorization. Parallel Forms X and Y are available.

2637
Iowa Algebra Aptitude Test: Third Edition. Greene, H.A.; Sabers, Darrell 1969
Subtests: Sequences; Lessons; Open Phrases; Dependence and Variation
Descriptors: Academic Aptitude; *Algebra; *Aptitude Tests; *Mathematics Tests; Secondary Education; *Secondary School Students; Timed Tests

Identifiers: IAAT
Availability: Bureau of Educational Research and Service, The University of Iowa; W. 325 Seashore Hall, Iowa City, IA 52242
Grade Level: 8-12
Notes: Time, 40; Items, 80
Designed to predict success of students in elementary algebra course.

2694
Inter-American Series: Test of General Ability, Preschool Level. Manuel, Herschel T. 1966
Subtests: Oral Vocabulary; Number; Association; Classification
Descriptors: *Academic Aptitude; *Aptitude Tests; *Cognitive Ability; Cognitive Tests; *Individual Testing; Language Acquisition; Number Concepts; *Preschool Children; Preschool Education; *Spanish; Spatial Ability
Identifiers: GAPDE; HGPDEs; Test Batteries
Availability: Guidance Testing Associates; P.O. Box 28096, San Antonio, TX 78228
Target Audience: 4-5
Notes: Time, 50 approx.; Items, 80
Subtests in oral vocabulary and number yield a Verbal-Numerical score. Subtests in association and classification yield a nonverbal score. Tests are individually administered in 2 testing sessions on different days. No oral response is required. Designed to provide an estimate of the ability to do academic work. Two forms are available in English and Spanish parallel editions.

2750
Cree Questionnaire. Thurstone, Thelma Gwinn; Mellinger, John 1959
Descriptors: *Adults; *Creative Thinking; Creativity; *Creativity Tests; Questionnaires; Work Attitudes
Availability: London House Management Consultants; 1550 Northwest Hwy., Park Ridge, IL 60068
Target Audience: 18-64
Notes: Time, 15 approx.; Items, 145
Designed to measure an individual's overall creative potential and the extent to which subject's behavior resembles that of identified creative individuals. Subject should not be told this is a test of creativity. Alternate Forms A and B may be used to discourage copying in large group test administrations and memorization when retesting is required.

2751
Intuitive Mechanics (Weights and Pulleys) Level B. Thurstone, L.L.; Jeffrey, T.E. 1959
Descriptors: Adults; *Aptitude Tests; Career Counseling; *Mechanical Skills; *Occupational Tests; Personnel Selection; Spatial Ability; Vocational Interests
Identifiers: *Mechanical Aptitude
Availability: London House Management Consultants, Inc.; 1550 Northwest Hwy., Park Ridge IL 60068
Target Audience: Adults
Notes: Time, 3
Designed to measure the ability to understand mechanical relationships; to visualize internal movement in a mechanical system. For use in identifying individuals with high mechanical interest and ability. May be used for vocational counseling or selection. A group or individual test.

2752
Mechanical Movements. Thurstone, L.L.; Jeffrey, T.E. 1963
Descriptors: Adults; *Aptitude Tests; Career Counseling; *Mechanical Skills; *Occupational Tests; Personnel Selection; Spatial Ability; Vocational Interests
Identifiers: *Mechanical Aptitude
Availability: London House Management Consultants, Inc.; 1550 Northwest Hwy., Park Ridge IL 60068
Target Audience: Adults
Notes: Time, 14
Designed to measure mechanical comprehension as indicated by the ability to visualize a mechanical system where there is internal movement or displacement of its parts. For identification of individuals with high mechanical interest and ability, either as an employee selection device or for vocational counseling. May be group or individually administered.

2753
Understanding Communication. Thurstone, Thelma Gwinn 1956
Descriptors: Achievement Tests; Adolescents; *Adults; Cognitive Processes; Communication Skills; Multiple Choice Tests; *Receptive Language; *Secondary School Students; Timed Tests; Verbal Ability; *Verbal Communication; *Verbal Learning; *Verbal Tests

Availability: London House Management Consultants; 1550 Northwest Hwy., Park Ridge, IL 60068
Target Audience: 12-65
Notes: Time, 15; Items, 40
Designed to measure comprehension of verbal material using the format of short sentences and phrases. Involves one's understanding of the sentences/phrases and their implications. The author feels that the test involves the solving of a problem presented in verbal form; and not the recognition of the answer, nor memory, speed, or simply vocabulary.

2754
Word Fluency Test. Corsini, Raymond J. 1957
Descriptors: Adults; *Communication Skills; *Constructed Response; *Employees; *Job Applicants; Job Skills; *Language Proficiency; Occupational Tests; Timed Tests; *Verbal Ability; Verbal Tests; Vocational Aptitude
Identifiers: WFT
Availability: London House Management Consultants; 1550 Northwest Hwy., Park Ridge, IL 60068
Target Audience: Adults
Notes: Time, 10; Items, 80
Timed, group administered instrument which measures only the speed or quickness of verbal associations. It does not measure verbal comprehension; the author feels that limited vocabulary does not have a significant bearing on the score. The subject is to write as many words as possible that fit into the named categories and that begin with the letters given. Used principally with those occupations in which accurate, rapid communication is important.

2755
Verbal Reasoning. Corsini, Raymond J.; Renck, Richard 1958
Descriptors: Adults; *Aptitude Tests; *Deduction; *Job Applicants; Job Skills; Occupational Tests; *Personnel; Personnel Selection; Problem Solving; Timed Tests; Verbal Tests; *Vocational Aptitude
Identifiers: *Reasoning; *Reasoning Ability
Availability: London House Management Consultants; 1550 Northwest Hwy., Park Ridge, IL 60068
Target Audience: Adults
Notes: Time, 15; Items, 12
Timed instrument to measure one's ability to reason logically from written material. The authors recommend its use in conjunction with an instrument which measures nonverbal reasoning ability. Each item describes the activities of 4 brothers; the 3-part answer must be deduced from the description. Used with various groups of employees: unskilled and semi-skilled, foremen, salespersons, engineers, chemists, executives, middle management, and white-collar executives.

2876
SRA Short Tests of Clerical Ability. Palormo, Jean Maier 1959
Subtests: Arithmetic; Business Vocabulary; Checking; Coding; Oral and Written Directions; Filing; Language
Descriptors: Adults; *Aptitude Tests; *Business Skills; Clerical Occupations; *Clerical Workers; Employment Potential; Job Applicants; Multiple Choice Tests; *Occupational Tests; Timed Tests; Vocational Aptitude
Identifiers: *Clerical Aptitude; *Clerical Skills; Maier (Jean); Short Tests of Clerical Ability; STCA
Availability: Science Research Associates, Inc.; 155 N. Wacker Dr., Chicago, IL 60606
Target Audience: Adults
Notes: Time, 39; Items, 347
A battery of 7 short tests, designed to measure the aptitudes or abilities that are important for the performance of various common office duties. The various tests may be used individually or in any combination. Measures the ability to solve simple arithmetic problems; to solve problems using percentages, decimals, and fractions; to check names and numbers accurately; to memorize rote material rapidly and to code this information correctly; to take useful notes, remember oral instructions, and to follow written directions; to alphabetize rapidly and to demonstrate good filing ability; to detect errors in spelling, grammar, punctuation, and capitalization; and general verbal ability and knowledge of business terms. Each test is timed separately.

2877
SRA Clerical Aptitudes. Richardson, Bellows, Henry and Co. Inc., New York, NY 1947
Subtests: Office Vocabulary; Office Arithmetic; Office Checking

Descriptors: Adults; Arithmetic; Clerical Occupations; *Clerical Workers; Computation; *Job Applicants; *Mathematics Achievement; Multiple Choice Tests; *Occupational Tests; Timed Tests; *Verbal Ability; Vocabulary; Vocational Aptitude
Identifiers: *Clerical Aptitude; *Clerical Checking; Clerical Skills
Availability: Science Research Associates, Inc.; 155 N. Wacker Dr., Chicago, IL 60606
Target Audience: 17-64
Notes: Time, 25; Items, 88

Measures 3 office job aptitudes: 1) the ability to understand words and ideas; 2) the ability to handle figures easily and accurately, and 3) the ability to recognize likenesses and differences rapidly. Used as an aid to the selection of office personnel.

2893
Space Relations (Paper Puzzles). Thurstone, L.L.; Jeffrey, T.E. 1956
Descriptors: Adults; *Aptitude Tests; *Mechanical Skills; *Occupational Tests; *Personnel Selection; *Spatial Ability; *Vocational Evaluation
Identifiers: Closure Flexibility; Embedded Figures; *Mechanical Aptitude
Availability: London House; 1550 Northwest Hwy., Park Ridge, IL 60068
Target Audience: Adults
Notes: Time, 9; Items, 30

Designed for use in identifying individuals with high mechanical interest and ability for vocational counseling and selection of personnel. It may be group or individually administered and is hand-scored. Measures closure flexibility, the ability to keep a configuration in mind that is hidden or embedded in a larger drawing. Also measures the "second space factor," the ability to visualize a diagram or drawing in which there is internal movement of parts.

2912
Ohio State University Psychological Exam, Form 26. Toops, Herbert A. 1959
Subtests: Synonyms and Antomyns; Analogies; Reading Comprehension
Descriptors: Academic Ability; *Aptitude Tests; *College Students; Higher Education; High Schools; *High School Students; *Intelligence; Reading Comprehension; Verbal Ability
Identifiers: Analogy; Antonyms; Synonyms
Availability: Wilbur L. Layton; 3604 Ross Rd., Ames, IA 50010
Grade Level: 9-16
Notes: Items, 150

Designed to assess academic aptitude and intelligence.

3034
Screening Test of Academic Readiness. Ahr, A. Edward 1966
Subtests: Picture Vocabulary; Letters; Picture Completion; Copying; Picture Description; Human Figure Drawing; Relationships; Numbers
Descriptors: Academic Ability; *Cognitive Development; Cognitive Measurement; Diagnostic Tests; *Preschool Children; Preschool Education; *School Readiness; *School Readiness Tests; *Screening Tests
Identifiers: Oral Testing; STAR
Availability: Priority Innovations; P.O. Box 792, Skokie, IL 60067
Target Audience: 2-5
Notes: Time, 60 approx.; Items, 50

Designed to assess readiness of preschool and kindergarten age children. STAR highlights strengths and weaknesses related to school readiness. Total score of 8 subtests may be converted to a deviation I.Q. score. Test should be administered in 2 sessions with a rest or activity period separating the sessions.

3035
Academic Aptitude Tests (Non-Verbal Intelligence). Kobal, Andrew; And Others 1957
Subtests: Spatial Relations; Comprehension of Physical Relations; Graphic Relations
Descriptors: *Abstract Reasoning; *Academic Aptitude; Adolescents; Adults; *Aptitude Tests; Career Counseling; Nonverbal Tests; Pictorial Stimuli; Predictive Measurement; Technical Occupations
Availability: Psychometric Affiliates; P.O. Box 807, Murfreesboro, TN 37133
Target Audience: 12-65
Notes: Time, 26 approx.; Items, 58

Designed to evaluate that aspect of intelligence related to aptitude for abstract academic work required in mathematical, engineering, designing, and other physical sciences.

3103
Early Detection Inventory. McGahan, F.E.; McGahan, Carolyn 1967
Subtests: Social-Emotional Behavior Responses; School Readiness Tasks; Motor Performance; Personal History
Descriptors: *Biographical Inventories; Child Development; Cognitive Development; Concept Formation; Developmental Disabilities; Educational Diagnosis; Individual Testing; *Learning Problems; *Maturity Tests; Motor Development; Observation; Perceptual Development; Perceptual Motor Coordination; Performance Tests; *Preschool Children; School Readiness; *School Readiness Tests; *Screening Tests; Young Children
Identifiers: EDI
Availability: N.E.T. Educational Services, Inc.; 3065 Clark Ln., Paris, TX 75460
Target Audience: 4-6
Notes: Items, 101

Screening instrument used to identify potential academic underachievers by evaluating a child's social, emotional, physical, and intellectual development. The social and emotional development are based upon observation; the physical development upon information supplied by parents; and the intellectual development upon the child's performance of motor tasks. Individually administered. While designed for preschool children, it is useful with children in ungraded primary classes and transitional classes.

3257
Goldstein-Scheerer Tests of Abstract and Concrete Thinking. Goldstein, Kurt; Scheerer, Martin 1951
Subtests: Cube; Color Sort; Object Sort; Color Form Sort; Stick
Descriptors: *Abstract Reasoning; Adults; Clinical Diagnosis; *Cognitive Style; Cognitive Tests; *Diagnostic Tests; *Individual Testing; Logical Thinking; *Neurological Impairments; *Patients; *Performance Tests; Problem Solving
Identifiers: Gelb Goldstein Color Sorting Test; Gelb Goldstein Weigl Scheerer Object Sorting Test; Goldstein Scheerer Cube Test; Goldstein Scheerer Stick Test; *Reasoning Ability; Test Batteries; Weigl Goldstein Scheerer Color Form Sorting Test
Availability: The Psychological Corp.; 555 Academic Ct., San Antonio, TX 78204-0952
Target Audience: Adults

Group of instruments to evaluate abstract and concrete reasoning of brain-damaged patients. Requires the use of specialized test materials or common household items. Copyright date of instruments varies from 1941 to 1951. Individually administered performance tests.

3289
Measurement of Skills. Clarke, Walter V.; And Others
Subtests: Skill with Vocabulary; Skill with Numbers; Skill with Shape; Speed and Accuracy; Skill in Orientation; Skill in Thinking; Skill with Memory; Skill with Fingers; Skill in Typing; Skill with Words; Test of Color Vision
Descriptors: *Academic Aptitude; Adolescents; Adults; *Aptitude Tests; *Cognitive Ability; *Employees; *Job Applicants; *Job Placement; Job Skills; Occupational Tests; Secondary School Students; Vocational Aptitude
Identifiers: Activity Vector Analysis; MOS; MOS Battery; Test Batteries
Availability: Walter V. Clarke Associates; 2 Jackson Walkway, Providence, RI 02903
Target Audience: 13-64
Notes: Time, 49; Items, 1200

Measures fundamental skills and basic thinking processes that appear to represent major abilities needed for successful performance on many jobs. Designed primarily as an aid in selection and classification of business and industrial employees. Also recommended as indicators of junior high and high school student strengths and weaknesses for an array of major abilities. Most subtests are timed for 5 minutes. Administration and interpretation restricted to psychologists or other people trained in psychological test administration. Restricted distribution.

3325
General Clerical Test. Psychological Corp., San Antonio, TX 1972
Subtests: Clerical; Numerical; Verbal
Descriptors: Adults; Alphabetizing Skills; *Aptitude Tests; *Clerical Workers; *Job Applicants; Language Skills; *Occupational Tests; Office Practice; Verbal Ability
Identifiers: *Clerical Aptitude; GCT
Availability: The Psychological Corp.; 555 Academic Ct., San Antonio, TX 78204-0952
Target Audience: Adults
Notes: Time, 49

Designed to measure aptitudes important in clerical work. All tests are timed, emphasizing speed and accuracy. Two editions are available. Regular edition consists of a single booklet which includes all subtests. Other edition is composed of 2 partial booklets. Booklet A includes items for clerical and numerical subscores. Booklet B includes items for verbal subscore. Contents of both editions are identical.

3329
Porch Index of Communicative Ability. Porch, Bruce E. 1981
Subtests: Writes Function in Sentences; Writes Names of Objects; Names (Spelling Dictated); Names (Copies); Geometric Forms; Demonstrates Function; Demonstrates Function (Ordered); Describes Function; Names Objects; Sentence Completion; Imitative Naming; Reads Function and Position; Reads Name and Position; Points to Object by Function; Points to Objects by Name; Matching Pictures with Object; Matching Objects with Object
Descriptors: *Adults; *Aphasia; Cognitive Development; *Cognitive Style; Communication (Thought Transfer); *Communication Disorders; Individual Development; *Individual Testing; Perception Tests; *Perceptual Handicaps; Perceptual Motor Learning; Performance Tests; Sensory Integration; Verbal Tests; Visual Stimuli
Identifiers: Oral Tests; PICA
Availability: Consulting Psychologists Press; 577 College Ave., Palo Alto, CA 94306
Target Audience: Adults

Designed to quantify and describe certain verbal, gestural, and graphic abilities in aphasic adults. Individually administered. Requires much training by the test administrator. Approximately 40 hours of work with the manual, etc., is suggested. Requires the use of specialized sets of cards, various items found in any home, etc.

3352
Flanagan Industrial Tests. Flanagan, John C. 1960
Descriptors: Adults; *Aptitude Tests; *Employees; *Job Applicants; Job Placement; *Job Skills; Occupational Tests; *Predictive Measurement
Identifiers: FIT; Self Administered Tests; Test Batteries
Availability: Science Research Associates; 155 N. Wacker Dr., Chicago, IL 60606
Target Audience: 18-64

Measures 18 aptitudes or functions important to supervisory, technical, office, skilled, and entry-level job demands. Separate booklets for each skill. Personnel administrator may choose specific tests appropriate to each job. The tests are Arithmetic (60 items, 5 minutes); Assembly (20 items, 5 minutes); Components (30 items, 5 minutes); Coordination (16 items, 5 minutes); Electronics (30 items, 15 minutes); Expression (30 items, 5 minutes); Ingenuity (20 items, 15 minutes); Inspection (36 items, 5 minutes); Judgment and Comprehension (26 items, 15 minutes); Mathematics & Reasoning (30 items, 15 minutes); Mechanics (30 items, 15 minutes); Memory (10 minutes); Patterns (15 items, 5 minutes); Planning (20 items, 15 minutes); Precision (60 items, 5 minutes); Scales (60 items, 5 minutes); Tables (60 items, 5 minutes) and Vocabulary (72 items, 15 minutes). Special adaptation of Flanagan Aptitude Classification Tests (FACT) for industry and business.

3418
Advanced Mental Alertness Test. Human Resources, International, Cleveland, OH 1957
Descriptors: Adults; *College Graduates; *Intelligence; *Intelligence Tests; *Recruitment; Timed Tests; Vocabulary
Identifiers: AMA; Speededness (Tests)
Availability: Human Resources, International; Test Service Div., 3 Commerce Park Square, 24100 Chagrin Blvd., Ste. 270, Cleveland, OH 44122
Target Audience: Adults
Notes: Time, 8; Items, 50

Designed to provide a quick measure of overall mental ability of potential employees. Items are difficult and designed for use with college graduates. Useful in college recruitment programs. Six types of items include numerical reasoning, vocabulary, scrambled sentences, number series, verbal analogies, and common knowledge.

3424
The School Readiness Checklist. Austin, John J. 1972
Descriptors: Check Lists; Childhood Interests; Cognitive Development; Developmental Stages; *Kindergarten Children; *Parent Participation; Primary Education; *School Readiness; Spanish
Availability: Research Concepts; 1368 E. Airport Rd., Muskegon, MI 49444
Grade Level: K
Notes: Items, 43

Checklist filled out by parents to help determine if a child is ready to enter school. Questions deal with child's growth and age; general activity related to growth; practical skills; remembering; understanding; general knowledge; attitudes and interests. Checklist is also available in Spanish.

3506
Curtis Object Completion Test. Curtis, James W. 1961
Descriptors: Adults; Aptitude Tests; Drafting; *Job Applicants; *Screening Tests; Skilled Workers; *Spatial Ability; *Visualization
Identifiers: Curtis Spatial Tests; *Mechanical Aptitude
Availability: Psychometric Affiliates; P.O. Box 807, Murfreesboro, TN 37133
Target Audience: 18-64
Notes: Time, 1; Items, 24
Designed to measure 2-dimensional perceptual efficiency. Suitable as part of battery to screen manual operators. May be administered to groups or individuals.

3507
Curtis Space—Form Test. Curtis, James W. 1960
Descriptors: Adults; Aptitude Tests; *Job Applicants; *Screening Tests; *Skilled Workers; *Spatial Ability; *Visualization
Identifiers: Curtis Spatial Tests; *Mechanical Aptitude
Availability: Psychometric Affiliates; P.O. Box 807, Murfreesboro, TN 37133
Target Audience: 18-64
Notes: Time, 1; Items, 16
Designed to measure 3-dimensional perceptual efficiency. Suitable as part of a battery to screen manual operators. May be administered to individuals or groups.

3511
Wechsler Memory Scale. Wechsler, David; Stone, C. P. 1974
Subtests: Personal and Current Information; Orientation; Mental Control; Logical Memory; Memory Span; Visual Reproduction; Associate Learning
Descriptors: Adults; *Clinical Diagnosis; *Cognitive Processes; Cognitive Tests; *Individual Testing; *Neurological Impairments; *Patients; *Short Term Memory
Identifiers: *Psychiatric Patients; WMS
Availability: The Psychological Corp.; 555 Academic Ct., San Antonio, TX 78204-0952
Target Audience: Adults
Notes: Time, 15 approx.
Individually administered instrument to measure adult memory. Used to detect memory defects in certain specific organic brain damage and with certain psychiatric patients, senile and other subjects. Available as Form I or II.

3515
General Information Survey. Gough, Harrison G. 1956
Descriptors: Adults; *Aptitude Tests; *Cognitive Ability; Cognitive Tests; *Intelligence; *Knowledge Level; *Leadership Qualities; Multiple Choice Tests; *Qualifications
Identifiers: GIS
Availability: Prof. Harrison G. Gough; Institute of Personality Assessment and Research, Dept. of Psychology, University of California, 2240 Piedmont Ave., Berkeley, CA 94720
Target Audience: Adults
Notes: Time, 30 approx.; Items, 70
Designed to measure one's range and breadth of knowledge while avoiding the conventional instrument's emphasis upon formal, intellectual, academic-acquired knowledge. Emphasizes cultural lore, folk knowledge, music, athletics, recreation, etc. Based upon the theory that the breadth of interests and range of knowledge are among the important factors which seem to characterize individuals of exceptional leadership and executive talent. Available in Forms A and B. Distribution of tests restricted.

3586
Fireman Entrance Aptitude Tests. McCann Associates, Inc., Huntington Valley, PA
Subtests: Verbal and Quantitative Learning Ability; Interest, Common Sense, Mechanical Aptitude
Descriptors: Adults; Aptitude Tests; *Fire Fighters; *Job Applicants; *Occupational Tests; *Vocational Aptitude
Availability: McCann Associates; 2755 Philmont Ave., Huntingdon Valley, PA 19006
Target Audience: 18-64
Designed to assess applicant's aptitude for firefighting and ability to learn firefighting skills quickly. Form 62A consists of 100 questions. Form 70A consists of 130 questions. Form 70A is easier and intended for users who are legally required to use 70 percent as minimum passing score. Tests are restricted and may be purchased only by Civil Service Commissions or other competent municipal officials.

3589
Police Officer Examination. McCann Associates, Inc., Huntington Valley, PA 1980
Descriptors: Adults; Aptitude Tests; *Job Applicants; *Occupational Tests; *Police; *Vocational Aptitude
Availability: McCann Associates; 2755 Philmont Ave., Huntington Valley, PA 19006
Target Audience: 18-64
Form 100 consists of 100 questions and requires 160 minutes. Areas assessed include observational ability; ability to exercise judgment and common sense; interest in police work; ability to exercise judgment in map reading and dealing with people; ability to read and comprehend police text material; and reasoning ability. Form 125 consists of 125 questions and requires 185 minutes. Areas assessed include observational ability; police aptitude; police public relations; and police judgment. Tests are restricted and are rented, not sold. User must return used and unused question booklets to publisher. Tests are available only to Civil Service Commissions and other responsible officials.

3609
Inventory II. Stevens, Thurow and Associates, Chicago, IL 1956
Descriptors: Adults; *Aptitude Tests; *Cognitive Ability; Cognitive Processes; Cognitive Tests; *Employees; Employment Potential; *Job Applicants; *Job Placement; Problem Solving; Timed Tests; *Vocational Aptitude
Identifiers: Inventory No II; Mental Ability Test (Inventory II)
Availability: Stevens, Thurow and Associates; 100 W. Monroe St., Chicago, IL 60603
Target Audience: Adults
Notes: Time, 15; Items, 50
Timed test designed to measure mental ability and alertness of literate persons over the age of 16 regardless of their level of education. Includes problem solving involving word meanings and verbally constructed conceptual relations, manipulations of number relationships, reasoning, and visualizing abilities. The authors feel that persons who obtain a high score on this instrument learn more quickly, have superior powers of conceptual manipulation and analysis, have a higher natural adaptability to new situations, and are able to solve a greater variety of problems. This instrument also used as a subtest for some of Stevens, Thurow and Associates' other occupational tests.

3610
Primary Mechanical Ability Tests. Hazelhurst, J.H. 1950
Subtests: Crosses; Bolts; Tools; Missing Lines
Descriptors: Ability Identification; Adults; Apprenticeship; *Aptitude Tests; *Employees; Hand Tools; *Job Applicants; Job Placement; *Job Skills; Occupational Tests; *Spatial Ability; Timed Tests; Trade and Industrial Education; *Visualization; Vocational Aptitude
Identifiers: *Mechanical Aptitude
Availability: Stevens, Thurow and Associates; 100 W. Monroe St., Chicago, IL 60603
Target Audience: Adults
Notes: Time, 22; Items, 185
Timed, group administered test that measures mechanical aptitude. Measures size discrimination, space perception, tool knowledge and visualization. Used for broadly classifying shop employees, placement of apprentices in appropriate mechanical trades, and for classifying individual differences among non-related factors which may appear to be related to mechanical aptitude.

3810
Leiter Adult Intelligence Scale. Leiter, Russell Graydon 1964
Subtests: Similarities-Differences; Digits Forward and Backward; Recall; Pathways; Stencil Design; Painted Cubes
Descriptors: *Adults; *Disabilities; Individual Testing; *Intelligence; *Intelligence Quotient; *Intelligence Tests; Psychological Evaluation; Verbal Ability
Identifiers: LAIS
Availability: Stoelting Co.; 620 Wheat Ln., Wood Dale, IL 60191
Target Audience: 18-64
Notes: Time, 40 approx.
Designed to measure general adult intelligence. Sensitive to deficits in cognitive, psycho-physical, or social areas; therefore, provides a measure of functional efficiency for psychologically disabled or superior subjects. Yield verbal, performance, and full scale intelligence quotient.

3818
Cornell Critical Thinking Test, Level X, and Z, Experimental Edition. Ennis, Robert H.; Millman, Jason 1961
Descriptors: Cognitive Processes; *Cognitive Tests; *Critical Thinking; Higher Education; Secondary Education; *Secondary School Students; *Undergraduate Students

Identifiers: Cornell Critical Thinking Test; Self Administered Tests
Availability: Illinois Thinking Project; University of Illinois, 1310 S. Sixth St., Champaign, IL 61820
Grade Level: 7-16
Notes: Time, 50 approx.
Developed to assess ability in several aspects of critical thinking, the reasonable assessment of statements. Level X is suitable for grades 7-12, Level Z for grades 13-16. Level X has 72 test items. Level Z has 52 items.

3832
Spelling and Word Meaning Test. Richardson, Bellows, Henry and Co., Washington, DC 1957
Subtests: Spelling; Word Meaning
Descriptors: *Achievement Tests; Adolescents; Adults; Business Education; Clerical Occupations; *Clerical Workers; Employment Potential; *High School Students; *Job Applicants; Job Skills; Office Occupations; *Spelling; Timed Tests; *Verbal Ability; Verbal Tests; *Vocabulary; Vocational Aptitude; Vocational Education
Identifiers: Antonyms; Clerical Aptitude; *Clerical Skills; RBH Spelling and Word Meaning Test; RBH Word Meaning Test; Synonyms; Word Meaning Test
Availability: Richardson, Bellows, Henry and Co., Inc.; 1140 Connecticut Ave., N.W., Washington, DC 20036
Target Audience: 16-65
Notes: Time, 10; Items, 120
Designed as a quick measure of the respondent's spelling ability and vocabulary. Actually 2 tests bound in a single booklet. The Spelling Test consists of 60 commonly misspelled words; the respondent is to determine whether the word is spelled correctly. The Word Meaning Test consists of 60 antonyms or synonyms, each pair expressed in a sentence. The respondent is to determine whether the statement made is right or wrong. Used as a quick measure of verbal ability for clerical and general office positions; also used by business education high school juniors and seniors.

3834
Vocabulary Test. Richardson, Bellows, Henry and Co., Washington, DC 1948
Descriptors: Adults; *Clerical Occupations; *Clerical Workers; Employment Potential; *Job Applicants; Job Skills; *Occupational Tests; Personnel Evaluation; Screening Tests; Semantics; Timed Tests; *Verbal Ability; Verbal Tests; Vocabulary; Vocational Aptitude
Identifiers: Antonyms; *Clerical Aptitude; Clerical Skills; RBH Vocabulary Test; *Synonyms
Availability: Richardson, Bellows, Henry and Co., Inc.; 1140 Connecticut Ave., N.W., Washington, DC 20036
Target Audience: Adults
Notes: Time, 5; Items, 64
Short, steeply scaled test designed to measure a person's ability to understand words. In each item 2 words are given; the respondent must decide whether the words mean the same, are opposite in meaning or neither the same or opposite. According to authors used successfully in the screening and selection of applicants for a variety of clerical positions.

3839
Test of Non-Verbal Reasoning, Long Form. Richardson, Bellows, Henry and Co., Washington, DC 1963
Descriptors: *Abstract Reasoning; *Adults; *Concept Formation; *Culture Fair Tests; *Educationally Disadvantaged; Intelligence Tests; Job Applicants; *Nonverbal Tests; *Skilled Workers
Identifiers: RBH Nonverbal Reasoning Test Long Form
Availability: Richardson, Bellows, Henry and Co., Inc.; 1140 Connecticut Ave., N.W., Washington, DC 20036
Target Audience: 18-64
Notes: Time, 15; Items, 45
A nonverbal and nonlanguage test of abstract reasoning and intelligence. Useful for low educational level personnel in the United States and foreign countries. Has also been useful with technical and managerial personnel with a high level of education. Examinee need not read English, but must read numbers to record answers properly. May be used as part of a test battery for industrial personnel for whom language presents a problem.

3840
Test of Learning Ability. Richardson, Bellows, Henry and Co., Washington, DC 1947
Subtests: Vocabulary; Block Counting; Arithmetic

Descriptors: Adults; Aptitude Tests; *Arithmetic; *Cognitive Ability; Cognitive Tests; *Employees; *Intelligence; *Job Applicants; Job Placement; Multiple Choice Tests; Occupational Tests; Screening Tests; *Spatial Ability; Timed Tests; *Verbal Ability; Verbal Tests; Vocational Aptitude
Identifiers: RBH Test of Learning Ability
Availability: Richardson, Bellows, Henry and Co.; 1140 Connecticut Ave., N.W., Washington, D.C. 20036
Target Audience: Adults
Notes: Time, 15; Items, 54

Designed to measure 3 major components of intelligence: vocabulary comprehension, arithmetic reasoning, and ability to perceive spatial relations. Used by personnel departments in a variety of screening, selection, placement, and promotion situations. Comes in 2 forms: Form S and Form T. Restricted distribution.

3842
Three Dimensional Space Test. Richardson, Bellows, Henry and Co., Washington, DC 1950
Descriptors: Adults; *Aptitude Tests; *Job Applicants; *Job Placement; Job Skills; Occupational Tests; Personnel Selection; *Spatial Ability; Timed Tests; *Visualization; *Visual Measures; Visual Perception; Visual Stimuli; *Vocational Aptitude
Identifiers: TDS
Availability: Richardson, Bellows, Henry and Co.; 1140 Connecticut Ave., N.W., Washington, D.C. 20036
Target Audience: Adults
Notes: Time, 10; Items, 10

Timed, group administered instrument to measure one's ability to visualize in space. In each item, 2 figures are given: a flattened out pattern with folding lines indicated and the finished box. The subject is to match the numbers given on each pattern with the appropriate letters on the finished box. Used as an aid in selection of industrial personnel, mainly mechanical and drafting type of occupations.

3853
Test of Learning Ability, Form ST. Richardson, Bellows, Henry and Co., Washington, DC 1957
Subtests: Vocabulary; Block Counting; Arithmetic
Descriptors: Adults; Aptitude Tests; *Arithmetic; *Cognitive Ability; Cognitive Tests; *Employees; *Intelligence; *Job Applicants; Job Placement; Multiple Choice Tests; Occupational Tests; Screening Tests; *Spatial Ability; Timed Tests; *Verbal Ability; Verbal Tests; Vocational Aptitude
Availability: Richardson, Bellows, Henry and Co.; 1140 Connecticut Ave., N.W., Washington, DC 20036
Target Audience: Adults
Notes: Time, 25; Items, 108

A combination of Test of Learning Ability, Form S and Form T (TC003840), designed to better accommodate and delimit the lower and upper ability levels. Basically measures the intelligence level of employees such as managers, executives, technical and professional employees, sales employees and applicants, clerical employees, industrial supervisors, mechanical and operating employees, etc. Used by personnel departments in a variety of screening, selection, placement, and promotion situations. Restricted distribution.

3854
Test of Non-Verbal Reasoning, Short Form. Richardson, Bellows, Henry and Co., Washington, DC 1963
Descriptors: *Abstract Reasoning; *Adults; *Concept Formation; *Culture Fair Tests; *Educationally Disadvantaged; Intelligence Tests; *Job Applicants; *Nonverbal Tests; *Unskilled Workers
Identifiers: RBH Non Verbal Reasoning Test Short Form
Availability: Richardson, Bellows, Henry and Co., Inc.; 1140 Connecticut Ave., N.W., Washington, DC 20036
Target Audience: 18-64
Notes: Time, 10; Items, 24

A shortened version of RBH Non-Verbal Reasoning Test (TC003839) designed for inclusion in industrial test batteries. Test measures intelligence and abstract reasoning ability with nonverbal and nonlanguage items. A mirror image of the test is available for cultures where reading is done from right to left.

4042
Stutsman Copying Test. Stutsman, Rachel 1948
Subtests: Copying a Circle; Copying a Cross; Copying a Star
Descriptors: Individual Testing; *Intelligence; Intelligence Tests; Performance Tests; *Preschool Children; Preschool Education; *Young Children

Identifiers: *Copying Ability; Merrill Palmer Scale of Mental Tests
Availability: Stoelting Co.; 620 Wheat Ln., Wood Dale, IL 60191
Target Audience: 2-5

One of several tests used to comprise the Merrill Palmer Scale of Mental Tests (TC011971). The series was designed to measure intelligence of young children. Used in many instances as a substitute for, or supplement to, the Binet Scale (TC001402). The tests included in the scale are Stutsman Copying Test (TC004042); Stutsman Little Pink Tower (TC004045); Stutsman Pyramid Test (TC004046); Stutsman Buttoning Test (TC004047); Stutsman Stick and String (TC004048); Stutsman Color Matching Test (TC004049); Wallin Pegboard A (TC004050); Wallin Pegboard B (TC004051); Stutsman Nested Cubes (TC004052); Pintner Manikin Test (TC004053); Decroly Matching Game (TC004054); Stutsman Picture Formboard 2 (TC004055); Stutsman Picture Formboard 3 (TC004056); Woodworth Wells Association Test (TC004057); Stutsman Language Test (TC004058); Kohs Block Design Test (TC004059); Stutsman Picture Formboard 1 (TC004060); Mare-Foal Formboard (TC004061); Seguin-Goddard Formboard (TC004062). Designed to assess young child's ability to copy a circle, cross or star. Child is given credit if he or she attempts a reasonable facsimile of the figure.

4043
Quick Word Test: Level II. Borgatta, Edgar F.; Corsini, Raymond J. 1967
Descriptors: *Adults; *Cognitive Ability; *Grade 11; *Grade 12; Higher Education; High Schools; High School Students; Intelligence Tests; Screening Tests; *Undergraduate Students; *Verbal Ability
Identifiers: QWT
Availability: F.E. Research Publishers, Inc.; 115 N. Prospect Ave., Itasca, IL 60143
Grade Level: 11-16
Target Audience: 15-64
Notes: Time, 15 approx.; Items, 100

Designed for use as a rapid screening or assessment of general mental ability. Developed for use with superior eleventh and twelfth grade students, college and professional groups, and select groups of adults. Two parallel forms are available. Rationale for this instrument is the theory that word knowledge is one of the best single indicators of mental ability.

4044
Quick Word Test: Elementary Level. Borgatta, Edgar F.; Corsini, Richard J. 1967
Descriptors: *Cognitive Ability; *Elementary School Students; Intelligence Tests; Intermediate Grades; Screening Tests; *Verbal Ability
Identifiers: QWT
Availability: F.E. Research Publishers, Inc.; 115 N. Prospect Ave., Itasca, IL 60143
Grade Level: 4-6
Notes: Time, 20 approx.; Items, 50

Designed as a rapid screening or assessment of general mental ability. Rationale for this instrument is the theory that word knowledge is one of the best single indicators of mental ability. Two parallel forms are available.

4045
Stutsman Little Pink Tower Test. Stutsman, Rachel 1948
Descriptors: Individual Testing; *Intelligence; Intelligence Tests; Performance Tests; *Preschool Children; Preschool Education; *Psychomotor Skills; *Short Term Memory; Timed Tests; *Young Children
Identifiers: Merrill Palmer Scale of Mental Tests
Availability: Stoelting Co.; 620 Wheat Ln., Wood Dale, IL 60191
Target Audience: 3-5

One of several tests used to comprise the Merrill Palmer Scale of Mental Tests (TC011971). The series was designed to measure intelligence of young children. Used in many instances as a substitute for, or supplement to, the Binet Scale (TC001402). The tests included in the scale are Stutsman Copying Test (TC004042); Stutsman Little Pink Tower (TC004045); Stutsman Pyramid Test (TC004046); Stutsman Buttoning Test (TC004047); Stutsman Stick and String (TC004048); Stutsman Color Matching Test (TC004049); Wallin Pegboard A (TC004050); Wallin Pegboard B (TC004051); Stutsman Nested Cubes (TC004052); Pintner Manikin Test (TC004053); Decroly Matching Game (TC004054); Stutsman Picture Formboard 2 (TC004055); Stutsman Picture Formboard 3 (TC004056); Woodworth Wells Association Test (TC004057); Stutsman Language Test (TC004058); Kohs Block Design Test (TC004059); Stutsman Picture Formboard 1 (TC004060); Mare-Foal Formboard (TC004061); Seguin-Goddard Formboard (TC004062). Examiner constructs a tower of 5 blocks behind screen and then shows child completed tower. Tower is destroyed and child must build it retaining the image of the object he or she is trying to copy. Blocks vary in size. Assesses intelligence and short term memory.

4046
Stutsman Pyramid Test. Stutsman, Rachel 1948
Descriptors: Individual Testing; *Intelligence; Intelligence Tests; Performance Tests; *Preschool Children; Preschool Education; *Psychomotor Skills; Timed Tests; Verbal Ability; *Young Children
Identifiers: Merrill Palmer Scale of Mental Tests
Availability: Stoelting Co.; 620 Wheat Ln., Wood Dale, IL 60191
Target Audience: 2-5

One of several tests used to comprise the Merrill Palmer Scale of Mental Tests (TC011971). The series was designed to measure intelligence of young children. Used in many instances as a substitute for, or supplement to, the Binet Scale (TC001402). The tests included in the scale are Stutsman Copying Test (TC004042); Stutsman Little Pink Tower (TC004045); Stutsman Pyramid Test (TC004046); Stutsman Buttoning Test (TC004047); Stutsman Stick and String (TC004048); Stutsman Color Matching Test (TC004049); Wallin Pegboard A (TC004050); Wallin Pegboard B (TC004051); Stutsman Nested Cubes (TC004052); Pintner Manikin Test (TC004053); Decroly Matching Game (TC004054); Stutsman Picture Formboard 2 (TC004055); Stutsman Picture Formboard 3 (TC004056); Woodworth Wells Association Test (TC004057); Stutsman Language Test (TC004058); Kohs Block Design Test (TC004059); Stutsman Picture Formboard 1 (TC004060); Mare-Foal Formboard (TC004061); Seguin-Goddard Formboard (TC004062). Examiner builds a pyramid out of 3 blocks as example. Child must create a 6-block pyramid. Assesses comprehension of directions, motor coordination, and ability to analyze placement of blocks.

4047
Stutsman Buttoning Test. Stutsman, Rachel 1948
Descriptors: Individual Testing; Intelligence Tests; Performance Tests; *Preschool Children; Preschool Education; Timed Tests; *Young Children
Identifiers: Manual Dexterity; Merrill Palmer Scale of Mental Tests
Availability: Stoelting Co.; 620 Wheat Ln., Wood Dale, IL 60191
Target Audience: 2-5

One of several tests used to comprise the Merrill Palmer Scale of Mental Tests (TC011971). The series was designed to measure intelligence of young children. Used in many instances as a substitute for, or supplement to, the Binet Scale (TC001402). The tests included in the scale are Stutsman Copying Test (TC004042); Stutsman Little Pink Tower (TC004045); Stutsman Pyramid Test (TC004046); Stutsman Buttoning Test (TC004047); Stutsman Stick and String (TC004048); Stutsman Color Matching Test (TC004049); Wallin Pegboard A (TC004050); Wallin Pegboard B (TC004051); Stutsman Nested Cubes (TC004052); Pintner Manikin Test (TC004053); Decroly Matching Game (TC004054); Stutsman Picture Formboard 2 (TC004055); Stutsman Picture Formboard 3 (TC004056); Woodworth Wells Association Test (TC004057); Stutsman Language Test (TC004058); Kohs Block Design Test (TC004059); Stutsman Picture Formboard 1 (TC004060); Mare-Foal Formboard (TC004061); Seguin-Goddard Formboard (TC004062). Child is shown how to fasten buttons into buttonholes. Examiner unfastens them and child must then repeat the process.

4048
Stutsman Stick and String Test. Stutsman, Rachel 1948
Descriptors: Individual Testing; *Intelligence; Intelligence Tests; Performance Tests; *Preschool Children; Preschool Education; Psychomotor Skills; Timed Tests; *Young Children
Identifiers: Merrill Palmer Scale of Mental Tests
Availability: Stoelting Co.; 620 Wheat Ln., Wood Dale, IL 60191
Target Audience: 1-4

One of several tests used to comprise the Merrill Palmer Scale of Mental Tests (TC011971). The series was designed to measure intelligence of young children. Used in many instances as a substitute for, or supplement to, the Binet Scale (TC001402). The tests included in the scale are Stutsman Copying Test (TC004042); Stutsman Little Pink Tower (TC004045); Stutsman Pyramid Test (TC004046); Stutsman Buttoning Test (TC004047); Stutsman Stick and String (TC004048); Stutsman Color Matching Test (TC004049); Wallin Pegboard A (TC004050); Wallin Pegboard B (TC004051); Stutsman Nested Cubes (TC004052); Pintner Manikin Test (TC004053); Decroly Matching Game (TC004054); Stutsman Picture Formboard 2 (TC004055); Stutsman Picture Formboard 3 (TC004056); Woodworth Wells Association Test (TC004057); Stutsman Language Test (TC004058); Kohs Block Design Test (TC004059); Stutsman Picture Formboard 1 (TC004060); Mare-Foal Formboard (TC004061); Seguin-Goddard Formboard (TC004062). Task is to pull stick toward oneself using the string attached to it. The child should grasp the string with both hands to pull the stick toward him or her. Success is attained if child definitely decreases distance between himself or herself and the stick by pulling on the string.

4049
Stutsman Color-Matching Test. Stutsman, Rachel 1948
Descriptors: *Classification; *Color; Individual Testing; *Intelligence; Intelligence Tests; Performance Tests; *Preschool Children; Preschool Education; Timed Tests; Visual Discrimination; *Young Children
Identifiers: Color Discrimination; Merrill Palmer Scale of Mental Tests
Availability: Stoelting Co.; 620 Wheat Ln., Wood Dale, IL 60191
Target Audience: 1-4
One of several tests used to comprise the Merrill Palmer Scale of Mental Tests (TC011971). The series was designed to measure intelligence of young children. Used in many instances as a substitute for, or supplement to, the Binet Scale (TC001402). The tests included in the scale are Stutsman Copying Test (TC004042); Stutsman Little Pink Tower (TC004045); Stutsman Pyramid Test (TC004046); Stutsman Buttoning Test (TC004047); Stutsman Stick and String (TC004048); Stutsman Color Matching Test (TC004049); Wallin Pegboard A (TC004050); Wallin Pegboard B (TC004051); Stutsman Nested Cubes (TC004052); Pintner Manikin Test (TC004053); Decroly Matching Game (TC004054); Stutsman Picture Formboard 2 (TC004055); Stutsman Picture Formboard 3 (TC004056); Woodworth Wells Association Test (TC004057); Stutsman Language Test (TC004058); Kohs Block Design Test (TC004059); Stutsman Picture Formboard 1 (TC004060); Mare-Foal Formboard (TC004061); Seguin-Goddard Formboard (TC004062). Designed to assess ability to discriminate color differences as well as to comprehend the task of sorting disks into boxes according to color.

4050
Wallin Pegboard A. Harcourt Brace Jovanovich, Inc., New York, NY 1948
Descriptors: Individual Testing; *Intelligence; Intelligence Tests; *Perceptual Motor Coordination; Performance Tests; *Preschool Children; Preschool Education; Spatial Ability; Timed Tests; *Young Children
Identifiers: Merrill Palmer Scale of Mental Tests
Availability: Stoelting Co.; 620 Wheat Ln., Wood Dale, IL 60191
Target Audience: 1-4
One of several tests used to comprise the Merrill Palmer Scale of Mental Tests (TC011971). The series was designed to measure intelligence of young children. Used in many instances as a substitute for, or supplement to, the Binet Scale (TC001402). The tests included in the scale are Stutsman Copying Test (TC004042); Stutsman Little Pink Tower (TC004045); Stutsman Pyramid Test (TC004046); Stutsman Buttoning Test (TC004047); Stutsman Stick and String (TC004048); Stutsman Color Matching Test (TC004049); Wallin Pegboard A (TC004050); Wallin Pegboard B (TC004051); Stutsman Nested Cubes (TC004052); Pintner Manikin Test (TC004053); Decroly Matching Game (TC004054); Stutsman Picture Formboard 2 (TC004055); Stutsman Picture Formboard 3 (TC004056); Woodworth Wells Association Test (TC004057); Stutsman Language Test (TC004058); Kohs Block Design Test (TC004059); Stutsman Picture Formboard 1 (TC004060); Mare-Foal Formboard (TC004061); Seguin-Goddard Formboard (TC004062). Child must replace pegs in board in their respective places after the examiner removes them.

4051
Wallin Pegboard B. Harcourt Brace Jovanovich, Inc., New York, NY 1948
Descriptors: Individual Testing; *Intelligence; Intelligence Tests; Perceptual Motor Coordination; Performance Tests; *Preschool Children; Preschool Education; *Spatial Ability; Timed Tests; *Young Children
Identifiers: Merrill Palmer Scale of Mental Tests
Availability: Stoelting Co.; 620 Wheat Ln., Wood Dale, IL 60191
Target Audience: 2-4
One of several tests used to comprise the Merrill Palmer Scale of Mental Tests (TC011971). The series was designed to measure intelligence of young children. Used in many instances as a substitute for, or supplement to, the Binet Scale (TC001402). The tests included in the scale are Stutsman Copying Test (TC004042); Stutsman Little Pink Tower (TC004045); Stutsman Pyramid Test (TC004046); Stutsman Buttoning Test (TC004047); Stutsman Stick and String (TC004048); Stutsman Color Matching Test (TC004049); Wallin Pegboard A (TC004050); Wallin Pegboard B (TC004051); Stutsman Nested Cubes (TC004052); Pintner Manikin Test (TC004053); Decroly Matching Game (TC004054); Stutsman Picture Formboard 2 (TC004055); Stutsman Picture Formboard 3 (TC004056); Woodworth Wells Association Test (TC004057); Stutsman Language Test (TC004058); Kohs Block Design Test (TC004059); Stutsman Picture Formboard 1 (TC004060); Mare-Foal Formboard (TC004061); Seguin-Goddard Formboard (TC004062). Instrument requires child to replace pegs in appropriate spaces. More difficult than Wallin Peg-Board A (TC004050).

4052
Stutsman Nested Cubes. Stutsman, Rachel 1948
Descriptors: Individual Testing; *Intelligence; Intelligence Tests; *Perceptual Motor Coordination; Performance Tests; Personality Assessment; *Preschool Children; Preschool Education; Timed Tests; *Young Children
Identifiers: Merrill Palmer Scale of Mental Tests
Availability: Stoelting Co.; 620 Wheat Ln., Wood Dale, IL 60191
Target Audience: 1-4
One of several tests used to comprise the Merrill Palmer Scale of Mental Tests (TC011971). The series was designed to measure intelligence of young children. Used in many instances as a substitute for, or supplement to, the Binet Scale (TC001402). The tests included in the scale are Stutsman Copying Test (TC004042); Stutsman Little Pink Tower (TC004045); Stutsman Pyramid Test (TC004046); Stutsman Buttoning Test (TC004047); Stutsman Stick and String (TC004048); Stutsman Color Matching Test (TC004049); Wallin Pegboard A (TC004050); Wallin Pegboard B (TC004051); Stutsman Nested Cubes (TC004052); Pintner Manikin Test (TC004053); Decroly Matching Game (TC004054); Stutsman Picture Formboard 2 (TC004055); Stutsman Picture Formboard 3 (TC004056); Woodworth Wells Association Test (TC004057); Stutsman Language Test (TC004058); Kohs Block Design Test (TC004059); Stutsman Picture Formboard 1 (TC004060); Mare-Foal Formboard (TC004061); Seguin-Goddard Formboard (TC004062). Designed to assess motor ability of young children. Task is to nest 4 progressively larger hollow cubes. Judgments about personality may be made by observing child's approach to this task.

4053
Pinter Manikin Test. Stutsman, Rachel 1948
Descriptors: Individual Testing; *Intelligence; Intelligence Tests; Perceptual Motor Coordination; Performance Tests; *Preschool Children; Preschool Education; Timed Tests; *Young Children
Identifiers: Merrill Palmer Scale of Mental Tests
Availability: Stoelting Co.; 620 Wheat Ln., Wood Dale, IL 60191
Target Audience: 3-5
One of several tests used to comprise the Merrill Palmer Scale of Mental Tests (TC011971). The series was designed to measure intelligence of young children. Used in many instances as a substitute for, or supplement to, the Binet Scale (TC001402). The tests included in the scale are Stutsman Copying Test (TC004042); Stutsman Little Pink Tower (TC004045); Stutsman Pyramid Test (TC004046); Stutsman Buttoning Test (TC004047); Stutsman Stick and String (TC004048); Stutsman Color Matching Test (TC004049); Wallin Pegboard A (TC004050); Wallin Pegboard B (TC004051); Stutsman Nested Cubes (TC004052); Pintner Manikin Test (TC004053); Decroly Matching Game (TC004054); Stutsman Picture Formboard 2 (TC004055); Stutsman Picture Formboard 3 (TC004056); Woodworth Wells Association Test (TC004057); Stutsman Language Test (TC004058); Kohs Block Design Test (TC004059); Stutsman Picture Formboard 1 (TC004060); Mare-Foal Formboard (TC004061); Seguin-Goddard Formboard (TC004062). Subject is presented with 6 components which may be assembled to represent a man. The test is scored according to the accuracy in completing the figure. Test seems to be of little interest to preschool children.

4054
Decroly Matching Game. Harcourt Brace Jovanovich, Inc., New York, NY Stutsman, Rachel 1948
Descriptors: Individual Testing; *Intelligence; Intelligence Tests; Performance Tests; *Preschool Children; Preschool Education; Timed Tests; Visual Measures; *Young Children
Identifiers: Merrill Palmer Scale of Mental Tests
Availability: Stoelting Co.; 620 Wheat Ln., Wood Dale, IL 60191
Target Audience: 3-5
One of several tests used to comprise the Merrill Palmer Scale of Mental Tests (TC011971). The series was designed to measure intelligence of young children. Used in many instances as a substitute for, or supplement to, the Binet Scale (TC001402). The tests included in the scale are Stutsman Copying Test (TC004042); Stutsman Little Pink Tower (TC004045); Stutsman Pyramid Test (TC004046); Stutsman Buttoning Test (TC004047); Stutsman Stick and String (TC004048); Stutsman Color Matching Test (TC004049); Wallin Pegboard A (TC004050); Wallin Pegboard B (TC004051); Stutsman Nested Cubes (TC004052); Pintner Manikin Test (TC004053); Decroly Matching Game (TC004054); Stutsman Picture Formboard 2 (TC004055); Stutsman Picture Formboard 3 (TC004056); Woodworth Wells Association Test (TC004057); Stutsman Language Test (TC004058); Kohs Block Design Test (TC004059); Stutsman Picture Formboard 1 (TC004060); Mare-Foal Formboard (TC004061); Seguin-Goddard Formboard (TC004062). Task is to match pictures on individual cards with pictures on larger cards, each of which has 4 pictures. Failures generally resulted from inability to understand that pictures were to be matched.

4055
Stutsman Picture Formboard 2. Stutsman, Rachel 1948
Descriptors: Individual Testing; *Intelligence; Intelligence Tests; Perceptual Motor Coordination; Performance Tests; *Preschool Children; Preschool Education; *Spatial Ability; Timed Tests; *Young Children
Identifiers: Merrill Palmer Scale of Mental Tests
Availability: Stoelting Co.; 620 Wheat Ln., Wood Dale, IL 60191
Target Audience: 2-5
Notes: Time, 1 approx.; Items, 3
One of several tests used to comprise the Merrill Palmer Scale of Mental Tests (TC011971). The series was designed to measure intelligence of young children. Used in many instances as a substitute for, or supplement to, the Binet Scale (TC001402). The tests included in the scale are Stutsman Copying Test (TC004042); Stutsman Little Pink Tower (TC004045); Stutsman Pyramid Test (TC004046); Stutsman Buttoning Test (TC004047); Stutsman Stick and String (TC004048); Stutsman Color Matching Test (TC004049); Wallin Pegboard A (TC004050); Wallin Pegboard B (TC004051); Stutsman Nested Cubes (TC004052); Pintner Manikin Test (TC004053); Decroly Matching Game (TC004054); Stutsman Picture Formboard 2 (TC004055); Stutsman Picture Formboard 3 (TC004056); Woodworth Wells Association Test (TC004057); Stutsman Language Test (TC004058); Kohs Block Design Test (TC004059); Stutsman Picture Formboard 1 (TC004060); Mare-Foal Formboard (TC004061); Seguin-Goddard Formboard (TC004062). The picture "Playing Mother" by Jessie Wilcox Smith was cut into 3 wooden pieces which child must assemble. The test is timed up to the point where child completes the puzzle.

4056
Stutsman Picture Formboard 3. Stutsman, Rachel 1948
Descriptors: Individual Testing; *Intelligence; Intelligence Tests; Perceptual Motor Coordination; Performance Tests; *Preschool Children; Preschool Education; *Spatial Ability; *Young Children
Identifiers: Merrill Palmer Scale of Mental Tests
Availability: Stoelting Co.; 620 Wheat Ln., Wood Dale, IL 60191
Target Audience: 2-5
Notes: Items, 4
One of several tests used to comprise the Merrill Palmer Scale of Mental Tests (TC011971). The series was designed to measure intelligence of young children. Used in many instances as a substitute for, or supplement to, the Binet Scale (TC001402). The tests included in the scale are Stutsman Copying Test (TC004042); Stutsman Little Pink Tower (TC004045); Stutsman Pyramid Test (TC004046); Stutsman Buttoning Test (TC004047); Stutsman Stick and String (TC004048); Stutsman Color Matching Test (TC004049); Wallin Pegboard A (TC004050); Wallin Pegboard B (TC004051); Stutsman Nested Cubes (TC004052); Pintner Manikin Test (TC004053); Decroly Matching Game (TC004054); Stutsman Picture Formboard 2 (TC004055); Stutsman Picture Formboard 3 (TC004056); Woodworth Wells Association Test (TC004057); Stutsman Language Test (TC004058); Kohs Block Design Test (TC004059); Stutsman Picture Formboard 1 (TC004060); Mare-Foal Formboard (TC004061); Seguin-Goddard Formboard (TC004062). The picture "Off To Play" by Jessie Wilcox Smith was cut into 4 pieces made of wood which child must assemble. There is no time limit and is scored as passed or failed. It is somewhat more difficult than Stutsman Picture Formboard 2 (TC004055).

4057
Woodworth-Wells Association Test. Woodworth, R.S.; Wells, F.L. 1948
Descriptors: Association Measures; Individual Testing; *Intelligence; Intelligence Tests; *Preschool Children; Preschool Education; Timed Tests; *Young Children
Identifiers: *Action Agent Test; Merrill Palmer Scale of Mental Tests
Availability: Stoelting Co.; 620 Wheat Ln., Wood Dale, IL 60191
Target Audience: 2-4
Notes: Items, 20
One of several tests used to comprise the Merrill Palmer Scale of Mental Tests (TC011971). The series was designed to measure intelligence of young children. Used in many instances as a substitute for, or supplement to, the Binet Scale (TC001402). The tests included in the scale are Stutsman Copying Test (TC004042); Stutsman Little Pink Tower (TC004045); Stutsman Pyramid Test (TC004046); Stutsman Buttoning Test (TC004047); Stutsman Stick and String (TC004048); Stutsman Color Matching Test (TC004049); Wallin Pegboard A (TC004050); Wallin Pegboard B (TC004051); Stutsman Nested Cubes (TC004052); Pintner Manikin Test (TC004053); Decroly Matching Game (TC004054); Stutsman Picture Form-

board 2 (TC004055); Stutsman Picture Formboard 3 (TC004056); Woodworth Wells Association Test (TC004057); Stutsman Language Test (TC004058); Kohs Block Design Test (TC004059); Stutsman Picture Formboard 1 (TC004060); Mare-Foal Formboard (TC004061); Seguin-Goddard Formboard (TC004062). Designed to assess intelligence in young children. Examiner asks child "What?" followed by 20 stimulus words. All responses should be recorded whether or not they are relevant. Child should be given blocks or toys to play with while being questioned, so that attention can be diverted from play to test items. He/she reverts to play when question is answered.

4058
Stutsman Language Test. Stutsman, Rachel 1948
Descriptors: Individual Testing; *Intelligence; Intelligence Tests; Language Tests; *Preschool Children; Preschool Education; Verbal Ability; *Young Children
Identifiers: Merrill Palmer Scale of Mental Tests; Simple Questions
Availability: Stoelting Co.; 620 Wheat Ln., Wood Dale, IL 60191
Target Audience: 1-4
Notes: Items, 10

One of several tests used to comprise the Merrill Palmer Scale of Mental Tests (TC011971). The series was designed to measure intelligence of young children. Used in many instances as a substitute for, or supplement to, the Binet Scale (TC001402). The tests included in the scale are Stutsman Copying Test (TC004042); Stutsman Little Pink Tower (TC004045); Stutsman Pyramid Test (TC004046); Stutsman Buttoning Test (TC004047); Stutsman Stick and String (TC004048); Stutsman Color Matching Test (TC004049); Wallin Pegboard A (TC004050); Wallin Pegboard B (TC004051); Stutsman Nested Cubes (TC004052); Pintner Manikin Test (TC004053); Decroly Matching Game (TC004054); Stutsman Picture Formboard 2 (TC004055); Stutsman Picture Formboard 3 (TC004056); Woodworth Wells Association Test (TC004057); Stutsman Language Test (TC004058); Kohs Block Design Test (TC004059); Stutsman Picture Formboard 1 (TC004060); Mare-Foal Formboard (TC004061); Seguin-Goddard Formboard (TC004062). Designed to assess verbal comprehension. Subjects' responses, to simple questions are recorded verbatim.

4059
Kohs Block Design. Kohs, Samuel C. 1948
Descriptors: *Adolescents; *Children; Disadvantaged Youth; Elementary Secondary Education; Hearing Impairments; Individual Testing; *Intelligence; Intelligence Tests; Language Handicaps; Non English Speaking; Performance Tests; *Preschool Children; Preschool Education; *Visual Perception; *Young Adults; *Young Children
Identifiers: Merrill Palmer Scale of Mental Tests
Availability: Stoelting Co.; 620 Wheat Ln., Wood Dale, IL 60191
Target Audience: 3-19
Notes: Time, 40 approx.

One of several tests used to comprise the Merrill Palmer Scale of Mental Tests (TC011971). The series was designed to measure intelligence of young children. Used in many instances as a substitute for, or supplement to, the Binet Scale (TC001402). The tests included in the scale are Stutsman Copying Test (TC004042); Stutsman Little Pink Tower (TC004045); Stutsman Pyramid Test (TC004046); Stutsman Buttoning Test (TC004047); Stutsman Stick and String (TC004048); Stutsman Color Matching Test (TC004049); Wallin Pegboard A (TC004050); Wallin Pegboard B (TC004051); Stutsman Nested Cubes (TC004052); Pintner Manikin Test (TC004053); Decroly Matching Game (TC004054); Stutsman Picture Formboard 2 (TC004055); Stutsman Picture Formboard 3 (TC004056); Woodworth Wells Association Test (TC004057); Stutsman Language Test (TC004058); Kohs Block Design Test (TC004059); Stutsman Picture Formboard 1 (TC004060); Mare-Foal Formboard (TC004061); Seguin-Goddard Formboard (TC004062). When this instrument is used as part of Merrill Palmer Scale, it assesses preschool children ages 18-35 months. Task is to duplicate designs on cards by manipulating 16 colored cubes.

4060
Stutsman Picture Formboard 1. Stutsman, Rachel 1948
Descriptors: Individual Testing; *Intelligence; Intelligence Tests; Perceptual Motor Coordination; Performance Tests; *Preschool Children; Preschool Education; *Spatial Ability; Timed Tests; *Young Children
Identifiers: Merrill Palmer Scale of Mental Tests
Availability: Stoelting Co.; 620 Wheat Ln., Wood Dale, IL 60191
Target Audience: 2-5

One of several tests used to comprise the Merrill Palmer Scale of Mental Tests (TC011971). The series was designed to measure intelligence of young children. Used in many instances as a substitute for, or supplement to, the Binet Scale (TC001402). The tests included in the scale are Stutsman Copying Test (TC004042); Stutsman Little

Pink Tower (TC004045); Stutsman Pyramid Test (TC004046); Stutsman Buttoning Test (TC004047); Stutsman Stick and String (TC004048); Stutsman Color Matching Test (TC004049); Wallin Pegboard A (TC004050); Wallin Pegboard B (TC004051); Stutsman Nested Cubes (TC004052); Pintner Manikin Test (TC004053); Decroly Matching Game (TC004054); Stutsman Picture Formboard 2 (TC004055); Stutsman Picture Formboard 3 (TC004056); Woodworth Wells Association Test (TC004057); Stutsman Language Test (TC004058); Kohs Block Design Test (TC004059); Stutsman Picture Formboard 1 (TC004060); Mare-Foal Formboard (TC004061); Seguin-Goddard Formboard (TC004062). The picture "Mother's Own" by Jessie Wilcox Smith was cut into 2 wooden pieces. The time a child requires to properly place the puzzle pieces is the measure of recording quality of success. No credit should be given for success which requires longer than 14 seconds.

4061
Mare-Foal Formboard. Healy, William; Fernald, G.M. 1948
Descriptors: Individual Testing; Intelligence Tests; Perceptual Motor Coordination; Performance Tests; Personality Assessment; *Preschool Children; Preschool Education; *Spatial Ability; Timed Tests; Visual Discrimination; *Young Children
Identifiers: Merrill Palmer Scale of Mental Tests
Availability: Stoelting Co.; 620 Wheat Ln., Wood Dale, IL 60191
Target Audience: 3-5
Notes: Items, 7

One of several tests used to comprise the Merrill Palmer Scale of Mental Tests (TC011971). The series was designed to measure intelligence of young children. Used in many instances as a substitute for, or supplement to, the Binet Scale (TC001402). The tests included in the scale are Stutsman Copying Test (TC004042); Stutsman Little Pink Tower (TC004045); Stutsman Pyramid Test (TC004046); Stutsman Buttoning Test (TC004047); Stutsman Stick and String (TC004048); Stutsman Color Matching Test (TC004049); Wallin Pegboard A (TC004050); Wallin Pegboard B (TC004051); Stutsman Nested Cubes (TC004052); Pintner Manikin Test (TC004053); Decroly Matching Game (TC004054); Stutsman Picture Formboard 2 (TC004055); Stutsman Picture Formboard 3 (TC004056); Woodworth Wells Association Test (TC004057); Stutsman Language Test (TC004058); Kohs Block Design Test (TC004059); Stutsman Picture Formboard 1 (TC004060); Mare-Foal Formboard (TC004061); Seguin-Goddard Formboard (TC004062). Instrument is of great interest to preschool children. It is somewhat more difficult for them than Segiun-Goddard Formboard (TC004062). Many personality tendencies are exhibited as children work at this task.

4062
Seguin-Goddard Formboard Test. Seguin, E.; And Others
Descriptors: Individual Testing; *Intelligence; Intelligence Tests; Perceptual Motor Coordination; Performance Tests; *Preschool Children; Preschool Education; *Spatial Ability; Timed Tests; Visual Discrimination; *Young Children
Identifiers: Merrill Palmer Scale of Mental Tests
Availability: Stoelting Co.; 620 Wheat Ln., Wood Dale, IL 60191
Target Audience: 2-5
Notes: Time, 5; Items, 10

One of several tests used to comprise the Merrill Palmer Scale of Mental Tests (TC011971). The series was designed to measure intelligence of young children. Used in many instances as a substitute for, or supplement to, the Binet Scale (TC001402). The tests included in the scale are Stutsman Copying Test (TC004042); Stutsman Little Pink Tower (TC004045); Stutsman Pyramid Test (TC004046); Stutsman Buttoning Test (TC004047); Stutsman Stick and String (TC004048); Stutsman Color Matching Test (TC004049); Wallin Pegboard A (TC004050); Wallin Pegboard B (TC004051); Stutsman Nested Cubes (TC004052); Pintner Manikin Test (TC004053); Decroly Matching Game (TC004054); Stutsman Picture Formboard 2 (TC004055); Stutsman Picture Formboard 3 (TC004056); Woodworth Wells Association Test (TC004057); Stutsman Language Test (TC004058); Kohs Block Design Test (TC004059); Stutsman Picture Formboard 1 (TC004060); Mare-Foal Formboard (TC004061); Seguin-Goddard Formboard (TC004062). Formboard consists of 10 recessed and 10 wooden blocks in geometrical forms. Child has 3 trials of 5 minutes each to match the block to the proper recess. The score is the shortest time of 3 trials.

4063
Foster Maze A. Foster, William S. 1923
Descriptors: *Adolescents; *Adults; *Children; Individual Testing; *Intelligence; Intelligence Tests; Nonverbal Tests; Performance Tests
Identifiers: Blind Tracing; *Mazes
Availability: Stoelting Co.; 620 Wheat Ln., Wood Dale, IL 60191
Target Audience: 5-64

Blindfolded subject must proceed through a grooved maze pattern using a stylus or pencil. Examiner indicates when subject has successfully completed the maze. Forms A and B provide different maze patterns.

4064
Foster Maze B. Foster, William S. 1923
Descriptors: *Adolescents; *Adults; *Children; Individual Testing; *Intelligence; *Intelligence Tests; Nonverbal Tests; Performance Tests
Identifiers: Blind Tracing; *Mazes
Availability: Stoelting Co.; 620 Wheat Ln., Wood Dale, IL 60191
Target Audience: 5-64

Blindfolded subject must proceed through a grooved maze pattern using a stylus or pencil. Examiner indicates when subject has successfully completed the maze. Forms A and B provide different maze patterns.

4114
Concept Assessment Kit—Conservation. Goldschmid, Marcel L.; Bentler, Peter M. 1968
Subtests: Two-Dimensional Space; Number; Substance; Continuous Quantity; Weight; Discontinuous Quantity
Descriptors: *Conservation (Concept); Individual Testing; *Intellectual Development; Performance Tests; Preschool Education; Primary Education; *Young Children
Identifiers: Piagetian Tasks
Availability: Educational and Industrial Testing Service; P.O. Box 7234, San Diego, CA 92107
Target Audience: 4-8
Notes: Time, 15 approx.; Items, 44

Designed to measure child's level of conservation as determined by his or her conservation behavior and his or her comprehension of the principle involved. Conservation behavior refers to child's judgment of the relative quantity of 2 objects, 1 of which has just been manipulated by the examiner. Comprehension is assessed by the child's explanation for his or her judgment. Forms A and B are parallel forms. Form C measures slightly different dimension of conservation and includes tasks of Area and Length.

4120
The Cornell Class-Reasoning Test, Form X. Ennis, Robert H.; And Others 1964
Descriptors: Cognitive Processes; *Cognitive Style; *Cognitive Tests; Critical Thinking; *Deduction; *Elementary School Students; Elementary Secondary Education; *Logical Thinking; *Secondary School Students
Identifiers: Cornell Critical Thinking Test Series; *Reasoning Ability
Availability: Illinois Thinking Project; University of Illinois, 1310 S. Sixth St., Champaign, IL 61820
Grade Level: 4-12
Notes: Items, 78

Designed to measure deductive logic ability of adolescents aged 10 through 18. Also available from: ERIC Document Reproduction Service; 3900 Wheeler Ave., Alexandria, VA 22304, (ED003818, 314 pages).

4121
The Cornell Conditional-Reasoning Test, Form X. Ennis, Robert H.; And Others 1964
Descriptors: Cognitive Processes; *Cognitive Style; *Cognitive Tests; Critical Thinking; *Deduction; *Elementary School Students; Elementary Secondary Education; *Logical Thinking; *Secondary School Students
Identifiers: Cornell Critical Thinking Test Series; *Reasoning Ability
Availability: Illinois Thinking Project; University of Illinois, 1310 S. Sixth St., Champaign, IL 61820
Grade Level: 4-12
Notes: Items, 78

Designed to assess ability in conditional reasoning or deductive logic of adolescents 10 through 18 years of age. Also available from: ERIC Document Reproduction Service; 3900 Wheeler Ave., Alexandria, VA 22304 (ED003818, 314 pages).

4135
Hiskey Nebraska Test of Learning Aptitude. Hiskey, Marshall S. 1966
Subtests: Bead Patterns; Memory for Colors; Picture Identification; Picture Association; Paper Folding Patterns; Visual Attention Span; Block Patterns; Completion of Drawings; Memory for Digits; Puzzle Blocks; Picture Analogies; Spatial Reasoning
Descriptors: Academic Ability; *Elementary School Students; Elementary Secondary Education; *Hearing Impairments; Individual Testing; Intelligence; *Intelligence Tests; *Language Handicaps; Nonverbal Tests; *Preschool Children; Preschool Education; *Secondary School Students; *Speech Handicaps

Identifiers: HNTLA
Availability: The Hiskey Nebraska Test; 5640 Baldwin, Lincoln, N.E. 68507
Target Audience: 2-18
Notes: Time, 60 approx.

Designed to evaluate learning potentials of hearing-impaired, speech-impaired, or language-impaired children. Separate norms for deaf and hearing subjects, ages 2.5 to 18.5 years. All responses are nonverbal. Is a revision and restandardization of the Nebraska Test of Learning Aptitude for Young Deaf Children.

4136
Haptic Intelligence Scale for Adult Blind. Shurrager, Harriet C.; Shurrager, Phil S. 1964
Subtests: Digit Symbol; Object Assembly; Block Design; Plan-of-Search; Object Completion; Pattern Board; Bead Arithmetic
Descriptors: *Adults; *Blindness; *Intelligence; *Intelligence Tests; *Nonverbal Tests; Performance Tests; *Tactual Perception; Visual Impairments
Identifiers: HISab
Availability: Stoelting Co.; 620 Wheat Ln., Wood Dale, IL 60191
Target Audience: 18-64
Notes: Time, 90 approx.; Items, 88

A nonverbal intelligence test designed to measure intelligence of blind adults. May be used in conjunction with the Verbal Scale of the Wechsler Adult Intelligence Scale (TC000413).

4142
Albert Einstein Scales of Sensori-Motor Development. Escalona, Sibylle K.; Corman, Harvey H. 1969
Subtests: Prehension; Object Permanence; Spatial Relationships
Descriptors: Behavior Rating Scales; *Cognitive Development; Cognitive Tests; Individual Testing; *Infants; *Intelligence; Perceptual Motor Coordination; Spatial Ability; Piagetian Theory
Availability: Library Administration; Albert Einstein College of Medicine of Yeshiva University, 1300 Morris Park Ave., Bronx, NY 10461
Target Audience: 0-2

Designed to assess cognitive development of infants. Items were designed to elicit the most mature behavior integrations of which the subject is capable. Based upon the theories on preverbal intelligence proposed by Piaget.

4145
Clerical Tests: Inventory R—Interpretation of Tabulated Material. Stevens, Thurow and Associates, Chicago, IL 1951
Descriptors: Adults; *Clerical Occupations; *Clerical Workers; Employment Potential; *Job Applicants; Job Placement; Job Skills; Office Occupations; Problem Solving; *Tables (Data); Timed Tests; Vocational Aptitude; *Work Sample Tests
Identifiers: *Clerical Aptitude; *Clerical Skills
Availability: Stevens, Thurow and Associates; 100 W. Monroe St., Chicago, IL 60603
Target Audience: Adults
Notes: Time, 7; Items, 19

Part of a series of clerical tests designed to test one's ability to locate specific items and extract material from a tabular form. Used to assist in the selection of employees for specific positions which require this type of skill. This series designed to be used in addition to the publisher's Series N (TC003611) and Series V (TC003612) batteries.

4146
Clerical Tests: Inventory M—Interpretation of Tabulated Material. Stevens, Thurow and Associates, Chicago, IL 1951
Descriptors: Adults; *Clerical Occupations; *Clerical Workers; Employment Potential; *Job Applicants; Job Placement; Job Skills; Office Occupations; Problem Solving; *Tables (Data); Timed Tests; Vocational Aptitude; *Work Sample Tests
Identifiers: *Clerical Aptitude; *Clerical Skills
Availability: Stevens, Thurow and Associates; 100 W. Monroe St., Chicago, IL 60603
Target Audience: Adults
Notes: Time, 3; Items, 50

Part of a series of clerical tests designed to test one's ability to locate specific items and extract material from a tabular form. Used to assist in the selection of employees for specific positions which require this type of skill. This series designed to be used in addition to the publisher's Series N (TC003611) and Series V (TC003612) batteries.

4148
Clerical Tests: Inventory J—Arithmetical Reasoning. Stevens, Thurow and Associates, Chicago, IL 1966

Descriptors: Adults; Aptitude Tests; Clerical Occupations; *Clerical Workers; Computation; Employment Potential; *Job Applicants; Job Placement; Job Skills; *Mathematical Concepts; *Occupational Tests; Office Occupations; Mathematics Tests; Timed Tests; Vocational Aptitude; *Work Sample Tests
Identifiers: Clerical Aptitude; *Clerical Skills; *Number Operations
Availability: Stevens, Thurow and Associates; 100 W. Monroe St., Chicago, IL 60603
Target Audience: Adults
Notes: Time, 7; Items, 10

Part of a series of clerical tests designed to test one's knowledge and ability in arithmetical reasoning. Used to assist in the selection of employees for specific positions which require this type of skill. This series designed to be used in addition to the publisher's Series N (TC003611) and Series V (TC003612) batteries.

4156
Parent Readiness Evaluation of Preschoolers. Ahr, A. Edward 1968
Subtests: General Information; Comprehension; Opposites; Identification; Verbal Associations; Verbal Description; Listening; Language; Concepts; Motor Coordination; Visual-Motor Association; Visual Interpretation; Auditory; Visual Memory
Descriptors: *Individual Testing; *Kindergarten Children; *Parent Participation; Performance; *Preschool Children; *School Readiness Tests; *Screening Tests; Verbal Ability; Young Children
Identifiers: PREP
Availability: Priority Innovations; P.O. Box 792, Skokie, IL 60076
Target Audience: 4-6

PREP is a parent-administered individual test for preschool and kindergarten children that assesses skills and abilities in 14 separate areas in addition to yielding verbal, performance, and total scores.

4163
O'Connor Wiggly Block. O'Connor, Johnson
Descriptors: Adolescents; Adults; Aptitude Tests; *Employees; *Job Applicants; *Occupational Tests; *Performance Tests; *Spatial Ability; Timed Tests; *Visualization; Vocational Aptitude
Identifiers: OWB
Availability: Stoelting Co.; 620 Wheat Ln., Wood Dale, IL 60191
Target Audience: 16-64
Notes: Time, 20 approx.

Designed to evaluate assemblage and other mechanical skills by assessing one's ability to visualize construction in the third dimension of space. Used for industrial personnel who require such visualization as in the development of mechanical parts from drawings, etc., or which give an estimate of required aptitudes as in occupations of mechanics, tool and die makers, draftsmen, engineers, and architects. To be given by experienced test administrators. Requires the use of the set of wiggly blocks (forms). The score is obtained by taking the average time of the 3 trials; the subject is required to reassemble the wiggly forms into 1 square block and is given 3 trials. Developed in the 1920s.

4192
Western Personnel Test: Spanish. Gunn, Robert L.; Manson, Morse P. 1964
Descriptors: Adults; Aptitude Tests; *Cognitive Ability; Cognitive Tests; Computation; Employment Qualifications; *Intelligence; *Learning; *Mathematical Applications; Mathematical Concepts; Multiple Choice Tests; Spanish; *Spanish Speaking; Timed Tests; *Verbal Ability; Vocational Aptitude
Identifiers: Los Tests Western Para Personal; WPT
Availability: Western Psychological Services; Order Dept., 12031 Wilshire Blvd., Los Angeles, CA 90025
Target Audience: Adults
Notes: Time, 5; Items, 24

A quickly administered instrument used to evaluate general mental ability and learning ability. Includes both verbal and mathematical abilities. Items require a brief answer based upon one's mathematical calculations or are multiple choice. Used with the general population, professional, college, clerical, skilled, and unskilled populations to evaluate general ability and for screening by personnel departments. Scores are given in terms of percentiles. This edition is in Spanish, but the manual is in English. Also available in English (TC000712).

4206
Test of Perceptual Organization. Martin, William T. 1969

Descriptors: Abstract Reasoning; *Adolescents; *Adults; Clinical Diagnosis; *Emotional Disturbances; *Handicap Identification; Psychomotor Skills; Spatial Ability; *Timed Tests
Identifiers: TPO
Availability: Psychologists and Educators; P.O. Box 513, St. Louis, MO 63017
Target Audience: 12-64
Notes: Time, 10

Designed to measure abstract reasoning, psychomotor functioning, and ability to follow specific, exacting instructions in an accurate manner. Disturbances in these areas are indicative of emotional and organic pathology. Useful as a clinical research tool and a screening instrument for use in clinical and counseling settings. May be administered to groups or individuals.

4245
Vane Kindergarten Test. Vane, Julia R. 1968
Subtests: Perceptual Motor; Man; Vocabulary
Descriptors: *Academic Aptitude; *Adjustment (to Environment); *Aptitude Tests; Kindergarten; *Kindergarten Children; Perceptual Motor Coordination; *Predictive Measurement; Primary Education; School Readiness; *Vocabulary Development
Identifiers: VKT
Availability: Clinical Psychology Publishing Co.; 4 Conant Square, Brandon, VT 05733-0315
Grade Level: K

Developed to evaluate intellectual and academic potential and behavior adjustment of young children. Most effective when administered any time after first 3 weeks of the kindergarten year. May be used with pre-kindergarten age children in special programs.

4282
Physiognomic Cue Test. Stein, Morris A. 1974
Subtests: Feeling Physiognomic; Thing-Physiognomic
Descriptors: *Adults; *Cognitive Style; Cognitive Tests; Creative Thinking; Forced Choice Technique; Higher Education; Pictorial Stimuli; *Undergraduate Students
Identifiers: PCT; Physiognomic Perception
Availability: Human Sciences Press; 72 Fifth Ave., New York, NY 10011
Grade Level: 13-16
Target Audience: 18-64
Notes: Time, 10 approx.; Items, 32

Designed to assess an individual's cognitive style. Measures physiognomic perception which is attributing human actions or feelings to pictorial stimuli.

4713
Illinois Test of Psycholinguistic Abilities: Revised Edition. Kirk, Samuel A; And Others 1968
Subtests: Auditory Reception; Visual Reception; Visual Sequential Memory; Auditory Association; Auditory Sequential Memory; Visual Association; Visual Closure; Verbal Expression; Grammatic Closure; Manual Expression; Auditory Closure; Sound Blending
Descriptors: Auditory Perception; Children; Cognitive Processes; *Diagnostic Tests; Elementary Education; *Elementary School Students; Expressive Language; Individual Testing; *Intelligence; Intelligence Tests; Pictorial Stimuli; *Preschool Children; Preschool Education; *Psycholinguistics; Receptive Language; Visual Perception
Identifiers: ITPA; Sequential Memory
Availability: University of Illinois Press; Urbana, IL 61801
Target Audience: 2-10

Designed to assess abilities in psycholinguistic functions in children between the ages of 2 and 10. Different starting points are specified for children of differing ability levels. If child is suspected of being retarded or gifted, the estimated mental age should determine the starting point. In average children, the chronological age is used to determine the starting point.

4716
SRA Verbal Form. Thurstone, Thelma Gwinn; Thurstone, L.L. 1956
Descriptors: Adults; *Aptitude Tests; *Cognitive Ability; *College Students; *Employees; Higher Education; High Schools; *High School Students; Mathematics Achievement; Occupational Tests; Secondary Education; *Secondary School Students
Availability: Science Research Associates; Business Programs Div., 155 N. Wacker Dr., Chicago, IL 60606
Target Audience: 13-64
Notes: Time, 15; Items, 84

Designed to measure general ability of students in junior high school through college, as well as adults from unskilled laborers to executives. SRA Verbal is a shorter version of Thurstone Test of Mental Alertness

(TC002081). A linguistic, quantitative, and total score may be derived. Personnel managers and educational counselors may use this instrument to determine individual's ability to learn, solve problems, foresee and plan, and think creatively. Forms A and B are available. Job tasks tested include ability to learn, comprehend, solve problems, follow instructions, and adjust effectively to changing situations.

4732
Word Association Test. Campbell, Joel T.; Belcher, Leon 1968
Descriptors: *Association Measures; *Black Students; *Cognitive Style; Cognitive Tests; Disadvantaged; Higher Education; *Undergraduate Students
Identifiers: Word Associations
Availability: Psychological Reports; v23 p119-34, 1968
Grade Level: 13-16
Notes: Items, 100

Designed to assess word association responses of Black college students. Subjects were asked to write their response to stimulus words.

4800
Wechsler Adult Intelligence Scale: Test Profile. Consulting Psychologists Press, Inc., Palo Alto, CA 1968
Descriptors: Adults; *Intelligence Tests; Older Adults; *Profiles; *Psychologists; Records (Forms); Scoring; *Test Interpretation
Identifiers: Supplementary Profile for the WAIS; WAIS Test Profile
Availability: Consulting Psychologists Press; 577 College Ave., Palo Alto, CA 94306
Target Audience: 18-75

Designed for use by psychologists in reporting test results to teachers or parents. The shortened form of reporting test scores provides for easy reference, graphic clarity, and a better understanding of subsections of the total test.

4801
Wechsler Preschool and Primary Scale of Intelligence: Test Profile. Consulting Psychologists Press, Inc., Palo Alto, CA 1968
Descriptors: Elementary School Students; Grade 1; *Intelligence Tests; *Preschool Children; Preschool Education; Primary Education; *Profiles; *Psychologists; Records (Forms); Scoring; *Test Interpretation
Identifiers: Supplementary Profile for the WPPSI; WPPSI Test Profile
Availability: Consulting Psychologists Press; 577 College Ave., Palo Alto, CA 94306
Target Audience: 4-6

Designed for use by psychologists in reporting test results to teachers or parents. The shortened form of reporting test scores provides for easy reference, graphic clarity and a better understanding of subsections of the total test.

4802
Wechsler Intelligence Scale for Children: Test Profile. Consulting Psychologists Press, Inc., Palo Alto, CA 1968
Descriptors: Adolescents; Children; *Elementary School Students; Elementary Secondary Education; *Intelligence Tests; *Profiles; *Psychologists; Records (Forms); Scoring; *Secondary School Students; *Test Interpretation
Identifiers: Supplementary Profile for the WISC; WISC Test Profile
Availability: Consulting Psychologists Press; 577 College Ave., Palo Alto, CA 94306
Target Audience: 5-15

Designed for use by psychologists in reporting test results to teachers, parents, or counselors. The shortened form of reporting test scores provides for easy reference, graphic clarity, and a better understanding of subsections of the total test.

4891
Wisconsin Card Sorting Test. Grant, David A.; Berg, Esta A.
Descriptors: *Abstract Reasoning; *Adolescents; *Adults; *Children; Computer Assisted Testing; Computer Software; Individual Testing; *Neurological Impairments; Performance Tests; *Preschool Children; *Screening Tests
Identifiers: WCST
Availability: Psychological Assessment Resources, Inc.; P.O. Box 998, Odessa, FL 33556
Target Audience: 4-64
Notes: Items, 64

Designed to assess preservation and abstract thinking in subjects from preschool children through adults. Provides objective measure of particular difficulty on card sorting task. Instrument is useful in identifying cerebral dysfunction, except where local lesions do not involve frontal areas. Useful screening test for brain damage. A computerized version is available for Apple IIe, II Plus and IIc.

4899
Account Clerk Test (70-A). Public Personnel Association, Chicago, IL 1959
Subtests: Number Checking; Error Detection; Commercial Arithmetic; Business Vocabulary; Business Theory; Applied Bookkeeping
Descriptors: Adults; *Aptitude Tests; *Bookkeeping; Business Skills; Occupational Tests; *Vocational Aptitude
Availability: International Personnel Management Association; 1313 E. 60th St., Chicago, IL 60637
Target Audience: Adults
Notes: Time, 120; Items, 130

Developed to aid in selection of personnel for sub-professional accounting work at entrance level. Measures specific aptitudes, involving both speed and accuracy, and job knowledge.

4948
Zip Test. Scott, Norval C.
Subtests: Language Facility Section; Word Recognition; Reading Comprehension; Word Opposites; Math Section; English Language Facility
Descriptors: Children; *Elementary School Students; English (Second Language); *Individual Testing; Language Fluency; Mathematics Achievement; *Migrant Children; Mathematics Tests; Reading Achievement; Reading Tests; *School Readiness Tests; *Screening Tests; *Spanish Speaking; *Student Placement
Availability: ASIS/NAPS, c/o Microfiche Publications; P.O. Box 3513, Grand Central Station, New York, NY 10163-3513 (NAPS Document 0070)
Target Audience: 5-12
Notes: Time, 30

Determines grade placement of a migrant child in reading and math and assesses the child's English language facility. The test locates the instructional level at which a child can effectively use a mathematics book and a reader and should not be used for chronological grade placement.

5003
Purdue Non-Language Personnel Test. Tiffin, Joseph 1969
Descriptors: Abstract Reasoning; *Adults; Career Guidance; *Cognitive Ability; *Culture Fair Tests; *Nonverbal Tests; *Personnel Selection
Identifiers: Purdue Personnel Tests
Availability: University Book Store; 360 State St., W. Lafayette, IN 47906
Target Audience: 18-64
Notes: Time, 10; Items, 24

Designed to measure mental ability through use of geometric forms. May be used with persons from various cultural and educational backgrounds. Useful in identifying mentally alert people among groups that cannot be fairly tested with verbal tests. Sale of test is restricted to industrial personnel departments and psychologists using tests for instruction or vocational guidance.

5008
Bennett Mechanical Comprehension Test, Form S. Bennett, George K. 1968
Descriptors: Adolescents; Adults; *Aptitude Tests; College Science; *College Students; Engineering Education; *High School Students; Industrial Education; *Job Applicants; *Mechanics (Physics); *Mechanics (Process); Occupational Tests; Secondary School Science; *Skilled Workers; Technical Education; Timed Tests; Trade and Industrial Education; Vocational Aptitude; Vocational High Schools
Identifiers: BMCT
Availability: The Psychological Corp.; 555 Academic Ct., San Antonio, TX 78204-0952
Target Audience: 14-64
Notes: Time, 30; Items, 68

Designed to measure the ability to perceive and comprehend the relationship of mechanical elements and physical law, and to apply this knowledge to new, practical situations. Administered to high school students, candidates and students in engineering schools, applicants and current employees of mechanical jobs, for other adult males of comparable ability and education, and for all women competing for or currently in comparable jobs or educational levels. Forms S and T are revisions of earlier Forms AA, BB, CC and W1. They have a wider range of difficulty, are for both men and women, and are timed. Scoring is the number correct, with no reduction of score for incorrect answers.

5009
Bennett Mechanical Comprehension Test, Form T. Bennett, George K. 1968

Descriptors: Adolescents; Adults; *Aptitude Tests; *College Applicants; College Science; *College Students; Engineering Education; *High School Students; Industrial Education; *Job Applicants; *Mechanics (Physics); *Mechanics (Process); Occupational Tests; Secondary School Science; *Skilled Workers; Technical Education; Timed Tests; Trade and Industrial Education; Vocational Aptitude; Vocational High Schools
Identifiers: BMCT
Availability: The Psychological Corp.; 555 Academic Ct., San Antonio, TX 78204-0952
Target Audience: 14-64
Notes: Time, 30; Items, 68

Designed to measure the ability to perceive and comprehend the relationship of mechanical elements and physical law, and to apply this knowledge to new, practical situations. Administered to high school students, candidates and students in engineering schools, applicants and current employees of mechanical jobs, for other adult males of comparable ability and education, and for all women competing for or currently in comparable jobs or educational levels. Forms S and T are revisions of earlier Forms AA, BB, CC and W1. They have a wider range of difficulty, are for both men and women, and are timed. Scoring is the number correct, with no reduction of score for incorrect answers.

5051
Test de Comprension Mecanica: Forma AA. Bennett, George K. 1957
Descriptors: Adolescents; Adults; *Aptitude Tests; High Schools; *High School Students; *Job Applicants; *Mechanics (Physics); *Mechanics (Process); Secondary School Science; *Skilled Workers; *Spanish; Technical Education; Trade and Industrial Education; Vocational Aptitude
Identifiers: Bennett Mechanical Comprehension Test
Availability: Manual Moderno; Av. Sonora 206, Col. Hipodromo, 06100 Mexico D.F., Mexico
Target Audience: 14-64
Notes: Time, 30 approx.; Items, 60

This instrument is a Spanish translation of the Bennett Mechanical Comprehension Test (TC001631). It measures the ability to understand mechanical relationships and physical laws in practical situations. For more recent edition, see Test de Comprension Mecanica Bennett (TC006998) available from the Psychological Corporation, 555 Academic Ct., San Antonio, TX 78204-0952. Form AA is usually administered to male high school students and job applicants; Form BB to male candidates or students of engineering schools and adult males of comparable ability and education.

5121
Children's Associative Responding Test. Achenbach, Thomas M. 1975
Descriptors: *Cognitive Style; Cognitive Tests; Intermediate Grades; Junior High Schools
Identifiers: Analogy Test Items; CART; *Free Associations; TIM(A)
Availability: Tests in Microfiche; Test Collection, Educational Testing Service, Princeton, NJ 08541
Grade Level: 5-8
Notes: Time, 30; Items, 68

A multiple choice analogy test designed to identify children who rely on associations to obvious cues rather than using their reasoning abilities.

5123
Neuro-Developmental Observation. Richardson, H. Burtt; And Others 1973
Subtests: Right-Left Tasks; Motor Tasks; Connecting Circles
Descriptors: Individual Testing; Learning Activities; *Learning Modalities; *Learning Problems; Learning Processes; Observation; *Parent Participation; Primary Education; *Problem Solving; *Teacher Participation; *Teaching Methods; *Young Children
Identifiers: Child Development Consultation; NDO; TIM(B)
Availability: Tests in Microfiche; Test Collection, Educational Testing Service, Princeton, NJ 08541
Grade Level: K-1
Notes: Time, 20 approx.

Carried out on a one-to-one basis, the NDO is designed to serve 4 objectives: provide data concerning the conditions under which the child can be successful; demonstrate these strategies in the presence of the parent or teacher; involve the child in problem solving and learning to seek help from his or her environment; and begin a practical problem-solving ongoing collaboration between the Child Development Consultant and the people who must carry out any recommendation. Length of test varies as it is dependent on the number of correct responses; failure is followed by training. Requires both pre- and post-testing sessions with the Child Development Consultant. The emphasis is not on the performance of specific tasks but on helping the child to learn through the use of a variety of strategies that involve auditory, visual and kinesthetic presentations. Observation by parents and/or teacher is an important part of the procedure. The 3 subtests demonstrate the following: 1) Right-Left Tasks—segmenting a task into component parts; 2) Motor Tasks—influence of auditory, visual, and kinesthetic types of presentation upon the child's action; and 3) Connecting Circles—influence of distractions.

5156
Cutrona Child Study Profile of Psycho-Educational Abilities. Cutrona, Michael P. 1970
Subtests: General Behavior; Gross Motor Development; Fine Motor Development; Body Image and Awareness; Tactile Kinesthetic Development; Visual Motor Perception; Auditory Perception; Time Orientation; Non Verbal Conceptualization; Numerical Conceptualization
Descriptors: Academic Aptitude; Child Development; *Elementary School Students; Handicap Identification; Individual Development; Individual Testing; *Learning Problems; Learning Readiness; *Observation; Performance; *Primary Education; Rating Scales; *School Readiness; School Readiness Tests; Screening Tests; *Student Adjustment; *Student Behavior; Student Evaluation
Availability: Cutronics Educational Institute Publications; 128 W. 56th St., Bayonne, NJ 07002
Grade Level: K-3
Notes: Items, 98
Screening device used to provide a psychoeducational profile of the child. Used as part of complete child study diagnostic evaluation, in planning pre-school and primary grade educational programs, and for special education programs. According to the author, the instrument indicates general behavioral trends and the child's adequacy of ability or competency in psychoeducational areas.

5178
Fruit Distraction Test. Santostefano, Sebastiano 1964
Descriptors: *Adolescents; Attention Control; *Children; *Cognitive Style; Cognitive Tests; Individual Testing; Visual Perception
Identifiers: Distractibility; FDT; *Field Articulation
Availability: Santostefano, Sebastiano. A Biodevelopmental Approach to Clinical Child Psychology. New York: John Wiley & Sons, 1978
Target Audience: 3-15
Designed to assess the cognitive control principle of field articulation or the selective deployment of attention. There are 4 test cards and 3 practice cards. The instrument requires knowledge of colors and good color perception. The child should be able to recognize and name primary colors.

5220
Test of Learning Ability Forms DS-12, DT-12. Richardson, Bellows, Henry and Co., Washington, DC 1961
Subtests: Vocabulary; Block Counting; Arithmetic
Descriptors: Adults; Aptitude Tests; *Arithmetic; *Cognitive Ability; Cognitive Tests; *Employees; *Intelligence; *Job Applicants; Job Placement; Multiple Choice Tests; Occupational Tests; Screening Tests; *Spatial Ability; Timed Tests; *Verbal Ability; Verbal Tests; Vocational Aptitude
Identifiers: RBH Test of Learning Ability
Availability: Richardson, Bellows, Henry and Co.; 1140 Connecticut Ave., N.W., Washington, DC 20036
Target Audience: Adults
Notes: Time, 12; Items, 54
Designed to measure 3 major components of intelligence: vocabulary comprehension, arithmetic reasoning, and ability to perceive spatial relations. Used by personnel departments in a variety of screening, selection, placement, and promotion situations. Contents are the same as in Test of Learning Ability (TC003840), but it differs in the amount of time spent reading directions and had been developed for use when the subjects are relatively unsophisticated in test taking or when the administrator anticipates the need for more instruction and time for taking the test.

5302
Asymmetrical Preference Test. Lindgren, Henry Clay 1964
Descriptors: Adults; *Art Appreciation; *Creativity; *Self Concept Measures; *Self Evaluation (Individuals)
Identifiers: Adjective Check Lists; APT; *Asocial Attitudes; Barron (Frank); Forced Choice Personality Questionnaire; TIM(B)
Availability: Tests in Microfiche; Test Collection, Educational Testing Service, Princeton, NJ 08541
Target Audience: Adults

Notes: Time, 10; Items, 30
Self-administered instrument is designed to determine if there is a relationship between asocial attitudes and creativity and one's preference for modern versus traditional art. The items comprising this questionnaire were derived from the self-descriptive adjectives employed by Barron in his studies on creativity.

5361
WISC-R Profile Form. Hobby, Kenneth L.
Descriptors: *Elementary School Students; Elementary Secondary Education; Intelligence Quotient; *Intelligence Tests; *Profiles; Records (Forms); *Secondary School Students; *Test Interpretation
Identifiers: Wechsler Intelligence Scale for Children (Revised); WISC R
Availability: Psychologists and Educators; P.O. Box 513, St. Louis, MO 63017
Target Audience: 6-16
Summary of all necessary information needed to interpret and understand WISC-R test results.

5378
Gilliland Learning Potential Examination: 1970 Revision. Gilliland, Hap 1970
Subtests: Visual Memory; Symbol Identification; Symbol Interpretation; Relationships; Listening Comprehension; Picture Completion; General Information and Interests; Symbol Representation
Descriptors: *Academic Aptitude; Adults; American Indians; *Aptitude Tests; *Culture Fair Tests; *Disadvantaged; Elementary School Students; Elementary Secondary Education; Intelligence; Nonverbal Tests; *Reading Difficulties; *Reservation American Indians; Secondary School Students
Identifiers: Culturally Specific Tests
Availability: Montana Council for Indian Education; 517 Rimrock Rd., P.O. Box 31215, Billings, MT 59107
Target Audience: 6-16
Designed to determine scholastic aptitude, particularly in reading. Designed for nonreaders and culturally different students from age 6 to 16. May be used with older teenagers and adults with reading difficulties. Areas assessed include visual memory, listening comprehension, ability to use symbols, and to see relationships. Non-Cultural and Non-Reading scores can be computed. A slightly adapted version is being used with Indian tribes north of the Arctic Circle and in the Amazon jungles.

5488
The Contemporary School Readiness Test. Sauer, Clara Elbert 1970
Subtests: Writing My Name; Colors of the Spectrum; Science, Health, and Social Studies; Numbers; Handwriting; Reading; Visual Discrimination; Auditory Discrimination; Listening Comprehension
Descriptors: Auditory Discrimination; Elementary School Students; *Grade 1; *Kindergarten Children; Listening Comprehension; Predictive Measurement; Primary Education; Reading Readiness; *School Readiness; *School Readiness Tests; Visual Discrimination
Availability: Montana Council for Indian Education; P.O. Box 31215, Billings, MT 59107
Grade Level: K-1
Notes: Time, 90 approx.; Items, 100
Designed to predict the success of children in first grade. Should be administered to children in kindergarten or early weeks of first grade.

5491
Picture Story Measure of Kindness Concept. Baldwin, Clara P. 1968
Descriptors: Adolescents; *Altruism; Attitude Measures; Children; Cognitive Development; *Elementary School Students; Elementary Secondary Education; Higher Education; *Interpersonal Relationship; *Secondary School Students; *Undergraduate Students
Availability: ASIS/NAPS; c/o Microfiche Publications, P. O. Box 3513, Grand Central Station, New York, NY 10163-3513 (Document 00653)
Grade Level: K-16
Notes: Items, 10
Designed to study the development of children's cognitive understanding of interpersonal relationships. Concepts of kindness are assessed by this instrument.

5535
Rhodes WISC Scatter Profile. Rhodes, Fen 1969
Subtests: Full Scale Scatter; Verbal Scale Scatter; Performance Scale Scatter
Descriptors: Adolescents; Children; *Intelligence Tests; *Profiles; Records (Forms); *Test Interpretation

Identifiers: *Wechsler Intelligence Scale for Children
Availability: Educational and Industrial Testing Service; P.O. Box 7234, San Diego, CA 92107
Target Audience: 5-15
Notes: Time, 1 approx.
Designed to assist user of the WISC in evaluating and interpreting the levels and patterns of performance of individual subjects on the various subtests. Enables administrator to determine which subtests deviate sufficiently from the composite to be considered as having possible diagnostic significance.

5569
Grassi Block Substitution Test for Measuring Organic Brain Pathology. Grassi, Joseph R. 1970
Descriptors: Adults; Cognitive Style; *Diagnostic Tests; Individual Testing; Minimal Brain Dysfunction; *Neurological Impairments; *Patients; Performance Tests; Psychiatric Hospitals; Psychological Evaluation
Identifiers: *Psychiatric Patients; Schizophrenic Patients
Availability: Charles C. Thomas, Publisher; 2600 S. First St., Springfield, IL 62717
Target Audience: 18-64
Designed to demonstrate impairment of concrete and abstract performance due to organic brain dysfunction. Especially useful to detect early and minimal organic changes so that defects may be diagnosed in early stages of the disease process.

5575
Test of Science Comprehension. Nelson, C.H.; Mason, J.M.
Descriptors: *Achievement Tests; *Critical Thinking; *Elementary School Students; *General Science; Intermediate Grades; Pretests Posttests; Problem Solving; *Science Tests
Availability: Science Education; v47 n4 p320-30, Oct 1963
Grade Level: 4-6
Notes: Items, 60
Designed to assess critical thinking in science. To obtain the most meaningful results, arrangements should be made to give the test as a pretest early in the school year and again as a posttest near the end of the academic year.

5577
New Uses. Hoepfner, Ralph; Guilford, J.P. 1969
Descriptors: Adolescents; *Adults; *Cognitive Style; *Cognitive Tests; *Divergent Thinking; Problem Solving; *Students; Timed Tests
Identifiers: Convergent Production of Semantic Transformations; NU; Picture Gestalt; *Reasoning Ability; Structure of Intellect
Availability: Sheridan Psychological Services, Inc.; P.O. Box 6101, Orange, CA 92667
Target Audience: 14-64
Notes: Time, 9
Measures the factor known as convergent production of semantic transformations, which is defined as the ability to redefine, a part of the structure-of-intellect ability. A low score may indicate functional fixedness, which inhibits problem solving and prevents insights. Revision of Picture Gestalt.

5579
Memory for Meanings. Hoepfner, Ralph; Guilford, J.P. 1969
Descriptors: Adolescents; *Adults; *Cognitive Tests; *Definitions; Memorization; *Semantics; *Short Term Memory; *Students; Timed Tests; Verbal Tests
Identifiers: Memory for Semantic Units; MM; *Synonyms
Availability: Sheridan Psychological Services, Inc.; P.O. Box 6101, Orange, CA 92667
Target Audience: 12-64
Notes: Time, 12
Measures the factor known as memory for semantic units. The respondent is to remember the meanings of a group of words. He or she then, by remembering, is able to recognize very close synonyms.

5582
Sketches. Gershon, Arthur; And Others 1967
Descriptors: Adolescents; *Adults; *Cognitive Tests; Constructed Response; *Creativity Tests; *Divergent Thinking; Nonverbal Tests; *Students; Timed Tests; *Visual Measures
Identifiers: Divergent Production of Figural Units; Structure of Intellect
Availability: Sheridan Psychological Services, Inc.; P.O. Box 6101, Orange, CA 92667
Target Audience: 12-64
Notes: Time, 8
Measures the factor known as figural fluency, or divergent production of figural units. This is the ability to produce with efficiency a number of visual-figural-information units when asked to make one into a recognizable object.

5584
Expression Grouping. O'Sullivan, Maureen; Guilford, J.P.
Descriptors: Adolescents; *Adults; *Affective Behavior; *Affective Measures; Cognitive Tests; *Human Posture; *Nonverbal Communication; Pictorial Stimuli; Social Cognition; *Students; Timed Tests; Visual Measures
Identifiers: Cognition of Behavioral Classes
Availability: Consulting Psychologists Press; 577 College Ave., Palo Alto, CA 94306
Target Audience: 14-64
Notes: Time, 10
Measures the factor known as cognition of behavioral classes, which is defined as the ability to view a multiple number of pictured expressions involving different parts of the body, and to decide what psychological state or momentary disposition they indicate in common.

5585
Missing Cartoons. DeMille, Richard; And Others
Descriptors: Adolescents; *Adults; *Behavior; Cartoons; *Cognitive Tests; Pictorial Stimuli; *Social Cognition; *Students; Timed Tests; Visual Measures
Identifiers: Cognition of Behavioral Implications; Cognition of Behavioral Systems; Cognition of Behavioral Units
Availability: Consulting Psychologists Press; 577 College Ave., Palo Alto, CA 94306
Target Audience: 14-64
Notes: Time, 16
Measures 3 factors of social cognition: cognition of behavioral systems (situations), cognition of behavioral units (momentary dispositions), and cognition of behavioral implications (predictions). From a 4-part cartoon strip with 1 picture missing, the respondent chooses the most appropriate, alternative cartoon to complete the meaning of the strip. No text is given with the cartoons.

5588
Social Translations. O'Sullivan, Maureen; Guilford, J.P.
Descriptors: Adolescents; *Adults; *Cognitive Tests; *Communication (Thought Transfer); *Interpersonal Relationship; *Social Cognition; *Students; Timed Tests
Identifiers: Cognition of Behavioral Relations; Cognition of Behavioral Transformations
Availability: Consulting Psychologists Press; 577 College Ave., Palo Alto, CA 94306
Target Audience: 14-64
Notes: Time, 8
Measures basically the cognition of behavioral transformations and, to some degree, cognition of behavioral relations; that is, being able to appreciate the type of psychological relation which occurs between 2 individuals in the act of communication.

5589
Cartoon Predictions. O'Sullivan, Maureen; Guilford, J.P.
Descriptors: Adolescents; *Adults; *Behavior; *Cartoons; Cognitive Tests; Pictorial Stimuli; *Predictive Measurement; *Social Cognition; *Students; Timed Tests; Visual Measures
Identifiers: Cognition of Behavioral Implications
Availability: Consulting Psychologists Press; 577 College Ave., Palo Alto, CA 94306
Target Audience: 14-64
Notes: Time, 8
Measures cognitive, behavioral implications, that is, the ability to predict what is most likely to happen next when dealing with a sequence of behaviors.

5602
Mehrabian Picture Vocabulary Test. Mehrabian, Albert
Descriptors: *Cognitive Measurement; Individual Testing; *Language Acquisition; *Pictorial Stimuli; *Preschool Children; *Psycholinguistics; *Verbal Ability; Verbal Development; Verbal Tests; Visual Measures; Vocabulary
Identifiers: Measures of Vocabulary and Gramm Skills to Age 6; MPVT; Oral Tests; Picture Vocabulary Test
Availability: Developmental Psychology; v2 n3 p439-46, 1970
Target Audience: 2-5
Notes: Time, 20 approx.; Items, 35
Measures a child's verbal ability, linguistic skill, and language acquisition. In each set of pictures, the child is asked to identify a specific item. Individually administered.

5613
Walker Readiness Test for Disadvantaged Pre-School Children in the United States. Walker, Wanda 1969
Subtests: Similarities; Differences; Numerical Analogies; Missing Parts
Descriptors: *Concept Formation; Culture Fair Tests; *Disadvantaged Youth; English; French; *Individual Testing; Nonverbal Tests; Number Concepts; *Preschool Children; *Preschool Tests; *School Readiness Tests; Spanish Speaking; Young Children
Identifiers: Project Head Start
Availability: ERIC Document Reproduction Service; 3900 Wheeler Ave., Alexandria, VA 22304 (ED037253, 147 pages)
Target Audience: 4-6
Notes: Items, 50
An individually administered culture-fair, nonverbal readiness test, directions for which are available in English, Spanish, or French. (Included in ERIC Document ED037253, 147 pages.) Test population is rural and urban disadvantaged preschool children.

5614
Gross Geometric Forms. Gross, Ruth Brill 1970
Descriptors: Cognitive Style; *Creativity; *Individual Testing; Performance Tests; *Preschool Children; Preschool Education
Identifiers: TIM(B)
Availability: Tests in Microfiche; Test Collection, Educational Testing Service, Princeton, NJ 08541
Target Audience: 3-7
Notes: Time, 20 approx.; Items, 10
Designed to assess creativity in young children. The child's manipulation of various flat, geometric forms is rated, yielding scores for productivity, communicability of ideas, and richness of thinking. Experimental instrument. Individually administered.

5719
Pre-Kindergarten Goal Card: 1968 Revision. Cincinnati Public Schools, Ohio Dept. of Instruction 1968
Subtests: Tested Qualities (106); Observed Qualities (43)
Descriptors: Behavior Rating Scales; *Concept Formation; Creativity; *Language Skills; *Preschool Children; Preschool Education; Psychomotor Skills; *School Readiness Tests
Identifiers: TIM(A)
Availability: Tests in Microfiche; Test Collection, Educational Testing Service, Princeton, NJ 08541
Target Audience: 2-5
Notes: Items, 149
This test is designed to measure various qualities in preschool aged children. Variables assessed are: physical coordination, relationship of people and things, auditory discrimination, concepts of size, concepts of color, visual discrimination, concept of weight, manipulation of materials, arithmetic skills, concepts of location and space, and listening skills. The teacher observes the child's performance of certain activities: Mental Alertness; Language Ability; Social Awareness; Health Habits; Creative Abilities; Motor Coordination.

5785
What Could It Be? Pilot Edition. Torrance, E. Paul; Phillips, Victor K. 1970
Descriptors: Children; Creativity; *Creativity Tests; *Divergent Thinking; Individual Testing; Performance Tests
Identifiers: TIM(B)
Availability: Tests in Microfiche; Test Collection, Educational Testing Service, Princeton, NJ 08541
Target Audience: 3-10
Notes: Time, 18; Items, 6
This test of originality for children aged 3 through 10 years consists of a set of wooden blocks of different shapes that are used as stimuli. For each block, the child is asked to think of as many things as he or she can that are suggested by the shape of that block. Administered individually.

5834
Career Ability Placement Survey. Knapp, Lila F.; Knapp, Robert R. 1976
Descriptors: Aptitude Tests; *Career Development; *Cognitive Ability; Higher Education; Secondary Education; *Secondary School Students; Semantics; Spatial Ability; *Undergraduate Students
Identifiers: CAPS; Manual Dexterity; Mechanical Comprehension; Perceptive Reasoning; *Reasoning Ability; Test Batteries
Availability: Educational and Industrial Testing Service; P.O. Box 7234, San Diego, CA 92107
Grade Level: 7-16
Notes: Time, 40 approx.
Designed to measure abilities through use of 8 5-minute ability tests. Test of Mechanical Reasoning has 20 items; Spatial Relations has 18 items; Verbal Reasoning has 6 items; Numerical Ability has 24 items; Language Usage has 30 items; Word Knowledge has 56 items; Perceptual

Speed and Accuracy has 150 items; and Manual Speed and Dexterity has 19 items. Machine Scoring and Self Scoring forms are available. Interpretation of CAPS in career development may be accomplished in terms of the COP System structure of occupations. Fourteen job family clusters are used in CAPS Self-Interpretation Profile and Guide.

5839
Mother Goose Problems Test: Revised Edition. Torrance, E. Paul 1969
Descriptors: *Creativity; *Divergent Thinking; Individual Testing; Verbal Communication; *Visual Measures; Young Children
Identifiers: TIM(B)
Availability: Tests in Microfiche; Test Collection, Educational Testing Service, Princeton, NJ 08541
Target Audience: 3-6
Notes: Time, 30 approx.; Items, 2
Designed to assess the creative thinking ability of young children from 3 to 6 years of age. Verbal flexibility, fluency, and originality are elicited by asking children to suggest alternative possibilities to various problems posed by 4 of the Mother Goose rhymes. Administered individually. Forms A and B available. Experimental instrument.

5882
Verbal Identification Test. Institute for Developmental Studies, New York, NY 1965
Subtests: Noun Enumeration Score; Action Enumeration Score; Combined Enumeration Score; Noun Gestalt Score; Action Gestalt Score; Combined Gestalt Score
Descriptors: Cognitive Tests; *Concept Formation; Disadvantaged Youth; Elementary Education; *Elementary School Students; Expressive Language; Language Acquisition; Pictorial Stimuli; *Verbal Development
Identifiers: Institute for Developmental Studies; Verbal Survey Language Tests
Availability: Institute for Developmental Studies; Press Bldg., New York University, Washington Square, New York, NY 10003
Grade Level: K-5
Notes: Time, 20 approx.; Items, 20
Designed to measure labeling function and conceptual ability. Assesses the child's ability to describe and identify pictorial representations of objects, events, and people in his/her environment.

5884
Word Association Test. Institute for Developmental Studies, New York, NY 1965
Descriptors: *Association (Psychology); Disadvantaged Youth; Elementary Education; *Elementary School Students; Language Tests; Oral Language; *Verbal Development
Identifiers: Institute for Developmental Studies; Verbal Survey Language Tests; *Word Associations
Availability: Institute for Developmental Studies; Press Bldg., New York University, Washington Square, New York, NY 10003
Grade Level: 1-5
Notes: Time, 5 approx.; Items, 14
Designed to sample student's partially structured speech, mid-way between spontaneous and structured associations.

5885
Word Distance Scale. Institute for Developmental Studies, New York, NY 1965
Descriptors: Association (Psychology); Disadvantaged Youth; Elementary Education; *Elementary School Students; Language Tests; *Verbal Development
Identifiers: Institute for Developmental Studies; *Semantic Distance; Verbal Survey Language Tests
Availability: Institute for Developmental Studies; Press Bldg., New York University, Washington Square, New York, NY 10003
Grade Level: 1-5
Notes: Time, 15 approx.; Items, 11
Designed to measure the degree of relatedness of words to other words in terms of associative belongingness, or "connotative spread."

5887
Concept Formation Test I. Institute for Developmental Studies, New York, NY 1965
Descriptors: Classification; Cognitive Tests; *Concept Formation; Disadvantaged Youth; Elementary Education; *Elementary School Students; Pictorial Stimuli; Verbal Communication
Identifiers: Institute for Developmental Studies
Availability: Institute for Developmental Studies; Press Bldg., New York University, Washington Square, New York, NY 10003
Grade Level: 1-5
Notes: Items, 8

Designed to measure classification ability on the basis of qualities in the stimulus field ranging from perceptual identity to class communality. Child is presented with a booklet consisting of pictorial stimuli representing concepts of identity, similarity, class specificity, and class generalization. Yields a "choice" score and a verbalization score.

5888
Concept Formation Test II. Institute for Developmental Studies, New York, NY 1965
Descriptors: Classification; Cognitive Tests; *Concept Formation; Elementary Education; *Elementary School Students; Geometric Constructions
Identifiers: Institute for Developmental Studies
Availability: Institute for Developmental Studies; Press Bldg., New York University, Washington Square, New York, NY 10003
Grade Level: 1-5
Notes: Items, 28

Designed to measure classification ability on the basis of qualities in the stimulus field ranging from perceptual identity to class communality. Instrument employs abstract geometrical figures so that choice behavior of subject would provide maximum information. Stimulus items cover 4 attributes which include form, color, size, and number.

5889
Concept Sorting Task. Institute for Developmental Studies, New York, NY 1965
Descriptors: *Abstract Reasoning; *Classification; Cognitive Tests; *Concept Formation; Elementary Education; Verbal Communication
Identifiers: Card Sort; CST; Institute for Developmental Studies
Availability: Institute for Developmental Studies; Press Bldg., New York University, Washington Square, New York, NY 10003
Grade Level: 1-5
Notes: Time, 10 approx.; Items, 16

Designed to elicit information concerning the logical basis children use in organizing conceptual stimuli. Child is presented with 16 cards in random order. Task is to sort them into piles and then explain his/her groupings.

5895
Hidden Figures Test. Institute for Developmental Studies, New York, NY 1965
Descriptors: Elementary Education; *Elementary School Students; *Neurological Impairments; Spatial Ability; Tachistoscopes; *Visual Discrimination; Visual Measures; Visual Perception
Identifiers: Institute for Developmental Studies
Availability: Institute for Developmental Studies; Press Bldg., New York University, Washington Square, New York, NY 10003
Grade Level: 1-5

Designed to measure subject's visual perceptual abilities. Subject must identify familiar objects or abstract figures embedded in other similar but more complex figures. Useful in evaluating retraining potential of brain-damaged children.

5919
Short Form Test of Academic Aptitude. Sullivan, Elizabeth T.; And Others 1970
Subtests: Vocabulary; Analogies; Sequences; Memory
Descriptors: *Academic Aptitude; *Aptitude Tests; *Elementary School Students; Elementary Secondary Education; Memory; Predictive Measurement; *Secondary School Students; Vocabulary
Identifiers: Analogies; Sequences; SFTAA
Availability: CTB/McGraw Hill; Del Monte Research Park, Monterey, CA 93940
Grade Level: 1-12
Notes: Time, 35

A measure of academic aptitude, i.e., knowledge and skills not directly taught in school, that have been shown to predict academic achievement. Users of this test are encouraged to change to the Test of Cognitive Skills (TC011526-TC011530). Machine scoring is no longer performed by the publisher.

5927
Guilford-Zimmerman Aptitude Survey: Verbal Comprehension. Guilford, J.P.; Zimmerman, Wayne S.
Descriptors: Adolescents; *Adults; *Aptitude Tests; *Language Aptitude; Language Tests; *Semantics; *Students; Timed Tests; *Verbal Ability
Identifiers: Cognition of Semantic Units; GZAS; VC
Availability: Consulting Psychologists Press; 577 College Ave., Palo Alto, CA 94306
Target Audience: 14-64
Notes: Time, 25; Items, 72

Measures the factor known as cognition of semantic units, or verbal comprehension; and is one of 7 parts in the Guilford-Zimmerman Aptitude Survey. The parts may be used separately or in a combined form.

5928
Guilford-Zimmerman Aptitude Survey: General Reasoning. Guilford, J.P.; Zimmerman, Wayne S.
Descriptors: Adolescents; *Adults; *Aptitude Tests; Cognitive Ability; *Problem Solving; *Students; Timed Tests
Identifiers: Cognition of Semantic Systems; GR; GZAS; *Reasoning; *Reasoning Ability
Availability: Consulting Psychologists Press; 577 College Ave., Palo Alto, CA 94306
Target Audience: 14-64
Notes: Time, 35

One of 7 parts of the Guilford-Zimmerman Aptitude Survey; the parts may be given separately, or in a combined form. This part measures the factor known as cognition of semantic systems, which is used in a variety of problem-solving tasks. The authors have reduced the amount of numerical computation to a minimum.

5929
Guilford-Zimmerman Aptitude Survey: Numerical Operations. Guilford, J.P.; Zimmerman, Wayne S.
Descriptors: Adolescents; *Adults; *Aptitude Tests; *Arithmetic; Children; *Computation; *Mathematics Tests; *Students; Timed Tests
Identifiers: GZAS; NO; *Number Operations
Availability: Consulting Psychologists Press; 577 College Ave., Palo Alto, CA 94306
Target Audience: 10-64
Notes: Time, 8

One part of 7 parts in the Guilford-Zimmerman Aptitude Survey. The parts may be used separately or in a combined form. This part measures numerical facility, an aptitude used for tasks involving work with numbers—accounting, making change, and many other types of clerical work. Problems include addition, subtraction, and multiplication in multiple-choice items.

5930
Guilford-Zimmerman Aptitude Survey: Perceptual Speed. Guilford, J.P.; Zimmerman, Wayne S.
Descriptors: Adolescents; *Adults; *Aptitude Tests; *Students; Timed Tests
Identifiers: *Clerical Aptitude; Clerical Skills; Evaluation of Figural Units; GZAS; *Perceptual Speed; PS
Availability: Consulting Psychologists Press; 577 College Ave., Palo Alto, CA 94306
Target Audience: 14-64
Notes: Time, 5

One of 7 parts in the Guilford-Zimmerman Aptitude Survey. The parts may be given separately, i.e., singly, or in a combined form. This part measures the ability to compare visual details quickly and accurately and to judge whether they are identical or not. This ability is known as evaluation of figural units. Many clerical positions, as well as inspectors or machine operators, depend upon this type of aptitude.

5931
Guilford-Zimmerman Aptitude Survey: Spatial Orientation. Guilford, J.P.; Zimmerman, Wayne S.
Descriptors: Adolescents; *Adults; *Aptitude Tests; Cognitive Ability; *Spatial Ability; *Students; Timed Tests; *Visual Measures; *Visual Stimuli
Identifiers: Cognition of Figural Systems; GZAS; SO
Availability: Consulting Psychologists Press; 577 College Ave., Palo Alto, CA 94306
Target Audience: 14-64
Notes: Time, 10

One part of the 7 part Guilford-Zimmerman Aptitude Survey. The parts may be used singly, or in a combined form. This part measures the factor known as cognition of figural systems, the ability to perceive spatial arrangements. This ability is used in the operation of machines when there is a choice of direction of movement in response to given signals.

5932
Guilford-Zimmerman Aptitude Survey: Spatial Visualization. Guilford, J.P.; Zimmerman, Wayne S.
Descriptors: Adolescents; *Adults; *Aptitude Tests; Cognitive Ability; *Spatial Ability; *Students; Timed Tests; *Visual Measures; *Visual Stimuli
Identifiers: Cognition of Figural Transformations; GZAS; SV
Availability: Consulting Psychologists Press; 577 College Ave., Palo Alto, CA 94306
Target Audience: 14-64
Notes: Time, 10

One part of the 7 part Guilford-Zimmerman Aptitude Survey; the parts may be used singly, or in a combined form. This part measures the factor known as cognition of figural transformations, the ability to manipulate ideas in a visual manner. This ability is used by many types of engineers, architects, and draftsmen.

5949
Florida Taxonomy of Cognitive Behavior. Brown, Bob Burton; And Others 1968
Subtests: Specifics (6); Ways and Means of Dealing with Specifics (7); Universals and Abstractions (4); Translation (6); Interpretation (6); Application (4); Analysis (11); Synthesis (9); Evaluation (2)
Descriptors: Adolescents; Adults; Behavior Rating Scales; Children; *Classroom Observation Techniques; *Cognitive Measurement; *Cognitive Style; Elementary Secondary Education; *Students; *Teachers
Identifiers: TIM(A)
Availability: Tests in Microfiche; Test Collection, Educational Testing Service, Princeton, NJ 08541
Target Audience: 2-65
Notes: Time, 30; Items, 55

Designed for describing cognitive behavior evidenced by teachers and pupils in classroom situations.

6040
WISC Mental Description Sheet. Blazer, John A. 1970
Subtests: Emotional Reactions; Consistency of Mental Activity; Content of Mental Activity; Intellectual Capacities and Responses
Descriptors: Children; *Elementary School Students; Elementary Secondary Education; Intelligence Quotient; *Intelligence Tests; *Profiles; Records (Forms); *Secondary School Students; *Test Interpretation
Identifiers: Wechsler Intelligence Scale for Children; WISC
Availability: Psychologists and Educators; P.O. Box 513, St. Louis, MO 63017
Target Audience: 5-15
Notes: Time, 10 approx.

Designed to reveal a graphic profile indicating subject's general functioning. Interpretive areas include emotional reactions, consistency of mental activity, content of mental activity, and intellectual capacities and responses.

6076
Cornell Critical Thinking Test, Level Z. Ennis, Robert H.; Millman, Jason 1971
Descriptors: *Achievement Tests; Cognitive Processes; Cognitive Tests; *Critical Thinking; Higher Education; *Undergraduate Students
Identifiers: Cornell Critical Thinking Test; Self Administered Tests
Availability: Illinois Thinking Project; University of Illinois, 1310 S. Sixth St., Champaign, IL 61820
Grade Level: 13-16
Notes: Time, 50 approx.; Items, 52

Developed to assess ability in several aspects of critical thinking, the reasonable assessment of statements. Level Z is best adapted to students in higher education. However, some high ability secondary students would be able to cope with it.

6077
Cornell Critical Thinking Test, Level X. Ennis, Robert H.; Millman, Jason 1971
Descriptors: Cognitive Processes; *Cognitive Tests; *Critical Thinking; Secondary Education; *Secondary School Students
Identifiers: Cornell Critical Thinking Test; Self Administered Tests
Availability: Illinois Thinking Project; University of Illinois, 1310 S. Sixth St., Champaign, IL 61820
Grade Level: 7-12
Notes: Time, 50 approx.; Items, 72

Developed to assess ability in several aspects of critical thinking, defined as the reasonable assessment of statements. Level X consists of 4 sections. The first section asks for bearing of information on a hypothesis. The second section assesses ability to judge reliability of information on the basis of its source. The third section assesses ability to judge whether statement follows from premises. The final section focuses on identification of assumptions.

6128
Stereognostic Recognition of Objects and Shapes. Piaget, Jean 1970
Descriptors: *Children; Concept Formation; Elementary Education; *Elementary School Students; Individual Testing; *Preschool Children; Preschool Education; *Spatial Ability; *Tactual Perception
Identifiers: Euclidian Concepts; Piaget (Jean); *Piagetian Tests

Availability: Laurendeau, Monique and Adrien Pinard. The Development of the Concept of Space in the Child. New York: International Universities Press, Inc., 1970.
Target Audience: 2-12

Designed to demonstrate development of the most elementary concepts of topological space and the genetic primacy of these concepts in relation to Euclidian concepts. Student identifies objects through sense of touch. This is an experimental test.

6129
Localization of Topographical Positions. Piaget, Jean 1970
Descriptors: *Children; Concept Formation; Elementary Education; *Elementary School Students; Individual Testing; *Preschool Children; Preschool Education; *Spatial Ability
Identifiers: Euclidian Concepts; Piaget (Jean); *Piagetian Tests
Availability: Laurendeau, Monique and Adrien Pinard. The Development of the Concept of Space in the Child. New York: International Universities Press, Inc., 1970.
Target Audience: 2-12

Designed to assess child's early spatial representations with emphasis on problem of the extension of topological concepts into projective and Euclidian concepts. Child must place objects on landscape in exact position shown by examiner. This is an experimental test.

6130
Construction of a Projective Straight Line. Piaget, Jean 1970
Descriptors: *Children; Concept Formation; Elementary Education; *Elementary School Students; Individual Testing; *Preschool Children; Preschool Education; *Spatial Ability
Identifiers: Piaget (Jean); *Piagetian Tests
Availability: Laurendeau, Monique and Adrien Pinard. The Development of the Concept of Space in the Child. New York: International Universities Press, Inc., 1970.
Target Audience: 2-12

Designed to measure child's ability to construct a straight line between 2 points. Child arranges a group of elements in a single constant direction. This ability illustrates the shift from topological representations to projective and Euclidian representations in the child's conception of space. This is an experimental test.

6131
Concepts of Left and Right. Piaget, Jean 1970
Descriptors: *Children; Concept Formation; Elementary Education; *Elementary School Students; Individual Testing; *Preschool Children; Preschool Education; *Spatial Ability
Identifiers: Piaget (Jean); *Piagetian Tests; *Right Left Discrimination
Availability: Laurendeau, Monique and Adrien Pinard. The Development of the Concept of Space in the Child. New York: International Universities Press, Inc., 1970.
Target Audience: 2-12

Designed to assess the development of the most basic concepts of projective space in an effort to understand the child's construction and progressive coordination of the major dimensions of this space. This is an experimental test.

6132
Coordination of Perspectives. Piaget, Jean 1970
Descriptors: *Children; Concept Formation; Elementary Education; *Elementary School Students; Individual Testing; Perception; *Preschool Children; Preschool Education; *Spatial Ability
Identifiers: Piaget (Jean); *Piagetian Tests
Availability: Laurendeau, Monique and Adrien Pinard. The Development of the Concept of Space in the Child. New York: International Universities Press, Inc., 1970.
Target Audience: 2-12

Designed to determine stages making the progressive development of projective space. Projective concepts develop later than topological concepts. This is an experimental test.

6136
Quantity Matching Inventory—1/Mathematics. Victor, Jack; Coller, Alan R. 1970
Descriptors: *Cognitive Measurement; Concept Formation; Early Childhood Education; *Elementary School Students; Individual Testing; *Number Concepts; *Preschool Children; Preschool Education; Primary Education
Identifiers: Institute for Developmental Studies; QMI 1M
Availability: Institute for Developmental Studies; Press Bldg., New York University, Washington Square, New York, NY 10003

Grade Level: K-3
Target Audience: 2-8
Notes: Items, 16

Designed to assess young child's quantitative concepts. Child is asked to match pictures with same number of objects. This instrument is also available from the author: Alan R. Coller; 12 Burlington Ave., Vorhees, NJ 08043

6137
Quantity Matching Inventory—1/Mathematics, Set A. Victor, Jack; Coller, Alan R. 1971
Descriptors: *Cognitive Measurement; Concept Formation; Early Childhood Education; *Elementary School Students; Individual Testing; *Number Concepts; *Preschool Children; Preschool Education; Primary Education
Identifiers: Institute for Developmental Studies; QMI 1M
Availability: Institute for Developmental Studies; Press Bldg., New York University, Washington Square, New York, NY 10003
Grade Level: K-3
Target Audience: 2-8

Designed to assess child's understanding of quantitative concepts. Instrument is also available from the author: Alan R. Coller; 12 Burlington Ave., Vorhees, NJ 08043

6140
Relational Concepts Inventory/Pre-Math. Institute for Developmental Studies, New York, NY 1970
Descriptors: Cognitive Measurement; *Concept Formation; *Elementary School Students; Individual Testing; Mathematical Concepts; Pictorial Stimuli; *Preschool Children; Preschool Education; Primary Education
Identifiers: Institute for Developmental Studies; RCI(PM)
Availability: Institute for Developmental Studies; Press Bldg., New York University, Washington Square, New York, NY 10003
Grade Level: K-1
Target Audience: 2-6

Designed to assess young child's mathematical concepts. Developed for preschool children through Grade one. Instrument is also available from Alan R. Coller, 12 Burlington Ave., Vorhees, NJ 08043.

6143
Same/Different Inventory—3. Victor, Jack; And Others 1970
Descriptors: Cognitive Measurement; *Concept Formation; Individual Testing; *Preschool Children; Preschool Education; Primary Education; *Visual Discrimination
Identifiers: Early Childhood Inventories; Institute for Developmental Studies; SDI 3
Availability: Institute for Developmental Studies; Press Bldg., New York University, Washington Square, New York, NY 10003
Grade Level: K-1
Target Audience: 2-6

Designed to assess child's ability to match objects or identify the object that is different. Instrument is also available from Alan R. Coller, 12 Burlington Ave., Vorhees, NJ 08043.

6144
Shape Name Inventory. Institute for Developmental Studies, New York, NY 1965
Subtests: Non-verbal Receptive; Verbal Expressive
Descriptors: Achievement Tests; *Concept Formation; Individual Testing; *Preschool Children; Preschool Education; Visual Perception
Identifiers: COPKI; Curriculum Oriented Prekindergarten Inventories; Institute for Developmental Studies; SNI
Availability: Institute for Developmental Studies; Press Bldg., New York University, Washington Square, New York, NY 10003
Target Audience: 2-5
Notes: Items, 16

Designed to evaluate preschool child's ability to identify 8 common shapes. The nonverbal receptive task requires the child to point to specific shapes. In the verbal expressive task, the child is asked to name each shape as it is presented. Instrument is also available from Alan R. Coller, 12 Burlington Ave., Vorhees, NJ 08043.

6145
Same/Different Inventory—1. Institute for Developmental Studies, New York, NY
Descriptors: Cognitive Measurement; *Concept Formation; Individual Testing; *Preschool Children; Preschool Education
Identifiers: COPKI; Curriculum Oriented Prekindergarten Inventories; Institute for Developmental Studies; SDI
Availability: Institute for Developmental Studies; Press Bldg., New York University, Washington Square, New York, NY 10003
Target Audience: 2-5

Notes: Items, 12

Designed to measure the child's ability to comprehend and utilize same-different concepts on the receptive level. Instrument is also available from Alan R. Coller, 12 Burlington Ave., Vorhees, NJ 08043.

6146
Color Name Inventory. Institute for Developmental Studies, New York, NY
Subtests: Non-verbal Receptive Task; Verbal Expressive Task
Descriptors: Achievement Tests; *Color; *Concept Formation; Individual Testing; *Preschool Children; Preschool Education
Identifiers: CNI; COPKI; Curriculum Oriented Prekindergarten Inventories; Institute for Developmental Studies
Availability: Institute for Developmental Studies; Press Bldg., New York University, Washington Square, New York, NY 10003
Target Audience: 2-5
Notes: Items, 24

Designed to evaluate a child's ability to identify 12 common colors. An extensive color vocabulary is basic to learning more complex concepts. Instrument is also available from Alan R. Coller, 12 Burlington Ave., Vorhees, NJ 08043.

6147
Prepositions Inventory/Linguistic Concepts. Victor, Jack; Coller, Alan R. 1970
Descriptors: *Concept Formation; Early Childhood Education; *Elementary School Students; Individual Testing; *Language Acquisition; Language Tests; *Preschool Children; Prepositions
Identifiers: Early Childhood Inventories; Institute for Developmental Studies; PILC
Availability: Institute for Developmental Studies; Press Bldg., New York University, Washington Square, New York, NY 10003
Target Audience: 2-6
Notes: Items, 32

Designed to assess child's ability to comprehend linguistic concepts, especially prepositions. Examinee is asked to indicate picture described by administrator. Instrument is also available from Alan R. Coller, 12 Burlington Ave., Vorhees, NJ 08043.

6148
Set Matching Inventory—Math. Institute for Developmental Studies, New York, NY 1970
Descriptors: Cognitive Measurement; *Concept Formation; Early Childhood Education; *Elementary School Students; Individual Testing; *Mathematical Concepts; *Preschool Children; Visual Perception
Identifiers: Early Childhood Inventories; Institute for Developmental Studies; SMIM
Availability: Institute for Developmental Studies; Press Bldg., New York University, Washington Square, New York, NY 10003
Target Audience: 2-6

Designed to assess child's ability to understand mathematical concepts and ability to match similar objects. Instrument is also available from Alan R. Coller, 12 Burlington Ave., Vorhees, NJ 08043.

6156
The Floating and Sinking of Objects. Laurendeau, Monique; Pinard, Adrien 1962
Descriptors: *Cognitive Development; *Concept Formation; Elementary Education; *Elementary School Students; Individual Testing; *Induction; Logical Thinking; Physical Sciences; *Preschool Children; Preschool Education
Identifiers: Causal Thinking; Piaget (Jean); Piagetian Tests
Availability: Laurendeau, Monique and Adrien Pinard. Casual Thinking in the Child. New York: International Universities Press, Inc., 1962.
Target Audience: 4-12

Designed to assess child's understanding of physical laws. This provides information about his or her logic and mental representations.

6162
Bannatyne System: Early Screening and Diagnostic Tests—Phase I. Bannatyne, Alexander D. 1975
Subtests: Symbol to Sound—Phonemes; Tactile Finger Sensing; Pictorial Mistakes Test; Sound Blending Test; Coding Speed Test; Symbol to Sound Words; Parent Questionnaire; Examiner's Checklist
Descriptors: *Elementary School Students; Gifted; Grade 1; *Handicap Identification; High Risk Students; Individual Testing; *Learning Disabilities; *Preschool Children; Preschool Education; Preschool Tests; Primary Education; Psychomotor Skills; *Screening Tests; Spatial Ability; Student Placement; *Talent Identification

Identifiers: BS ESDT; Test Batteries
Availability: Learning Systems Press; P.O. Box 91108, Lafayette, LA 70509
Target Audience: 3-6
Notes: Time, 25 approx.

Designed for individual screening of all students before, on, or immediately after school entry. Determines which students are "at risk," potentially learning disabled, or gifted. These students identified in Phase I screening assessment are then specifically diagnosed using Bannatyne System: Early Screening and Diagnostic Tests—Phase II (TC008030).

6179
Eliot-Price Test. Eliot, John; Price, Lewis 1974
Descriptors: Adults; Children; Individual Testing; *Spatial Ability; *Visualization; Visual Measures
Identifiers: TIM(B)
Availability: Tests in Microfiche; Test Collection, Educational Testing Service, Princeton, NJ 08541
Target Audience: 9-65
Notes: Time, 20 approx.; Items, 30

Research instrument designed to measure the ability to perceive and to imagine object arrangements from different viewpoints. It is a pictorial adaptation of Piaget's 3-mountain task. Intended for children and adults in grade 4 and above. However, if administered individually, the test may be used with children in grades 2 and 3.

6244
Zeitlin Early Identification Screening. Zeitlin, Shirley 1974
Descriptors: Body Image; Cognitive Development; *Individual Testing; Language Acquisition; *Learning Problems; Memory; *Preschool Children; Questionnaires; *Screening Tests; Young Children
Identifiers: TIM(B); ZEIS
Availability: Tests in Microfiche; Test Collection, Educational Testing Service, Princeton, NJ 08541
Target Audience: 3-7
Notes: Items, 12

Individually administered instrument is designed to identify children who may have special learning needs. The screening consists of items relating to language, cognitive development, visual motor, auditory and visual memory, gross motor, body image, directionality, and laterality. The questions are divided into 3 parts, including verbal tasks, paper and pencil tasks, and nonverbal performance. Checklists for recording relevant observable behaviors and emotional indicators are included. Research instrument.

6355
Language Development Inventory for Kindergarten or Preschool. Lamar Consolidated Independent School District 1976
Subtests: Object Recognition; Oral Comprehension; Form Discrimination and Categorizing; Picture Interpretation; Follow Simple Instructions
Descriptors: *Basic Skills; *Comprehension; *Interpretive Skills; *Language Acquisition; *Preschool Children; Reading Readiness; *Receptive Language; *Recognition (Psychology)
Identifiers: TIM(E)
Availability: Tests in Microfiche; Test Collection, Educational Testing Service, Princeton, NJ 08541
Target Audience: Preschool Children
Notes: Items, 31

Designed to determine a pupil's eligibility for kindergarten or preschool due to inability to use and understand the common English language words that are necessary for normal progress in the first grade. The inventory consists of 5 areas: object recognition, oral comprehension, form discrimination and categorizing, picture interpretation, and follow simple instructions.

6400
Tests de Aptitud Diferencial, Forms A and B. Bennett, George K.; And Others 1959
Subtests: Razonamiento Verbal; Habilidad Numerica; Razonamiento Abstracto; Relaciones Espaciales; Razonamiento Mecanico; Velocidad y Exactitud; Uso de lenguaje
Descriptors: Abstract Reasoning; *Adults; *Aptitude Tests; *Career Guidance; *Educational Counseling; Language Usage; Mathematical Applications; Mechanical Skills; Secondary Education; *Secondary School Students; *Spanish; Spatial Ability; Spelling; Verbal Ability
Identifiers: Differential Aptitude Tests
Availability: Dr. Robert B. MacVean; Colegio Americano de Guatemala, Apartado Postal No. 82, Guatemala City, Guatemala, C.A.
Grade Level: 8-12
Target Audience: 12-64

Spanish version of an early edition of the Differential Aptitude Tests. This Spanish version is a separate booklet form, one booklet for each of the subtests. DAT is used to assess the basic intellectual aptitude of secondary school and college students for vocational and educational guidance. May also be used to select employees.

6404
Optometry College Admission Test. Psychological Corp., San Antonio, TX
Subtests: Verbal Ability; Quantitative Ability; Biology; Chemistry; Physics; Study and Reading
Descriptors: *Academic Ability; *Academic Aptitude; *Achievement Tests; Adults; Aptitude Tests; College Admission; *College Applicants; *College Entrance Examinations; Computation; Multiple Choice Tests; *Natural Sciences; *Optometry; Timed Tests
Identifiers: Association of Schools and Colleges of Optometry; OCAT
Availability: The Psychological Corp.; 555 Academic Ct., San Antonio, TX 78204-0952
Target Audience: Adults
Notes: Time, 240

Designed as an entrance exam for those seeking admission to colleges of optometry. Measures both general academic ability and scientific knowledge. Administered by The Psychological Corporation for the Association of Schools and Colleges of Optometry. Restricted distribution; tests given only at designated test centers throughout the U.S. and Canada. Instrument is under constant revision; thus, the number of items and time (3-1/2 to 4 hours) varies.

6451
Rhodes WAIS Scatter Profile. Rhodes, Fen 1969
Subtests: Full Scale Scatter; Verbal Scale Scatter; Performance Scale Scatter
Descriptors: Adolescents; Adults; *Intelligence Tests; *Profiles; Records (Forms); *Test Interpretation
Identifiers: *Wechsler Adult Intelligence Scale
Availability: Educational and Industrial Testing Services; P.O. Box 7234, San Diego, CA 92107
Target Audience: 16-64
Notes: Time, 1 approx.

Designed to assist user of the WAIS in evaluating and interpreting the levels and patterns of performance of individual subjects on the various subtests. Enables administrator to determine which subtests deviate sufficiently from the composite to be considered as having possible diagnostic significance.

6453
Children's Embedded Figures Test: 1971 Edition. Karp, Stephen A.; Konstadt, Norma 1971
Subtests: Tent; House
Descriptors: Children; *Cognitive Measurement; *Cognitive Style; *Elementary School Students; *Individual Testing; *Perception Tests; *Field Dependence Independence
Availability: CEFT; *Figure Ground; Gestalt Psychology
Grade Level: Consulting Psychologists Press; 577 College Ave., Palo Alto, CA 94036
Notes: Time, 5-12; Items, 25

An individually administered, perceptual test in which the subject locates a previously seen simple figure within a larger complex figure which has been organized to obscure or embed the simple figure. In addition to serving as indicator of cognitive functioning and cognitive style, tests have been used in assessment studies relating to analytic ability in other tasks, social behavior, body concept, preferred defense mechanisms and other processes.

6454
Kansas Reflection Impulsivity Scale for Preschoolers. Wright, John C. 1971
Descriptors: *Cognitive Style; *Individual Testing; *Preschool Children; Timed Tests
Identifiers: *Impulsiveness; KRISP; *Reflective Thinking
Availability: John C. Wright; Dept. of Human Development, University of Kansas, Lawrence, KS 66045
Target Audience: 3-5
Notes: Items, 15

An individually administered test designed to identify children ages 3 to 5.5 who are unusually reflective or impulsive in their cognitive style/tempo. Two forms are available. Child selects from a group of drawings one which matches an example. Test is timed.

6464
The Group Embedded Figures Test. Oltman, Philip K.; And Others 1971
Descriptors: *Field Dependence Independence; Adolescents; Adults; Children; Cognitive Measurement; *Cognitive Style; *Group Testing; Older Adults; *Perception Tests
Identifiers: *Figure Ground; GEFT; Gestalt Psychology

Availability: Consulting Psychologists Press; 577 College Ave., Palo Alto, CA 94036
Target Audience: 10-70
Notes: Time, 20 approx.; Items, 18

Embedded figure design test designed for group measure. Measures cognitive style through the use of perceptual tasks.

6499
National Security Agency Professional Qualification Test. National Security Agency, Fort George Meade, MD 1956
Subtests: English Usage; Interactions; Directions; Digit Identification; Artificial Language; Number Series; Matrices; Judgment
Descriptors: Adults; College Graduates; English; Evaluative Thinking; Grammar; Language Acquisition; Language Aptitude; Language Usage; Number Concepts; *Occupational Tests; *Personnel Selection; Professional Occupations; Verbal Ability
Identifiers: *National Security Agency; Reasoning Ability
Availability: National Security Agency; Fort George G. Meade, MD 20755, ATTN: Office of Employment (M322)
Target Audience: 21-64
Notes: Time, 240

Designed to measure ability to reason logically, verbal ability, quantitative ability. Used for the selection of college graduates with Bachelor's degrees for employment in the National Security Agency.

6503
Preliminary Scholastic Aptitude Test/National Merit Scholarship Qualifying Test. Educational Testing Service, Princeton, NJ 1982
Subtests: Verbal; Quantitative
Descriptors: *Academic Aptitude; *Aptitude Tests; Braille; High Schools; *High School Students; Large Type Materials; Mathematics Tests; *Scholarships; Verbal Ability
Identifiers: National Merit Scholarship Corporation; Scholastic Aptitude Test
Availability: Educational Testing Service; PSAT/NMSQT, P.O. Box 589, Princeton, NJ 08541
Grade Level: 11
Notes: Time, 100

Designed to measure verbal and mathematical reasoning abilities. Can be used by school counselors for educational planning and to estimate student performance on the Scholastic Aptitude Test required by many colleges for admission. Used as the qualifying tests for students who wish to participate in nationwide scholarship competitions. Special editions are available in large type and braille. Tests are updated regularly.

6560
Test of Directional Skills. Sterritt, Graham M. 1973
Descriptors: *Preschool Children; Preschool Education; *Reading Readiness; Reading Readiness Tests; *Spatial Ability
Identifiers: TIM(D)
Availability: Tests in Microfiche; Test Collection, Educational Testing Service, Princeton, NJ 08541
Target Audience: 2-5
Notes: Items, 12

Measures spatial orientation abilities prerequisite to learning to read: orienting to the beginning of a sentence or block of text, tracking words from left to right, and tracking lines of text from top to bottom. Consists of 12 cards bearing 1 to 4 lines of printing in primary size type.

6586
Pennsylvania Preschool Inventory. Dusewicz, R.A.; Lutz, C.H. 1973
Descriptors: *Cognitive Development; Human Body; Individual Testing; Number Concepts; *Preschool Children; *Preschool Tests; *School Readiness Tests; Self Concept; Spatial Ability; Young Children
Identifiers: Analogies; *Picture Identification Test; Picture Inventory; PPI
Availability: Pennsylvania State Dept. of Education; P.O. Box 911, Harrisburg, PA 17126
Target Audience: 3-6
Notes: Time, 15 approx.; Items, 61

Test designed to assess the cognitive development of preschool children, serving as a rapid but reliable means of evaluation. Space is provided on each score sheet for subjective comments relevant to the child's performances on the test. Areas covered include: passive vocabulary, complementary relationships, non-complementary relationships, number concepts, verbal analogies, and awareness of self.

6603
Territorial Decentration Test. Stoltman, Joseph P. 1971

Subtests: Verbal Territorial Identification (10); Verbal Territorial Relationship (9); Territorial Inclusion Using Written Symbols (9); Territorial Inclusion Using Props (10)
Descriptors: Children; *Cognitive Development; *Cognitive Tests; Individual Testing
Identifiers: *Piagetian Tests; *Territorial Decentration; TIM(A)
Availability: Tests in Microfiche; Test Collection, Educational Testing Service, Princeton, NJ 08541
Target Audience: 5-12
Notes: Time, 20; Items, 38

Individually administered Piagetian measure designed to assess a child's comprehension of particular territorial relationships. Props consisting of colored rectangles and discs are used. Sets of maps are needed.

6690
Similes Test. Schaefer, Charles E. 1971
Descriptors: *Creativity; *Creativity Tests; *Elementary School Students; Higher Education; Intermediate Grades; Secondary Education; *Secondary School Students; Talent; *Talent Identification; *Undergraduate Students; Verbal Stimuli
Identifiers: Sentence Completion Tests
Availability: Research Psychologists Press, Inc.; P.O. Box 984, Port Huron, MI 48060
Grade Level: 4-16
Notes: Time, 15; Items, 10

Designed to identify literary talent and originality in children and adolescents. Subject must complete 10 incomplete simile forms. Each stem requires 3 different endings. The uniqueness of the response determines the originality scoring weights. Two alternate forms are available.

6694
Matching Familiar Figures Test. Kagan, Jerome 1965
Descriptors: Cognitive Measurement; *Conceptual Tempo; Elementary Education; *Elementary School Students; Individual Testing; Pictorial Stimuli; *Preschool Children; Preschool Education
Identifiers: MFF
Availability: Jerome Kagan; Dept. of Psychology and Social Relations, William James Hall, Harvard University, Cambridge, MA 02138
Grade Level: K-6
Target Audience: 2-12

Designed to assess conceptual tempo in preschool and elementary age children. Child must match pictures of familiar objects.

6700
Preschool and Early Primary Skill Survey. Long, John A.; And Others 1971
Subtests: Picture Recognition; Picture Relationship; Picture Sequences; Form Completion
Descriptors: *Disadvantaged; *Elementary School Students; Grade 1; Grade 2; Individual Testing; Kindergarten; Perceptual Motor Coordination; *Preschool Children; Preschool Education; Primary Education; *School Readiness; *School Readiness Tests; *Slow Learners; Visual Discrimination; *Visual Perception
Identifiers: PEPSS
Availability: Stoelting Co.; 620 Wheat Ln., Wood Dale, IL 60191
Target Audience: 3-7
Notes: Time, 100 approx.; Items, 54

Designed to measure skills considered significant for children in achieving early school success. The skills assessed are visual recognition, discrimination and association, cognition of pictured sequences, and perceptual motor abilities. May be used with small groups of children or individually administered. Analysis of survey results will enable early childhood teachers to identify strengths and weaknesses in preschool skills.

6750
Preschool Embedded Figures Test. Coates, Susan 1972
Descriptors: *Field Dependence Independence; *Cognitive Measurement; *Cognitive Style; *Individual Testing; *Perception; *Preschool Children; Preschool Education
Identifiers: *Figure Ground; *Gestalt Psychology; PEFT
Availability: Consulting Psychologists Press; 577 College Ave., Palo Alto, CA 94306
Target Audience: 3-5

An individually administered, perceptual test in which the subject locates a previously seen simple figure within a larger complex figure which has been organized to obscure or embed the simple figure. In addition to serving as indicator of cognitive functioning and cognitive style, tests have been used in assessment studies relating to analytic ability in other tasks, social behavior, body concept, preferred defense mechanisms, and other processes.

6796
School and College Ability Tests—Series II, Level 2. Educational Testing Service, Princeton, NJ 1969
Subtests: Verbal; Mathematics
Descriptors: *Academic Aptitude; *Aptitude Tests; High Schools; *High School Students; *Mathematics; Nonverbal Ability; *Predictive Measurement; *Verbal Ability
Identifiers: *SCAT Series II
Availability: CTB/McGraw Hill; Del Monte Research Park, 2500 Garden Rd., Monterey, CA 93940
Grade Level: 9-12
Notes: Time, 45 approx.; Items, 100

Designed to provide estimates of basic verbal and mathematical ability. Forms A and B are available.

6797
School and College Ability Tests: Series II, Level 3. Educational Testing Service, Princeton, NJ 1969
Subtests: Verbal; Mathematics
Descriptors: *Academic Aptitude; *Aptitude Tests; *Grade 6; Intermediate Grades; Junior High Schools; *Junior High School Students; *Mathematics; Nonverbal Ability; *Predictive Measurement; *Verbal Ability
Identifiers: *SCAT Series II
Availability: CTB/McGraw Hill; Del Monte Research Park, 2500 Garden Rd., Monterey, CA 93940
Grade Level: 6-9
Notes: Time, 45 approx.; Items, 100

Designed to provide estimates of basic verbal and mathematical ability for students in late grade 6 through early grade 9. Forms A and B are available.

6798
School and College Ability Tests—Series II, Level 4. Educational Testing Service, Princeton, NJ 1969
Subtests: Verbal; Mathematics
Descriptors: *Academic Aptitude; *Aptitude Tests; Elementary Education; *Elementary School Students; *Mathematics; Nonverbal Ability; *Predictive Measurement; *Verbal Ability
Identifiers: *SCAT Series II
Availability: CTB/McGraw Hill; Del Monte Research Park, 2500 Garden Rd., Monterey, CA 93940
Grade Level: 3-6
Notes: Time, 45 approx.; Items, 100

Designed to provide estimates of basic verbal and mathematical ability for students in grade 3 through early grade 6. Forms A and B are available.

6818
Columbia Mental Maturity Scale—Levels A-H. Third Edition. Burgemeister, Bessie B. 1972
Descriptors: Children; *Cognitive Ability; *Cognitive Tests; *Disabilities; *Disadvantaged; Individual Testing; *Neurological Impairments; *Non English Speaking; Nonverbal Tests; *Pictorial Stimuli; *Preschool Children; Spanish; Spanish Speaking
Identifiers: CMMS; *Reasoning Ability
Availability: The Psychological Corp.; 555 Academic Ct., San Antonio, TX 78204-0952
Target Audience: 3-10
Notes: Time, 20 approx.; Items, 92

Designed to yield estimate of general reasoning ability of children aged 3.5 to 9.11. Child takes level indicated for his or her chronological age. From 51 to 65 items are actually presented depending upon level administered. Requires no verbal response and a minimal motor response. CMMS is suitable for use with brain damaged children, as well as those with mental retardation, visual handicaps, speech impairment, or hearing loss. Instrument does not depend on reading or language skills, making it suitable for non-English speakers. Spanish directions are included in manual.

6822
Communicative Evaluation Chart from Infancy to Five Years. Anderson, Ruth M.; And Others 1963
Descriptors: Ability Identification; Child Development; *Communication Skills; Individual Testing; *Infants; *Language Skills; Perceptual Development; *Preschool Children; Psychomotor Skills; *Screening Tests
Availability: Educators Publishing Service; 75 Moulton St., Cambridge, MA 02238-9101
Target Audience: 0-5

Designed for quick appraisal of child's overall abilities or disabilities in language and beginning visual-motor-perceptual skills. Contains language and performance levels for the child of 3 months, 6 months, 9 months, 12 months, 18 months, 24 months, 3 years, 4 years, and 5 years of age.

6829
Iowa Geometry Aptitude Test: Third Edition. Maxey, James; Sabers, Darrell 1969
Subtests: Logical Deduction; Visualization
Descriptors: *Aptitude Tests; *College Bound Students; *Geometry; High Schools; *High School Students; *Logical Thinking; Mathematics Tests; *Spatial Ability
Identifiers: IGAT
Availability: Bureau of Educational Research and Service; The University of Iowa, W. 325 Seashore Hall, Iowa City, IA
Grade Level: 9-12
Notes: Time, 55 approx.; Items, 55

Designed to assess student's potential success in geometry. May be used in educational planning.

6903
McCarthy Scales of Children's Abilities. McCarthy, Dorothea 1972
Subtests: Verbal; Perceptual-Performance; Quantitative; General Cognitive; Memory, and Motor
Descriptors: Academic Aptitude; Cognitive Tests; Elementary Education; *Elementary School Students; *Handicap Identification; Motor Development; Predictive Measurement; *Preschool Children; Preschool Education; Psychomotor Skills; *Talent Identification
Identifiers: MSCA
Availability: The Psychological Corp.; 555 Academic Ct., San Antonio, TX 78204-0952
Target Audience: 2-9
Notes: Time, 60 approx.

Designed to assess the intellectual and motor development of children 2.5 through 8.5 years of age. Useful in identification of children with learning disabilities, or auditory, visual or speech defects, or gifted children. Eighteen tests have been grouped into 6 scales—Verbal, Perceptual-Performance, Quantitative, General Cognitive, Memory, and Motor.

6923
Test of Concept Utilization. Crager, Richard L. 1972
Subtests: Color; Shape; Homogeneous Function; Abstract; Stimulus Bound; Object Bound; Relational Function; Minor Relational; Unilateral; Negation; Infusion; Creation
Descriptors: *Cognitive Style; *Cognitive Tests; *Concept Formation; Diagnostic Teaching; *Elementary School Students; Elementary Secondary Education; Language Acquisition; Learning Disabilities; *Secondary School Students
Identifiers: TCU
Availability: Western Psychological Services; 12031 Wilshire Blvd., Los Angeles, CA 90025
Target Audience: 5-18
Notes: Time, 15 approx.; Items, 50

Designed to determine an individual child's level of thinking and use of language, indicating the direction educational activities should take to help that child learn. Provides qualitative and quantitative assessments of five areas of conceptual thinking: Color; Shape; Relational Function; Homogeneous Function; and Abstract Function.

6927
Meeting Street School Screening Test. Hainsworth, Peter K.; Siqueland, Marian L. 1969
Subtests: Motor Patterning; Visual Perceptual and Motor; Language
Descriptors: Child Development; Cognitive Development; Elementary School Students; *Grade 1; Individual Development; *Individual Testing; *Kindergarten Children; Learning Disabilities; Learning Readiness; Performance; Performance Tests; *Primary Education; Reading Readiness; School Readiness; School Readiness Tests; *Screening Tests
Identifiers: MSSST; Oral Tests
Availability: Easter Seal Society of Rhode Island, Inc.; Meeting St. School, 667 Waterman Ave., E. Providence, RI 02914
Grade Level: K-1
Notes: Time, 20 approx.

Untimed, individually administered screening test designed to identify kindergarten and first grade students with learning disabilities and thus avoid a mismatch of the student's skill and the school curriculum. Requires the use of specialized set of cards with pictures, designs, etc.

6998
Test de Comprension Mecanica Bennett. Bennett, George K. 1970

Descriptors: Adolescents; Adults; *Aptitude Tests; College Applicants; College Science; College Students; Engineering Education; *High School Students; Industrial Education; Job Applicants; *Mechanics (Physics); *Mechanics (Process); Occupational Tests; Secondary School Science; *Skilled Workers; *Spanish; *Spanish Speaking; Technical Education; Timed Tests; Trade and Industrial Education; Vocational Aptitude; Vocational High Schools
Identifiers: Bennett Mechanical Comprehension Test; BMCT
Availability: The Psychological Corp.; 555 Academic Ct., San Antonio, TX 78204-0952
Target Audience: 14-64
Notes: Time, 30; Items, 68

In Spanish. Designed to measure the ability to perceive and comprehend the relationship of mechanical elements and physical law, and to apply this knowledge to new, practical situations. Administered to high school students, candidates and students in engineering schools, applicants and current employees of mechanical jobs, for other adult males of comparable ability and education, and for all women competing for or currently in comparable jobs or educational levels. Includes both Form S and Form T, which are revisions of earlier Forms AA, BB, CC and W1. Forms S and T have a wider range of difficulty, are for both men and women, and are timed. Scoring is the number correct, with no reduction of score for incorrect answers. Directions and instructions are available as Spanish Language Tape Recording.

7012
Academic Readiness Scale. Burks, Harold F. 1968
Subtests: Motor; Perceptual-Motor; Cognitive; Motivational; Social Adjustment
Descriptors: *Grade 1; *Handicap Identification; *Intellectual Development; *Kindergarten Children; Learning Readiness; Primary Education; Rating Scales; *School Readiness; *School Readiness Tests; Slow Learners; Student Evaluation; Young Children
Identifiers: ARS
Availability: Arden Press; P.O. Box 2084, Palm Springs, CA 92262
Grade Level: K-1

Developed for identification of students with potential learning handicaps. To be administered at end of kindergarten year or beginning of first grade year.

7121
Purdue Elementary Problem Solving Inventory. Feldhusen, John F.; And Others
Subtests: Sensing and Identifying; Clarification I; Clarification II; Problem Parts; Presolution; Solving Problems I; Solving Problems II; Solving Problems III
Descriptors: Audiotape Recordings; Cognitive Processes; *Cognitive Tests; *Disadvantaged; Elementary Education; *Elementary School Students; Filmstrips; Group Testing; Individual Testing; Multiple Choice Tests; *Problem Solving
Identifiers: TIM(C)
Availability: Tests in Microfiche; Test Collection, Educational Testing Service, Princeton, NJ 08541
Grade Level: 2-6
Notes: Time, 45 approx.; Items, 49

Designed to assess the general problem-solving ability of culturally different disadvantaged children. Real-life problem situations are used to measure the following abilities: sensing that a problem exists, identifying and defining the problem, asking questions, guessing causes, clarifying the goal of the problem situation, judging if more information is needed, analyzing details of the problem and identifying critical elements, redefining familiar objects for unusual uses, seeing implications, solving single- and multiple-solution problems, and verifying solutions. Cartoons presented on a film strip are used as the stimuli for each problem task and all the instructions are presented on an audio tape. Individual or group administration.

7127
Spatial Orientation Memory Test. Wepman, Joseph M.; Turaids, Dainis 1971
Descriptors: Child Development; Children; *Elementary School Students; *Individual Development; *Individual Testing; *Learning Readiness; Multiple Choice Tests; Perception Tests; *Recall (Psychology); Retention (Psychology); *Spatial Ability; Visual Measures; *Visual Perception; Visual Stimuli
Identifiers: Oral Tests; SOMT
Availability: Western Psychological Services; 12031 Wilshire Blvd., Los Angeles, CA 90025
Target Audience: 5-9
Notes: Time, 20 approx.; Items, 20

Individually administered instrument that assesses a child's ability to retain and to recall the directional relationships of visually presented forms. Includes the basic recognition of horizontality and verticality as well as the retention and recall of oblique spatially oriented figures. The subject responds by pointing to one of the multiple choices. Available as Form I and Form II.

7148
Primary School Behavior Q-Sort. Baumrind, Diana 1972
Descriptors: Behavior Rating Scales; Cognitive Style; *Elementary School Students; *Interpersonal Competence; Peer Relationship; Primary Education; Student Behavior
Identifiers: Card Sort; Parental Authority Research Project
Availability: Dr. Diana Baumrind; Institute of Human Development, University of California, Tolman Hall 1203, Berkeley, CA 94720
Grade Level: 1-3
Notes: Items, 82

Designed to assess personal, interpersonal, and cognitive behavior of primary grade children. Many items were derived from Preschool Behavior Q Sort (TC005939).

7170
Differential Aptitude Tests: Forms S and T. Bennett, George K.; And Others 1972
Subtests: Verbal Reasoning; Numerical Ability; Abstract Reasoning; Clerical Speed and Accuracy; Mechanical Reasoning; Space Relations; Spelling; Language Usage
Descriptors: Abstract Reasoning; *Aptitude Tests; Arithmetic; *Career Counseling; *Educational Counseling; Language Usage; Large Type Materials; Mechanical Skills; Problem Solving; Secondary Education; *Secondary School Students; Spatial Ability; Spelling; Verbal Ability; Visual Acuity; Visual Impairments
Identifiers: Analogies; Clerical Aptitude; DAT; Test Batteries
Availability: The Psychological Corp.; 555 Academic Ct., San Antonio, TX 78204-0952
Grade Level: 8-12
Notes: Time, 180 approx.; Items, 630

Integrated battery of aptitude tests designed for educational and vocational guidance in junior and senior high schools. Yields 8 scores dealing with various facets of intelligence. Each of the tests in the battery can be separately administered. Test battery is given over a period of time, preferably within a 1- or 2-week period. Form S is available in large print for visually impaired subjects from American Printing House for the Blind, 1839 Frankfort Ave., Louisville, KY 40206.

7171
Escala de Inteligencia Wechsler para Adultos. Green, R.F.; Martinez, J.N. 1968
Subtests: Informacion; Comprension; Aritmetica; Analogias; Repeticion de Digitos; Vocabulario; Digito Simbolo; Dibujos para Completar; Disenos con Cubos; Ordenamiento de Dibujos; Composicion de Objetos
Descriptors: Adults; *Cognitive Ability; Cognitive Tests; Hispanic Americans; *Individual Testing; Intelligence Quotient; *Intelligence Tests; Latin Americans; *Spanish; *Spanish Americans; *Spanish Speaking; Timed Tests
Identifiers: EIWA; WAIS; Wechsler Adult Intelligence Scale
Availability: The Psychological Corp.; 555 Academic Ct., San Antonio, TX 78204-0952
Target Audience: 16-64
Notes: Time, 60 approx.; Items, 305

An authorized Spanish/American version of the Wechsler Adult Intelligence Scale. Type of item varies; some require computation, completion, or performance. The translators call attention to the fact that the Spanish and English language materials for WAIS are not interchangeable. Not all subtests are timed.

7189
Semantic Features Test. Evanechko, Peter O.; Maguire, T.O. 1975
Descriptors: Children; *Cognitive Measurement; *Elementary School Students; Intermediate Grades; Junior High Schools; *Semantics; *Vocabulary Development
Identifiers: TIM(A)
Availability: Tests in Microfiche; Test Collection, Educational Testing Service, Princeton, NJ 08541
Grade Level: 5-8
Notes: Items, 276

Used to identify the dimensions of an individual's meaning space. The items represent 24 categories of meaning which are arranged in 5 logical groupings: similarity group (synonym, similarity, supraordinate, whole-part, part-part); relation group (coordinate, attribute, contrast, free association, connotation); action group (action upon action-on, common-use, use-of, repetition); explanation group (contiguity, analysis, synthesis, ostensive definition); and class membership group (extension of a class, denotation in context, generic definition, class membership implied, intension of a class).

7198
Index of Perceptual-Motor Laterality. Berman, Allan 1973
Descriptors: *Brain Hemisphere Functions; *Children; Cognitive Ability; Individual Testing; *Lateral Dominance; Perceptual Motor Coordination; Performance Tests
Identifiers: Index of Cerebral Dominance (ICD); Test Batteries
Availability: Perceptual and Motor Skills; v39 p599-605, 1973
Target Audience: 8-13
Notes: Time, 45 approx.; Items, 54

Designed to measure cerebral dominance and its relationship to intellectual ability. Instrument is also available from the author, Dr. Allen Berman, Department of Psychology, University of Rhode Island, Chafee Bldg., Kingston, RI 02881

7229
Black Intelligence Test of Cultural Homogeneity. Williams, Robert L. 1972
Descriptors: Adolescents; Adults; *Black Culture; *Black Dialects; *Blacks; Cultural Awareness; *Intelligence Tests; Multiple Choice Tests; Vocabulary
Identifiers: BITCH; *Culturally Specific Tests
Availability: Williams and Associates, Inc.; Educational and Psychological Services, 6374 Del Mar Blvd., St. Louis, MO 63130
Target Audience: 13-64
Notes: Time, 30 approx.; Items, 100

Culturally specific, multiple choice, vocabulary and intelligence test which uses items drawn from the Black Experience. The test may be used as a measure of learning potential, or as a measure of sensitivity and responsiveness of Whites to the Black Experience.

7274
Category Width Scale. Pettigrew, Thomas F. 1958
Descriptors: *Adults; *Classification; *Cognitive Style; Cognitive Tests; Estimation (Mathematics); Multiple Choice Tests
Identifiers: CW Scale; Estimation Questionnaire
Availability: Thomas F. Pettigrew, Dept. of Psychology and Social Relations; William James Hall, Harvard University, 33 Kirkland St., Cambridge, MA 02138
Target Audience: Adults
Notes: Items, 20

Assesses individual's ability to estimate extremes of categories of objects. Subjects are consistent in defining narrow or broad ranges of categories. High scores correlate positively with quantitative ability. Males seem to score higher than females.

7284
Auditory Sequential Memory Test. Wepman, Joseph M.; Morency, Anne 1973
Descriptors: Academic Aptitude; Cognitive Ability; Cognitive Tests; *Elementary School Students; Individual Testing; Learning Disabilities; *Learning Processes; *Learning Readiness; *Primary Education; *Retention (Psychology); *School Readiness; Young Children; Short Term Memory
Identifiers: Memory for Digits; Perceptual Test Battery (PTB)
Availability: Western Psychological Services; 12031 Wilshire Blvd., Los Angeles, CA 90025
Target Audience: 5-8
Notes: Time, 5 approx.; Items, 14

Individualized test to measure a perceptual auditory ability, more specifically, ability to recall the exact order of group of digits which are given orally. Sometimes called Memory-for-Digits. Used to determine a student's readiness for learning to read, speak, and to do arithmetic processes. Also useful in determining specific auditory learning disabilities. According to the author, the longer span of immediate memory in exact order a child can use, the more accurate, more intelligible, and more adaptive his or her learning is likely to be. Comes in Form I and II. The 6 perceptual tests may be used in combination as a Perceptual Test Battery consisting of Spatial Orientation Memory Test (TC007127), Auditory Discrimination Test (TC007283), Auditory Memory Span Test (TC007285), Auditory Sequential Memory Test (TC007284), Visual Discrimination Test (TC008090), Visual Memory Test (TC008091).

7285
Auditory Memory Span Test. Wepman, Joseph M.; Morency, Anne 1973
Descriptors: *Auditory Stimuli; Child Development; *Elementary School Students; *Individual Testing; *Learning Readiness; Perception Tests; *Perceptual Development; *Primary Education; School Readiness; *Short Term Memory; Verbal Tests; Young Children
Identifiers: AMST; Oral Tests

Availability: Western Psychological Services; 12031 Wilshire Blvd., Los Angeles, CA 90025
Target Audience: 5-8
Notes: Time, 5 approx.; Items, 15

Individually administered instrument to measure a child's ability to recall single syllable spoken words when given in progressively increasing number of words. Based on the theory that, as a perceptual process, there is strong, positive relationship between auditory memory ability and the child's development of speech, language, and learning-to-learn to read. Available as Form I and Form II.

7296
Children's Mirth Response Test. Zigler, Edward; And Others
Descriptors: Adolescents; *Cartoons; Children; *Cognitive Development; *Cognitive Tests; *Humor
Identifiers: CMRT; TIM(A)
Availability: Tests in Microfiche; Test Collection, Educational Testing Service, Princeton, NJ 08541
Target Audience: 7-15
Notes: Items, 25

An experimental device designed to investigate the relation between cognitive development and humor appreciation. The test consists of 25 cartoons and yields 3 scores: a measure of whether or not the child thought the cartoon was funny, employing a simple yes-no response; a facial mirth score employing 5 scoring categories; and a comprehension score, employing 3 categories.

7314
Test of Creative Potential. Hoepfner, Ralph; Hemenway, Judith 1973
Subtests: Writing Words; Picture Decoration; License Plate Words
Descriptors: Adolescents; Adults; Aptitude Tests; Children; *Creativity; *Creativity Tests; *Elementary School Students; Elementary Secondary Education; *Secondary School Students; Timed Tests; *Verbal Ability
Identifiers: TCP
Availability: Monitor; P.O. Box 2337, Hollywood, CA 90028
Target Audience: 7-64
Notes: Time, 30 approx.

Designed to assess general creative potential of subjects from 7 years of age through adolescence and adulthood. Assesses factors of fluency, flexibility, and elaboration of verbal, symbolic, and figural materials. Available in 2 parallel forms.

7321
Thinking Creatively with Sounds and Words: Level I. Torrance, E. Paul; And Others 1973
Subtests: Sounds and Images; Onomatopoeia and Images
Descriptors: *Auditory Stimuli; *Creativity; *Creativity Tests; *Elementary School Students; Elementary Secondary Education; *Secondary School Students; Verbal Ability; *Verbal Stimuli
Identifiers: TCSW; Test Batteries
Availability: Scholastic Testing Service, Inc.; 480 Meyer Rd., Bensenville, IL 60106
Grade Level: 3-12
Notes: Time, 30 approx.

A battery of 2 tests, Sounds and Images (SI) and Onomatopoeia and Images (OI), is designed to assess creativity by measuring the originality of ideas stimulated by abstract sounds and spoken onomatopoeic words. Tests must be administered using 2 long playing records on which are presented instructions to the subjects and the auditory and verbal stimuli. The recordings also maintain the timing of the tests. Parallel forms are available for Level I.

7322
Thinking Creatively with Sounds and Words: Level II. Torrance, E. Paul; And Others 1973
Subtests: Sounds and Images; Onomatopoeia and Images
Descriptors: *Adults; *Auditory Stimuli; *Creativity; *Creativity Tests; Verbal Ability; *Verbal Stimuli
Identifiers: TCSW; Test Batteries
Availability: Scholastic Testing Service, Inc.; 480 Meyer Rd., Bensenville, IL 60106
Target Audience: 18-64
Notes: Time, 30 approx.

A battery of 2 tests, Sounds and Images (SI) and Onomatopoeia and Images (OI), is designed to assess creativity by measuring the originality of ideas stimulated by abstract sounds and spoken onomatopoeic words. Tests must be administered using 2 long playing records on which are presented instructions to the subjects and the auditory and verbal stimuli. The recordings also maintain the timing of the tests. Parallel forms are available for Level II.

7388
Symbol Gestalt Test: Form A Revised. Stein, Kenneth B. 1970

Descriptors: Adults; *Cognitive Style; Cognitive Tests; Group Testing; *Individual Testing; *Neurological Impairments; *Perception Tests; *Perceptual Motor Coordination; Timed Tests
Identifiers: SG; TIM(B)
Availability: Tests in Microfiche; Test Collection, Educational Testing Service, Princeton, NJ 08541
Target Audience: Adults
Notes: Time, 3; Items, 120

Perceptual motor test for brain damage involves the duplication of a series of geometrical designs and figures. Completion of the task emphasizes both speed and accuracy and reveals individual differences in perception, cognitive ordering, and processing stimuli.

7391
Motoric Ideational Sensory Test. Stein, Kenneth B.; Lenrow, Peter 1970
Subtests: Sensory Dimension; Ideational Dimension; Motoric Dimension
Descriptors: *Cognitive Style; Cognitive Tests; *College Students; Higher Education; Interest Inventories; Rating Scales; Student Interests
Identifiers: MIST
Availability: Journal of Personality and Social Psychology; v16 n4 p656-64, 1970
Grade Level: 13-20
Notes: Items, 45

Designed to measure the motoric, ideational, and sensory perceptual expressive dimensions. These dimensions are defined by self-endorsed statements pertaining to activity preferences. Individual's expressive style may be determined from test results.

7461
Wechsler Intelligence Scale for Children—Revised. Wechsler, David 1974
Subtests: Information; Similarities; Arithmetic; Vocabulary; Comprehension; Picture Completion; Picture Arrangement; Block Design; Object Assembly; Coding (or Mazes); Digit Span
Descriptors: Adolescents; Children; *Elementary School Students; Elementary Secondary Education; *Gifted; Hearing Impairments; Individual Testing; *Intelligence; Intelligence Quotient; *Intelligence Tests; Performance Tests; *Secondary School Students; Talent Identification; Verbal Ability
Identifiers: Test Batteries; WISCR
Availability: The Psychological Corp.; 555 Academic Ct., San Antonio, TX 78204-0952
Target Audience: 6-16
Notes: Time, 60 approx.; Items, 328

Designed for use by school psychologists and other trained clinical examiners to measure intelligence of children ages 6.0 to 16.11. WISC-R is a revision of the earlier WISC (TC000414) and requires new materials. It cannot be administered with WISC materials. The verbal and performance subtests are administered alternately. WISC-R may be used as part of System of Multicultural Pluralistic Assessment (SOMPA) (TC009044). Available in special edition for hearing impaired subjects from Office of Demographic Studies, Gallaudet College, Washington, DC 20002.

7489
Thumin Test of Mental Dexterity. Thumin, Fred J. 1973
Descriptors: Academic Ability; *Adults; Cognitive Ability; *Employees; Higher Education; *Intelligence; *Intelligence Tests; Mathematical Concepts; *Undergraduate Students; Verbal Ability
Identifiers: MDT
Availability: Applied Psychology Center; P.O. Box 11283, St. Louis, MO 63105
Grade Level: 13-16
Target Audience: Adults
Notes: Time, 60 approx.; Items, 100

Designed as a group test of mental ability to be used for discriminating individuals of higher than average intelligence. A greater emphasis is placed upon general information than is usually found in intelligence tests. May be used by business and industrial organizations to evaluate current and prospective employees at various levels of responsibility. Author is currently preparing an administration manual.

7542
Goyer Organization of Ideas Test. Goyer, Robert S. 1955
Descriptors: *Abstract Reasoning; *Cognitive Measurement; *Cognitive Processes; *College Students; *Convergent Thinking; Higher Education; *Logical Thinking; Norm Referenced Tests; *Perception
Identifiers: TIM(A)
Availability: Tests in Microfiche; Test Collection, Educational Testing Service, Princeton, NJ 08541

Grade Level: Higher Education
Notes: Time, 50 approx.; Items, 50

Designed to measure the ability to organize ideas which is defined as the skill whereby an individual perceives verbal stimuli, analyzes and abstracts from those stimuli the cues consistent with his or her purposes in perceiving them, and synthesizes and generalizes the ideas selected. The test items pertain to 4 skill categories: component (part whole) relationships, material to purpose (relevance) relationships, and transitional (connective) relationships. Appropriate for use with college students. There are 3 forms of the test; form S has 30 items and is dated 1968.

7570
The Kindergarten Questionnaire. Perlman, Evelyn; Berger, Susan 1976
Descriptors: Cognitive Development; Emotional Development; *Kindergarten; Language Acquisition; Learning Problems; *Maturity (Individuals); Physical Health; *Preschool Children; Preschool Education; Psychomotor Skills; *School Readiness; *Screening Tests
Availability: Evelyn Perlman; 10 Tyler Rd., Lexington, MA 02173
Target Audience: 4-5
Notes: Time, 30; Items, 65

Designed for use in identifying children who might have learning, emotional, behavioral, or language deficiencies. Used in the spring of the year prior to kindergarten entrance so that they may be deferred. Consists of a parent report of health and physical information, and a series of drawing, copying, and gross motor tasks to be performed by the child.

7588
Henmon-Nelson Tests of Mental Ability: Primary Battery. Nelson, Martin J.; French, Joseph L. 1973
Subtests: Listening Test; Picture Vocabulary Test; Size and Number Test
Descriptors: Abstract Reasoning; *Academic Aptitude; *Aptitude Tests; Elementary School Students; *Grade 1; *Grade 2; *Kindergarten Children; Number Concepts; Primary Education; *School Readiness; Spatial Ability; Verbal Ability
Identifiers: Oral Tests; Reasoning Ability
Availability: Riverside Publishing Co.; 8420 Bryn Mawr Ave., Chicago, IL 60631
Grade Level: K-2
Notes: Time, 30 approx.

Designed to measure those aspects of mental ability which are important for success in school work. Requires efficient utilization of verbal and numerical symbols and ability to acquire and retain information in common symbol form. Instructions and questions are orally administered.

7589
Henmon-Nelson Tests of Mental Ability: 1973 Revision, Form 1. Lamke, Tom A.; Nelson, Martin J. 1973
Descriptors: *Academic Aptitude; *Aptitude Tests; *Elementary School Students; Elementary Secondary Education; Mathematical Concepts; *Secondary School Students; Verbal Ability; Vocabulary
Availability: Riverside Publishing Co.; 8420 Bryn Mawr Ave., Chicago, IL 60631
Grade Level: 3-12
Notes: Time, 30 approx.; Items, 90

Designed to measure those aspects of mental ability which are important for success in academic work. Items at each of 3 overlapping levels are arranged in recurring omnibus cycles of increasing difficulty. Levels are grades 3-6, 6-9, and 9-12.

7591
Altus Information Inventory. Gorsuch, Richard 1964
Descriptors: Adults; Higher Education; High Schools; *High School Students; *Intelligence; *Screening Tests; *Undergraduate Students
Identifiers: TIM(C)
Availability: Tests in Microfiche; Test Collection, Educational Testing Service, Princeton, NJ 08541
Grade Level: 9-16
Notes: Time, 5 approx.; Items, 13

Designed to measure general intelligence for screening purposes. It is a shorter version of the Altus-Bell test.

7621
Geriatric Interpersonal Evaluation Scale. Plutchik, Robert; And Others
Descriptors: Adults; Cognitive Processes; *Cognitive Style; *Geriatrics; Individual Testing; Interviews; *Older Adults; *Patients; Psychiatric Hospitals
Identifiers: GIES; *Psychiatric Patients
Availability: Dr. Robert Plutchik; 1131 N. Ave., New Rochelle, NY 10804

Target Audience: 18-99
Notes: Items, 16

Designed to assess the degree of cognitive functioning of highly regressed patients through the use of a semi-structured interview. Also measures perceptual motor ability. Used primarily with geriatric ward patients.

7675
Auditory Pointing Test. Fudala, Janet B.; And Others 1974
Subtests: Memory Span; Sequential Memory
Descriptors: Auditory Perception; Auditory Tests; Cognitive Processes; *Diagnostic Tests; Educational Diagnosis; Elementary Education; *Elementary School Students; *Individual Testing; *Learning Disabilities; *Learning Problems; Pictorial Stimuli; *Sensory Integration; Sequential Learning; *Short Term Memory; Visual Perception
Identifiers: APT; Oral Tests
Availability: United Educational Services; P.O. Box 605, East Aurora, NY 10452
Grade Level: K-5
Notes: Items, 151

Individually administered instrument which measures and distinguishes between span and sequential short term memory. The subject is shown a picture containing many objects and, first, asked to point out a specific object; then, asked to point out 2 objects in the same order as the test administrator said them. The test is stopped when the number of errors is too high. The longest list of named objects is 10. Comes in Form A and B; requires the use of set of cards depicting the objects. Used as an aid in identifying specific learning disabilities such as deficiencies in auditory and visual sequential memory.

7687
Schematic Concept Formation Task. Evans, Selby H. 1973
Descriptors: Adolescents; Adults; *Aptitude Tests; Children; *Cognitive Ability; Concept Formation; Culture Fair Tests; *Disadvantaged; Elementary Secondary Education; Higher Education; Nonverbal Tests; *Predictive Measurement
Identifiers: SCF; TIM(B)
Availability: Tests in Microfiche; Test Collection, Educational Testing Service, Princeton, NJ 08541
Target Audience: 6-65
Notes: Items, 210

Designed to measure aptitude for spontaneous classification of stimuli on the basis of similarity, this nonverbal cognitive aptitude measure may be useful in predicting a person's learning ability or academic potential independently of his or her cultural background or educational level. The items consist of computer generated graph-like and language-like patterns.

7695
Behavioral Developmental Profile. Donahue, Michael; And Others 1972
Descriptors: Cognitive Development; *Developmental Stages; *Disabilities; *Disadvantaged; Emotional Development; Language Acquisition; *Physical Development; Social Development; *Young Children
Availability: ERIC Document Reproduction Service; 3900 Wheeler Ave., Alexandria, VA 22304 (ED079917, 35p)
Target Audience: 0-6

Developed for use with handicapped and disadvantaged children ages 0-6. Covers receptive and expressive language, cognitive, fine, and gross motor skills, personal-social skills, self-help skills and emotions. Profile format used with a guide listing behaviors occurring at set ages. Establishes a baseline and ceiling while indicating areas for intervention. Not timed. From 2 to 10 items of behavior are listed for each age range.

7729
Uncritical Inference Test. Haney, William V. 1972
Descriptors: *Adults; Cognitive Tests; *College Students; Critical Thinking; Higher Education; Induction; *Logical Thinking
Identifiers: Reasoning Ability
Availability: International Society for General Semantics; P.O. Box 2469, San Francisco, CA 94126
Grade Level: 13-16
Target Audience: Adults
Notes: Items, 75

Designed to assess respondent's ability to think accurately and carefully. Examinee reads a story and answers a series of true or false statements. The respondent is instructed to use only information specifically given in the story.

7741
TAB Science Test: An Inventory of Science Methods. Butts, David P. 1966

Descriptors: *Cognitive Processes; *Cognitive Tests; Elementary School Science; *Elementary School Students; Intermediate Grades; *Problem Solving; Science Tests
Identifiers: TAB Inventory of Science Processes; TIM(C)
Availability: Tests in Microfiche; Test Collection, Educational Testing Service, Princeton, NJ 08541
Grade Level: 4-6

Developed to assess a student's inquiry behaviors including searching, data processing, verifying, discovering, assimilating, and accommodating. The test samples inquiry behaviors by presenting the student with a specific problem, a list of clues to help him solve the problem, and the opportunity to gather clue data when they are needed. Two forms of the test are available.

7770
Means-End Problem Solving Procedure. Platt, Jerome J.; Spivack, George 1975
Descriptors: Adolescents; Adults; Interpersonal Relationship; Logical Thinking; *Patients; *Problem Solving; Projective Measures; *Psychiatric Hospitals
Identifiers: *Psychiatric Patients; Self Administered Tests; The MEPS Procedure
Availability: George Spivack, Hahnemann University (MS 626), Broad & Vine St., Philadelphia, PA 19102
Target Audience: 15-64
Notes: Items, 10

Designed to assess appropriate problem solving methods. Subject is presented with a situation involving an interpersonal conflict. The beginning and end of the situation are given. The patient must supply the means of achieving the goal. Stories may be scored for relevant means, obstacles, enumeration of means, time, irrelevant means, no-means responses, as well as for story content.

7797
Hess School Readiness Scale. Hess, Richard J. 1975
Subtests: Pictorial Identification; Discrimination of Animal Pictures; Picture Memory; Form Perception and Discrimination; Comprehension and Discrimination; Copying Geometric Forms; Paper Folding; Number Concepts; Digit Memory Span; Opposite Analogies; Comprehension; Sentence Memory Span
Descriptors: *Cognitive Ability; *Individual Testing; *Intelligence; Intelligence Tests; Preschool Children; Preschool Education; *School Readiness; *School Readiness Tests; Screening Tests; *Young Children
Identifiers: HSRS
Availability: Media Materials; 2936 Remington Ave., Baltimore, MD 21211-8891
Target Audience: 3-7
Notes: Time, 10 approx.; Items, 45

Designed to measure general intelligence for screening purposes. Measures intellectual readiness to attend school. A personal-social scale provides information regarding school readiness in areas other than intellect. Examiner must be trained in administration of individual psychological tests in order to use HSRS effectively.

7802
Essential Math and Language Skills. Sternberg, Les; And Others 1978
Subtests: Language Skills; Sets and Operations; Numbers and Operations; Part and Whole Relations; Spatial Relations; Measurement; Patterns
Descriptors: Academic Aptitude; Children; *Cognitive Ability; Cognitive Development; Cognitive Tests; *Concept Formation; *Diagnostic Tests; Disabilities; *Individual Testing; Language Skills; Learning Readiness; Mathematical Concepts; *Preschool Children; *Primary Education; *School Readiness; School Readiness Tests; Visual Measures; Visual Stimuli
Identifiers: EMLS Program; Numbers and Operations; Part Whole Relations; Pattern Recognition Skills Inventory; Sets and Operations; Spatial Relations
Availability: Hubbard; 1946 Raymond Dr., N.brook, IL 60062
Target Audience: 4-10

Individually administered instrument used to 1) assess a student's ability to recognize various pattern sequences and 2) measure the cognitive readiness of handicapped (or nonhandicapped) students relating to mathematical and language concepts. Pattern Recognition Skills Inventory was incorporated into the Program.

7822
Readiness for Kindergarten: A Coloring Book for Parents. Massey, J.D. 1975

Descriptors: Emotional Development; Intellectual Development; *Parent Participation; Physical Development; *Preschool Children; *School Readiness Tests; *Screening Tests; Social Development
Availability: Consulting Psychologists Press; 577 College Ave., Palo Alto, CA 94306
Target Audience: 5
Notes: Items, 62

Using a coloring book format, this device enables parents to evaluate their preschool child's school readiness in the areas of intellectual, physical, and social-emotional development.

7827
Vocabulary Comprehension Scale. Bangs, Tina E. 1975
Subtests: Pronouns; Quality; Position; Size; Quantity
Descriptors: Achievement Tests; *Diagnostic Tests; Individual Testing; *Learning Disabilities; Performance Tests; Preschool Tests; *School Readiness; School Readiness Tests; *Verbal Development; Verbal Tests; *Vocabulary Development; *Young Children
Identifiers: Oral Tests
Availability: DLM Teaching Resources; P.O. Box 4000, 1 DLM Park, Allen, TX 75002
Target Audience: 2-6

Orally and individually administered test to determine a child's comprehension of various words regarding size, position, number, etc. Used to give teachers of language or learning handicapped children baseline information needed to plan activities for helping these children develop vocabulary acquired for kindergarten or first grade. Requires the child to manipulate various materials upon spoken directions by the test administrator. Test packet includes the materials (tea set, trees, people, fence, ladder, cubes, buttons, etc.) to be manipulated.

7872
Ordinal Scales of Psychological Development. Uzgiris, Ina C.; Hunt, J. McV. 1975
Subtests: The Development of Visual Pursuit and the Permanence of Objects; The Development of Means for Obtaining Desired Environmental Events; The Development of Imitation: Vocal and Gestural; The Development of Operational Causality; The Construction of Object Relations in Space; The Development of Schemes for Relating to Objects
Descriptors: Behavior Rating Scales; *Cognitive Development; Concept Formation; Developmental Stages; *Infant Behavior; *Infants; *Psychological Evaluation
Identifiers: Ordinal Scales
Availability: Uzgiris, Ina C.; Hunt, J. McV. Assessment in Infancy. Urbana: University of Illinois Press, 1975
Target Audience: 0-2

Designed to measure infant's level of cognitive development. Ordinal scales are designed to elicit specific behaviors. Assesses development fostering quality of differing child rearing regimes by comparing mean age of infants at successive levels of development who are living under differing child-rearing regimes.

7897
Comprehensive Ability Battery. Hakstian, A. Ralph; Cattell, Raymond B. 1975
Subtests: Verbal Ability; Numerical Ability; Spatial Ability; Perceptual Completion; Clerical Speed and Accuracy; Reasoning; Hidden Shapes; Rote Memory; Mechanical Ability; Meaningful Memory; Memory Span; Spelling; Auditory Ability; Esthetic Judgment; Organizing Ideas; Production of Ideas; Verbal Fluency; Originality; Tracking; and Drawing
Descriptors: Abstract Reasoning; Aptitude Tests; Audiotape Recordings; *Auditory Discrimination; *Career Counseling; *Cognitive Ability; Creativity; High Schools; *High School Students; Memory; *Spatial Ability; Verbal Ability
Identifiers: CAB; Test Batteries; Thurstone Primary Mental Abilities Schema
Availability: Institute for Personality and Ability Testing; P.O. Box 188, Champaign, IL 61820
Grade Level: 9-12

Designed to measure primary ability factors important in industrial settings, and career and vocational counseling. Battery consists of 20 tests in 4 test booklets. Each test measures a single ability and may be used individually or in combination. Timed tests require approximately 5 to 7 minutes each.

7904
Comprehensive Identification Process. Zehrbach, R. Reid 1975

Descriptors: Cognitive Ability; *Disabilities; Expressive Language; *Handicap Identification; Hearing (Physiology); Individual Testing; Interviews; *Parent Participation; *Preschool Children; Preschool Education; Psychomotor Skills; Screening Tests; *Special Education; Vision
Identifiers: CIP
Availability: Scholastic Testing Service; 480 Meyer Rd., Bensenville, IL 60106
Target Audience: 2-5
Notes: Time, 30 approx.

Developed to identify all children in a community who are eligible for special preschool programs or need medical attention or therapy to function at full potential in kindergarten or grade one. Parent and child are individually interviewed. Areas of child's ability which are assessed include cognitive-verbal, fine motor, gross motor, speech and expressive language, hearing, vision, social/effective behavior, and medical history.

7912
Allied Health Aptitude Test. Psychological Corp., San Antonio, TX
Subtests: Verbal Ability; Numerical Ability; Arithmetic Processes; Science; Reading Skill; Scholastic Aptitude Total
Descriptors: Academic Ability; *Academic Achievement; *Academic Aptitude; *Achievement Tests; *Admission (School); Adults; *Allied Health Occupations Education; Allied Health Personnel; *Aptitude Tests; *College Entrance Examinations; Computation; Multiple Choice Tests; *Sciences; *Technical Education; Timed Tests
Identifiers: AHAT; Aptitude Test for Allied Health Programs
Availability: The Psychological Corp.; 555 Academic Ct., San Antonio, TX 78204-0952
Target Audience: Adults
Notes: Time, 240

Designed as an exam for those seeking admission to various allied health programs such as inhalation therapy, medical record administration, respiratory therapy, laboratory assistants, radiologic technologists, surgical nursing technologists, medical record technologists. This exam differed from the Allied Health Entrance Examination (TC007913) in the length of the program. The AHAT program is typically a 1 year or 2 year program. Not distributed to individuals, given only at specified testing centers. Instrument under constant revision; thus, the number of items and time vary (from 3-1/2 to 4 hours). Restricted.

7913
Allied Health Entrance Examination. Psychological Corp., San Antonio, TX
Subtests: Verbal Ability; Numerical Ability; Arithmetic Fundamentals; Science; Reading Skill; Reading Speed; Academic Ability
Descriptors: Academic Ability; *Academic Achievement; *Academic Aptitude; *Achievement Tests; *Admission (School); Adults; *Allied Health Occupations Education; Allied Health Personnel; Aptitude Tests; College Entrance Examinations; Computation; High School Students; Multiple Choice Tests; *Sciences; Timed Tests; *Vocational Education
Identifiers: AHEE
Availability: The Psychological Corp.; 555 Academic Ct., San Antonio, TX 78204-0952
Grade Level: 12
Target Audience: Adults
Notes: Time, 240

Designed as an exam for those seeking admission to various allied health programs such as dental assistant, surgical technician, medical record technician, and other similar programs which lead to certification but require one year or less of training. Restricted distribution; tests given only at specified testing centers throughout the U.S. and Canada. Instrument under constant revision; thus, the number of items and time vary (from 3-1/2 to 4 hours).

7914
Predictive Ability Test: Adult Edition. Friedman, Myles I. 1974
Descriptors: *Adults; *Culture Fair Tests; High Schools; *High School Seniors; *Intelligence; Intelligence Tests; Pictorial Stimuli; *Prediction; *Predictive Validity
Identifiers: PAT
Availability: Dr. Myles I. Friedman; College of Education, University of S.Carolina, Columbia, SC 29208
Target Audience: 17-64
Notes: Items, 30

Designed to measure intelligence by requiring respondent to make predictions about events. Based upon the theory that people who can predict events more accurately are more intelligent than those who cannot. The instrument consists of pictures and instructions written at a sixth

grade reading level. It is culture fair and may be administered orally to nonreaders or non-English speaking subjects.

7929
Wisconsin Test of Adult Basic Education. Wisconsin University, Madison, University Extension 1971
Subtests: Word Meaning, Reading; Arithmetic; Life Coping Skills; the World around Me
Descriptors: Achievement Tests; Adult Basic Education; Adults; Cognitive Style; *Computation; *Daily Living Skills; *Functional Literacy; *Rural Population; *Verbal Ability
Identifiers: Rural Family Development Project; TIM(C); WITABE
Availability: Tests in Microfiche; Test Collection, Educational Testing Service, Princeton, NJ 08541
Target Audience: Adults
Notes: Time, 90 approx.; Items, 68

Developed for use in monitoring the achievement of basic educational and coping skills by persons enrolled in the Rural Family Development Program. It consists of 3 subtests. Subtests 1 and 2 focus on basic reading and computational skills. Subtest 3 deals with the coping skills an adult normally needs in his or her daily life. It includes such tasks as using a road map, ordering by mail, filling out a tax return, using a phone book, and writing a letter of application.

7933
Scales for Rating the Behavioral Characteristics of Superior Students. Renzulli, Joseph S. 1976
Subtests: Learning Characteristics; Motivational Characteristics; Creativity Characteristics; Leadership Characteristics; Artistic Characteristics; Musical Characteristics; Dramatics Characteristics; Communication Characteristics-Precision; Communication Characteristics-Expressiveness; Planning
Descriptors: *Ability Identification; Academically Gifted; Behavior Rating Scales; *Diagnostic Teaching; *Elementary School Students; *Gifted; Intermediate Grades; Screening Tests; Special Education; *Student Characteristics
Identifiers: SRBCSS
Availability: Creative Learning Press; P.O. Box 320, Mansfield Center, CT 06250
Grade Level: 4-6

Designed to provide an objective and systematic instrument to be used as an aid to guiding teacher judgment in identification of superior students. Learning experiences should be developed to capitalize on student's strengths. The scores obtained for each dimension yield a profile. They should not be added to yield a total score.

7976
Employee Aptitude Survey: Prueba 2—Habilidad Numerica. Grimsley, G.; And Others 1969
Subtests: Integers; Decimals; Fractions
Descriptors: Adults; *Aptitude Tests; Career Choice; Career Counseling; College Students; Computation; Employees; Employment Potential; *High School Seniors; *Job Applicants; Job Placement; Job Skills; Mathematics; Multiple Choice Tests; *Occupational Tests; *Mathematics Tests; *Spanish; Spanish Speaking; Timed Tests; Vocational Aptitude; Vocational Education
Identifiers: EAS; *Mathematical Aptitude; Number Operation
Availability: Psychological Services, Inc.; 3450 Wilshire Blvd., Ste. 1200, Los Angeles, CA 90010
Target Audience: 17-64
Notes: Time, 10; Items, 75

A battery of 3 tests: integers, decimal fractions, and common fractions, each is timed separately. Designed to measure skill in the 4 basic operations of addition, subtraction, multiplication, and division. Also measures the ability to work easily with numbers, and to do arithmetic fast and accurately. Executives, supervisory engineering, accounting, sales, and many types of clerical jobs require good ability in this area. Also available in English. Scoring is the number right minus 1/4 the wrong answers.

7979
Employee Aptitude Survey: Prueba 5—Visualizacion De Espacio (Forma A Rev.). Grimsley, G.; And Others
Descriptors: Adults; *Aptitude Tests; Career Choice; Career Counseling; Cognitive Ability; Cognitive Tests; College Students; Employees; Employment Potential; *High School Seniors; *Job Applicants; Job Placement; Job Skills; *Occupational Tests; *Spanish; Spanish Speaking; *Spatial Ability; Timed Tests; Visual Measures; *Visual Perception; Vocational Aptitude; Vocational Education
Identifiers: EAS

Availability: Psychological Services, Inc.; 3450 Wilshire Blvd., Ste. 1200, Los Angeles, CA 90010
Target Audience: 17-64
Notes: Time, 5; Items, 50

Designed to measure the ability to visualize forms in space and to manipulate these forms or objects mentally. The test taker is shown a group of numbered, piled blocks and must determine, for a specifically numbered block, how many other blocks touch it. The authors feel that this test is a requirement for draftsmen, engineers, and personnel in technical positions. They refer to space visualization as a strong component of mechanical aptitude. Comes in both English and Spanish.

7980
Employee Aptitude Survey: Prueba 6—Razonamiento Numerico (Forma A, Revisada). Grimsley, G.; And Others 1969
Descriptors: Adults; *Aptitude Tests; Career Choice; Career Counseling; Cognitive Ability; Cognitive Tests; College Students; Employees; Employment Potential; *High School Seniors; *Induction; Intelligence; *Job Applicants; Job Placement; Job Skills; *Occupational Tests; Mathematics Tests; *Serial Ordering; *Spanish; Spanish Speaking; Timed Tests; Vocational Aptitude; Vocational Education
Identifiers: EAS; *Reasoning Ability
Availability: Psychological Services, Inc.; 3450 Wilshire Blvd., Ste. 1200, Los Angeles, CA 90010
Target Audience: 17-64
Notes: Time, 5; Items, 20

Designed to measure the ability to analyze logical relationships and to see the underlying principles of such relationships. This is also known as the process of inductive reasoning—making generalizations from specific instances. The authors feel that this ability is an important part of general intelligence and is a valuable ability in technical, supervisory, and executive positions. The test taker is given a series of numbers and determines what the next number will be. Scoring is the number right minus 1/4 the number wrong. Comes in 2 English Forms (A and B) and in Spanish.

7981
Employee Aptitude Survey: Prueba 7—Razonamiento Verbal (Forma A Rev.). Grimsley, G.; And Others 1969
Descriptors: Adults; *Aptitude Tests; Career Choice; Career Counseling; Cognitive Ability; Cognitive Tests; College Students; *Decision Making Skills; Employees; Employment Potential; *High School Seniors; *Job Applicants; Job Placement; Job Skills; *Logical Thinking; *Occupational Tests; *Spanish; Spanish Speaking; Timed Tests; Verbal Tests; Vocational Aptitude; Vocational Education
Identifiers: EAS; Reasoning; *Reasoning Ability
Availability: Psychological Services, Inc.; 3450 Wilshire Blvd., Ste. 1200, Los Angeles, CA 90010
Target Audience: 17-64
Notes: Time, 5; Items, 30

Designed to measure the ability to analyze verbally stated facts and to make valid judgments on the basis of the logical implications of such facts; and thus, the ability to analyze available information in order to make practical decisions. An important feature of the test is the measurement of the ability to determine whether the available facts provide sufficient information to draw a definite conclusion. The authors recommend this ability for executive, administrative, supervisory, scientific, accounting, and technical maintenance personnel. Scoring is the number of right answers minus 1/2 the wrong answers. Comes in both English and Spanish.

7983
Employee Aptitude Survey: Prueba 10—Razonamiento Simbolico (Forma A). Ruch, F.L.; Ford, J.S. 1969
Descriptors: *Abstract Reasoning; Adults; *Aptitude Tests; Career Choice; Career Counseling; Cognitive Ability; Cognitive Tests; College Students; Employees; Employment Potential; *High School Seniors; *Job Applicants; Job Placement; Job Skills; *Logical Thinking; Occupational Tests; *Spanish; Spanish Speaking; Timed Tests; Vocational Aptitude; Vocational Education
Identifiers: EAS; Reasoning Ability
Availability: Psychological Services, Inc.; 3450 Wilshire Blvd., Ste. 1200, Los Angeles, CA 90010
Target Audience: 17-64
Notes: Time, 5; Items, 30

Designed to measure the ability to think and reason abstractly, using symbols rather than words or numbers; to manipulate abstract symbols mentally; and to make judgments and decisions which are logical and valid. Each problem contains a statement and a conclusion, and uses certain symbols such as the equal sign and mathematical symbols for greater than and smaller than, etc. The test taker determines whether the conclusion is definitely true, definitely false, or impossible to determine on the basis of the statement. Scoring is the number of right answers minus 1/2 the wrong answers. Comes in 2 English language forms and in Spanish.

8007
Sigel Conceptual Style Sorting Task. Sigel, Irving E. 1970
Subtests: Descriptive; Relational-Contextual; Categorical-Inferential
Descriptors: *Classification; *Cognitive Style; *Cognitive Tests; Elementary Education; *Elementary School Students; Pictorial Stimuli; Visual Measures
Identifiers: SCST; TIM(D)
Availability: Tests in Microfiche; Test Collection, Educational Testing Service, Princeton, NJ 08541
Grade Level: 2-6
Notes: Time, 43 approx.; Items, 34
Designed to indicate an elementary school child's conceptual style, the task consists of a series of 3-picture sets. For each set, the child must select 2 pictures and provide a reason why they go together. The scoring categories are: descriptive (part-whole, global); relational-contextual (thematic, geographic, temporal, comparative, functional, interpersonal relationship, institutional relationship); categorical-inferential (common behavior or function, common role or attribute, moral or aesthetic judgment, common affect state, common geographic location, inferred common attribute, value judgment). Form F and Form M are available.

8008
Pupil Evaluation Measure. Evans, Velma; Whitney, Edward N. 1973
Descriptors: *Cognitive Development; *Cognitive Measurement; Concept Formation; Criterion Referenced Tests; *Disadvantaged; *Elementary School Students; *Preschool Children; Preschool Education; Primary Education
Identifiers: PEM; Piagetian Stages; TIM(C)
Availability: Tests in Microfiche; Test Collection, Educational Testing Service, Princeton, NJ 08541
Target Audience: 2-7
Notes: Items, 9
Measure based on Piagetian stages of cognitive development. Each of the 9 tasks provides for observation of the students' growth as they master simple concrete tasks and proceed to a more abstract level. Observations are conducted once a month.

8012
Developmental Patterns in Elemental Reading Skills. Stennett, Richard G.; And Others
Subtests: Visual; Auditory; Auditory/Visual; Visual/Motor; Language Background Factors; Test Behavior and Attitude; Instructional Exposure; Mastery
Descriptors: Audiolingual Skills; Auditory Perception; Basic Skills; *Beginning Reading; Decoding (Reading); *Kindergarten Children; Language Acquisition; *Objective Tests; *Primary Education; Psychomotor Skills; *Reading Readiness; *Reading Readiness Tests; Retention (Psychology); Student Attitudes; Student Behavior; Visual Discrimination
Identifiers: Canada; Test Batteries; TIM(C)
Availability: Tests in Microfiche; Test Collection, Educational Testing Service, Princeton, NJ 08541
Grade Level: K-3
Used to measure the normal development of several of the basic skills children must acquire if they are to become skilled readers.

8030
Bannatyne System: Early Screening and Diagnostic Tests—Phase II. Bannatyne, Alexander D. 1975
Subtests: Recall Vocabulary; Design Matching; Balance Test; Auditory Closure; Form/Motor Memory; Auditory Vocal Sequencing Memory; Dexterity Parallels; Spatial Form Recognition; Echo Words
Descriptors: *Diagnostic Teaching; Diagnostic Tests; Elementary School Students; Grade 1; *High Risk Students; Individual Testing; Intelligence Quotient; Language Skills; *Learning Disabilities; *Memory; *Preschool Children; Preschool Education; Preschool Tests; Primary Education; Spatial Ability
Identifiers: BS ESDT; Test Batteries
Availability: Learning Systems Press; P.O. Box 91108, Lafayette, LA 70509
Target Audience: 3-6
Notes: Time, 25 approx.

Designed to obtain an accurate diagnostic profile of the strengths and deficits of "at risk," learning disabled, and gifted students. Profile may be used in prescriptive planning of student's academic program. Assesses skills in reading, spelling, language, and spatial ability. Composite quotients may be derived for intelligence, language, or spatial ability.

8033
Hd Km Non-Verbal Test. Forms A and B. Kalyan-Masih, Violet 1962
Subtests: Classifications; Analogies
Descriptors: Group Testing; *Indians; *Intelligence Tests; Junior High Schools; *Junior High School Students; *Nonverbal Tests; *Reservation American Indians
Identifiers: TIM (C)
Availability: Tests in Microfiche; Test Collection, Educational Testing Service, Princeton, NJ 08541
Grade Level: 7-9
Notes: Time, 70 approx.; Items, 120
Designed to measure intelligence which is defined operationally as the ability to interpret and use symbols, the usual and familiar, as well as the unusual and unfamiliar ones. Forms A and B of the test may be given together or independently. Each form consists of 60 items divided into 2 sections. Part I consists of 23 classifications, suggestions for solving and practice exercises. Part II consists of 37 analogies, suggestions for solving, and practice exercises.

8050
Inventory of Symptoms of Cognitive Development: Pre-Mathematical Skills. Goolsby, T.M.; And Others 1969
Subtests: Imitating; Recognizing; Shapes; Size; Classifying; Matching; Comparing; Understanding; Counting; Computing; Measuring
Descriptors: *Mathematical Concepts; Preschool Children; *Mathematics Tests; *School Readiness Tests
Availability: ERIC Document Reproduction Service; 3900 Wheeler Ave., Alexandria, VA 22304 (ED046989, 33 pages)
Target Audience: 3-5
Designed to identify and record children's development in various areas of pre-mathematics skills. Included in Thomas M. Goolsby's Evaluation of Cognitive Development: An Observational Technique in Pre-Mathematics Skills. Research Paper No. 11, June 1969. (ED046989).

8091
Visual Memory Test. Wepman, Joseph M.; And Others 1975
Descriptors: *Elementary School Students; Individual Testing; Nonverbal Tests; Pictorial Stimuli; Primary Education; Reading Difficulties; *Reading Readiness; *Short Term Memory; *Visual Measures; *Young Children
Availability: Western Psychological Services; 12031 Wilshire Blvd., Los Angeles, CA 90025
Target Audience: 5-8
Notes: Items, 16
Designed to measure ability to retain visually presented nonalphabetic forms in immediate memory. Verbal responses are not required. Students experiencing difficulty in this perceptual task may have problems in learning to read. Low score may indicate necessity of further evaluation.

8190
Hidden Figures Test: CF-1 (Revised). Ekstrom, Ruth B.; And Others 1976
Descriptors: Aptitude Tests; Cognitive Measurement; *Cognitive Style; *Cognitive Tests; Higher Education; *Retention (Psychology); Secondary Education; *Secondary School Students; *Spatial Ability; Timed Tests; *Undergraduate Students; Visual Perception
Identifiers: *Closure Flexibility; *Field Independence; Kit of Referenced Tests for Cognitive Factors; Test Batteries
Availability: Educational Testing Service; R 122, Princeton, NJ 08541
Grade Level: 8-16
Notes: Time, 24 approx.; Items, 32
The Kit of Factor Referenced Cognitive Tests consists of 72 cognitive tests intended as markers for 23 aptitude factors to which they are referenced. The factors assessed are Flexibility of Closure, Speed of Closure, Verbal Closure, Associational Fluency, Expressional Fluency, Figural Fluency, Ideational Fluency, Word Fluency, Induction, Integrative Process, Associative Memory, Memory Span, Visual Memory, Number, Perceptual Speed, General Reasoning, Logical Reasoning, Spatial Orientation, Spatial Scanning, Verbal Comprehension, Visualization, Figural Flexibility, and Flexibility of Use. The kit is designed for research purposes. Hidden Figures Test is an adaptation of the Gottschaldt Figures type test. One of 3 tests to measure flexibility of closure. May be used to study field independence. Instrument has some variance on factors of

Spatial Orientation and Visualization. Flexibility of closure is the ability to retain a given visual configuration in mind so as to disembed it from other well defined perceptual material.

8191
Hidden Patterns Test: CF-2 (Revised). Ekstrom, Ruth B.; And Others 1976
Descriptors: Aptitude Tests; Cognitive Measurement; *Cognitive Style; *Cognitive Tests; *Grade 6; Higher Education; Intermediate Grades; *Retention (Psychology); Secondary Education; *Secondary School Students; *Spatial Ability; Timed Tests; *Undergraduate Students; Visual Perception
Identifiers: *Closure Flexibility; Kit of Referenced Tests for Cognitive Factors; Speededness (Tests); Test Batteries
Availability: Educational Testing Service; R 122, Princeton, NJ 08541
Grade Level: 6-16
Notes: Time, 6 approx.; Items, 400
The Kit of Factor Referenced Cognitive Tests consists of 72 cognitive tests intended as markers for 23 aptitude factors to which they are referenced. The factors assessed are Flexibility of Closure, Speed of Closure, Verbal Closure, Associational Fluency, Expressional Fluency, Figural Fluency, Ideational Fluency, Word Fluency, Induction, Integrative Process, Associative Memory, Memory Span, Visual Memory, Number, Perceptual Speed, General Reasoning, Logical Reasoning, Spatial Orientation, Spatial Scanning, Verbal Comprehension, Visualization, Figural Flexibility, and Flexibility of Use. The kit is designed for research purposes. This instrument was suggested by Thurstone's Designs. One of 3 tests to measure the flexibility of closure. Subject must identify whether or not a given configuration is embedded in each of several geometric patterns. Flexibility of closure is the ability to retain a given visual configuration in mind so as to disembed it from other well defined perceptual material.

8192
Copying Test: CF-3. Ekstrom, Ruth B.; And Others 1976
Descriptors: Aptitude Tests; Cognitive Measurement; *Cognitive Style; *Cognitive Tests; Eye Hand Coordination; *Grade 6; Higher Education; Intermediate Grades; *Retention (Psychology); Secondary Education; *Secondary School Students; Timed Tests; *Undergraduate Students
Identifiers: *Closure Flexibility; Kit of Referenced Tests for Cognitive Factors; Test Batteries
Availability: Educational Testing Service; R 122, Princeton, NJ 08541
Grade Level: 6-16
Notes: Time, 6 approx.; Items, 64
The Kit of Factor Referenced Cognitive Tests consists of 72 cognitive tests intended as markers for 23 aptitude factors to which they are referenced. The factors assessed are Flexibility of Closure, Speed of Closure, Verbal Closure, Associational Fluency, Expressional Fluency, Figural Fluency, Ideational Fluency, Word Fluency, Induction, Integrative Process, Associative Memory, Memory Span, Visual Memory, Number, Perceptual Speed, General Reasoning, Logical Reasoning, Spatial Orientation, Spatial Scanning, Verbal Comprehension, Visualization, Figural Flexibility, and Flexibility of Use. The kit is designed for research purposes. Instrument was suggested by Thurstone's adaptation of a subtest similarly named in Mac Quarrie's Test for Mechanical Ability. One of 3 tests to measure flexibility of closure, which is assessed in this instrument in the act of superimposing a configuration on a strong visual field. Flexibility of closure is the ability to retain a given visual configuration in mind so as to disembed it from other well defined perceptual material.

8193
Gestalt Completion Test: CS-1. Ekstrom, Ruth B.; And Others 1976
Descriptors: Aptitude Tests; Cognitive Measurement; *Cognitive Style; *Cognitive Tests; *Grade 6; Higher Education; Intermediate Grades; Secondary Education; *Secondary School Students; Timed Tests; *Undergraduate Students; Visualization
Identifiers: *Closure Speed; *Gestalt Completion; Kit of Referenced Tests for Cognitive Factors; Test Batteries
Availability: Educational Testing Service; R 122, Princeton, NJ 08541
Grade Level: 6-16
Notes: Time, 4 approx.; Items, 20
The Kit of Factor Referenced Cognitive Tests consists of 72 cognitive tests intended as markers for 23 aptitude factors to which they are referenced. The factors assessed are Flexibility of Closure, Speed of Closure, Verbal Closure, Associational Fluency, Expressional Fluency, Figural Fluency, Ideational Fluency, Word Fluency, Induction, Integrative Process, Associative Memory, Memory Span, Visual Memory, Number, Perceptual Speed, General Reasoning, Logical Reasoning, Spatial Orientation, Spatial Scanning, Verbal Comprehension, Visualization, Figural Flexi-

bility, and Flexibility of Use. The kit is designed for research purposes. One of 3 tests to measure speed of closure, the ability to unite an apparently disparate perceptual field into a single concept. Drawings are presented representing parts of objects being portrayed. Subject records the name of object. Test was suggested by the Street Gestalt Completion Test.

8194
Concealed Words Test: CS-2. Ekstrom, Ruth B.; And Others 1976
Descriptors: Aptitude Tests; Cognitive Measurement; *Cognitive Style; *Cognitive Tests; *Grade 6; Higher Education; Intermediate Grades; Secondary Education; *Secondary School Students; Timed Tests; *Undergraduate Students; Visualization
Identifiers: *Closure Speed; Kit of Referenced Tests for Cognitive Factors; Test Batteries
Availability: Educational Testing Service; R 122, Princeton, NJ 08541
Grade Level: 6-16
Notes: Time, 8 approx.; Items, 50
The Kit of Factor Referenced Cognitive Tests consists of 72 cognitive tests intended as markers for 23 aptitude factors to which they are referenced. The factors assessed are Flexibility of Closure, Speed of Closure, Verbal Closure, Associational Fluency, Expressional Fluency, Figural Fluency, Ideational Fluency, Word Fluency, Induction, Integrative Process, Associative Memory, Memory Span, Visual Memory, Number, Perceptual Speed, General Reasoning, Logical Reasoning, Spatial Orientation, Spatial Scanning, Verbal Comprehension, Visualization, Figural Flexibility, and Flexibility of Use. The kit is designed for research purposes. One of 3 tests to measure speed of closure, the ability to unite an apparently disparate perceptual field into a single concept. Words are presented with parts of each letter missing. Subject must write out the complete word. This test has some variance on Factor of Verbal Closure. Instrument suggested by Thurstone's Mutilated Words.

8195
Snowy Pictures: CS-3. Ekstrom, Ruth B.; And Others 1976
Descriptors: Aptitude Tests; Cognitive Measurement; *Cognitive Style; *Cognitive Tests; *Grade 6; Higher Education; Intermediate Grades; Secondary Education; *Secondary School Students; Timed Tests; *Undergraduate Students; *Visual Acuity
Identifiers: Closure Speed; Kit of Referenced Tests for Cognitive Factors; Test Batteries
Availability: Educational Testing Service; R 122, Princeton, NJ 08541
Grade Level: 6-16
Notes: Time, 6 approx.; Items, 24
The Kit of Factor Referenced Cognitive Tests consists of 72 cognitive tests intended as markers for 23 aptitude factors to which they are referenced. The factors assessed are Flexibility of Closure, Speed of Closure, Verbal Closure, Associational Fluency, Expressional Fluency, Figural Fluency, Ideational Fluency, Word Fluency, Induction, Integrative Process, Associative Memory, Memory Span, Visual Memory, Number, Perceptual Speed, General Reasoning, Logical Reasoning, Spatial Orientation, Spatial Scanning, Verbal Comprehension, Visualization, Figural Flexibility, and Flexibility of Use. The kit is designed for research purposes. One of 3 tests to measure speed of closure, the ability to unite an apparently disparate perceptual field into a single concept. Subject is asked to identify objects which are partly obliterated by snow-like spatters.

8196
Scrambled Words: CV-1. Ekstrom, Ruth B.; And Others 1976
Descriptors: Aptitude Tests; Cognitive Measurement; *Cognitive Style; *Cognitive Tests; Higher Education; Secondary Education; *Secondary School Students; Timed Tests; *Undergraduate Students
Identifiers: Kit of Referenced Tests for Cognitive Factors; Test Batteries; *Verbal Closure
Availability: Educational Testing Service; R 122, Princeton, NJ 08541
Grade Level: 8-16
Notes: Time, 10 approx.; Items, 50
The Kit of Factor Referenced Cognitive Tests consists of 72 cognitive tests intended as markers for 23 aptitude factors to which they are referenced. The factors assessed are Flexibility of Closure, Speed of Closure, Verbal Closure, Associational Fluency, Expressional Fluency, Figural Fluency, Ideational Fluency, Word Fluency, Induction, Integrative Process, Associative Memory, Memory Span, Visual Memory, Number, Perceptual Speed, General Reasoning, Logical Reasoning, Spatial Orientation, Spatial Scanning, Verbal Comprehension, Visualization, Figural Flexibility, and Flexibility of Use. The kit is designed for research purposes. One of 3 tests to measure verbal closure, the ability to solve problems requiring the identifica-

tion of visually presented words when some of the letters are scrambled. Subject is asked to write a common English word from a group of scrambled letters.

8197
Hidden Words: CV-2. Ekstrom, Ruth B.; And Others 1976
Descriptors: Aptitude Tests; Cognitive Measurement; *Cognitive Style; *Cognitive Tests; Higher Education; Secondary Education; *Secondary School Students; Timed Tests; *Undergraduate Students
Identifiers: Kit of Referenced Tests for Cognitive Factors; Test Batteries; *Verbal Closure
Availability: Educational Testing Service; R 122, Princeton, NJ 08541
Grade Level: 8-16
Notes: Time, 8 approx.; Items, 40
The Kit of Factor Referenced Cognitive Tests consists of 72 cognitive tests intended as markers for 23 aptitude factors to which they are referenced. The factors assessed are Flexibility of Closure, Speed of Closure, Verbal Closure, Associational Fluency, Expressional Fluency, Figural Fluency, Ideational Fluency, Word Fluency, Induction, Integrative Process, Associative Memory, Memory Span, Visual Memory, Number, Perceptual Speed, General Reasoning, Logical Reasoning, Spatial Orientation, Spatial Scanning, Verbal Comprehension, Visualization, Figural Flexibility, and Flexibility of Use. The kit is designed for research purposes. One of 3 tests to measure verbal closure, the ability to solve problems requiring the identification of visually presented words when some of the letters are embedded among other letters. Subject is asked to find and circle one or more 4-letter words in apparently random lines of letters.

8198
Incomplete Words: CV-3. Ekstrom, Ruth B.; And Others 1976
Descriptors: Aptitude Tests; Cognitive Measurement; *Cognitive Style; *Cognitive Tests; Higher Education; Secondary Education; *Secondary School Students; Timed Tests; *Undergraduate Students
Identifiers: Kit of Referenced Tests for Cognitive Factors; Missing Data; Test Batteries; *Verbal Closure
Availability: Educational Testing Service; R 122, Princeton, NJ 08541
Grade Level: 8-16
Notes: Time, 6 approx.; Items, 36
The Kit of Factor Referenced Cognitive Tests consists of 72 cognitive tests intended as markers for 23 aptitude factors to which they are referenced. The factors assessed are Flexibility of Closure, Speed of Closure, Verbal Closure, Associational Fluency, Expressional Fluency, Figural Fluency, Ideational Fluency, Word Fluency, Induction, Integrative Process, Associative Memory, Memory Span, Visual Memory, Number, Perceptual Speed, General Reasoning, Logical Reasoning, Spatial Orientation, Spatial Scanning, Verbal Comprehension, Visualization, Figural Flexibility, and Flexibility of Use. The kit is designed for research purposes. One of 3 tests to measure verbal closure, the ability to solve problems requiring the identification of visually presented words when some of the letters are missing. Subject is asked to provide one or more letters to complete common words.

8199
Controlled Associations Test: FA-1. Ekstrom, Ruth B.; And Others 1976
Descriptors: Aptitude Tests; Association (Psychology); Cognitive Measurement; *Cognitive Style; *Cognitive Tests; *Grade 6; Higher Education; Intermediate Grades; Secondary Education; *Secondary School Students; Timed Tests; *Undergraduate Students; Verbal Stimuli
Identifiers: *Associational Fluency; Kit of Referenced Tests for Cognitive Factors; *Synonyms; Test Batteries
Availability: Educational Testing Service; R 122, Princeton, NJ 08541
Grade Level: 6-16
Notes: Time, 12 approx.; Items, 8
The Kit of Factor Referenced Cognitive Tests consists of 72 cognitive tests intended as markers for 23 aptitude factors to which they are referenced. The factors assessed are Flexibility of Closure, Speed of Closure, Verbal Closure, Associational Fluency, Expressional Fluency, Figural Fluency, Ideational Fluency, Word Fluency, Induction, Integrative Process, Associative Memory, Memory Span, Visual Memory, Number, Perceptual Speed, General Reasoning, Logical Reasoning, Spatial Orientation, Spatial Scanning, Verbal Comprehension, Visualization, Figural Flexibility, and Flexibility of Use. The kit is designed for research purposes. One of 3 tests to measure associational fluency, the ability to produce rapidly words which share a given area of meaning or some other common semantic property. Instrument was adapted from Thurstone's test of this name. Task is to write as many synonyms as possible for each stimulus word.

8200
Opposites Test: FA-2. Ekstrom, Ruth B.; And Others 1976
Descriptors: Aptitude Tests; Association (Psychology); Cognitive Measurement; *Cognitive Style; *Cognitive Tests; *Grade 6; Higher Education; Intermediate Grades; Secondary Education; *Secondary School Students; Timed Tests; *Undergraduate Students; Verbal Stimuli
Identifiers: *Antonyms; *Associational Fluency; Kit of Referenced Tests for Cognitive Factors; Test Batteries
Availability: Educational Testing Service; R 122, Princeton, NJ 08541
Grade Level: 6-16
Notes: Time, 10 approx.; Items, 8
The Kit of Factor Referenced Cognitive Tests consists of 72 cognitive tests intended as markers for 23 aptitude factors to which they are referenced. The factors assessed are Flexibility of Closure, Speed of Closure, Verbal Closure, Associational Fluency, Expressional Fluency, Figural Fluency, Ideational Fluency, Word Fluency, Induction, Integrative Process, Associative Memory, Memory Span, Visual Memory, Number, Perceptual Speed, General Reasoning, Logical Reasoning, Spatial Orientation, Spatial Scanning, Verbal Comprehension, Visualization, Figural Flexibility, and Flexibility of Use. The kit is designed for research purposes. One of 3 tests to measure associational fluency, the ability to produce rapidly words which share a given area of meaning or some other common semantic property. Subject is asked to write as many antonyms as possible for each stimulus word.

8201
Figures of Speech: FA-3. Ekstrom, Ruth B.; And Others 1976
Descriptors: Aptitude Tests; Cognitive Measurement; *Cognitive Style; *Cognitive Tests; *Figurative Language; Higher Education; High Schools; *High School Students; Timed Tests; *Undergraduate Students; Verbal Stimuli
Identifiers: *Associational Fluency; Kit of Referenced Tests for Cognitive Factors; Test Batteries
Availability: Educational Testing Service; R 122, Princeton, NJ 08541
Grade Level: 9-16
Notes: Time, 10 approx.; Items, 10
The Kit of Factor Referenced Cognitive Tests consists of 72 cognitive tests intended as markers for 23 aptitude factors to which they are referenced. The factors assessed are Flexibility of Closure, Speed of Closure, Verbal Closure, Associational Fluency, Expressional Fluency, Figural Fluency, Ideational Fluency, Word Fluency, Induction, Integrative Process, Associative Memory, Memory Span, Visual Memory, Number, Perceptual Speed, General Reasoning, Logical Reasoning, Spatial Orientation, Spatial Scanning, Verbal Comprehension, Visualization, Figural Flexibility, and Flexibility of Use. The kit is designed for research purposes. One of 3 tests to measure associational fluency, the ability to produce rapidly words which share a given area of meaning or some other common semantic property. Subject is asked to provide up to 3 words or phrases to complete each of 10 figures of speech.

8202
Making Sentences: FE-1. Ekstrom, Ruth B.; And Others 1976
Descriptors: Aptitude Tests; Cognitive Measurement; *Cognitive Style; *Cognitive Tests; *Grade 6; Higher Education; Intermediate Grades; Language Skills; Secondary Education; *Secondary School Students; Timed Tests; *Undergraduate Students; *Verbal Ability
Identifiers: *Expressional Fluency; Kit of Referenced Tests for Cognitive Factors; Test Batteries
Availability: Educational Testing Service; R 122, Princeton, NJ 08541
Grade Level: 6-16
Notes: Time, 10 approx.; Items, 20
The Kit of Factor Referenced Cognitive Tests consists of 72 cognitive tests intended as markers for 23 aptitude factors to which they are referenced. The factors assessed are Flexibility of Closure, Speed of Closure, Verbal Closure, Associational Fluency, Expressional Fluency, Figural Fluency, Ideational Fluency, Word Fluency, Induction, Integrative Process, Associative Memory, Memory Span, Visual Memory, Number, Perceptual Speed, General Reasoning, Logical Reasoning, Spatial Orientation, Spatial Scanning, Verbal Comprehension, Visualization, Figural Flexibility, and Flexibility of Use. The kit is designed for research purposes. One of 3 tests to measure expressional fluency, the ability to think rapidly of word groups or phrases. Subject must make sentences of a specified length when the initial letter or some of the words is provided.

8203
Arranging Words: FE-2. Ekstrom, Ruth B.; And Others 1976

Descriptors: Aptitude Tests; Cognitive Measurement; *Cognitive Style; *Cognitive Tests; *Grade 6; Higher Education; Intermediate Grades; Language Skills; Secondary Education; *Secondary School Students; Sentences; Timed Tests; *Undergraduate Students; Verbal Ability
Identifiers: *Expressional Fluency; Kit of Referenced Tests for Cognitive Factors; Test Batteries
Availability: Educational Testing Service; R 122, Princeton, NJ 08541
Grade Level: 6-16
Notes: Time, 10 approx.; Items, 8

The Kit of Factor Referenced Cognitive Tests consists of 72 cognitive tests intended as markers for 23 aptitude factors to which they are referenced. The factors assessed are Flexibility of Closure, Speed of Closure, Verbal Closure, Associational Fluency, Expressional Fluency, Figural Fluency, Ideational Fluency, Word Fluency, Induction, Integrative Process, Associative Memory, Memory Span, Visual Memory, Number, Perceptual Speed, General Reasoning, Logical Reasoning, Spatial Orientation, Spatial Scanning, Verbal Comprehension, Visualization, Figural Flexibility, and Flexibility of Use. The kit is designed for research purposes. One of 3 tests to measure expressional fluency, the ability to think rapidly of word groups or phrases. Subject is asked to write up to 40 different sentences using 8 key words.

8204
Rewriting: FE-3. Ekstrom, Ruth B.; And Others 1976
Descriptors: Aptitude Tests; Cognitive Measurement; *Cognitive Style; *Cognitive Tests; *Grade 6; Higher Education; Intermediate Grades; Secondary Education; *Secondary School Students; Timed Tests; *Undergraduate Students; Verbal Ability; *Writing Skills
Identifiers: *Expressional Fluency; Kit of Referenced Tests for Cognitive Factors; Test Batteries
Availability: Educational Testing Service; R 122, Princeton, NJ 08541
Grade Level: 6-16
Notes: Time, 10 approx.; Items, 6

The Kit of Factor Referenced Cognitive Tests consists of 72 cognitive tests intended as markers for 23 aptitude factors to which they are referenced. The factors assessed are Flexibility of Closure, Speed of Closure, Verbal Closure, Associational Fluency, Expressional Fluency, Figural Fluency, Ideational Fluency, Word Fluency, Induction, Integrative Process, Associative Memory, Memory Span, Visual Memory, Number, Perceptual Speed, General Reasoning, Logical Reasoning, Spatial Orientation, Spatial Scanning, Verbal Comprehension, Visualization, Figural Flexibility, and Flexibility of Use. The kit is designed for research purposes. One of 3 tests designed to measure expressional fluency, the ability to think rapidly of word groups or phrases. Examinee is asked to rewrite each of 6 sentences in 2 different ways.

8205
Ornamentation Test: FF-1. Ekstrom, Ruth B.; And Others 1976
Descriptors: Aptitude Tests; Cognitive Measurement; *Cognitive Style; *Cognitive Tests; Creative Art; *Creativity; *Grade 6; Higher Education; Intermediate Grades; Secondary Education; *Secondary School Students; Timed Tests; *Undergraduate Students
Identifiers: *Figural Fluency; Kit of Referenced Tests for Cognitive Factors; Test Batteries
Availability: Educational Testing Service; R 122, Princeton, NJ 08541
Grade Level: 6-16
Notes: Time, 4 approx.; Items, 48

The Kit of Factor Referenced Cognitive Tests consists of 72 cognitive tests intended as markers for 23 aptitude factors to which they are referenced. The factors assessed are Flexibility of Closure, Speed of Closure, Verbal Closure, Associational Fluency, Expressional Fluency, Figural Fluency, Ideational Fluency, Word Fluency, Induction, Integrative Process, Associative Memory, Memory Span, Visual Memory, Number, Perceptual Speed, General Reasoning, Logical Reasoning, Spatial Orientation, Spatial Scanning, Verbal Comprehension, Visualization, Figural Flexibility, and Flexibility of Use. The kit is designed for research purposes. One of 3 tests designed to measure figural fluency, the ability to draw quickly a number of examples, elaborations or restructurings based on a given visual or descriptive stimulus. Subject is asked to make as many different decorations as possible on common objects.

8206
Elaboration Test: FF-2. Ekstrom, Ruth B.; And Others 1976
Descriptors: Aptitude Tests; Cognitive Measurement; *Cognitive Style; *Cognitive Tests; Creative Art; Creative Thinking; *Creativity; *Grade 6; Higher Education; Intermediate Grades; Secondary Education; *Secondary School Students; Timed Tests; *Undergraduate Students
Identifiers: *Figural Fluency; Kit of Referenced Tests for Cognitive Factors; Test Batteries
Availability: Educational Testing Service; R 122, Princeton, NJ 08541
Grade Level: 6-16
Notes: Time, 4 approx.; Items, 40

The Kit of Factor Referenced Cognitive Tests consists of 72 cognitive tests intended as markers for 23 aptitude factors to which they are referenced. The factors assessed are Flexibility of Closure, Speed of Closure, Verbal Closure, Associational Fluency, Expressional Fluency, Figural Fluency, Ideational Fluency, Word Fluency, Induction, Integrative Process, Associative Memory, Memory Span, Visual Memory, Number, Perceptual Speed, General Reasoning, Logical Reasoning, Spatial Orientation, Spatial Scanning, Verbal Comprehension, Visualization, Figural Flexibility, and Flexibility of Use. The kit is designed for research purposes. One of 3 tests designed to measure figural fluency, the ability to draw quickly a number of examples, elaborations, or restructurings based on a given visual or descriptive stimulus. Subject is asked to add to the existing decoration, as many different decorations as possible.

8207
Symbols Test: FF-3. Ekstrom, Ruth B.; And Others 1976
Descriptors: Aptitude Tests; Cognitive Measurement; *Cognitive Style; *Cognitive Tests; Creative Thinking; *Creativity; Higher Education; High Schools; *High School Students; Timed Tests; *Undergraduate Students
Identifiers: *Figural Fluency; Kit of Referenced Tests for Cognitive Factors; Test Batteries
Availability: Educational Testing Service; R 122, Princeton, NJ 08541
Grade Level: 9-16
Notes: Time, 10 approx.; Items, 10

The Kit of Factor Referenced Cognitive Tests consists of 72 cognitive tests intended as markers for 23 aptitude factors to which they are referenced. The factors assessed are Flexibility of Closure, Speed of Closure, Verbal Closure, Associational Fluency, Expressional Fluency, Figural Fluency, Ideational Fluency, Word Fluency, Induction, Integrative Process, Associative Memory, Memory Span, Visual Memory, Number, Perceptual Speed, General Reasoning, Logical Reasoning, Spatial Orientation, Spatial Scanning, Verbal Comprehension, Visualization, Figural Flexibility, and Flexibility of Use. The kit is designed for research purposes. One of 3 tests designed to measure figural fluency, the ability to draw quickly a number of examples, elaborations, or restructurings based on a given visual or descriptive stimulus. Subject is asked to draw up to 5 different symbols for each of 10 words or phrases.

8208
Topics Test: FI-1. Ekstrom, Ruth B.; And Others 1976
Descriptors: Aptitude Tests; Cognitive Measurement; *Cognitive Style; *Cognitive Tests; *Divergent Thinking; Higher Education; Secondary Education; *Secondary School Students; Timed Tests; *Undergraduate Students
Identifiers: Ideas; *Ideational Fluency; Kit of Referenced Tests for Cognitive Factors; Test Batteries
Availability: Educational Testing Service; R 122, Princeton, NJ 08541
Grade Level: 8-16
Notes: Time, 8; Items, 2

The Kit of Factor Referenced Cognitive Tests consists of 72 cognitive tests intended as markers for 23 aptitude factors to which they are referenced. The factors assessed are Flexibility of Closure, Speed of Closure, Verbal Closure, Associational Fluency, Expressional Fluency, Figural Fluency, Ideational Fluency, Word Fluency, Induction, Integrative Process, Associative Memory, Memory Span, Visual Memory, Number, Perceptual Speed, General Reasoning, Logical Reasoning, Spatial Orientation, Spatial Scanning, Verbal Comprehension, Visualization, Figural Flexibility, and Flexibility of Use. The kit is designed for research purposes. Instrument was adapted from Calvin Taylor's version of a test by R.B. Cattell. Subject must write as many ideas as possible about a given topic. One of 3 instruments which measure ideational fluency, the facility to write a number of ideas about a given topic. The quantity, rather than quality, of ideas is emphasized.

8209
Theme Test: FI-2. Ekstrom, Ruth B.; And Others 1976
Descriptors: Aptitude Tests; Cognitive Measurement; *Cognitive Style; *Cognitive Tests; Higher Education; Secondary Education; *Secondary School Students; Timed Tests; *Undergraduate Students; *Writing (Composition)
Identifiers: *Ideational Fluency; Kit of Referenced Tests for Cognitive Factors; Test Batteries
Availability: Educational Testing Service; R 122, Princeton, NJ 08541
Grade Level: 8-16
Notes: Time, 8; Items, 2

The Kit of Factor Referenced Cognitive Tests consists of 72 cognitive tests intended as markers for 23 aptitude factors to which they are referenced. The factors assessed are Flexibility of Closure, Speed of Closure, Verbal Closure, Associational Fluency, Expressional Fluency, Figural Fluency, Ideational Fluency, Word Fluency, Induction, Integrative Process, Associative Memory, Memory Span, Visual Memory, Number, Perceptual Speed, General Reasoning, Logical Reasoning, Spatial Orientation, Spatial Scanning, Verbal Comprehension, Visualization, Figural Flexibility, and Flexibility of Use. The kit is designed for research purposes. Instrument was adapted from C. Taylor's version of a test by R.B. Cattell. Subject must write as much as possible about a given theme. One of 3 instruments which measure ideational fluency, the facility to write a number of ideas about a given topic. The quantity of ideas produced within broad constraints rather than the quality of ideas is emphasized.

8210
Thing Categories Test: FI-3. Ekstrom, Ruth B.; And Others 1976
Descriptors: Aptitude Tests; Cognitive Measurement; *Cognitive Style; *Cognitive Tests; *Creative Thinking; Higher Education; Secondary Education; *Secondary School Students; Timed Tests; *Undergraduate Students
Identifiers: *Ideational Fluency; Kit of Referenced Tests for Cognitive Factors; Test Batteries
Availability: Educational Testing Service; R 122, Princeton, NJ 08541
Grade Level: 8-16
Notes: Time, 6

The Kit of Factor Referenced Cognitive Tests consists of 72 cognitive tests intended as markers for 23 aptitude factors to which they are referenced. The factors assessed are Flexibility of Closure, Speed of Closure, Verbal Closure, Associational Fluency, Expressional Fluency, Figural Fluency, Ideational Fluency, Word Fluency, Induction, Integrative Process, Associative Memory, Memory Span, Visual Memory, Number, Perceptual Speed, General Reasoning, Logical Reasoning, Spatial Orientation, Spatial Scanning, Verbal Comprehension, Visualization, Figural Flexibility, and Flexibility of Use. The kit is designed for research purposes. Instrument was adapted from Taylor's Things Round, a version of a test by R.B. Cattell. Subject is asked to list the names of things that are alike in a specified way. One of 3 instruments which measure ideational fluency, the facility to write a number of exemplars of a given class of objects. The quantity, rather than quality, of ideas produced within broad constraints is emphasized.

8211
Word Endings Test: FW-1. Ekstrom, Ruth B.; And Others 1976
Descriptors: Aptitude Tests; Cognitive Measurement; *Cognitive Style; *Cognitive Tests; *Grade 6; Higher Education; Intermediate Grades; Secondary Education; *Secondary School Students; *Suffixes; Timed Tests; *Undergraduate Students
Identifiers: Kit of Referenced Tests for Cognitive Factors; Test Batteries
Availability: Educational Testing Service; R 122, Princeton, NJ 08541
Grade Level: 6-16
Notes: Time, 6

The Kit of Factor Referenced Cognitive Tests consists of 72 cognitive tests intended as markers for 23 aptitude factors to which they are referenced. The factors assessed are Flexibility of Closure, Speed of Closure, Verbal Closure, Associational Fluency, Expressional Fluency, Figural Fluency, Ideational Fluency, Word Fluency, Induction, Integrative Process, Associative Memory, Memory Span, Visual Memory, Number, Perceptual Speed, General Reasoning, Logical Reasoning, Spatial Orientation, Spatial Scanning, Verbal Comprehension, Visualization, Figural Flexibility, and Flexibility of Use. The kit is designed for research purposes. Instrument is similar to Thurstone's Suffixes. Subject must write as many words as possible ending with certain given letters. One of 3 instruments measuring word fluency, the facility to produce words that fit one or more structural, phonetic, or orthographic restrictions that are not relevant to the meaning of the words.

8212
Word Beginnings Test: FW-2. Ekstrom, Ruth B.; And Others 1976
Descriptors: Aptitude Tests; Cognitive Measurement; *Cognitive Style; *Cognitive Tests; *Grade 6; Higher Education; Intermediate Grades; Secondary Education; *Secondary School Students; Timed Tests; *Undergraduate Students

Identifiers: Kit of Referenced Tests for Cognitive Factors; *Prefixes; Test Batteries
Availability: Educational Testing Service; R 122, Princeton, NJ 08541
Grade Level: 6-16
Notes: Time, 6

The Kit of Factor Referenced Cognitive Tests consists of 72 cognitive tests intended as markers for 23 aptitude factors to which they are referenced. The factors assessed are Flexibility of Closure, Speed of Closure, Verbal Closure, Associational Fluency, Expressional Fluency, Figural Fluency, Ideational Fluency, Word Fluency, Induction, Integrative Process, Associative Memory, Memory Span, Visual Memory, Number, Perceptual Speed, General Reasoning, Logical Reasoning, Spatial Orientation, Spatial Scanning, Verbal Comprehension, Visualization, Figural Flexibility and Flexibility of Use. The kit is designed for research purposes. Instrument is similar to Thurstone's Prefixes. Subject is to write as many words as possible beginning with certain given letters. One of 3 instruments which measure word fluency, the facility to produce words that fit one or more structural, phonetic, or orthographic restrictions that are not relevant to the meaning of the words.

8213
Word Beginnings and Endings Test: FW-3. Ekstrom, Ruth B.; And Others 1976
Descriptors: Aptitude Tests; Cognitive Measurement; *Cognitive Style; *Cognitive Tests; *Grade 6; Higher Education; Intermediate Grades; Phonemes; Secondary Education; *Secondary School Students; Timed Tests; *Undergraduate Students
Identifiers: Kit of Referenced Tests for Cognitive Factors; Test Batteries
Availability: Educational Testing Service; R 122, Princeton, NJ 08541
Grade Level: 6-16
Notes: Time, 6

The Kit of Factor Referenced Cognitive Tests consists of 72 cognitive tests intended as markers for 23 aptitude factors to which they are referenced. The factors assessed are Flexibility of Closure, Speed of Closure, Verbal Closure, Associational Fluency, Expressional Fluency, Figural Fluency, Ideational Fluency, Word Fluency, Induction, Integrative Process, Associative Memory, Memory Span, Visual Memory, Number, Perceptual Speed, General Reasoning, Logical Reasoning, Spatial Orientation, Spatial Scanning, Verbal Comprehension, Visualization, Figural Flexibility, and Flexibility of Use. The kit is designed for research purposes. Instrument is similar to Thurstone's First and Last Letters. Subject is asked to write as many words as possible beginning with one given letter and ending with another. One of 3 instruments which measure word fluency, the facility to produce words that fit one or more structural, phonetic, or orthographic restrictions that are not relevant to the meaning of the words.

8214
Letter Sets Test: I-1. Ekstrom, Ruth B.; And Others 1976
Descriptors: Aptitude Tests; Cognitive Measurement; *Cognitive Style; *Cognitive Tests; Concept Formation; Higher Education; *Induction; Secondary Education; *Secondary School Students; Timed Tests; *Undergraduate Students
Identifiers: Kit of Referenced Tests for Cognitive Factors; Test Batteries
Availability: Educational Testing Service; R 122, Princeton, NJ 08541
Grade Level: 8-16
Notes: Time, 14; Items, 30

The Kit of Factor Referenced Cognitive Tests consists of 72 cognitive tests intended as markers for 23 aptitude factors to which they are referenced. The factors assessed are Flexibility of Closure, Speed of Closure, Verbal Closure, Associational Fluency, Expressional Fluency, Figural Fluency, Ideational Fluency, Word Fluency, Induction, Integrative Process, Associative Memory, Memory Span, Visual Memory, Number, Perceptual Speed, General Reasoning, Logical Reasoning, Spatial Orientation, Spatial Scanning, Verbal Comprehension, Visualization, Figural Flexibility, and Flexibility of Use. The kit is designed for research purposes. Instrument was suggested by Thurstone's Letter Grouping. Subject must use inductive reasoning to determine relationship between sets of letters. One of 3 tests to identify types of reasoning abilities involved in forming and testing hypotheses that will fit a set of data.

8215
Locations Test: I-2. Ekstrom, Ruth B.; And Others 1976
Descriptors: Aptitude Tests; Cognitive Measurement; *Cognitive Style; *Cognitive Tests; Concept Formation; Higher Education; *Induction; Secondary Education; *Secondary School Students; Timed Tests; *Undergraduate Students
Identifiers: Kit of Referenced Tests for Cognitive Factors; Test Batteries
Availability: Educational Testing Service; R 122, Princeton, NJ 08541

Grade Level: 8-16
Notes: Time, 12; Items, 28

The Kit of Factor Referenced Cognitive Tests consists of 72 cognitive tests intended as markers for 23 aptitude factors to which they are referenced. The factors assessed are Flexibility of Closure, Speed of Closure, Verbal Closure, Associational Fluency, Expressional Fluency, Figural Fluency, Ideational Fluency, Word Fluency, Induction, Integrative Process, Associative Memory, Memory Span, Visual Memory, Number, Perceptual Speed, General Reasoning, Logical Reasoning, Spatial Orientation, Spatial Scanning, Verbal Comprehension, Visualization, Figural Flexibility, and Flexibility of Use. The kit is designed for research purposes. Instrument was suggested by Thurstone's Marks. One of 3 tests to identify types of reasoning abilities involved in forming and testing hypotheses that will fit a set of data.

8216
Figure Classification: I-3. Ekstrom, Ruth B.; And Others 1976
Descriptors: Aptitude Tests; Classification; Cognitive Measurement; *Cognitive Style; *Cognitive Tests; Concept Formation; Higher Education; *Induction; Secondary Education; *Secondary School Students; Timed Tests; *Undergraduate Students
Identifiers: Kit of Referenced Tests for Cognitive Factors; Test Batteries
Availability: Educational Testing Service; R 122, Princeton, NJ 08541
Grade Level: 8-16
Notes: Time, 16; Items, 28

The Kit of Factor Referenced Cognitive Tests consists of 72 cognitive tests intended as markers for 23 aptitude factors to which they are referenced. The factors assessed are Flexibility of Closure, Speed of Closure, Verbal Closure, Associational Fluency, Expressional Fluency, Figural Fluency, Ideational Fluency, Word Fluency, Induction, Integrative Process, Associative Memory, Memory Span, Visual Memory, Number, Perceptual Speed, General Reasoning, Logical Reasoning, Spatial Orientation, Spatial Scanning, Verbal Comprehension, Visualization, Figural Flexibility, and Flexibility of Use. The kit is designed for research purposes. Instrument was suggested by Thurstone's Figure Classification Test. One of 3 tests to identify types of reasoning abilities involved in forming and testing hypotheses that will fit a set of data.

8217
Calendar Test: IP-1. Ekstrom, Ruth B.; And Others 1976
Descriptors: Aptitude Tests; Cognitive Measurement; *Cognitive Style; *Cognitive Tests; Higher Education; *Logical Thinking; Problem Solving; Secondary Education; *Secondary School Students; Timed Tests; *Undergraduate Students
Identifiers: *Integrative Processes; Kit of Referenced Tests for Cognitive Factors; Test Batteries
Availability: Educational Testing Service; R 122, Princeton, NJ 08541
Grade Level: 8-16
Notes: Time, 14; Items, 20

The Kit of Factor Referenced Cognitive Tests consists of 72 cognitive tests intended as markers for 23 aptitude factors to which they are referenced. The factors assessed are Flexibility of Closure, Speed of Closure, Verbal Closure, Associational Fluency, Expressional Fluency, Figural Fluency, Ideational Fluency, Word Fluency, Induction, Integrative Process, Associative Memory, Memory Span, Visual Memory, Number, Perceptual Speed, General Reasoning, Logical Reasoning, Spatial Orientation, Spatial Scanning, Verbal Comprehension, Visualization, Figural Flexibility, and Flexibility of Use. The kit is designed for research purposes. Subject is asked to select certain dates on a calendar by following fairly complex sets of directions. One of 2 instruments to measure integrative processes, the ability to mentally retain simultaneously or combine several conditions, premises, or rules in order to produce a correct response.

8218
Following Directions: IP-2. Ekstrom, Ruth B.; And Others 1976
Descriptors: Aptitude Tests; Cognitive Measurement; *Cognitive Style; *Cognitive Tests; Higher Education; High Schools; *High School Students; *Logical Thinking; Problem Solving; Timed Tests; *Undergraduate Students
Identifiers: *Integrative Processes; Kit of Referenced Tests for Cognitive Factors; Test Batteries
Availability: Educational Testing Service; R 122, Princeton, NJ 08541
Grade Level: 9-16
Notes: Time, 14; Items, 20

The Kit of Factor Referenced Cognitive Tests consists of 72 cognitive tests intended as markers for 23 aptitude factors to which they are referenced. The factors assessed are Flexibility of Closure, Speed of Closure, Verbal Closure, Associational Fluency, Expressional Fluency, Figural

Fluency, Ideational Fluency, Word Fluency, Induction, Integrative Process, Associative Memory, Memory Span, Visual Memory, Number, Perceptual Speed, General Reasoning, Logical Reasoning, Spatial Orientation, Spatial Scanning, Verbal Comprehension, Visualization, Figural Flexibility, and Flexibility of Use. The kit is designed for research purposes. Subject is asked to determine the point in a matrix of letters that would be reached by following a complex set of directions. One of 2 instruments to measure integrative processes, the ability to mentally retain simultaneously or combine several conditions, premises, or rules in order to produce a correct response.

8219
Picture Number Test: MA-1. Ekstrom, Ruth B.; And Others 1976
Descriptors: Aptitude Tests; Association (Psychology); Cognitive Measurement; *Cognitive Style; *Cognitive Tests; *Grade 6; Higher Education; Intermediate Grades; Memory; *Recall (Psychology); Secondary Education; *Secondary School Students; Timed Tests; *Undergraduate Students
Identifiers: *Associative Memory; Kit of Referenced Tests for Cognitive Factors; Test Batteries
Availability: Educational Testing Service; R 122, Princeton, NJ 08541
Grade Level: 6-16
Notes: Time, 14 approx.; Items, 42

The Kit of Factor Referenced Cognitive Tests consists of 72 cognitive tests intended as markers for 23 aptitude factors to which they are referenced. The factors assessed are Flexibility of Closure, Speed of Closure, Verbal Closure, Associational Fluency, Expressional Fluency, Figural Fluency, Ideational Fluency, Word Fluency, Induction, Integrative Process, Associative Memory, Memory Span, Visual Memory, Number, Perceptual Speed, General Reasoning, Logical Reasoning, Spatial Orientation, Spatial Scanning, Verbal Comprehension, Visualization, Figural Flexibility, and Flexibility of Use. The kit is designed for research purposes. Instrument was adapted from a test by Anne Anastasi. One of 3 instruments which measure associate memory, the ability to recall 1 part of a previously learned, but otherwise unrelated, pair of items when the other part of the pair is presented.

8220
Object Number Test: MA-2. Ekstrom, Ruth B.; And Others 1976
Descriptors: Aptitude Tests; Association (Psychology); Cognitive Measurement; *Cognitive Style; *Cognitive Tests; *Grade 6; Higher Education; Intermediate Grades; Memory; *Recall (Psychology); Secondary Education; *Secondary School Students; Timed Tests; *Undergraduate Students
Identifiers: *Associative Memory; Kit of Referenced Tests for Cognitive Factors; Test Batteries
Availability: Educational Testing Service; R 122, Princeton, NJ 08541
Grade Level: 6-16
Notes: Time, 10 approx.; Items, 30

The Kit of Factor Referenced Cognitive Tests consists of 72 cognitive tests intended as markers for 23 aptitude factors to which they are referenced. The factors assessed are Flexibility of Closure, Speed of Closure, Verbal Closure, Associational Fluency, Expressional Fluency, Figural Fluency, Ideational Fluency, Word Fluency, Induction, Integrative Process, Associative Memory, Memory Span, Visual Memory, Number, Perceptual Speed, General Reasoning, Logical Reasoning, Spatial Orientation, Spatial Scanning, Verbal Comprehension, Visualization, Figural Flexibility, and Flexibility of Use. The kit is designed for research purposes. Instrument was adapted from Thurstone's word-number. One of 3 instruments which measure associate memory, the ability to recall one part of a previously learned, but otherwise unrelated, pair of items when the other part of the pair is presented.

8221
First and Last Names Test: MA-3. Ekstrom, Ruth B.; And Others 1976
Descriptors: Aptitude Tests; Association (Psychology); Cognitive Measurement; *Cognitive Style; *Cognitive Tests; *Grade 6; Higher Education; Intermediate Grades; Memory; *Recall (Psychology); Secondary Education; *Secondary School Students; Timed Tests; *Undergraduate Students
Identifiers: *Associative Memory; Kit of Referenced Tests for Cognitive Factors; Test Batteries
Availability: Educational Testing Service; R 122, Princeton, NJ 08541
Grade Level: 6-16
Notes: Time, 10 approx.; Items, 30

The Kit of Factor Referenced Cognitive Tests consists of 72 cognitive tests intended as markers for 23 aptitude factors to which they are referenced. The factors assessed are Flexibility of Closure, Speed of Closure, Verbal Closure, Associational Fluency, Expressional Fluency, Figural

Fluency, Ideational Fluency, Word Fluency, Induction, Integrative Process, Associative Memory, Memory Span, Visual Memory, Number, Perceptual Speed, General Reasoning, Logical Reasoning, Spatial Orientation, Spatial Scanning, Verbal Comprehension, Visualization, Figural Flexibility, and Flexibility of Use. The kit is designed for research purposes. Instrument was adpated from Thurstone's First Names. One of 3 instruments which measure associate memory, the ability to recall one part of a previously learned, but otherwise unrelated, pair of items when the other part of the pair is presented.

8222
Auditory Number Span Test: MS-1. Ekstrom, Ruth B.; And Others 1976
Descriptors: Aptitude Tests; Auditory Stimuli; Cognitive Measurement; *Cognitive Style; *Cognitive Tests; *Grade 6; Higher Education; Intermediate Grades; Secondary Education; *Secondary School Students; *Short Term Memory; *Undergraduate Students
Identifiers: Kit of Referenced Tests for Cognitive Factors; *Memory Span; Number Sequence; Test Batteries
Availability: Educational Testing Service; R 122, Princeton, NJ 08541
Grade Level: 6-16
Notes: Time, 10 approx.; Items, 24

The Kit of Factor Referenced Cognitive Tests consists of 72 cognitive tests intended as markers for 23 aptitude factors to which they are referenced. The factors assessed are Flexibility of Closure, Speed of Closure, Verbal Closure, Associational Fluency, Expressional Fluency, Figural Fluency, Ideational Fluency, Word Fluency, Induction, Integrative Process, Associative Memory, Memory Span, Visual Memory, Number, Perceptual Speed, General Reasoning, Logical Reasoning, Spatial Orientation, Spatial Scanning, Verbal Comprehension, Visualization, Figural Flexibility, and Flexibility of Use. The kit is designed for research purposes. Digit span test with digits in series of varying length being read at a speed of 1-digit per second. One of 3 instruments to measure memory span, the ability to recall a number of distinct elements for immediate reproduction. Instrument was developed by Kelley (1954).

8223
Visual Number Span Test: MS-2. Ekstrom, Ruth B.; And Others 1976
Descriptors: Aptitude Tests; Cognitive Measurement; *Cognitive Style; *Cognitive Tests; *Grade 6; Higher Education; Intermediate Grades; Secondary Education; *Secondary School Students; *Short Term Memory; *Undergraduate Students; Visual Stimuli
Identifiers: Kit of Referenced Tests for Cognitive Factors; *Memory Span; Number Sequences; Test Batteries
Availability: Educational Testing Service; R 122, Princeton, NJ 08541
Grade Level: 6-16
Notes: Time, 10 approx.; Items, 24

The Kit of Factor Referenced Cognitive Tests consists of 72 cognitive tests intended as markers for 23 aptitude factors to which they are referenced. The factors assessed are Flexibility of Closure, Speed of Closure, Verbal Closure, Associational Fluency, Expressional Fluency, Figural Fluency, Ideational Fluency, Word Fluency, Induction, Integrative Process, Associative Memory, Memory Span, Visual Memory, Number, Perceptual Speed, General Reasoning, Logical Reasoning, Spatial Orientation, Spatial Scanning, Verbal Comprehension, Visualization, Figural Flexibility, and Flexibility of Use. The kit is designed for research purposes. Digit span test with digits in series of varying length presented individually on large cards. Digits are exposed at the rate of 1 per second. One of 3 instruments designed to measure memory span, the ability to recall a number of distinct elements for immediate reproduction. Instrument was developed by Kelley (1954).

8224
Auditory Letter Span Test: MS-3. Ekstrom, Ruth B.; And Others 1976
Descriptors: Aptitude Tests; Auditory Stimuli; Cognitive Measurement; *Cognitive Style; *Cognitive Tests; *Grade 6; Higher Education; Intermediate Grades; Letters (Alphabet); Secondary Education; *Secondary School Students; *Short Term Memory; *Undergraduate Students
Identifiers: Kit of Referenced Tests for Cognitive Factors; *Memory Span; Test Batteries
Availability: Educational Testing Service; R 122, Princeton, NJ 08541
Grade Level: 6-16
Notes: Time, 10 approx.; Items, 24

The Kit of Factor Referenced Cognitive Tests consists of 72 cognitive tests intended as markers for 23 aptitude factors to which they are referenced. The factors assessed are Flexibility of Closure, Speed of Closure, Verbal Closure, Associational Fluency, Expressional Fluency, Figural Fluency, Ideational Fluency, Word Fluency, Induction, Integrative Process, Associative Memory, Memory Span, Visual Memory, Number, Perceptual Speed, General Reasoning, Logical Reasoning, Spatial Orientation, Spatial Scanning, Verbal Comprehension, Visualization, Figural Flexibility, and Flexibility of Use. The kit is designed for research purposes. Letter span test with letters in series of varying length being read at a speed of one letter per second. One of 3 instruments designed to measure memory span, the ability to recall a number of distinct elements for immediate reproduction. Instrument was developed by Kelley (1954).

8225
Shape Memory Test: MV-1. Ekstrom, Ruth B.; And Others 1976
Descriptors: Aptitude Tests; Cognitive Measurement; *Cognitive Style; *Cognitive Tests; *Grade 6; Higher Education; Intermediate Grades; Secondary Education; *Secondary School Students; *Short Term Memory; Timed Tests; *Undergraduate Students; Visual Stimuli
Identifiers: Iconic Storage; Kit of Referenced Tests for Cognitive Factors; Test Batteries; *Visual Memory
Availability: Educational Testing Service; R 122, Princeton, NJ 08541
Grade Level: 6-16
Notes: Time, 16 approx.; Items, 32

The Kit of Factor Referenced Cognitive Tests consists of seventy two cognitive tests intended as markers for twenty three aptitude factors to which they are referenced. The factors assessed are Flexibility of Closure, Speed of Closure, Verbal Closure, Associational Fluency, Expressional Fluency, Figural Fluency, Ideational Fluency, Word Fluency, Induction, Integrative Process, Associative Memory, Memory Span, Visual Memory, Number, Perceptual Speed, General Reasoning, Logical Reasoning, Spatial Orientation, Spatial Scanning, Verbal Comprehension, Visualization, Figural Flexibility, and Flexibility of Use. The kit is designed for research purposes. Subject is asked to identify those irregular forms which were previously seen in the same orientation on a study page. One of three instruments designed to measure visual memory, the ability to remember the configuration, location, and orientation of figural material.

8226
Building Memory: MV-2. Ekstrom, Ruth B.; And Others 1976
Descriptors: Aptitude Tests; *Buildings; Cognitive Measurement; *Cognitive Style; *Cognitive Tests; *Grade 6; Higher Education; Intermediate Grades; Maps; Secondary Education; *Secondary School Students; *Short Term Memory; Timed Tests; *Undergraduate Students
Identifiers: Iconic Storage; Kit of Referenced Tests for Cognitive Factors; Test Batteries; *Visual Memory
Availability: Educational Testing Service; R 122, Princeton, NJ 08541
Grade Level: 6-16
Notes: Time, 16 approx.; Items, 24

The Kit of Factor Referenced Cognitive Tests consists of 72 cognitive tests intended as markers for 23 aptitude factors to which they are referenced. The factors assessed are Flexibility of Closure, Speed of Closure, Verbal Closure, Associational Fluency, Expressional Fluency, Figural Fluency, Ideational Fluency, Word Fluency, Induction, Integrative Process, Associative Memory, Memory Span, Visual Memory, Number, Perceptual Speed, General Reasoning, Logical Reasoning, Spatial Orientation, Spatial Scanning, Verbal Comprehension, Visualization, Figural Flexibility, and Flexibility of Use. The kit is designed for research purposes. Subject is asked to indicate the location of a number of buildings seen on a previously studied map. One of 3 instruments designed to measure visual memory, the ability to remember the configuration, location, and orientation of figural material.

8227
Map Memory: MV-3. Ekstrom, Ruth B.; And Others 1976
Descriptors: Aptitude Tests; Cognitive Measurement; *Cognitive Style; *Cognitive Tests; *Grade 6; Higher Education; Intermediate Grades; *Maps; Secondary Education; *Secondary School Students; *Short Term Memory; *Undergraduate Students
Identifiers: Iconic Storage; Kit of Referenced Tests for Cognitive Factors; Test Batteries; *Visual Memory
Availability: Educational Testing Service; R 122, Princeton, NJ 08541
Grade Level: 6-16
Notes: Time, 12 approx.; Items, 24

The Kit of Factor Referenced Cognitive Tests consists of 72 cognitive tests intended as markers for 23 aptitude factors to which they are referenced. The factors assessed are Flexibility of Closure, Speed of Closure, Verbal Closure, Associational Fluency, Expressional Fluency, Figural Fluency, Ideational Fluency, Word Fluency, Induction, Integrative Process, Associative Memory, Memory Span, Visual Memory, Number, Perceptual Speed, General Reasoning, Logical Reasoning, Spatial Orientation, Spatial Scanning, Verbal Comprehension, Visualization, Figural Flexibility, and Flexibility of Use. The kit is designed for research purposes. Subject is asked to identify those maps which were previously presented on a study page. One of 3 instruments designed to measure visual memory, the ability to remember the configuration, location, and orientation of figural material.

8228
Addition Test: N-1. Ekstrom, Ruth B.; And Others 1976
Descriptors: *Addition; Aptitude Tests; Arithmetic; Cognitive Measurement; *Cognitive Style; *Cognitive Tests; *Grade 6; Higher Education; Intermediate Grades; *Mathematics Tests; Secondary Education; *Secondary School Students; Timed Tests; *Undergraduate Students
Identifiers: Accuracy; Kit of Referenced Tests for Cognitive Factors; *Numerical Ability; Speededness (Tests); Test Batteries
Availability: Educational Testing Service; R 122, Princeton, NJ 08541
Grade Level: 6-16
Notes: Time, 4; Items, 120

The Kit of Factor Referenced Cognitive Tests consists of 72 cognitive tests intended as markers for 23 aptitude factors to which they are referenced. The factors assessed are Flexibility of Closure, Speed of Closure, Verbal Closure, Associational Fluency, Expressional Fluency, Figural Fluency, Ideational Fluency, Word Fluency, Induction, Integrative Process, Associative Memory, Memory Span, Visual Memory, Number, Perceptual Speed, General Reasoning, Logical Reasoning, Spatial Orientation, Spatial Scanning, Verbal Comprehension, Visualization, Figural Flexibility, and Flexibility of Use. The kit is designed for research purposes. A speed test of the addition of sets of three 1- or 2-digit numbers. One of a series of 4 instruments to measure number facility, the ability to perform basic arithmetic operations with speed and accuracy. This factor is not a major component in mathematical reasoning or higher mathematical skills.

8229
Division Test: N-2. Ekstrom, Ruth B.; And Others 1976
Descriptors: Aptitude Tests; Arithmetic; Cognitive Measurement; *Cognitive Style; *Cognitive Tests; *Division; *Grade 6; Higher Education; Intermediate Grades; *Mathematics Tests; Secondary Education; *Secondary School Students; Timed Tests; *Undergraduate Students
Identifiers: Accuracy; Kit of Referenced Tests for Cognitive Factors; *Numerical Ability; Speededness (Tests); Test Batteries
Availability: Educational Testing Service; R 122, Princeton, NJ 08541
Grade Level: 6-16
Notes: Time, 4; Items, 120

The Kit of Factor Referenced Cognitive Tests consists of 72 cognitive tests intended as markers for 23 aptitude factors to which they are referenced. The factors assessed are Flexibility of Closure, Speed of Closure, Verbal Closure, Associational Fluency, Expressional Fluency, Figural Fluency, Ideational Fluency, Word Fluency, Induction, Integrative Process, Associative Memory, Memory Span, Visual Memory, Number, Perceptual Speed, General Reasoning, Logical Reasoning, Spatial Orientation, Spatial Scanning, Verbal Comprehension, Visualization, Figural Flexibility, and Flexibility of Use. The kit is designed for research purposes. A speed test in dividing 2- or 3-digit numbers by single-digit numbers. One of a series of 4 instruments designed to measure number facility, the ability to perform basic arithmetic operations with speed and accuracy. This factor is not a major component in mathematical reasoning or higher mathematical skills.

8230
Subtraction and Multiplication Test: N-3. Ekstrom, Ruth B.; And Others 1976
Descriptors: Aptitude Tests; Arithmetic; Cognitive Measurement; *Cognitive Style; *Cognitive Tests; *Grade 6; Higher Education; Intermediate Grades; *Multiplication; Mathematics Tests; Secondary Education; *Secondary School Students; *Subtraction; Timed Tests; *Undergraduate Students
Identifiers: Accuracy; Kit of Referenced Tests for Cognitive Factors; *Numerical Ability; Speededness (Tests); Test Batteries
Availability: Educational Testing Service; R 122, Princeton, NJ 08541
Grade Level: 6-16
Notes: Time, 4; Items, 120

The Kit of Factor Referenced Cognitive Tests consists of 72 cognitive tests intended as markers for 23 aptitude factors to which they are referenced. The factors assessed are Flexibility of Closure, Speed of Closure, Verbal Closure, Associational Fluency, Expressional Fluency, Figural Fluency, Ideational Fluency, Word Fluency, Induction, Integrative Process, Associative Memory, Memory Span, Visual Memory, Number, Perceptual Speed, General Reasoning, Logical Reasoning, Spatial Orientation, Spatial Scanning, Verbal Comprehension, Visualization, Figural Flexibility, and Flexibility of Use. The kit is designed for research purposes. A speed test alternating 10 items of subtracting 2-digit numbers from 2-digit numbers and 10 items of multiplying 2-digit numbers by single-digit numbers. One of a series of 4 instruments designed to measure number faculty, the ability to perform basic arithmetic operations with speed and accuracy. This factor is not a major component in mathematical reasoning or higher mathematical skills.

8231
Addition and Subtraction Correction: N-4. Ekstrom, Ruth B.; And Others 1976
Descriptors: *Addition; Aptitude Tests; Arithmetic; Cognitive Measurement; *Cognitive Style; *Cognitive Tests; *Grade 6; Higher Education; Intermediate Grades; *Mathematics Tests; Secondary Education; *Secondary School Students; *Subtraction; Timed Tests; *Undergraduate Students
Identifiers: Accuracy; Kit of Referenced Tests for Cognitive Factors; *Numerical Ability; Speededness (Tests); Test Batteries
Availability: Educational Testing Service; R 122, Princeton, NJ 08541
Grade Level: 6-16
Notes: Time, 4; Items, 120
The Kit of Factor Referenced Cognitive Tests consists of 72 cognitive tests intended as markers for 23 aptitude factors to which they are referenced. The factors assessed are Flexibility of Closure, Speed of Closure, Verbal Closure, Associational Fluency, Expressional Fluency, Figural Fluency, Ideational Fluency, Word Fluency, Induction, Integrative Process, Associative Memory, Memory Span, Visual Memory, Number, Perceptual Speed, General Reasoning, Logical Reasoning, Spatial Orientation, Spatial Scanning, Verbal Comprehension, Visualization, Figural Flexibility, and Flexibility of Use. The kit is designed for research purposes. Subject is asked to indicate whether the answer shown for simple addition and subtraction problems is correct. One of a series of 4 instruments designed to measure number facility, the ability to perform basic arithmetic operations with speed and accuracy. This factor is not a major component in mathematical reasoning or higher mathematical skills.

8232
Finding A's Test: P-1. Ekstrom, Ruth B.; And Others 1976
Descriptors: Aptitude Tests; Cognitive Measurement; *Cognitive Style; *Cognitive Tests; *Grade 6; Higher Education; Intermediate Grades; Secondary Education; *Secondary School Students; Timed Tests; *Undergraduate Students; *Visual Perception
Identifiers: Kit of Referenced Tests for Cognitive Factors; *Perceptual Speed; *Scanning; Speededness (Tests); Test Batteries
Availability: Educational Testing Service; R 122, Princeton, NJ 08541
Grade Level: 6-16
Notes: Time, 4; Items, 1640
The Kit of Factor Referenced Cognitive Tests consists of 72 cognitive tests intended as markers for 23 aptitude factors to which they are referenced. The factors assessed are Flexibility of Closure, Speed of Closure, Verbal Closure, Associational Fluency, Expressional Fluency, Figural Fluency, Ideational Fluency, Word Fluency, Induction, Integrative Process, Associative Memory, Memory Span, Visual Memory, Number, Perceptual Speed, General Reasoning, Logical Reasoning, Spatial Orientation, Spatial Scanning, Verbal Comprehension, Visualization, Figural Flexibility, and Flexibility of Use. The kit is designed for research purposes. Instrument was suggested by Thurstone's Letter "A." Subject must check the 5 words in a column of 41 words that contain the letter "A." One of 3 instruments designed to measure perceptual speed, which is the speed in comparing figures or symbols, scanning to find figures or symbols, or carrying out other simple tasks involving visual perception. Three components of this factor are perceptual fluency, decision speed, and immediate perceptual memory.

8233
Number Comparison Test: P-2. Ekstrom, Ruth B.; And Others 1976
Descriptors: Aptitude Tests; Cognitive Measurement; *Cognitive Style; *Cognitive Tests; *Grade 6; Higher Education; Intermediate Grades; Secondary Education; *Secondary School Students; Timed Tests; *Undergraduate Students; Visual Discrimination; *Visual Perception
Identifiers: Kit of Referenced Tests for Cognitive Factors; *Perceptual Speed; Speededness (Tests); Test Batteries
Availability: Educational Testing Service; R 122, Princeton, NJ 08541
Grade Level: 6-16
Notes: Time, 3; Items, 96
The Kit of Factor Referenced Cognitive Tests consists of 72 cognitive tests intended as markers for 23 aptitude factors to which they are referenced. The factors assessed are Flexibility of Closure, Speed of Closure, Verbal Clo-

sure, Associational Fluency, Expressional Fluency, Figural Fluency, Ideational Fluency, Word Fluency, Induction, Integrative Process, Associative Memory, Memory Span, Visual Memory, Number, Perceptual Speed, General Reasoning, Logical Reasoning, Spatial Orientation, Spatial Scanning, Verbal Comprehension, Visualization, Figural Flexibility, and Flexibility of Use. The kit is designed for research purposes. Instrument was suggested by the Minnesota Vocational Test for Clerical Workers. The subject inspects pairs of multi-digit numbers and indicates whether the 2 numbers in each pair are the same or different. One of 3 instruments designed to measure perceptual speed, which is the speed in comparing figures or symbols, or carrying out other simple tasks involving visual perception. Three components of this factor are perceptual fluency, decision speed, and immediate perceptual memory.

8234
Identical Pictures Test: P-3. Ekstrom, Ruth B.; And Others 1976
Descriptors: Aptitude Tests; Cognitive Measurement; *Cognitive Style; *Cognitive Tests; *Grade 6; Higher Education; Intermediate Grades; Secondary Education; *Secondary School Students; Timed Tests; *Undergraduate Students; *Visual Perception
Identifiers: Kit of Referenced Tests for Cognitive Factors; *Perceptual Speed; Speededness (Tests); Test Batteries
Availability: Educational Testing Service; R 122, Princeton, NJ 08541
Grade Level: 6-16
Notes: Time, 3; Items, 96
The Kit of Factor Referenced Cognitive Tests consists of 72 cognitive tests intended as markers for 23 aptitude factors to which they are referenced. The factors assessed are Flexibility of Closure, Speed of Closure, Verbal Closure, Associational Fluency, Expressional Fluency, Figural Fluency, Ideational Fluency, Word Fluency, Induction, Integrative Process, Associative Memory, Memory Span, Visual Memory, Number, Perceptual Speed, General Reasoning, Logical Reasoning, Spatial Orientation, Spatial Scanning, Verbal Comprehension, Visualization, Figural Flexibility, and Flexibility of Use. The kit is designed for research purposes. Suggested by similar tests by Thurstone. Subject is to check which 1 of the 5 numbered geometrical figures or pictures in a row is identical to the given figure. One of 3 instruments designed to measure perceptual speed, defined as the speed in comparing figures or symbols, or carrying out other simple tasks involving visual perception. Three components of this factor are perceptual fluency, decision speed, and immediate perceptual memory.

8235
Arithmetic Aptitude Test: RG-1. Ekstrom, Ruth B.; And Others 1976
Descriptors: Aptitude Tests; Arithmetic; Cognitive Measurement; *Cognitive Style; *Cognitive Tests; *Grade 6; Intermediate Grades; Multiple Choice Tests; *Problem Solving; *Mathematics Tests; Secondary Education; *Secondary School Students; Timed Tests
Identifiers: Kit of Referenced Tests for Cognitive Factors; *Reasoning Ability; Test Batteries
Availability: Educational Testing Service; R 122, Princeton, NJ 08541
Grade Level: 6-12
Notes: Time, 20; Items, 30
The Kit of Factor Referenced Cognitive Tests consists of 72 cognitive tests intended as markers for 23 aptitude factors to which they are referenced. The factors assessed are Flexibility of Closure, Speed of Closure, Verbal Closure, Associational Fluency, Expressional Fluency, Figural Fluency, Ideational Fluency, Word Fluency, Induction, Integrative Process, Associative Memory, Memory Span, Visual Memory, Number, Perceptual Speed, General Reasoning, Logical Reasoning, Spatial Orientation, Spatial Scanning, Verbal Comprehension, Visualization, Figural Flexibility, and Flexibility of Use. The kit is designed for research purposes. Multiple choice test of word problems requiring only arithmetic for solution. One of 3 instruments to measure general reasoning, the ability to select and organize relevant information for the solution of a problem.

8236
Mathematics Aptitude Test: RG-2. Ekstrom, Ruth B.; And Others 1976
Descriptors: Algebra; Aptitude Tests; Arithmetic; Cognitive Measurement; *Cognitive Style; *Cognitive Tests; Higher Education; High Schools; *High School Students; Multiple Choice Tests; *Problem Solving; *Mathematics Tests; Secondary Education; Timed Tests; *Undergraduate Students
Identifiers: Kit of Referenced Tests for Cognitive Factors; *Reasoning Ability; Test Batteries
Availability: Educational Testing Service; R 122, Princeton, NJ 08541
Grade Level: 11-16
Notes: Time, 20; Items, 30

The Kit of Factor Referenced Cognitive Tests consists of 72 cognitive tests intended as markers for 23 aptitude factors to which they are referenced. The factors assessed are Flexibility of Closure, Speed of Closure, Verbal Closure, Associational Fluency, Expressional Fluency, Figural Fluency, Ideational Fluency, Word Fluency, Induction, Integrative Process, Associative Memory, Memory Span, Visual Memory, Number, Perceptual Speed, General Reasoning, Logical Reasoning, Spatial Orientation, Spatial Scanning, Verbal Comprehension, Visualization, Figural Flexibility, and Flexibility of Use. The kit is designed for research purposes. Multiple Choice test of word problems requiring arithmetic or very simple algebraic concepts for solution. One of 3 instruments designed to measure general reasoning, the ability to select and organize relevant information for the solution of a problem.

8237
Necessity Arithmetic Operations: RG-3. Ekstrom, Ruth B.; And Others 1976
Descriptors: Aptitude Tests; Arithmetic; Cognitive Measurement; *Cognitive Style; *Cognitive Tests; *Grade 6; Higher Education; Intermediate Grades; *Problem Solving; *Mathematics Tests; Secondary Education; *Secondary School Students; Timed Tests; *Undergraduate Students
Identifiers: Kit of Referenced Tests for Cognitive Factors; *Reasoning Ability; Test Batteries
Availability: Educational Testing Service; R 122, Princeton, NJ 08541
Grade Level: 6-16
Notes: Time, 10; Items, 30
The Kit of Factor Referenced Cognitive Tests consists of 72 cognitive tests intended as markers for 23 aptitude factors to which they are referenced. The factors assessed are Flexibility of Closure, Speed of Closure, Verbal Closure, Associational Fluency, Expressional Fluency, Figural Fluency, Ideational Fluency, Word Fluency, Induction, Integrative Process, Associative Memory, Memory Span, Visual Memory, Number, Perceptual Speed, General Reasoning, Logical Reasoning, Spatial Orientation, Spatial Scanning, Verbal Comprehension, Visualization, Figural Flexibility, and Flexibility of Use. The kit is designed for research purposes. Instrument is based on a similar test by Guilford. Subject must determine what numerical operations are required to solve arithmetic problems without doing the computations. One of 3 instruments designed to measure general reasoning, the ability to select and organize relevant information for the solution of a problem.

8238
Nonsense Syllogisms Test: RL-1. Ekstrom, Ruth B.; And Others 1976
Descriptors: Abstract Reasoning; Aptitude Tests; Cognitive Measurement; *Cognitive Style; *Cognitive Tests; Higher Education; High Schools; *High School Students; *Logical Thinking; Secondary Education; Timed Tests; *Undergraduate Students
Identifiers: Kit of Referenced Tests for Cognitive Factors; *Reasoning Ability; Syllogisms; Test Batteries
Availability: Educational Testing Service; R 122, Princeton, NJ 08541
Grade Level: 11-16
Notes: Time, 8; Items, 30
The Kit of Factor Referenced Cognitive Tests consists of 72 cognitive tests intended as markers for 23 aptitude factors to which they are referenced. The factors assessed are Flexibility of Closure, Speed of Closure, Verbal Closure, Associational Fluency, Expressional Fluency, Figural Fluency, Ideational Fluency, Word Fluency, Induction, Integrative Process, Associative Memory, Memory Span, Visual Memory, Number, Perceptual Speed, General Reasoning, Logical Reasoning, Spatial Orientation, Spatial Scanning, Verbal Comprehension, Visualization, Figural Flexibility, and Flexibility of Use. The kit is designed for research purposes. One of 4 instruments to measure logical reasoning, the ability to reason from premise to conclusion or to evaluate the correctness of a conclusion. This instrument was suggested by Thurstone's False Premises. Subjects are presented with formal syllogisms using nonsensical content so they cannot be solved by reference to past learning. Subject must evaluate the logical correctness of the stated conclusion.

8239
Diagramming Relationships: RL-2. Ekstrom, Ruth B.; And Others 1976
Descriptors: Aptitude Tests; Cognitive Measurement; *Cognitive Style; *Cognitive Tests; Higher Education; High Schools; *High School Students; *Logical Thinking; Relationship; Secondary Education; Timed Tests; *Undergraduate Students
Identifiers: Kit of Referenced Tests for Cognitive Factors; *Reasoning Ability; Test Batteries
Availability: Educational Testing Service; R 122, Princeton, NJ 08541
Grade Level: 9-16
Notes: Time, 8; Items, 30

The Kit of Factor Referenced Cognitive Tests consists of 72 cognitive tests intended as markers for 23 aptitude factors to which they are referenced. The factors assessed are Flexibility of Closure, Speed of Closure, Verbal Closure, Associational Fluency, Expressional Fluency, Figural Fluency, Ideational Fluency, Word Fluency, Induction, Integrative Process, Associative Memory, Memory Span, Visual Memory, Number, Perceptual Speed, General Reasoning, Logical Reasoning, Spatial Orientation, Spatial Scanning, Verbal Comprehension, Visualization, Figural Flexibility, and Flexibility of Use. The kit is designed for research purposes. One of 4 instruments to measure logical reasoning, the ability to reason from premise to conclusion. This instrument requires examinee to select 1 of 5 diagrams which best illustrates the interrelationship among sets of 3 objects.

8240
Inference Test: RL-3. Ekstrom, Ruth B.; And Others 1976
Descriptors: Inferences; Aptitude Tests; Cognitive Measurement; *Cognitive Style; *Cognitive Tests; Higher Education; High Schools; *High School Students; *Logical Thinking; Secondary Education; Timed Tests; *Undergraduate Students
Identifiers: *Inferential Reasoning; Kit of Referenced Tests for Cognitive Factors; *Reasoning Ability; Test Batteries
Availability: Educational Testing Service; R 122, Princeton, NJ 08541
Grade Level: 11-16
Notes: Time, 12; Items, 20

The Kit of Factor Referenced Cognitive Tests consists of 72 cognitive tests intended as markers for 23 aptitude factors to which they are referenced. The factors assessed are Flexibility of Closure, Speed of Closure, Verbal Closure, Associational Fluency, Expressional Fluency, Figural Fluency, Ideational Fluency, Word Fluency, Induction, Integrative Process, Associative Memory, Memory Span, Visual Memory, Number, Perceptual Speed, General Reasoning, Logical Reasoning, Spatial Orientation, Spatial Scanning, Verbal Comprehension, Visualization, Figural Flexibility, and Flexibility of Use. The kit is designed for research purposes. One of 4 instruments to measure logical reasoning, the ability to reason from premise to conclusion, or to evaluate the correctness of a conclusion. This instrument was suggested by a similarly named test by Guilford. Examinee must select 1 of 5 conclusions that can be drawn from each given statement.

8241
Deciphering Languages: RL-4. Ekstrom, Ruth B.; And Others 1976
Descriptors: Abstract Reasoning; Aptitude Tests; Cognitive Measurement; *Cognitive Style; *Cognitive Tests; Higher Education; High Schools; *High School Students; *Logical Thinking; Secondary Education; Timed Tests; *Undergraduate Students
Identifiers: Kit of Referenced Tests for Cognitive Factors; *Reasoning Ability; Test Batteries
Availability: Educational Testing Service; R 122, Princeton, NJ 08541
Grade Level: 11-16
Notes: Time, 16; Items, 24

The Kit of Factor Referenced Cognitive Tests consists of 72 cognitive tests intended as markers for 23 aptitude factors to which they are referenced. The factors assessed are Flexibility of Closure, Speed of Closure, Verbal Closure, Associational Fluency, Expressional Fluency, Figural Fluency, Ideational Fluency, Word Fluency, Induction, Integrative Process, Associative Memory, Memory Span, Visual Memory, Number, Perceptual Speed, General Reasoning, Logical Reasoning, Spatial Orientation, Spatial Scanning, Verbal Comprehension, Visualization, Figural Flexibility, and Flexibility of Use. The kit is designed for research purposes. One of 4 instruments to measure logical reasoning, the ability to reason from premise to conclusion, or to evaluate the correctness of a conclusion. This instrument requires examinee to use reasoning to determine the English translation of artificial languages.

8242
Card Rotations Test: S-1. Ekstrom, Ruth B.; And Others 1976
Descriptors: Aptitude Tests; Cognitive Measurement; *Cognitive Style; *Cognitive Tests; Higher Education; Secondary Education; *Secondary School Students; *Spatial Ability; Timed Tests; *Undergraduate Students
Identifiers: Kit of Referenced Tests for Cognitive Factors; Test Batteries; Visual Memory
Availability: Educational Testing Service; R 122, Princeton, NJ 08541
Grade Level: 8-16
Notes: Time, 6; Items, 20

The Kit of Factor Referenced Cognitive Tests consists of 72 cognitive tests intended as markers for 23 aptitude factors to which they are referenced. The factors assessed are Flexibility of Closure, Speed of Closure, Verbal Closure, Associational Fluency, Expressional Fluency, Figural Fluency, Ideational Fluency, Word Fluency, Induction, Integrative Process, Associative Memory, Memory Span, Visual Memory, Number, Perceptual Speed, General Reasoning, Logical Reasoning, Spatial Orientation, Spatial Scanning, Verbal Comprehension, Visualization, Figural Flexibility, and Flexibility of Use. The kit is designed for research purposes. One of 2 instruments designed to measure spatial orientation, the ability to perceive spatial patterns or to maintain orientation with respect to objects in space. Instrument was suggested by Thurstone's Cards. Subject must mentally rotate the configurations.

8243
Cube Comparisons Test: S-2. Ekstrom, Ruth B.; And Others 1976
Descriptors: Aptitude Tests; Cognitive Measurement; *Cognitive Style; *Cognitive Tests; Higher Education; Secondary Education; *Secondary School Students; *Spatial Ability; Timed Tests; *Undergraduate Students
Identifiers: Kit of Referenced Tests for Cognitive Factors; Test Batteries; Visual Memory
Availability: Educational Testing Service; R 122, Princeton, NJ 08541
Grade Level: 8-16
Notes: Time, 6; Items, 42

The Kit of Factor Referenced Cognitive Tests consists of 72 cognitive tests intended as markers for 23 aptitude factors to which they are referenced. The factors assessed are Flexibility of Closure, Speed of Closure, Verbal Closure, Associational Fluency, Expressional Fluency, Figural Fluency, Ideational Fluency, Word Fluency, Induction, Integrative Process, Associative Memory, Memory Span, Visual Memory, Number, Perceptual Speed, General Reasoning, Logical Reasoning, Spatial Orientation, Spatial Scanning, Verbal Comprehension, Visualization, Figural Flexibility, and Flexibility of Use. The kit is designed for research purposes. One of 2 instruments designed to measure spatial orientation, the ability to perceive spatial patterns or to maintain orientation with respect to objects in space. Instrument was suggested by Thurstone's Cubes. Subject must mentally rotate the configurations.

8244
Maze Tracing Speed Test: SS-1. Ekstrom, Ruth B.; And Others 1976
Descriptors: Aptitude Tests; Cognitive Measurement; *Cognitive Style; *Cognitive Tests; *Grade 6; Higher Education; Intermediate Grades; Secondary Education; *Secondary School Students; *Spatial Ability; Timed Tests; *Undergraduate Students
Identifiers: Kit of Referenced Tests for Cognitive Factors; Mazes; *Spatial Scanning; Test Batteries
Availability: Educational Testing Service; R 122, Princeton, NJ 08541
Grade Level: 6-16
Notes: Time, 6; Items, 8

The Kit of Factor Referenced Cognitive Tests consists of 72 cognitive tests intended as markers for 23 aptitude factors to which they are referenced. The factors assessed are Flexibility of Closure, Speed of Closure, Verbal Closure, Associational Fluency, Expressional Fluency, Figural Fluency, Ideational Fluency, Word Fluency, Induction, Integrative Processes, Associative Memory, Memory Span, Visual Memory, Number, Perceptual Speed, General Reasoning, Logical Reasoning, Spatial Orientation, Spatial Scanning, Verbal Comprehension, Visualization, Figural Flexibility, and Flexibility of Use. The kit is designed for research purposes. One of 3 tests to measure spatial scanning, the speed in exploring visually a wide or complicated spatial field. The examinee must find and mark a path through a moderately complex series of printed mazes.

8245
Choosing a Path: SS-2. Ekstrom, Ruth B.; And Others 1976
Descriptors: Aptitude Tests; Cognitive Measurement; *Cognitive Style; *Cognitive Tests; Higher Education; Pattern Recognition; Secondary Education; *Secondary School Students; *Spatial Ability; Timed Tests; *Undergraduate Students
Identifiers: Kit of Referenced Tests for Cognitive Factors; *Spatial Scanning; Test Batteries
Availability: Educational Testing Service; R 122, Princeton, NJ 08541
Grade Level: 8-16
Notes: Time, 14; Items, 32

The Kit of Factor Referenced Cognitive Tests consists of 72 cognitive tests intended as markers for 23 aptitude factors to which they are referenced. The factors assessed are Flexibility of Closure, Speed of Closure, Verbal Closure, Associational Fluency, Expressional Fluency, Figural Fluency, Ideational Fluency, Word Fluency, Induction, Integrative Processes, Associative Memory, Memory Span, Visual Memory, Number, Perceptual Speed, General Reasoning, Logical Reasoning, Spatial Orientation, Spatial Scanning, Verbal Comprehension, Visualization, Figural Flexibility, and Flexibility of Use. The kit is designed for research purposes. One of 3 tests to measure spatial scanning, the speed in exploring visually a wide or complicated spatial field. This test was suggested by one of the AAF Printed Classification Tests. Each item consists of a network of lines having many intersecting and intermeshed wires with several sets of terminals. Task is to trace lines and determine for which 1 of 5 pairs of terminals there is a complete circuit through a circle at the top. Comprehension of the pattern by scanning rather than simple visual pursuit of lines is encouraged.

8246
Map Planning Test: SS-3. Ekstrom, Ruth B.; And Others 1976
Descriptors: Aptitude Tests; Cognitive Measurement; *Cognitive Style; *Cognitive Tests; *Grade 6; Higher Education; Intermediate Grades; Map Skills; Secondary Education; *Secondary School Students; *Spatial Ability; Timed Tests; *Undergraduate Students
Identifiers: Kit of Referenced Tests for Cognitive Factors; *Spatial Scanning; Test Batteries
Availability: Educational Testing Service; R 122, Princeton, NJ 08541
Grade Level: 6-16
Notes: Time, 6; Items, 4

The Kit of Factor Referenced Cognitive Tests consists of 72 cognitive tests intended as markers for 23 aptitude factors to which they are referenced. The factors assessed are Flexibility of Closure, Speed of Closure, Verbal Closure, Associational Fluency, Expressional Fluency, Figural Fluency, Ideational Fluency, Word Fluency, Induction, Integrative Processes, Associative Memory, Memory Span, Visual Memory, Number, Perceptual Speed, General Reasoning, Logical Reasoning, Spatial Orientation, Spatial Scanning, Verbal Comprehension, Visualization, Figural Flexibility, and Flexibility of Use. The kit is designed for research purposes. One of 3 tests to measure spatial scanning, the speed in exploring visually a wide or complicated spatial field. Suggested by one of the AAF Printed Classification Tests. Examinee must plan routes between given points so that no roadblocks need to be crossed. Task is to find shortest available route as quickly as possible.

8247
Vocabulary I: V-1. Ekstrom, Ruth B.; And Others 1976
Descriptors: Aptitude Tests; Cognitive Measurement; *Cognitive Style; *Cognitive Tests; Higher Education; Long Term Memory; Secondary Education; *Secondary School Students; Timed Tests; *Undergraduate Students; Vocabulary
Identifiers: Carroll (John B); Kit of Referenced Tests for Cognitive Factors; Synonyms; Test Batteries; *Verbal Comprehension
Availability: Educational Testing Service; R 122, Princeton, NJ 08541
Grade Level: 7-12
Notes: Time, 8; Items, 36

The Kit of Factor Referenced Cognitive Tests consists of 72 cognitive tests intended as markers for 23 aptitude factors to which they are referenced. The factors assessed are Flexibility of Closure, Speed of Closure, Verbal Closure, Associational Fluency, Expressional Fluency, Figural Fluency, Ideational Fluency, Word Fluency, Induction, Integrative Processes, Associative Memory, Memory Span, Visual Memory, Number, Perceptual Speed, General Reasoning, Logical Reasoning, Spatial Orientation, Spatial Scanning, Verbal Comprehension, Visualization, Figural Flexibility, and Flexibility of Use. The kit is designed for research purposes. One of 5 tests designed to measure verbal comprehension, the ability to understand the English language. A 4-choice synonym test adapted from a test by J. B. Carroll, who believed verbal comprehension is almost exclusively dependent on the contents of the lexicosemantic long-term memory store.

8248
Vocabulary II: V-2. Ekstrom, Ruth B.; And Others 1976
Descriptors: Aptitude Tests; Cognitive Measurement; *Cognitive Style; *Cognitive Tests; Higher Education; Long Term Memory; Secondary Education; *Secondary School Students; Timed Tests; *Undergraduate Students; Vocabulary
Identifiers: Kit of Referenced Tests for Cognitive Factors; Synonyms; Test Batteries; *Verbal Comprehension
Availability: Educational Testing Service; R 122, Princeton, NJ 08541
Grade Level: 7-12
Notes: Time, 8; Items, 36

The Kit of Factor Referenced Cognitive Tests consists of 72 cognitive tests intended as markers for 23 aptitude factors to which they are referenced. The factors assessed are Flexibility of Closure, Speed of Closure, Verbal Closure, Associational Fluency, Expressional Fluency, Figural Fluency, Ideational Fluency, Word Fluency, Induction, Integrative Processes, Associative Memory, Memory Span, Visual Memory, Number, Perceptual Speed, General Reasoning, Logical Reasoning, Spatial Orientation, Spatial Scanning, Verbal Comprehension, Visualization, Figural Flexibility, and Flexibility of Use. The kit is designed for research purposes. One of 5 tests designed to measure verbal comprehension, the ability to understand the English language. A 5-choice synonym test adapted from a Cooperative Vocabulary Test. Format is intentionally different from V-1 (TC008247).

8249
Extended Range Vocabulary Test: V-3. Ekstrom, Ruth B.; And Others 1976
Descriptors: Aptitude Tests; Cognitive Measurement; *Cognitive Style; *Cognitive Tests; Higher Education; Long Term Memory; Secondary Education; *Secondary School Students; Timed Tests; *Undergraduate Students; Vocabulary
Identifiers: Kit of Referenced Tests for Cognitive Factors; Synonyms; Test Batteries; *Verbal Comprehension
Availability: Educational Testing Service; R 122, Princeton, NJ 08541
Grade Level: 7-16
Notes: Time, 12; Items, 48

The Kit of Factor Referenced Cognitive Tests consists of 72 cognitive tests intended as markers for 23 aptitude factors to which they are referenced. The factors assessed are Flexibility of Closure, Speed of Closure, Verbal Closure, Associational Fluency, Expressional Fluency, Figural Fluency, Ideational Fluency, Word Fluency, Induction, Integrative Processes, Associative Memory, Memory Span, Visual Memory, Number, Perceptual Speed, General Reasoning, Logical Reasoning, Spatial Orientation, Spatial Scanning, Verbal Comprehension, Visualization, Figural Flexibility, and Flexibility of Use. The kit is designed for research purposes. One of 5 tests designed to measure verbal comprehension, the ability to understand the English language. A 5-choice synonym test adapted from a Cooperative Vocabulary Test, items range from very easy to very difficult.

8250
Advanced Vocabulary Test I: V-4. Ekstrom, Ruth B.; And Others 1976
Descriptors: Aptitude Tests; Cognitive Measurement; *Cognitive Style; *Cognitive Tests; Higher Education; *High School Students; Long Term Memory; Secondary Education; Timed Tests; *Undergraduate Students; Vocabulary
Identifiers: Kit of Referenced Tests for Cognitive Factors; Synonyms; Test Batteries; *Verbal Comprehension
Availability: Educational Testing Service; R 122, Princeton, NJ 08541
Grade Level: 11-16
Notes: Time, 8; Items, 36

The Kit of Factor Referenced Cognitive Tests consists of 72 cognitive tests intended as markers for 23 aptitude factors to which they are referenced. The factors assessed are Flexibility of Closure, Speed of Closure, Verbal Closure, Associational Fluency, Expressional Fluency, Figural Fluency, Ideational Fluency, Word Fluency, Induction, Integrative Processes, Associative Memory, Memory Span, Visual Memory, Number, Perceptual Speed, General Reasoning, Logical Reasoning, Spatial Orientation, Spatial Scanning, Verbal Comprehension, Visualization, Figural Flexibility, and Flexibility of Use. The kit is designed for research purposes. One of 5 tests designed to measure verbal comprehension, the ability to understand the English language. A 5-choice synonym test adapted from a Cooperative Vocabulary Test, items are mainly very difficult.

8251
Advanced Vocabulary Test II: V-5. Ekstrom, Ruth B.; And Others 1976
Descriptors: Aptitude Tests; Cognitive Measurement; *Cognitive Style; *Cognitive Tests; Higher Education; *High School Students; Long Term Memory; Secondary Education; Timed Tests; *Undergraduate Students; Vocabulary
Identifiers: Carroll (John B); Kit of Referenced Tests for Cognitive Factors; Synonyms; Test Batteries; *Verbal Comprehension
Availability: Educational Testing Service; R 122, Princeton, NJ 08541
Grade Level: 11-16
Notes: Time, 8; Items, 36

The Kit of Factor Referenced Cognitive Tests consists of 72 cognitive tests intended as markers for 23 aptitude factors to which they are referenced. The factors assessed are Flexibility of Closure, Speed of Closure, Verbal Closure, Associational Fluency, Expressional Fluency, Figural Fluency, Ideational Fluency, Word Fluency, Induction, Integrative Processes, Associative Memory, Memory Span, Visual Memory, Number, Perceptual Speed, General Reasoning, Logical Reasoning, Spatial Orientation, Spatial Scanning, Verbal Comprehension, Visualization, Figural Flexibility, and Flexibility of Use. The kit is designed for research purposes. One of 5 tests designed to measure verbal comprehension, the ability to understand the English language. A 4-choice synonyms test adapted from a test by J. B. Carroll, this instrument contains mainly difficult items.

8252
Form Board Test: VZ-1. Ekstrom, Ruth B.; And Others 1976

Descriptors: Aptitude Tests; Cognitive Measurement; *Cognitive Style; *Cognitive Tests; Higher Education; *High School Students; Secondary Education; *Spatial Ability; Timed Tests; *Undergraduate Students; *Visualization
Identifiers: Kit of Referenced Tests for Cognitive Factors; Test Batteries
Availability: Educational Testing Service; R 122, Princeton, NJ 08541
Grade Level: 9-16
Notes: Time, 16; Items, 48

The Kit of Factor Referenced Cognitive Tests consists of 72 cognitive tests intended as markers for 23 aptitude factors to which they are referenced. The factors assessed are Flexibility of Closure, Speed of Closure, Verbal Closure, Associational Fluency, Expressional Fluency, Figural Fluency, Ideational Fluency, Word Fluency, Induction, Integrative Processes, Associative Memory, Memory Span, Visual Memory, Number, Perceptual Speed, General Reasoning, Logical Reasoning, Spatial Orientation, Spatial Scanning, Verbal Comprehension, Visualization, Figural Flexibility, and Flexibility of Use. The kit is designed for research purposes. One of 3 measures designed to assess the subject's visualization, the ability to manipulate, or transform, the image of spatial patterns into other arrangements. Visualization requires the figure be mentally restructured into components for manipulation while the whole figure is manipulated in spatial orientation.

8253
Paper Folding Test: VZ-2. Ekstrom, Ruth B.; And Others 1976
Descriptors: Aptitude Tests; Cognitive Measurement; *Cognitive Style; *Cognitive Tests; Higher Education; *High School Students; Secondary Education; *Spatial Ability; Timed Tests; *Undergraduate Students; *Visualization
Identifiers: Kit of Referenced Tests for Cognitive Factors; Paper Folding; Test Batteries
Availability: Educational Testing Service; R 122, Princeton, NJ 08541
Grade Level: 9-16
Notes: Time, 6; Items, 20

The Kit of Factor Referenced Cognitive Tests consists of 72 cognitive tests intended as markers for 23 aptitude factors to which they are referenced. The factors assessed are Flexibility of Closure, Speed of Closure, Verbal Closure, Associational Fluency, Expressional Fluency, Figural Fluency, Ideational Fluency, Word Fluency, Induction, Integrative Processes, Associative Memory, Memory Span, Visual Memory, Number, Perceptual Speed, General Reasoning, Logical Reasoning, Spatial Orientation, Spatial Scanning, Verbal Comprehension, Visualization, Figural Flexibility, and Flexibility of Use. The kit is designed for research purposes. One of 3 instruments designed to measure visualization, the ability to manipulate, or transform, the image of spatial patterns into other arrangements. Visualization requires the figure be mentally restructured into components for manipulation while the whole figure is manipulated in spatial orientation. This instrument was suggested by Thurstone's Punched Holes Test.

8254
Surface Development Test: VZ-3. Ekstrom, Ruth B.; And Others 1976
Descriptors: Aptitude Tests; Cognitive Measurement; *Cognitive Style; *Cognitive Tests; Higher Education; *High School Students; Secondary Education; *Spatial Ability; Timed Tests; *Undergraduate Students; *Visualization
Identifiers: Kit of Referenced Tests for Cognitive Factors; Test Batteries
Availability: Educational Testing Service; R 122, Princeton, NJ 08541
Grade Level: 9-16
Notes: Time, 12; Items, 12

The Kit of Factor Referenced Cognitive Tests consists of 72 cognitive tests intended as markers for 23 aptitude factors to which they are referenced. The factors assessed are Flexibility of Closure, Speed of Closure, Verbal Closure, Associational Fluency, Expressional Fluency, Figural Fluency, Ideational Fluency, Word Fluency, Induction, Integrative Processes, Associative Memory, Memory Span, Visual Memory, Number, Perceptual Speed, General Reasoning, Logical Reasoning, Spatial Orientation, Spatial Scanning, Verbal Comprehension, Visualization, Figural Flexibility, and Flexibility of Use. The kit is designed for research purposes. One of 3 instruments designed to measure visualization, the ability to manipulate, or transform, the image of spatial patterns into other arrangements. Visualization requires the figure be mentally restructured into components for manipulation while the whole figure is manipulated in spatial orientation. This instrument was suggested by Thurstone's Surface Development Test.

8255
Toothpicks Test: XF-1. Ekstrom, Ruth B.; And Others 1976
Descriptors: Aptitude Tests; Cognitive Measurement; *Cognitive Style; *Cognitive Tests; Higher Education; *High School Students; Problem Solving; Secondary Education; *Spatial Ability; Timed Tests; *Undergraduate Students

Identifiers: *Figural Flexibility; Kit of Referenced Tests for Cognitive Factors; Test Batteries
Availability: Educational Testing Service; R 122, Princeton, NJ 08541
Grade Level: 11-16
Notes: Time, 12; Items, 10

The Kit of Factor Referenced Cognitive Tests consists of 72 cognitive tests intended as markers for 23 aptitude factors to which they are referenced. The factors assessed are Flexibility of Closure, Speed of Closure, Verbal Closure, Associational Fluency, Expressional Fluency, Figural Fluency, Ideational Fluency, Word Fluency, Induction, Integrative Processes, Associative Memory, Memory Span, Visual Memory, Number, Perceptual Speed, General Reasoning, Logical Reasoning, Spatial Orientation, Spatial Scanning, Verbal Comprehension, Visualization, Figural Flexibility, and Flexibility of Use. The kit is designed for research purposes. One of 3 instruments designed to measure figural flexibility, the ability to change set in order to generate new and different solutions to figural problems. Subject is requested to present different arrangements of toothpicks according to sets of specified rules.

8256
Planning Patterns: XF-2. Ekstrom, Ruth B.; And Others 1976
Descriptors: Abstract Reasoning; Aptitude Tests; Cognitive Measurement; *Cognitive Style; *Cognitive Tests; Higher Education; *High School Students; Problem Solving; Secondary Education; *Spatial Ability; Timed Tests; *Undergraduate Students
Identifiers: Figural Flexibility; Kit of Referenced Tests for Cognitive Factors; Test Batteries
Availability: Educational Testing Service; R 122, Princeton, NJ 08541
Grade Level: 10-16
Notes: Time, 4; Items, 6

The Kit of Factor Referenced Cognitive Tests consists of 72 cognitive tests intended as markers for 23 aptitude factors to which they are referenced. The factors assessed are Flexibility of Closure, Speed of Closure, Verbal Closure, Associational Fluency, Expressional Fluency, Figural Fluency, Ideational Fluency, Word Fluency, Induction, Integrative Processes, Associative Memory, Memory Span, Visual Memory, Number, Perceptual Speed, General Reasoning, Logical Reasoning, Spatial Orientation, Spatial Scanning, Verbal Comprehension, Visualization, Figural Flexibility, and Flexibility of Use. The kit is designed for research purposes. One of 3 instruments designed to measure figural flexibility, the ability to change set in order to generate new and different solutions to figural problems. Subject is asked to arrange a certain number of specified capital letters in different positions or orientations on matrices of dots.

8257
Storage Test: XF-3. Ekstrom, Ruth B.; And Others 1976
Descriptors: *Abstract Reasoning; Aptitude Tests; Cognitive Measurement; *Cognitive Style; *Cognitive Tests; Higher Education; *High School Students; Problem Solving; Secondary Education; Spatial Ability; Timed Tests; *Undergraduate Students
Identifiers: Figural Flexibility; Kit of Referenced Tests for Cognitive Factors; Test Batteries
Availability: Educational Testing Service; R 122, Princeton, NJ 08541
Grade Level: 10-16
Notes: Time, 6; Items, 2

The Kit of Factor Referenced Cognitive Tests consists of 72 cognitive tests intended as markers for 23 aptitude factors to which they are referenced. The factors assessed are Flexibility of Closure, Speed of Closure, Verbal Closure, Associational Fluency, Expressional Fluency, Figural Fluency, Ideational Fluency, Word Fluency, Induction, Integrative Processes, Associative Memory, Memory Span, Visual Memory, Number, Perceptual Speed, General Reasoning, Logical Reasoning, Spatial Orientation, Spatial Scanning, Verbal Comprehension, Visualization, Figural Flexibility, and Flexibility of Use. The kit is designed for research purposes. One of 3 instruments designed to measure figural flexibility, the ability to change set in order to generate new and different solutions to figural problems. Subject is asked to show various ways small boxes can be arranged inside of a larger container.

8258
Combining Objects: XV-1. Ekstrom, Ruth B.; And Others 1976
Descriptors: Aptitude Tests; Cognitive Measurement; *Cognitive Style; *Cognitive Tests; Creativity; Creativity Tests; *Divergent Thinking; Higher Education; High Schools; *High School Students; Timed Tests; *Undergraduate Students
Identifiers: *Flexibility (Cognitive); Kit of Referenced Tests for Cognitive Factors; Test Batteries
Availability: Educational Testing Service; R 122, Princeton, NJ 08541
Grade Level: 9-16

Notes: Time, 10; Items, 20

The Kit of Factor Referenced Cognitive Tests consists of 72 cognitive tests intended as markers for 23 aptitude factors to which they are referenced. The factors assessed are Flexibility of Closure, Speed of Closure, Verbal Closure, Associational Fluency, Expressional Fluency, Figural Fluency, Ideational Fluency, Word Fluency, Induction, Integrative Processes, Associative Memory, Memory Span, Visual Memory, Number, Perceptual Speed, General Reasoning, Logical Reasoning, Spatial Orientation, Spatial Scanning, Verbal Comprehension, Visualization, Figural Flexibility, and Flexibility of Use. The kit is designed for research purposes. One of 4 instruments designed to measure flexibility of use, the mental set necessary to think of different uses for objects. Subject is asked to name 2 objects which, when used together, would fulfill a particular request.

8259
Substitute Uses: XU-2. Ekstrom, Ruth B.; And Others 1976
Descriptors: Aptitude Tests; Cognitive Measurement; *Cognitive Style; *Cognitive Tests; Creativity; Creativity Tests; *Divergent Thinking; Higher Education; High Schools; *High School Students; Timed Tests; *Undergraduate Students
Identifiers: Flexibility (Cognitive); Kit of Referenced Tests for Cognitive Factors; Test Batteries
Availability: Educational Testing Service; R 122, Princeton, NJ 08541
Grade Level: 9-16
Notes: Time, 10; Items, 20
The Kit of Factor Referenced Cognitive Tests consists of 72 cognitive tests intended as markers for 23 aptitude factors to which they are referenced. The factors assessed are Flexibility of Closure, Speed of Closure, Verbal Closure, Associational Fluency, Expressional Fluency, Figural Fluency, Ideational Fluency, Word Fluency, Induction, Integrative Processes, Associative Memory, Memory Span, Visual Memory, Number, Perceptual Speed, General Reasoning, Logical Reasoning, Spatial Orientation, Spatial Scanning, Verbal Comprehension, Visualization, Figural Flexibility, and Flexibility of Use. The kit is designed for research purposes. One of 4 instruments designed to measure flexibility of use, the mental set necessary to think of different uses for objects. Subject is asked to think of a common object that could serve as a substitute for the given object or purpose.

8260
Making Groups: XU-3. Ekstrom, Ruth B.; And Others 1976
Descriptors: Aptitude Tests; Cognitive Measurement; *Cognitive Style; *Cognitive Tests; Creativity; Creativity Tests; *Divergent Thinking; Higher Education; High Schools; *High School Students; Timed Tests; *Undergraduate Students
Identifiers: *Flexibility (Cognitive); Kit of Referenced Tests for Cognitive Factors; Test Batteries
Availability: Educational Testing Service; R 122, Princeton, NJ 08541
Grade Level: 9-16
Notes: Time, 10; Items, 4
The Kit of Factor Referenced Cognitive Tests consists of 72 cognitive tests intended as markers for 23 aptitude factors to which they are referenced. The factors assessed are Flexibility of Closure, Speed of Closure, Verbal Closure, Associational Fluency, Expressional Fluency, Figural Fluency, Ideational Fluency, Word Fluency, Induction, Integrative Processes, Associative Memory, Memory Span, Visual Memory, Number, Perceptual Speed, General Reasoning, Logical Reasoning, Spatial Orientation, Spatial Scanning, Verbal Comprehension, Visualization, Figural Flexibility, and Flexibility of Use. The kit is designed for research purposes. One of 4 instruments designed to measure flexibility of use, the mental set necessary to think of different uses for objects. Subject is asked to combine 3 or more items from a list of 7 into groups and to provide a reason for each grouping.

8261
Different Uses: XU-4. Ekstrom, Ruth B.; And Others 1976
Descriptors: Aptitude Tests; Cognitive Measurement; *Cognitive Style; *Cognitive Tests; Creativity; Creativity Tests; *Divergent Thinking; *Grade 6; Higher Education; Intermediate Grades; Secondary Education; *Secondary School Students; Timed Tests; *Undergraduate Students
Identifiers: *Flexibility (Cognitive); Kit of Referenced Tests for Cognitive Factors; Test Batteries
Availability: Educational Testing Service; R 122, Princeton, NJ 08541
Grade Level: 6-16
Notes: Time, 10; Items, 8

The Kit of Factor Referenced Cognitive Tests consists of 72 cognitive tests intended as markers for 23 aptitude factors to which they are referenced. The factors assessed are Flexibility of Closure, Speed of Closure, Verbal Closure, Associational Fluency, Expressional Fluency, Figural Fluency, Ideational Fluency, Word Fluency, Induction, Integrative Processes, Associative Memory, Memory Span, Visual Memory, Number, Perceptual Speed, General Reasoning, Logical Reasoning, Spatial Orientation, Spatial Scanning, Verbal Comprehension, Visualization, Figural Flexibility, and Flexibility of Use. The kit is designed for research purposes. One of 4 instruments designed to measure flexibility of use, the mental set necessary to think of different uses for objects. Subject is asked to think of up to 6 different uses for 4 common objects. Score is based on number of changes of use, not on total number of responses.

8265
Ross Test of Higher Cognitive Processes. Ross, John D.; Ross, Catherine M. 1976
Subtests: Analogies; Deductive Reasoning; Missing Premises; Abstract Relations; Sequential Synthesis; Questioning Strategies; Analysis of Relevant and Irrelevant Information; Analysis of Attributes
Descriptors: *Abstract Reasoning; *Academically Gifted; *Cognitive Style; Cognitive Tests; *Critical Thinking; *Elementary School Students; Intermediate Grades; Program Evaluation; *Screening Tests
Identifiers: Blooms Taxonomy; Ross Test
Availability: Academic Therapy Publications; 20 Commercial Blvd., Novato, CA 94947
Grade Level: 4-6
Notes: Time, 105 approx.; Items, 105
Designed to assess abstract and critical thinking skills among gifted and non-gifted students in grades 4 to 6. May be administered to individuals or groups. Useful in evaluation of program or curriculum effectiveness. Measures abilities referred to in Bloom's Taxonomy of Educational Objectives, Handbook I as Analysis, Synthesis, and Evaluation.

8266
Khatena—Torrance Creative Perception Inventory. Khatena, Joe; Torrance, E. Paul 1976
Subtests: What Kind of Person Are You?; Something about Myself
Descriptors: *Adults; Biographical Inventories; *Creative Thinking; Creativity Tests; *Gifted; Personality Traits; Secondary Education; *Secondary School Students; *Self Concept Measures; Student Placement
Identifiers: KTCPI; SAM; Test Batteries; WKOPAY
Availability: Stoelting Co.; 620 Wheat Ln., Wood Dale, IL 60191
Grade Level: 7-12
Target Audience: 12-64
Notes: Time, 45 approx.; Items, 100
Designed to identify creative individuals. May be used to select individuals for participation in special educational programs or job assignments. Two biographical components may be administered independently or together as a test battery. "What Kind of Person Are You?" assesses acceptance of authority, self-confidence, inquisitiveness, awareness of others, and discipline imagination. "Something about Myself" assesses environmental sensitivity, initiative, self-strength, intellectuality, individuality, and artistry.

8297
Motor Academic Perceptual Skill Development Checklist. Smith, Donna K. 1973
Subtests: Motor Skills; Academic Skills; Perceptual Skills
Descriptors: *Academic Aptitude; Behavior Rating Scales; Children; *Multiple Disabilities; Observation; *Perceptual Development; *Psychomotor Skills; Reading Readiness; *School Readiness; Visual Discrimination; *Young Children
Identifiers: MAP; TIM(D)
Availability: Tests in Microfiche; Test Collection, Educational Testing Service, Princeton, NJ 08541
Target Audience: 2-8
Designed to provide the teacher of multiply handicapped children with a behavior-oriented evaluation of the child's existing skills in the following areas: motor (gross motor, manipulative, self-care, exhibiting body awareness), academic (general readiness, communication, early skill development), and perceptual (visual discrimination, non-visual discrimination). The checklist is completed through teacher observation of children as they are involved in classroom activities.

8298
Scientific New Uses Test. Gough, Harrison G. 1975

Descriptors: Adults; Creative Thinking; *Creativity; Creativity Tests; *Engineers; *Scientists
Availability: Journal of Creative Behavior; v9 n4 p245-52, Fourth Quarter 1975
Target Audience: 18-64
Notes: Time, 30; Items, 20
Designed to measure creativity of scientists and engineers. Examinees are asked to think of as many new scientific uses as possible for each of 20 items.

8299
Scientific Word Association Test. Gough, Harrison G. 1976
Descriptors: Adults; *Association (Psychology); *Creativity; Divergent Thinking; *Engineers; Projective Measures; *Scientists
Identifiers: TIM(E)
Availability: Tests in Microfiche; Test Collection, Educational Testing Service, Princeton, NJ 08541
Target Audience: Adults
Notes: Time, 10 approx.; Items, 200
Employs the word association technique to provide a measure of associational fluency and creative thinking in scientists.

8312
R-B Number Readiness Test. Roberts, Dorothy M.; Bloom, Irving 1974
Descriptors: *Kindergarten Children; *Number Concepts; Numbers; Pictorial Stimuli; Preschool Education; *Mathematics Tests; School Readiness; *School Readiness Tests
Identifiers: *Numerical Ability; Oral Testing; TIM(D)
Availability: Tests in Microfiche; Test Collection, Educational Testing Service, Princeton, NJ 08541
Grade Level: Kindergarten
Notes: Items, 19
Employs pictorial items to measure specific aspects of number readiness: counting, cardinality, ordinality, one-to-one correspondence, vocabulary, writing single numerals, recognition of shapes and patterns, and recognition and matching of numerals. It should be administered orally to small groups of children.

8328
Four Music Conservation Tasks. Zimmerman, Marilyn P.; Sechrest, Lee
Descriptors: *Audiotape Recorders; Audiotape Recordings; *Auditory Discrimination; Children; *Elementary School Students; Individual Testing; *Junior High School Students; *Music Appreciation; Perception Tests
Identifiers: Music Identification; *Music Tests; Piagetian Tasks; TIM(D)
Availability: Tests in Microfiche; Test Collection, Educational Testing Service, Princeton, NJ 08541
Target Audience: 5-13
Notes: Time, 30; Items, 4
Designed to assess the development of simple conservation skills in music listening. They consist of 4 musical phrases in which systematic deformations are made. The deformations include change of instrument, mode, tempo, harmony, rhythm, contour, and interval. The respondent must indicate whether the second tune is the same as or different from the first and describe how it is the same or different.

8329
Six Music Conservation Tasks. Zimmerman, Marilyn P.; Sechrest, Lee 1966
Descriptors: *Audiotape Recorders; Audiotape Recordings; *Auditory Discrimination; Children; Concept Formation; *Conservation (Concept); *Elementary School Students; Individual Testing; *Junior High School Students; *Music Appreciation; Perception Tests
Identifiers: Music Identification; *Music Tests; Piagetian Tasks; TIM(D)
Availability: Tests in Microfiche; Test Collection, Educational Testing Service, Princeton, NJ 08541
Target Audience: 5-13
Notes: Time, 60 approx.; Items, 6
Developed to assess children's acquisition of the Piagetian concept of conservation in musical development. The 6 tasks are: conservation of duration, conservation of meter, conservation of rhythm pattern under deformation of tone, conservation of tonal pattern under deformation of pitch, conservation of melody under deformation of tempo, and conservation of tonal pattern under deformation of rhythm.

8331
Creative Response Matrices Test. Vernon, Philip E. 1969

Descriptors: *Cognitive Processes; Cognitive Style; *Culture Fair Tests; Elementary Education; *Elementary School Students; *English (Second Language); *Logical Thinking; Nonverbal Tests
Identifiers: Oral Testing; TIM(D)
Availability: Tests in Microfiche; Test Collection, Educational Testing Service, Princeton, NJ 08541
Target Audience: 6-12
Notes: Time, 15 approx.; Items, 24

A general reasoning test developed for use with culturally different children who would understand instructions presented in oral (but not written) English and who are probably unfamiliar with the multiple-choice format. Each item involves the completion of a figural series. The test is intended to be self-instructing since the respondent learns the instructions by having earlier test items explained.

8367
Psycho-Educational Battery. Pope, Lillie 1976
Subtests: Gross Motor Performance; Fine Motor Coordination; Awareness of Place and Time; Probe of Interests; Sight Words; Decoding and Reading Comprehension; Basic Reading Skills; Spelling; Concept Development; Ability to Classify and Language Usage; Auditory Memory; Auditory Word Discrimination; Speech; Handicapping Behavior; Helpful Characteristics; Physical Status and Appearance
Descriptors: Adolescents; Adults; Children; Cognitive Tests; *Diagnostic Tests; Educational Diagnosis; High Risk Students; Individual Testing; *Learning Problems; *Psychoeducational Methods; Psychological Characteristics; Psychological Evaluation; *Screening Tests; *Student Evaluation; Student Problems; *Students
Identifiers: Oral Tests; PEB
Availability: Stoelting Co.; 620 Wheat Ln., Wood Dale, IL 60191
Target Audience: 5-64

Designed to help improve educational planning for individual learners by providing performance data that enable the teacher to pinpoint the needs of the individual. Used for 1) early screening and identification of children who are likely to have learning problems, sometimes called high risk children; 2) psycho-educational assessment of skills and deficits of children who can not seem to handle the demands of kindergarten or the early grades; and 3) psycho-educational assessment of skills and deficits of learners of any age who seem to have difficulty with reading skills, etc., with a view to educational planning for remediation and avoidance of further problems. Available in 2 forms: Level Y for kindergarten through 6 grade; and Level O for grade 7 through adult years; subtests vary slightly for each form. In Form Y the first section is a group, orally administered test. Those whose responses are inadequate, unusual or questionable are further tested individually. Reading sections are the same as those in Deborah Edel's Informal Evaluation of Oral Reading.

8372
Schenectady Kindergarten Rating Scales. Conrad, W. Glenn; Tobiessen, Jon E. 1969
Subtests: Degree of Deviance in Ability; Impulse Control; Social Adjustment; Inhibition; Speech
Descriptors: Behavior Rating Scales; *Cognitive Development; Emotional Adjustment; *Kindergarten Children; *Language Acquisition; Motor Development; *Predictive Measurement; Preschool Education; Social Development; *Student Evaluation; Teachers
Identifiers: SKRS; TIM(D)
Availability: Tests in Microfiche; Test Collection, Educational Testing Service, Princeton, NJ 08541
Grade Level: Kindergarten
Notes: Time, 10 approx.; Items, 13

A battery of 13 teacher rating scales developed to measure behavioral dimensions related to school achievement and emotional adjustment. It provides a method for screening children so that preventive or remedial programs can be provided for those who are deficient in language, motor, social, or cognitive development.

8373
Matric Test of Referential Communication. Greenspan, Stephen; Barenboim, Carl 1974
Descriptors: *Cognitive Development; *Egocentrism; Elementary Education; *Elementary School Students; Emotional Adjustment; *Emotional Disturbances; *Individual Testing; Nonverbal Tests; Residential Schools; *Verbal Communication
Identifiers: *Piagetian Stages; TIM(D)
Availability: Tests in Microfiche; Test Collection, Educational Testing Service, Princeton, NJ 08541
Grade Level: 1-6

Assesses communicative egocentrism using a 3x3 matrix board and colored, geometric shapes. The child is asked to dictate instructions that would enable a hypothetical other child who is unable to see the subject's board to replicate

a design that the subject has made on his or her matrix board. Scoring of these instructions provides a measure of the child's cognitive-developmental level in an area of functioning significant to Piagetian theory.

8416
Time Understanding Inventory. Forer, Ruth K.; Keogh, Barbara K. 1970
Subtests: Subjective Time; Objective Time; Historic Time; Time Estimation; Draw a Clock; Tell Time; Clock Matching; Fill in Time
Descriptors: *Achievement Tests; *Concept Formation; Elementary Education; *Elementary School Students; Individual Testing; *Time; *Time Perspective
Identifiers: Oral Tests; Perceptual Time Inventory
Availability: Barbara Keogh; UCLA Graduate School of Education; Los Angeles, CA 90024
Grade Level: 1-6
Notes: Time, 30 approx.; Items, 53

Evaluates a student's understanding of time and his or her ability to apply this knowledge. Individually administered and untimed. Type of answer varies from subtest to subtest: oral answer, multiple choice, and drawing in clock hands.

8422
Formal Operations Test-Biology. Bart, William M. 1972
Descriptors: Adolescents; *Biology; *Cognitive Measurement; *Deduction; *Logical Thinking; Multiple Choice Tests; Secondary Education; *Secondary School Students
Identifiers: Piagetian Tasks; TIM(D)
Availability: Tests in Microfiche; Test Collection, Educational Testing Service, Princeton, NJ 08541
Target Audience: 13-19
Notes: Items, 30

Measures formal reasoning ability using 30 logic items with biological content. Each item requires a simple deduction through use of logical rules of inference in order for the validly deductible response to be recognized. One of 3 tests covering different subject areas.

8423
Formal Operations Test-History. Bart, William M. 1972
Descriptors: Adolescents; *Cognitive Measurement; *Deduction; *History; *Logical Thinking; Multiple Choice Tests; Secondary Education; *Secondary School Students; Social Studies
Identifiers: Piagetian Tasks; TIM(D)
Availability: Tests in Microfiche; Test Collection, Educational Testing Service, Princeton, NJ 08541
Target Audience: 13-19
Notes: Items, 30

Measures formal reasoning ability using 30 logic items with historical content. Each item requires a simple deduction through use of logical rules of inference in order for the validly deductible response to be recognized. One of 3 tests covering different subject areas.

8424
Formal Operations Test-Literature. Bart, William M. 1972
Descriptors: Adolescents; *Cognitive Measurement; *Deduction; *Literature; *Logical Thinking; Multiple Choice Tests; Secondary Education; *Secondary School Students
Identifiers: Piagetian Tasks; TIM(D)
Availability: Tests in Microfiche; Test Collection, Educational Testing Service, Princeton, NJ 08541
Target Audience: 13-19
Notes: Items, 30

Measures formal reasoning ability using 30 logic items with literary content. Each item requires a simple deduction through use of logical rules of inference in order for the validly deductible response to be recognized. One of 3 tests covering different subject areas.

8426
Application of Generalizations Test. Wallen, Norman E. 1969
Subtests: Test Score; Reasoning Score
Descriptors: *Cognitive Tests; *Elementary School Students; *Generalization; *Induction; Intermediate Grades; Secondary Education; *Secondary School Students
Identifiers: AGT; *Taba (Hilda) Teaching Strategies; TIM(D)
Availability: Tests in Microfiche; Test Collection, Educational Testing Service, Princeton, NJ 08541
Grade Level: 4-12
Notes: Items, 65

Designed to measure the ability to apply generalizations to new situations in order to make defensible inferences. The focus of the test is on generalizations emphasized in the Taba Social Studies Curriculum. It is appropriate in grades 4 and above.

8428
Two Alternative Perception Test. Goodman, Lisl M.
Descriptors: Adolescents; Adults; Children; *Cognitive Style; *Perception Tests; Personality Traits; *Visual Perception
Identifiers: APT; *Spatial Visualization; TIM(D)
Availability: Tests in Microfiche; Test Collection, Educational Testing Service, Princeton, NJ 08541
Target Audience: 4-60
Notes: Time, 2 approx.; Items, 27

Designed to investigate whole vs. part perception, the test consists of 3 parallel sets of 9 drawings. Each drawing can be seen as a representation of 1 whole object or as a collection of separate objects. On the basis of perceptual scores, respondents are classified into 1 of 3 categories: whole-dominant, part-dominant, and neutral.

8434
CTBS Readiness Test, Form S, Level A. CTB/McGraw-Hill, Monterey, CA 1977
Subtests: Letter Forms; Letter Names; Listening for Information; Letter Sounds; Visual Discrimination; Sound Matching; Language; Mathematics
Descriptors: Achievement Tests; *Grade 1; *Kindergarten Children; Primary Education; *Reading Readiness; *Reading Readiness Tests
Availability: CTB/McGraw Hill; Del Monte Research Park, Monterey, CA 93940
Grade Level: K-1
Notes: Items, 168

Assesses many of the skills included in prereading programs. There are 8 subtests. Letter names measures students' ability to identify orally named letters of the alphabet. Letter forms test provides an estimate of the extent to which a student can distinguish forms of letters. Listening for information assesses students' ability to obtain information from the spoken word. Letter sounds subtest requires the student to select the letter sound heard at the beginning of a word. Visual discrimination measures students' ability to discern similarities and differences in words, shapes, and other visual stimuli. In the sound matching subtest, students must determine whether 2 orally presented words are the same or different. The language test assesses students' ability to recognize correct and incorrect grammar and syntax when presented orally. The mathematics section is not used to estimate readiness levels. Test is used for grades K-1.3.

8444
Preschool Interpersonal Problem-Solving Test. Shure, Myrna B.; Spivack, George 1974
Descriptors: Cognitive Processes; Females; Individual Testing; *Interpersonal Competence; Interpersonal Relationship; Males; Mothers; *Parent Child Relationship; *Peer Relationship; Pictorial Stimuli; *Preschool Children; Preschool Education; *Problem Solving; Projective Measures; Young Children
Identifiers: PIPS
Availability: George Spivack, Director; Dept. of Mental Health Sciences, Hahnemann Medical College, 112 N. Broad St., Philadelphia, PA 19102
Target Audience: 4-5
Notes: Time, 30 approx.

Designed to measure preschool child's cognitive ability to solve real life interpersonal problems. Differentiates among young children who differ in social adjustment. Instrument is divided into 2 sections. The first presents a series of stories describing a problem between peers. The second part presents situations in which child has done something to make his or her mother angry and he or she must devise ways to avoid her anger. Boys are shown pictures of boys at play, while girls are shown pictures of girls.

8458
Singer-Brunk Figure Reproduction Test. Singer, Robert N.; Brunk, Jason W. 1967
Descriptors: Elementary Education; *Elementary School Students; *Perceptual Motor Coordination; *Performance Tests; *Problem Solving; Spatial Ability
Identifiers: Singer Brunk Perceptual Motor Test
Availability: Robert N. Singer; Movement Science Program, 201 Montgomery Gymnasium, Florida State University, Tallahassee, FL 32306
Target Audience: 6-12
Notes: Items, 14

Designed to measure problem-solving ability as represented by perceptual motor activity. Subjects are asked to replicate geometrical patterns which appear on paper or screen, to a wooden board containing 4 rows and 4 columns of nails, with the use of a rubber band.

8467
A Test for Inquiry Social Studies. Muir, Sharon Pray 1976
Descriptors: Aptitude Tests; *Cognitive Development; Cognitive Style; Cognitive Tests; *Elementary School Students; *Inquiry; Intermediate Grades; *Learning Processes; *Logical Thinking; Multiple Choice Tests; Problem Solving; *Social Studies
Identifiers: TISS
Availability: Sharon Pray Muir; Dept. of Curriculum Instruction, Oklahoma State University, Stillwater, OK 74078
Grade Level: 5-6
Notes: Time, 50 approx.; Items, 40
Measures a fifth or sixth grader's application of either inquiry social studies or higher cognitive thinking with the student's prior knowledge minimized. This untimed instrument may be used in a criterion referenced manner. Based upon the theory that the relationship of the inquiry process and higher cognitive thought is established in social studies literature.

8489
Parent Discipline Inventory. Dlugokinski, Eric L. 1973
Descriptors: Adolescents; Children; *Discipline Policy; Elementary Secondary Education; *Empathy; *Induction; Mother Attitudes; *Mothers; Parent Child Relationship; *Peer Relationship; Rating Scales; Situational Tests
Identifiers: TIM(D)
Availability: Tests in Microfiche; Test Collection, Educational Testing Service, Princeton, NJ 08541
Target Audience: 8-15
Notes: Items, 6
Designed to assess children's perceptions of maternal disciplinary style in terms of inductive responses to peer-conflict situations. Induction refers to attempts at communicating to the child the consequences of his or her actions for others and involves using reasoning to develop empathy or perception of the needs of others.

8523
Creativity Self Report Scale. Feldhusen, John F.; and Others 1965
Descriptors: *Creativity; *Creativity Tests; Higher Education; Secondary Education; *Secondary School Students; Self Evaluation (Individuals); *Undergraduate Students
Identifiers: CR; Survey
Availability: John F. Feldhusen; Purdue University-SCC-G, Educational Psychology Section, W. Lafayette, IN 47906
Grade Level: 7-16
Notes: Time, 15 approx.; Items, 67
Designed to assess creative behavior and attributes of students. Eight factor scores are applicable to junior and senior high school populations: self-descriptive items; socially conforming self image; socially non-conforming self image; dynamic, energetic aspects of self image; fluency; diffidence in self image; flexibility; global items. Seven factor scores are applicable to college level populations: self-descriptive items; cognitive complexity, innovation, and curiosity; risk-taking, inpulsive behavior; creative imagination; fluency; flexibility, global items. Instrument is titled "Survey" to avoid revelation of its purpose to examinee.

8528
Kahn Intelligence Test: A Culture-Minimized Experience. Kahn, Theodore C. 1975
Subtests: Brief Placement Scale; Main Scale; Concept Formation; Recall; Motor Coordination; Sign Language; Scale for Use with Blind Subjects
Descriptors: Adolescents; Adults; *Blindness; Children; Concept Formation; *Culture Fair Tests; Deafness; Disadvantaged; Individual Testing; Infants; *Intelligence Tests; *Mental Retardation; Performance Tests; Retention (Psychology); *Sign Language
Identifiers: KIT EXP
Availability: Psychological Test Specialists; P.O. Box 9229, Missoula, MT 59807
Target Audience: 0-64
Designed to assess intelligence requiring a minimum of verbalization and no reading, writing, or verbal knowledge. Consists of a brief placement scale to determine entry into the main scale and special shorter scales to estimate ability in areas of concept formation, recall, and motor coordination. Special scales are suggested for administration by sign language and for testing sight-handi-

capped and blind persons. Distribution is restricted to psychologists, psychiatrists, counselors and others with comparable training, as well as qualified researchers.

8530
SRA Test of Mechanical Concepts. Stanard, Steven J.; Bode, Kathleen Wahl 1976
Subtests: Mechanical Interrelationships; Mechanical Tools and Devices; Spatial Relations
Descriptors: *Adults; *Counseling Techniques; Hand Tools; *Mechanical Skills; Occupational Tests; Secondary Education; *Secondary School Students; *Spatial Ability
Identifiers: *Mechanical Aptitude; Mechanical Comprehension
Availability: Science Research Associates; 155 N. Wacker Dr., Chicago, IL 60606
Target Audience: 13-64
Notes: Time, 45 approx.; Items, 78
Designed to measure skills and abilities necessary for performance in jobs requiring mechanical ability. Forms A and B are available. May be used in educational levels from junior high school through college as well as in industrial settings. Useful in measuring individual differences in mechanical aptitudes.

8538
The Magic Kingdom: A Preschool Screening Program. Kallstrom, Christine 1975
Descriptors: Concept Formation; Diagnostic Tests; *Handicap Identification; Interpersonal Competence; Kindergarten; *Kindergarten Children; Language Acquisition; *Learning Disabilities; *Preschool Children; Preschool Education; Psychomotor Skills; *Screening Tests
Identifiers: Screening Programs
Availability: Red River Human Services Foundation; 15 Broadway, Ste. 510, Fargo, ND 58126
Target Audience: 3-6
Notes: Time, 90 approx.
Screening program for preschool children in several developmental areas. These include motor, visual, auditory, language, conceptual, and social-emotional. Designed primarily to identify children with special needs. Parents are involved in the screening process.

8636
Classroom Creativity Observation Schedule: 1969 Revision. Denny, David A. 1969
Subtests: Motivational Climate; Pupil Interest; Teacher Pupil Relationship; Pupil Relationship; Pupil Initiative; Teacher Approach; Encouragement of Pupil Divergency; Unusual Response
Descriptors: Classroom Environment; Classroom Observation Techniques; *Creative Thinking; *Elementary School Students; *Elementary School Teachers; *Interaction Process Analysis; *Observation; *Primary Education; Student Behavior; Teacher Student Relationship; Teacher Behavior
Identifiers: CCOS
Availability: David A. Denny; Professor Of Education, State University College, Oneonta, NY 13820
Grade Level: K-3
Designed to record verbal and nonverbal classroom behaviors hypothesized to be related to pupil creativity. Based upon recorded observation for various periods of time.

8671
Triple Mode Test of Categorization. Silverman-Dresner, Toby R. 1966
Subtests: Functional; Associative; Superordinate
Descriptors: Adolescents; Children; *Classification; *Cognitive Measurement; Cognitive Processes; *Deafness; *Pictorial Stimuli; Visual Measures
Identifiers: Silverman (Toby R); TIM(D); Vygotsky (Lev S)
Availability: Tests in Microfiche; Test Collection, Educational Testing Service, Princeton, NJ 08541
Target Audience: 7-15
Notes: Time, 45 approx.; Items, 126
Based upon Lev S. Vygotsky's 3 major roles of categorization. Designed to reveal the ways in which deaf children categorize stimuli and to determine if there are different developmental patterns in deaf vs. hearing children. Each item consists of 3 pictures; the child is to place the center picture (an object) into either the right or left picture, i.e., where he thinks the center picture belongs.

8677
SORTS Test for Sampling Children's Organization and Recall Strategies. Riegel, R. Hunt 1976
Descriptors: *Classification; *Cluster Grouping; Concept Formation; *Elementary School Students; *Individual Testing; Learning Disabilities; *Learning Strategies; Mild Mental Retardation; Perceptual Handicaps; Primary Education; *Recall (Psychology); Visual Measures
Identifiers: SORTS Test (Riegel)

Availability: Montage Press; P.O. Box 4322, Hamden, CT 06514
Grade Level: K-3
Series of picture cards presented to a child with instructions to identify and sort animals/objects, to give reasons for groupings, to test recall and organizational skills. Not to be group-administered or used with children with severe visual or physical handicaps; test requires good vision, and physical coordination to handle cards.

8678
Micro Tower System of Vocational Evaluation. ICD Rehabilitation & Research Center, New York, NY 1977
Subtests: Electronic Connector Assembly; Bottle Capping and Packing; Lamp Assembly; Blueprint Reading; Graphics Illustration; Mail Sorting; Filing; Zip Coding; Record Checking; Message Taking; Want Ads Comprehension; Payroll Computation; Making Change
Descriptors: *Adolescents; *Adults; Aptitude Tests; Clerical Occupations; *Disabilities; Mathematical Concepts; Mental Retardation; Physical Disabilities; Psychomotor Skills; *Semiskilled Occupations; Spatial Ability; *Unskilled Occupations; Verbal Ability; *Vocational Aptitude; *Vocational Evaluation; *Work Sample Tests
Availability: International Center for the Disabled; Micro Tower Research, 340 E. 24th St., New York, NY 10010
Target Audience: 15-64
A series of work sample tests designed to measure aptitudes required in unskilled and semi-skilled jobs. Assesses motor skills, clerical perception, spatial perception, as well as job-related verbal and numerical skills. Designed for vocational guidance for clients in vocational rehabilitation programs, as well as students.

8679
Santa Clara Inventory of Developmental Tasks. Santa Clara Unified School District, CA 1974
Subtests: Social-Emotional; Motor Coordination; Visual Motor Performance; Visual Perception; Visual Memory; Auditory Perception; Auditory Memory; Language Development; Conceptual Development
Descriptors: Auditory Perception; *Child Development; *Classroom Observation Techniques; Concept Formation; *Developmental Tasks; Interpersonal Competence; Language Acquisition; Motor Development; Perceptual Motor Coordination; *Primary Education; Recall (Psychology); *Screening Tests; Visual Perception; *Young Children
Identifiers: Elementary Secondary Education Act Title I; IDT; TIM(N)
Availability: Tests in Microfiche; Test Collection, Educational Testing Service, Princeton, NJ 08541
Grade Level: K-2
Target Audience: 5-7
Notes: Items, 72
Developed as an ESEA Title I project of the Santa Clara Unified School District. Consists of 72 tasks which represent milestones in children's development. Tasks are sequenced by chronological age and arranged into 9 skill areas. Inventory can be used as a screening device; as a basis for parent conferences; or as a record of a child's performance to facilitate correct placement by student's next teacher.

8696
Woodcock-Johnson Psycho-Educational Battery. Woodcock, Richard W.; Johnson, Mary B. 1977
Subtests: Picture Vocabulary; Spatial Relations; Memory for Sentences; Visual-Auditory Learning; Blending; Quantitative Concepts; Visual Matching; Antonyms and Synonyms; Analysis-Synthesis; Numbers Reversed; Concept Formation; Analogies; Letter Word-Identification; Word Attack; Passage Comprehension; Calculations; Applied Problems; Dictation; Proofing; Science; Social Studies; Humanities; Reading Interest; Mathematics Interest; Written Language Test; Physical Interest; Social Interest
Descriptors: *Achievement Tests; Adolescents; Adults; *Aptitude Tests; Children; *Cognitive Tests; Individual Testing; *Interest Inventories; Older Adults; Standardized Tests; Testing Programs
Identifiers: Antonyms; Quantitative Thinking; Synonyms; Test Batteries
Availability: DLM Teaching Resources; P.O. Box 4000, 1 DLM Park, Allen, TX 75002
Target Audience: 2-70
Notes: Time, 120 approx.
Individually administered battery is comprised of 27 subtests (over 877 items), divided according to 3 major areas of assessment: cognitive ability/scholastic aptitude, scholastic achievement and interest level. Norms are provided from preschool to the geriatric level. Cassette recorder and

stop watch are required for portions of the test. Primary application is student evaluation. May also be used for vocational rehabilitation counseling and as a research instrument. Special feature: Part I subtests Quantitative Concepts and Antonyms-Synonyms, requiring about 15 minutes to administer and score, correlate highly with measures of intelligence as well as with school achievement.

8721
Method for Assessing Mastery in One-Year Old Infants. Morgan, George A.; And Others 1976
Subtests: Effectance Production; Practicing Emerging Skills; Problem Solving
Descriptors: Achievement Need; Behavior Rating Scales; *Infant Behavior; *Infants; *Motivation; Performance; Performance Tests; *Persistence; *Problem Solving
Identifiers: TIM(D)
Availability: Tests in Microfiche; Test Collection, Educational Testing Service, Princeton, NJ 08541
Target Audience: 1
Notes: Time, 40 approx.; Items, 11
A series of tasks and an observational scoring system developed to measure mastery motivation in infants. The child completes 11 tasks categorized into 3 types: effectance production, practicing emerging skills, and problem solving.

8728
Tests of Group Learning Skills. Watson, Michael A. 1976
Subtests: Visual-Motor; Visual-Memory; Visual Discrimination; Visual Association; Auditory Memory; Auditory Discrimination; Auditory Association; Auditory-Visual Association
Descriptors: Academic Achievement; Audiotape Cassettes; *Auditory Discrimination; *Cognitive Style; Cognitive Tests; *Diagnostic Teaching; *Elementary School Students; Filmstrips; Learning Disabilities; *Preschool Children; Preschool Education; Primary Education; *Visual Discrimination; Young Children
Identifiers: GLS
Availability: Educational Activities, Inc.; P.O. Box 392, Freeport, NY 11520
Target Audience: 3-11
Notes: Time, 240 approx.; Items, 140
Designed to evaluate information processing skills required in most mechanical academic tasks. Measures the most important developmental learning skills in a group setting.

8729
Drawing Completion Task. Greenberg, Judith W.
Subtests: Originality; Popularity of Subject Matter; Spontaneous Flexibility; Asymmetry; Dynamism; Complexity; Fit to Stimulus
Descriptors: Children; *Creativity; *Divergent Thinking; *Elementary School Students; *Nonverbal Tests
Identifiers: TIM(D)
Availability: Tests in Microfiche; Test Collection, Educational Testing Service, Princeton, NJ 08541
Target Audience: 8-12
Notes: Items, 8
Measures creativity and divergent production in an unstructured nonverbal context. The child's drawings are scored on 7 dimensions: originality, popularity of subject matter, spontaneous flexibility, asymmetry, dynamism, complexity, and fit to stimulus.

8732
Visual Synthesis and Memory Tasks. Greenberg, Judith W.
Descriptors: *Individual Testing; *Pattern Recognition; Perception Tests; Preschool Education; *Recognition (Psychology); *Visual Perception; *Young Children
Identifiers: TIM(D)
Availability: Tests in Microfiche; Test Collection, Educational Testing Service, Princeton, NJ 08541
Target Audience: 5-7
Notes: Time, 80 approx.; Items, 25
A series of tasks assessing the child's ability to recognize a whole geometric figure after the parts have been shown and then removed. Test was individually administered in 2 sessions of approximately 40 minutes each.

8796
Test of Ability to Explain. Sawin, Enoch I. 1969
Subtests: Recognition of Events Connected by Causality; Recognition of Principles that Explain Events; Application of Principles that Explain Cause-and-Effect Relations
Descriptors: Deduction; Elementary School Students; Essay Tests; *Grade 6; Intermediate Grades; *Logical Thinking; Multiple Choice Tests; Social Studies

Identifiers: ABEX; Explanations; Reasoning
Availability: ERIC Document Reproduction Service; 3900 Wheeler Ave., Alexandria, VA 22304 (ED040106, 374 pages)
Grade Level: 6
Notes: Time, 50 approx.; Items, 33
Designed to assess student's ability to explain ideas involving social studies content. Forms available as multiple choice or essay. Essay test consists of 8 items which yield 3-part scores—ability to explain relationships, recognition of relevant facts, and recognition of relevant generalizations.

8797
Interpretation of Data Test. Crawford, William
Descriptors: *Cognitive Tests; *Deduction; Elementary School Students; *Grade 6; Intermediate Grades; Logical Thinking; *Social Studies
Identifiers: IDT; Inference Skills
Availability: ERIC Document Reproduction Service; 3900 Wheeler Ave., Alexandria, VA 22304 (ED040106, 374 pages)
Grade Level: 6
Notes: Items, 27
Instrument is intended to measure the student's ability to make logically defensible deductions (inferences) from information provided. Test format consists of an archaeological site map of a bushman settlement and accompanying identification of symbols found on the map.

8798
Visual Aural Digit Span Test. Koppitz, Elizabeth M. 1978
Subtests: Aural-Oral; Visual-Oral; Aural-Written; Visual-Written
Descriptors: Auditory Stimuli; *Diagnostic Tests; Elementary Education; *Elementary School Students; *Individual Testing; Learning Disabilities; *Memory; Mental Retardation; School Readiness; Screening Tests; *Short Term Memory; Visual Stimuli
Identifiers: VADS
Availability: Grune and Stratton; 111 Fifth Ave., New York, NY 10003
Grade Level: K-6
Designed to assess intersensory integration, sequencing, and recall and serve as a diagnostic instrument for identifying learning disabilities in school age children. Useful for students from end of kindergarten to grade 6. Useful as part of screening battery for school readiness.

8803
Science Process Instrument: Experimental Edition. American Association for the Advancement of Science, Washington, DC 1970
Subtests: Observing; Classifying; Measuring; Using Numbers; Using Space/Time Relationships; Inferring; Communicating and Predicting
Descriptors: *Concept Formation; Elementary Education; Elementary School Science; *Elementary School Students; Individual Testing; Learning Processes; *Scientific Concepts
Identifiers: Science a Process Approach
Availability: American Association for the Advancement of Science; 1515 Massachusetts Ave. NW, Washington, DC 20005
Grade Level: K-6
Developed to determine processes by which students learn scientific concepts. Student begins tasks at a level comparable to his or her age and continues to the level at which he or she fails.

8833
The Selected Creativity Tasks. Abraham, Eugene C.
Subtests: Instances; Alternate Uses
Descriptors: *Creativity; *Creativity Tests; Divergent Thinking; Elementary School Students; *Grade 6; Individual Testing; Measures (Individuals); *Verbal Tests
Identifiers: SCT; TIM(E)
Availability: Tests in Microfiche; Test Collection, Educational Testing Service, Princeton, NJ 08541
Grade Level: 6
Notes: Items, 8
Designed to identify creative ability. Verbal responses are assessed according to the following criteria: fluency, flexibility, originality, and elaboration. The administrator asks the questions verbally and the child answers verbally. The administrator records the answer exactly as stated.

8835
Classroom Observational Record. Reynolds, William A.; And Others 1971
Descriptors: *Classroom Observation Techniques; *Cognitive Processes; *Elementary School Students; Elementary Secondary Education; *Secondary School Students; Teacher Student Relationship; *Verbal Communication
Identifiers: COR

Availability: Eugene C. Abraham, Associate Professor; Science Education, Temple University Rm. 250, Ritter Hall, Philadelphia, PA 19122
Grade Level: 1-12
Notes: Items, 22
Designed to permit observers to analyze the cognitive levels on which classroom verbal interactions take place.

8867
Tick Tack Toe Test. Sutton-Smith, Brian; Roberts, John M. 1967
Descriptors: *Cognitive Style; Cognitive Tests; Cross Cultural Studies; *Culture Fair Tests; Elementary Education; *Elementary School Students; Games; Logical Thinking; Problem Solving
Identifiers: Reasoning
Availability: Genetic Psychology Monographs; v75 p3-42, 1967
Grade Level: K-8
Notes: Time, 5 approx.; Items, 6
Designed to assess strategic competence by inference from subject's performance in playing Tick Tack Toe. Game requires no verbal ability and is a pure game of strategy. For this reason it is a suitable measure for use in cross cultural research.

8868
Checklist for Kindergarten. Dade County Public Schools, Hialeah, FL, Dept. of Exceptional Child Education
Descriptors: *Check Lists; Creativity; *Gifted; Interpersonal Competence; *Kindergarten Children; Language Skills; Mathematics; Primary Education; Psychomotor Skills; Talent Identification
Availability: Dade County Public Schools; Coordination for Gifted Programs, 733 E. 57th St., Hialeah, FL 33013
Grade Level: K
Notes: Items, 27
Instrument designed to assist in the identification of gifted kindergarten students. The device in the form of a checklist permits teacher evaluation in the areas of language, psychomotor abilities, mathematics, creativity, and general characteristics.

8875
Revised Beta Examination, Second Edition. Kellogg, C.E.; Morton, N.W. 1978
Subtests: Mazes; Coding; Paper Form Boards; Picture Completion; Clerical Checking; Picture Absurdities
Descriptors: Adolescents; Adults; Aptitude Tests; *Cognitive Ability; Cognitive Tests; *Educationally Disadvantaged; Employees; Employment Potential; *Illiteracy; Job Applicants; Job Skills; *Nonverbal Ability; Nonverbal Tests; Spanish; Spanish Speaking; Timed Tests; Visual Measures; *Visual Stimuli; *Vocational Aptitude
Identifiers: Army Group Examination Beta; BETA II
Availability: The Psychological Corp.; 555 Academic Ct., San Antonio, TX 78204-0952
Target Audience: 13-64
Notes: Items, 210
Nonverbal measure of mental abilities; thus, useful with illiterate, non-English speaking, or handicapped persons employed in unskilled jobs in industrial organizations. Revision of Army Group Examination Beta (1920). Also available in Spanish BETA (TC885031). Scores yield percentile rank and deviation IQ. Instructions in this version are also given in Spanish.

8889
Known Word Test. Levinson, Elizabeth J.
Descriptors: Cognitive Ability; Cognitive Development; *Cognitive Tests; *Definitions; *Individual Testing; Intelligence; Intelligence Differences; Language Acquisition; Learning Processes; *Preschool Children; Semantics; *Verbal Ability; Verbal Learning; Verbal Tests; *Vocabulary Development; Vocabulary Skills; Word Lists
Identifiers: Oral Tests
Availability: Elizabeth J. Levinson; 78 N. Main St., Orono, ME 04473
Target Audience: 5
Notes: Time, 50 approx.; Items, 30
Measures the cognitive level of a child's definitions, as distinct from that child's knowledge of the words' meanings. The author states that the instrument was devised to test the following hypothesis: encouraging and teaching 5-year olds to define words in a cognitively more mature fashion, and giving them experience in doing so, will raise the functional IQ's of these 5-year olds above the level gained by 5-year olds who did not receive this training and experience. Individually administered with a short rest period after each 10 words.

8911
Mathematical Problem Solving Test. Wearne, Diana C. 1975
Descriptors: *Aptitude Tests; *Creative Thinking; *Elementary School Mathematics; Elementary School Students; *Grade 4; *Individual Testing; *Information Utilization; Intermediate Grades; *Problem Solving; Productive Thinking
Availability: ERIC Document Reproduction Service; 3900 Wheeler Ave., Alexandria, VA 22304, (ED144958, 174 pages)
Grade Level: 4
Notes: Items, 22
Individually administered test developed to provide information regarding the child's mastery of the prerequisites for problem solving. Information is obtained by asking 3 questions regarding a problem situation to assess a student's understanding of vocabulary and mastery of prerequisite concepts. The test was designed to produce 3 scores: a comprehension score, an application score, and a problem solving score.

8913
Social Interaction and Creativity in Communication System. Johnson, David L. 1975
Descriptors: Audiotape Recordings; *Classroom Observation Techniques; *Communication Skills; *Creativity; *Elementary School Students; Elementary Secondary Education; Gifted; *Secondary School Students; Student Behavior; Teacher Student Relationship; *Talent Identification; Videotape Recordings
Identifiers: SICCS
Availability: Stoelting Co.; 620 Wheat Ln., Wood Dale, IL 60191
Grade Level: K-12
Designed to identify and evaluate creativity, leadership, and communication skills through structured observation of student-teacher verbal interactions.

8921
Focal Point Location Test. Strang, Harold R.
Descriptors: *Elementary School Students; Individual Testing; Pattern Recognition; Perception Tests; *Preschool Children; Preschool Education; Primary Education; *Spatial Ability; Visual Perception; *Visual Stimuli
Availability: Harold R. Strang; Foundations of Education, University of Virginia, 260 Ruffner Hall, 405 Emmet St., Charlottesville, VA 22903
Target Audience: 2-8
Notes: Items, 10
Designed to assess the relationship between the location of focal points in nonrealistic figures and inversion perception. Examinee is instructed to indicate which of 2 identical figures is upside down.

8932
Science Reasoning Level Test. Duszynska, Anna
Descriptors: *Piagetian Theory; Academic Achievement; Achievement Tests; *Cross Cultural Studies; *Elementary School Students; Foreign Countries; Intermediate Grades; *Logical Thinking; *Science Tests; *Scientific Literacy
Identifiers: Poland; SRLT
Availability: ERIC Document Reproduction Service; 3900 Wheeler Ave., Alexandria, VA 22304 (ED144988, 28 pages)
Grade Level: 4-6
Notes: Items, 16
Designed to determine whether a test based on Piaget model of development of thought processes could be used to study the development of scientific reasoning in elementary school students. Relationship between reasoning and academic achievement and patterns in development of thought processes were compared for students in Poland and United States.

8933
Creativity Checklist. Johnson, David L.
Descriptors: Classroom Observation Techniques; *College Students; *Creativity; *Creativity Tests; *Elementary School Students; Elementary Secondary Education; Higher Education; Rating Scales; *Secondary School Students; *Talent Identification
Identifiers: CCh
Availability: Stoelting Co.; 620 Wheat Ln., Wood Dale, IL 60191
Grade Level: K-20
Notes: Time, 15 approx.; Items, 8
Designed to assess individual's creativity on the basis of observation by a teacher or someone else familiar with the subject's behavior. May be used in conjunction with Gifted and Talented Screening Form (TC008980).

8950
Instruments for Measuring Cognitive Abilities at the Intermediate Grade Level. Harris, Margaret L.; Harris, Chester W. 1974
Descriptors: *Cognitive Ability; Cognitive Style; Cognitive Tests; *Elementary School Students; Induction; Intermediate Grades; Memory; Number Concepts; Spatial Ability; *Verbal Ability
Identifiers: Guilford (JP)
Availability: ERIC Document Reproduction Service; 3900 Wheeler Ave., Alexandria, VA 22304 (ED150148, 209 pages)
Grade Level: 4-6
A series of instruments to measure cognitive abilities in the areas of verbal ability, induction, numerical ability, word fluency, memory, perceptual speed, simple visualization, spatial ability, evaluation, and seeing relationships. Many instruments are adaptations of Guilford's work. Related material in ERIC Document ED107470. Test instruments and manual are intended to accompany authors' 1973 monograph "A Structure of Concept Attainment Abilities."

8980
Gifted and Talented Screening Form. Johnson, David L.
Descriptors: *Academically Gifted; Creativity; Elementary Education; *Elementary School Students; Gifted; Intelligence; Junior High Schools; *Junior High School Students; Leadership; Psychomotor Skills; Rating Scales; *Screening Tests; *Talent Identification
Identifiers: GTSF
Availability: Stoelting Co.; 620 Wheat Ln., Wood Dale, IL 60191
Grade Level: K-9
Notes: Time, 10 approx.; Items, 24
Designed to screen individuals and groups for gifted and talented school programs. Students are observed and assessed in talent areas of academics, intelligence, creativity, leadership, visual-performing arts, and psychomotor ability.

9011
Reading Test for Vocational Education. Weiss, Lucile 1976
Subtests: Autosense; How to Change a Gasket; Communications; Television; The Drill Press; Sources of Electrical Energy
Descriptors: Aptitude Tests; *Cloze Procedure; High Schools; *High School Students; *Reading Comprehension; *Screening Tests; *Vocational Aptitude; Vocational Education
Identifiers: TIM(E)
Availability: Tests in Microfiche; Test Collection, Educational Testing Service, Princeton, NJ 08541
Grade Level: 9-12
Notes: Items, 300
Designed to function as a screening procedure to identify students who lack academic skills but who, because of interest and knowledge in nonacademic areas, will succeed in vocational education programs. It was developed to serve as an alternative to academically oriented tests used for screening purposes.

9044
System of Multicultural Pluralistic Assessment. Mercer, Jane R.; Lewis, June F. 1978
Descriptors: *Adjustment (to Environment); Auditory Perception; Biographical Inventories; Black Youth; Children; *Cognitive Ability; *Culture Fair Tests; Disabilities; Elementary Education; *Elementary School Students; Exceptional Persons; Hispanic Americans; Intelligence; Interpersonal Competence; Nondiscriminatory Education; Parents; *Perceptual Motor Learning; Physical Development; Physical Health; Psychomotor Skills; Sociocultural Patterns; *Spanish; Special Education; Student Evaluation; Talent Identification; Visual Acuity; White Students
Identifiers: Adaptive Behavior Inventory for Children; Bender Visual Motor Gestalt Test; SOMPA; Wechsler Intelligence Scale for Children (Revised); Wechsler Preschool Primary Scale of Intelligence
Availability: The Psychological Corp.; 555 Academic Ct., San Antonio, TX 78204-0952
Target Audience: 5-11
Notes: Time, 80 approx.
Comprehensive system for assessment of cognitive and sensorimotor abilities, and adaptive behavior of children ages 5 to 11 years of age. Parent Interview Materials and Student Assessment Materials are 2 major components. Each component is available as a separate package. Parent Interview is conducted in the home with the principal caretaker of the child, usually the mother. May be conducted in English or Spanish and requires 1 hour to complete. The measures used in the interview include the Adaptive Behavior Inventory for Children (TC011756); Sociocultural Scales; and Health History Inventories. Student Assessment Materials include Physical Dexterity Tasks; Bender Visual Motor Gestalt Test (TC001319); Weight by Height; Visual Acuity; Auditory Acuity; and WISC-R (TC007461). The system is racially and culturally nondiscriminatory and thus fulfills the requirements of the Education for All Handicapped Children Act. Normative data are available for Black, Hispanic, and White Children.

9050
Wachs Analysis of Cognitive Structures. Wachs, Harry; Vaughan, Lawrence J. 1977
Subtests: Identification of Objects; Object Design; Graphic Design; General Movement
Descriptors: *Cognitive Development; Culture Fair Tests; *Disadvantaged; Hearing Impairments; Individual Testing; Language Handicaps; *Learning Disabilities; Performance Tests; Piagetian Theory; *Preschool Children; Preschool Education; Psychomotor Skills; School Readiness
Identifiers: WACS
Availability: Western Psychological Services; 12031 Wilshire Blvd., Los Angeles, CA 90025
Target Audience: 3-6
Notes: Time, 45 approx.
Designed to detect quality of a child's actual performance of high level thinking for various body and sense thinking tasks. Fifteen clusters of tasks are grouped into 4 subjects. Inventory activities are presented as challenging games.

9055
Griffiths Mental Development Scale. Griffiths, Ruth 1955
Subtests: Locomotor; Personal-Social; Hearing and Speech; Eye and Hand; Performance
Descriptors: Cognitive Ability; *Cognitive Development; *Cognitive Tests; Eye Hand Coordination; Hearing (Physiology); Individual Testing; Infant Behavior; *Infants; Intelligence; Intelligence Tests; Psychomotor Skills
Availability: Test Center, Inc.; Snug Harbor Village, 7721 Holiday Dr., Sarasota, FL 33581
Target Audience: 0-2
Notes: Items, 27
Designed to measure cognitive development which is significant for intelligence or indicative of mental growth.

9056
Griffiths Mental Development Scales, Extension. Griffiths, Ruth 1970
Subtests: Locomotor; Personal-Social; Hearing and Speech; Eye and Hand Coordination; Performance; Practical Reasoning
Descriptors: Abstract Reasoning; *Cognitive Development; *Cognitive Tests; Elementary School Students; Eye Hand Coordination; Individual Testing; Intelligence; Intelligence Tests; Interpersonal Competence; *Preschool Children; Preschool Education; Primary Education; Psychomotor Skills; Speech Skills; *Young Children
Availability: Test Center, Inc.; Snug Harbor Village, 7721 Holiday Dr., Sarasota, FL 33581
Target Audience: 3-8
Notes: Items, 22
Designed as an upward extension of Griffiths Mental Development Scales (TC 009055). Designed to assess intelligence and cognitive development of children ages 3 to 8.

9075
Test Procedures for Preschool Children. Graham, Frances K.; Ernhart, Claire B. 1962
Subtests: Vocabulary Scale; Block-Sort; Copy-Forms; Motor Coordination; Figure-Ground; Tactual-Localization; Mark-Car Accuracy; Mark-Car Mark; Distraction-Variable Error; Distraction-Constant Error; Parent Questionnaire (Personality)
Descriptors: *Concept Formation; Diagnostic Tests; Individual Testing; *Neurological Impairment; *Perceptual Motor Coordination; Performance Tests; Personality Assessment; *Preschool Children; Preschool Education; *Vocabulary Skills
Identifiers: Test Batteries
Availability: Dr. Frances K. Graham; Dept. of Psychology, University of Delaware, Newark, DE 19716
Target Audience: 2-5
Notes: Time, 60 approx.
Developed to measure vocabulary skills, conceptual ability, perceptual-motor ability, and personality characteristics of preschool children. Designed for use in differentiating brain injured from normal population. Personality characteristics were assessed by parent-completed questionnaires and rating scales completed by examiner.

9078
Draw-a-Person. Golomb, Claire 1972
Descriptors: Child Development; *Concept Formation; *Elementary School Students; *Freehand Drawing; *Preschool Children; Preschool Education; Primary Education; Projective Measures; *Sculpture
Identifiers: Representational Modeling

Availability: Claire Golomb; Dept. of Psychology, University of Massachusetts, Harbor Campus, Boston, MA 02125
Target Audience: 2-7
Designed to assess the relationship between representation and cognition in children's drawings and sculptings of human figures.

9098
Naming Category Instances. Shipman, Virginia C. 1969
Descriptors: Cognitive Measurement; *Concept Formation; Individual Testing; *Preschool Children; Preschool Education
Availability: Virginia C. Shipman; 41 Riverside Dr., Princeton, NJ 08540
Target Audience: 3-4
Child is asked to name all the things he or she can that belong to a simple category. The first subtest is used to communicate the nature of the task by child and examiner alternating naming instances. In the second subtest, the child alone names instances of a category. Examiner times child's responses from the time instructions are complete to the discontinuance of the task.

9121
Arthur Adaptation of the Leiter International Performance Scale. Arthur, Grace 1952
Subtests: Two Year Tests; Three Year Tests; Four Year Tests; Five Year Tests; Six Year Tests; Seven Year Tests; Eight Year Tests; Nine Year Tests; Ten Year Tests; Eleven Year Tests; Twelve Year Tests
Descriptors: Culture Fair Tests; *Elementary School Students; Individual Testing; *Intelligence; *Intelligence Tests; *Nonverbal Tests; Performance Tests; *Preschool Children; Preschool Education; Primary Education; Speech Handicaps; Young Children
Identifiers: Arthur Adaptation of Leiter Intl Performance Scale; Leiter International Performance Scale
Availability: Western Psychological Services; 12031 Wilshire Blvd., Los Angeles, CA 90025
Target Audience: 3-7
Designed as a nonverbal Binet scale for young children. Tests are untimed and those at lower end of scale measure ability to learn rather than acquired skills or learned material. Ratings obtained from combining scores on this instrument with the Revised Form II of Point of Scale Performance Tests (TC000842) yield a reliable measurement of general intelligence except in areas of oral and written response. Results are especially useful with children with a foreign language handicap or delayed speech.

9133
Conceptual Learning and Development Assessment Series I: Equilateral Triangle. DiLuzio, Geneva J.; And Others 1975
Descriptors: Abstract Reasoning; *Cognitive Development; Cognitive Tests; *Concept Formation; Difficulty Level; *Elementary School Students; Elementary Secondary Education; *Geometric Concepts; *Secondary School Students
Identifiers: CLD; Equilateral Triangle; Klausmeier (HJ); Oral Testing; Test Batteries
Availability: ERIC Document Reproduction Service; 3900 Wheeler Ave., Alexandria, VA 22304 (ED 103 482, 80 pages)
Grade Level: K-12
Target Audience: 4-18
Developed as part of research on the Conceptual Learning and Development model. Measures the level of attainment of the concept, equilateral triangle, and uses of that concept. The Conceptual Learning and Development model specifies 4 successive levels of concept attainment. These include concrete level, identity level, classificatory level, and formal level. A concept attained at the classificatory or formal levels may be used in 4 ways. These are horizontal transfer, cognizing supraordinate-subordinate relations, cognizing various other relations among concepts, and generalizing to problem solving situations.

9134
Conceptual Learning and Development Assessment Series IV: Tree. Klausmeier, Herbert J.; And Others 1974
Descriptors: Abstract Reasoning; Cognitive Development; Cognitive Processes; Cognitive Tests; *Concept Formation; Difficulty Level; *Elementary School Students; Elementary Secondary Education; Fundamental Concepts; Identification; *Secondary School Students; *Trees
Identifiers: CLD; Oral Testing; Test Batteries
Availability: ERIC Document Reproduction Service; 3900 Wheeler Ave., Alexandria, VA 22304 (ED 103 485, 131 pages)
Grade Level: K-12
Target Audience: 4-18

Developed as part of research on the Conceptual Learning and Development Model. Measures the level of attainment of the concept, tree. The Conceptual Learning and Development model specifies 4 successive levels of concept attainment. These include concrete level, and formal level. A concept attained at the classificatory or formal levels may be used in 4 ways. These are horizontal transfer, cognizing supraordinate-subordinate relations, cognizing various other relations among concepts, and generalizing to problem solving situations.

9135
Kindergarten Screening Instrument. Houston Independent School District, TX 1975
Subtests: Vision; Hearing; Eye Hand Coordination; Language Learning; Gross Motor
Descriptors: Child Development; *Cognitive Development; *Individual Development; Individual Testing; *Kindergarten Children; Learning Readiness; *Performance Tests; Primary Education; *Psychomotor Skills; School Readiness; *Screening Tests; Spanish; *Spanish Speaking; Visual Measures; Visual Stimuli; Volunteers
Identifiers: HISD Kindergarten Screening Instrument; in Public Schools (Houston); Oral Tests
Availability: ERIC Document Reproduction Service; 3900 Wheeler Ave., Alexandria, VA 22304 (ED153999, 84 pages)
Grade Level: K
Screening device developed by the Board of Education of the Houston Independent School District through the Volunteers in Public Schools. Used to detect possible difficulties in such areas as perception, discrimination, physical development, and cognitive development. Individually administered by the trained volunteers. Requires the use of numerous items, such as eye chart, cassette tape playback, various drawings and pictures, scissors, a 24-inch hoop, etc. Instructions that are to be given to the child are written in both Spanish and English.

9145
ITPA Profile Form. Hobby, Kenneth L. 1974
Descriptors: Elementary Education; *Elementary School Students; *Intelligence Tests; *Preschool Children; Preschool Education; *Profiles; *Psycholinguistics; Records (Forms); *Test Interpretation
Identifiers: Illinois Test of Psycholinguistic Abilities; ITPA
Availability: Psychologists and Educators; P.O. Box 513, St. Louis, MO 63017
Target Audience: 2-10
Designed to create a visual profile of student's ITPA scores simplifying interpretation of test results. Profile may be completed using scaled scores and raw scores.

9149
WAIS Profile Form. Hobby, Kenneth L.
Descriptors: Adolescents; *Adults; High Schools; *High School Students; Intelligence Quotient; *Intelligence Tests; Older Adults; *Profiles; Records (Forms); *Test Interpretation
Identifiers: WAIS; Wechsler Adult Intelligence Scale
Availability: Psychologists and Educators; P.O. Box 513, St. Louis, MO 63017
Target Audience: 16-74
Summary of all necessary information needed to interpret and understand WAIS test results. Creates a visual display of subject's assets and weaknesses.

9150
WPPSI Profile Form. Hobby, Kenneth L.
Descriptors: *Elementary School Students; *Grade 1; Intelligence Quotient; *Intelligence Tests; *Preschool Children; Preschool Education; Primary Education; *Profiles; Records (Forms); *Test Interpretation
Identifiers: Wechsler Preschool Primary Scale of Intelligence; WPPSI
Availability: Psychologists and Educators; P.O. Box 513, St. Louis, MO 63017
Target Audience: 4-6
Summary of all necessary information needed to interpret and understand WPPSI test results. Creates a visual display of child's assets and weaknesses.

9152
WAIS Mental Description Sheet. Blazer, John A. 1974
Subtests: Emotional Reactions; Consistency of Mental Activity; Context of Mental Activity; Intellectual Capacities and Responses
Descriptors: *Adults; Intelligence Quotient; *Intelligence Tests; Older Adults; *Profiles; Records (Forms); *Test Interpretation
Identifiers: WAIS; Wechsler Adult Intelligence Scale
Availability: Psychologists and Educators; P.O. Box 513, St. Louis, MO 63017
Target Audience: 16-74
Notes: Time, 10 approx.

Designed to reveal a graphic profile indicating subject's general functioning. Interpretive areas include emotional reactions, consistency of mental activity, content of mental activity, and intellectual capacities and responses.

9199
Purdue Spatial Visualization Tests. Guay, Ronald B. 1976
Subtests: Visualization of Developments; Visualization of Rotations; Visualization of Views
Descriptors: Adults; *Aptitude Tests; Multiple Choice Tests; *Spatial Ability; Timed Tests; *Visualization; Visual Measures; *Visual Perception; *Visual Stimuli
Identifiers: PSVT
Availability: Dr. Ronald B. Guay; 315-Industrial Education Bldg., Purdue University, W. Lafayette, IN 47907
Target Audience: Adults
Notes: Items, 90
Measures the subject's ability to visualize the folding into 3-dimensional objects, the rotation of 3-dimensional objects and how 3-dimensional objects look from various viewing positions. Comes in 2 forms: the longer form has 90 questions; the shorter version 36 items.

9202
SRA Achievement Series, Forms 1 and 2, 1978 Edition: Level A. Naslund, Robert A.; And Others 1978
Subtests: Reading; Mathematics
Descriptors: *Academic Achievement; *Academic Aptitude; *Achievement Tests; Auditory Discrimination; *Elementary School Mathematics; Elementary School Students; *Grade 1; *Kindergarten Children; Mathematical Concepts; Primary Education; *Reading Skills; *Visual Discrimination
Identifiers: ACH; Test Batteries
Availability: Science Research Associates, Inc.; 155 N. Wacker Dr., Chicago, IL 60606
Grade Level: K-1
Notes: Time, 180 approx.; Items, 140
Designed to measure basic skills taught in kindergarten in reading readiness and mathematics concepts. No reading is required of students. Recommended for administration in spring of kindergarten year or fall grade one. Educational Ability Series (EAS) provides an estimate of educational ability. EAS is optional and designed to be used in conjunction with the Achievement Series. Has new norms collected for 1983-84.

9203
SRA Achievement Series, Forms 1 and 2, 1978 Edition: Level B. Naslund, Robert A.; And Others 1978
Subtests: Reading; Mathematics
Descriptors: *Academic Achievement; *Academic Aptitude; *Achievement Tests; Computation; *Elementary School Mathematics; *Elementary School Students; *Grade 1; *Grade 2; Mathematical Concepts; Primary Education; *Reading Skills
Identifiers: ACH; Test Batteries
Availability: Science Research Associates, Inc.; 155 N. Wacker Dr., Chicago, IL 60606
Grade Level: 1-2
Notes: Time, 195 approx.; Items, 176
Designed to measure basic skills taught in grade 1 in reading and mathematics. Recommended for administration in spring grade 1 and fall grade 2. Educational Ability Series (EAS) provides an estimate of educational ability. EAS is optional and designed for use in conjunction with the Achievement Series. Items are read aloud and measure vocabulary, number concepts, picture grouping, and manipulation of forms in space. A Reading only edition is also available at this level. Has new norms collected for 1983-84.

9204
SRA Achievement Series, Forms 1 and 2, 1978 Edition: Level C. Naslund, Robert A.; And Others 1978
Subtests: Reading; Mathematics; Language Arts
Descriptors: *Academic Achievement; *Academic Aptitude; *Achievement Tests; *Elementary School Mathematics; Elementary School Students; Grade 2; Grade 3; *Language Arts; Primary Education; *Reading Skills
Identifiers: ACH; Test Batteries
Availability: Science Research Associates, Inc.; 155 N. Wacker Dr., Chicago, IL 60606
Grade Level: 2-3
Notes: Time, 220 approx.; Items, 220
Designed to measure basic skills in reading, mathematics, and language arts. Recommended for administration in spring grade 2 and fall grade 3. Educational Ability Series (EAS) provides an estimate of educational ability. EAS is optional and designed for use in conjunction with the Achievement Series. Items are read aloud and measure vocabulary, number concepts, picture grouping, and ma-

nipulation of forms in space. A Reading only edition is also available at this level. Has new norms collected for 1983-84.

9205
SRA Achievement Series, Forms 1 and 2, 1978 Edition: Level D. Naslund, Robert A.; And Others 1978
Subtests: Reading, Mathematics; Language Arts
Descriptors: *Academic Achievement; *Academic Aptitude; *Achievement Tests; Elementary Education; *Elementary School Mathematics; *Elementary School Students; Grade 3; Grade 4; *Language Arts; Reading Skills
Identifiers: ACH; Test Batteries
Availability: Science Research Associates, Inc.; 155 N. Wacker Dr., Chicago, IL 60606
Grade Level: 3-4
Notes: Time, 197 approx.; Items, 256
Designed to measure basic skills in reading, mathematics, and language arts. Recommended for administration in spring grade 3 and fall grade 4. Educational Ability Series (EAS) provides an estimate of educational ability. EAS is optional and designed for use in conjunction with the Achievement Series. Items are read aloud and measure vocabulary, number concepts, picture grouping, and manipulation of forms in space. A Reading only edition is also available at this level. Has new norms collected for 1983-84.

9206
SRA Achievement Series, Forms 1 and 2, 1978 Edition: Level E. Naslund, Robert A.; And Others 1978
Subtests: Reading; Mathematics; Language Arts; Reference Materials; Social Studies; Science
Descriptors: *Academic Achievement; *Academic Aptitude; *Achievement Tests; Elementary School Mathematics; Elementary School Science; *Elementary School Students; Intermediate Grades; Language Arts; Library Skills; Reading Skills; Social Studies
Identifiers: ACH; Test Batteries
Availability: Science Research Associates, Inc.; 155 N. Wacker Dr., Chicago, IL 60606
Grade Level: 4-6
Notes: Time, 305 approx.; Items, 465
Designed to measure basic skills in reading, mathematics, language arts, use of reference materials, social studies, and science. A shorter version of the test, the 3R edition, includes tests in reading, mathematics, and language arts only. Educational Ability Series is optional and designed for use in conjunction with the Achievement series. EAS provides an estimate of educational ability. Has new norms collected for 1983-84.

9207
SRA Achievement Series, Forms 1 and 2, 1978 Edition: Level F. Naslund, Robert A.; And Others 1978
Subtests: Reading; Mathematics; Language Arts; Reference Materials; Social Studies; Science
Descriptors: *Academic Achievement; *Academic Aptitude; *Achievement Tests; *Elementary School Students; Elementary Secondary Education; Grade 6; Grade 7; Grade 8; Language Arts; Library Skills; *Mathematics; *Reading Skills; Secondary School Science; Social Studies
Identifiers: ACH; Test Batteries
Availability: Science Research Associates, Inc.; 155 N. Wacker Dr., Chicago, IL 60606
Grade Level: 6-8
Notes: Time, 305 approx.; Items, 465
Designed to measure basic skills in reading, mathematics, social studies, and science. A shorter version of the test, the 3R edition, includes tests in reading, mathematics, and language arts only. Educational Ability Series is optional and designed for use in conjunction with the Achievement series. EAS provides an estimate of educational ability. Has new norms collected for 1983-84.

9208
SRA Achievement Series, Forms 1 and 2, 1978 Edition: Level G. Naslund, Robert A.; And Others 1978
Subtests: Reading; Mathematics; Language Arts; Reference Materials; Social Studies; Science
Descriptors: *Academic Achievement; *Academic Aptitude; *Achievement Tests; Language Arts; Library Skills; *Reading Skills; Secondary Education; Secondary School Mathematics; Secondary School Science; *Secondary School Students; Social Studies
Identifiers: ACH; Test Batteries
Availability: Science Research Associates, Inc.; 155 N. Wacker Dr., Chicago, IL 60606
Grade Level: 8-10
Notes: Time, 305 approx.; Items, 465
Designed to measure basic skills in reading, mathematics, language arts, use of reference materials, social studies, and science. A shorter version of the test, the 3R edition, includes tests in reading, mathematics, and language arts

only. Educational Ability Series is optional and designed for use in conjunction with the Achievement series. EAS provides an estimate of educational ability. Has new norms collected for 1983-84.

9209
SRA Achievement Series, Forms 1 and 2, 1978 Edition: Level H. Naslund, Robert A.; And Others 1978
Subtests: Reading; Mathematics; Language Arts; Reference Materials; Social Studies; Science; Applied Skills
Descriptors: *Academic Achievement; *Academic Aptitude; *Achievement Tests; Consumer Economics; High Schools; *High School Students; Language Arts; Library Skills; Reading Skills; Secondary School Mathematics; Secondary School Science; Social Studies
Identifiers: ACH; Test Batteries
Availability: Science Research Associates, Inc.; 155 N. Wacker Dr., Chicago, IL 60606
Grade Level: 9-12
Notes: Time, 305 approx.; Items, 420
Designed to measure basic skills in reading, mathematics, language arts, use of reference materials, social studies and science. The Educational Ability Series (EAS) is optional and designed for use in conjunction with the Achievement series. EAS provides an estimate of educational ability. The subtest, Applied Skills, measures the following areas of adult life: consumer economics, health and safety, employment, and community resources. Has new norms collected for 1983-84.

9214
Pennsylvania Preschool Inventory, 1978 Revision. Dusewicz, R.A.; Lutz, C.H. 1978
Descriptors: *Cognitive Development; Human Body; Individual Testing; Number Concepts; *Preschool Children; *Preschool Tests; *School Readiness Tests; Self Concept; Spatial Ability; Young Children
Identifiers: Analogies; Picture Identification Test; Picture Inventory; PPI
Availability: Pennsylvania State Dept. of Education; Harrisburg, PA 17108
Target Audience: 3-6
Notes: Time, 15 approx; Items, 61
1978 Revised Edition of a test designed to assess the cognitive development of preschool children, serving as a rapid but reliable means of evaluation. Space is provided on each score sheet for subjective comments relevant to the child's performance on the test. Areas covered include: passive vocabulary; complementary relationships, noncomplementary relationships, number concepts, verbal analogies, and awareness of self.

9264
SOI Learning Abilities Test. Meeker, Mary; Meeker, Robert 1975
Subtests: Memory Divergent Production; Evaluation; Cognition; Convergent Production
Descriptors: Academic Ability; Adults; *Cognitive Ability; Convergent Thinking; Creativity; Decision Making; Diagnostic Teaching; *Diagnostic Tests; Divergent Thinking; *Educational Diagnosis; *Elementary School Students; Elementary Secondary Education; Mathematical Concepts; Memory; Reading Skills; *Secondary School Students; Spatial Ability
Identifiers: Guilford (JP); SOI (LA); *Structure of Intellect
Availability: SOI Systems; P.O. Box D, Vida, OR 97488
Grade Level: 2-12
Target Audience: Adults
Designed to assess specific learning abilities which research has shown to be foundational cluster for a student's learning of reading and arithmetic. Three levels of difficulty are: beginning level, intermediate level, and advanced level. All students should begin at first level to establish a basal level of performance and to ensure student understands what is to be done for each subtest. Subtests are based on Guilford's Structure of Intellect (SI) factors.

9265
SOI Learning Abilities Test: Special Edition, K-1. Meeker, Mary; And Others 1975
Subtests: Memory; Divergent Production; Evaluation; Cognition; Convergent Production
Descriptors: *Cognitive Ability; *Diagnostic Teaching; *Diagnostic Tests; *Educational Diagnosis; Elementary School Students; Gifted; *Grade 1; *Kindergarten Children; Learning Disabilities; Mathematical Concepts; Primary Education; Reading Skills; *Special Education
Identifiers: Guilford (JP); *Structure of Intellect
Availability: SOI Systems; P.O. Box D, Vida, OR 97488
Grade Level: K-1

Basal level of achievement drawn from regular version of SOI Learning Abilities Test. Designed for young children and those with special needs such as mentally gifted and learning handicapped children. Students who pass all items on any subtest or do extremely well on test in general should be tested on regular revision of SOI-LA where there are 2 higher levels of difficulty.

9266
SOI Learning Abilities Test: Reading Readiness. Meeker, Mary; Meeker, Robert 1975
Descriptors: *Cognitive Ability; Convergent Thinking; Diagnostic Teaching; Divergent Thinking; Pictorial Stimuli; *Preschool Children; Preschool Education; *Reading Diagnosis; *Reading Readiness; *Reading Readiness Tests
Identifiers: Guilford (JP); *Structure of Intellect
Availability: SOI Systems; P.O. Box D, Vida, OR 97488
Target Audience: 2-5
Designed to measure level of student's reading readiness. May be used to derive a reading readiness training program. Any student who gets all items correct should be administered SOI Basic test to establish upper limits.

9267
SOI Screening Form for Gifted. Meeker, Mary; Meeker, Robert 1975
Descriptors: *Ability Identification; *Cognitive Ability; Convergent Thinking; Divergent Thinking; Elementary Education; *Elementary School Students; *Gifted; *Screening Tests
Identifiers: Guilford (JP); *Structure of Intellect
Availability: SOI Systems; P.O. Box D, Vida, OR 97488
Grade Level: 1-6
Notes: Time, 30 approx.
Designed to identify those students who should be tested further for gifted qualification.

9364
Inventory of Piaget's Developmental Tasks. Furth, Hans 1970
Subtests: Quantity; Levels; Sequence; Weight; Matrix; Symbols; Perspective; Movement; Volume; Seriation; Rotation; Angles; Shadows; Classes; Inclusion; Inference; Probability
Descriptors: Adolescents; Children; *Cognitive Tests; *Concept Formation; *Developmental Stages; Multiple Choice Tests
Identifiers: *Piagetian Tasks; TIM(E)
Availability: Tests in Microfiche; Test Collection, Educational Testing Service, Princeton, NJ 08541
Target Audience: 8-14
Notes: Items, 72
A paper and pencil version of Piaget's tasks. It is intended for children from age 8 to mid-adolescence. There are 18 problem areas each consisting of 1 example and 4 questions. The inventory is untimed.

9371
Minnesota Spatial Relations Test. Davis, Rene V. 1979
Descriptors: *Adults; High Schools; *High School Students; Individual Testing; *Spatial Ability
Identifiers: MSRT
Availability: American Guidance Service; Publishers' Bldg., Circle Pines, MN 55014
Target Audience: 14-64
Notes: Time, 20 approx.
Designed to assess speed and accuracy in the discrimination of 3-dimensional geometric shapes. Used to assess spatial visualization ability.

9450
School and College Ability Tests: Series III, Elementary Level. Educational Testing Service, Princeton, NJ 1979
Subtests: Verbal; Quantitative
Descriptors: *Academic Aptitude; *Aptitude Tests; Elementary Education; *Elementary School Students; Intermediate Grades; *Mathematics; Nonverbal Ability; *Predictive Measurement; *Verbal Ability
Identifiers: SCAT Series III
Availability: Publishers Test Service; 2500 Garden Rd., Monterey, CA 93940
Grade Level: 3-6
Notes: Time, 40 approx.; Items, 100
Designed to measure verbal and quantitative concept development. Forms X and Y are available. Standardized concurrently with STEP III.

9451
School and College Ability Tests: Series III, Intermediate Level. Educational Testing Service, Princeton, NJ 1979
Subtests: Verbal; Quantitative

Descriptors: *Academic Aptitude; *Aptitude Tests;
*Grade 6; Intermediate Grades; Junior High
Schools; *Junior High School Students;
*Mathematics; Nonverbal Ability; *Predictive
Measurement; *Verbal Ability
Identifiers: SCAT Series III
Availability: Publishers Test Service; 2500 Garden
Rd., Monterey, CA 93940
Grade Level: 6-9
Notes: Time, 40 approx.; Items, 100

Designed to measure verbal and quantitative concept development. Forms X and Y are available. Standardized
concurrently with STEP III.

9452
**School and College Ability Tests: Series III, Ad-
vanced Level.** Educational Testing Service,
Princeton, NJ 1979
Subtests: Verbal; Quantitative
Descriptors: *Academic Aptitude; *Aptitude Tests;
High Schools; *High School Students;
*Mathematics; Nonverbal Ability; *Predictive
Measurement; *Verbal Ability
Identifiers: SCAT Series III
Availability: Publishers Test Service; 2500 Garden
Rd., Monterey, CA 93940
Grade Level: 9-12
Notes: Time, 40 approx.; Items, 100

Designed to measure verbal and quantitative concept development. Forms X and Y are available. Standardized
concurrently with STEP III.

9455
**Cognitive Abilities Test Multilevel Edition, Form
3.** Thorndike, Robert L.; Hagen, Elizabeth 1978
Subtests: Verbal; Quantitative; Nonverbal
Descriptors: Academic Aptitude; *Cognitive Abil-
ity; *Cognitive Tests; *Elementary School Stu-
dents; Elementary Secondary Education; Math-
ematics Tests; *Secondary School Students;
*Spatial Ability; Verbal Tests
Availability: Riverside Publishing Co.; 3 O'Hare
Towers, 8420 Bryn Mawr Ave., Chicago, IL
60631
Grade Level: 3-12
Notes: Time, 98; Items, 240

Consists of 3 test batteries. Verbal battery is composed of
vocabulary, sentence completion, verbal classification, and
verbal analogies. The quantitative battery is composed of
quantitative relations, number series, and equation building. The Nonverbal battery consists of figure classification,
figure analogies and figure synthesis. The verbal battery
has 100 items and requires 34 minutes working time. The
quantitative battery has 60 items and requires 32 minutes.
The nonverbal battery has 80 items and requires 32 minutes.

9488
Measure of Object Permanence. Bell, Silvia M.
Descriptors: Child Development; *Concept Forma-
tion; Infant Behavior; *Infants; *Object Perma-
nence; Performance Tests
Identifiers: Piaget (Jean)
Availability: ASIS/NAPS; c/o Microfiche Publica-
tions, P.O. Box 3513, Grand Central Station,
New York NY 10163-3513 (Document œ00965)
Target Audience: 0-2

Designed to assess infant's ability to find an object which
attracted his/her attention when it is hidden behind a
"screen." Infant is observed to see if he/she indicates
location of object.

9489
Measure of Person Permanence. Bell, Silvia M.
Descriptors: Child Development; *Concept Forma-
tion; Infant Behavior; *Infants; Mothers; Perfor-
mance Tests
Identifiers: Person Performance; Piaget (Jean)
Availability: ASIS/NAPS; c/o Microfiche Publica-
tions, P.O. Box 3513, Grand Central Station,
New York NY 10163-3513 (Document œ00965)
Target Audience: 0-2

Designed to assess infant's ability to locate his/her mother
when she hides behind a "screen." Infant is observed to
watch for indications mother has been located.

9512
Impression Formation Test. Streufert, Siegfried;
Driver, Michael J. 1967
Descriptors: *Concept Formation; Higher Educa-
tion; Human Relations; *Individual Characteris-
tics; Perception; *Personality Assessment; Social
Influences; Undergraduate Students
Identifiers: *Complexity Theory; *Perceptual So-
cial Complexity
Availability: Educational and Psychological Mea-
surement; v27 n4 p1025-39, Win 1967
Grade Level: 13-16
Notes: Time, 50; Items, 15

Sentence completion designed to measure perceptual social
complexity. Subject describes 2 individuals using separate
sets of 3 adjectives and then must use both sets to describe a third person. Subjects are scored on the degree to
which their descriptions show integration and differentiation.

9535
Piaget—Poincare Test. Meeker, Mary 1963
Descriptors: Cognitive Development; *Cognitive
Tests; *Compensation (Concept); *Concept For-
mation; *Conservation (Concept); Elementary
Education; Elementary School Students; Perfor-
mance Tests; Preschool Children; Preschool
Education
Identifiers: *Piaget (Jean)
Availability: SOI Systems; P.O. Box D, Vida, OR
97488
Target Audience: 2-12

The Piagetian tasks are analyzed in terms of Guilford's
structure of intellect.

9536
A Rating Scale for Identifying Creative Potential.
Meeker, Mary
Descriptors: *Creativity; Creativity Tests; Elemen-
tary Secondary Education; Identification; Rating
Scales; Talent; Talent Identification
Availability: SOI Systems; P.O. Box D, Vida, OR
97488
Grade Level: K-12
Target Audience: 5-17
Notes: Items, 11

For rating students in sensitivity, fluency, flexibility, originality, organizing and synthesizing ability, perseverance,
energy, impatience with routine.

9537
FSM SOI Group Memory Test. Meeker, Mary
1973
Descriptors: *Aptitude Tests; Auditory Stimuli;
*Memory; Numbers; Pictorial Stimuli; Primary
Education; Retention (Psychology); Verbal Stim-
uli; Young Children
Identifiers: *Guilfords Structure of Intellect
Availability: SOI Systems; P.O. Box D, Vida, OR
97488
Grade Level: K-3
Target Audience: 5-8
Notes: Time, 5; Items, 19

Measures memory span, using figural, symbolic, and semantic stimuli.

9552
Adaptability Test. Tiffin, Joseph; Lawshe, C.H.
1942
Descriptors: *Adjustment (to Environment);
Adults; *Aptitude Tests; Managerial Occupa-
tions; Multiple Choice Tests; Office Occupa-
tions; *Personnel Selection; Sales Occupations;
Verbal Tests
Identifiers: *Adaptability; Factory Occupations
Availability: Science Research Associates, Inc.;
155 N. Wacker Dr., Chicago, IL 60606
Target Audience: Adults
Notes: Time, 15; Items, 35

Designed to measure mental adaptability or alertness. Can
be used to distinguish between adaptable employees and
those more suited to routine jobs. Not for poor readers or
high level executives.

9567
Extended Merrill-Palmer Scale. Ball, Rachel Stut-
sman; And Others 1978
Descriptors: *Divergent Thinking; *Evaluative
Thinking; Individual Testing; Intelligence;
*Intelligence Tests; *Preschool Children; Pro-
ductive Thinking
Identifiers: Structure of Intellect
Availability: Stoelting Co.; 620 Wheat Ln., Wood
Dale, IL 60191
Target Audience: 3-5
Notes: Items, 16

Profile yields a composite score for each of 4 dimensions:
semantic production, figural production, semantic evaluation, and figural evaluation. Individually administered.

9577
Check-List Description of Nations. Scott, William
A.; Blight, Charles 1970
Subtests: Rating of Nations for Check-List De-
scription (10)
Descriptors: *Adults; *Check Lists; *Cognitive
Measurement; *Cognitive Processes; Theories
Availability: William A. Scott; Dept. of Psychol-
ogy, University of Colorado, Boulder, CO
80302
Target Audience: Adults
Notes: Items, 720

Measures the structural properties of cognition about a
particular domain of events (nations).

9578
**Checklist of Similarities and Differences between
Nations.** Scott, William A. 1970
Descriptors: *Adults; *Check Lists; *Cognitive
Measurement; *Cognitive Processes; Theories
Availability: William A. Scott; Dept. of Psychol-
ogy, University of Colorado, Boulder, CO
80302
Target Audience: Adults
Notes: Items, 10

Measures structural properties of cognition about a particular domain of events (nations).

9579
Grouping Nations on Specified Attributes. Scott,
William A. 1970
Descriptors: *Adults; *Classification; *Cognitive
Measurement; *Cognitive Processes; Objective
Tests; Rating Scales; Theories
Availability: William A. Scott; Dept. of Psychol-
ogy, University of Colorado, Boulder, CO
80302
Target Audience: Adults
Notes: Items, 30

Measures structural properties of cognition about a particular domain of events (nations).

9580
Homogenizing Sets of Nations. Scott, William A.
1970
Descriptors: Adults; Attitude Measures; *Cognitive
Measurement; *Cognitive Processes; *Foreign
Countries
Availability: William A. Scott; Dept. of Psychol-
ogy, University of Colorado, Boulder, CO
80302
Target Audience: Adults
Notes: Items, 29

Designed to measure the structural properties of cognition
about a particular domain of events, specifically nations of
the world. Subjects indicate why they feel certain ones are
grouped together on a prepared list and then rate a list of
others on a 7-point scale of like-dislike.

9581
Listing and Comparing Nations. Scott, William
A.; Laver, John E. 1970
Descriptors: *Adults; *Classification; *Cognitive
Measurement; *Cognitive Processes; Computer
Software; Objective Tests; Theories
Availability: William A. Scott; Dept. of Psychol-
ogy, University of Colorado, Boulder, CO
80302
Target Audience: Adults
Notes: Items, 12

Measures the structural properties of cognition about a
particular domain of events (nations).

9582
Most Similar Pairs of Nations. Scott, William A.
1970
Descriptors: *Adults; *Cognitive Measurement;
*Cognitive Processes; Computer Software;
*Objective Tests; Theories
Availability: William A. Scott; Dept. of Psychol-
ogy, University of Colorado, Boulder, CO
80302
Target Audience: Adults
Notes: Items, 3

Measures the structural properties of cognition about a
particular domain of events (nations).

9583
Open Description and Rating—Nations. Scott,
William A. 1970
Descriptors: *Adults; *Cognitive Measurement;
*Cognitive Processes; Computer Software;
*Essay Tests; Rating Scales; Theories
Availability: William A. Scott; Dept. of Psychol-
ogy, University of Colorado, Boulder, CO
80302
Target Audience: Adults
Notes: Items, 34

Measures the structural properties of cognition about a
particular domain of events (nations).

9584
Rating of Nations. Scott, William A.; And Others
1970
Descriptors: Likert Scales; *Adults; *Cognitive
Measurement; *Cognitive Processes; Computer
Software; Theories
Availability: William A. Scott; Dept. of Psychol-
ogy, University of Colorado, Boulder, CO
80302
Target Audience: Adults
Notes: Items, 40

Measures the structural properties of cognition about a
particular domain of events (nations).

9585
Similarities and Differences between Nations.
Scott, William A. 1970
Descriptors: *Adults; *Classification; *Cognitive
Measurement; *Cognitive Processes; Computer
Software; Theories
Availability: William A. Scott; Dept. of Psychol-
ogy, University of Colorado, Boulder, CO
80302
Target Audience: Adults
Notes: Items, 5
Measures the structural properties of cognition about a
particular domain of events (nations).

9586
Similarity of Paired Nations. Scott, William A.
1970
Descriptors: *Adults; *Cognitive Measurement;
*Cognitive Processes; Computer Software;
*Rating Scales; Theories
Availability: William A. Scott; Dept. of Psychol-
ogy, University of Colorado, Boulder, CO
80302
Target Audience: Adults
Notes: Items, 40
Measures structural properties of cognition about a par-
ticular domain of events (nations).

9666
Barrio Test of Primary Abilities (Form A).
Oliveria, Arnulfo L. 1972
Descriptors: Adults; Cultural Awareness;
*Elementary School Teachers; *Intelligence
Tests; *Spanish Speaking; *Testing Problems
Availability: Educational Leadership; p169-70,
Nov 1972
Target Audience: Adults
Notes: Items, 16
An intelligence test for teachers working with Spanish-
speaking students. Designed to raise the consciousness of
teachers about the problems of students from the barrio.

9672
The You Test. Maw, Wallace H.; Maw, Ethel W.
1961
Subtests: What Would You Do (26); Which Say-
ing Do You Believe (16); You Find the Answer
(1); Can You Solve the Code (12); You Ask the
Questions (1)
Descriptors: Academic Aptitude; *Aptitude Tests;
Curiosity; Elementary Education; *Elementary
School Students; *Problem Solving; Question-
naires; Student Attitudes
Availability: Wallace H. Maw; College of Human
Resources, Dept. of Individual and Family
Studies, 101 Alison Hall, University of Dela-
ware, Newark, DE 19711
Grade Level: K-6
Notes: Items, 54
Measures children's problem-solving ability, curiosity, and
interests.

9696
Letter Association Scale. Browman, Carl P.; And
Others 1977
Descriptors: *Association (Psychology); Higher
Education; *Letters (Alphabet); *Rating Scales;
Undergraduate Students
Availability: Carl P. Browman; Psychiatry and Be-
havioral Science, State University of New York,
Stony Brook, NY 11794
Grade Level: 13-16
Notes: Items, 111
Designed to measure subjects' perceptions of the relative
associative strength of single letters and ordered letter
sequences.

9708
Information Test of Intelligence. Guthrie, George
M. 1970
Descriptors: *Adults; Cultural Influences; *Culture
Fair Tests; Foreign Countries; *Intelligence
Tests; *Rural Population; Test Bias; Testing
Problems
Identifiers: *Philippines
Availability: ERIC Document Reproduction Ser-
vice; 3900 Wheeler Ave., Alexandria, VA 22304
(ED054212, 11 pages)
Target Audience: Adults
Notes: Items, 25
Constructed for use with rural Filipinos. Questions are
based on experiences common to this population. Cannot
be used to compare groups from markedly different cul-
tural backgrounds.

9711
Object Sorting Task. Dunn, James A. 1969
Descriptors: *Cognitive Development; *Cognitive
Measurement; Concept Formation; Elementary
Education; Elementary School Students;
*Intelligence; Intelligence Tests

Availability: ERIC Document Reproduction Service; 3900 Wheeler Ave., Alexandria, VA 22304
(ED036808, 26 pages)
Grade Level: K-6
Notes: Time, 20 approx
Model underlying this test assumes that one's intellect at
any moment is the set of all information one has at one's
disposal at that moment. The test involves object sorting
tests based on a variety of attribute dimensions of the 6
plastic blocks.

9713
Number Series. Form A. Robinson, Pamela Eliza-
beth 1970
Descriptors: *Cognitive Ability; *Cognitive Tests;
Correlation; Grade 5; *Induction; *Intelligence;
Intermediate Grades; Learning; Measurement
Techniques
Availability: ERIC Document Reproduction Ser-
vice; 3900 Wheeler Ave., Alexandria, VA 22304
(ED043086, 101 pages)
Grade Level: 5
Notes: Time, 20; Items, 35
One of 2 measures of cognitive ability to be used in
studying the nature of intelligence. Test is characterized by
a task requiring a student to find an underlying rule or
principle for each item. Test is based on Guilford's Cogni-
tion of Symbolic Systems factors. Form B consists of 30
items.

9714
Circle Reasoning. Form A. Robinson, Pamela
Elizabeth 1970
Descriptors: *Cognitive Ability; *Cognitive Tests;
Correlation; Grade 5; *Induction; *Intelligence;
Intermediate Grades; Learning; Measurement
Techniques
Availability: ERIC Document Reproduction Ser-
vice; 3900 Wheeler Ave., Alexandria, VA 22304
(ED043086, 101 pages)
Grade Level: 5
Notes: Time, 20; Items, 30
One of 2 measures of cognitive ability to be used in
studying the nature of intelligence. Test is characterized by
a task requiring a student to find an underlying rule or
principle for each item. Test is based on Guilford's Cogni-
tion of Symbolic Systems factors. Form B consists of 25
items.

9716
Test Wiseness Scale. Diamond, James J.; Evans,
W. 1972
Subtests: Longest Alternative; Grammatical Clues;
Specific Determiners; Association; Overlapping
Distractors
Descriptors: *Cognitive Ability; *Elementary
School Students; Guessing (Tests); Intentional
Learning; Intermediate Grades; *Multiple
Choice Tests; Problem Solving; *Test Wiseness
Identifiers: TIM(F)
Availability: Tests in Microfiche; Test Collection,
Educational Testing Service, Princeton, NJ
08541
Grade Level: 5-6
Notes: Items, 30
Designed to test children's ability to use extraneous clues
to answer test questions. Uses fictitious material.

9743
The Springs Task. Linn, Marcia C.; Rica, Marian
R. 1978
Descriptors: *Ability Identification; Adolescents;
Children; *Critical Thinking; *Experiments;
*Logical Thinking
Identifiers: *Reasoning
Availability: ERIC Document Reproduction Ser-
vice; 3900 Wheeler Ave., Alexandria, VA 22304
(ED163092, 13 pages)
Target Audience: 11-16
Notes: Time, 15; Items, 5
Individually administered apparatus-based task to measure
ability to criticize and control experiments, to name vari-
ables, and to analyze results.

9756
Langdon Adult Intelligence Test. Langdon, Kevin
1978
Descriptors: *Adults; Intelligence Quotient;
*Intelligence Tests; Multiple Choice Tests
Identifiers: Four Sigma Society
Availability: Four Sigma Society; P.O. Box 795,
Berkeley, CA 94701
Target Audience: Adults
Notes: Items, 56
Untimed self-administered 56-item test purported to mea-
sure intelligence quotients (IQ) in the 130-170 range. Test
is sent to Four Sigma Society for scoring.

9757
Preschool Inventory, Spanish Edition. Caldwell,
Bettye M. 1974

Descriptors: Academic Achievement; *Learning
Readiness; Preschool Education; *School Readi-
ness Tests; *Spanish Speaking
Availability: Publishers Test Service; 2500 Garden
Rd., Monterey, CA 93940
Target Audience: 3-5
Notes: Time, 30; Items, 64
Screening test for achievement in areas necessary for suc-
cess in school. Reveals degree of disadvantage of a child
entering school. Covers self-knowledge, ability to follow
directions, verbal expression, basic numerical concepts,
and sensory attributes. Fall norms are based on a Head
Start population.

9761
Cognitive Abilities Test. Primary Battery, Form 3.
Thorndike, Robert L.; Hagen, Elizabeth 1978
Subtests: Cognitive Abilities Test, Level 1: Cog-
nitive Abilities Test, Level 2
Descriptors: *Academic Aptitude; *Cognitive Abil-
ity; Elementary School Students; *Learning
Readiness; Mathematical Concepts; Pictorial
Stimuli; Primary Education; *Visual Measures;
Vocabulary
Identifiers: *Oral Tests
Availability: Riverside Publishing Co.; 8420 Bryn
Mawr Ave., Chicago, IL 60631
Grade Level: K-3
Notes: Time, 60 approx.; Items, 182
Orally administered. Designed to provide information on
the development of skills necessary to function in school.
Subtests include relational concepts, object classification,
quantitative, concepts, oral vocabulary.

9781
School Readiness Test, Spanish Language Edition.
Anderhalter, O.F. 1977
Subtests: Word Recognition (15); Identifying Let-
ters (20): Visual Discrimination (15); Handwrit-
ing Readiness (10); Auditory Discrimination
(13); Comprehension and Interpretation (12);
Number Readiness (30)
Descriptors: Auditory Discrimination; Comprehen-
sion; Early Childhood Education; Handwriting;
Writing Readiness; *Kindergarten; Letters
(Alphabet); Numbers; *School Readiness Tests;
*Spanish Speaking; Visual Discrimination;
Word Recognition
Availability: Scholastic Testing Service; 480 Meyer
Rd. Bensenville, IL 60106
Grade Level: K-1
Notes: Time, 60; Items, 115
Group administered at end of grade K or before third full
week of grade 1. Test results place child at 1 of 6 readi-
ness levels: Long Delay, Short Delay, Marginal, Average
Ready, Superior Ready, Gifted Ready

9817
Cognitive Complexity Test. Bieri, James
Descriptors: Adults; *Cognitive Measurement;
*Cognitive Style; Cognitive Tests; *Interpersonal
Relationship; Social Behavior
Availability: Bieri, James and Others. The Discrimination of Behavioral Information. Huntington, NY: Robert E. Krieger Publishing Co.,
1975
Target Audience: Adults
Notes: Items, 10
Modified version of the Rep Test for assessing cognitive
complexity. Uses a 10 by 10 grid. Each of 10 columns is
identified by a different role type selected to be representative of persons who are important in rater's social
environment. After identifying 10 people who best correspond to 10 role types, rater uses 6-point Likert scale to
rate those individuals selected.

9818
Instruments for Assessing Creativity. Wallach,
Michael A.; Kogan, Nathan
Descriptors: Children; Creativity; *Creativity Re-
search; *Creativity Tests; *Grade 5; Intermedi-
ate Grades; Verbal Stimuli; Visual Stimuli
Availability: Wallach, Michael A. and Nathan
Kogan. Modes of Thinking in Young Children:
A Study of the Creativity-Intelligence Distinc-
tion. New York: Holt, Rinehart and Winston,
1965
Grade Level: 5
Five procedures used to explore creativity; 2 are visual
and 3 verbal. Verbal techniques are called instances, alternate uses, and similarities. The 2 visual techniques are
pattern meanings and line meanings.

9820
Measures of Breadth of Categorization. Wallach,
Michael A.; Caron, A.J.
Descriptors: Children; *Cognitive Style; Creativity;
*Creativity Tests; *Grade 5; Intermediate
Grades; Personality Assessment
Identifiers: *Choice Behavior; *Classification
(Cognitive Process)

Availability: Wallach, Michael A. and Nathan Kogan. Modes of Thinking in Young Children: A Study of the Creativity-Intelligence Distinction. New York: Holt, Rinehart and Winston, 1965
Grade Level: 5
Notes: Items, 12
Children's version of the 1958 Pettigrew category-width test (TC007274). Used to assess children's categorizing and conceptualizing processes.

9821
Measures of Conceptual Style. Kogan, Jerome; And Others
Descriptors: *Children; *Cognitive Style; Creativity; *Creativity Tests; *Grade 5; Intermediate Grades
Identifiers: Choice Behavior; *Classification (Cognitive Process)
Availability: Wallach, Michael A. and Nathan Kogan. Modes of Thinking in Young Children: A Study of the Creativity-Intelligence Distinction. New York: Holt, Rinehart and Winston, 1965
Grade Level: 5
Categories used in scoring reasons provided by child for sorting objects are descriptive, inferential, and relational. For thematic integration, children use set of 4 words to make up a study.

9822
Fantasy Measure. Miller, D.R.; Swanson, G.E.
Descriptors: *Children; Creativity; Creativity Tests; Failure; *Grade 5; Intermediate Grades; Personality; *Personality Measures; *Story Telling
Identifiers: Defensiveness
Availability: Wallach, Michael A. and Nathan Kogan. Modes of Thinking in Young Children: A Study of the Creativity-Intelligence Distinction. New York: Holt, Rinehart and Winston, 1965
Grade Level: 5
Notes: Items, 5
Children complete stories in which main character is a child under stress of failure.

9823
Measures of Physiognomic Sensitivity. Sarbin, T.; Hardyck, C.D.
Descriptors: *Children; Creativity; *Creativity Tests; *Grade 5; Intermediate Grades; *Projective Measures; Visual Measures
Identifiers: *Physiognomy
Availability: Wallach, Michael A. and Nathan Kogan. Modes of Thinking in Young Children: A Study of the Creativity-Intelligence Distinction. New York: Holt, Rinehart and Winston, 1965
Grade Level: 5
Notes: Items, (73)
Four procedures explore child's ability to describe affective properties of visual data: free descriptions of stick figures; free descriptions of paths; emotive connotations of abstract patterns; bizarre emotive attributions for stick figures.

9825
Body Image Rating Scale. Cratty, Bryant J.
Descriptors: *Body Image; Elementary School Students; Motor Development; Perceptual Development; *Rating Scales; *Young Children
Availability: Cratty, Bryant J. Perceptual and Motor Development in Infants and Children. New York: Macmillan, 1970
Target Audience: 4-7
Notes: Items, 16
Two major concepts underlie this scale: the body image is formed at the conceptual, as well as the dynamic, level as the body interacts with objects in the environment and correct assessment of developmental stages in the acquisition of body image requires both static and dynamic judgments.

9830
Precausal Thinking Questionnaires. Laurendeau, Monique; Pinard, Adrien 1962
Subtests: The Concept of Dream; The Concept of Life; The Origin of Night; The Movement of Clouds; The Floating and Sinking of Objects
Descriptors: Children; *Cognitive Processes; *Intellectual Development; Motion; Questionnaires; Realism; Verbal Tests
Identifiers: Animism; Piagetian Measures; Precausal Thinking
Availability: Laurendeau, Monique and Adrien Pinard. Causal Thinking in the Child: A Genetic and Experimental Approach. New York: International Universities Press, 1962
Target Audience: 4-12
Notes: Items, (161)

Series of verbal interview type measures in which a series of problems are discussed with the child such as "Why doesn't a marble float?" The child's responses indicate the age at which stages of intellectual evolution are reached. Part of a study to verify Piaget's conclusions on forms of precausal thinking; realism; animism; artificialism; dynamism; and understanding of physical laws.

9837
Liquid Quantity Conservation Task. Hess, Robert D.; Shipman, Virginia C. 1967
Descriptors: Academic Achievement; Black Mothers; *Black Students; Cognitive Development; Conceptual Tempo; Economic Factors; Family Environment; Individual Testing; Longitudinal Studies; *Parent Child Relationship; Parent Influence; *Preschool Children; Preschool Education; Questionnaires; Reading Readiness
Identifiers: Project Head Start
Availability: ERIC Document Reproduction Service; 3900 Wheeler Ave., Alexandria, VA 22304 (ED022550, 68 pages)
Target Audience: 2-5
One of a series of instruments designed to measure child's cognitive abilities, impulsivity, and reading readiness and the mother's attitudes about school, her intelligence level, and her flexibility of thought. The instruments were developed for use in a study of mothers and their preschool children to determine the differential effects of middle and lower socioeconomic group cognitive environments on Black urban preschool children.

9838
Length Conservation Task. Hess, Robert D.; Shipman, Virginia C. 1967
Descriptors: *Black Mothers; *Black Students; Cognitive Development; Conservation (Concept); Economic Factors; Family Environment; Longitudinal Studies; *Parent Child Relationship; Parent Influence; *Preschool Children; Preschool Education
Identifiers: Length; Project Head Start
Availability: ERIC Document Reproduction Service; 3900 Wheeler Ave., Alexandria, VA 22304 (ED022550, 68 pages)
Target Audience: 4-5
Notes: Items, 6
One of a series of instruments designed to measure child's cognitive abilities, impulsivity, and reading readiness and the mother's attitudes about school, her intelligence level, and her flexibility of thought. The instruments were developed for use in a study of mothers and their preschool children to determine the differential effects of middle and lower socioeconomic group cognitive environments on Black urban preschool children.

9839
Number Constancy Test. Hess, Robert D.; Shipman, Virginia C. 1967
Descriptors: *Black Mothers; *Black Students; Cognitive Development; Economic Factors; Family Environment; Longitudinal Studies; Numbers; *Parent Child Relationship; Parent Influence; *Preschool Children; Preschool Education
Identifiers: Project Head Start
Availability: ERIC Document Reproduction Service; 3900 Wheeler Ave., Alexandria, VA 22304 (ED022550, 68 pages)
Target Audience: 4-5
Notes: Items, 3
One of a series of instruments designed to measure child's cognitive abilities, impulsivity, and reading readiness and the mother's attitudes about school, her intelligence level, and her flexibility of thought. The instruments were developed for use in a study of mothers and their preschool children to determine the differential effects of middle and lower socioeconomic group cognitive environments on Black urban preschool children.

9840
Ring Segment Task. Hess, Robert D.; Shipman, Virginia C. 1967
Descriptors: *Black Mothers; *Black Students; Cognitive Development; Economic Factors; Family Environment; Longitudinal Studies; *Parent Child Relationship; Parent Influence; *Preschool Children; Preschool Education
Identifiers: Measurement (Mathematics); Project Head Start
Availability: ERIC Document Reproduction Service; 3900 Wheeler Ave., Alexandria, VA 22304 (ED022550, 68 pages)
Target Audience: 4-5
Notes: Items, 5
One of a series of instruments designed to measure child's cognitive abilities, impulsivity, and reading readiness and the mother's attitudes about school, her intelligence level, and her flexibility of thought. The instruments were developed for use in a study of mothers and their preschool

children to determine the differential effects of middle and lower socioeconomic group cognitive environments on Black urban preschool children.

9841
Generic Identity Task. Hess, Robert D.; Shipman, Virginia C. 1967
Descriptors: *Black Mothers; *Black Students; Cognitive Development; Concept Formation; Economic Factors; Family Environment; Longitudinal Studies; *Parent Child Relationship; Parent Influence; *Preschool Children; Preschool Education
Identifiers: Generic Identity; Project Head Start
Availability: ERIC Document Reproduction Service; 3900 Wheeler Ave., Alexandria, VA 22304 (ED022550, 68 pages)
Target Audience: 4-5
Notes: Items, 6
One of a series of instruments designed to measure child's cognitive abilities, impulsivity, and reading readiness and the mother's attitudes about school, her intelligence level, and her flexibility of thought. The instruments were developed for use in a study of mothers and their preschool children to determine the differential effects of middle and lower socioeconomic group cognitive environments on Black urban preschool children.

9842
Class Inclusion Task. Hess, Robert D.; Shipman, Virginia C. 1967
Descriptors: *Black Mothers; *Black Students; Classification; Cognitive Development; Economic Factors; Family Environment; Longitudinal Studies; *Parent Child Relationship; Parent Influence; *Preschool Children; Preschool Education
Identifiers: Project Head Start
Availability: ERIC Document Reproduction Service; 3900 Wheeler Ave., Alexandria, VA 22304 (ED022550, 68 pages)
Target Audience: 4-5
Notes: Items, 7
One of a series of instruments designed to measure child's cognitive abilities, impulsivity, and reading readiness and the mother's attitudes about school, her intelligence level, and her flexibility of thought. The instruments were developed for use in a study of mothers and their preschool children to determine the differential effects of middle and lower socioeconomic group cognitive environments on Black urban preschool children.

9843
Dream Interview. Hess, Robert D.; Shipman, Virginia C. 1967
Descriptors: *Black Mothers; *Black Students; Cognitive Development; Economic Factors; Family Environment; Interviews; Longitudinal Studies; *Parent Child Relationship; Parent Influence; *Preschool Children; Preschool Education
Identifiers: *Dreams; Project Head Start; Reality
Availability: ERIC Document Reproduction Service; 3900 Wheeler Ave., Alexandria, VA 22304 (ED022550, 68 pages)
Target Audience: 4-5
One of a series of instruments designed to measure child's cognitive abilities, impulsivity, and reading readiness and the mother's attitudes about school, her intelligence level, and her flexibility of thought. The instruments were developed for use in a study of mothers and their preschool children to determine the differential effects of middle and lower socioeconomic group cognitive environments on Black urban preschool children. Interview technique designed to assess preschool child's comprehension of dreams versus reality.

9844
Draw a Circle Slowly. Hess, Robert D.; Shipman, Virginia C. 1967
Descriptors: *Black Mothers; *Black Students; Cognitive Development; Economic Factors; Family Environment; Longitudinal Studies; *Parent Child Relationship; Parent Influence; *Preschool Children; Preschool Education
Identifiers: Project Head Start
Availability: ERIC Document Reproduction Service; 3900 Wheeler Ave., Alexandria, VA 22304 (ED022550, 68 pages)
Target Audience: 4-5
One of a series of instruments designed to measure child's cognitive abilities, impulsivity, and reading readiness and the mother's attitudes about school, her intelligence level, and her flexibility of thought. The instruments were developed for use in a study of mothers and their preschool children to determine the differential effects of middle and lower socioeconomic group cognitive environments on Black urban preschool children.

9845
Curiosity Task. Hess, Robert D.; Shipman, Virginia C. 1967

Descriptors: *Black Mothers; *Black Students; Cognitive Development; *Curiosity; Economic Factors; Family Environment; Individual Testing; Longitudinal Studies; *Parent Child Relationship; Parent Influence; *Preschool Children; Preschool Education
Identifiers: Project Head Start
Availability: ERIC Document Reproduction Service; 3900 Wheeler Ave., Alexandria, VA 22304 (ED022550, 68 pages)
Target Audience: 4-5
Notes: Items, 16
One of a series of instruments designed to measure child's cognitive abilities, impulsivity, and reading readiness and the mother's attitudes about school, her intelligence level, and her flexibility of thought. The instruments were developed for use in a study of mothers and their preschool children to determine the differential effects of middle and lower socioeconomic group cognitive environments on Black urban preschool children. Designed to assess preschool child's curiosity through use of 8 pairs of simple and complex drawings which child examined with a viewing apparatus.

9864
Abstract Ability Test. Harvard University, Graduate School of Education; Preschool Project Shapiro, Bernice; Kaban, Barbara 1976
Descriptors: *Abstract Reasoning; *Cognitive Ability; *Concept Formation; Developmental Stages; *Developmental Tasks; Infant Behavior; Infants; Preschool Children
Identifiers: TIM(F)
Availability: Tests in Microfiche; Test Collection, Educational Testing Service, Princeton, NJ 08541
Target Audience: 1-3
Notes: Items, 32
Developed through the Harvard Preschool Project, this instrument is designed to measure the child's ability to deal with abstraction. Consists of a series of tasks, developmentally ordered into 8 levels. Tasks consist of finding, following, dropping, and locating objects and understanding concepts such as gravity and equilibrium. Items for levels I-IV selected from scales I and V of the Hunt-Uzgiris Scales of Infant Development. Items for levels V-VIII selected from Pacific Test Series and Stanford-Binet Intelligence Scales.

9894
Pupil Communication Skills Inventory. Brentwood Union School District, CA
Descriptors: Bilingualism; *Bilingual Students; Children; *Communication Skills; Comprehension; Concept Formation; Grammar; Rating Scales; *Spanish Speaking; Speech Communication
Identifiers: TIM(F)
Availability: Tests in Microfiche; Test Collection, Educational Testing Service, Princeton, NJ 08541
Target Audience: Children
Teacher rating of the frequency with which a child performs a list of behaviors in Spanish or in English. Behaviors are concerned with oral communication, conceptual knowledge, knowledge of grammar, and comprehension skill. Orientation form has 46 items. Transitional form has 47 items.

10002
Specific Aptitude Test Battery for Ward Clerk (Medical Services). Manpower Administration (DOL), Washington, DC, U.S. Training and Employment Service 1974
Subtests: General Learning Ability; Numerical Aptitude; Clerical Perception; Motor Coordination
Descriptors: Adults; *Aptitude Tests; Career Guidance; Computation; *Culture Fair Tests; Employment Potential; Employment Qualifications; Ethnic Groups; *Hospital Personnel; Job Applicants; Job Skills; *Job Training; Minority Groups; Multiple Choice Tests; Occupational Tests; Personnel Evaluation; Personnel Selection; Predictive Measurement; Mathematics Tests; Timed Tests; *Vocational Aptitude
Identifiers: GATB; General Aptitude Test Battery; SATB; Specific Aptitude Test Battery; USES; *Ward Clerks (Medical Services)
Availability: Local U.S. Employment Service Office
Target Audience: Adults
Notes: Time, 39; Items, 480
Battery of tests selected from the General Aptitude Test Battery (TC001422). Used in the selection of inexperienced or untrained individuals for training as a ward clerk in a hospital. Through research it has been determined that these, combined subtests, used together, are a significant aptitude measure and do predict job performance. Research also indicates that this instrument does not discriminate among minorities nor ethnic groups. Number of items excludes the subtest on manual dexterity, which is scored according to the number of successfully completed

moves; this subtest requires the use of equipment. Available as Form A or B. A report describing the development of this test can be found in the ERIC system, document ED100969.

10003
Specific Aptitude Test Battery for Drafter, Civil (Profes. and Kin.). Manpower Administration (DOL), Washington, DC, U.S. Training and Employment Service 1974
Subtests: General Learning Ability; Numerical Aptitude; Spatial Aptitude; Clerical Perception
Descriptors: Adults; *Aptitude Tests; Career Guidance; *Culture Fair Tests; *Drafting; Employment Potential; Employment Qualifications; Ethnic Groups; Job Applicants; Job Skills; *Job Training; Minority Groups; Multiple Choice Tests; Occupational Tests; Personnel Evaluation; Personnel Selection; Predictive Measurement; Timed Tests; *Vocational Aptitude
Identifiers: *Civil Draftsmen; GATB; General Aptitude Test Battery; SATB; USES Specific Aptitude Test Battery
Availability: Local U.S. Employment Service Office
Target Audience: Adults
Notes: Time, 44; Items, 390
Battery of tests selected from the General Aptitude Test Battery (TC001422). Used in the selection of inexperienced or untrained individuals for training civil drafters. Through research it has been determined that these, combined subtests, used together, are a significant aptitude measure and do predict job performance. Research also indicates that this instrument does not discriminate among minorities nor ethnic groups. Comes as Form A or Form B. A report describing the development of this test can be found in the ERIC system, document ED103489.

10004
Specific Aptitude Test Battery for Teacher Aid, Elementary School. Manpower Administration (DOL), Washington, DC, U.S. Training and Employment Service 1974
Subtests: Verbal Aptitude; Numerical Aptitude; Clerical Perception; Motor Coordination
Descriptors: Adults; *Aptitude Tests; Career Guidance; Computation; *Culture Fair Tests; *Elementary Schools; Employment Potential; Employment Qualifications; Ethnic Groups; Job Applicants; Job Skills; *Job Training; Minority Groups; Multiple Choice Tests; Occupational Tests; Personnel Evaluation; Personnel Selection; Predictive Measurement; Mathematics Tests; *Teacher Aides; Timed Tests; *Vocational Aptitude
Identifiers: GATB; General Aptitude Test Battery; SATB; USES Specific Aptitude Test Battery
Availability: Local U.S. Employment Service Office
Target Audience: Adults
Notes: Time, 33; Items, 415
Battery of tests selected from the General Aptitude Test Battery (TC001422). Used in the selection of inexperienced or untrained individuals for training as an elementary school teacher aid. Through research it has been determined that these, combined subtests, used together, are a significant aptitude measure and do predict job performance. Research also indicates that this instrument does not discriminate among minorities nor ethnic groups. Comes in Forms A and B. A report describing the development of this test can be found in the ERIC system, document ED103456.

10005
Specific Aptitude Test Battery for Electronics Assembler (Electronics). Manpower Administration (DOL), Washington, DC, U.S. Training and Employment Service 1974
Subtests: Spatial Aptitude; Form Perception; Clerical Perception; Manual Dexterity
Descriptors: Adults; *Aptitude Tests; *Assembly (Manufacturing); Career Guidance; *Culture Fair Tests; *Electronics Industry; Employment Potential; Employment Qualifications; Ethnic Groups; Job Applicants; Job Skills; *Job Training; Minority Groups; Multiple Choice Tests; Occupational Tests; Performance Tests; Personnel Evaluation; Personnel Selection; Predictive Measurement; Timed Tests; *Vocational Aptitude
Identifiers: *Electronics Assemblers; GATB; General Aptitude Test Battery; SATB; USES Specific Aptitude Test Battery
Availability: Local U.S. Employment Service Office
Target Audience: Adults
Notes: Time, 26; Items, 299
Battery of tests selected from the General Aptitude Test Battery (TC001422). Used in the selection of inexperienced or untrained individuals for training as electronics assemblers. Through research it has been determined that these, combined subtests, used together, are a significant

aptitude measure and do predict job performance. Research also indicates that this instrument does not discriminate among minorities nor ethnic groups. Number of items does not include the subtest on manual dexterity, which is scored according to the number of completed moves and which requires the use of equipment. Comes as Form A or Form B. A report describing the development of this test can be found in the ERIC system, document ED103492.

10006
Specific Aptitude Test Battery for Teller (Banking). Manpower Administration (DOL), Washington, DC, U.S. Training and Employment Service 1975
Subtests: Numerical Aptitude; Form Perception; Clerical Perception
Descriptors: Adults; *Aptitude Tests; *Banking; Career Guidance; Computation; *Culture Fair Tests; Employment Potential; Employment Qualifications; Ethnic Groups; Job Applicants; Job Skills; *Job Training; Minority Groups; Multiple Choice Tests; Occupational Tests; Personnel Evaluation; Personnel Selection; Predictive Measurement; Mathematics Tests; Timed Tests; *Vocational Aptitude
Identifiers: Aptitude Test Battery for Teller (Banking); *Bank Tellers; GATB; General Aptitude Test Battery; SATB; USES Specific Aptitude Test Battery
Availability: Local U.S. Employment Service Office
Target Audience: Adults
Notes: Time, 31; Items, 334
Battery of tests selected from the General Aptitude Test Battery (TC001422). Used in the selection of inexperienced or untrained individuals for training as bank tellers. Through research it has been determined that these, combined subtests, used together, are a significant aptitude measure and do predict job performance. Research also indicates that this instrument does not discriminate among minorities nor ethnic groups. Comes in Forms A and B. A report describing the development of this test can be found in the ERIC system, document ED103495.

10007
Specific Aptitude Test Battery for Utility Hand (Paper Goods). Manpower Administration (DOL), Washington, DC, U.S. Training and Employment Service 1975
Subtests: Form Perception; Clerical Perception; Manual Dexterity
Descriptors: Adults; *Aptitude Tests; Career Guidance; *Culture Fair Tests; Employment Potential; Employment Qualifications; Ethnic Groups; Job Applicants; Job Skills; *Job Training; Minority Groups; Multiple Choice Tests; Occupational Tests; *Paper (Material); Performance Tests; Personnel Evaluation; Personnel Selection; Predictive Measurement; Timed Tests; *Vocational Aptitude
Identifiers: GATB; General Aptitude Test Battery; SATB; USES Specific Aptitude Test Battery; *Utility Hands (Paper Goods)
Availability: Local U.S. Employment Service Office
Target Audience: Adults
Notes: Time, 20; Items, 259
Battery of tests selected from the General Aptitude Test Battery (TC001422). Used in the selection of inexperienced or untrained individuals for training as a utility hand, working with paper goods. Through research it has been determined that these, combined subtests, used together, are a significant aptitude measure and do predict job performance. Research also indicates that this instrument does not discriminate among minorities nor ethnic groups. Number of items does not include the manual dexterity subtest, which is scored according to the number of moved objects; this subtest requires the use of equipment. Comes in Forms A and B. A report describing the development of this test can be found in the ERIC system, document ED117132.

10008
Specific Aptitude Test Battery for Nurse, Licensed, Practical (Medical Ser.). Manpower Administration (DOL), Washington, DC, U.S. Training and Employment Service 1975
Subtests: Verbal Aptitude; Clerical Perception; Motor Coordination; Manual Dexterity
Descriptors: Adults; *Aptitude Tests; Career Guidance; *Culture Fair Tests; Employment Potential; Employment Qualifications; Ethnic Groups; Job Applicants; Job Skills; *Job Training; Minority Groups; Multiple Choice Tests; *Nursing; Occupational Tests; Performance Tests; Personnel Evaluation; Personnel Selection; *Practical Nursing; Predictive Measurement; Timed Tests; *Vocational Aptitude

Identifiers: Aptitude Test for Nurse (Licensed Practical); GATB; General Aptitude Test Battery; SATB; USES Specific Aptitude Test Battery
Availability: Local U.S. Employment Service Office
Target Audience: Adults
Notes: Time, 15; Items, 340
Battery of tests selected from the General Aptitude Test Battery (TC001422). Used in the selection of inexperienced or untrained individuals for training as a licensed practical nurse in medical services. Through research it has been determined that these, combined subtests, used together, are a significant aptitude measure and do predict job performance. Research also indicates that this instrument does not discriminate among minorities nor ethnic groups. Number of items does not include subtest for manual dexterity, which requires the use of equipment and is scored according to the number of items manipulated. Comes in Forms A and B. A report describing the development of this test can be found in the ERIC system, document ED117159.

10009
Specific Aptitude Test Battery for Maintenance Repairer, Factory or Mill (Any Industry). Manpower Administration (DOL), Washington, DC, U.S. Training and Employment Service 1975
Subtests: Spatial Aptitude; Clerical Perception; Manual Dexterity
Descriptors: Adults; *Aptitude Tests; Career Guidance; *Culture Fair Tests; Employment Potential; Employment Qualifications; Ethnic Groups; Job Applicants; Job Skills; *Job Training; *Machine Repairers; Minority Groups; Multiple Choice Tests; Occupational Tests; Performance Tests; Personnel Evaluation; Personnel Selection; Predictive Measurement; Timed Tests; *Vocational Aptitude
Identifiers: Aptitude Test Battery for Maintenance Repairer; GATB; General Aptitude Test Battery; SATB; USES Specific Aptitude Test Battery
Availability: Local U.S. Employment Service Office
Target Audience: Adults
Notes: Time, 14; Items, 190
Battery of tests selected from the General Aptitude Test Battery (TC001422). Used in the selection of inexperienced or untrained individuals for training as a factory or mill (any industry) maintenance repairer. Through research it has been determined that these, combined subtests, used together, are a significant aptitude measure and do predict job performance. Research also indicates that this instrument does not discriminate among minorities nor ethnic groups. Number of items does not include the subtest on manual dexterity, which is scored according to the number of successfully completed moves; this subtest requires the use of equipment. Comes in Form A and B. A report describing the development of this test can be found in the ERIC system, document ED117160.

10010
Specific Aptitude Test Battery for Nurse Aid (Medical Service). Manpower Administration (DOL), Washington, DC, U.S. Training and Employment Service 1975
Subtests: General Learning Ability; Form Perception; Clerical Perception
Descriptors: Adults; *Aptitude Tests; Career Guidance; *Culture Fair Tests; Employment Potential; Employment Qualifications; Ethnic Groups; Job Applicants; Job Skills; *Job Training; Minority Groups; Multiple Choice Tests; *Nurses Aides; Occupational Tests; Personnel Evaluation; Personnel Selection; Predictive Measurement; Timed Tests; *Vocational Aptitude
Identifiers: GATB; General Aptitude Test Battery; SATB; USES Specific Aptitude Test Battery
Availability: Local U.S. Employment Service Office
Target Audience: Adults
Notes: Time, 37; Items, 384
Battery of tests selected from the General Aptitude Test Battery (TC001422). Used in the selection of inexperienced or untrained individuals for training as a nurse aid in the medical service. Through research it has been determined that these, combined subtests, used together, are a significant aptitude measure and do predict job performance. Research also indicates that this instrument does not discriminate among minorities nor ethnic groups. Available as Form A or B. A report describing the development of this test can be found in the ERIC system, document ED118597.

10011
Specific Aptitude Test Battery for Proof-Machine Operator (Banking). Manpower Administration (DOL), Washington, DC, U.S. Training and Employment Service 1975
Subtests: Numerical Aptitude; Clerical Perception; Motor Coordination

Descriptors: Adults; *Aptitude Tests; *Banking; Career Guidance; Computation; *Culture Fair Tests; Employment Potential; Employment Qualifications; Ethnic Groups; Job Applicants; Job Skills; *Job Training; Minority Groups; Multiple Choice Tests; Occupational Tests; Personnel Evaluation; Personnel Selection; Predictive Measurement; Mathematics Tests; Timed Tests; *Vocational Aptitude
Identifiers: GATB; General Aptitude Test Battery; *Proof Machine Operator; SATB; USES Specific Aptitude Test Battery
Availability: Local U.S. Employment Service Office
Target Audience: Adults
Notes: Time, 20; Items, 355
Battery of tests selected from the General Aptitude Test Battery (TC001422). Used in the selection of inexperienced or untrained individuals for training as a proof machine operator in banking. Through research it has been determined that these, combined subtests, used together, are a significant aptitude measure and do predict job performance. Research also indicates that this instrument does not discriminate among minorities nor ethnic groups. Comes in Forms A and B. A report describing the development of this test can be found in the ERIC system, document ED118598.

10012
Specific Aptitude Test Battery for Plumber (const.)/Pipe Fitter (const.). Manpower Administration (DOL), Washington, DC, U.S. Training and Employment Service 1978
Subtests: Verbal Aptitude; Form Perception; Manual Dexterity
Descriptors: Adults; *Aptitude Tests; Career Guidance; *Construction Industry; *Culture Fair Tests; Employment Potential; Employment Qualifications; Ethnic Groups; Job Applicants; Job Skills; *Job Training; Minority Groups; Multiple Choice Tests; Occupational Tests; Performance Tests; Personnel Evaluation; Personnel Selection; *Plumbing; Predictive Measurement; Timed Tests; *Vocational Aptitude
Identifiers: GATB; General Aptitude Test Battery; SATB; USES Specific Aptitude Test Battery
Availability: Local U.S. Employment Service Office
Target Audience: Adults
Notes: Time, 20; Items, 169
Battery of tests selected from the General Aptitude Test Battery (TC001422). Used in the selection of inexperienced or untrained individuals for training as plumbers or pipefitters in the construction industry. Through research it has been determined that these, combined subtests, used together, are a significant aptitude measure and do predict job performance. Research also indicates that this instrument does not discriminate among minorities nor ethnic groups. Number of items does not include the subtest for manual dexterity; manual dexterity subtest requires the use of equipment. Available in Forms A and B. A report describing the development of this test can be found in the ERIC system, document ED 158 039.

10024
Checklist for Early Recognition of Problems in Classrooms. Schleichkorn, Jacob 1972
Subtests: Coordination and Motor Activities; Behavior Responses (Aural); Communication (Verbal); Conceptual Ability; Perception
Descriptors: Behavior Rating Scales; Check Lists; *Communication Skills; *Elementary School Students; Elementary School Teachers; *Handicap Identification; Perceptual Development; Primary Education; *Psychomotor Skills; *Screening Tests; *Student Behavior
Availability: Journal of Learning Disabilities; v5 n8 p501-03, Oct 1972
Grade Level: K-3
Notes: Items, 121
Designed to assist primary grade teachers to recognize developing problems of students. The checklist is to be used only as a screening device to identify children who are in need of further evaluation.

10096
Modified Version of the Infant Psychological Development Scale. McElroy, Evelyn M. 1973
Subtests: Visual Pursuit and Permanence of Objects; the Construction of Objects in Space; Development of Schemas in Relation to Objects; Localization of an Object by Its Sound in the Waking State
Descriptors: Piagetian Theory; Individual Testing; Infants; Intelligence Tests; Motor Development; *Neonates; *Perceptual Development; Sensory Integration; Spatial Ability
Availability: ERIC Document Reproduction Service; 3900 Wheeler Ave., Alexandria, VA 22304 (ED171763, 842 pages)
Target Audience: 0-1

Notes: Time, 5 approx.; Items, 18
This volume consists of a series of psychosocial and physiological clinical nursing instruments. The instruments were selected from the published literature in health care, education, psychology, and the social sciences. Instruments focus upon nursing practice and stress patient variables. Instrument is designed to measure neonate's (birth-2 months) sensorimotor intelligence. This is a modified version of the Uzgiris-Hunt Infant Psychological Development Scale. Must be administered by an investigator trained to reliably judge neonate responses. Instrument is based upon Piaget's theory of sensorimotor intelligence.

10141
Otis-Lennon School Ability Test, Primary I. Forms R and S. Otis, Arthur S.; Lennon, Roger T. 1982
Descriptors: Abstract Reasoning; *Academic Aptitude; *Aptitude Tests; Cognitive Ability; Elementary School Students; *Grade 1; Primary Education; Verbal Development
Identifiers: OLSAT; Oral Tests; Otis Lennon Mental Ability Test
Availability: The Psychological Corp.; 555 Academic Ct., San Antonio, TX 78204-0952
Grade Level: 1
Notes: Time, 50 approx.; Items, 60
Designed to provide an accurate and efficient measure of the abilities needed to acquire the desired cognitive outcomes of formal education. Concentrates on assessing the verbal educational factor through a series of tasks that call for the application of several processes to verbal, quantitative, and pictorial content. For the primary I level, test items are all pictorial and sample the mental processes of analogizing, classification, following directions, quantitative reasoning, and verbal comprehension. All items are presented orally; no reading is required. Tests on this series are a revision of the Otis-Lennon Mental Ability Test (O-LMAT). Form R is dated 1979 and form S is dated 1982. Yields a "School Ability Index" score similar to a deviation I.Q. as to statistical properties.

10142
Otis-Lennon School Ability Test, Primary II. Forms R and S. Otis, Arthur S.; Lennon, Roger T. 1982
Descriptors: Abstract Reasoning; *Academic Aptitude; *Aptitude Tests; Cognitive Ability; Elementary School Students; *Grade 2; *Grade 3; Primary Education; Verbal Development
Identifiers: OLSAT; Oral Tests; Otis Lennon Mental Ability Test
Availability: The Psychological Corp.; 555 Academic Ct., San Antonio, TX 78204-0952
Grade Level: 2-3
Notes: Time, 50 approx.; Items, 75
Designed to provide an accurate and efficient measure of the abilities needed to acquire the desired cognitive outcomes of formal education. Tests concentrate on assessing the verbal educational factor through a variety of tasks that call for the application of several processes to verbal, quantitative, and pictorial content. Test items are all pictorial in nature and sample the mental processes of analogizing, classification, following directions, quantitative reasoning, and verbal comprehension. All items are presented orally and no reading is required. Tests in this series are a revision of the Otis-Lennon Mental Ability Test (O-LMAT). Form R is dated 1979; form S is dated 1982. Yields a "School Ability Index" score similar to a deviation I.Q. as to statistical properties.

10143
Otis-Lennon School Ability Test, Elementary. Forms R and S. Otis, Arthur S.; Lennon, Roger T. 1982
Descriptors: Abstract Reasoning; *Academic Aptitude; *Aptitude Tests; Cognitive Ability; *Elementary School Students; *Grade 4; *Grade 5; Intermediate Grades; Verbal Development
Identifiers: OLSAT; Otis Lennon Mental Ability Test
Availability: The Psychological Corp.; 555 Academic Ct., San Antonio, TX 78204-0952
Grade Level: 4-5
Notes: Time, 45 approx.; Items, 70
Designed to provide an accurate and efficient measure of the abilities needed to acquire the desired cognitive outcomes of formal education. Tests concentrate on assessing the verbal educational factor through a variety of tasks that call for the application of several processes to verbal, quantitative, and pictorial content. In the elementary level test, item content samples verbal, figural, and quantitative reasoning, and verbal comprehension ability. This test series is a revision of the Otis-Lennon Mental Ability Test (O-LMAT). Form R is dated 1979 and form S is dated 1982. Yields a "School Ability Index" score similar to a deviation I.Q. as to statistical properties.

10144
Otis-Lennon School Ability Test, Intermediate. Forms R and S. Otis, Arthur S.; Lennon, Roger T. 1982

Descriptors: Abstract Reasoning; *Academic Aptitude; *Aptitude Tests; Cognitive Ability; *Grade 6; Junior High Schools; *Junior High School Students; Verbal Development
Identifiers: OLSAT; Otis Lennon Mental Ability Test
Availability: The Psychological Corp.; 555 Academic Ct., San Antonio, TX 78204-0952
Grade Level: 6-8
Notes: Time, 45 approx.; Items, 80

Designed to provide an accurate and efficient measure of the abilities needed to acquire the desired cognitive outcomes of formal education. Tests concentrate on assessing the verbal-educational factor through a variety of tasks that call for the application of several processes to verbal, quantitative, and pictorial content. In the intermediate level test, item content samples verbal, figural, and quantitative reasoning and verbal comprehension ability. This test series is a revision of the Otis-Lennon Mental Ability Test (O-LMAT). Form R is dated 1979, and form S is dated 1982. Yields a "School Ability Index" score similar to a deviation I.Q. as to statistical properties.

10145
Otis-Lennon School Ability Test, Advanced. Forms R and S. Otis, Arthur S.; Lennon, Roger T. 1982
Descriptors: Abstract Reasoning; *Academic Aptitude; *Aptitude Tests; Cognitive Ability; High Schools; *High School Students; Verbal Development
Identifiers: OLSAT; Otis Lennon Mental Ability Test
Availability: The Psychological Corp.; 555 Academic Ct., San Antonio, TX 78204-0952
Grade Level: 9-12
Notes: Time, 40 approx.; Items, 80

Designed to provide an accurate and efficient measure of the abilities needed to acquire the desired cognitive outcomes of formal education. Tasks concentrate on the verbal-educational factor through a variety of tasks which call for application of several processes to verbal, quantitative, and pictorial content. In the advanced level test, item content samples verbal, figural, and quantitative reasoning, and verbal comprehension ability. This test series is a revision of the Otis-Lennon Mental Ability Test (O-LMAT). Form R is dated 1979 and Form S is dated 1982. Yields a "School Ability Index" score similar to a deviation I.Q. as to statistical properties.

10177
Modes of Learning a Second Language. Bowen, J. Donald 1978
Subtests: Derivational Morphology; Reading List-Monosyllables; Reading List-Polysyllables; Reading List-Letters and Numbers; Imitation-Short Sentences; Response-One Word
Descriptors: Adolescents; *Auditory Stimuli; Cognitive Style; Individual Testing; *Language Acquisition; *Language Tests; Literacy; *Second Language Learning; *Visual Stimuli
Availability: Alatis, James E., ed., International Dimensions of Bilingual Education. Washington, DC: Georgetown University Press, 1978
Target Audience: Adolescents
Notes: Time, 15 approx.; Items, 96

Used to determine method of acquisition of a second language, taking into account the influence of literacy. Designed to evaluate the English of 3 groups whose language learning experience differs in ways that can perhaps be assigned literacy correlates. Measures certain skills using aural and visual techniques, after which correlations between test performance and cognitive style can be attempted, specifically as related to preliteracy and postliteracy.

10188
Deductive Reasoning Test. Ross, G. Robert; Fletcher, Harold J. 1974
Descriptors: Cognitive Tests; *Deduction; Higher Education; Logical Thinking; Secondary Education; *Secondary School Students; *Undergraduate Students
Identifiers: Syllogisms
Availability: ERIC Document Reproduction Service; 3900 Wheeler Ave., Alexandria, VA 22304 (ED090315, 30 pages)
Grade Level: 8-14
Notes: Items, 16

Designed to assess deductive reasoning capabilities of students in grades 8, 10, 12, and 14.

10251
Test for Analytical Cognition of Mathematical Content. Cangelosi, James S. 1971
Descriptors: Algebra; Cognitive Processes; *Cognitive Style; High Schools; *High School Students; *Mathematics; Multiple Choice Tests
Identifiers: TIM(E)
Availability: Tests in Microfiche; Test Collection, Educational Testing Service, Princeton, NJ 08541
Grade Level: 9-12
Notes: Items, 40

Designed to measure the cognitive processes involved in analyzing numerical and algebraic mathematical situations. Difficulty level is suitable for students who have completed one algebra course.

10271
Formal Operations Measure. Tomlinson-Keasey, Carol Ann; Campbell, Thomas
Descriptors: Cognitive Processes; *Cognitive Tests; *College Students; Deduction; Higher Education; *Logical Thinking; *Pretests Posttests; *Problem Solving
Identifiers: TIM(G)
Availability: Tests in Microfiche; Test Collection, Educational Testing Service, Princeton, NJ 08541
Grade Level: 13-16
Notes: Time, 60 approx.; Items, 14

Pretest and posttest designed to measure logical thinking in college students. Requires subjects to perform the following kinds of formal operations: proportionality, systematic searches, isolation of variables, correlation, probability, and multiple transformation of information.

10322
Expressive One-Word Picture Vocabulary Test. Gardner, Morrison F. 1979
Descriptors: Age Grade Placement; Basic Vocabulary; Bilingual Students; Children; *Cognitive Development; *Elementary School Students; *Expressive Language; Individual Testing; *Intelligence Tests; *Mental Age; Pictorial Stimuli; Preschool Children; School Readiness; *Screening Tests; Student Placement; *Verbal Ability; Verbal Tests; *Visual Measures
Identifiers: EOWPVT; Oral Tests
Availability: Academic Therapy Publications; 20 Commercial Blvd., Novato, CA 94947
Target Audience: 2-12
Notes: Time, 20 approx.; Items, 110

Untimed measure of verbal intelligence for children ages 2 to 12; may also be used with older persons. May also be used for screening of possible speech defects or potential learning disorders, estimation of bilingual students' fluency in English, screening for kindergarten and for kindergarten readiness or placement, and as an appraisal of a student's definitional and interpretational skills. The respondent is presented with 110 pictures, 1 at a time, and is asked to name each picture. The objects depicted fall into 4 categories of language: general concepts, groupings (plurals), abstract concepts, and descriptive concepts. Distribution is restricted.

10327
Job Performance Scale. E.F. Wonderlic and Associates, Northfield, IL 1977
Subtests: General Ability to Learn and Perform on Job; General Attitude Toward Job
Descriptors: Ability; Adults; Behavior Rating Scales; *Employee Attitudes; *Employees; *Job Performance; Occupational Tests; Personnel Evaluation; Supervisors
Availability: E.F. Wonderlic and Associates; 820 Frontage Rd., Northfield, IL 60093
Target Audience: 18-64
Notes: Items, 55

Designed to enable ranking of employees on 3 scales: general ability to learn and perform on the job, general attitude toward job, and combined productivity-attitude ranking. Two rating forms are used. Form 2 is shorter, but more detailed than Form 1.

10334
Basic Educational Skills Test. Segel, Ruth; Golding, Sandra 1979
Subtests: Reading; Writing; Mathematics
Descriptors: *Aural Learning; Basic Skills; Diagnostic Tests; Elementary Education; *Elementary School Mathematics; Elementary School Students; *Learning Disabilities; Learning Modalities; *Reading Tests; *Screening Tests; *Speech Skills; *Tactual Perception; *Visual Learning; *Writing Skills
Identifiers: BEST
Availability: United Educational Services; P.O. Box 357, East Aurora, NY 14052
Grade Level: 1-5
Notes: Time, 60; Items, 75

Individually administered assessment of perceptual abilities and academic skills. May be administered by teacher, aide, or parent. Recording form correlates performance on each item with relevant perceptual modalities.

10348
Learning Style Inventory. Dunn, Rita; And Others 1978
Subtests: Sound; Light; Temperature; Design; Self-Motivated; Adult- Motivated; Teacher-Motivated; Unmotivated; Persistent; Responsible; Structure; Prefers Learning Alone; Peer Oriented Learner; Prefers Learning with Adults; Prefers Learning through Several Ways; Auditory Preferences; Visual Preferences; Tactile and Kinesthetic Preferences; Food; Morning; Late Morning; Afternoon; Evening; Mobility
Descriptors: Academic Persistence; Classroom Environment; *Cognitive Style; Cognitive Tests; *Elementary School Students; Elementary Secondary Education; Learning Modalities; *Secondary School Students; Social Influences; Student Motivation
Identifiers: LSI
Availability: Price Systems, Inc.; P.O. Box 3067, Lawrence, KS 66044
Grade Level: 3-12
Notes: Time, 30 approx.; Items, 104

Designed to diagnose student's individual learning style. Computerized results are available in 3 forms—individual summary, class summary, and subscale summary. Assesses individual's learning preferences in areas of immediate environment, emotionality, sociological needs, and physical needs.

10351
Preschool Language Assessment Instrument. Blank, Marion; And Others 1978
Descriptors: *Abstract Reasoning; *Classroom Communication; Cognitive Tests; Individual Testing; Language Acquisition; *Language Processing; *Language Skills; Learning Readiness; Perceptual Development; *Pictorial Stimuli; *Preschool Children; *Preschool Tests; School Readiness; *Screening Tests; Verbal Tests; Visual Measures; Young Children
Identifiers: Experimental Tests; Oral Tests; PLAI
Availability: Grune and Stratton, Inc; 111 Fifth Ave., New York, NY 10003
Target Audience: 3-6
Notes: Time, 20 approx.; Items, 60

Experimental, individually administered tests to 1) assess the child's language skills so that teaching encounters can be structured to match the child's level of functioning; and 2) to provide the earliest identification of those children who may encounter severe difficulties in the school setting. May also be used for children up to the age of 10 if poor school performance is present or the child's language skills are questionable. According to the authors, the instrument is based upon the level of abstraction as determined by the degree of distance (i.e., the perceptions) available to the child and the language that he or she must understand and use in dealing with those materials. Contains 15 items of each perceptual-language distance: matching perceptions, selective analysis of perception, reordering perception, and reasoning about perception.

10383
Productivity Environmental Preference Survey. Dunn, Rita; And Others 1979
Subtests: Sound; Light; Warmth; Formal Design; Motivated/Unmotivated; Persistent; Responsible; Structure; Learning Alone; Peer Oriented Learner; Authority Oriented; Several Ways; Auditory Preferences; Visual Preferences; Tactile Preferences; Kinesthetic Preferences; Requires Intake; Morning/Evening; Late Morning; Afternoon; Needs Mobility
Descriptors: *Adults; Adult Students; *Cognitive Style; Cognitive Tests; *Educational Environment; Employees; Higher Education; *Individual Differences; Learning Modalities; Motivation; *Productivity; *Social Influences; *Work Environment
Identifiers: PEPS
Availability: Price Systems; P.O. Box 3271, Lawrence, KS 66044
Target Audience: Adults
Notes: Time, 30 approx.; Items, 100

Designed to assess an adult's individual productivity and learning style. Assesses individual preferences in adult's occupational or educational activities in 4 areas. These include immediate environment, emotionality, sociological needs, and physical needs. Computerized scoring may provide printouts of individual profiles, group summary, or subscale summary.

10384
Concept Evaluation Test. Privette, Jerry A. 1972
Descriptors: *Christianity; Cognitive Tests; *Concept Formation; Elementary Education; *Elementary School Students; Multiple Choice Tests; Religion; *Religious Education
Identifiers: Approaches to Measurement in Religious Education
Availability: ERIC Document Reproduction Service; 3900 Wheeler Ave., Alexandria, VA 22304 (ED170300, 30 pages)
Grade Level: K-6

Notes: Items, 12

Designed to assess development of religious conceptualization using an instrument of ordinal measurement.

10390
Pre-School Screening Instrument. Cohen, Stephen Paul 1979
Subtests: Human Figure Drawing; Visual Fine Motor Perception; Visual Gross Motor Perception; Language Development; Speech; Behavior
Descriptors: *Behavior Development; Individual Testing; Language Acquisition; *Learning Problems; Observation; Performance Tests; *Preschool Children; *Psychomotor Skills; Questionnaires; *School Readiness; School Readiness Tests; *Screening Tests; Verbal Communication; *Verbal Development; Verbal Tests; Visual Perception; Young Children
Identifiers: Oral Tests; PSSI
Availability: Stoelting Co.; 620 Wheat Ln., Wood Dale, IL 60191
Target Audience: 4-5
Notes: Time, 10 approx.; Items, 32

Individually administered screening test for pre-kindergarten children to identify those with potential learning problems. Includes observations by administrator, performance and some verbal responses by the testee, and a Parental Questionnaire on which the parent gives developmental, medical, behavioral and general information about the child. Comes with the equipment needed to carry out the performance parts of the test.

10438
McCarron-Dial Evaluation System. Dial, Jack G.; And Others 1975
Subtests: Wechsler Adult Intelligence Scale (180); Peabody Picture Vocabulary Test (175); Bender Visual Motor Gestalt Test (9); Haptic Visual Discrimination Test; McCarron Assessment of Neuromuscular Development; Observational Emotional Inventory; Dial Behavior Rating Scale
Descriptors: Adolescents; Adults; *Clinical Diagnosis; *Cognitive Ability; Coping; Diagnostic Tests; *Disabilities; *Educational Diagnosis; Emotional Adjustment; Learning Disabilities; Perceptual Development; Psychomotor Skills; Vocational Aptitude; *Vocational Rehabilitation; Work Sample Tests
Identifiers: Psychiatric Patients; Sensory Motor Skills
Availability: Common Market Press; P.O. Box 45628, Dallas, TX 75245
Target Audience: Adolescents, Adults

Component tests evaluate disabled person's cognitive, emotional-coping and sensorimotor functioning in a neuropsychological approach to vocational, clinical, or educational evaluation.

10471
Tactile Test of Basic Concepts. Caton, Hilda R. 1971
Descriptors: *Blindness; *Classroom Communication; *Cognitive Development; Cognitive Tests; Concept Formation; Criterion Referenced Tests; *Elementary School Students; Individual Testing; Primary Education; Raised Line Drawings; *School Readiness Tests; *Tactile Adaptation
Identifiers: *Boehm Test of Basic Concepts; BTBC; Oral Tests; TTBC
Availability: American Printing House for the Blind, Inc.; 1839 Frankfort Ave., Louisville, KY 40206-0085
Grade Level: K-2
Notes: Time, 50 approx.; Items, 50

Tactile test designed to evaluate a student's mastery of concepts needed to understand oral classroom communication and which are usually found in commonly used instructional materials. Concepts are classed as Space (location, direction, orientation, dimensions), quantity and number, time, and miscellaneous. Adapted from the Boehm Test of Basic Concepts (TC009434), Form A.

10487
Brigance Diagnostic Inventory of Basic Skills. Brigance, Albert H. 1977
Subtests: Readiness; Reading; Language Arts; Math
Descriptors: *Basic Skills; *Diagnostic Tests; Elementary Education; Elementary School Mathematics; *Elementary School Students; *Geometry; Grammar; *Handwriting; Writing Skills; *Individualized Instruction; Individual Testing; *Language Arts; *Learning Readiness; *Mathematics; *Oral Reading; Reading Comprehension; *Reading Readiness Tests; Reading Skills; *Spelling; Vocabulary Skills; Word Recognition; Word Study Skills
Availability: Curriculum Associates, Inc.; 5 Esquire Rd., N. Billerica, MA 01862
Grade Level: K-6

Notes: Time, 20; Items, 2890

Individually administered inventory designed to assess basic readiness and academic skills, measure and record performance, and as an aid in individualizing instruction.

10490
Watson-Glaser Critical Thinking Appraisal, Forms A and B. Watson, Goodwin; Glaser, Edward M. 1980
Subtests: Inference; Recognition of Assumptions; Deduction; Interpretation; Evaluation of Arguments
Descriptors: *Adults; *Cognitive Tests; *Critical Thinking; Deduction; Higher Education; High Schools; *High School Students; *Undergraduate Students
Identifiers: CTA
Availability: The Psychological Corp.; 555 Academic Ct., San Antonio, TX 78204-0952
Grade Level: 9-16
Notes: Time, 50 approx.; Items, 80

Designed to measure 5 aspects of ability to think critically. This ability is a major goal of academic instruction as well as an essential part of many occupations. Forms A and B are equivalent.

10530
Uniform Performance Assessment System. Child Development and Mental Retardation Center; University of Washington, Seattle 1978
Subtests: Pre-Academic/Fine Motor; Communication; Social/Self Help; Gross Motor; Behavior Management
Descriptors: Behavior Patterns; *Child Development; Cognitive Development; *Disabilities; *Individualized Education Programs; Individual Testing; *Infants; *Language Processing; Mental Retardation; *Preschool Children; Preschool Education; Psychomotor Skills; Young Children
Identifiers: UPAS
Availability: Child Development and Mental Retardation Center, WJ-10; Experimental Education Unit, University of Washington, Seattle, WA 98105
Target Audience: 0-6

A curriculum-referenced instrument designed for use with handicapped children. Assesses skills normally acquired between birth and 6 years of age.

10591
Self Scoring I.Q. Test. Munzert, Alfred W. 1977
Descriptors: *Adolescents; *Adults; *Children; Intelligence; *Intelligence Quotient; *Intelligence Tests
Identifiers: Reasoning Ability; Self Scoring Tests
Availability: E.P. Dutton Co.; 2 Park Ave., New York, NY 10016, Attn: Frank Heidelberger
Target Audience: 9-64
Notes: Time, 45 approx.; Items, 60

Designed to assess general intelligence level of children aged 9 and above, as well as adults. Instructions are given for computing intelligence quotient. Answers and explanations for them are given in the test booklet. Instrument is also available from: Hemisphere Publications; 20 Elm Street, Franklinville, NY 14737

10601
Manual for Administering the Analysis of Developmental Learning Skills. Revised 1977. S. Bend Community School Corp., IN 1977
Subtests: Motor Coordination; Visual Performance; Visual Perception; Visual Memory; Auditory Perception; Auditory Memory; Language Development; Conceptual Development Social Development
Descriptors: Developmental Tasks; *Diagnostic Teaching; Diagnostic Tests; *Individual Development; Individual Testing; Kindergarten; *Kindergarten Children; Learning Disabilities; Perceptual Development; Primary Education; Psychomotor Skills; *School Readiness Tests
Identifiers: ADLS; *Analysis of Developmental Learning Skills
Availability: ERIC Document Reproduction Service; 3900 Wheeler Ave., Alexandria, VA 22304 (ED177175 microfiche only)
Target Audience: 4-5

Designed to identify children with lags in developmental skills. Useful in identification of children with learning disabilities, retardation, social, or emotional problems. Instrument combined Learning Style Screening Instrument (LSSI) and the Inventory of Developmental Tasks (IDT). Available from EDRS only in microfiche.

10648
Bateria de Examenes de Aptitud General. United States Dept. of Labor, Employment and Training Administration, Washington, DC 1974

Subtests: Name Comparison; Computation; Three-Dimensional Space; Vocabulary; Tool Matching; Arithmetic Reasoning; Form Matching; Mark Making; Pegboard; Finger Dexterity Board
Descriptors: *Adults; *Aptitude Tests; Career Guidance; High School Students; Perceptual Motor Coordination; Personnel Evaluation; *Personnel Selection; Professional Occupations; Semiskilled Occupations; Skilled Occupations; Spanish; *Spanish Speaking; Spatial Ability; Unskilled Occupations; Verbal Ability; *Vocational Aptitude; *Vocational Interests
Identifiers: Clerical Aptitude; Finger Dexterity; Manual Dexterity; Mathematical Aptitude
Availability: State Employment Service Offices
Target Audience: 18-64

A Spanish language version of the General Aptitude Test Battery (GATB) (TC001422) designed for use by State Employment Service Offices for evaluation of applicants for jobs and training programs. Aptitudes measured are: general learning ability, verbal aptitude, numerical aptitude, spatial aptitude, form perception, clerical perception, motor coordination, finger dexterity, manual dexterity. Scores on part 1, name comparison, and part 4, vocabulary, are not translations. They use Spanish surnames and vocabulary words and are not comparable to the English version.

10673
Luria-Nebraska Neuropsychological Test Battery. Luria, A.R.; And Others 1980
Subtests: Motor Functions; Rhythm; Tactile Functions; Visual Functions; Receptive Speech; Expressive Speech; Writing; Reading; Arithmetic; Memory; Intellectual Processes; Pathognomonic Scale; Left Hemisphere; Right Hemisphere
Descriptors: Adolescents; Adults; Arithmetic; *Clinical Diagnosis; Cognitive Processes; *Diagnostic Tests; Expressive Language; Individual Testing; Memory; *Neurological Impairments; Psychomotor Skills; Reading Skills; Receptive Language; Standardized Tests; Tactual Visual Tests; Writing Skills
Identifiers: *Normal Persons; *Schizophrenic Patients
Availability: Western Psychological Services; 12031 Wilshire Blvd., Los Angeles, CA 90025
Target Audience: 13-64
Notes: Time, 150; Items, 269

Standardized version for use with normal, schizophrenic and brain damaged patients to identify and localize specific areas of brain dysfunction. Picture cards, cassette tape recorder, and simple objects are required. Individually administered.

10684
Psychological Differentiation Inventory. Evans, Frederick J. 1967
Subtests: Embeddedness; Ego Functioning; Social Awareness; Controls and Defenses; Body Image
Descriptors: *Cognitive Style; *College Students; Higher Education; Individual Testing; *Psychological Testing; Rating Scales
Identifiers: Embedded Figures Test; *Field Dependence; TIM(G)
Availability: Tests in Microfiche; Test Collection, Educational Testing Service, Princeton, NJ 08541
Grade Level: 13-16
Notes: Items, 50

A paper and pencil inventory empirically developed to correlate with the Embedded Figures Test as a measure of field dependence. Measures 5 selected areas of cognitive functioning involved in field dependence: embeddedness, ego functioning, social awareness, controls and defenses, and body image. Individually administered.

10694
The Callier-Azusa Scale, G. Edition. Stillman, Robert 1978
Subtests: Postural Control; Locomotion; Fine Motor; Visual Motor; Visual Development; Auditory Development; Tactile Development; Undressing and Dressing; Personal Hygiene; Development of Feeding Skills; Toileting; Cognitive Development; Receptive Communication; Expressive Communication; Development of Speech; Interactions with Adults; Interactions with Peers; Interactions with the Environment
Descriptors: Children; *Cognitive Development; *Daily Living Skills; *Deaf Blind; Expressive Language; *Motor Development; *Perceptual Development; *Physical Disabilities; Rating Scales; Receptive Language; *Severe Disabilities; *Social Development; *Speech Communication
Identifiers: *Developmental Scales
Availability: Callier Center for Communication Disorders; 1966 Inwood Rd., Dallas, TX 75235
Target Audience: 0-12
Notes: Items, 800

This edition of the scale now covers cognitive development through the pre-operational period. New items were added to the Receptive and Expressive Communication subscales. Designed to aid in the assessment of deaf-blind and severely and profoundly handicapped children so that developmentally appropriate activities can be provided.

10719
Lexington Developmental Scales: Long Form. United Cerebral Palsey of the Bluegrass, Inc., Lexington, KY 1977
Subtests: Motor—Gross and Fine; Language—Receptive and Expressive; Cognitive; Personal-Social
Descriptors: Behavior Rating Scales; *Child Development; *Cognitive Development; *Daily Living Skills; *Disabilities; *Expressive Language; Individual Testing; *Preschool Children; Preschool Education; Profiles; *Psychomotor Skills; *Receptive Language; Special Education; *Young Children
Identifiers: LDS
Availability: Child Development Centers of the Bluegrass, Inc.; 465 Springhill Dr., P.O. Box 8003, Lexington, KY 40503
Target Audience: 0-6
Notes: Time, 120 approx.; Items, 424
Designed to provide meaningful profiles of the attainment levels of individual children from birth to 6 years of age. Development is assessed in the areas of motor, language, cognitive, and personal-social skills. Scales are arranged according to age levels from birth to 6 years. The scales consist of behavioral and experiential items. Behavioral items may be assessed by direct observation and are primarily in the motor, language, and cognitive scales. The personal-social scale consists primarily of experiential items. These items consist of information which must be obtained from anecdotal records or from parents.

10720
Lexington Developmental Scales: Short Form. United Cerebral Palsey of the Bluegrass, Inc., Lexington, KY 1977
Subtests: Motor; Language; Cognitive; Personal-Social
Descriptors: Behavior Rating Scales; *Child Development; *Cognitive Development; *Daily Living Skills; *Disabilities; Expressive Language; Individual Testing; *Preschool Children; Preschool Education; Psychomotor Skills; *Receptive Language; Screening Tests; Special Education; *Young Children
Identifiers: LDS
Availability: Child Development Centers of the Bluegrass, Inc.; 465 Springhill Dr., P.O. Box 8003, Lexington, KY 40503
Target Audience: 0-6
Notes: Time, 45 approx.; Items, 212
Designed as a screening tool for assessment of young children's development in the areas of motor, language, cognitive, and personal social skills. May be used by teachers, nurses, social workers, and homemakers during clinic or home visit. Scales are arranged according to age levels from birth to 6 years of age. The scale is composed of behavioral and experiential items.

10734
Child Observation Guide. Stone, Mark 1980
Descriptors: Attention; *Behavior Rating Scales; *Child Development; Children; Cognitive Development; Daily Living Skills; Emotional Development; *Interpersonal Competence; *Observation; Psychomotor Skills
Identifiers: COG
Availability: Psychologists and Educators; P.O. Box 513, St. Louis, MO 63017
Target Audience: 5-12
Notes: Items, 10
Designed for use with children of all ages through adolescence to determine a general level of functioning in 10 areas. Manual provides a rationale and directions for making and recording observations.

10737
Washington Pre-College Test. Washington Pre-College Testing Program, Seattle, WA 1979
Descriptors: Achievement Tests; Aptitude Tests; Career Counseling; *College Bound Students; High Schools; Interest Inventories; *Language Skills; *Mathematics Achievement; Spatial Ability; Testing Programs; *Vocational Interests
Identifiers: Test Batteries; *Washington Precollege Testing Program; WPC
Availability: Washington Pre-College Testing Program; 1400 N.E. Campus Pwy., Seattle, WA 98105
Grade Level: 11-12
Notes: Items, 352
Designed to assist college bound students and their guidance counselors to determine areas of interest and ability. WPC yields 2 composite scores—verbal and quantitative and requires approximately 140 minutes to complete. The

Vocational Interest Inventory (VII) is a 112 item questionnaire that has been part of the WPC Test since 1970. It is untimed. Tests are updated periodically. See ERIC document ED185074 for other information.

10756
Bay Area Functional Performance Evaluation, Research Edition. Bloomer, Judith; Williams, Susan K. 1979
Subtests: Task Oriented Assessment (11); Social Interaction Scale (35)
Descriptors: Adults; *Behavior Rating Scales; Cognitive Measurement; *Daily Living Skills; *Institutionalized Persons; Interpersonal Competence; Mental Disorders; *Perception; Psychomotor Skills; *Social Behavior; Verbal Communication
Identifiers: Dependency (Personality); Independence (Personality)
Availability: Consulting Psychologists Press, Inc.; 577 College Ave.; Palo Alto, CA 94306
Target Audience: Adults
Notes: Items, 46
Developed to assess, in a consistent and measurable way, some of the functions that people must be able to perform in general activities of daily living. The combined results of the 2 subtests are used as indicators of overall functional performance and provide information about cognitive, affective, and perceptual motor characteristics. Standardized on an adult psychiatric inpatient population.

10777
Learning Potential Assessment Device. Feuerstein, Reuven; And Others 1979
Subtests: Organization of Data (2); Plateaux Test (4); LPAD Variations I (5); Representational Stencil Design Test (20)
Descriptors: Adolescents; Children; *Cognitive Ability; Diagnostic Tests; *Disabilities; Disadvantaged; Disadvantaged Youth; Group Testing; *Individual Testing; *Intelligence Tests; *Learning Processes; *Mild Mental Retardation; *Nonverbal Tests; Training Methods
Identifiers: LPAD
Availability: Feuerstein, Reuven; and Others. The Dynamic Assessment of Retarded Performers. Baltimore: University Park Press, 1979
Target Audience: 12-17
Notes: Items, 49
Battery of nonverbal tests designed to measure intellectual potential of handicapped and disadvantaged adolescents. Examinee is given training to master series of tasks concerning elementary cognitive principles. Tests the individual in the process of learning.

10778
Psychoeducational Profile. Schopler, Eric 1979
Subtests: Imitation (10); Perception (11); Fine Motor (10); Gross Motor (11); Eye-Hand Integration (14); Cognitive Performance (14); Cognitive Verbal Skills (39); Pathology Scale (44)
Descriptors: *Autism; Children; *Cognitive Development; *Developmental Disabilities; Diagnostic Tests; Individualized Education Programs; Individual Testing; *Motor Development; *Perceptual Motor Coordination; *Psychosis
Availability: Schopler, Eric. Individualized Assessment and Treatment for Autistic and Developmentally Disabled Children. Baltimore: University Park Press, 1979
Target Audience: 1-12
Notes: Time, 60; Items, 139
This inventory of behavior skills utilizes a set of developmentally ordered toy and play activities to provide information on developmental functioning and degree of psychosis in autistic, psychotic, and developmentally disabled children functioning at a preschool level. Aids in planning individual programs.

10783
Butch and Slim. Ward, J. 1972
Descriptors: Adolescents; Children; Deduction; *Gifted; Individual Testing; *Intelligence Tests; Logic
Identifiers: Combinatorial Analysis; Great Britain; Piaget
Availability: British Journal of Educational Psychology; v42 p267-89, 1972
Target Audience: 10-18
Notes: Time, 24; Items, 32
Individually administered game of propositional logic based on Piaget's combinatorial analysis of children's thinking in adolescence. Discriminates children of high intelligence. Uses theme of 2 bankrobbers.

10789
Cognitive Training Test Battery. Corter, Harold M.; And Others 1968

Subtests: Similarities-Differences Test; Cognitive Flexibility Test; Productivity Responsiveness Test; Perceptual Organization Test; Judgment Test; Deutero Learning Test; Creativity-Originality Test; Problem Solving Test
Descriptors: *Auditory Perception; Children; *Cognitive Ability; *Concept Formation; *Creativity; Group Testing; *Logical Thinking; *Mild Mental Retardation; *Problem Solving; Program Evaluation; Summative Evaluation; *Tactual Perception; *Verbal Ability; *Visual Perception
Identifiers: *Deutero Learning; *Flexibility (Cognitive); *Following Directions; Normal Persons; Training Programs
Availability: Harold M. Corter; Dept. of Psychology, North Carolina State University, P.O. Box 5096, Raleigh, NC 27650
Target Audience: 5-12
Notes: Items, 499
Series of brief, timed and untimed, group or individual tests used with both normal and educable mentally retarded children, to evaluate the effects of a training program. Covers concept formation, flexibility (perceptual, conceptual, spontaneous); verbal fluency; following directions; perceptual and motor manipulative abilities; visual, tactile, and auditory perception; logical reasoning, conservation, problem solving, deutero learning and creativity. Some sections of the test allow from 30 seconds to 3 minutes for completion. Each subtest listed contains a number of shorter subtests.

10794
Industrial Arts Aptitude Battery: Woodworking Test, Forms A and B. Raff, Carl; And Others
Subtests: Knowledge of Terms (25); Relationships (25); Comprehension and Problem Solving (25)
Descriptors: *Aptitude Tests; Hand Tools; High Schools; *Industrial Arts; Junior High Schools; Knowledge Level; Problem Solving; Relationship; Two Year Colleges; *Woodworking
Availability: Bureau of Educational Measurements; Kansas State Teachers College, Emporia, KS 66801
Grade Level: 7-14
Notes: Items, 75
Part of a battery including tests in metalworking, power mechanics and electricity-electronics. Multiple choice items, cover tool identification, tool-related analogies, and woodworking related problem solving.

10877
Peabody Picture Vocabulary Test—Revised, Form L. Dunn, Lloyd M.; Dunn, Leota M. 1981
Descriptors: *Academic Ability; Academic Aptitude; *Achievement Tests; Adolescents; Adults; Children; *Gifted; Job Placement; *Mental Retardation; *Non English Speaking; Preschool Children; *Screening Tests; *Verbal Ability; Vocabulary Skills
Identifiers: *Aural Vocabulary; PPVT
Availability: American Guidance Service; Publishers' Bldg., Circle Pines, MN 55014
Target Audience: 2-40
Notes: Time, 15; Items, 175
Nationally standardized, individually administered measure of hearing vocabulary. Designed to measure verbal ability or scholastic aptitude. Used for screening special students, job candidates, and to assess vocabulary of non-English speaking students, ranging in age from 2.5 years to 40.

10878
Peabody Picture Vocabulary Test—Revised, Form M. Dunn, Lloyd M.; Dunn, Leota M. 1981
Descriptors: *Academic Ability; *Achievement Tests; Adolescents; Adults; Children; *Gifted; Job Placement; *Mental Retardation; *Non English Speaking; Preschool Children; *Screening Tests; *Verbal Ability; *Vocabulary Skills
Identifiers: *Aural Vocabulary; PPVT
Availability: American Guidance Service; Publishers' Bldg., Circle Pines, MN 55014
Target Audience: 2-40
Notes: Time, 15; Items, 175
Nationally standardized, individually administered measure of hearing vocabulary. Designed to measure verbal ability or scholastic aptitude. Used for screening special students, job candidates, and to assess vocabulary of non-English speaking students, ranging in age from 2.5 years to 40.

10909
Individual Assessment. Alpha Plus Corp., Piedmont, CA 1977
Subtests: Language; Cognitive; Gross Motor; Fine Motor; Socio-Emotional; Self-Help

Descriptors: Child Development; *Cognitive Style; *Developmental Disabilities; Early Childhood Education; *Elementary School Students; Exceptional Persons; *Language Skills; Observation; *Preschool Children; Preschool Education; *Psychomotor Skills
Availability: Circle Preschool; 9 Lake Ave., Piedmont, CA 94611
Target Audience: 2-8

Designed to assess 6 skill areas of child development. Observer rates child on skills based upon observation. Assessment is appropriate for children with exceptionalities or developmental delays. Useful in setting objectives for educational development of this population.

10911
Design Blocks and Patterns. Special Education Materials, Inc., Yonkers, NY 1969
Descriptors: Adolescents; Children; Elementary School Students; Elementary Secondary Education; Memory; *Perception Tests; *Perceptual Motor Coordination; Performance Tests; Secondary School Students; *Spatial Ability; *Special Education; *Visual Discrimination
Identifiers: Fine Motor Skills; Visual Memory
Availability: Special Education Materials, Inc.; 484 S. Broadway, Yonkers, NY 10705
Target Audience: 5-15

Designed to evaluate visual discrimination, perception of spatial relationships; visual memory, and fine motor development. Set consists of 9 blocks and 12 design cards printed on both sides.

10912
Color Pattern Board. Special Education Materials, Inc., Yonkers, NY 1969
Descriptors: Elementary School Students; Elementary Secondary Education; Mental Retardation; *Perception Tests; Perceptual Handicaps; *Perceptual Motor Coordination; Secondary School Students; Spatial Ability; *Special Education; Visual Perception
Identifiers: Visual Memory
Availability: Special Education Materials, Inc.; 484 S. Broadway, Yonkers, NY 10705
Grade Level: 1-12

Designed to evaluate perceptual abilities of educable and trainable mentally retarded children and perceptually handicapped individuals. Assesses color perception, spatial relationship, visual discrimination and memory, and eye-hand coordination.

10915
Test de Comprension Mecanica: Forma BB. Bennett, George K. 1957
Descriptors: Adults; *Aptitude Tests; College Science; *Engineering Education; Higher Education; *Job Applicants; *Mechanics (Physics); *Mechanics (Process); *Skilled Workers; *Spanish; Vocational Aptitude
Identifiers: Bennett Mechanical Comprehension Test
Availability: The Psychological Corp.; 555 Academic Ct., San Antonio, TX 78204-0952
Target Audience: 18-64
Notes: Time, 30 approx.; Items, 60

A Spanish translation of the Bennett Mechanical Comprehension Test, Form BB, 1951. Instrument was designed to measure the ability to perceive and comprehend the relationship of mechanical elements and physical forces in practical applications. For more recent edition, see Test de Comprehension Mecanica Bennett (TC006998) available from the Psychological Corporation, 7500 Old Oak Blvd., Cleveland, OH 44130. Form AA is usually administered to male high school students and job applicants; Form BB to male candidates or students of engineering schools and adult males of comparable ability and education.

10918
Test of Verbal Absurdities. Maw, Wallace H.; Maw, Ethel W. 1972
Descriptors: *Cognitive Measurement; *Curiosity; *Elementary School Students; *Grade 5; Intermediate Grades; *Verbal Stimuli
Identifiers: *Absurdities; *Hyperbole; TIM(G)
Availability: Tests in Microfiche; Test Collection, Educational Testing Service, Princeton, NJ 08541
Grade Level: 5
Notes: Items, 52

A test administered to children to test the hypothesis that high curiosity children exceed low curiosity children in recognizing verbal absurdities.

10940
Word and Number Assessment Inventory. Johansson, Jean C.; Johansson, Charles B. 1976
Subtests: Words; Numbers

Descriptors: Adults; Aptitude Tests; Career Counseling; *Computation; High Schools; *High School Students; Mathematical Concepts; *Vocabulary Skills; *Vocational Aptitude
Identifiers: WNAI
Availability: NCS/Interpretive Scoring Systems; P.O. Box 1416, Minneapolis, MN 55440
Target Audience: 14-64
Notes: Time, 60 approx.; Items, 80

Measures examinee's verbal and mathematical skills and helps match skills to appropriate career areas. Provides career information relevant to scores and offers suggestions for skill improvement.

10949
Inventory for Measuring Individual Differences in Learning Processes. Schmeck, Ronald Ray; And Others 1977
Subtests: Synthesis-Analysis; Study Methods; Fact Retention; Elaborative Processing
Descriptors: Cognitive Processes; *College Students; Encoding (Psychology); Higher Education; *Learning Processes; Retention (Psychology); Study Habits; Synthesis
Identifiers: Self Report Measures
Availability: Applied Psychological Measurement; v1 n3 p413-31, Sum 1977
Grade Level: 13-16
Notes: Items, 62

A self-report inventory of learning behaviors requiring a true/false response. Items cover organizational processes, approaches to encoding, adherence to systematic, traditional study techniques, and retention of detailed factual information.

10956
Group Inventory for Finding Creative Talent. Second Edition. Rimm, Sylvia B. 1980
Subtests: Primary Level (32); Elementary Level (34); Upper Elementary Level (33)
Descriptors: Children; *Creativity; Elementary Education; *Elementary School Students; *Gifted; Personality Traits; *Screening Tests
Identifiers: GIFT
Availability: Educational Assessment Service, Inc.; Rte. One, P.O. Box 139-A, Watertown, WI 53094
Grade Level: K-6
Target Audience: 5-12
Notes: Time, 45 approx.; Items, 99

Used to screen elementary school students for programs for the creatively gifted by identifying attitudes and values associated with creativity. Validity studies have been conducted with various socioeconomic, ethnic, and special learning groups as well as with several foreign populations.

10962
Gifted Identification Chart. Alexander, Patricia; Muia, Joseph A. 1980
Descriptors: Abstract Reasoning; Check Lists; Communication (Thought Transfer); *Creativity; Elementary Education; *Gifted; Leadership; Reading Interests
Availability: Reading Horizons; v20 n4 p302-10, Sum 1980
Grade Level: 1-6
Notes: Items, 61

Observational checklist for classroom use to determine the presence of positive behaviors which have been identified as creativity or creative end products. For use with culturally dominant and subdominant students.

10963
The Hoeflin Intelligence Test. Form H. Hoeflin, Ronald K. 1980
Subtests: Number Series (12); Verbal Analogies (24); Spatial Problems (12)
Descriptors: Adults; *High Achievement; *Intelligence Tests
Availability: Ronald K. Hoeflin; 439 W. 50th St., New York, NY 10019
Target Audience: Adults
Notes: Items, 48

An intelligence test for those interested in high IQ societies.

10971
Group Inventory for Finding Interests. Level I. Rimm, Sylvia B.; Davis, Gary A. 1979
Descriptors: *Creativity; *Gifted; *Interest Inventories; Junior High Schools; *Screening Tests; Student Interests; *Talent Identification
Availability: Educational Assessment Service; Rte. 1, P.O. Box 139-A, Watertown, WI 53094
Grade Level: 6-9
Notes: Time, 35 approx.; Items, 60

Screening test to help select junior high school students for programs for the creatively gifted. Identifies students with attitudes and interests usually associated with creativity, such as independence, curiosity, perseverance, flexibility, breadth of interest, risk taking, and sense of humor.

10976
Learning Disability Rating Procedure. Spadafore, Gerald J.; Spadafore, Sharon J. 1981
Descriptors: Attention Span; Decoding (Reading); Elementary Secondary Education; Intelligence Quotient; Interpersonal Competence; *Learning Disabilities; Learning Motivation; Listening Comprehension; Rating Scales; Severe Disabilities; *Student Evaluation; *Student Placement; Verbal Development; Writing Skills
Availability: Academic Therapy Publications; 20 Commercial Blvd., Novato, CA 94947
Grade Level: K-12

Evaluation method by which a student is systematically rated on each of 10 indicators associated with learning disabilities. Yields a placement score which indicates student's suitability for inclusion in a program for learning disabled students.

10979
Group Inventory for Finding Interests. Level 2. Rimm, Sylvia B.; Davis, Gary A. 1979
Descriptors: *Creativity; *Gifted; High Schools; *Interest Inventories; *Screening Tests; Student Interests; *Talent Identification
Availability: Educational Assessment Service; Rte. 1, P.O. Box 139-A, Watertown, WI 53094
Grade Level: 9-12
Notes: Time, 35 approx.; Items, 60

Screening test to help select senior high school students for creatively gifted programs. Identifies students with attitudes and interests usually associated with creativity, such as independence, curiosity, perseverance, flexibility, breadth of interest, risk taking, and sense of humor.

11014
Expressive One-Word Picture Vocabulary Test. Spanish Edition. Gardner, Morrison F. 1980
Descriptors: Children; Expressive Language; *Spanish Speaking; *Verbal Ability; *Verbal Development; *Verbal Tests; *Vocabulary
Availability: Academic Therapy Publications; 20 Commercial Blvd., Novata, CA 94947
Target Audience: 2-12
Notes: Time, 20; Items, 110

Estimates child's verbal intelligence through child's ability to form and to express an idea or concept of a picture or object. May also be used to screen for possible speech defects, estimate bilingual student's fluency in English; screen for prekindergarten or kindergarten readiness or placement. Is individually administered. May be used with subjects older than standardization population.

11025
Muma Assessment Program. Muma, John R.; Muma, Diane Bush 1979
Descriptors: Children; *Cognitive Ability; *Communication Skills; Individualized Education Programs; *Informal Assessment; *Language Acquisition
Identifiers: Descriptive Method; MAP
Availability: Natural Child Publishing Co.; P.O. Box 3452, Lubbock, TX 79452
Target Audience: Children

Program of descriptive procedures which allows clinicians a means of assessing an individual's cognitive-linguistic-communicative systems and processes. Provides criterion-referenced, prescriptive assessment which can be used to generate individualized educational programs.

11039
Preschool Language Scale. Revised Edition. Zimmerman, Irla Lee; And Others 1979
Subtests: Auditory Comprehension Scale (40); Verbal Ability Scale (40)
Descriptors: Bilingual Students; Diagnostic Tests; Language Acquisition; *Language Tests; *Listening Comprehension; *Spanish Speaking; *Verbal Ability; Verbal Development; Young Children
Availability: The Psychological Corp.; 555 Academic Ct., San Antonio, TX 78204-0952
Target Audience: 1-7
Notes: Time, 20; Items, 80

Evaluation and screening instrument for children of all ages who function at a preschool or primary language level. Diagnoses areas of strengths and deficiencies in auditory comprehension and verbal ability. Consists of a series of auditory and verbal language tasks assigned to age levels. A Spanish version is included.

11050
Screening Manual: A Project APT Resource Manual. Gendreau, Joan C.; And Others 1980
Subtests: Hearing; Vision; Physical Function; Oral Motor; Maladaptive Behavior; Cognition Checklist; Home Information Questionnaire

Descriptors: Auditory Tests; Cognitive Development; *Elementary School Students; Elementary Secondary Education; Family Environment; *Multiple Disabilities; Physical Examinations; Psychomotor Skills; *Screening Tests; *Secondary School Students; *Severe Mental Retardation; Social Adjustment; Vision Tests
Identifiers: Project APT
Availability: ERIC Document Reproduction Service; 3900 Wheeler Ave., Alexandria, VA 22304 (ED192474, 74 pages)
Grade Level: K-12

Part of a series of materials developed for a program designed to foster home-school coordination in educational planning and program implementation for severely mentally retarded and/or multiply handicapped students. Provides 5 screening tools in the areas of hearing, vision, physical functioning, oral motor, and maladaptive behavior. Also available are a cognition checklist and a home information questionnaire.

11051
Developmental Achievement Wheel: A Project APT Assessment Manual. Gendreau, Joan C.; And Others 1975
Subtests: Cognition; Communication-Verbal Expressive; Communication-Nonverbal Expressive; Communication-Receptive; Gross Motor; Fine Motor; Self Help-Grooming and Toileting; Self Help-Dressing; Self Help-Feeding; Socialization
Descriptors: *Child Development; Cognitive Measurement; Daily Living Skills; Interpersonal Competence; Measures (Individuals); *Multiple Disabilities; Nonverbal Communication; Physical Disabilities; Psychomotor Skills; *Severe Mental Retardation; Verbal Ability; Young Children
Identifiers: Developmental Assessment Wheel; Project APT
Availability: ERIC Document Reproduction Service; 3900 Wheeler Ave., Alexandria, VA 22304 (ED192475, 51 pages)
Target Audience: 0-6
Notes: Items, 363

Assesses functional age level of multiply handicapped or severely mentally retarded students in 6 major areas: cognition, language, gross motor, fine motor, self-help, and socialization. The wheel consists of 5 concentric rings—0 to 6 months, 6 months-1 year, 1 year-2 years, 2-4 years, and 4-6 years. Permits recording student's past, present, and future levels of performance. For some skills, there are alternative sequences for physically handicapped children.

11080
Developmental Tasks for Kindergarten Readiness. Lesiak, Walter J. 1978
Subtests: Social Interaction; Name Printing; Body Concepts; Auditory Sequencing; Auditory Association; Visual Discrimination; Visual Memory; Visual Motor; Color Naming; Relational Concepts; Number Knowledge; Alphabet Knowledge
Descriptors: Cognitive Development; *Developmental Tasks; Diagnostic Tests; *Kindergarten; Oral Language; Perceptual Motor Learning; *Preschool Children; *School Readiness Tests; Screening Tests; Social Development
Identifiers: DTKR
Availability: Clinical Psychology Publishing Co.; 4 Conant Square, Brandon, VT 05733
Target Audience: 4-6
Notes: Time, 30 approx.; Items, 177

Administered prior to a child's entrance into kindergarten or during first weeks of enrollment. Standardized for children ranging in age from 4 years 6 months, to 6 years 2 months. Provides data about child's skills and abilities as they relate to successful performance in kindergarten. Instrument is multivariate in format, and subtests were selected from a child development model, instructional objectives in kindergarten curriculum guides, and research studies.

11093
Cognitive Skills Assessment Battery. Second Edition. Boehm, Ann E.; Slater, Barbara R. 1981
Descriptors: *Cognitive Ability; *Cognitive Measurement; Concept Formation; Human Body; Individual Testing; *Kindergarten Children; Memory; *Preschool Children; Preschool Education; Psychomotor Skills; Self Concept; Visual Discrimination
Identifiers: CSAB
Availability: Teachers College Press; P.O. Box 939, Wolfeboro, NH 03894-0939
Target Audience: Preschool Children
Notes: Time, 25 approx.; Items, 98

Administered to each child individually by teachers, aides, school psychologists, or learning disability specialists to provide a profile of prekindergarten or kindergarten children's skill competencies for purposes of curriculum planning. Five broad categories of skills are included: orientation towards one's environment, discrimination of similarities and differences, comprehension and concept formation, coordination, and immediate and delayed memory.

11108
Figural Relations Diagnostic Test. Forms A and B. Willis, Sherry L.; Plemons, Judy 1977
Descriptors: *Cognitive Development; *Cognitive Measurement; Intelligence; *Older Adults; Pretests Posttests; *Spatial Ability; *Transfer of Training
Identifiers: ADEPT; *Fluid Intelligence; TIM(I)
Availability: Tests in Microfiche; Test Collection, Educational Testing Service, Princeton, NJ 08541
Target Audience: 65-99
Notes: Items, 42

Used in a study of the intellectual functioning of older adults to measure transfer of training as part of the Adult Development and Enrichment Project (ADEPT) at the Pennsylvania State University. Each form contains 4 subtests of from 7-14 nonverbal items. Item types include series classifications, matrices, and conditions. Form A is a pretest and Form B a posttest.

11111
ADEPT Induction Diagnostic Test. Baltes, Paul B.; Willis, Sherry L. 1979
Subtests: Letter Sets Test; Number Series; Letter Series
Descriptors: *Cognitive Tests; *Induction; *Intelligence Differences; *Older Adults
Identifiers: ADEPT; *Fluid Intelligence; TIM(I)
Availability: Tests in Microfiche; Test Collection, Educational Testing Service, Princeton, NJ 08541
Target Audience: 65-99

Used to examine the degree to which fluid intelligence can be modified in older adults through a cognitive training program. Induction is one of the primary mental abilities to be measured in determining fluid intelligence. Two forms of the Letter Sets and Number Series are available. Used as part of the Adult Development and Enrichment Project (ADEPT).

11112
Early Identification Screening Program. Kindergarten Screening. Baltimore City Schools, MD 1982
Subtests: X's in Circles; XO Pattern; Counting Number Sets; See-Say Letters; Matching Colors; Naming Pictures; Hear-Touch (Body Parts)
Descriptors: Auditory Stimuli; Individual Testing; *Kindergarten Children; *Learning Modalities; *Learning Problems; Primary Education; *Screening Tests; Visual Stimuli
Availability: Modern Curriculum Press; 13900 Prospect Rd., Cleveland, OH 44136
Grade Level: Kindergarten
Notes: Time, 9 approx.

Meant to be used at beginning of school year to measure individual child's performance of specific tasks in order to predict which children may develop learning problems. It measures child's written or oral response to visual or auditory stimuli. Consists of 3 1-minute frequency measures and is given to each child over a period of 3 days. It takes approximately 20 minutes per child to complete the process and 9 minutes of screening per child. Three learning modalities which are screened are hear-write, see-write, and see-say.

11117
Light's Retention Scale: Revised Edition. Light, H. Wayne 1981
Descriptors: Attendance Patterns; Behavior Problems; *Elementary School Students; Elementary Secondary Education; *Grade Repetition; Intelligence; Physical Characteristics; *Rating Scales; *Secondary School Students; Sex; Student Motivation
Availability: Academic Therapy Publications; 20 Commercial Blvd., Novato, CA 94947
Grade Level: K-12
Notes: Time, 15; Items, 19

Assists the school professional in deciding whether a student would benefit from grade retention. Considers factors such as attendance, intelligence, size, age, sex, history, parent participation, student motivation, and emotional or behavior problems.

11119
Valett Inventory of Critical Thinking Abilities. Valett, Robert E. 1981
Subtests: Imagination; Evaluation; Humor; Application; Comprehension; Synthesis; Verbal Concepts; Calculation; Analysis; Knowledge
Descriptors: Children; Comprehension; Computation; Criterion Referenced Tests; *Critical Thinking; Evaluative Thinking; Humor; Imagination; Knowledge Level; *Problem Solving; Synthesis; Verbal Ability; *Piagetian Theory
Identifiers: Analysis; VICTA
Availability: Academic Therapy Publications; 20 Commercial Blvd., Novato, CA 94947
Target Audience: 4-12
Notes: Time, 40; Items, 100

Criterion-referenced instrument designed to assess problem solving skills and abilities. Based on a neo-Piagetian model emphasizing developmental stages. Consists of a series of problem solving tasks.

11120
Learning Efficiency Test. Webster, Raymond E. 1981
Subtests: Visual Memory; Auditory Memory
Descriptors: Auditory Stimuli; *Cognitive Style; *Diagnostic Tests; *Elementary School Students; Elementary Secondary Education; *Individual Testing; *Recall (Psychology); *Secondary School Students; Visual Stimuli
Identifiers: LET
Availability: Academic Therapy Publications; 20 Commercial Blvd., Novato, CA 94947
Grade Level: 1-12
Target Audience: 6-18
Notes: Time, 15 approx.; Items, 18

A norm-referenced diagnostic test which is individually administered to provide a measure of the visual and auditory memory characteristics of students. Through a comparison of scores obtained on the subtests, a student's perferred learning style can be identified. For each subtest, both ordered and unordered recall are assessed under 3 recall conditions: immediate, short term, and long term. This test is not designed for use with children younger than 6 or with students who are severely hearing impaired, deaf, trainable mentally retarded, or severely and profoundly mentally retarded. Auditory sections may be administered to blind or visually impaired students.

11134
Knox's Cube Test (KCT). Stone, Mark H.; Wright, Benjamin D. 1980
Descriptors: Adolescents; Adults; *Attention Span; Children; Deafness; Non English Speaking; *Nonverbal Tests; *Short Term Memory
Identifiers: KCT; Tapping Test
Availability: Stoelting Co.; 620 Wheat Ln., Wood Dale, IL 60191
Target Audience: 2-65
Notes: Items, 51

A nonverbal test measuring attention span and short-term memory. Incorporates all previous versions. Can be used with deaf, nonverbal and non-English speaking persons. A Junior Form and a Senior Form are available with 16 and 22 items respectively.

11135
Kaufman Infant and Preschool Scale. Kaufman, H. 1979
Subtests: General Reasoning; Storage; Verbal Communication
Descriptors: *Cognitive Development; *Cognitive Measurement; Intervention; Mental Age; *Mental Retardation; Screening Tests; Verbal Communication; Young Children
Identifiers: KIPS; Reasoning Ability
Availability: Stoelting Co.; 620 Wheat Ln., Wood Dale, IL 60191
Target Audience: 0-4
Notes: Time, 30; Items, 20

Designed to measure early high level cognition in general reasoning, storage, verbal communication. Indicates need for intervention and suggests activities. Can be used with mentally retarded subjects of all ages whose mental age using KIPS does not exceed 48 months.

11139
Early Identification Screening Program First-Grade Screening. Baltimore City Schools, MD 1982
Subtests: X's in Circles; XO Pattern; Counting Number Sets; See-Say Letters; Matching Colors; Naming Pictures; Hear-Touch (Body Parts); See-Write Letters; See-Say Numbers
Descriptors: Auditory Stimuli; *Grade 1; Individual Testing; *Learning Modalities; *Learning Problems; Primary Education; *Screening Tests; Visual Stimuli
Availability: Modern Curriculum Press; 13900 Prospect Rd., Cleveland, OH 44136
Grade Level: 1
Notes: Time, 9 approx.

Meant to be used at the beginning of the school year to measure individual child's performance of specific tasks in order to predict which children may develop learning problems. It measures child's written or oral response to visual or auditory stimuli. Consists of 3 1-minute frequency measures and is given to each child over a period of 3 days. It takes approximately 20 minutes per child to complete the process and 9 minutes of screening per child. Three learning modalities which are screened are hear-write, see-write, and see-say.

11140
Behavioral Deviancy Profile. Ball, Betty; Weinberg, Rita 1980
Descriptors: *Adolescents; *Behavior Rating Scales; *Children; Cognitive Development; Emotional Development; *Emotional Problems; Graphs; Interpersonal Competence; Language Acquisition; Motor Development; *Social Adjustment
Availability: Stoelting Co.; 620 Wheat Ln., Wood Dale, IL 60191
Target Audience: 3-21
Notes: Time, 120 approx.; Items, 18

Comprehensive assessment of emotionally and socially disturbed children and adolescents in 18 areas: physical growth, gross motor development, fine motor development, motor activity, sensory perception, cognition, intelligence, speech, language, affect, aggression, relationship with mother, relationship with father, relationship with siblings, relationship with peers, relationship with adults, ego-self, superego-conscience. The 4 major areas encompassed by these 18 factors include physical and motor development, cognitive development, speech and language, and social and emotional development.

11141
Prereading Skills Test for Kindergarten. Nale, Nell; And Others 1975
Subtests: Visual Perception; Letter Identification-Capital; Letter Identification-Lower Case; Auditory Perception-Rhyming Words; Auditory Perception-Vowel Sounds; Auditory Perception-Initial Consonant Sounds; Concept Development; Listening Comprehension
Descriptors: Concept Formation; *Kindergarten Children; Listening Comprehension; Perceptual Development; Primary Education; *Reading Readiness; *Reading Readiness Tests; *Reading Skills
Availability: Economy Co.; P.O. Box 25308, 1901 N. Walnut St., Oklahoma City, OK 73125
Grade Level: Kindergarten
Notes: Items, 100

Measures pupil mastery of certain prereading skills presented in The Caterpillar Caper reader. Test should be administered in at least 3 sessions.

11146
General Inventory for Kindergarten. Nale, Nell; And Others 1975
Subtests: Social Concepts; Motor Development; General Concepts; Memory and Problem Solving; Self Concept and Independence; Attitude and Interest in School; Social Relationships
Descriptors: Concept Formation; *Individual Testing; *Kindergarten Children; Language Acquisition; Perceptual Motor Coordination; Primary Education; *School Readiness Tests; Social Development
Availability: Economy Co.; P.O. Box 25308, 1901 N. Walnut St., Oklahoma City, OK 73125
Grade Level: Kindergarten
Notes: Time, 30 approx.; Items, 60

Individually administered inventory to be given at the beginning of the kindergarten year. Assesses student's current level of conceptual development, language development, social/emotional development, and perceptual/motor development.

11154
The Hill Performance Test of Selected Positional Concepts. Hill, Everett W. 1981
Subtests: Ability to Identify Positional Relationships of Body Parts; Ability to Move Various Body Parts to Demonstrate Positional Concepts; Ability to Move the Body in Relationship to Objects to Demonstrate Positional Concepts; Ability to Manipulate Objects to Demonstrate Positional Concepts
Descriptors: Children; Individual Testing; Perceptual Handicaps; *Performance Tests; *Spatial Ability; *Visual Impairments; *Visually Handicapped Mobility
Availability: Stoelting Co.; 620 Wheat Ln., Wood Dale, IL 60191
Target Audience: 6-10
Notes: Items, 72

Individually administered test designed to assess spatial conceptual strengths and weaknesses of visually impaired children through their response to a series of directions. Children must have basic language abilities, be mobile and recognize body part names.

11157
The Visual-Verbal Test. 1981 Edition. Feldman, Marvin J.; Drasgow, James 1981
Descriptors: *Abstract Reasoning; Adults; *Cognitive Measurement; *Concept Formation; Diagnostic Tests; *Individual Testing; *Pictorial Stimuli; *Schizophrenia
Identifiers: VVT
Availability: Western Psychological Services; 12031 Wilshire Blvd., Los Angeles, CA 90025
Target Audience: Adults
Notes: Time, 120 approx.; Items, 42

Measures various aspects of conceptual thought in schizophrenics. Involves a concept formation task which requires individuals to formulate 2 different concepts for a given set of stimuli. Six concepts used in the test are color, form, size, structural similarities, position, and naming objects. Test is individually administered and easy to administer but only a qualified psychologist or therapist should interpret results and make a differential diagnosis.

11162
Wide Range Intelligence and Personality Test. Jastak, Joseph F. 1978
Subtests: Arithmetic; Spelling; Vocabulary; Verbal Reasoning; Social Concept; Picture Reasoning; Space Series; Space Completion; Coding; Number Series
Descriptors: Adolescents; Adults; Arithmetic; Behavior Patterns; Children; Cognitive Ability; *Emotional Adjustment; *Intelligence Tests; *Language Skills; Logical Thinking; Middle Aged Adults; *Motivation; Multiple Choice Tests; Older Adults; *Personality Measures; Personality Traits; *Psychomotor Skills; *Social Adjustment; Spatial Ability; Spelling; Verbal Ability; Vocabulary Skills
Identifiers: Coding Test; Number Sequences; WRIPT
Availability: Jastak Associates, Inc.; 1526 Gilpin Ave., Wilmington, DE 19806
Target Audience: 9-65
Notes: Time, 35; Items, 143

Designed to provide information about an individual's intelligence, ability, personality structure, and behaviors. Results in a global intelligence score and scores for language, reality set, motivation, and psychomotor skills.

11164
Developing Cognitive Abilities Test. Level 2. Scott, Foresman and Co., Glenview, IL 1980
Subtests: Picture Opposites; Excluding Information; Finding Causes; Drawing Conclusions; Visual Analogies; Visual Reasoning; Pattern Extension; Developmental Mathematics; Mathematics
Descriptors: *Cognitive Ability; *Cognitive Tests; Elementary School Students; *Grade 2; *Mathematical Concepts; Primary Education; *Spatial Ability; *Verbal Ability
Identifiers: DCAT
Availability: American Testronics; P.O. Box 2270, Iowa City, IA 52244
Grade Level: 2
Notes: Items, 80

Part of the Comprehensive Assessment Program. Is a measure of learning characteristics and abilities which contribute to academic performance. An important use of the test, in combination with the Achievement Series (TC011066-TC011067 and TC011069-TC011075), is to identify students achieving at a statistically higher or lower level than other students with similar abilities. For each level, the following scores are available: raw score, percent correct, local percentile, national percentile, local stanine, national stanine. The Level 2 test is examiner paced. Reports scores in 3 categories: verbal, quantitative, and spatial.

11165
Developing Cognitive Abilities Test. Level 3. Scott, Foresman and Co., Glenview, IL 1980
Subtests: Knowledge; Comprehension; Application; Analysis; Synthesis; Verbal; Quantitative; Spatial
Descriptors: *Cognitive Ability; *Cognitive Tests; Elementary School Students; *Grade 3; *Mathematical Concepts; Primary Education; *Spatial Ability; *Verbal Ability
Identifiers: DCAT
Availability: American Testronics; P.O. Box 2270, Iowa City, IA 52244
Grade Level: 3
Notes: Time, 50; Items, 80

Part of the Comprehensive Assessment Program. Is a measure of learning characteristics and abilities which contribute to academic performance. An important use of the tests, in combination with the Academic Series (TC011066-TC011067 and TC011069-TC011075), is to identify students achieving at a statistically higher or lower level than other students with similar abilities. For each level, the following scores are available: raw score, percent correct, local percentile, national percentile, local stanine, national stanine.

11166
Developing Cognitive Abilities Test. Level 4. Scott, Foresman and Co., Glenview, IL 1980
Subtests: Knowledge; Comprehension; Application; Analysis; Synthesis; Verbal; Quantitative; Spatial
Descriptors: *Cognitive Ability; *Cognitive Tests; Elementary School Students; *Grade 4; Intermediate Grades; *Mathematical Concepts; *Spatial Ability; *Verbal Ability
Identifiers: DCAT
Availability: American Testronics; P.O. Box 2270, Iowa City, IA 52244
Grade Level: 4
Notes: Time, 50; Items, 80

Part of the Comprehensive Assessment Program. Is a measure of learning characteristics and abilities which contribute to academic performance. An important use of the tests, in combination with the Achievement Series (TC011066-TC011067 and TC011069-TC011075), is to identify students achieving at a statistically higher or lower level than other students with similar abilities. For each level, the following scores are available: raw score, percent correct, local percentile, national percentile, local stanine, national stanine.

11167
Developing Cognitive Abilities Test. Form 5/6. Scott, Foresman and Co., Glenview, IL 1980
Subtests: Knowledge; Comprehension; Application; Analysis; Synthesis; Verbal; Quantitative; Spatial
Descriptors: *Cognitive Ability; *Cognitive Tests; Elementary School Students; *Grade 5; *Grade 6; Intermediate Grades; *Mathematical Concepts; *Spatial Ability; *Verbal Ability
Identifiers: DCAT
Availability: American Testronics; P.O. Box 2270, Iowa City, IA 52244
Grade Level: 5-6
Notes: Time, 50; Items, 80

Part of the Comprehensive Assessment Program. Is a measure of learning characteristics and abilities which contribute to academic performance. An important use of the test, in combination with the Achievement Series (TC011066-TC011067 and TC011069-TC011075), is to identify students achieving at a statistically higher or lower level than other students with similar abilities. For each level, the following scores are available: raw score, percent correct, local percentile, national percentile, local stanine, national stanine. Two forms of the test are available.

11168
Developing Cognitive Abilities Test. Level 7/8. Scott, Foresman and Co., Glenview, IL 1980
Subtests: Knowledge; Comprehension; Application; Analysis; Synthesis; Verbal; Quantitative; Spatial
Descriptors: *Cognitive Ability; *Cognitive Tests; Junior High Schools; *Junior High School Students; *Mathematical Concepts; *Spatial Ability; *Verbal Ability
Identifiers: DCAT
Availability: American Testronics; P.O. Box 2270, Iowa City, IA 52244
Grade Level: 7-8
Notes: Time, 50; Items, 80

Part of the Comprehensive Assessment Program. Is a measure of learning characteristics and abilities which contribute to academic performance. An important use of the test, in combination with the Academic Series (TC011066-TC011067 and TC011069-TC011075), is to identify students achieving at a statistically higher or lower level than other students with similar abilities. For each level, the following scores are available: raw score, percent correct, local percentile, national percentile, local stanine, national stanine. Two forms of the test are available.

11169
Developing Cognitive Abilities Test. Level 9/12. Scott, Foresman and Co., Glenview, IL 1980
Subtests: Knowledge; Comprehension; Application; Analysis; Synthesis; Verbal; Quantitative; Spatial
Descriptors: *Cognitive Ability; *Cognitive Tests; High Schools; *High School Students; *Mathematical Concepts; *Spatial Ability; *Verbal Ability
Identifiers: DCAT
Availability: American Testronics; P.O. Box 2270, Iowa City, IA 52244
Grade Level: 9-12
Notes: Time, 50; Items, 80

Part of the Comprehensive Assessment Program. Is a measure of learning characteristics and abilities which contribute to academic performance. An important use of the test, in combination with the Achievement Series (TC011066-TC011067 and TC011069-TC011075), is to identify students achieving at a statistically higher or lower level than other students with similar abilities. For each level, the following scores are available: raw score, percent correct, local percentile, national percentile, local stanine, national stanine. Two forms of the test are available.

11171
Perceptual Acuity Test. Gough, Harrison G.; And Others 1967

Descriptors: Adolescents; Adults; Children; College Students; *Culture Fair Tests; Intelligence Tests; Nonverbal Tests; Perception Tests; *Visual Perception
Identifiers: Field Independence; Geometric Forms; Optical Illusions; TIM (H)
Availability: Tests in Microfiche; Test Collection, Educational Testing Service, Princeton, NJ 08541
Target Audience: 8-65
Notes: Time, 20; Items, 30

A group test of visual perception of geometrical forms and optical illusions. Observer determines which figure is largest, which of several lines are equal in length, etc. Has been found to also measure field independence and academic intelligence. Test is said to be culture fair.

11187
Slosson Intelligence Test (SIT) and Oral Reading Test (SORT) for Children and Adults. Second Edition. Slosson, Richard L. 1981
Descriptors: Adolescents; Adults; Children; Elementary Secondary Education; Individual Testing; Infants; *Intelligence Tests; *Oral Reading; *Reading Tests
Identifiers: SIT; SORT
Availability: Academic Therapy Publications; 20 Commercial Blvd., Novato, CA 94947
Target Audience: 0-64
Notes: Time, 30 approx.

Individually administered test that assesses general intelligence of infants through adults. The Slosson Oral Reading Test (SORT) is included with the Slosson Intelligence Test (SIT) and assesses ability of students from primary grades through high school to pronounce correctly words of increasing difficulty. Test is administered verbally and number of items and content of test questions vary according to age range. Can also be used with blind subjects or those with other visual impairments.

11190
Wechsler Adult Intelligence Scale—Revised. Wechsler, David 1981
Subtests: Information; Digit Span; Vocabulary; Arithmetic; Comprehension; Similarities; Picture Completion; Picture Arrangement; Block Design; Object Assembly; Digit Symbol
Descriptors: Adolescents; Adults; Individual Testing; *Intelligence Tests; Nonverbal Tests; Older Adults
Identifiers: WAIS (R)
Availability: The Psychological Corp.; 555 Academic Ct., San Antonio, TX 78204-0952
Target Audience: 16-74
Notes: Time, 60 approx.; Items, 258

Individually administered intelligence scale for use with adolescents and adults. This scale is a revision and complete restandardization of the 1955 WAIS. Comprises 6 verbal and 5 nonverbal tests which may be administered separately or together to yield verbal, performance, and full-scale IQ scores.

11201
The Booklet Category Test. DeFilippis, Nick A.; McCampbell, Elizabeth 1979
Descriptors: *Abstract Reasoning; Adults; Computer Assisted Testing; Computer Software; *Concept Formation; *Neurological Impairments; *Screening Tests; *Visual Measures
Identifiers: BCT; *Halstead Category Test; *Halstead Reitan Neuropsychological Tests
Availability: Psychological Assessment Resources; P.O. Box 998, Odessa, FL 33556
Target Audience: Adults
Notes: Items, 208

A booklet version of the Halstead Category Test. A visually presented test of concept formation, abstract reasoning which is a sensitive indicator of brain dysfunction in the Halstead-Reitan Neuropsychological Test Battery and is about as valid as the complete battery in detecting the presence or absence of brain damage. A review of this test by Cecil R. Reynolds appears in School Psychology Review; v12 n4 p487-88, Fall 1983. A computerized version is available for Apple IIe, II Plus and IIc.

11202
Halstead-Reitan Neuropsychological Test Battery: Spanish Version. Manual. Melendez, Fernando; Prado, Hydee 1981
Descriptors: *Abstract Reasoning; Adults; *Concept Formation; *Neurological Impairments; Psychological Evaluation; *Screening Tests; *Spanish; Visual Stimuli
Identifiers: *Halstead Reitan Neuropsychological Tests
Availability: Psychological Assessment Resources; P.O. Box 998, Odessa, FL 33556
Target Audience: Adults

General instructions in Spanish for administering the Halstead Category Test which is a visually presented test of concept formation and abstract reasoning used to indicate brain dysfunction. Part of the Halstead-Reitan Neuropsychological Test Battery.

11203
Halstead Category Test for Young Children. Reitan, Ralph M. 1979
Subtests: Matching; Quality; Uniqueness; Lesser Quantity; Summary
Descriptors: *Abstract Reasoning; *Concept Formation; *Neurological Impairments; Psychological Evaluation; *Screening Tests; Visual Stimuli; *Young Children
Identifiers: *Halstead Reitan Neuropsychological Tests; *Reitan Indiana Neuropsychological Test Battery
Availability: Neuropsychology Laboratory; 1338 E. Edison St., Tuscon, AZ 85719
Target Audience: 5-8
Notes: Items, 80

A visually presented test of concept formation and abstract reasoning that indicates brain dysfunction. Part of the Reitan Indiana Neuropsychological Test Battery for Children which is based on the Halstead Reitan Neuropsychological Tests. The complete battery for children includes Wechsler Intelligence Scale for Children, sensory perceptual tests, a modification of the Halstead-Wepman Aphasia Screening Test and the Reitan-Indiana Neuropsychological Test Battery for Children.

11212
The Pupil Rating Scale Revised. Screening for Learning Disabilities. Myklebust, Helmer R. 1981
Subtests: Auditory Comprehension; Spoken Language; Orientation; Motor Coordination; Personal-Social Behavior
Descriptors: *Academic Failure; Adolescents; *Behavior Rating Scales; Children; Elementary Education; *Elementary School Students; *High Risk Students; Interpersonal Competence; Language Proficiency; *Learning Disabilities; Listening Comprehension; Perceptual Development; Psychomotor Skills; *Screening Tests
Availability: Western Psychological Services; 12031 Wilshire Blvd., Los Angeles, CA 90025
Grade Level: K-6
Target Audience: 5-14
Notes: Time, 10 approx.; Items, 24

Identifies children with good mental ability, hearing and vision, adequate emotional adjustment, and without overriding physical handicaps but who have a high risk of failing in school. The auditory comprehension and spoken language scores indicate the degree of success of verbal learning. The orientation, motor coordination, and personal-social behavior scores indicate nonverbal learning. Ratings should not be made until teachers have had at least one month of experience with the children, and not more than 30 children should be rated by one teacher.

11217
Quickscreen. Second Grade. Fudala, Janet B. 1979
Subtests: Name Writing; Figures; Story; Cognitive; Sentences
Descriptors: Auditory Perception; Cognitive Development; *Grade 2; *Handicap Identification; *Learning Disabilities; *Learning Problems; Listening Comprehension; Perceptual Motor Coordination; Primary Education; *Screening Tests
Availability: Western Psychological Services; 12031 Wilshire Blvd., Los Angeles, CA 90025
Grade Level: 2
Notes: Time, 25 approx.; Items, 5

Brief classroom procedure designed to screen for speech language, and learning problems. The procedure can be administered to an average classroom at 1 time. The grade 2 level has 2 parallel forms. The subtests measure auditory comprehension, cognitive skills, visual motor, and auditory vocal development.

11236
WISC-R Split-Half Short Form. Hobby, Kenneth L. 1980
Subtests: Information; Picture Completion; Similarities; Picture Arrangement; Arithmetic; Block Design; Vocabulary; Object Assembly; Comprehension; Coding; Digit Span; Mazes
Descriptors: *Adolescents; *Children; *Intelligence Tests
Identifiers: Wechsler Intelligence Scale for Children (Revised)
Availability: Western Psychological Services; 12031 Wilshire Blvd., Los Angeles, CA 90025
Target Audience: 6-16
Notes: Time, 45 approx.

Differs from WISC-R in that only selected items are administered on 9 of the subtests. All standard administration procedures outlined in the WISC-R manual (1974) are used with the Split-Half Short Form (S-H). The ad-

ministration of selected items requires some modifications in the starting points, basals, ceilings, and methods of computing raw scores. Split-half procedures are used on all subtests except coding, digit-span, and mazes. Items to be administered in each of the 9 subtests depend on age of child.

11270
Creativity Tests for Children. Guilford, J.P.; And Others 1971
Subtests: Names for Stories; What to Do with It; Similar Meanings; Writing Sentences; Kinds of People; Make Something out of It; Different Letter Groups; Making Objects; Hidden Letters; Adding Decorations
Descriptors: *Creativity Tests; *Elementary School Students; Intermediate Grades; *Verbal Ability; Visual Measures; *Visual Perception; Visual Stimuli
Identifiers: *Divergent Production Battery; Figural Creativity
Availability: SOI Institute; 343 Richmond St., El Segundo, CA 90245
Grade Level: 4-6
Notes: Time, 100

Designed to measure aspects of divergent production. Assesses verbal and visual-figural abilities. Seven of the tests are adaptations of adult forms: Plot Titles (TC001972); Alternate Uses (TC001533); Associational Fluency I (TC001678); Possible Jobs (TC001681); Alternate Letter Groups (not available); Making Objects (TC001682); Decorations (TC001684).

11274
Comprehensive Language Program. Peoria Association for Retarded Citizens, IL 1981
Subtests: Attending; Manipulation of Objects; Mimicking; Matching; Identifying; Labeling; Following Directions; Word Combinations
Descriptors: Adults; *Check Lists; Children; Identification; Imitation; *Language Acquisition; Language Fluency; *Language Handicaps; Listening Comprehension; Motor Development; Perceptual Development; *Student Evaluation
Identifiers: CLP
Availability: Scholastic Testing Service; 480 Meyer Rd., Bensenville, IL 60106
Target Audience: 5-64
Notes: Items, 125

An inventory of speech and language behaviors which enables administrator to systematically document language-handicapped students' language abilities and progress. Profile can be used to group students for language stimulation, to develop long- and short-term goals, and to choose specific lesson plans for each student. Used with children and adults.

11275
Thinking Creatively in Action and Movement. Torrance, E. Paul 1981
Subtests: How Many Ways; Can You Move Like; What Other Ways; What Can You Do with a Paper Cup
Descriptors: *Creativity; *Creativity Tests; *Motion; *Preschool Children; *Young Children
Identifiers: TCAM
Availability: Scholastic Testing Service; 480 Meyer Rd., Bensenville, IL 60106
Target Audience: 3-8
Notes: Time, 30 approx.; Items, 96

To assess creativity of young children, especially preschoolers. Responses are physical in nature, although verbal responses are acceptable. Activities which comprise instrument are designed to sample some of the more important kinds of creative thinking abilities of preschool children.

11282
Nonverbal Test of Cognitive Skills. Johnson, G. Orville; Boyd, Herbert F. 1981
Subtests: Paper Folding; Cube Building; Figure Identification; Figure Completion; Figure Discrimination; Figure Drawing; Figure Memory; Picture Completion I; Picture Completion II; Color Patterns; Knox Cubes; Dominoes; Tapping; Figure Association
Descriptors: *Cognitive Ability; *Cognitive Tests; Elementary Education; *Elementary School Students; Individual Testing; *Nonverbal Tests; Predictive Measurement
Identifiers: NTCS
Availability: The Psychological Corp.; 555 Academic Ct., San Antonio, TX 78204-0952
Grade Level: K-7
Target Audience: 6-13
Notes: Time, 30 approx.; Items, 126

Individually administered test of cognitive skills which are essential to academic learning, have little or no dependence upon specific social and school-learned skills and knowledge, but will predict the degree to which a child will profit from instruction in those skills. Intended to test those skills essential to academic learning and performance: memory, association, recognition, discrimination, space and spatial relationships, conceptual thinking, reasoning, perception, and ability to recognize and to deal with quantities. A review of this test by Cecil R. Reynolds appears in School Psychology Review; v12 n4 p485-87, Fall 1983.

11299
Halstead Category Test for Older Children.
Reitan, Ralph M. 1979
Subtests: Matching; Quantity; Uniqueness; Proportion; Summary
Descriptors: *Abstract Reasoning; *Adolescents; *Children; *Concept Formation; *Neurological Impairments; Psychological Evaluation; *Screening Tests; Visual Stimuli
Identifiers: *Halstead Reitan Neuropsychological Tests
Availability: Neuropsychology Laboratory; 1338 E. Edison St., Tucson, AZ 85719
Target Audience: 9-14
Notes: Items, 168
A visually presented test of concept formation and abstract reasoning which indicates brain dysfunction. Part of the Halstead Reitan Neuropsychological Tests. Battery for children aged 9 to 14 is very similar to adult version (TC011300). The Wechsler Intelligence Scale for Children is used in place of the Wechsler Bellevue Scale and the Minnesota Multiphasic Personality Inventory is omitted.

11300
Halstead Category Test for Adults. Reitan, Ralph M. 1979
Subtests: Matching; Quantity; Uniqueness; Identification; Proportion; Summary
Descriptors: *Abstract Reasoning; Adults; *Concept Formation; *Neurological Impairments; Psychological Evaluation; *Screening Tests; Visual Stimuli
Identifiers: *Halstead Reitan Neuropsychological Tests
Availability: Neuropsychology Laboratory; 1338 E. Edison St., Tucson, AZ 85719
Target Audience: Adults
Notes: Items, 208
A visually presented test of concept formation and abstract reasoning which indicates brain dysfunction. Part of the Halstead Reitan Neuropsychological Tests which also includes Wechsler Bellevue Scale (Form I), Trail Making Test, Reitan's modification of the Halstead Wepman Aphasia Screening Test, various tests of sensory-perceptual functions, and the Minnesota Multiphasic Personality Inventory.

11301
The Nelson Denny Reading Test. Form F. Brown, James I.; And Others 1981
Subtests: Vocabulary; Comprehension and Rate
Descriptors: Academic Aptitude; *Achievement Tests; Adults; *College Students; Higher Education; High Schools; *High School Students; *Reading Achievement; *Reading Comprehension; Reading Diagnosis; Reading Rate; *Reading Tests; Screening Tests; *Vocabulary Development
Availability: Riverside Publishing; 8420 Bryn Mawr Ave., Chicago, IL 60631
Grade Level: 9-16
Notes: Time, 35; Items, 136
Used primarily to assess student ability in reading comprehension, vocabulary development, and reading rate. May also be used as a screening test, for predicting academic success, and as a diagnostic tool. Available in 2 forms.

11313
The Goodman Lock Box. Goodman, Joan F. 1979
Subtests: Competence; Organization; Aimless Actions
Descriptors: *Attention Control; Behavior Problems; Developmental Disabilities; *Goal Orientation; Individual Testing; Learning Disabilities; *Object Manipulation; Perceptual Motor Coordination; *Preschool Children; *Problem Solving
Availability: Stoelting Co.; 620 Wheat Ln., Wood Dale, IL 60191
Target Audience: 2-5
Notes: Time, 6 approx.; Items, 10
Designed to evaluate preschool child's spontaneous approach to a novel, problematic situation. Primary clinical purpose is to identify preschool children who have difficulty controlling their attention and organizing their explorations and whose random and repetitive movements lack any apparent goal direction. Can also be used to identify children with perceptual-motor deficits. Recommended for use with children suspected of developmental delay, specific learning disability, or behavioral problem. Must always be included as part of a larger test battery

because it supplements existing instruments. Except under unusual conditions, it is expected that the examiner will be a psychologist. Individually administered.

11357
Cartoon Conservation Scales. DeAvila, Edward A. 1980
Subtests: Conservation of Number; Conservation of Length; Conservation of Substance; Conservation of Distance; Horizontality of Water; Conservation of Volume; Egocentricity-Perspective; Probability
Descriptors: *Cartoons; *Cognitive Measurement; *Conservation (Concept); Elementary Education; *Elementary School Students; *Intellectual Development; *Pictorial Stimuli
Identifiers: CCS; *Piagetian Tasks
Availability: Publishers Test Service; 2500 Garden Rd., Monterey, CA 93940
Grade Level: 1-6
Notes: Time, 25 approx.; Items, 32
Measure of intellectual development derived from the theory of Jean Piaget. Developed as a means of assessing intellectual development of children of diverse linguistic and ethnic backgrounds. Although the CCS is not a timed test, children should be able to complete it in 20 to 25 minutes. At grade 1, it is recommended that tests be administered to 1 or 2 students at a time; at grades 2 through 6, groups of up to 10 students may be tested.

11359
Carrow Auditory-Visual Abilities Test. Carrow-Woolfolk, Elizabeth 1981
Subtests: Visual Discrimination Matching; Visual Discrimination Memory; Visual Motor Copying; Visual Motor Memory; Motor Speed; Picture Memory; Picture Sequence Selection; Digits Forward; Digits Backward; Sentence Repetition; Word Repetition; Auditory Blending; Auditory Discrimination in Quiet; Auditory Discrimination in Noise
Descriptors: *Auditory Perception; *Children; *Cognitive Ability; *Elementary School Students; Individual Testing; Memory; Norm Referenced Tests; *Perception Tests; Perceptual Motor Learning; *Visual Perception
Identifiers: CAVAT
Availability: DLM Teaching Resources; P.O. Box 4000, 1 DLM Park, Allen, TX 75002
Target Audience: 4-10
Notes: Time, 90 approx.; Items, 312
Individually administered, norm referenced test which measures auditory and visual perceptual, motor, and memory skills. The test allows for identification and description of language-learning problems; allows comparison of individual performances in auditory and visual abilities by providing data on interrelationships among discrimination, memory and motor skills; allows analysis of the source of an auditory or visual problem; and clarifies a child's unique strengths and weaknesses and helps to determine particular areas of deficiency.

11360
Inventory of Readiness Skills. Revised. Third Edition. Shelquist, Jack 1973
Subtests: Auditory Memory Sequential; Word Discrimination; Body Awareness; Locational and Directional Concepts; Color Discrimination; Visual-Motor Coordination; Visual Memory; Letter Perception; Letter Names
Descriptors: Concept Formation; Educationally Disadvantaged; *Grade 1; Individual Testing; *Kindergarten Children; Learning Disabilities; Mental Retardation; Perceptual Development; *Preschool Children; Preschool Education; Primary Education; Remedial Programs; *School Readiness Tests; *Student Placement
Availability: Educational Programmers; P.O. Box 332, Roseburg, OR 97470
Target Audience: 2-6
Notes: Time, 20 approx.; Items, 82
Individually administered test designed to assist the teacher in making a diagnostic assessment of a child's understanding of selected fundamental skills before a formalized instructional program is begun. Provides pretest and posttest measurement and can be used for preschool, kindergarten, first grade, Headstart, primary mentally retarded, and learning disabled children or for placement in remedial programs.

11365
The Child's Intellectual Progress Scale. Form B. Maxwell, William 1979
Subtests: Visual Perception; Visual Discrimination; Visual Memory; Mathematical Learning; Arithmetic; Words; Logic and Deduction; Pattern Discovery; Spelling; Mathematical Operations
Descriptors: Individual Testing; Intelligence Quotient; *Intelligence Tests; *Young Children
Identifiers: CHIPS

Availability: William Maxwell; IQ Co., P.O. Box 1534, Suva, Fiji Islands
Target Audience: 3-7
Notes: Time, 6 approx.; Items, 105
Individually administered, simplified intelligence test for parents or other nonprofessionals to administer to children.

11436
Orleans-Hanna Algebra Prognosis Test (Revised). Hanna, Gerald S.; Orleans, Joseph B. 1982
Descriptors: *Algebra; Predictive Measurement; *Prognostic Tests; Secondary Education; *Secondary School Students
Availability: The Psychological Corp.; 555 Academic Ct., San Antonio, TX 78204-0952
Grade Level: 7-12
Notes: Time, 60 approx.; Items, 60
Designed to identify before instruction begins, those students who may achieve relative success in an algebra course and those most likely to encounter difficulties. Test is useful for counseling, selecting, and grouping algebra students. Test is structured to tap selected aspects of 3 important variables: aptitude, achievement, and interest and motivation.

11437
Differential Aptitude Tests. Forms V and W. Bennett, George K.; And Others 1982
Subtests: Verbal Reasoning; Numerical Ability; Abstract Reasoning; Clerical Speed and Accuracy; Mechanical Reasoning; Space Relations; Spelling; Language Usage
Descriptors: Abstract Reasoning; *Aptitude Tests; *Career Guidance; *Educational Counseling; Language Usage; Mathematical Applications; Mechanical Skills; Secondary Education; *Secondary School Students; Spatial Ability; Spelling; Verbal Ability
Identifiers: Clerical Aptitude; DAT
Availability: The Psychological Corp.; 555 Academic Ct., San Antonio, TX 78204-0952
Grade Level: 8-12
Notes: Time, 171; Items, 605
Integrated battery of aptitude tests designed for educational and vocational guidance in junior and senior high schools. Yields 9 scores including an index of scholastic ability.

11457
Inventario de Santa Clara de Tareas de Desenvolvimiento. Santa Clara Unified School District, CA 1978
Subtests: Coordinacion Muscular; Coordinacion Visual Muscular; Percepcion Visual; Memoria Visual; Discriminacion Auditiva; Memoria Auditiva; Desarrollo del Idioma; Desarrollo de Conceptos
Descriptors: Auditory Perception; Bilingual Education Programs; *Child Development; *Classroom Observation Techniques; Concept Formation; *Developmental Tasks; Language Acquisition; Limited English Speaking; Motor Development; Non English Speaking; Perceptual Motor Coordination; *Primary Education; Recall (Psychology); *Screening Tests; *Spanish; *Spanish Speaking; Visual Perception; *Young Children
Identifiers: Elementary Secondary Education Act Title I; Inventory of Developmental Tasks; ITD
Availability: Zweig Associates; 1711 McGaw Ave., Irvine, CA 92714
Grade Level: K-2
Target Audience: 5-7
Notes: Items, 60
Spanish version of the Santa Clara Inventory of Developmental Tasks which was developed as an ESEA Title I project. Consists of 60 tasks chosen because they represent milestones in children's development. The 60 tasks are arranged in 8 skill areas: motor coordination; visual motor performance; visual perception; visual memory; auditory perception; auditory memory; language development; conceptual development. The inventory can be used as a screening device; as a basis for parent conferences; and as a record of child's development to facilitate correct placement by student's next teacher.

11466
The Blind Learning Aptitude Test. Newland, T. Ernest 1971
Descriptors: *Academic Aptitude; Adolescents; *Aptitude Tests; *Blindness; Children; Individual Testing; *Manipulative Materials; Tactual Perception
Identifiers: BLAT
Availability: University of Illinois Press; 54 E. Gregory Dr., P.O. Box 5081, Station A, Champaign, IL 61820
Target Audience: 6-20
Notes: Time, 45 approx.; Items, 61

Test of learning potential designed specifically to meet the needs of blind children. Is a tactile discrimination test involving dots and lines similar to those used in Braille characters but not requiring the fine tactile discrimination needed for Braille reading.

11488
Functional Educability Index. McGahan, F.E.; McGahan, Carolyn 1969
Subtests: Personal Identity; Abstract Reasoning; Visual Perception; Immediate Recall; Naming of Objects; Mathematical Reasoning; Spelling; Figure Copying; Make a Picture of a Person
Descriptors: Abstract Reasoning; Adolescents; Adults; *Basic Skills; Children; *Cognitive Development; *Cognitive Measurement; *Curriculum Design; *Illiteracy; Individual Testing; Language Skills; Mathematical Concepts; *Perceptual Handicaps; Perceptual Motor Learning; Recall (Psychology); Spelling; Visual Perception
Availability: N.E.T. Educational Services; 3065 Clark Ln., Paris, TX 75460
Target Audience: 10-65
Notes: Time, 15 approx.

Individually administered instrument used to determine functional or operational academic level; to establish educational baseline of individuals; and to provide criteria for curriculum design. Originally developed to provide basic criteria for teachers to use in making judgments relative to functional educational level of illiterate adults. Later extended to use with students from upper elementary grades through high school. Instruments probe 6 basic areas necessary to the learning process. It is not intended for IQ assessment.

11489
Indice de Funcion Educativa. McGahan, F.E.; McGahan, Carolyn 1969
Subtests: Identidad Personal; Razonamiento Abstracto; Percepcion Visual; Recordatario Inmediato; Nombramiento de Objectos; Razonamiento Matematico; Deletreo; Reproducion de Figuras; Dibuje la Imagen de Una Persona
Descriptors: Abstract Reasoning; Adolescents; Adults; *Basic Skills; Children; *Cognitive Development; *Cognitive Measurement; *Curriculum Design; *Illiteracy; Individual Testing; Language Skills; Mathematical Concepts; *Perceptual Handicaps; Perceptual Motor Learning; Recall (Psychology); *Spanish; Spelling; Visual Perception
Availability: N.E.T. Educational Services; 3065 Clark Ln., Paris, TX 75460
Target Audience: 10-65
Notes: Time, 15 approx.

Individually administered instrument used to determine functional or operational academic level; to establish educational baseline of individuals; and to provide criteria for curriculum design. Originally developed to provide basic criteria for teachers to use in making judgments relative to functional educational level of illiterate adults. Later extended to use with students from upper elementary grades through high school. Instruments probe 6 basic areas necessary to the learning process. It is not intended for IQ assessment.

11498
The First Grade Readiness Checklist. Austin, John J. 1972
Descriptors: Check Lists; Childhood Interests; Cognitive Development; Developmental Stages; *Grade 1; *Parent Participation; Primary Education; *School Readiness
Availability: Research Concepts; 1368 E. Airport Rd., Muskegon, MI 49444
Grade Level: 1
Notes: Items, 54

Checklist filled out by parents to help determine if child is ready to enter grade one. Questions deal with growth and age; general activity related to growth; practical skills; remembering; understanding; general knowledge; attitudes and interests. This is a research edition.

11503
The Three-R's Test. Levels 9-12, Forms A and B. Achievement Edition. Cole, Nancy S.; And Others 1982
Subtests: Reading; Language; Mathematics
Descriptors: *Language Usage; *Achievement Tests; *Aptitude Tests; Capitalization (Alphabetic); Cognitive Measurement; Culture Fair Tests; Elementary Education; *Elementary School Mathematics; *Elementary School Students; Grammar; *Language Proficiency; *Mathematics Achievement; Punctuation; *Reading Achievement; Spelling
Availability: Riverside Publishing Co.; 3 O'Hare Towers, 8420 Bryn Mawr Ave., Chicago, IL 60631
Grade Level: 3-6
Notes: Time, 130 approx.; Items, 125

Designed to measure students' proficiency in reading, language arts, and mathematics. All items are based on objectives commonly used at these grade levels. The achievement edition of the tests are available in two forms, A and B. The achievement and abilities edition combines Form A of the achievement test with a 95-item verbal and quantitative abilities test. The abilities portion can be administered in about 60 minutes. The abilities portion consists of a verbal part comprised of 2 subtests, verbal classification and verbal analogies, and a quantitative part, comprised of 2 subtests, quantitative relations and number series. Also at levels 9-12, a class period edition is available. This is an achievement test designed to be administered in a single class period. One form of the test is available at each grade level.

11504
The Three-R's Test. Levels 13-14, Forms A and B. Achievement Edition. Cole, Nancy S.; And Others 1982
Subtests: Reading; Language; Mathematics
Descriptors: *Language Usage; *Achievement Tests; *Aptitude Tests; Capitalization (Alphabetic); Cognitive Measurement; Culture Fair Tests; Grammar; Junior High Schools; *Junior High School Students; *Language Proficiency; *Mathematics Achievement; Punctuation; *Reading Achievement; *Secondary School Mathematics; Spelling
Availability: Riverside Publishing Co.; 3 O'Hare Towers, 8420 Bryn Mawr Ave., Chicago, IL 60631
Grade Level: 7-8
Notes: Time, 130 approx.; Items, 125

Designed to measure students' proficiency in reading, language arts, and mathematics. All items are based on objectives commonly used at these grade levels. The achievement and abilities edition combines Form A of the achievement edition with a 95-item verbal and quantitative abilities test. The abilities portion can be administered in approximately 60 minutes. The abilities portion consists of a verbal part comprised of 2 subtests, verbal classification and verbal analogies, and a quantitative part, comprised of 2 subtests, quantitative relations and number series. Also at levels 13-14, a class period edition is available. This is an achievement test designed to be administered in a single class period. One form of the test is available at each grade level.

11505
The Three-R's Test. Levels 15-18, Forms A and B. Achievement Edition. Cole, Nancy S.; And Others 1982
Subtests: Reading; Language; Mathematics
Descriptors: *Language Usage; *Achievement Tests; *Aptitude Tests; Capitalization (Alphabetic); Cognitive Measurement; Culture Fair Tests; Grammar; High Schools; *High School Students; *Language Proficiency; *Mathematics Achievement; Punctuation; *Reading Achievement; *Secondary School Mathematics; Spelling
Availability: Riverside Publishing Co.; 3 O'Hare Towers, 8420 Bryn Mawr Ave., Chicago, IL 60631
Grade Level: 9-12
Notes: Time, 130 approx.; Items, 125

Designed to measure students' proficiency in reading, language arts, and mathematics. All items are based on objectives commonly used at these grade levels. The achievement editions are available in Forms A and B. The achievement and abilities edition combines Form A of the achievement edition with a 95-item verbal and quantitative abilities test. The abilities portion can be administered in approximately 60 minutes. The abilities portion consists of a verbal part comprised of 2 subtests, verbal classification and verbal analogies, and a quantitative part, comprised of 2 subtests, quantitative relations and number series. Also at levels 15-18, a class period edition is available. This is an achievement test designed to be administered in a single class period. One form of the test is available at each grade level.

11507
Comprehensive Testing Program II, Levels 3, 4, and 5. Educational Testing Service, Princeton, NJ 1982
Subtests: Verbal Aptitude; Quantitative Aptitude; Mathematics Concepts; Mathematics Computation; Vocabulary; Reading Mechanics of Writing; English Expression; Algebra; Geometry; General Mathematics
Descriptors: *Academic Ability; *Achievement Tests; *Algebra; *Aptitude Tests; Computation; Elementary School Students; Elementary Secondary Education; *Geometry; Grammar; Intermediate Grades; *Language Arts; Mathematical Concepts; *Mathematics; Private Schools; *Reading Tests; Secondary Education; Secondary School Students; Suburban Schools; *Verbal Ability; *Vocabulary Skills; Writing Skills
Identifiers: CTPII; Educational Records Bureau NY; *Quantitative Aptitude
Availability: Educational Records Bureau; P.O. Box 619, Princeton, NJ 08541
Grade Level: 4-12
Notes: Time, 300; Items, 440

Levels 3, 4, and 5 consist of an achievement and an aptitude test. The aptitude test is designed to predict academic performance and has a verbal and quantitative section. An accompanying achievement battery covers: reading, mathematics concepts and computation (levels 3 and 4), algebra (levels 4 and 5), geometry and general mathematics (level 5), vocabulary, mechanics of writing and English expression. Provides norms for use with independent schools and suburban schools as well as national norms.

11511
Humanics National Child Assessment Form: Ages 3 to 6. Humanics Limited, Atlanta, Ga. 1982
Subtests: Social Emotional; Motor Skills; Language; Cognitive; Hygiene-Self Help
Descriptors: Check Lists; *Child Development; Cognitive Development; Emotional Development; Language Proficiency; Preschool Children; Psychomotor Skills; Self Care Skills; Socialization; *Young Children
Availability: Humanics Limited; 1182 W. Peachtree St., P.O. Box 7447, Atlanta, GA 30309
Target Audience: 3-6
Notes: Items, 90

Designed to help teacher or teacher aide to observe child in different areas of development and to follow changes over a period of time. May also be used by parents to help them understand and relate to individual needs of child. Intended as a tool to aid in planning educational and developmental experiences for child. It is not designed for diagnostic or clinical evaluations.

11526
Test of Cognitive Skills, Level 1. CTB/McGraw-Hill, Monterey, CA 1981
Subtests: Sequences; Analogies; Memory; Verbal Reasoning
Descriptors: Abstract Reasoning; *Academic Aptitude; *Aptitude Tests; Classification; *Cognitive Measurement; Culture Fair Tests; *Elementary School Students; Logical Thinking; Primary Education; Recall (Psychology)
Identifiers: TCS
Availability: CTB/McGraw-Hill; Del Monte Research Park, Monterey, CA 93940
Grade Level: 2-3
Notes: Time, 47 approx.; Items, 79

Series of ability tests designed to assess academic aptitude of students. Not intended to measure all aspects of mental ability nor do tests include only those aptitudes and skills that are functions of formal school training. Emphasis is placed on abilities of a relatively abstract nature that are important to success in an educational program. Such abilities include understanding verbal and nonverbal concepts and comprehending relationships among ideas presented in a variety of forms. Test is a major revision of, and successor to, the Short Form Test of Academic Aptitude (SFTAA).

11527
Test of Cognitive Skills, Level 2. CTB/McGraw-Hill, Monterey, CA 1981
Subtests: Sequences; Analogies; Memory; Verbal Reasoning
Descriptors: Abstract Reasoning; *Academic Aptitude; *Aptitude Tests; Classification; *Cognitive Measurement; Culture Fair Tests; Elementary Education; *Elementary School Students; Logical Thinking; Recall (Psychology)
Identifiers: TCS
Availability: CTB/McGraw Hill; Del Monte Research Park, Monterey, CA 93940
Grade Level: 3-5
Notes: Time, 53 approx.; Items, 80

Series of ability tests designed to assess academic aptitude of students. Not intended to measure all aspects of mental ability nor do tests include only those aptitudes and skills that are functions of formal school training. Emphasis is placed on abilities of a relatively abstract nature that are important to success in an educational program. Such abilities include understanding verbal and nonverbal concepts and comprehending relationships among ideas presented in a variety of forms. Test is a major revision of, and successor to, the Short Form Test of Academic Aptitude (SFTAA).

11528
Test of Cognitive Skills, Level 3. CTB/McGraw-Hill, Monterey, CA 1981
Subtests: Sequences; Analogies; Memory; Verbal Reasoning

Descriptors: Abstract Reasoning; *Academic Aptitude; *Aptitude Tests; Classification; *Cognitive Measurement; Culture Fair Tests; *Elementary School Students; *Grade 7; Intermediate Grades; Logical Thinking; Recall (Psychology)
Identifiers: TCS
Availability: CTB/McGraw-Hill; Del Monte Research Park, Monterey, CA 93940
Grade Level: 5-7
Notes: Time, 53 approx.; Items, 80

Series of ability tests designed to assess academic aptitude of students. Not intended to measure all aspects of mental ability nor do tests include only those aptitudes and skills that are functions of formal school training. Emphasis is placed on abilities of a relatively abstract nature that are important to success in an educational program. Such abilities include understanding verbal and nonverbal concepts and comprehending relationships among ideas presented in a variety of forms. Test is a major revision of, and successor to, the Short Form Test of Academic Aptitude (SFTAA).

11529
Test of Cognitive Skills, Level 4. CTB/McGraw-Hill, Monterey, CA 1981
Subtests: Sequences; Analogies; Memory; Verbal Reasoning
Descriptors: Abstract Reasoning; *Academic Aptitude; *Aptitude Tests; Classification; *Cognitive Measurement; Culture Fair Tests; Junior High Schools; *Junior High School Students; Logical Thinking; Recall (Psychology)
Identifiers: TCS
Availability: CTB/McGraw Hill; Del Monte Research Park, Monterey, CA 93940
Grade Level: 7-9
Notes: Time, 53 approx.; Items, 80

Series of ability tests designed to assess academic aptitude of students. Not intended to measure all aspects of mental ability nor do tests include only those aptitudes and skills that are functions of formal school training. Emphasis is placed on abilities of a relatively abstract nature that are important to success in an educational program. Such abilities include understanding verbal and nonverbal concepts and comprehending relationships among ideas presented in a variety of forms. Test is a major revision of, and successor to, the Short Form Test of Academic Aptitude (SFTAA).

11530
Test of Cognitive Skills, Level 5. CTB/McGraw-Hill, Monterey, CA 1981
Subtests: Sequences; Analogies; Memory; Verbal Reasoning
Descriptors: Abstract Reasoning; *Academic Aptitude; *Aptitude Tests; Classification; *Cognitive Measurement; Culture Fair Tests; High Schools; *High School Students; Logical Thinking; Recall (Psychology)
Identifiers: TCS
Availability: CTB/McGraw-Hill; Del Monte Research Park, Monterey, CA 93940
Grade Level: 9-12
Notes: Time, 53 approx.; Items, 80

Series of ability tests designed to assess academic aptitude of students. Not intended to measure all aspects of mental ability nor do tests include only those aptitudes and skills that are functions of formal school training. Emphasis is placed on abilities of a relatively abstract nature that are important to success in an educational program. Such abilities include understanding verbal and nonverbal concepts and comprehending relationships among ideas presented in a variety of forms. Test is a major revision of, and successor to, the Short Form Test of Academic Aptitude (SFTAA).

11531
Humanics National Child Assessment Form: Birth to 3. Kaufman, Marsha; McMurrain, T. Thomas 1982
Subtests: Social Emotional; Language; Cognitive; Gross Motor; Fine Motor
Descriptors: Check Lists; *Child Development; Cognitive Development; Emotional Development; *Infants; Language Proficiency; Psychomotor Skills; Socialization; *Young Children
Identifiers: CDAF
Availability: Humanics Limited; 1182 W. Peachtree St., P.O. Box 7447, Atlanta, GA 30309
Target Audience: 0-3
Notes: Items, 90

Designed to help teacher or parent observe child in different areas of development and to follow changes over a period of time. Used to help them understand and relate to individual needs of child. Checklist contains selected skills and behaviors which a child is likely to manifest in first 3 years of life. It is not intended for use in clinical and diagnostic evaluation, but can be used as a tool in planning educational and developmental experiences for child.

11533
McCarron-Dial Work Evaluation System. Evaluation of the Mentally Disabled—A Systematic Approach. McCarron, Lawrence T.; Dial, Jack G. 1976
Subtests: Verbal-Cognitive; Sensory; Motor; Emotional; Integration-Coping; Work Competency
Descriptors: Adjustment (to Environment); Adults; Cognitive Ability; Emotional Development; *Job Performance; *Mental Retardation; Perceptual Motor Learning; *Predictive Measurement; Psychological Patterns; *Standardized Tests
Identifiers: Haptic Visual Discrimination Test; HVDT; MDWES
Availability: Common Market Press; 2880 LBJ Freeway, Ste. 255, Dallas, TX 75234
Target Audience: Adults

Developed as a means of predicting vocational competency of mentally disabled individuals. Five basic predictor factors, which are considered essential for effective performance in a work environment, are assessed with specific tests. Factors and tests are verbal-cognitive (Wechsler Adult Intelligence Scale or Stanford Binet Intelligence Scale and Peabody Picture Vocabulary Test); Sensory (Bender Visual Motor Gestalt Test and Haptic Visual Discrimination Test); Motor (McCarron Assessment of Neuromuscular Development: Fine and Gross Motor Abilities); emotional (Observational Emotional Inventory); integration-coping (Behavior Rating Scale). System can be used to determine vocational functioning of mentally disabled individuals within the following areas: day care, work activities, extended shelter employment, transitional sheltered employment, community employment.

11579
Screening Test of Adolescent Language. Prather, Elizabeth M.; And Others 1980
Subtests: Vocabulary; Auditory Memory Span; Language Processing; Proverb Explanation
Descriptors: Auditory Stimuli; Comprehension; *Expressive Language; Individual Testing; *Language Handicaps; Language Processing; Memory; *Receptive Language; *Screening Tests; Secondary Education; *Secondary School Students; Vocabulary
Identifiers: STAL
Availability: University of Washington Press; Seattle, WA 98105
Grade Level: 7-12
Notes: Time, 7 approx.; Items, 23

Screening instrument for language disorders and linguistic development of junior and senior high school students. Test is individually administered to identify those students who may warrant further diagnostic evaluation. However, test results should not be interpreted as a comprehensive diagnostic evaluation of linguistic development. Instrument measures both receptive and expressive language through 4 subtests.

11586
Miller Assessment for Preschoolers. Miller, Lucy Jane 1982
Descriptors: *Child Development; *Cognitive Development; *Individual Testing; *Preschool Children; *Psychomotor Skills; *Screening Tests
Identifiers: MAP
Availability: Foundation for Knowledge in Development; 4857 S. Albion, Littleton, CO 80121
Target Audience: 2-5
Notes: Time, 30 approx.; Items, 27

Individually administered screening tool for children from the ages of 2 years 9 months to 5 years 8 months. Provides a comprehensive overview of child's developement status with respect to other children of the same age. Developed to provide short screening tool for educators and clinicians to identify children in need of further evaluation and to provide comprehensive structured clinical framework for evaluation and remediation. For the latter, there is a MAP Supplemental Observations which requires broad clinical knowledge and is a separate entity from the 27 core items. For MAP, there are 5 performance indices: foundations (basic motor and sensory abilities); coordination (complex fine and oral motor abilities); verbal (cognitive language abilities); nonverbal (cognitive abilities not requiring spoken language); and complex tasks (interaction of sensory, motor, and cognitive abilities).

11599
The ABC Inventory. Adair, Normand; Blesch, George 1978
Subtests: Draw a Man; Characteristics of Objects; General Topics; Numbers and Shapes
Descriptors: Individual Testing; *Kindergarten Children; Maturity (Individuals); Predictive Measurement; *Preschool Children; Preschool Education; *School Readiness; *School Readiness Tests; *Screening Tests
Availability: Research Concepts; 1368 E. Airport Rd., Muskegon, MI 49444
Target Audience: 3-6
Notes: Time, 9 approx.; Items, 18

Designed to assess child's readiness for kindergarten or first grade. May be used to yield a readiness age thereby reducing possibility of early school failure.

11601
The Lollipop Test: A Diagnostic Screening Test of School Readiness. Chew, Alex L. 1981
Subtests: Identification of Colors and Shapes, and Copying Shapes; Picture Description, Position, and Spatial Recognition; Identification of Numbers, and Counting; Identification of Letters, and Writing
Descriptors: Culture Fair Tests; *Educational Diagnosis; *Individual Testing; *Kindergarten Children; Number Concepts; *School Readiness; *Screening Tests; Spatial Ability; Visual Discrimination; Visual Perception
Availability: Stoelting Co.; 620 Wheat Ln., Wood Dale, IL 60191
Grade Level: K
Notes: Time, 15 approx.; Items, 52

Used primarily as a screening test to identify children's deficits and strengths in readiness skills necessary to obtain maximum benefit from first-grade experiences and to identify those children who may require additional psychoeducational evaluation. It is not intended as a device to exclude or postpone admission to school, but as an aid in developing the most appropriate programs for children's individual needs. Individually administered test.

11602
Fuld Object Memory Evaluation. Fuld, Paula Altman 1977
Subtests: Storage; Retrieval; Consistent Retrieval; Recall Failure-Ineffective Reminders
Descriptors: Blindness; Children; *Cognitive Measurement; Deafness; *Learning; *Memory; *Older Adults; Recall (Psychology); Schizophrenia
Availability: Stoelting Co.; 620 Wheat Ln., Wood Dale, IL 60191
Target Audience: 70-90

Allows evaluation of memory and learning of older adults under conditions which insure attention and minimize anxiety. Also measures ability to retrieve words rapidly from familiar semantic categories, used for dementia screening. Test has also proved easy to give to young school-age children, and to blind and deaf persons.

11612
Clinical Language Intervention Program. Semel, Eleanor; Wiig, Elisabeth 1982
Descriptors: Elementary Education; Expressive Language; *Informal Assessment; *Language Processing; *Language Proficiency; Memory; *Pragmatics; Pretests Posttests; Receptive Language; *Semantics; Syntax
Identifiers: CLIP
Availability: The Psychological Corp.; 555 Academic Ct., San Antonio, TX 78204-0952
Grade Level: K-8
Notes: Items, 359

Designed as an informal assessment of a child's facility in processing and/or production of critical linguistic concepts, relationships, structures and pragmatic variables. Covers: semantics, syntax, memory, pragmatics. Also useful as a pretest/posttest to document progress.

11620
Armed Services Vocational Aptitude Battery Forms 5-10. Air Force Human Resources Lab., Lackland AFB, TX, Personnel Research Div. 1976
Subtests: Attention to Detail; Numerical Operations; Word Knowledge; Arithmetic Reasoning; Space Perception; Mathematics Knowledge; Electronics Information; Mechanical Comprehension; Automotive Information; Shop Information; General Science; General Information; Classification Inventory
Descriptors: Adolescents; Adults; Algebra; *Aptitude Tests; *Armed Forces; *Career Guidance; *Electronics; *General Science; Geometry; High Schools; *Interest Inventories; *Job Placement; *Mathematical Concepts; *Spatial Ability; *Verbal Ability
Identifiers: ASVAB; Attention to Detail; Automotive Information; Mechanical Comprehension; *Numerical Ability; Shop Information
Availability: Testing Directorate; Headquarters, Military Enlistment Processing Command, ATTN: MERCT, Fort Sheridan, IL 60037
Target Audience: 14-64
Notes: Time, 195; Items, 382

Used for the classification and assignment of enlisted personnel and as a guidance tool in high schools. Testing is obtained by contacting your local recruiting station. Other information can be obtained at the availability address.

11622
WPT Wolfe Screening Test for Programming Aptitude. Wolfe Computer Aptitude Testing Ltd., Oradell, NJ 1982
Descriptors: Adolescents; Adults; *Aptitude Tests; *Career Guidance; *Computer Software; Elementary Secondary Education; Job Placement; Mathematical Logic; *Programing; *Screening Tests; *Simulation; Specifications
Availability: Wolfe Computer Aptitude Testing Ltd.; P.O. Box 319, Oradell, NJ 07649
Target Audience: 14-64

Series of simulated on-the-job tasks evaluates documentation ability, logical ability, and interpretation of specifications. For use by schools, placement agencies and vocational institutes.

11687
Aptitude Tests for Policemen. McCann Associates, Inc., Huntington Valley, PA
Descriptors: Adults; *Aptitude Tests; *Job Applicants; *Occupational Tests; *Police; *Vocational Aptitude
Availability: McCann Associates; 2755 Philmont Ave., Huntingdon Valley, PA 19006
Target Audience: 18-64

Designed to measure ability of candidates to learn police work. Form 62 contains 100 items. Form 70 contains 130 items and is an easier version. Tests assess verbal and quantitative learning ability, as well as interest, common sense, and public relations. Tests are restricted and sold only to Civil Service Commission or to other competent municipal officials. For a statistically validated version see Police Officer Examination (TC003589).

11693
The Word Processing Operator Assessment Battery. Harvard Personnel Testing, Oradell, NJ 1982
Descriptors: Adults; Alphabetizing Skills; English; Filing; French; *Occupational Tests; *Problem Solving; *Screening Tests; *Word Processing
Identifiers: Coding; *Manual Dexterity; *Numerical Ability
Availability: Harvard Personnel Testing; P.O. Box 319, Oradell, NJ 07649
Target Audience: Adults

Screening test for applicants to the position. Measures: attention to detail, ability to solve problems, manual dexterity, numerical skills, alphabetizing, filing, and coding. Used along with interviews, reference checking, and machine tests. Available in English and French.

11718
Berger Aptitude for Programming Test. Berger, Frances; Berger, Raymond M.
Descriptors: Adults; *Aptitude Tests; Chinese; *Data Processing Occupations; Employees; French; German; Italian; Japanese; Job Applicants; Personnel Evaluation; *Personnel Selection; *Programers; *Programing; Spanish; *Work Sample Tests
Identifiers: BAPT
Availability: Psychometrics, Inc.; Sales Dept., 13245 Riverside, Sherman Oaks, CA 91423
Target Audience: 18-64
Notes: Time, 100 approx.; Items, 30

Designed to measure ability to write short computer programs. It is a tutorial test which teaches elements of the job prior to presenting test questions. Examinees are taught a simple programing language to be used in solving test problems. Administration time is divided into 2 segments. Approximately 60 minutes is spent in tutorial instruction and practice items, 40 minutes of acutal test taking. Individuals will have been taught to code, loop, increment, and branch. Forms available in Italian, French, German, Spanish, Japanese and Chinese translations. Sale of tests is restricted to personnel directors, data processing training directors, and data processing managers. Not sold to individuals.

11731
Berger Computer Operator Aptitude Test. Berger, Frances; Berger, Raymond M.
Descriptors: Adults; *Aptitude Tests; *Data Processing Occupations; Employees; *Job Applicants; Personnel Evaluation; *Personnel Selection
Identifiers: BCOAT; *Computer Operators
Availability: Psychometrics, Inc.; Sales Dept., 13245 Riverside, Sherman Oaks, CA 91423
Target Audience: 18-64
Notes: Time, 90 approx.; Items, 20

Designed to measure one's potential as a computer operator. Examinee learns rules and commands necessary to communicate with a hypothetical computer. Operator routes jobs through a computer using concepts of job priority, job time limitations, job status, and appropriate responses to job status. Used to select computer operator trainees. Sale of tests is restricted to personnel directors, data processing training directors, and data processing managers. Not sold to individuals.

11738
Creativity Assessment Packet. Williams, Frank 1980
Descriptors: *Creativity; Creativity Tests; *Divergent Thinking; *Elementary School Students; Elementary Secondary Education; Gifted; Rating Scales; *Screening Tests; *Secondary School Students; Self Evaluation (Individuals); Visual Measures
Identifiers: CAP; Guilfords Structure of Intellect; Structure of Intellect
Availability: D.O.K. Publishers; P.O. Box 605, East Aurora, NY 14052
Grade Level: 3-12
Target Audience: 8-18

Initially developed to screen for gifted or talented students in schools providing federal, state, or local programs aimed at developing creative abilities. Is now available for measuring all children's creative potential. Packet consists of 2 group-administered tests plus a rating scale for parents and teachers of the same tested factors among children. The test of Divergent Thinking is a 12-item instrument which measures a combination of verbal, left brain abilities along with nonverbal, right brain visual perceptive abilities. It yields 4 scores based on Guilford's Structure of Intellect: fluency, flexibility, originality, and elaboration. The test of Divergent Feeling is a 50-item, multiple choice instrument which evaluates how curious, imaginative, complex, and risk-taking children think they are. It yields a total weighted raw score and 4 subscores: curiosity, imagination, complexity, and risk-taking. The Williams Scale is an observational checklist of 8 creativity factors measured by the tests. For each factor, the parent or teacher rates the child on 6 characteristics. There are also 4 open-ended items.

11748
A Test of Graphicacy. Wainer, Howard 1980
Descriptors: *Comprehension; Concept Formation; *Elementary School Students; *Graphs; Intermediate Grades; Multiple Choice Tests; Nonverbal Learning; *Teaching Methods; *Visual Measures; *Visual Stimuli
Availability: Applied Psychological Measurement; v4 n3 p331-40, Sum 1980
Grade Level: 3-5
Notes: Items, 8

Used in a study to investigate the extent to which children learn to use graphic displays and at what age this learning is complete. Study also examined other aspects: kinds of questions for which graphs can be used, what sorts of displays work best and for what kinds of questions, do all children become graphically literate.

11753
Entrance Examination for Schools of Health Related Technologies. Psychological Corp., San Antonio, TX
Subtests: Verbal Ability; Quantitative Ability; Science; Reading Comprehension; Space Relations
Descriptors: *Academic Ability; *Admission Criteria; Adults; *Allied Health Occupations Education; Blood Circulation; *College Entrance Examinations; Dental Technicians; Dietetics; Electroencephalography; Medical Laboratory Assistants; Medical Technologists; Pharmacology; Physical Therapy; Radiologic Technologists; Reading Comprehension; Science Tests; Spatial Ability; Surgical Technicians; Verbal Ability
Identifiers: Electrocardiography; *Entrance Examinations; Optometric Technicians; *Quantitative Ability; Respiratory Therapists; Schools of Health Technology; Ultrasound Technologists
Availability: The Psychological Corp.; 555 Academic Ct., San Antonio, TX 78204-0952
Target Audience: Adults
Notes: Time, 240

For applicants seeking admission to 1- or 2-year post-high school programs in health-related technologies. Measures general academic ability and scientific knowledge, emphasizing the physical sciences. Used for candidates for the following health areas: circulation, dental, dietetic, electrocardiography and encephalography, medical lab and records, nuclear and radiologic, operating room, optometry, pharmacy, physical therapy, pulmonary and respiratory, ultrasound, vision and others.

11757
Pharmacy College Admission Test. American Association of Colleges of Pharmacy, Bethesda, MD
Subtests: Verbal Ability; Quantitative Ability; Biology; Chemistry; Reading comprehension
Descriptors: Adults; Biology; Chemistry; *College Entrance Examinations; High Schools; *High School Seniors; Pharmaceutical Education; *Pharmacology; Reading Comprehension; Verbal Ability
Identifiers: Quantitative Ability
Availability: The Psychological Corp.; 555 Academic Ct., San Antonio, TX 78204-0952
Grade Level: 12
Notes: Time, 240

Measures general academic ability and scientific knowledge of applicants seeking admission to colleges of pharmacy. Test is administered at established testing centers on specific dates. Periodically updated.

11759
Advanced Personnel Test. Psychological Corp., San Antonio, TX 1975
Descriptors: *Administrators; Adults; *Cognitive Ability; *Occupational Tests; *Researchers; *Verbal Ability
Identifiers: Analogies; APT; Miller Analogies Test; *Reasoning Ability
Availability: The Psychological Corp.; 555 Academic Ct., San Antonio, TX 78204-0952
Target Audience: Adults

A difficult test of verbal reasoning ability using the same items as the Miller Analogies Test (TC002078). Used by business, industry and government for employment testing for hiring and upgrading of management and research personnel. The test is administered at testing centers around the country. Requires the solution of a series of problems stated in the form of analogies.

11764
Hay Aptitude Test Battery. Hay, Edward N. 1977
Subtests: Warm-Up; Hay Number Perception Test; Hay Name Finding Test; Hay Number Series Completions
Descriptors: Adults; *Aptitude Tests; *Clerical Occupations; *Occupational Tests; *Vocational Aptitude
Identifiers: Clerical Checking; *Clerical Skills; *Numerical Ability; Practice Tests
Availability: E.F. Wonderlic and Associates; P.O. Box 7, Northfield, IL 60093
Target Audience: Adults
Notes: Time, 13; Items, 286

Designed for use in selecting job applicants for positions requiring numerical ability and precision in working with names and numbers. Includes an unscored practice test. Originally developed to use in selecting applicants for clerical positions. Has also proven valid for plant jobs and operating positions.

11765
Harshman Figures. Harshman, Richard A.; Harshman, Louise 1982
Descriptors: Adolescents; Adults; *Cognitive Ability; Pictorial Stimuli; *Spatial Ability
Identifiers: *Closure Ability; Closure Speed; Gestalt Closure; Perceptual Closure; TIM(I)
Availability: Tests in Microfiche; Test Collection, Educational Testing Service, Princeton, NJ 08541
Target Audience: 13-38
Notes: Time, 3; Items, 11

A test of closure ability (called closure speed, Gestalt closure, perceptual closure) for a wide range of persons having poor to excellent closure abilities. Utilizes large pictures of familiar items or animals. Two forms are available. Both should be administered to reduce the influence of state-dependent fluctuations on performance.

11768
Cognitive Diagnostic Battery. Kay, Stanley R. 1982
Subtests: Color Form Preference Test; Color Form Representation Test; Egocentricity of Thought Test; Progressive Figure Drawing Test; Span of Attention Test
Descriptors: Abstract Reasoning; Adolescents; Adults; Attention Span; Children; *Cognitive Ability; *Cognitive Measurement; Concept Formation; *Diagnostic Tests; Individual Testing; *Mental Disorders; Mental Retardation; *Nonverbal Tests; Perceptual Motor Coordination; Social Development
Identifiers: *Cognitive Evaluation; *Psychiatric Patients
Availability: Psychological Assessment Resources; P.O. Box 998, Odessa, FL 33556
Target Audience: 2-64
Notes: Time, 30 approx.; Items, 46

Series of 5 tests to evaluate nature and degree of intellectual disorders and to aid in differential diagnosis. Wide range assessment of intellectual functions which helps to distinguish between mental subnormality and abnormality, assess cognitive deficits due to impaired development versus later regression, and differentially diagnose mental retardation versus psychosis. Designed to be suitable for a psychiatric population. Tests are brief, easily administered, self-paced, require no verbal response, demand little attention or informational knowledge and are valid for repeated use. Suitable for psychiatric patients who are intellectually limited, nonverbal, inattentive, overtly psychotic or otherwise untestable by conventional means. Five tests examine areas of concept formation, symbolic thinking, socialization of thought, perceptual development, and temporal attention.

11772
Trites Neuropsychological Test. Trites, D.R. 1975
Subtests: Halstead Category Test; Halstead Tactual Performance Test; Motor Steadiness Battery; Roughness Discrimination Test; Dynamometer Grip Strength Test; Finger Tapping Test; Knox Cube Test; Tactile Form Recognition Test; Grooved Pegboard Test; Foot Tapping Test
Descriptors: Academic Achievement; Adolescents; Adults; Attention Span; Children; *Diagnostic Tests; Language Skills; Memory; *Minimal Brain Dysfunction; *Neurological Impairments; *Psychomotor Skills; Visual Perception
Identifiers: Halstead Reitan Neuropsychological Tests; Reasoning Ability
Availability: Lafayette Instrument Co.; P.O. Box 5729, Sagamore Pwy., Lafayette, IN 47903
Target Audience: 6-64

Designed to detect or confirm the presence of brain dysfunction and to describe the extent of impairment and document a patient's capabilities. Consists of a variety of measures of psychomotor ability, academic achievement, reasoning ability, language functions, visual perceptual ability, attention span, and memory. Some of the tests are derived from the Halstead-Reitan Battery, the Wisconsin Motor Steadiness Battery and the Wechsler Adult Intelligence Scale.

11774
IPI Hiring Manual and Job-Tests Program. Industrial Psychology, Inc., New York, NY 1981
Descriptors: Adults; Aptitude Tests; Biographical Inventories; Clerical Occupations; Employee Attitudes; *Employees; *Job Applicants; Job Performance; *Job Skills; Personality Measures; Professional Occupations; Semiskilled Workers; Skilled Workers; Supervisors
Identifiers: Test Batteries
Availability: Industrial Psychology, Inc.; 515 Madison Ave., New York, NY 10022
Target Audience: 18-64

Series of 23 test forms used in different combinations for 24 job-test fields. Lower level jobs use 5 or 6 tests, while upper level jobs will use 10 to 12 tests. Tests A-N are aptitude-intelligence tests. Tests O, P, and R are personality or temperament tests. Tests T through X are biography or weighted application forms. Most job tests require about 5 minutes each. Testing at lower level jobs requires about 30 minutes. Testing at higher levels requires about 1 hour.

11777
School Readiness Test. Gesell Institute of Child Development 1978
Subtests: Visuals 1 and 3; Face Sheet; Initial Interview; Cube Tests; Pencil and Paper; Right and Left; Incomplete Man
Descriptors: Age Grade Placement; Attention Span; Child Development; Eye Hand Coordination; Grade 1; Grade 2; Grade 3; Kindergarten; Psychomotor Skills; School Readiness; *School Readiness Tests; Verbal Development; Visual Perception; *Young Children
Availability: Programs for Education; 1200 Broadway, New York, NY 10001
Target Audience: 4-9

Designed for use as a measure of school readiness based on developmental not chronological age. Tests include: figure copying, completing a figure; and handedness. Tests measure: eye-hand coordination, motor skill, attention span, level of functioning in a structured fine-motor task, visual perception, and verbal ability.

11779
Scholastic Level Exam. Revised 1981. Wonderlic, Charles F. 1981
Descriptors: Abstract Reasoning; *Cognitive Ability; Cognitive Tests; *College Students; Counseling Techniques; Higher Education; High Schools; *High School Students; Mathematical Concepts; Postsecondary Education; *Vocational Schools
Identifiers: SLE; Wonderlic Personnel Test
Availability: E.F. Wonderlic and Associates; P.O. Box N7, Northfield, IL 60093
Grade Level: 11-16
Notes: Time, 12; Items, 50

Reformat of Wonderlic Personnel Test. Designed for use in student admissions at technical schools and counseling at colleges and universities. Scholastic Level Exam name and format was selected to differentiate test use between school and employer. Normative information is identical to Wonderlic Personnel Test (TC000404).

11781
Sentence Imitation Screening Tests. Mecham, Merlin J.; Jones, J. Dean 1979
Subtests: Easy Special Sentences; Intermediate Special Sentences; More Difficult Special Sentences

Descriptors: Audiotape Recordings; Individual Testing; *Language Acquisition; Language Processing; Memory; *Screening Tests; *Speech Skills; Young Children
Identifiers: SIST; Verbal Imitation
Availability: Communication Research Associates; P.O. Box 11012, Salt Lake City, UT 84147
Target Audience: 3-6
Notes: Time, 5 approx.; Items, 90

Designed to assess performance in sequencing language structures and handling syntactic transformational rules; language processing memory span; and verbal imitative performance. Responses should be recorded on tape for later scoring.

11787
Psychological Stimulus Response Test. Mullen, Eileen M. 1977
Subtests: Auditory Language Scale; Visual Motor Scale
Descriptors: *Children; *Cognitive Development; *Cognitive Measurement; Concept Formation; Individual Testing; *Learning Modalities; *Multiple Disabilities; *Severe Disabilities; Tactual Perception; Verbal Ability; Visual Perception
Identifiers: PSR; PSR Test
Availability: Meeting St. School; 667 Waterman Ave., E. Providence, RI 02914
Target Audience: 1-10

Designed to assess the cognitive abilities of severely, multiply handicapped children. The stimulus and response item content is designed to minimize the physical aspects of the tasks while tapping behavior which demonstrates acquisition of concepts traditionally associated with levels of intellectual development. PSR Test introduces concept of functional age (F.A.) instead of mental age. Test is particularly effective with severely multiply handicapped children, ages 1 to 5, and with older, retarded, severely multiply handicapped children, ages 6 to 10. In addition to the 2 scales comprising the test, there is also a tactile differentiation section.

11789
Allied Health Professions Admission Test. Psychological Corp., San Antonio, TX
Subtests: Verbal Ability; Quantitative Ability; Biology; Chemistry; Reading Comprehension
Descriptors: *Academic Ability; Academic Aptitude; *Achievement Tests; Adults; *Allied Health Occupations; *Allied Health Occupations Education; Allied Health Personnel; Aptitude Tests; College Admission; *College Applicants; *College Entrance Examinations; Computation; *Degrees (Academic); Multiple Choice Tests; *Natural Sciences; Timed Tests
Identifiers: AHPAT
Availability: The Psychological Corp.; 555 Academic Ct., San Antonio, TX 78204-0952
Target Audience: Adults
Notes: Time, 240

Designed as an entrance exam for applicants seeking admission to baccalaureate and post-baccalaureate programs in allied health schools. Measures general academic ability and scientific knowledge. Not distributed to individuals, given only at specified testing centers. Instrument under constant revision; thus, the number of items and the time vary from (3-1/2 to 4 hours). Restricted.

11791
Rhode Island Profile of Early Learning Behavior. Novack, Harry S.; And Others 1982
Subtests: Observable Behavior; Written Work
Descriptors: Classroom Observation Techniques; *Cognitive Processes; Elementary School Students; *Grade 1; *Grade 2; *Kindergarten Children; *Learning Problems; Primary Education; *Screening Tests; *Student Behavior
Identifiers: Rhode Island Pupil Identification Scale; RIPELB; RIPIS
Availability: Jamestown Publishers; P.O. Box 6743, Providence, RI 02940
Grade Level: K-2
Notes: Items, 40

Scale for identifying children with learning problems in grades K-2. Can also be used to show strengths and weaknesses of children who have no serious learning problems. Test items are divided into 2 parts. Part I deals with behavior observable in the classroom and includes body perception, sensory-motor coordination, attention, memory for events, and self concept. Part II deals with behavior which may be observed and evaluated through a review of the pupil's written work and includes memory for reproduction of symbols, directional or positional constancy, spatial and sequential arrangements of letters and symbols, and memory for symbols for cognitive operations.

11794
Adelphi Parent Administered Readiness Test. Klein, Pnina S. 1982

Subtests: Concept Formation; Letter Discrimination; Writing Ability; Knowledge of Numbers; Visual Perception; Visual Memory; Comprehension and Memory; Auditory Sequential Memory; Creative Ability; Recognition of Facial Expression of Emotions
Descriptors: Cognitive Development; Educational Diagnosis; English (Second Language); *Kindergarten Children; Language Handicaps; Learning Disabilities; *Parent Participation; Parent School Relationship; Primary Education; Remedial Instruction; *School Readiness Tests
Identifiers: APART; Public Law 94 142
Availability: Media Materials; 2936 Remington Ave., Baltimore, MD 21211
Grade Level: K
Notes: Time, 20 approx.

Provides for building a home school relationship by enrolling parents in testing their own children. Objectives of test are to assure direct parental involvement in preschool evaluation activities; to provide parents with profile of child's learning abilities; to show parents relationship between specific abilities and various academic subjects; to guide parents toward activities providing necessary educational remediation; to allow for involvement of non-English speaking or bilingual parents; to provide a means of identifying specific learning disabilities and to discriminate between children with learning disabilities and children with language problems; to present teachers and school psychologists opportunity to observe parent-child interaction patterns.

11795
Zaner-Bloser Kindergarten Screening Inventory. Milone, Michael N.; Lucas, Virginia H. 1980
Subtests: Naming Objects; Matching Objects; Naming Money; Matching Money; Naming Colors; Matching Colors; Naming Shapes; Matching Shapes; Naming Sets; Matching Sets; Naming Numerals; Matching Numerals; Naming Letters; Matching Letters; Spatial Relationship Words; Sequence Words; Sequencing; Counting; Writing Name; Tracing Strokes; Copying Strokes; Tracing Letters; Copying Letters
Descriptors: *Cognitive Development; *Criterion Referenced Tests; *Individual Testing; *Kindergarten Children; Primary Education; *School Readiness; *Screening Tests
Identifiers: KSI; Zaner Bloser Kindergarten Program
Availability: Zaner-Bloser; 1459 King Ave., Columbus, OH 43212
Grade Level: K

Developed to help teachers identify educationally relevant differences among kindergarten children to allow for appropriate curriculum planning. KSI comprises skills which appear on the Zaner-Bloser Kindergarten Program Foundations for Formal Learning and the Check Lists of Kindergarten Skills. KSI focuses on skills important to prereading, pre-writing, and pre-arithmetic. One skill prominent in KSI is left-to-right progression. Individually administered. KSI also allows for teacher observation and comments.

11798
Kranz Talent Identification Instrument. Kranz, Bella 1982
Descriptors: Abstract Reasoning; Academically Gifted; Creativity; *Culture Fair Tests; Elementary Education; *Elementary School Students; *Gifted; Junior High Schools; *Junior High School Students; Leadership; Psychomotor Skills; *Screening Tests; Spatial Ability; *Talent Identification; Theater Arts; Underachievement; Visual Arts
Identifiers: KTII; Multidimensional Screening Device
Availability: Kranz Talent Identification Instrument; P.O. Box 2450 44, Brooklyn, NY 11224
Grade Level: 3-8

A device to assist teachers, both in raising their awareness of the multiple criteria of giftedness and in screening talented children in their classes. Identifies children from all ethnic and sociological backgrounds. Involves a 3-stage procedure in which teachers are trained as raters; all children are appraised before any selections are made; a screening committee evaluates teacher ratings and pupil data to make final selections for a gifted program. Entire class is rated on each of the following areas: visual arts, performing arts, creative talent, one-sided talent, academic talent, leadership and organizing talent, psychomotor talent, spatial and abstract thinking, underachievement talent, hidden talent.

11799
Ennis-Weir Argumentation Test, Level X: An Essay Test of Rational Thinking Ability. Ennis, Robert H.; Weir, Eric 1982

Descriptors: *Cognitive Measurement; *College Students; *Essay Tests; Grade 6; Higher Education; High Schools; *High School Students; Junior High School Students; *Logical Thinking; *Persuasive Discourse; Writing (Composition)
Identifiers: EWAT(X)
Availability: Illinois Thinking Project; University of Illinois, 1310 S. Sixth St., Champaign, IL 61820
Grade Level: 9-16
Notes: Time, 40; Items, 9

A general test of rational thinking ability in the context of argumentation. Intended to help evaluate a person's ability to appraise an argument and to formulate, in writing, an argument in response. Calls for both critical and creative dimensions of rational thinking ability. Test consists of reading a letter to the editor and responding, paragraph by paragraph, to the logic of the letter's content, plus giving an overall evaluation of the letter. Most appropriate for use with high school and college students but may also be suitable for use in grades 6-8.

11802
Torrance Tests of Creative Thinking, Revised Edition. Torrance, E. Paul 1974
Subtests: Fluency; Flexibility; Originality; Elaboration
Descriptors: Cognitive Processes; *Creativity; *Creativity Tests; *Elementary School Students; Elementary Secondary Education; Gifted; *Graduate Students; Higher Education; Individual Testing; *Kindergarten Children; Pictorial Stimuli; *Secondary School Students; *Undergraduate Students
Identifiers: Thinking Creatively with Pictures; Thinking Creatively with Words; TTCT
Availability: Scholastic Testing Service; 480 Meyer Rd., Bensenville, IL 60106
Grade Level: K-20

Measures creativity by assessing 4 important mental characteristics: fluency, flexibility, originality, elaboration. Comes in 2 forms, verbal and figural, which may both be administered, preferably in 2 separate sittings. The verbal forms (Forms A and B) require written responses and may be administered to groups of students from grade 4 through graduate school. The verbal test may be individually administered to young children. The verbal test takes approximately 45 minutes. The figural test requires responses that are mainly drawing or pictorial in nature. Use of the figural test is recommended from kindergarten through graduate school and requires approximately 30 minutes. Streamlined scoring procedures for the figural form is a new alternative scoring procedure and yields norm referenced measures for fluency, originality, abstractness of titles, elaboration, and resistance to premature closure.

11829
Famous Writers School: Your Aptitude and Interest Profile. Famous Schools, Westport, CT. 1981
Descriptors: Adults; *Aptitude Tests; Attitude Measures; Correspondence Study; Interest Inventories; *Writing (Composition)
Availability: Famous Schools; P.O. Box 900, Westport, CT 06880
Target Audience: Adults
Notes: Items, 40

Designed to determine whether one has the abilities, attitudes and interests that most writers have. For use in evaluating clients for a mail order writing course.

11830
Famous Photographers School Aptitude Test. Famous Schools, Westport, CT. 1974
Descriptors: Adults; *Aptitude Tests; Correspondence Study; Diagnostic Tests; *Photography
Availability: Famous Schools; P.O. Box 900, Westport, CT 06880
Target Audience: Adults
Notes: Items, 45

Designed to determine if the test-taker has the ability to use photographic taste and judgment, and to indicate areas where further instruction is needed.

11831
Famous Artists School Aptitude Test. Famous Schools, Westport, CT. 1975
Descriptors: Adults; *Aptitude Tests; *Art; Correspondence Study
Availability: Famous Schools; P.O. Box 900, Westport, CT 06880
Target Audience: Adults

Designed to determine if the test-taker has ability to select a more interesting design or composition and exhibit pencil control and drawing ability.

11833
Color Matching Aptitude Test (1978 Edition). Inter-Society Color Council, Troy, NY 1978
Descriptors: Adults; *Aptitude Tests; *Color; Discrimination Learning; *Individual Testing; *Job Applicants; Occupational Tests; *Personnel; Personnel Selection; Visual Measures; *Visual Perception; Visual Stimuli; *Vocational Aptitude
Identifiers: Color Aptitude Test
Availability: Federation of Societies for Coatings Technology; 1315 Walnut St., Philadelphia, PA 19107
Target Audience: Adults
Notes: Items, 40

Individually administered instrument to aid in determining one's color-matching ability, NOT to be used to indicate color blindness. Used for those for whom color perception is an important part of their job. The authors recommend retesting at regular intervals. Untimed. Requires the use of the color chips, a chip dispenser and matching loose chips, carrying case. Earlier editions have title: Color Aptitude Test.

11862
Marshalltown Preschool Developmental Package. Donahue, Michael; And Others 1980
Descriptors: *Cognitive Development; Developmental Tasks; Diagnostic Teaching; *Disabilities; *Infants; Language Acquisition; *Preschool Children; Preschool Education; Psychomotor Skills; Screening Tests; Socialization
Identifiers: MBDP; MDSI
Availability: Marshalltown Project Area Education Agency 6; Preschool Div., 210 S. 12th St., Marshalltown, IA 50158
Target Audience: 0-6

Three-part system designed for screening, assessment and curriculum retrieval. Useful for preschool handicapped population. Developmental Profile (MBDP-S) contains 216 items which evaluate development in areas of motor, cognitive and socialization skills. Yields developmental quotient. Screening instrument (MDSI) has 24 items, requires about 15 minutes to administer and was developed for quick screening. Curriculum Management system enables teacher to develop teaching prescriptions.

11864
Basic School Skills Inventory—Diagnostic. Hammill, Donald D.; Leigh, James E. 1983
Subtests: Daily Living Skills; Spoken Language; Reading Readiness; Writing Readiness; Mathematics Readiness; Classroom Behavior
Descriptors: *Basic Skills; Criterion Referenced Tests; Daily Living Skills; *Diagnostic Tests; Elementary School Mathematics; Handwriting; Writing Readiness; Individual Testing; Norm Referenced Tests; *Preschool Children; Primary Education; Reading Readiness; *School Readiness Tests; Speech Communication; Student Behavior
Identifiers: BSSI D
Availability: PRO-ED; 8700 Shoal Creek Blvd., Austin, TX 78758
Target Audience: 4-6
Notes: Time, 30 approx.; Items, 110

Used to assist teachers and other educational personnel in assessing abilities of young children. Test has 4 main uses: to identify children performing significantly below their peers in the areas measured; to reveal specific strengths and weaknesses for instructional purposes; to document progress resulting from intervention programs; to use in research studies involving young children. Also suitable for use with older children who function within the developmental range of 4 to 6 years, such as retarded, underachievers, slow learners, learning disabled, educationally handicapped, or developmentally young. There are no time limits on test; time will vary but generally should not exceed 30 minutes.

11871
Kuhlmann-Anderson Tests, Level K. Eighth Edition. Kuhlmann, F.; Anderson, Rose G. 1982
Subtests: Verbal; Non-Verbal
Descriptors: *Academic Aptitude; Aptitude Tests; *Cognitive Ability; *Cognitive Tests; *Kindergarten Children; Nonverbal Ability; Predictive Measurement; Primary Education; Verbal Ability
Identifiers: Oral Tests
Availability: Scholastic Testing Service; 480 Meyer Rd., Bensenville, IL 60106
Grade Level: K
Notes: Time, 75 approx.; Items, 80

Designed to provide a measure of an individual's academic potential through assessing those cognitive skills related to the learning process. Uses 8 subtests, 4 of which employ item types primarily nonverbal in nature and which are based more upon an understanding of numbers and figures rather than upon vocabulary and reading skills. The other 4 subtests are more dependent upon verbal skills. The verbal cognitive skills quotient (CSQ) may be used as an estimate of potential in such areas as reading, language arts, social studies, and other areas heavily dependent on verbal skills. The nonverbal CSQ provides a measure for predicting achievement in such areas as mathematics, art, and physical sciences. Level K is administered orally and should be given over 2 days, 1 session each day.

11872
Kuhlmann-Anderson Tests, Level A. Eighth Edition. Kuhlmann, F.; Anderson, Rose G. 1982
Subtests: Verbal; Non-Verbal
Descriptors: *Academic Aptitude; Aptitude Tests; *Cognitive Ability; *Cognitive Tests; Elementary School Students; *Grade 1; Nonverbal Ability; Predictive Measurement; Primary Education; Verbal Ability
Availability: Scholastic Testing Service; 480 Meyer Rd., Bensenville, IL 60106
Grade Level: 1
Notes: Time, 75 approx.; Items, 80

Designed to provide a measure of an individual's academic potential through assessing those cognitive skills related to the learning process. Uses 8 subtests, 4 of which employ item types primarily nonverbal in nature and which are based more upon an understanding of numbers and figures rather than upon vocabulary and reading skills. The other 4 subtests are more dependent upon verbal skills. The level A test is administered orally. Test should be administered over a 2-day period. The verbal cognitive skills quotient (CSQ) may be used as an estimate of potential in such areas as reading, language arts, social studies and other areas heavily dependent on verbal skills. The nonverbal CSQ provides a measure for predicting achievement in such areas as mathematics, art, and the physical sciences. Level A is administered orally. Test is given in 2 days, 1 session each day.

11873
Kuhlmann-Anderson Tests, Level BC. Eighth Edition. Kuhlmann, F.; Anderson, Rose G. 1982
Subtests: Verbal; Non-Verbal
Descriptors: *Academic Aptitude; Aptitude Tests; *Cognitive Ability; *Cognitive Tests; Elementary School Students; *Grade 2; *Grade 3; Nonverbal Ability; Predictive Measurement; Primary Education; Verbal Ability
Identifiers: Oral Tests
Availability: Scholastic Testing Service; 480 Meyer Rd., Bensenville, IL 60106
Grade Level: 2-3
Notes: Time, 75 approx.; Items, 105

Designed to provide a measure of an individual's academic potential through assessing those cognitive skills related to the learning process. Uses 8 subtests, 4 of which employ item types primarily nonverbal in nature and which are based more upon an understanding of numbers and figures rather than upon vocabulary and reading skills. The other 4 subtests are more dependent upon verbal skills. The verbal cognitive skills quotient (CSQ) may be used as an estimate of potential in such areas as reading, language arts, social studies, and other areas heavily dependent on verbal skills. The nonverbal CSQ provides a measure for predicting achievement in such areas as mathematics, art, and physical sciences. Level BC is administered orally. Test should be given in 2 days, 1 session each day.

11874
Kuhlmann-Anderson Tests, Level CD. Eighth Edition. Kuhlmann, F.; Anderson, Rose G. 1982
Subtests: Verbal; Non-Verbal
Descriptors: *Academic Aptitude; Aptitude Tests; *Cognitive Ability; *Cognitive Tests; Elementary Education; Elementary School Students; *Grade 3; *Grade 4; Nonverbal Ability; Predictive Measurement; Verbal Ability
Availability: Scholastic Testing Service; 480 Meyer Rd., Bensenville, IL 60106
Grade Level: 3-4
Notes: Time, 75 approx.; Items, 120

Designed to provide a measure of an individual's academic potential through assessing those cognitive skills related to the learning process. Uses 8 subtests, 4 of which employ item types primarily nonverbal in nature and which are based more upon an understanding of numbers and figures rather than upon vocabularly and reading skills. The other 4 subtests are more dependent upon verbal skills. The verbal cognitive skills quotient (CSQ) may be used as an estimate of potential in such areas as reading, language arts, social studies, and other areas heavily dependent on verbal skills. The nonverbal CSQ provides a measure for predicting achievement in such areas as mathematics, art, and physical sciences.

11875
Kuhlmann-Anderson Tests, Level EF. Eighth Edition. Kuhlmann, F.; Anderson, Rose G. 1982
Subtests: Verbal; Non-Verbal
Descriptors: *Academic Aptitude; Aptitude Tests; *Cognitive Ability; *Cognitive Tests; *Elementary School Students; *Grade 5; *Grade 6; Intermediate Grades; Nonverbal Ability; Predictive Measurement; Verbal Ability
Availability: Scholastic Testing Service; 480 Meyer Rd., Bensenville, IL 60106
Grade Level: 5-6

Notes: Time, 75 approx.; Items, 130

Designed to provide a measure of an individual's academic potential through assessing those cognitive skills related to the learning process. Uses 8 subtests, 4 of which employ item types primarily nonverbal in nature and which are based more upon an understanding of numbers and figures rather than upon vocabularly and reading skills. The other 4 subtests are more dependent upon verbal skills. The verbal cognitive skills quotient (CSQ) may be used as an estimate of potential in such areas as reading, language arts, social studies, and other areas heavily dependent on verbal skills. The nonverbal CSQ provides a measure for predicting achievement in such areas as mathematics, art, and physical sciences.

11876
Kuhlmann-Anderson Tests, Level G. Eighth Edition. Kuhlmann, F.; Anderson, Rose G. 1982
Subtests: Verbal; Non-Verbal
Descriptors: *Academic Aptitude; Aptitude Tests; *Cognitive Ability; *Cognitive Tests; Junior High Schools; *Junior High School Students; Nonverbal Ability; Predictive Measurement; Verbal Ability
Availability: Scholastic Testing Service; 480 Meyer Rd., Bensenville, IL 60106
Grade Level: 7-9
Notes: Time, 75 approx.; Items, 130

Designed to provide a measure of an individual's academic potential through assessing those cognitive skills related to the learning process. Uses 8 subtests, 4 of which employ item types primarily nonverbal in nature and which are based more upon an understanding of numbers and figures rather than upon vocabularly and reading skills. The other 4 subtests are more dependent upon verbal skills. The verbal cognitive skills quotient (CSQ) may be used as an estimate of potential in such areas as reading, language arts, social studies, and other areas heavily dependent on verbal skills. The nonverbal CSQ provides a measure for predicting achievement in such areas as mathematics, art, and physical sciences.

11877
Kuhlmann-Anderson Tests, Level H. Eighth Edition. Kuhlmann, F.; Anderson, Rose G. 1982
Subtests: Verbal; Non-Verbal
Descriptors: *Academic Aptitude; Aptitude Tests; *Cognitive Ability; *Cognitive Tests; High Schools; *High School Students; Nonverbal Ability; Predictive Measurement; Verbal Ability
Availability: Scholastic Testing Service; 480 Meyer Rd., Bensenville, IL 60106
Grade Level: 9-12
Notes: Time, 75 approx.; Items, 130

Designed to provide a measure of an individual's academic potential through assessing those cognitive skills related to the learning process. Uses 8 subtests, 4 of which employ item types primarily nonverbal in nature and which are based more upon an understanding of numbers and figures rather than upon vocabulary and reading skills. The other 4 subtests are more dependent upon verbal skills. The verbal cognitive skills quotient (CSQ) may be used as an estimate of potential in such areas as reading, language arts, social studies, and other areas heavily dependent on verbal skills. The nonverbal CSQ provides a measure for predicting achievement in such areas as mathematics, art, and physical sciences.

11891
Stellern-Show Informal Learning Inventory. Stellern, John 1982
Descriptors: Auditory Perception; Elementary Education; *Elementary School Students; Expressive Language; Informal Assessment; *Learning Disabilities; Memory; *Screening Tests; Tactual Perception; Visual Perception
Identifiers: Graphic Ability; SILI
Availability: John Stellern; Special Education, P.O. Box 3374, University of Wyoming, Laramie, WY 82070
Grade Level: K-8
Notes: Items, 82

An informal assessment of a child's auditory, visual, haptic and multi-sensory input, memory and meaning processes and verbal, graphic and haptic output processes for use by classroom teachers, special educators, educational diagnosticians, etc. Consists of tasks to be performed by the child that can be observed and which may indicate presence of learning difficulties. Some sections require manipulative materials such as blocks.

11907
Wechsler Intelligence Scale for Children-Revised Test Profile. Consulting Psychologists Press, Inc., Palo Alto, CA 1975
Descriptors: Adolescents; Children; Elementary School Students; Elementary Secondary Education; *Intelligence Tests; *Profiles; *Psychologists; Records (Forms); Scoring; *Secondary School Students; *Test Interpretation
Identifiers: Supplementary Profile for the WISCR; WISCR Test Profile
Availability: Consulting Psychologists Press; 577 College Ave., Palo Alto, CA 94306
Target Audience: 6-17

Designed for use by psychologists in reporting test results to teachers, parents or counselors. The shortened form of reporting test scores provides for easy reference, graphic clarity, and a better understanding of subsections of the total test.

11908
Wechsler Intelligence Scale for Children-Revised: Scoring Criteria. Massey, James O.; And Others 1978
Descriptors: Adolescents; Children; *Elementary School Students; Elementary Secondary Education; *Intelligence Tests; *Scoring; *Secondary School Students; Test Interpretation; Verbal Tests
Identifiers: Wechsler Intelligence Scale for Children (Revised); WISC R
Availability: Consulting Psychologists Press, Inc.; 577 College Ave., Palo Alto, CA 94306
Target Audience: 6-16

A monograph containing a list of possible item responses to the verbal scales in the revised Wechsler Intelligence Scale for Children, WISC-R (TC007461). Designed for use by examiners to assist in subjective scoring of the verbal scales.

11913
Hill Medical Terminology Training Assessment Sample. Hill, Steven 1974
Descriptors: *Academic Ability; Adults; *Allied Health Occupations; *Aptitude Tests; High School Graduates; High School Students; Interest Inventories; *Medical Laboratory Assistants; *Medical Record Technicians; *Medical Vocabulary; *Nurses; *Practical Nursing; *Radiologic Technologists; *Work Sample Tests
Availability: Materials Development Center; Work Sample Manual Clearinghouse, Stout Vocational Rehabilitation Institute, University of Wisconsin-Stout, Menomonie, WI 54751
Target Audience: 16-64
Notes: Items, 100

Designed to assess post-high school student's or above-average high school student's interest in paramedical-related training programs and ability to perform tasks requiring academic skills; learn, retain and recall terminology; and study from a programed text, which is required prior for testing. For use with medical laboratory assistants and practical nurses. A multiple choice paper and pencil test.

11917
Test of Nonverbal Intelligence: A Language Free Measure of Cognitive Ability. Brown, Linda; And Others 1982
Descriptors: Adolescents; Adults; Bilingualism; Children; *Cognitive Ability; Individual Testing; *Intelligence Tests; Language Handicaps; Learning Disabilities; Mental Retardation; Non English Speaking; *Nonverbal Tests; Older Adults; Physical Disabilities; *Problem Solving
Identifiers: TONI
Availability: PRO-ED; 8700 Shoal Creek Blvd., Austin, TX 78758
Target Audience: 5-85
Notes: Time, 15 approx.; Items, 50

A language-free intelligence test used to evaluate the intellectual capacity of those individuals who are difficult or impossible to test with traditional pencil and paper tests. These include mentally retarded, stroke patients, bilingual and non-English speaking, speech or language handicapped, or learning disabled subjects. The basis of all the test items is problem solving and requires subjects to solve problems by identifying relationships among abstract figures. The examiner pantomimes the instructions and the subject points to the appropriate response. Test is not timed and requires approximately 15 minutes to administer. Available in 2-equivalent forms. Administered individually or to small groups.

11919
Occupational Aptitude Survey and Interest Schedule: Aptitude Survey. Parker, Randall M. 1983
Subtests: Vocabulary; Computation; Spatial Relations; Word Comparison; Making Marks
Descriptors: Adolescents; *Aptitude Tests; Computation; Motor Reactions; Secondary Education; *Secondary School Students; Spatial Ability; Visual Discrimination; Vocabulary; *Vocational Aptitude
Identifiers: Manual Dexterity; OASIS
Availability: PRO-ED; 8700 Shoal Creek Blvd., Austin, TX 78758
Grade Level: 8-12
Target Audience: 13-18
Notes: Time, 35 approx.; Items, 185

One of 2 separate instruments comprising the Occupational Aptitude Survey and Interest Schedule (OASIS). The aptitude test was developed to assist students in making career decisions by providing them with information regarding their relative strength in several aptitude areas related to the world of work. Scores are keyed directly to the Dictionary of Occupational Titles, Guide for Occupational Exploration, and the Worker Trait Group Guide. In addition to the 185 items of the first 4 subtests, the Making Marks subtest is a speeded task requiring the examinee to draw an asterisk-like figure in each of 160 boxes. May be administered to individuals or to groups.

11924
Learning Accomplishment Profile: Diagnostic Screening Edition. Chapel Hill Training-Outreach Project, NC; Kentucky State Dept. of Education, Frankfort 1981
Subtests: Fine Motor; Cognitive; Language; Gross Motor
Descriptors: Cognitive Ability; *High Risk Students; *Individual Testing; *Kindergarten Children; Language Skills; Primary Education; Psychomotor Skills; *Screening Tests
Identifiers: LAP(D)
Availability: Kaplan School Supply Corp.; 1310 Lewisville-Clemmons Rd., Lewisville, NC 27023
Grade Level: K
Notes: Time, 15 approx.; Items, 17

Developed for early identification of children potentially at-risk in learning and developmental areas. All items must be administered. Results obtained should be considered first or initial phase of the screening, referral, diagnostic, individualized programing, and instructional process. Items were selected from the Learning Accomplishment Profile-Diagnostic and includes items from the following subscales: fine motor, cognitive, language, and gross motor.

11928
Modified Weigl Test and Recognition Test of Bases of Groupings. Ward, Lionel O. 1980
Subtests: Modified Weigl I; Modified Weigl II; Modified Weigl III
Descriptors: *Aptitude Tests; Children; *Classification
Identifiers: *Abstraction Responses; TIM(I); Weigl Colour Form Sorting Test
Availability: Tests in Microfiche; Test Collection, Educational Testing Service, Princeton, NJ 08541
Target Audience: 7-11

Designed to measure the ability of children to classify objects according to 1, 2, or 3 different criteria. One instrument is a modification of the Weigl Colour-Form Sorting Test (1941). The other measures the child's recognition of the basis on which other figures are grouped, e.g., by size, color, material, shape.

11930
Swassing-Barbe Modality Index. Barbe, Walter B.; Swassing, Raymond H. 1979
Subtests: Visual; Auditory; Kinesthetic
Descriptors: Adults; Auditory Stimuli; Elementary Education; *Elementary School Students; English (Second Language); *Individual Testing; Kinesthetic Perception; *Learning Modalities; Objective Tests; Preschool Children; Visual Learning
Identifiers: SBMI; Zaner Bloser Modality Kit
Availability: Zaner-Bloser; 1459 King Ave., Columbus, OH 43212
Grade Level: K-6
Notes: Time, 20 approx.

Matching-to-sample task used to assess the modality or modalities children employ in learning, specifically the visual, auditory, and kinesthetic modes. Individually administered instrument in which a stimulus item or sample is presented and the respondent is asked to duplicate the sample. Instrument can be used with preschool age children, children whose first language is not English, older children and adults, as well as with the primary group of elementary school students.

11931
Bateria Woodcock Psico-Educativa en Espanol. Woodcock, Richard W. 1982
Subtests: Vocabulario Sobre Dibujos; Relaciones Espaciales; Aprendizaje Visual-Auditivo; Conceptos Cuantitativos; Pareo Visual; Antonimos-Sinonimos; Analisis-Sintesis; Inversion de Numeros; Formacion de Conceptos; Analogias; Identificacion de Letras y Palabras; Analisis de Palabras; Comprension de Textos; Calculo; Problemas Aplicados; Dictado; Comprobacion; Puncuacion y Empleo de Letras Mayusculas
Descriptors: *Academic Achievement; *Academic Aptitude; Adolescents; Adults; Bilingualism; Children; Clinical Diagnosis; *Cognitive Ability; *Cognitive Measurement; Handicap Identification; Individualized Education Programs; Individual Testing; Older Adults; Screening Tests; *Spanish; Spanish Speaking

Identifiers: Test Batteries; Woodcock Johnson Psycho Educational Battery
Availability: DLM Teaching Resources; P.O. Box 4000, 1 DLM Park, Allen, TX 75002
Target Audience: 3-80

Consists of 17 subtests which measure cognitive functions, expected scholastic achievement and actual academic achievement. To determine whether to assess a subject's psychoeducational abilities in English or Spanish, examiner may administer Oral Language Cluster (vocabulario sobre dibujos, antonimos-sinonimos, analogras) in Spanish from Bateria or in English from the Woodcock Language Proficiency Battery-English (1980). Battery may be used for clinical assessment, program evaluation or research purposes with individuals ranging from preschool age through the geriatric level. Within the school-age range, a primary application is for students having learning and/or adjustment problems. Uses of the battery include individual evaluation, selection and placement, individual program planning, guidance, recording individual growth, program evaluation, research studies, and psychometric training.

11934
Grimes Pharmacy Helper Work Sample. Grimes, Richard T. 1979
Descriptors: Adults; *Aptitude Tests; Medical Vocabulary; *Pharmacy; *Work Sample Tests
Identifiers: Clerks; Drugs; *Finger Dexterity; *Manual Dexterity
Availability: Materials Development Center; Work Sample Manual Clearinghouse, Stout Vocational Rehabilitation Institute, School of Education, University of Wisconsin-Stout, Menomonie, WI 54751
Target Audience: 18-64
Notes: Items, 15

Designed to assess the interest and ability to perform tasks required of a pharmacy helper, e.g., use medical terminology, transcribe drug information onto labels, select proper drugs, and fill containers with correct quantities. Also measures manual and finger dexterity, and ability to count, follow directions and record information legibly. Useful with those having an assessed reading level of grade 6. A pill counter and other common pharmacy items are necessary. Use with a clerical aptitude measure is suggested.

11935
Money Handling Assessment Sample. Shields, Marilyn 1974
Descriptors: Adults; *Aptitude Tests; Arithmetic; *Work Sample Tests
Identifiers: Clerks; *Money Skills
Availability: Materials Development Center; Work Sample Manual Clearinghouse, Stout Vocational Rehabilitation Institute, School of Education, University of Wisconsin-Stout, Menomonie, WI 54751
Target Audience: 18-64
Notes: Items, 10

Designed for use in vocational evaluation. Measures skills in money recognition and handling and basic arithmetic operations. For use with cash clerks; toll collectors and related jobs. Clients should be pretested for ability to recognize coins and perform arithmetic operations. Household items and play money are needed for administration.

11936
Shipping and Receiving Freight Handler Work Sample. Henderson, Merri Lee 1974
Descriptors: Adults; *Aptitude Tests; Decision Making Skills; Knowledge Level; *Work Sample Tests
Identifiers: *Clerks; *Freight Handlers; Postal Service
Availability: Materials Development Center; Work Sample Manual Clearinghouse, Stout Vocational Rehabilitation Institute, School of Education, University of Wisconsin-Stout, Menomonie, WI 54751
Target Audience: 18-64
Notes: Time, 60; Items, 15

Designed to assess ability to route packages and mail for shipment and to determine cost of shipment. Measures ability to make related judgments and use postal charts. For use with receiving, manifest, receipt, distributing, returned goods clerks and related jobs. Sixth grade reading level is necessary. Various stationery items are required.

11937
The Radio Announcing Work Sample. Boland, Kevin M. 1974
Descriptors: Adults; *Aptitude Tests; *Career Counseling; Communication Skills; High School Students; Language Skills; Public Speaking; *Radio; Secondary Education; *Television; *Work Sample Tests
Identifiers: Actors; *Announcers; Organizational Skills

Availability: Materials Development Center; Work Sample Manual Clearinghouse, Stout Vocational Rehabilitation Institute, School of Education, University of Wisconsin-Stout, Menomonie, WI 54751
Target Audience: 17-64
Notes: Time, 45; Items, 9

Designed for use with high school graduates or students near graduation to assess their ability to perform the tasks of a radio announcer. Examinees must have a reading level of at least 10th grade and must organize a 5 minute broadcast according to a prescribed format. Measures planning and organizational abilities, facility with language and vocabulary, poise and originality, and ability to relate to an audience. For vocational counseling of those interested in becoming television announcers, masters of ceremonies, dramatic readers, actors, and narrators. A tape recorder, clock, 2 commercial scripts and several more common items are required.

11943
Graduate Management Admission Test. Graduate Management Admission Council, Princeton, NJ 1982
Subtests: Verbal; Quantitative
Descriptors: *Academic Aptitude; *Administrator Education; *Aptitude Tests; Braille; *College Entrance Examinations; *College Seniors; *Graduate Students; Higher Education; Large Type Materials; Mathematics; Mathematics Tests; Reading Comprehension; Verbal Ability; Writing Skills
Identifiers: GMAT
Availability: Educational Testing Service; GMAT; P.O. Box 966-R; Princeton, NJ 08541
Grade Level: 16
Notes: Time, 180

Designed to provide counselors and admissions officers with a predictor of academic performance in the first year of graduate management school. Measures general verbal and mathematical abilities, including reading comprehension, writing ability and questions requiring analysis of situations, basic math skills, understanding of math concepts, quantitative reasoning and interpretation of data in charts and graphs, etc. Tests are updated periodically. Editions are available in large print and Braille editions and via cassette. Tests are updated regularly.

11944
Prueba de Admision para Estudios Graduados. Educational Testing Service, Princeton, NJ 1980
Subtests: Verbal Ability; Quantitative Ability; English as a Second Language; Writing
Descriptors: *Academic Ability; *Aptitude Tests; *College Entrance Examinations; *College Seniors; *English (Second Language); *Graduate Students; Higher Education; *Spanish Speaking; Verbal Ability; Writing Skills
Identifiers: PAEG; Puerto Rico
Availability: Educational Testing Service; International Office, Princeton, NJ 08541
Grade Level: 16
Notes: Time, 225; Items, 205

An aptitude test designed and constructed to measure academic ability at the graduate level for use in making decisions about the admission of applicants to graduate schools in Puerto Rico. Includes a measure of English as a second language.

11953
Kaufman Assessment Battery for Children. Kaufman, Alan S.; Kaufman, Nadeen L. 1983
Subtests: Hand Movements; Number Recall; Word Order; Magic Window; Face Recognition; Gestalt Closure; Triangles; Matrix Analogies; Spatial Memory; Photo Series; Expressive Vocabulary; Faces and Places; Arithmetic; Riddles; Reading Decoding; Reading Understanding
Descriptors: *Academic Achievement; *Achievement Tests; *Children; Elementary School Mathematics; *Individual Testing; *Intelligence; *Intelligence Tests; Knowledge Level; Problem Solving; Reading Skills; Recall (Psychology); Spatial Ability; Vocabulary
Identifiers: Analogies; KABC; Test Batteries
Availability: American Guidance Service; Publishers' Bldg., Circle Pines, MN 55014
Target Audience: 2-12
Notes: Time, 85 approx.

Individually administered intelligence and achievement battery for children aged 2.5 to 12.5 years. Time varies according to age of children: 35-50 minutes for preschool child; 50-70 minutes for 5-6 year olds; and 75-85 minutes for a child aged 7 or above. Although the battery includes 16 subtests, no child is given more than 13. The subtests fall into 3 areas: sequential processing with emphasis on the process used to produce correct solutions; simultaneous processing in which the problems are primarily spatial or analogic in nature; and achievement which focuses on acquired facts and applied skills. Intended for psychological and clinical assessment, psychoeducational evaluation of learning disabled and other exceptional

children, educational planning and placement, minority group assessment, preschool assessment, neuropsychological assessment and research. A review of the K-ABC by C.M. Narrett can be found in Reading Teacher; v37 p626-31, Mar 1984.

11955
Florida Kindergarten Screening Battery. Satz, Paul; Fletcher, Jack 1982
Descriptors: *Academic Achievement; Individual Testing; *Kindergarten Children; *Predictive Measurement; Primary Education; *Screening Tests
Identifiers: FKSB; Test Batteries
Availability: Psychological Assessment Resources; P.O. Box 998, Odessa, FL 33556
Grade Level: K
Notes: Time, 20 approx.

Brief screening device used to predict the likelihood that a kindergarten child will manifest learning problems 3 years later by the end of grade 2. Serves as an early warning device which permits early identification of learning problems. Consists of 4 tests and an optional fifth test: The Peabody Picture Vocabulary Rest-Revised (TC010877-TC010878), the Beery Developmental Test of Visual Motor Integration (TC002624); Recognition Discrimination Test by Small, Finger Localization Test by Benton, and Alphabet Recitation.

11956
Escala de Inteligencia Wechsler para Ninos—Revisada Edicion de Investigacion. Wechsler, David 1982
Subtests: Informacion; Semejanzas; Arithmetica; Vocabulario; Comprehension; Retencion de Digitos; Figuras Incompletas; Arreglo de Dibujos; Disenos con Bloques; Composicion de Objetos; Claves; Laberintos
Descriptors: Adolescents; *Bilingual Students; Children; *Elementary School Students; *Individual Testing; *Intelligence; *Intelligence Tests; *Secondary School Students; *Spanish; *Spanish Speaking
Identifiers: EIWN(R); Wechsler Intelligence Scale for Children (Revised); WISC(R)
Availability: The Psychological Corp.; 555 Academic Ct., San Antonio, TX 78204-0952
Target Audience: 6-16

Spanish adaption of the WISC-R for use with Chicano, Puerto Rican, and Cuban children. Currently a research edition published without norms. Is an individually administered measure of a child's capacity to understand and cope with the world. Intended for use by school psychologists and other trained clinical examiners. Child should not be penalized if he or she offers an acceptable response in English. Examiners should consider a bilingual administration of the test. However, the vocabulary and digit span items should be administered in Spanish only.

11965
Wallach-Kogan Creativity Tests. Wallach, Michael A.; Kogan, Nathan 1965
Subtests: Instances-uniqueness; Instances-number; Alternate Uses-uniqueness; Alternate uses-number; Similarities-uniqueness; Similarities-number; Pattern Meaning-uniqueness; Pattern Meaning-number; Line Meanings-uniqueness; Line Meanings-number
Descriptors: *Creative Thinking; *Creativity Tests; Elementary Education; Elementary School Students; *Grade 5; Intermediate Grades; Pictorial Stimuli; Verbal Tests
Identifiers: *Oral Tests; Semantic Flexibility; Semantic Redefinition
Availability: Wallach, Michael A.; Kogan, Nathan. Modes of Thinking in Young Children. New York: Holt, Rinehart and Winston, Inc., 1965
Grade Level: 5
Notes: Items, 40

A series of verbal and visual measures of creativity presented as games. Children supply lists of items, tell how many uses can be made of each, discuss likenesses between pairs of objects, and supply meanings to abstract drawings and lines.

11967
Computerized Information Processing Test Battery. Barrett, Gerald B. and Others 1982
Subtests: Choice Reaction Time; Sequential Memory; Simultaneous Memory; Visual Search; Multiple Item Access; Linear Scanning; Matrix Scanning; Array Memory; Vector Memory; Stimulus Pace; Stimulus Variety; Response Variety
Descriptors: Adults; Aptitude Tests; *Cognitive Processes; *Computer Assisted Testing; Decision Making; Memory; Minicomputers; Reaction Time; Visual Learning
Identifiers: Job Tasks; Sequential Memory
Availability: Applied Psychological Measurement; v6 n1 p13-29, Win 1982
Target Audience: 18-21

Notes: Time, 240

Describes a battery of computerized information-processing-based ability measures that could be group administered for possible use in applied settings. Also describes computerized measures of preferences for various task dimensions for use in measuring preferences for job dimensions. TV monitors interfacing with a minicomputer are necessary. Most tasks include responding in a prescribed manner to numerical or figural stimuli presented on the screen.

11971
Merrill-Palmer Scale of Mental Tests. Harcourt Brace Jovanovich, Inc., New York, NY 1948
Subtests: Stutsman Copying Test; Stutsman Little Pink Tower; Stutsman Pyramid Test; Stutsman Buttoning Test; Stutsman Stick and String; Stutsman Color Matching Test; Wallin Pegboard A and B; Stutsman Nested Cubes; Pinter Manikin Test; Decroly Matching Game; Stutsman Picture Formboard 1, 2, and 3; Woodworth Wells Association Test; Stutsman Language Test; Kohs Block Design Test; Mare-Foal Formboard; Seguin-Goddard Formboard
Descriptors: Individual Testing; *Intelligence; *Intelligence Tests; Nursery Schools; Performance Tests; *Preschool Children; Preschool Education; Spatial Ability; Timed Tests; Young Children
Identifiers: Test Batteries
Availability: Stoelting Co.; 620 Wheat Ln., Wood Dale, IL 60191
Target Audience: 1-4

A series of tests designed to measure the intelligence of young children. Useful as a substitute for, or supplement to, the Binet Scale (TC001402). The tests included in the scale are Stutsman Copying Test (TC004042); Stutsman Little Pink Tower (TC004045); Stutsman Pyramid Test (TC004046); Stutsman Buttoning Test (TC004047); Stutsman Stick and String (TC004048); Stutsman Color-Matching Test (TC004049); Wallin Pegboard A (TC004050); Wallin Pegboard B (TC004051); Stutsman Nested Cubes (TC004052); Pintner Manikin Test (TC004053); Decroly Matching Game (TC004054); Stutsman Picture Formboard 2 (TC004055); Stutsman Picture Formboard 3 (TC004056); Woodworth-Wells Association Test (TC004057); Stutsman Language Test (TC004058); Kohs Block Design Test (TC004059); Stutsman Picture Formboard 1 (TC004060); Mare-Foal Formboard (TC004061); Seguin-Goddard Formboard (TC004062).

11972
Law School Admission Test. Law School Admission Services; Newtown, PA. 1982
Descriptors: *Academic Aptitude; *Aptitude Tests; *College Applicants; *College Entrance Examinations; *Critical Reading; Critical Thinking; *Graduate Students; Higher Education; *Law Schools; Logical Thinking; Prognostic Tests; Reading Comprehension
Identifiers: LSAT; *Reasoning Ability; Writing Sample
Availability: Law School Admission Services; P.O. Box 2000, Newtown, PA 18940
Grade Level: 16
Notes: Time, 245; Items, 110

A standardized test designed to assist law schools in making decisions about the academic ability of their applicants. Assists in the prediction of performance during the first school year. Measures the ability to read with understanding and insight, understand relationships and draw conclusions, reason effectively, understand, analyze, use, and criticize arguments. A writing sample is forwarded to each law school the candidate designates. Updated and revised regularly.

11975
Mental Rotations Test. Vandenberg, S.G. 1971
Descriptors: Adolescents; Adults; Multiple Choice Tests; *Spatial Ability; Young Adults
Identifiers: Figure Rotations
Availability: S.G. Vandenberg; Institute for Behavioral Genetics, University of Colorado, Boulder, CO 80309
Target Audience: 14-64
Notes: Time, 10; Items, 20

Uses 3-dimensional objects displayed in 2-dimensional drawings produced by a computer to measure spatial visualization. Based on the Shepard-Metzler mental rotation study in Science; v171 p701-03, 1971.

11977
Talent Assessment Program. Revised Edition. Nighswonger, Wilton E. 1981
Subtests: Visualizing Structured Detail; Sorting (Size and Shape); Sorting (Color); Sorting by Touch; Handling Small Materials; Handling Large Materials; Using Small Tools; Using Large Tools; Visualizing Flow Paths; Memory for Structural Detail
Descriptors: Adolescents; Adults; *Aptitude Tests; Learning Disabilities; *Performance Tests; Secondary Education; *Secondary School Students; Skilled Occupations; Spatial Ability; Tactual Perception; Unskilled Occupations; Visual Discrimination; Visualization; *Vocational Aptitude
Identifiers: Manual Dexterity; TAP; Test Batteries
Availability: Talent Assessment, Inc.; P.O. Box 5087, Jacksonville, FL 32207
Grade Level: 7-12
Target Audience: 13-64
Notes: Time, 150 approx.

Consists of 10 tests which require hands-on work by client. Used to measure innate vocational aptitudes of all types of individuals, including handicapped, disadvantaged, and nonhandicapped vocational students. Tests measure skills applicable to work in trade, industrial, technical and professional technical lines, including skilled and unskilled occupations. Measures aptitudes in the general categories of visualization and retention, visual discrimination and manual dexterity.

11983
Order Picking Work Sample. Perkins, Eileen 1973
Descriptors: Adults; Clerical Workers; Job Skills; *Occupational Tests; Spatial Ability; Verbal Ability; *Work Sample Tests
Identifiers: Manual Dexterity; Mathematical Aptitude; *Order Fillers
Availability: Materials Development Center; Work Sample Manual Clearinghouse, Stout Vocational Rehabilitation Institute, School of Education, University of Wisconsin-Stout, Menomonie, WI 54751
Target Audience: Adults
Notes: Items, 5

For use in vocational evaluation with clients interested in preparing orders for shipment, as in the jobs of order filler, distributing clerk, packing and shipping clerk, delivery person. Measures verbal and numerical ability, spatial perception, finger and manual dexterity, ability to reach. Simple office supplies are needed.

12008
Hook Parts Salesperson Work Sample. Hook, Charles R. 1979
Descriptors: Ability; Adults; Handwriting; Writing Skills; Individual Testing; *Interpersonal Competence; Money Management; Reading Comprehension; Role Playing; *Sales Occupations; *Vocational Evaluation; *Work Sample Tests
Identifiers: Automotive Parts; Numerical Ability
Availability: Materials Development Center; Work Sample Manual Clearinghouse, Stout Vocational Rehabilitation Institute, School of Education, University of Wisconsin-Stout, Menomonie, WI 54751
Target Audience: 18-64
Notes: Items, 12

Designed to measure ability to perform sales related work, including dealing with customers, filling out forms, counting money, writing legibly, and reading. A role-playing situation is performed. Test is untimed but work pace is noted.

12014
Nonreading Aptitude Test Battery, 1982 Edition. United States Employment Service, Div. of Testing, Salem, OR 1982
Subtests: Oral Vocabulary; Number Comparison; Design Completion; Tool Matching; 3-Dimensional Space; Form Matching; GATB Mark Making; GATB Assemble; GATB Disassemble; GATB Place; GATB Turn
Descriptors: Adults; *Aptitude Tests; Career Guidance; Cognitive Ability; *Disadvantaged; *Occupational Tests; Personnel Selection; Psychomotor Skills; Spatial Ability; Verbal Ability; Visual Discrimination; Vocabulary
Identifiers: General Aptitude Test Battery; Manual Dexterity; NATB; Numerical Ability; Oral Tests; Perceptual Speed Finger Dexterity; United States Employment Service
Availability: State Employment Service Offices only
Target Audience: Adults
Notes: Time, 107; Items, 468

Developed for use with disadvantaged individuals. This revision is shorter than earlier versions and is purported to be easier to understand and administer, without loss of internal validity. Aptitudes measured are general learning ability, verbal ability, numerical ability, spatial aptitude, form perception, clerical perception, motor coordination, finger dexterity, manual dexterity. Administered by offices of the U.S. Employment Service for vocational guidance and employee selection.

12015
Specific Aptitude Test Batteries. United States Employment Service, Div. of Testing, Salem, OR 1967
Subtests: Name Comparison; Computation; 3-Dimensional Space; Vocabulary; Tool Matching; Arithmetic Reason; Form Matching; Mark Making; Place; Turn; Assemble; Disassemble
Descriptors: Adults; *Aptitude Tests; Job Placement; *Occupational Tests; Perceptual Motor Coordination; *Personnel Selection; Professional Occupations; Semiskilled Occupations; Skilled Occupations; Spatial Ability; Unskilled Occupations; Verbal Ability; Vocational Aptitude
Identifiers: SATB
Availability: State Employment Service Offices only
Target Audience: 18-64

Combinations of 2, 3 or 4 aptitudes and associated tests of the General Aptitude Test Battery (TC001422). Cutting scores are supplied. Used for selection of applicants to a specific job that has been identified as having duties similar to that for which the test is designed. Batteries are available for use in measuring aptitudes for professional, skilled, semi-, and unskilled occupations. For examples see TC010002-TC010012. Timing and numbers of items vary. Not available to the general public. For information, contact a state employment service agency, which is responsible for administering the tests.

12016
The Boder Test of Reading-Spelling Patterns. Boder, Elena; Jarrico, Sylvia 1982
Subtests: Oral Reading Test; Written Spelling Test
Descriptors: Adolescents; Children; Clinical Diagnosis; *Cognitive Ability; *Diagnostic Tests; *Dyslexia; *Individual Testing; *Reading Difficulties; *Reading Processes; *Spelling
Identifiers: BTRSP
Availability: Slosson Educational Publications; P.O. Box 280, East Aurora, NY 14052
Target Audience: 6-18
Notes: Time, 30 approx.

Test is based on premise that dyslexic reader has a characteristic pattern of cognitive strengths and weaknesses in 2 components of the reading process: the visual gestalt function and the auditory analytic function. Test is designed to clarify child's characteristic pattern of cognitive strengths and weaknesses in reading and spelling. Diagnostic purposes of test are to differentiate specific reading disability, or developmental dyslexia, from nonspecific reading disability, to classify dyslexic readers into 1 of 3 subtypes on basis of reading-spelling patterns, and to provide guidelines for remediation of the reading disability subtypes. The test should not be used alone to make a definitive diagnosis of developmental dyslexia but should be part of a multidisciplinary neuropsychoeducational evaluation and in conjunction with other diagnostic instruments. A review of the test by M.O. Smith can be found in Journal of Reading; v27 p22-26, Oct 1983.

12019
Pretesting Orientation Techniques. United States Employment Service, Div. of Testing, Salem, OR 1970
Descriptors: Adults; *Aptitude Tests; *Educationally Disadvantaged; Job Placement; *Occupational Tests; Perceptual Motor Coordination; *Personnel Selection; Spanish; Verbal Ability; Vocational Aptitude
Identifiers: Clerical Aptitude; Mathematical Aptitude; Practice Tests
Availability: U.S. Employment Service Offices only
Target Audience: 18-64
Notes: Time, 30

For use in pretesting with disadvantaged individuals who may be unfamiliar with testing procedures. Contains a brief test similar to the General Aptitude Test Battery (TC001412). A Spanish version is available. Not available to the general public. Contact a state employment service agency for further information.

12034
Test Lessons in Primary Reading, Second Enlarged and Revised Edition. McCall, William A.; Harby, Mary Lourita 1980
Descriptors: Critical Thinking; Elementary Education; *Elementary School Students; *Reading Ability; *Reading Comprehension; *Reading Tests
Availability: Slosson Educational Publications; P.O. Box 280, East Aurora, NY 14052
Grade Level: 2-6
Notes: Items, 62

Consists of 62 short stories followed by questions designed to evaluate students' reading progress and thinking skills. Teacher's manual also contains 8 questions for each story. These questions are designed to encourage such thinking skills as inference, drawing conclusions, making comparisons, recognizing cause and effect, understanding emotional reactions, and criticizing aspects of the story.

12035
Analytic Learning Disability Assessment. Gnagey, Thomas; Gnagey, Patricia 1982
Descriptors: Adolescents; Attention Span; Auditory Discrimination; *Basic Skills; Children; Concept Formation; *Diagnostic Tests; Handwriting; *Individual Testing; *Learning Disabilities; Long Term Memory; Mathematics Achievement; Psychomotor Skills; Reading Skills; Short Term Memory; Spatial Ability; Spelling; Visual Discrimination
Identifiers: ALDA
Availability: Slosson Educational Publications; P.O. Box 280, East Aurora, NY 14052
Grade Level: K-12
Target Audience: 5-17
Notes: Time, 75 approx.; Items, 77
Used to distinguish those students with specific learning skills deficits from those not having those deficits. Tests 77 skills which underlie basic school subjects, to reveal how students go about individual processes of learning. Summary scores include conceptualization and generalization, neuropsychological efficiency and organization, subject achievement potential; grade level achievement; educational lag; age level achievement; learning lag; neuropsychological lag; neuropsychological achievement potential; mean achievement level; neuropsychological achievement proficiency; failed unit score total; pervasive school readiness dysfunction; content achievement potential.

12065
Piagetian Measures of Cognitive Development for Children up to Age 2. Mehrabian, Albert; Williams, Martin 1971
Descriptors: *Cognitive Development; Individual Testing; Infants; Language Skills
Identifiers: *Piagetian Tests
Availability: Albert Mehrabian; 17141 Rayen St., Northridge, CA 91325
Target Audience: 0-2
Notes: Time, 30 approx.; Items, 28
Designed for use in exploring the effect of level of cognitive development on linguistic functioning. Based on Piaget's concepts. Administered individually in one session.

12123
SRA Nonverbal Form. McMurry, Robert N.; King, Joseph E. 1973
Descriptors: Adults; *Aptitude Tests; *Clerical Occupations; *Job Placement; *Limited English Speaking; *Nonverbal Ability; Nonverbal Tests; Occupational Tests; Pictorial Stimuli; *Sales Occupations
Identifiers: *Learning Ability
Availability: Science Research Associates; 155 N. Wacker Dr., Chicago, IL 60606
Target Audience: 18-64
Notes: Time, 10; Items, 60
Designed to measure general learning ability. Uses pictorial items. Does not require reading ability. Used in industry with claims processors, office personnel and route salespersons. Suitable for use with persons having difficulty in reading or understanding English. For placement of workers in entry level positions. Most useful for persons with less than 12 years of education.

12145
Frostig Pictures and Patterns, Revised Edition: Beginning. Frostig, Marianne 1972
Descriptors: *Elementary School Students; *Perceptual Handicaps; Perceptual Motor Coordination; Preschool Children; Preschool Education; Primary Education; Spatial Ability; Vision Tests; *Visual Perception
Identifiers: Frostig Developmental Program of Visual Perception
Availability: Modern Curriculum Press; 13900 Prospect Rd., Cleveland, OH 44136
Grade Level: K-3
Target Audience: 3-8
Notes: Items, 80
Sequentially arranged exercises designed to develop visual perception skills. Skill areas include visual-motor coordination, figure-ground perception, perceptual constancy, and perception of spatial relationships.

12146
Frostig Pictures and Patterns, Revised Edition: Intermediate. Frostig, Marianne 1972
Descriptors: *Elementary School Students; *Perceptual Handicaps; Perceptual Motor Coordination; Primary Education; Spatial Ability; Vision Tests; *Visual Perception
Identifiers: Frostig Developmental Program of Visual Perception
Availability: Modern Curriculum Press; 13900 Prospect Rd., Cleveland, OH 44136
Grade Level: K-3
Notes: Items, 112

A series of sequentially arranged exercises designed to develop visual perception skills. Skill areas include visual motor coordination, figure-ground perception, perceptual constancy, and perception of spatial relationships.

12147
Frostig Pictures and Patterns, Revised Edition: Advanced. Frostig, Marianne 1972
Descriptors: *Elementary School Students; *Perceptual Handicaps; Perceptual Motor Coordination; Primary Education; Spatial Ability; Vision Tests; *Visual Perception
Identifiers: Frostig Developmental Program of Visual Perception
Availability: Modern Curriculum Press; 13900 Prospect Rd., Cleveland, OH 44136
Grade Level: K-3
Notes: Items, 128
A series of sequentially arranged exercises designed to develop visual perception skills. Skill areas include visual-motor coordination, figure-ground perception, perceptual constancy, and perception of spatial relationships.

12149
Spielman Bicycle Wheel Truing Work Sample. Spielman, Roger A. 1975
Descriptors: Adults; Aptitude Tests; Psychomotor Skills; Repair; *Work Sample Tests
Identifiers: *Bicycles; Finger Dexterity; Manual Dexterity
Availability: Materials Development Center; Work Sample Manual Clearinghouse, Stout Vocational Rehabilitation Institute, School of Education, University of Wisconsin-Stout, Menomonie, WI 54751
Target Audience: 18-64
Notes: Items, 1
Designed to measure a person's aptitude for performing the tasks of bicycle repair. Requires eye-hand coordination, dexterity (finger and manual), use of hand tools, following directions. Test is timed.

12150
Electric Foot Stapler Work Sample. Neistadt, Jerry 1979
Descriptors: Adults; Aptitude Tests; Interests; *Machine Repairers; Psychomotor Skills; *Work Sample Tests
Identifiers: Foot Stapler
Availability: Materials Development Center; Work Sample Manual Clearinghouse, Stout Vocational Rehabilitation Institute, School of Education, University of Wisconsin-Stout, Menomonie, WI 54751
Target Audience: 18-64
Notes: Items, 11
Designed to measure ability and interest in machine-tending. Requires eye-hand-foot coordination, and ability to follow instructions. Machine is required.

12151
Dahl-Holmes Small Engine Work Sample. Dahl, Kathleen; Holmes, Reginald 1974
Descriptors: Adults; Aptitude Tests; Machine Repairers; *Work Sample Tests
Identifiers: *Engine Repair; Finger Dexterity; Manual Dexterity
Availability: Materials Development Center; Work Sample Manual Clearinghouse, Stout Vocational Rehabilitation Institute, School of Education, University of Wisconsin-Stout, Menomonie, WI 54751
Target Audience: 18-64
Notes: Time, 60; Items, 19
Designed to measure an individual's ability to disassemble and assemble a small engine. Requires ability to use hand tools, knowledge of the order in which parts should be removed, manual dexterity, and eye-hand coordination. Tools and small engine are required.

12152
Minor Tune-Up Work Sample. Iverson, John C. 1979
Descriptors: Adults; Aptitude Tests; *Auto Mechanics; Psychomotor Skills; Repair; *Work Sample Tests
Identifiers: Finger Dexterity; Manual Dexterity; Tune Up (Engine)
Availability: Materials Development Center; Work Sample Manual Clearinghouse, Stout Vocational Rehabilitation Institute, School of Education, University of Wisconsin-Stout, Menomonie, WI 54751
Target Audience: 18-64
Notes: Time, 72; Items, 8
Designed to measure ability to perform a minor tune-up on a car. Requires finger-dexterity, and tool handling ability.

12153
Russo Carburetor Disassembly-Assembly Work Sample. Russo, Robert H. 1979
Descriptors: Adults; Aptitude Tests; *Auto Mechanics; Psychomotor Skills; Repair; Spatial Ability; *Work Sample Tests
Identifiers: Carburetors; Finger Dexterity; Manual Dexterity
Availability: Materials Development Center; Work Sample Manual Clearinghouse, Stout Vocational Rehabilitation Institute, School of Education, University of Wisconsin-Stout, Menomonie, WI 54751
Target Audience: 18-64
Notes: Items, 20
Designed to measure ability to disassemble a 4-barrel carburetor. Requires ability to follow instructions, manual and finger dexterity, eye-hand coordination, spatial and organizational ability. Ninth grade reading level is required. Time is recorded.

12154
PSB-Health Occupations Aptitude Examination. Psychological Services Bureau, St. Thomas, PA 1983
Subtests: Academic Aptitude; Spelling; Reading Comprehension; Information in the Natural Sciences; Vocational Adjustment
Descriptors: *Academic Aptitude; *Allied Health Occupations; Anatomy; Aptitude Tests; Attitude Measures; Biology; Career Counseling; Chemistry; Curriculum Development; Dental Assistants; Health; Job Skills; Knowledge Level; Medical Technologists; Natural Sciences; Nonverbal Ability; Nurses Aides; Personality Traits; Pharmacology; Physics; Physiology; Postsecondary Education; Radiologic Technologists; Reading Comprehension; Safety; Secondary Education; Spelling; Student Placement; Surgical Technicians; Verbal Ability; *Vocational Adjustment; *Vocational Aptitude
Identifiers: Cytotechnologists; Electroencephalographic Technicians; Quantitative Ability; Recreational Therapists; Respiratory Therapists; *Test Batteries
Availability: Psychological Services Bureau; P.O. Box 4, St. Thomas, PA 17252
Grade Level: 10-16
Notes: Time, 120; Items, 385
A battery of tests designed to measure abilities, skills, knowledge, and attitudes important for the successful performance of students in the allied health education programs. Predictive of readiness for instruction. Also useful for placement, counseling, and curriculum planning. Measures verbal, quantitative and nonverbal ability, spelling, reading comprehension, knowledge, of biology, chemistry, physics, pharmacology, anatomy, physiology, health and safety, and personal qualities indicative of adjustment.

12155
PSB Nursing School Aptitude Examination. Psychological Services Bureau, St. Thomas, PA 1980
Subtests: Academic Aptitude; Spelling; Reading Comprehension; Information in the Natural Sciences; Vocational Adjustment Index
Descriptors: *Academic Aptitude; Admission (School); Anatomy; Attitude Measures; Biology; Career Counseling; Chemistry; Health; Knowledge Level; Microbiology; Nonverbal Ability; *Nurses; Personality Traits; Pharmacology; Physics; Physiology; Postsecondary Education; Reading Comprehension; Safety; Secondary Education; Spelling; Student Placement; Verbal Ability; Vocational Adjustment; *Vocational Aptitude
Identifiers: Quantitative Ability; *Test Batteries
Availability: Psychological Services Bureau; P.O. Box 4, St. Thomas, PA 17252
Grade Level: 10-16
Notes: Time, 165; Items, 445
A battery of 5 tests for use by 2 year associate degree programs and diploma schools of nursing in admission, placement and guidance procedures. May be used for high school counseling. Measures abilities, skills, knowledge and attitudes of students in educational programs preparing professional nurses. Measures learning ability, spelling, reading comprehension, knowledge of biology, microbiology, chemistry, physics, pharmacology, anatomy, physiology, health and safety, and personal qualities indicative of adjustment.

12156
PSB Aptitude for Practical Nursing Examination. Psychological Services Bureau, St. Thomas, PA 1980
Subtests: General Mental Ability; Spelling; Information in the Natural Sciences; Judgment in Practical Nursing Situations; Personal Adjustment Index

Descriptors: *Academic Aptitude; Adolescents; Adults; *Aptitude Tests; Attitude Measures; Biological Sciences; Chemistry; Cognitive Ability; Decision Making Skills; Earth Science; Health; Knowledge Level; Natural Sciences; Nonverbal Ability; Personality Traits; Physics; *Practical Nursing; Safety; Spelling; Verbal Ability; Vocational Adjustment; *Vocational Aptitude
Identifiers: Quantitative Ability; *Test Batteries
Availability: Psychological Services Bureau; P.O. Box 4, St. Thomas, PA 17252
Target Audience: 16-64
Notes: Time, 180; Items, 450

A battery of 5 tests for use by schools of practical nursing in admissions, placement and guidance procedures. Measures abilities, skills, knowledge and attitudes important for successful performance of students in educational programs that prepare practical nurses. Measures learning ability, spelling, knowledge of life science, physics, chemistry, earth science, health and safety, decision making related to nursing and personal qualities indicative of adjustment.

12173
Adult Neuropsychological Evaluation. Swiercinsky, Dennis 1978
Subtests: Hand/Foot Dominance Survey; Visual Acuity; Visual Dominance; Screening Survey of Motor Functions; Finger Tapping; Hand Dynamometer; Grooved Pegboard; Trail Making Tests; Auditory Sensitivity Survey; Rhythm Test; Tactile Sensitivity Survey; Stereognosis Survey; Finger Agnosia; Graphesthesia; Visual Sensitivity and Perimetry; Spatial Relations; Tactual Performance Test; Aphasia Language Performance Scales; Speech Sounds Perception; Wechsler Adult Intelligence Scale; Shipley Institute of Living Scale; Modified Wechsler Memory Scale
Descriptors: Adults; *Aphasia; Auditory Perception; Diagnostic Tests; *Individual Testing; Intelligence Tests; Lateral Dominance; Memory; *Neurological Impairments; Psychomotor Skills; Spatial Ability; Tactual Perception; Visual Acuity
Identifiers: *Neuropsychology; Test Batteries
Availability: Charles C. Thomas Publisher; 2600 S. First St., Springfield, IL 62717
Target Audience: 18-64
Notes: Time, 480

A battery of standardized tests assembled for use in clinical neuropsychology to aid in the diagnosis of brain damage. Assesses areas of mental functioning sensitive to brain impairment. Must be administered individually by trained personnel.

12175
Your Style of Learning and Thinking, Adult Form. Torrance, E. Paul; And Others 1977
Subtests: Right Hemisphere Specialization; Left Hemisphere Specialization; Integration
Descriptors: Adults; *Cognitive Processes; *Cognitive Style; Multiple Choice Tests; Research
Identifiers: *Hemispheric Dominance
Availability: Gifted Child Quarterly; v21 n4 p563-73, Win 1977
Target Audience: 18-64
Notes: Items, 36

A self-report measure of right-left hemispheric specialization or dominance and integration. Based on the rationale that learning is a function of cerebral hemispheric orientation. For research use. Two forms are available. Each item has 3 choices, 1 representing a specialized function of each hemisphere, and a third indicating integration. A children's version is available (TC012176).

12176
Your Style of Learning and Thinking, Children's Form. Reynolds, Cecil R.; And Others 1979
Subtests: Right Hemisphere Specialization; Left Hemisphere Specialization; Integration
Descriptors: *Cognitive Processes; *Cognitive Style; Elementary Education; *Elementary School Students; Multiple Choice Tests; Research
Identifiers: *Hemispheric Dominance
Availability: Gifted Child Quarterly; v23 n4 p757-67, Win 1979
Grade Level: 1-6
Notes: Items, 40

A measure of right-left hemispheric specialization or dominance, and integration. Based on the rationale that learning is a function of cerebral hemispheric orientation. For research use. Two forms are available. Each item has 3 choices, 1 representing a specialized function of each hemisphere and a third indicating integration. Read aloud to respondents. An adolescent/adult version is available (TC012175).

12181
Learning Style Identification Scale. Malcolm, Paul J.; And Others 1981
Descriptors: Behavior Rating Scales; Classroom Environment; *Cognitive Development; *Cognitive Style; Decision Making; Elementary Education; *Elementary School Students; *Problem Solving; *Self Concept; *Student Behavior
Identifiers: LSIS
Availability: Publishers Test Service; 2500 Garden Rd., Monterey, CA 93940
Grade Level: 1-6
Notes: Items, 24

Developed to make identification of students' learning styles more efficient and accurate. Learning style is the method students use to solve problems they face and is determined by the amount of intrapersonal and extrapersonal information received and used. Intrapersonal information comes from one's thoughts, values, ideas, beliefs and attitudes. Sources of extrapersonal information include people, events, and institutions. Use of intrapersonal information is influenced by one's self concept; use of extrapersonal information is determined by an individual's cognitive development. Five learning styles have been identified and assimilate various amounts of intrapersonal and extrapersonal data, influenced by individual's self concept and cognitive style or development. Objective of scale is to help students receive more intrapersonal and extrapersonal information, so that valid decisions on effective instruction can be made.

12205
WISC-R Performance Scale for Deaf Children. Anderson, Richard J.; Sisco, Frankie H. 1976
Subtests: Picture Completion; Picture Arrangement; Block Design; Object Assembly; Coding; Mazes
Descriptors: Adolescents; Children; Finger Spelling; *Hearing Impairments; Individual Testing; *Intelligence Tests; Nonverbal Tests; Performance Tests; Sign Language; Total Communication
Identifiers: Oral Testing; Wechsler Intelligence Scale for Children (Revised)
Availability: Office of Demographic Studies, Gallaudet College; Washington, DC 20002
Target Audience: 6-17

A standardization of the 5 performance scales of the WISC-R for use with hearing impaired children. Administered via total communication, oral communication, finger spelling with speech, gestures, and pantomime. The test itself is available from Psychological Corporation, San Antonio, TX. Normative data are provided by the source listed here.

12230
Basic Visual Motor Association Test. Battle, James 1982
Descriptors: Elementary Education; *Elementary School Students; Junior High Schools; *Junior High School Students; *Short Term Memory; Visual Measures; *Visual Perception; *Visual Stimuli
Identifiers: BVMAT
Availability: Special Child Publications; P.O. Box 33548, Seattle, WA 98133
Grade Level: 1-9
Notes: Time, 15 approx.; Items, 60

A test of visual short-term memory for children in grades 1 through 9. Assesses the following: recall of visual symbols, visual sequencing ability, visual association skills, visual motor ability, visual integrative ability, symbol integration skills. There are 2 alternate forms: Form A has 60 upper-case or capital letters; Form B has 60 lower-case or small letters. The test can be administered to individuals or to groups. It is recommended that individual administration be used for children below grade 2. Test results should be scored and interpreted by someone knowledgeable in assessment and visual-perceptual skills.

12231
Silver Drawing Test of Cognitive and Creative Skills. Silver, Rawley A. 1983
Subtests: Predictive Drawing; Drawing from Observation; Drawing from Imagination
Descriptors: Adolescents; Adults; Art Therapy; Children; *Cognitive Ability; *Cognitive Tests; Concept Formation; *Creativity; Culture Fair Tests; Deafness; Freehand Drawing; *Pictorial Stimuli; Rehabilitation; Spatial Ability; Speech Therapy
Identifiers: SDT; Sequencing Skills; Silver Test
Availability: Special Child Publications; P.O. Box 33548, Seattle, WA 98133
Target Audience: 6-64
Notes: Time, 15 approx.

Used to bypass language in assessing cognitive and creative skills and to assess ability to solve conceptual problems graphically. Three subtests are based on 3 reading categories: conceptual, spatial, and sequential. The Predictive Drawing subtest assesses sequential concepts; Drawing

from Observation assesses spatial concepts and relationships of height, width, and depth; Drawing from Imagination subtest assesses the ability to associate and form concepts, both concrete and abstract, and creativity. Test is based on premise that art can be a language of cognition parallel to the spoken word and that cognitive skills can be evidenced in visual as well as verbal contexts. Scoring and interpretation should be performed only by certified personnel experienced in testing diagnosis and remediation. Recommended for school psychologists, art therapists, and also for speech and hearing specialists, resource teachers, art teachers, rehabilitation counselors, and other professionals. Visual stimuli are designed in a culture-free freehand-sketch format.

12240
Problem Solving Inventory. Heppner, P. Paul; Petersen, Chris H. 1982
Subtests: Problem Solving Confidence; Approach Avoidance Style; Personal Control
Descriptors: Likert Scales; *College Students; Higher Education; *Problem Solving; Rating Scales; Self Evaluation (Individuals)
Identifiers: PSI
Availability: Journal of Counseling Psychology; v29 n1 p66-75, 1982
Grade Level: 13-16
Notes: Items, 32

A research instrument developed to investigate the dimensions of college students' real-life, personal, problem-solving processes. Three factors were identified for the problem-solving technique: confidence of the subject in solving his or her problems; whether subject attempts or avoids different problem solving activities; and the degree of self control exercised by the subject in problem solving activities. Research instrument is easily administered and scored.

12244
Radiator Flushing and Winterizing Work Sample. Tollander, Timothy 1979
Descriptors: Adults; *Auto Mechanics; *Occupational Tests; Spatial Ability; Vocational Aptitude; Vocational Interests; *Work Sample Tests
Identifiers: Manual Dexterity
Availability: Materials Development Center; Work Sample Manual Clearinghouse, Stout Vocational Rehabilitation Institute, School of Education, University of Wisconsin-Stout, Menomonie, WI 54751
Target Audience: 18-64
Notes: Items, 17

Designed for use in vocational evaluation with clients showing interest and potential for work in auto mechanics, specifically as a radiator mechanic. An actual auto cooling system is used. Clients should have sixth grade reading level. Requires ability to follow directions, use drawings of systems, manual and finger dexterity, eye-hand coordination, spatial perception, organizing ability, ability to use tools.

12288
Developmental Communication Inventory. Hanna, Rosemarie P.; And Others 1982
Descriptors: Cognitive Development; *Communication Disorders; Communication Skills; Criterion Referenced Tests; Individual Testing; Informal Assessment; Language Acquisition; Language Handicaps; Speech Handicaps; *Young Children
Identifiers: DCI; Developmental Communication Curriculum
Availability: The Psychological Corp.; 555 Academic Ct., San Antonio, TX 78204-0952
Target Audience: 1-7

Part of the Developmental Communication Curriculum developed at the Rehabilitation Institute of Pittsburgh. The inventory is a 2-part informal survey of the most important aspects of a child's development of cognition, language, and communication. Results of the survey can be used in making programatic decisions. Administration time varies. The activities manual gives curricular strategies and more than 300 activities to help the children learn.

12293
MKM Alphabet Printing Test. Michael, Leland D.; And Others 1978
Descriptors: *Alphabets; Cognitive Processes; Diagnostic Tests; Elementary Education; *Elementary School Students; Visualization
Availability: MKM, Inc.; 809 Kansas City St., Rapid City, SD 57701
Grade Level: 1-6

Child is given a blank sheet of paper and a pencil without an eraser. Student is then instructed to write the alphabet. Child may cross out any errors and then correct them. Instrument assesses student's ability to think in sequence, visualize and reproduce letters. Observer should note writing posture, pencil grip, and motor overflow. The Phonic

Mnemonic Method of Teaching Reading Manual of Instructions for use with this instrument is available from MKM, Inc.; 809 Kansas City St., Rapid City, SD 57701.

12320
Adams Construction Layout Work Sample. Adams, Jack 1974
Descriptors: Adults; Aptitude Tests; *Building Trades; *Vocational Evaluation; *Work Sample Tests
Availability: Materials Development Center; Work Sample Manual Clearinghouse, Stout Vocational Rehabilitation Institute, School of Education, University of Wisconsin-Stout, Menomonie, WI 54751
Target Audience: 18-64
Notes: Time, 120; Items, 7

Designed to assess an individual's ability to lay out an area in preparation for construction and to estimate potential for jobs such as bricklayer, stone mason, cement worker and other jobs requiring a layout. Measures ability to use layout tools, follow pictorial and written instructions, use job related tools, measure accurately, and make judgments. A reading level of grade 4 or 5 is required. Sample requires various pieces of common equipment.

12322
Pioneer Pen Assembly Job Sample. Gollan, Thomas R. 1974
Descriptors: Adults; Aptitude Tests; *Assembly (Manufacturing); *Vocational Evaluation; *Work Sample Tests
Availability: Materials Development Center; Work Sample Manual Clearinghouse, Stout Vocational Rehabilitation Institute, School of Education, University of Wisconsin-Stout, Menomonie, WI 54751
Target Audience: 18-64
Notes: Time, 70; Items, 100

Designed for use in vocational evaluation to measure a client's ability to perform multiple-step small parts assembly tasks. Client will select materials in proper sequence, manipulate small parts, test product, count and store finished products. Can be administered to clients with disabilities who have use of both hands and minimal visual acuity. A variety of simple materials is required.

12323
Revised Tomcheck/Brown Eye-Hand-Foot Coordination Work Sample. Banks, John J. 1974
Descriptors: Adults; Aptitude Tests; *Assembly (Manufacturing); *Eye Hand Coordination; *Vocational Evaluation; *Work Sample Tests
Identifiers: Eye Hand Foot Coordination; Finger Dexterity; Manual Dexterity
Availability: Materials Development Center; Work Sample Manual Clearinghouse, Stout Vocational Rehabilitation Institute, School of Education, University of Wisconsin-Stout, Menomonie, WI 54751
Target Audience: 18-64
Notes: Time, 110; Items, 90

Designed for use in vocational evaluation to measure client's ability to perform manipulative and assembly type tasks. Requires assembly of a nut and bolt device using a foot controlled power screwdriver. Abilities necessary are: eye-hand-foot coordination, finger and manual dexterity, work rhythm, and sitting tolerance. Various pieces of equipment are required.

12324
Giese Electrical Wiring Work Sample. Giese, Anita 1974
Descriptors: Adults; Aptitude Tests; *Electrical Occupations; Eye Hand Coordination; Individual Testing; *Vocational Evaluation; *Work Sample Tests
Identifiers: Finger Dexterity; Manual Dexterity
Availability: Materials Development Center; Work Sample Manual Clearinghouse, Stout Vocational Rehabilitation Institute, School of Education, University of Wisconsin-Stout, Menomonie, WI 54751
Target Audience: 18-64
Notes: Time, 30; Items, 2

Designed for use in vocational evaluation to assess a client's interest and potential for employment in assembly, appliance repair, or related fields. Requires completion of a wiring task. Necessary abilities are proficiency with a ruler, hand tools, ability to follow verbal and diagrammatic instructions, manual and finger dexterity, eye-hand coordination. For individuals with average or low intelligence. A variety of equipment is required.

12325
Wire Harness Assembly Work Sample. Behm, Pauline 1973
Descriptors: Adults; Aptitude Tests; *Assembly (Manufacturing); Eye Hand Coordination; Individual Testing; *Vocational Evaluation; *Work Sample Tests
Identifiers: Color Discrimination; Finger Dexterity; Manual Dexterity; *Wire Harness Assembly
Availability: Materials Development Center; Work Sample Manual Clearinghouse, Stout Vocational Rehabilitation Institute, School of Education, University of Wisconsin-Stout, Menomonie, WI 54751
Target Audience: 18-64
Notes: Time, 30; Items, 25

Designed for use in vocational evaluation with clients who indicate interest in or potential for bench assembly or related fields such as electrical assembly. Requires manipulation of wire into bundles. Necessary skills are manual and finger dexterity, eye-hand coordination, color discrimination, accuracy in detail work, ability to tolerate routine, repetitive tasks. A variety of equipment is needed.

12326
Strand Resistor Inspection and Testing Work Sample. Strand, Kevin 1973
Descriptors: Adults; Aptitude Tests; Individual Testing; *Inspection; Mathematics; Measurement; *Vocational Evaluation; Work Attitudes; *Work Sample Tests
Identifiers: *Strand Resistors
Availability: Materials Development Center; Work Sample Manual Clearinghouse, Stout Vocational Rehabilitation Institute, School of Education, University of Wisconsin-Stout, Menomonie, WI 54751
Target Audience: 18-64
Notes: Time, 90; Items, 20

Designed to measure clients' ability to inspect, determine value of, and accept or reject resistors, based on mathematical calculations. Also covers ability to measure accurately and follow instructions, and attitudes toward this type of work. Eighth grade reading and math levels are required. Meters and resistors are required for administration. For use in vocational evaluation.

12327
Tire Balancing Work Sample. Honeck, Lynn 1975
Descriptors: Adults; Aptitude Tests; Auto Mechanics; *Vocational Evaluation; Vocational Interests; *Work Sample Tests
Identifiers: *Tires
Availability: Materials Development Center; Work Sample Manual Clearinghouse, Stout Vocational Rehabilitation Institute, School of Education, University of Wisconsin-Stout, Menomonie, WI 54751
Target Audience: 18-64
Notes: Items, 4

Designed for use in vocational evaluation to determine an individual's interest in and potential for employment as a tire repairman. Requires ability to follow verbal instructions, to operate a tire balancer and record weights, as well as visual acuity. Client must be able to lift 30 lbs.

12329
Specific Aptitude Test Battery S-473 R82. Gambling Dealer (amuse. and rec.) 343.467-018. Employment and Training Administration (DOL), Washington, DC 1982
Subtests: General Learning Ability; Verbal Aptitude; Numerical Aptitude; Spatial Aptitude; Form Perception; Clerical Perception; Motor Coordination; Finger Dexterity; Manual Dexterity
Descriptors: Adults; *Aptitude Tests; Career Guidance; *Culture Fair Tests; *Employment Potential; Employment Qualifications; *Ethnic Groups; *Job Applicants; Job Skills; Job Training; *Minority Groups; Object Manipulation; Personnel Evaluation; *Personnel Selection; Predictive Measurement; Spatial Ability; Timed Tests; *Vocational Aptitude
Identifiers: *Gambling Dealer; GATB; General Aptitude Test Battery; Manual Dexterity; SATB; USES Specific Aptitude Test Battery
Availability: Local U.S. Employment Service Office
Target Audience: Adults

A series of aptitude tests for specific job skills. Designed to select inexperienced, or untrained, personnel for training and to predict their job proficiency. Instruments were developed to be culture fair for minorities and ethnic groups. Subtests were drawn from the General Aptitude Test Battery (TC001422). Use of these instruments is restricted to state employment agencies. Designed to assess individual's aptitude for training as a gambling dealer. Data from 4 different jobs were combined to form this test battery. The jobs were dealers for dice, roulette, bacarat, and twenty-one. A report describing the development of this test can be found in the ERIC system, document ED223707.

12330
Specific Aptitude Test Battery S200 R82. Ticket Agent (any ind.) 238.367-026. Employment and Training Administration (DOL), Washington, DC 1982
Subtests: General Learning Ability; Verbal Aptitude; Numerical Aptitude; Spatial Aptitude; Clerical Perception
Descriptors: Adults; *Aptitude Tests; Career Guidance; *Culture Fair Tests; *Employment Potential; Employment Qualifications; *Ethnic Groups; Job Analysis; *Job Applicants; Job Skills; Job Training; *Minority Groups; Personnel Evaluation; *Personnel Selection; Predictive Measurement; Spatial Ability; Timed Tests; *Vocational Aptitude
Identifiers: GATB; General Aptitude Test Battery; SATB; *Ticket Agents; USES Specific Aptitude Test Battery
Availability: Local U.S. Employment Service Office
Target Audience: Adults

A series of aptitude tests for specific job skills. Designed to select inexperienced, or untrained, personnel for training and to predict their job proficiency. Instruments were developed to be culture fair for minorities and ethnic groups. Subtests were drawn from the General Aptitude Test Battery (TC001422). Use of these instruments is restricted to state employment agencies. Designed to assess individual's aptitude for training as a ticket agent. A report describing the development of this test can be found in the ERIC system, document ED223718.

12331
Specific Aptitude Test Battery S-179 R82. Waiter/Waitress, Informal (hotel and rest.) 311.477-030. Employment and Training Administration (DOL), Washington, DC 1982
Subtests: Verbal Aptitude; Numerical Aptitude; Clerical Perception; Motor Coordination; Manual Dexterity
Descriptors: Adults; *Aptitude Tests; Career Guidance; *Culture Fair Tests; *Employment Potential; Employment Qualifications; *Ethnic Groups; Job Analysis; *Job Applicants; Job Skills; Job Training; *Minority Groups; Object Manipulation; Personnel Evaluation; *Personnel Selection; Predictive Measurement; Psychomotor Skills; Timed Tests; *Vocational Aptitude
Identifiers: GATB; General Aptitude Test Battery; Manual Dexterity; SATB; USES Specific Aptitude Test Battery; *Waiters Waitresses
Availability: Local U.S. Employment Service Office
Target Audience: Adults

A series of aptitude tests for specific job skills. Designed to select inexperienced, or untrained, personnel for training and to predict their job proficiency. Instruments were developed to be culture fair for minorities and ethnic groups. Subtests were drawn from the General Aptitude Test Battery (TC001422). Use of these instruments is restricted to state employment agencies. Instrument was designed to assess aptitude for employment as a waiter or waitress. A report describing the development of this test can be found in the ERIC system, document ED223714.

12332
Specific Aptitude Test Battery S-11 R82. Carpenter (const.) 860.381-022. Employment and Training Administration (DOL), Washington, DC 1982
Subtests: General Learning Ability; Numerical Aptitude; Spatial Manual Dexterity
Descriptors: Adults; *Aptitude Tests; Building Trades; Career Guidance; *Carpentry; *Construction (Process); *Culture Fair Tests; *Employment Potential; Employment Qualifications; *Ethnic Groups; Job Analysis; *Job Applicants; Job Skills; Job Training; *Minority Groups; Object Manipulation; Personnel Evaluation; *Personnel Selection; Predictive Measurement; Timed Tests; *Vocational Aptitude
Identifiers: GATB; General Aptitude Test Battery; Manual Dexterity; SATB; USES Specific Aptitude Test Battery
Availability: Local U.S. Employment Service Office
Target Audience: Adults

A series of aptitude tests for specific job skills. Designed to select inexperienced, or untrained, personnel for training and to predict their job proficiency. Instruments were developed to be culture fair for minorities and ethnic groups. Subtests were drawn from the General Aptitude Test Battery (TC001422). Use of these instruments is restricted to state employment agencies. Designed to assess individual's aptitude for training and employment as a carpenter. A report describing the development of this test can be found in the ERIC system, document ED223695.

12333
Specific Aptitude Test Battery S-474R82. Customer-Service Representative (Light, Heat, & Power; Telephone & Telegraph; Waterworks) 239.367-010. Employment and Training Administration (DOL), Washington, DC 1982
Subtests: General Learning Ability; Verbal Aptitude; Numerical Aptitude; Clerical Perception; Motor Coordination
Descriptors: Adults; *Aptitude Tests; Career Guidance; *Culture Fair Tests; *Employment Potential; Employment Qualifications; *Ethnic Groups; Job Analysis; *Job Applicants; Job Skills; Job Training; *Minority Groups; Personnel Evaluation; *Personnel Selection; Predictive Measurement; Timed Tests; *Utilities; *Vocational Aptitude
Identifiers: *Customer Services; GATB; General Aptitude Test Battery; SATB; USES Specific Aptitude Test Battery
Availability: Local U.S. Employment Service Office
Target Audience: Adults

A series of aptitude tests for specific job skills. Designed to select inexperienced, or untrained, personnel for training and to predict their job proficiency. Instruments were developed to be culture fair for minorities and ethnic groups. Subtests were drawn from the General Aptitude Test Battery (TC001422). Use of these instruments is restricted to state employment agencies. This instrument was designed to assess individual's aptitude for training and employment as a customer service representative. A report describing the development of this test can be found in the ERIC system, document ED223696.

12334
Specific Aptitude Test Battery S-68 R82. Refinery Operator (petrol. refin.) 549.260-010. Employment and Training Administration (DOL), Washington, DC 1982
Subtests: General Learning Ability; Numerical Aptitude; Spatial Aptitude; Form Perception; Clerical Perception; Manual Dexterity
Descriptors: Adults; *Aptitude Tests; Career Guidance; *Culture Fair Tests; *Employment Potential; Employment Qualifications; *Ethnic Groups; Job Analysis; *Job Applicants; Job Skills; Job Training; *Minority Groups; Personnel Evaluation; *Personnel Selection; Predictive Measurement; Timed Tests; *Vocational Aptitude
Identifiers: GATB; General Aptitude Test Battery; Manual Dexterity; *Refinery Operator; SATB; USES Specific Aptitude Test Battery
Availability: Local U.S. Employment Service Office
Target Audience: Adults

A series of aptitude tests for specific job skills. Designed to select inexperienced, or untrained, personnel for training and to predict their job proficiency. Instruments were developed to be culture fair for minorities and ethnic groups. Subtests were drawn from the General Aptitude Test Battery (TC001422). Use of these instruments is restricted to state employment agencies. Designed to assess aptitude for training and employment as a refinery operator. A report describing the development of this test can be found in the ERIC system, document ED223722.

12335
Specific Aptitude Test Battery S 326R82. Respiratory Therapist (medical ser.) 079.361-010. Employment and Training Administration (DOL), Washington, DC 1982
Subtests: General Learning Ability; Spatial Aptitude; Form Perception; Motor Coordination
Descriptors: Adults; *Aptitude Tests; Career Guidance; *Culture Fair Tests; *Employment Potential; Employment Qualifications; *Ethnic Groups; Therapists; *Respiratory Therapy; Job Analysis; *Job Applicants; Job Skills; Job Training; *Minority Groups; Personnel Evaluation; *Personnel Selection; Predictive Measurement; Psychomotor Skills; Timed Tests; *Vocational Aptitude
Identifiers: GATB; General Aptitude Test Battery; SATB; USES Specific Aptitude Test Battery
Availability: Local U.S. Employment Service Office
Target Audience: Adults

A series of aptitude tests for specific job skills. Designed to select inexperienced, or untrained, personnel for training and to predict their job proficiency. Instruments were developed to be culture fair for minorities and ethnic groups. Subtests were drawn from the General Aptitude Test Battery (TC001422). Use of these instruments is restricted to state employment agencies. Designed to assess individual's aptitude for training and employment as a respiratory therapist. A report describing the development of this test can be found in the ERIC system, document ED223723.

12337
Conceptual Learning and Development Assessment Series II: Cutting Tool. Klausmeier, Herbert J.; And Others 1973
Descriptors: Abstract Reasoning; Classification; Cognitive Development; Cognitive Processes; Cognitive Tests; *Concept Formation; Difficulty Level; *Elementary School Students; Elementary Secondary Education; Fundamental Concepts; Identification; *Secondary School Students
Identifiers: CLD; *Cutting Tools; Oral Testing; Test Batteries
Availability: ERIC Document Reproduction Service; 3900 Wheeler Ave., Alexandria, VA 22304 (ED103483, 87 pages)
Grade Level: K-12
Target Audience: 4-18

Developed as part of research on the Conceptual Learning and Development Model. Measures the level of attainment of the concept, cutting tool, as well as use of this concept. The Conceptual Learning and Development model specifies 4 successive levels of concept attainment. These include concrete level, identity level, classificatory level, and formal level. A concept attained at the classificatory or formal levels may be used in 4 ways. These are horizontal transfer, cognizing supraordinate-subordinate relations, cognizing various other relations among concepts, and generalizing to problem solving situations.

12338
Conceptual Learning and Development Assessment Series III: Noun. Klausmeier, Herbert J.; And Others 1973
Descriptors: Abstract Reasoning; Cognitive Development; Cognitive Processes; Cognitive Tests; *Concept Formation; Difficulty Level; *Elementary School Students; Elementary Secondary Education; Fundamental Concepts; Language Acquisition; *Nouns; *Secondary School Students
Identifiers: CLD; Oral Testing; Test Batteries
Availability: ERIC Document and Reproduction Service; 3900 Wheeler Ave., Alexandria, VA 22304 (ED 103 484, 91 pages)
Grade Level: K-12
Target Audience: 4-18

Developed as part of research on the Conceptual Learning and Development Model. Assesses the level of attainment of the concept, noun, as well as the use of this concept. The Conceptual Learning and Development model specifies four successive levels of concept attainment. These include concrete level, identity level, classificatory level, and formal level. A concept attained at the classificatory or formal levels may be used in 4 ways. These are horizontal transfer, cognizing supraordinate-subordinate relations, cognizing various other relations among concepts, and generalizing to problem solving situations.

12341
The Need for Cognition Scale. Cacioppo, John T.; Petty, Richard E. 1982
Descriptors: Adults; Attitude Measures; *Cognitive Processes; Needs; Rating Scales
Availability: Journal of Personality and Social Psychology; v42 n1 p116-31, 1982
Target Audience: 18-64
Notes: Items, 34

Designed to measure the tendency for an individual to engage in and enjoy thinking. One major factor was found. Scale consists of items that assess the tendency for individuals to gain intrinsic rewards from thinking, in a variety of situations.

12352
Specific Aptitude Test Battery S-471 R81 Semiconductor Occupations (Electronics). Employment and Training Administration (DOL), Washington, DC 1982
Subtests: Numerical Aptitude; Motor Coordination; Finger Dexterity; Manual Dexterity; Form Perception; Clerical Perception
Descriptors: Adults; *Aptitude Tests; Career Guidance; *Culture Fair Tests; *Electronic Technicians; *Employment Potential; Employment Qualifications; *Ethnic Groups; Job Analysis; *Job Applicants; Job Skills; Job Training; *Minority Groups; Personnel Evaluation; *Personnel Selection; Predictive Measurement; Timed Tests; *Vocational Aptitude
Identifiers: GATB; General Aptitude Test Battery; Manual Dexterity; SATB; USES Specific Aptitude Test Battery
Availability: Local U.S. Employment Service Office
Target Audience: Adults

A series of aptitude tests for specific job skills. Designed to select inexperienced, or untrained, personnel for training and to predict their job proficiency. Instruments were developed to be culture fair for minorities and ethnic groups. Subtests were drawn from the General Aptitude Test Battery (TC001422). Use of these instruments is restricted to state employment agencies. Designed to assess individual's aptitude for training or employment in electronics occupations. A report describing the development of this test can be found in the ERIC system, document ED224826.

12378
Plumbing Maintenance Work Sample. Saltzman, Douglas J. 1974
Descriptors: Adults; Aptitude Tests; Job Skills; Occupational Tests; *Plumbing; Spatial Ability; *Vocational Evaluation; *Work Sample Tests
Identifiers: Manual Dexterity
Availability: Materials Development Center; Work Sample Manual Clearinghouse, Stout Vocational Rehabilitation Institute, School of Education, University of Wisconsin-Stout, Menomonie, WI 54751
Target Audience: 18-64
Notes: Items, 8

Designed to measure spatial aptitude for positioning parts, form perception, motor coordination, manual dexterity, and ability to learn a plumbing task. Fourth grade reading level is required. Common plumbing parts are required.

12379
Oxy-Acetylene Welding and Cutting Work Sample. Buchkoski, David J. 1975
Descriptors: Adults; Aptitude Tests; Job Skills; Occupational Tests; *Vocational Evaluation; *Welding; *Work Sample Tests
Availability: Materials Development Center; Work Sample Manual Clearinghouse, Stout Vocational Rehabilitation Institute, School of Education, University of Wisconsin-Stout, Menomonie, WI 54751
Target Audience: 18-64
Notes: Items, 8

Designed to assess interest in and potential for jobs requiring work with an oxy-acetylene welding unit. Measures ability to comprehend written, oral and pictorial directions, and operate welding equipment. Measures ability to perform routine, repetitive tasks with little social contact.

12380
Schneck Arc Welding Work Sample. Schneck, Gerald R. 1971
Descriptors: Adults; Aptitude Tests; Job Skills; Occupational Tests; *Vocational Evaluation; *Welding; *Work Sample Tests
Availability: Materials Development Center; Work Sample Manual Clearinghouse, Stout Vocational Rehabilitation Institute, School of Education, University of Wisconsin-Stout, Menomonie, WI 54751
Target Audience: 18-64
Notes: Items, 15

Measures manual and finger dexterity, eye-hand coordination, ability to produce work meeting prescribed tolerances and standards, ability to operate and handle welding equipment, and ability to apply basic welding principles. An orientation and training session using a cassette and filmstrip is provided prior to testing. Sixth grade reading level is necessary.

12381
Johnson Machine Packaging Work Sample. Johnson, John G. 1973
Descriptors: Adults; Aptitude Tests; Job Skills; Machine Tool Operators; Occupational Tests; Psychomotor Skills; *Vocational Evaluation; *Work Sample Tests
Identifiers: *Packaging; *Packers
Availability: Materials Development Center; Work Sample Manual Clearinghouse, Stout Vocational Rehabilitation Institute, School of Education, University of Wisconsin-Stout, Menomonie, WI 54751
Target Audience: 18-64
Notes: Items, 50

Designed to assess the client's interest and ability in performing simple, repetitive machine packing operations. The following abilities are evaluated: eye-hand coordination, manual dexterity, ability to follow a diagram, form discrimination, and ability to follow verbal instructions. A variety of industrial items are required for administration.

12388
Expressive One-Word Picture Vocabulary Test-Upper Extension. Gardner, Morrison F. 1983
Descriptors: *Adolescents; Bilingual Students; *Cognitive Processes; *Concept Formation; Diagnostic Tests; *Expressive Language; Group Testing; Individual Testing; Intelligence; *Language Tests; Norm Referenced Tests; Pictorial Stimuli; Spanish Speaking; *Vocabulary
Identifiers: EOWPVT; *Verbal Intelligence
Availability: Academic Therapy Publications; 20 Commercial Blvd., Novato, CA 94947-6191
Target Audience: 12-16
Notes: Time, 15 approx.; Items, 70

Purpose is to obtain a basal estimate of a student's verbal intelligence by means of his or her acquired one-word expressive picture vocabulary. Can be valuable in obtaining a valid estimate of child's verbal intelligence through child's ability to form an idea or concept from a picture. This is an upward extension of the original Expressive One-Word Picture Vocabulary Test (TC010322), published in 1979. Can also yield information on possible speech defects, possible learning disorders, bilingual child's fluency in English, auditory processing, and auditory-visual association ability. Although normed on children whose primary language is English, may also be used with bilingual students to determine extent of their English vocabulary. A Spanish version is also available. The pictures are arranged in increasing order of difficulty and range from single concrete objects to collections of objects representing abstract concepts. Students respond to each item with a single word. May be administered individually or to small groups.

12396
DIAL-R. Mardell-Czudnowski, Carol D.; Goldenberg, Dorothea S. 1983
Subtests: Motor; Concepts; Language
Descriptors: *Ability Identification; Concept Formation; *Gifted; Individual Testing; Language Skills; *Learning Disabilities; Performance Tests; *Preschool Children; Preschool Education; *Psychomotor Skills; *Screening Tests
Availability: Childcraft Education Corp.; 20 Kilmer Rd., Edison, NJ 08818
Target Audience: 2-6
Notes: Time, 30 approx.; Items, 24

An early childhood screening test designed to identify children who may have special educational needs. Useful in identification of gifted and learning disabled students. Measures early motoric, conceptual, and language development. Separate norms are available for various minority groups.

12402
New Jersey Test of Reasoning Skills, Form A. Shipman, Virginia 1983
Descriptors: *Abstract Reasoning; College Students; Elementary School Students; Elementary Secondary Education; Induction; Language Processing; *Logical Thinking; Postsecondary Education; Questionnaires; Secondary School Students
Identifiers: New Jersey; Reasoning
Availability: Dr. Mathew Lipman; Institute for the Advancement of Philosophy for Children, Test Div., Montclair State College, Montclair, NJ 07043
Grade Level: 5-16
Notes: Time, 60; Items, 50

A measure of elementary reasoning and inquiry skills which concentrates on reasoning in language. For use at grade-5 reading level and above. Content of items is said to be juvenile but the test is useful for making comparisons across age levels. Scoring is done by the distributor of the test. Twenty-three reasoning skill areas are represented in the test, including inductive reasoning, syllogistic reasoning (conditional), part-whole reasoning, and analogical reasoning.

12405
Survey of Peer Relations, Form DQ. Wilson, Clark L. 1981
Descriptors: *Administrators; Adults; Communication Skills; *Employees; *Interpersonal Competence; *Occupational Tests; Peer Relationship; Problem Solving; Rating Scales; Surveys
Availability: Clark L. Wilson; P.O. Box 471, New Canaan, CT 06840
Target Audience: Adults
Notes: Items, 80

Designed for use by employee, employee's supervisor, and peers. Each responds to questions covering: organization of work, problem-solving approach, communication, work style, interpersonal skills. All statements are rated on a 7-point scale, indicating the extent to which the statement is true of the individual being rated.

12413
Classroom Behavior Description Checklist. Aaronson, May; And Others 1979
Descriptors: Academic Ability; Adjustment (to Environment); Affective Behavior; Behavior Problems; *Behavior Rating Scales; *Preschool Children; Social Behavior; *Student Behavior; Teacher Attitudes; Young Children
Identifiers: CBD; Task Orientation
Availability: ERIC Document Reproduction Service; 3900 Wheeler Ave., Alexandria, VA 22304 (ED183599, 46 pages)
Target Audience: 2-6
Notes: Items, 10

Checklist for obtaining teacher ratings of preschool children's behavior considered likely to influence school performance. Useful to identify children needing intervention. Covers child's ability, classroom adjustment and social, emotional and task-oriented behaviors. Suggested for use as a companion measure to the Preschool Preposition Test (TC 005 994), a screening measure for developmental delay.

12425
IEP Educational Diagnostic Inventories. Sedlak, Joseph E. 1979
Descriptors: *Diagnostic Tests; *Educational Diagnosis; Elementary Education; *Elementary School Students; Emotional Disturbances; Exceptional Persons; Gifted; Individualized Education Programs; Individual Testing; Intelligence; Learning Disabilities; Learning Modalities; Learning Problems; Mathematics Achievement; Mild Mental Retardation; Preschool Children; Preschool Education; Reading Skills; Screening Tests; Student Behavior
Identifiers: IEP Educational Diagnostic Inventories
Availability: National Press Publishing Co.; P.O. Box 237, Belle Vernon, PA 15012
Grade Level: K-6
Target Audience: 3-12

Developed to enable classroom teachers to screen and diagnose those students with potential learning problems. The teacher may administer the entire battery or only those sections deemed suitable for the problem objectives. The instruments are individually administered and may be used for normal, gifted, educable mentally retarded, emotionally disturbed, and learning disabled students. The battery results will yield information useful in developing an Individual Education Program for each student. The battery includes Diagnostic History Form (TC012531), National Intelligence Test (TC012532), Behavior Reinforcement Inventory (TC012533), Near-Point Visual Screening Inventory (TC012534), Reading Inventory (TC012535-TC012540), Math Inventory (TC012541-TC012543), Spelling Inventory (TC012544-TC012545), Handwriting Inventory (TC012546), Psycholinguistic Inventory (TC012547), and Modality Inventory (TC012548).

12434
Classroom Behavior Inventory. 42 Item Research Version. Schaefer, Earl S.; And Others 1978
Subtests: Extraversion; Creativity and Curiosity; Distractibility; Independence; Hostility; Verbal Intelligence; Task Orientation; Introversion; Consideration; Dependence
Descriptors: *Behavior Patterns; *Behavior Rating Scales; Cognitive Ability; *Kindergarten Children; Peer Relationship; Primary Education; Psychological Patterns; Teacher Student Relationship
Identifiers: CBI
Availability: Earl S. Schaefer; Dept. of Maternal and Child Health, University of North Carolina, Chapel Hill, NC 27514
Grade Level: K
Notes: Items, 42

Teachers complete behavior rating scales of kindergarten students. Factor structure of scale shows 3-dimensions: considerateness vs. hostility, academic competence, and extraversion vs. introversion. Goal of scale was to integrate social adjustment concepts, psychopathological concepts, and academic competence concepts.

12437
The Five P's: Parent Professional Preschool Performance Profile. Pre-Schooler's Workshop, Syosset, NY 1982
Subtests: Self-Help; Perceptual-Motor; Language Development; Social Development; Cognitive Development
Descriptors: Adjustment (to Environment); Behavior Problems; *Behavior Rating Scales; *Child Development; Cognitive Development; *Developmental Tasks; Individualized Education Programs; Interpersonal Competence; Language Acquisition; Language Handicaps; Learning Problems; *Preschool Children; Psychomotor Skills; Self Care Skills; *Young Children
Availability: Pre-Schooler's Workshop; 47 Humphrey Dr., Syosset, NY 11791
Target Audience: 2-8
Notes: Items, 338

Assessment instrument based on developmental landmarks and observable behaviors of children. Used to record behavior of preschool child who is labeled untestable or who is delayed or deviant or older child functioning at preschool level. The checklist is completed twice yearly, each time over a 2-week period by both parents and teachers. Can be used as a basis for developing individualized education plans. Assesses children in the areas of classroom adjustment; self help; motor skills; language, social and cognitive development.

12441
Cardboard Partition Assembly Work Sample. Hernandez, John 1974
Descriptors: Adults; Aptitude Tests; *Assembly (Manufacturing); *Disabilities; Individual Testing; *Work Sample Tests
Availability: Materials Development Center; Work Sample Manual Clearinghouse, Stout Vocational Rehabilitation Institute, School of Education, University of Wisconsin-Stout, Menomonie, WI 54751
Target Audience: 18-64
Notes: Time, 30; Items, 30

Designed for use in vocational evaluation with clients indicating interest in and potential for bench assembly work. Assesses a client's interest in fields involving manual dexterity, and gross assembly of products. Covers assembly and fitting of slotted cardboard pieces together to form partitions according to a prescribed plan. Useful with handicapped individuals.

12442
Rudd Tubeless Tire Repair Work Sample. Rudd, Herbert K. 1979
Descriptors: Adults; Aptitude Tests; *Auto Mechanics; Individual Testing; *Vocational Evaluation; *Work Sample Tests
Identifiers: Tires
Availability: Materials Development Center; Work Sample Manual Clearinghouse, Stout Vocational Rehabilitation Institute, School of Education, University of Wisconsin-Stout, Menomonie, WI 54751
Target Audience: 18-64
Notes: Time, 25; Items, 4

Developed for use in vocational evaluation with clients expressing an interest in auto mechanics. Assesses client's interest and potential for employment as a tire mounter or balancer. Covers ability to follow pictorial and written instructions and to repair a tire using required tools. Requires: manual and finger dexterity, stamina, frustration tolerance, accuracy and attention to detail, use of hand tools, eye-hand coordination, spatial and form perception. Sixth-grade reading level is necessary.

12443
Revised Reisterer Mechanical Aptitude Work Sample. Chambers, Elzabeth Lee 1974
Descriptors: Adults; Aptitude Tests; Individual Testing; *Visual Impairments; *Vocational Evaluation; *Work Sample Tests
Identifiers: *Mechanical Aptitude
Availability: Materials Development Center; Work Sample Manual Clearinghouse, Stout Vocational Rehabilitation Institute, School of Education, University of Wisconsin-Stout, Menomonie, WI 54751
Target Audience: 18-64
Notes: Time, 10; Items, 30

Designed to measure mechanical aptitude in visually impaired and nonvisually impaired persons. Evidence of ability in the area of spatial relations, form perception, and manual and finger dexterity are observed. Also useful with handicapped individuals having mental, physical or emotional disabilities. Subject assembles blocks, bolts, and rubber tubing.

12444
Inserting Cards, Folding and Packing Plastic Wallet Inserts. Kranick, Jack; And Others 1974
Descriptors: Adults; Aptitude Tests; Individual Testing; *Vocational Evaluation; *Work Sample Tests
Identifiers: *Packers
Availability: Materials Development Center; Work Sample Manual Clearinghouse, Stout Vocational Rehabilitation Institute, School of Education, University of Wisconsin-Stout, Menomonie, WI 54751
Target Audience: 18-64
Notes: Time, 15

Designed for use in vocational evaluation with clients interested or having the potential for bench assembly work. Measures client's interest and potential for employment in such fields as hand packager, inserter, or folder. Abilities observed are manual and finger dexterity, eye-hand coordination, spatial and form perception, accuracy of detail, ability to follow a sequence, tolerate routine tasks, and follow directions.

12445
The Road Map Reading Work Sample. Bodien, Jack M. 1974
Descriptors: Adults; Aptitude Tests; Individual Testing; *Map Skills; *Vocational Evaluation; *Work Sample Tests
Identifiers: *Road Maps
Availability: Materials Development Center; Work Sample Manual Clearinghouse, Stout Vocational Rehabilitation Institute, School of Education, University of Wisconsin-Stout, Menomonie, WI 54751
Target Audience: 18-64
Notes: Time, 20; Items, 13

Designed to be used in vocational evaluation with persons interested in truck or cab driving, general delivery work, or jobs requiring scheduling or dispatching. Includes ability to use coordinates to locate specific places, calculate mileage, use a map key or legend, determine direction, plan a route.

12446
Ogren Automobile Washing Work Sample. Ogren, Kenneth E. 1974
Descriptors: Adults; Aptitude Tests; Individual Testing; Mild Disabilities; *Vocational Evaluation; *Work Sample Tests
Identifiers: *Automobile Workers
Availability: Materials Development Center; Work Sample Manual Clearinghouse, Stout Vocational Rehabilitation Institute, School of Education, University of Wisconsin-Stout, Menomonie, WI 54751
Target Audience: 18-64
Notes: Time, 200

Designed to measure an individual's ability to wash the interior and exterior of an automobile. Can be used with clients having minor disabilities. Visual acuity is necessary. Washing and waxing of an entire auto is required.

12449
AGP Student Evaluation Checklist. O'Tuel, Frances S.; And Others 1983
Subtests: Critical Thinking Skills; Creative Thinking Skills; Research Skills; Social Skills; Task Commitment; Regular Classroom Participation
Descriptors: *Academically Gifted; Behavior Rating Scales; *Cognitive Processes; *Elementary School Students; Elementary Secondary Education; Grade 4; Grade 7; Grade 10; *Interpersonal Competence; *Secondary School Students; *Student Evaluation
Identifiers: Academically Gifted Program
Availability: Gifted Child Quarterly; v27 n3 p126-34, Sum 1983
Grade Level: 1-12
Notes: Items, 22

Designed to evaluate areas in which gifted students would perform in a program for the academically gifted. Teacher rates his/her students on 22 variables at the end of the academic year. The score is the total points circled by the teacher on a 4-point rating scale for each variable. The scale is constructed so that the lower the score, the more successful the student. Creative and critical thinking skills, research and social skills, task commitment, and regular classroom participation are assessed. Developed for a study of gifted students in grades 4, 7 and 10.

12463
Contributions to Neuropsychological Assessment: Serial Digit Learning. Benton, Arthur L.; And Others 1983
Descriptors: Adults; Cognitive Tests; Individual Testing; Mental Disorders; *Neurological Impairments; Older Adults; *Patients; *Short Term Memory
Identifiers: Neuropsychological Assessment
Availability: Oxford University Press; 1600 Pollitt Dr., Fairlawn, NJ 07410
Target Audience: 18-75
Notes: Time, 10 approx.; Items, 3

Designed to measure short term memory to be used in the clinical assessment of mental status. Examiner presents 8 or 9 randomly selected digits for the patient to repeat accurately for a varying number of trials up to 12. Form SD8 consists of an 8-digit sequence given to patients 65 years of age or older and those under 65 who have less than 12 years of education. Form SD9 consists of a 9-digit sequence which is given to patients under age 65 who have 12 or more years of education. In addition to ordering the tests separately, the 12 tests by Benton are also available in the book *Contributions to Neuropsychological Assessment: A Clinical Manual* by Arthur L. Benton and others, 1983. The book is published by Oxford University Press, 200 Madison Ave., New York, NY 10016. The book serves as a manual for the 12 related tests (TC012461-TC012472).

12464
Contributions to Neuropsychological Assessment: Facial Recognition. Benton, Arthur L.; And Others 1983
Subtests: Matching of Identical Front View Photographs. Matching of Front View with 3 Quarter View Photographs. Matching of Front View Photographs under Different Lighting Conditions
Descriptors: Adolescents; Adults; Children; Individual Testing; *Neurological Impairments; Older Adults; *Patients; Recognition (Psychology); Visual Measures; *Visual Perception
Identifiers: *Agnosia; Neuropsychological Assessment
Availability: Oxford University Press; 1600 Pollitt Dr., Fairlawn, NJ 07410
Target Audience: 6-74
Notes: Items, 54

Designed to provide a standardized objective procedure for assessing the capacity to identify and discriminate photographs of unfamiliar human faces. Facial agnosia was associated with other signs of right hemisphere dysfunction. A short form of 27 items is also available for use when examination time is limited. In addition to ordering the tests separately, the 12 tests by Benton are also available in the book *Contributions to Neuropsychological Assessment: A Clinical Manual* by Arthur L. Benton and others, 1983. The book is published by Oxford University Press, 200 Madison Ave., New York, NY 10016. The book serves as a manual for the 12 related tests (TC012461-TC012472).

12465
Contributions to Neuropsychological Assessment: Judgment of Line Orientation. Benton, Arthur L.; And Others 1983
Descriptors: Adolescents; Adults; Children; Individual Testing; Mental Disorders; *Neurological Impairments; Older Adults; *Patients; Perception Tests; *Spatial Ability
Identifiers: Neuropsychological Assessment
Availability: Oxford University Press; 1600 Pollitt Dr., Fairlawn, NJ 07410
Target Audience: 7-74
Notes: Items, 30

Designed to measure visuospatial judgment. Measures a single aspect of spatial thinking. Discriminates between patients with right hemisphere lesions and those with left hemisphere lesions. In addition to ordering the tests separately, the 12 tests by Benton are also available in the book *Contributions to Neuropsychological Assessment: A Clinical Manual* by Arthur L. Benton and others, 1983. The book is published by Oxford University Press, 200 Madison Ave., New York, NY 10016. The book serves as a manual for the 12 related tests (TC012461-TC012472).

12467
Contributions to Neuropsychological Assessment: Pantomime Recognition. Benton, Arthur L.; And Others 1983
Descriptors: Adults; *Aphasia; Individual Testing; Neurological Impairments; *Pantomime; *Patients; Perception Tests; Videotape Recordings
Identifiers: Neuropsychological Assessment
Availability: Oxford University Press; 1600 Pollitt Dr., Fairlawn, NJ 07410
Target Audience: Adults
Notes: Items, 30

Designed to provide an objective, standardized procedure for assessing a patient's ability to understand meaningful, nonlinguistic pantomimed actions. Impaired pantomime recognition was found to be closely related to defective reading comprehension in aphasic patients. In addition to ordering the tests separately, the 12 tests by Benton are also available in the book *Contributions to Neuropsychological Assessment: A Clinical Manual* by Arthur L. Benton and others, 1983. The book is published by Oxford University Press, 200 Madison Ave., New York, NY 10016. The book serves as a manual for the 12 related tests (TC012461-TC012472).

12468
Contributions to Neuropsychological Assessment: Tactile Form Perception. Benton, Arthur L.; And Others 1983
Descriptors: Adolescents; Adults; Children; Individual Testing; Mental Disorders; *Neurological Impairments; Older Adults; *Patients; Perception Tests; *Spatial Ability; *Tactual Perception
Identifiers: Neuropsychological Assessment
Availability: Oxford University Press; 1600 Pollitt Dr., Fairlawn, NJ 07410
Target Audience: 8-80
Notes: Time, 15 approx.; Items, 10

Designed to assess nonverbal tactile information processing. Failing performance was associated with other indications of impaired spatial thinking in patients with brain disease. Parallel forms A and B are available. In addition to ordering the tests separately, the 12 tests by Benton are also available in the book *Contributions to Neuropsychological Assessment: A Clinical Manual* by Arthur L. Benton and others, 1983. The book is published by Oxford University Press, 200 Madison Ave., New York, NY 10016. The book serves as a manual for the related tests (TC012461-TC012472).

12471
Contributions to Neuropsychological Assessment: 3 Dimensional Block Construction. Benton, Arthur L.; And Others 1983
Descriptors: Adolescents; Adults; Aphasia; Children; Individual Testing; *Neurological Impairments; *Patients; Performance Tests; Spatial Ability
Identifiers: Neuropsychological Assessment
Availability: Oxford University Press; 1600 Pollitt Dr., Fairlawn, NJ 07410
Target Audience: 6-64
Notes: Items, 3

Designed to assess visual constructional ability. Patient must reproduce 3 block models of increasing complexity. Two alternate forms are available. An experimental version using photographs as stimuli is also available. In addition to ordering the tests separately, the 12 tests by Benton are also available in the book *Contributions to Neuropsychological Assessment: A Clinical Manual* by Arthur L. Benton and others, 1983. The book is published by Oxford University Press, 200 Madison Ave., New York, NY 10016. The book serves as a manual for the related tests (TC012461-TC012472).

12484
Body Schema-Tempo Regulation Test. Santostefano, Sebastiano 1978
Subtests: Assessment of Body Ego and Associated Representations; Assessments of Regulation of Body Tempos
Descriptors: *Adolescents; *Body Image; *Children; Cognitive Style; Individual Testing; Performance Tests
Identifiers: BSTR
Availability: Santostefano, Sebastiano. A Biodevelopmental Approach to Clinical Child Psychology. New York: John Wiley & Sons, 1978.
Target Audience: 3-15

Designed to assess the unique and habitual ways a child constructs cognitive schemata of body positions, motility, and tempos.

12485
Object Sort Test II. Santostefano, Sebastiano 1978
Descriptors: *Adolescents; *Children; *Cognitive Style; *Cognitive Tests; Concept Formation; Individual Testing; Performance Tests
Identifiers: Cognitive Controls; OS II
Availability: Santostefano, Sebastiano. A Biodevelopmental Approach to Clinical Child Psychology. New York: John Wiley & Sons, 1978.
Target Audience: 4-17
Notes: Items, 46

Designed to assess the cognitive principle of equivalence range. Forty-six objects representing many materials, sizes, colors, shapes, and contents are presented to the child in a predetermined array. The child is given the task of arranging the objects into groups as he or she sees the relationship between objects.

12486
Circles Test of Focal Attention. Santostefano, Sebastiano 1978
Descriptors: *Adolescents; *Attention Control; *Children; Cognitive Style; *Cognitive Tests; Individual Testing
Identifiers: Piaget (Jean); Scanning
Availability: Santostefano, Sebastiano. A Biodevelopmental Approach to Clinical Child Psychology. New York: John Wiley & Sons, 1978.
Target Audience: 5-15
Notes: Items, 33

Designed to assess cognitive principle of focal attention. Respondents who scan items broadly and actively show better performance on this instrument.

12487
Leveling-Sharpening Circle and Wagon Tests. Santostefano, Sebastiano 1978
Descriptors: *Adolescents; *Children; *Cognitive Style; *Cognitive Tests; Individual Testing; *Short Term Memory; Visual Perception; Visual Stimuli
Identifiers: Cognitive Controls; Leveling Sharpening Dimension
Availability: Santostefano, Sebastiano. A Biodevelopmental Approach to Clinical Child Psychology. New York: John Wiley & Sons, 1978.
Target Audience: 3-15
Notes: Time, 30 approx.; Items, 122

Designed to assess the cognitive control processes of leveling-sharpening. The child is shown a series of circles increasing in size from 7 to 20 millimeters. The cognitive control process of sharpening is indicative of a child who perceives changes in size early in the series. Sharpening denotes articulate images of information held in memory over time and are differentiated from existing information. Leveling is a process where global images of information are held in memory over time and fused with existing information.

12488
Continuous Performance Test of Attention. Santostefano, Sebastiano 1978
Descriptors: *Adolescents; *Attention Span; *Children; *Cognitive Tests; Individual Testing; *Visual Perception; Visual Stimuli
Identifiers: Cognitive Controls; Scanning

Availability: Santostefano, Sebastiano. A Biodevelopmental Approach to Clinical Child Psychology. New York: John Wiley & Sons, 1978.
Target Audience: 3-15

Designed to provide a measure of continuous attention. The degree of activity and breadth of visual scanning are also assessed.

12489
Autokinetic Test. Santostefano, Sebastiano 1978
Descriptors: Children; *Cognitive Style; *Cognitive Tests; Elementary Education; *Elementary School Students; Individual Testing
Identifiers: Cognitive Controls
Availability: Santostefano, Sebastiano. A Biodevelopmental Approach to Clinical Child Psychology. New York: John Wiley & Sons, 1978.
Target Audience: 5-12
Notes: Time, 5 approx.

Designed to measure child's tolerance for unrealistic experiences.

12490
Memory for Spatial Orientation of Designs. Santostefano, Sebastiano 1978
Descriptors: *Adolescents; *Children; Cognitive Processes; *Cognitive Tests; Projection Equipment; Short Term Memory; Slides; *Spatial Ability; Visual Discrimination
Identifiers: Cognitive Controls
Availability: Santostefano, Sebastiano. A Biodevelopmental Approach to Clinical Child Psycholog. New York: John Wiley & Sons, 1978.
Target Audience: 3-15
Notes: Time, 4 approx.; Items, 48

Designed to assess accuracy of memory for spatial orientation of geometric designs. A slide is shown with a standard geometric shape. A second slide is shown with 4 illustrations of the shape. Three of the shapes on response slide have been rotated 45 degrees, 90 degrees or 180 degrees, while the fourth shape is the same as the first picture. Respondent must choose the design that is exactly like the first. Each slide is projected for 5 seconds.

12491
Exploded Block Design Test. Santostefano, Sebastiano 1978
Descriptors: *Cognitive Tests; Individual Testing; Performance Tests; Spatial Ability; *Visual Perception; *Young Children
Identifiers: Cognitive Controls
Availability: Santostefano, Sebastiano. A Biodevelopmental Approach to Clinical Child Psychology. New York: John Wiley & Sons, 1978.
Target Audience: 3-8
Notes: Items, 10

Designed to measure field articulation. Child must duplicate 10 designs created with colored cubes placed in a form board. The designs are taken from the Goldstein-Scheerer Cube Test, a component of the Goldstein-Scheerer Test of Abstract and Concrete thinking. (TC003257). Forms A and B are available.

12492
Incomplete Figures Test. Santostefano, Sebastiano 1978
Descriptors: *Attention Control; *Cognitive Tests; Individual Testing; Visual Perception; *Young Children
Identifiers: Cognitive Controls
Availability: Santostefano, Sebastiano. A Biodevelopmental Approach to Clinical Child Psychology. New York: John Wiley & Sons, 1978.
Target Audience: 3-8
Notes: Items, 6

Designed to assess cognitive principle of field articulation. Subject must complete figure partially drawn by discontinuous lines.

12493
Marble Board Test. Santostefano, Sebastiano 1978
Descriptors: *Cognitive Tests; Individual Testing; Performance Tests; Visual Perception; *Young Children
Identifiers: Cognitive Controls
Availability: Santostefano, Sebastiano. A Biodevelopmental Approach to Clinical Child Psychology. New York: John Wiley & Sons, 1978.
Target Audience: 3-8
Notes: Items, 8

Designed to assess cognitive control principle of field articulation. Child must reproduce a design with marbles and formboard. Stimulus is present throughout child's performance.

12494
Scattered Scanning Test. Santostefano, Sebastiano 1978
Descriptors: *Adolescents; *Attention Control; *Children; *Cognitive Style; Cognitive Tests; Psychomotor Skills; Visual Discrimination
Identifiers: Scanning; SST
Availability: Santostefano, Sebastiano. A Biodevelopmental Approach to Clinical Child Psychology. New York: John Wiley & Sons, 1978.
Target Audience: 3-15
Notes: Time, 1 approx.; Items, 50

Designed to assess focal attention cognitive control. Respondent must scan a sheet containing 50 geometric shapes and mark the circles and crosses as quickly as possible. A time limit of 30 seconds is established for this instrument. Form 1 contains 50 shapes. Form 2 contains 200 shapes. The examiner records the sequence of the child's markings on an identical test form. The Motor Tempo Test is included in the assessment to determine fine motor ability.

12495
Leveling-Sharpening House Test. Santostefano, Sebastiano 1978
Descriptors: Adolescents; Children; *Cognitive Style; *Cognitive Tests; Individual Testing; *Short Term Memory; Visual Perception; Visual Stimuli
Identifiers: Cognitive Controls; Leveling Sharpening Dimension; LSHT
Availability: Santostefano, Sebastiano. A Biodevelopmental Approach to Clinical Child Psychology. New York: John Wiley & Sons, 1978.
Target Audience: 3-15
Notes: Time, 15 approx.; Items, 60

Designed to assess the cognitive control processes of leveling and sharpening. Child must direct attention to a series of 60 pictures of a house displayed in succession and report when details in picture change.

12502
Teacher Rating Scale of Student Performance. Santostefano, Sebastiano 1978
Subtests: Academic Skills; Cognitive-Coping Skills; Regulation of Aggression and Tensions
Descriptors: Academic Achievement; Aggression; *Behavior Rating Scales; Cognitive Processes; Elementary Education; *Elementary School Students; Elementary School Teachers; *Student Behavior; *Student Evaluation
Availability: Santostefano, Sebastiano. A Biodevelopmental Approach to Clinical Child Psychology. New York: John Wiley & Sons, 1978.
Grade Level: K-6
Notes: Items, 15

Designed to assess developmental level of children. Teacher completes rating scale with respect to student's performance in comparison with all students teacher has taught at that age level.

12511
Perkins-Binet Tests of Intelligence for the Blind. Davis, Carl J. 1980
Descriptors: *Adolescents; *Blindness; *Children; Diagnostic Tests; Intelligence; *Intelligence Tests; Standardized Tests
Identifiers: Stanford Binet Intelligence Scale
Availability: Perkins School for the Blind; Howe Press, Watertown, MA 02172
Target Audience: 3-18

This test was adopted primarily from the Stanford Binet Intelligence Scale, third revision, forms L-M with the permission of Houghton Mifflin. Intent was to develop a scale of intelligence for blind subjects that would be an age level scale approximating the Stanford Binet structure and content. Two final forms of the test were developed. Form N consists of items for ages 4-18 and consists of 94 items, including alternate items. Form U is for ages 3-18 and consists of 99 items including alternate items. The Perkins-Binet is constructed so that serial tasks come first. Due to limited sampling, test-items below age 6 have limited statistical validity.

12532
IEP Educational Diagnostic Inventories: National Intelligence Test. Sedlak, Joseph E. 1979
Descriptors: Educational Diagnosis; Elementary Education; *Elementary School Students; Emotional Disturbances; *Exceptional Persons; Gifted; *Individualized Education Programs; Individual Testing; *Intelligence; Intelligence Quotient; Intelligence Tests; Learning Disabilities; Mild Mental Retardation; *Preschool Children; Preschool Education; *Screening Tests
Identifiers: IEP Educational Diagnostic Inventories

Availability: National Press Publishing Co.; P.O. Box 237, Belle Vernon, PA 15012
Target Audience: 3-12
Notes: Time, 5 approx.; Items, 78

One instrument in a test battery developed to enable classroom teachers to screen and diagnose those students with potential learning problems. The instrument may be used to develop an Individual Education Program for gifted, educable mentally retarded, emotionally disturbed, or learning disabled students. Designed as a screening device to estimate a student's general intellectual ability.

12535
IEP Educational Diagnostic Inventories: Pre-Reading Screening I and II. Sedlak, Joseph E. 1979
Descriptors: *Auditory Discrimination; *Diagnostic Tests; Educational Diagnosis; *Elementary School Students; Emotional Disturbances; *Exceptional Persons; Gifted; *Grade 1; *Individualized Education Programs; Individual Testing; *Kindergarten Children; Learning Disabilities; *Long Term Memory; Mild Mental Retardation; Primary Education; *Reading Readiness; Reading Readiness Tests; Reading Skills; Screening Tests; *Short Term Memory; *Visual Discrimination
Identifiers: IEP Educational Diagnostic Inventories
Availability: National Press Publishing Co.; P.O. Box 237, Belle Vernon, PA 15012
Grade Level: K-1

One instrument in a test battery developed to enable classroom teachers to screen and diagnose those students with potential learning problems. The instrument may be used to develop an Individual Education Program for gifted, educable mentally retarded, emotionally disturbed, or learning disabled students. Instruments are designed to assess the skills necessary for formal reading instruction. Pre-reading I assesses visual discrimination and long term memory. Pre-reading II assesses auditory discrimination and short term memory.

12547
IEP Educational Diagnostic Inventories: Psycholinguistic Inventory. Sedlak, Joseph E. 1979
Subtests: Reception; Memory; Expression
Descriptors: Auditory Discrimination; *Diagnostic Tests; Educational Diagnosis; Elementary Education; *Elementary School Students; Emotional Disturbances; *Exceptional Persons; Expressive Language; Gifted; *Individualized Education Programs; Individual Testing; Language Processing; Learning Disabilities; Mild Mental Retardation; *Psycholinguistics; *Receptive Language; *Short Term Memory
Identifiers: IEP Educational Diagnostic Inventories
Availability: National Press Publishing Co.; P.O. Box 237, Belle Vernon, PA 15012
Grade Level: K-6

One instrument in a test battery developed to enable classroom teachers to screen and diagnose those students with potential learning problems. The instrument may be used to develop an Individual Education Program for gifted, educable mentally retarded, emotionally disturbed, or learning disabled students. Instrument designed to assess student's ability to communicate. The receptive process is assessed by measuring auditory and visual reception, as well as auditory discrimination. The memory process is assessed by the visual sequential memory for numbers and words and the auditory sequential memory for numbers and words. The expressive process is assessed by the expressive grammar, verbal expression, and manual expression inventories.

12548
IEP Educational Diagnostic Inventories: Modality Inventory. Sedlak, Joseph E. 1979
Subtests: Visual Learning Approach; Auditory Learning Approach; Kinesthetic Learning Approach; Eclectic Learning Approach
Descriptors: *Cognitive Style; *Diagnostic Tests; Educational Diagnosis; Elementary Education; *Elementary School Students; Emotional Disturbances; *Exceptional Persons; Gifted; *Individualized Education Programs; Individual Testing; Kinesthetic Methods; Learning Disabilities; *Learning Modalities; Mild Mental Retardation; Word Recognition
Identifiers: IEP Educational Diagnostic Inventories
Availability: National Press Publishing Co.; P.O. Box 237, Belle Vernon, PA 15012
Grade Level: K-6
Notes: Items, 40

One instrument in a test battery developed to enable classroom teachers to screen and diagnose those students with potential learning problems. The instrument may be used to develop an Individual Education Program for gifted, educable mentally retarded, emotionally disturbed, or learning disabled students. This instrument was designed to assess student's cognitive style. Student is taught

10 unknown words through a specific approach-visual, auditory, kinesthetic, or eclectic. After all 40 words have been learned, student is tested on all 40 words. The results of this posttest, recommended for administration 1 or 2 weeks after learning, will be a measure of method in which student best learns new words for long-term retention.

12592
The Gross Geometric Forms Creativity Test for Children. Gross, Ruth Brill; And Others 1982
Descriptors: *Art Activities; *Children; *Creativity; *Creativity Tests; Performance Tests
Identifiers: GGF; *Pictorial Creativity
Availability: Stoelting Co.; 620 Wheat Ln., Wood Dale, IL 60191
Target Audience: 3-12
Notes: Items, 10

A work sample assessment of pictorial creativity in children. Based on a theoretical rationale taken from developmental psychology and art theory. Work presumes that creativity is a manifestation of child's total personality, involving cognitive, conative, and affective dimensions. The GGF method consists of 48 felt forms (circles, rectangles, half circles, triangles, squares) in 3 colors (red, blue, yellow) from which child makes 10 spontaneous pictorial constructions according to a standardized set and inquiry. Scoring is based on productivity, communicability of ideas, and richness of thinking. Instrument is experimental and intended primarily for research purposes.

12610
Kent Infant Development Scale. Reuter, Jeanette; Katoff, Lewis 1978
Subtests: Cognitive; Motor; Social; Language; Self Help
Descriptors: Behavior Rating Scales; Cognitive Development; *Disabilities; Dutch; German; High Risk Persons; *Infant Behavior; *Infants; Language Acquisition; Motor Development; Parents; Self Care Skills; Social Development; Spanish; Young Children
Identifiers: KID Scale
Availability: Kent Developmental Metrics; P.O. Box 845, 126 W. College Ave., Kent, OH 44240-0017
Target Audience: 0-1
Notes: Items, 252

Designed to assess behavioral development of infants and young handicapped children chronologically or developmentally below one year of age. Behavior assessment is completed by child's parent or primary caregiver. Computerized scoring and printout furnished developmental ages; a profile of strengths and weaknesses; and a timetable indicating which developmental milestones will be acquired next. May be used in developing a prescriptive educational program. Also for infants and handicapped children functioning below one year of age. Also available in German, Dutch, Hispanic (TC013170) and Castilian Spanish.

12612
PRIDE: Preschool and Kindergarten Interest Descriptor. Rimm, Sylvia B. 1983
Descriptors: *Creativity; *Gifted; *Kindergarten Children; *Preschool Children; Preschool Education; Rating Scales; *Screening Tests; Talent Identification
Identifiers: PRIDE
Availability: Educational Assessment Service; Rte. 1, Box 139A, Watertown, WI 53094
Target Audience: 3-6
Notes: Time, 35 approx.; Items, 50

Developed to provide an easily administered, reliable, and valid instrument to screen preschool and kindergarten children for programs for the creatively gifted. Purpose of PRIDE is to identify children with attitudes and interests usually associated with preschool and kindergarten creativity, such as a variety of interests, curiosity, independence, perseverance, imagination, playfulness, humor, and originality. It is recommended that parents complete the inventory at a parent meeting or during a preschool or kindergarten screening for their child. There is no time limit to complete the inventory but it usually takes between 20 and 35 minutes.

12638
Differential Imagery Questionnaire. Welsh, D. Kent 1979
Descriptors: *Behavior Rating Scales; College Students; Creativity; Fantasy; Higher Education; Visualization
Identifiers: DIQ
Availability: ERIC Document Reproduction Service; 3900 Wheeler Ave., Alexandria, VA 22304 (ED182314, 13 pages)
Grade Level: 13-16

The Differential Imagery Questionnaire (DIQ) is a new questionnaire on mental imagery and taps 4 types of imagery: work imagery (WI), picture memory (PM), imagery manipulation (IM), and fantasy (F). It is an attempt to develop an instrument that offers greater precision in the assessment of visual imagery.

12688
The TLC Learning Style Inventory. Silver, Harvey F.; Hanson, J. Robert 1980
Subtests: Sensing Feeling; Sensing Thinking; Intuitive Thinking; Intuitive Feeling
Descriptors: *Adults; *Cognitive Style; *College Students; Higher Education; Rating Scales; *Self Evaluation (Individuals)
Identifiers: Jung (Carl G); LSI; Self Administered Tests; TLC Learning Preference Inventory Kit
Availability: Educational Performance Associates; 600 Broad Ave., Ridgefield, NJ 07657
Grade Level: 13-16
Target Audience: Adults
Notes: Items, 80

A self descriptive test based on Carl Jung's Theory of Psychological Types (1921). Designed to help learners identify their own learning profile based on preferences for how information is collected and what judgments are made about its significance. Inventory contains 20 sets of 4 behaviors which are ranked by subject based on his or her own preferences. Four information processing behaviors are sensing, intuition, thinking, feeling.

12689
The TLC Learning Preference Inventory. Silver, Harvey F.; Hanson, J. Robert 1978
Subtests: Sensing Feeling; Sensing Thinking; Intuitive Thinking; Intuitive Feeling; Introversion; Extraversion
Descriptors: *Adults; Adult Students; *Cognitive Style; *College Students; *Elementary School Students; Elementary Secondary Education; Higher Education; Rating Scales; *Secondary School Students; *Self Evaluation (Individuals)
Identifiers: Jung (Carl G); LPI; Self Administered Tests; TLC Learning Preference Inventory Kit
Availability: Educational Performance Associates; 600 Broad Ave., Ridgefield, NJ 07657
Grade Level: 4-16
Target Audience: Adults
Notes: Items, 144

Designed to assist teachers in identifying individual students' learning preferences or styles. Self assessment tool based on Carl Jung's theory of Psychological Types (1921) which defined behavior as the result of 2 opposite but interdependent sets of functions: sensing and intuition (perceiving) versus thinking and feeling (judgments). Jung's theory also included an attitudinal dimension which modifies the perceiving and judgments functions. These attitudes are called introversion and extraversion and are reflected in a person's preferred way of treating ideas and tasks. The Learning Preference Inventory is an untimed, diagnostic assessment of how the student perceives himself or herself as a learner. It has been used with elementary, secondary, college and adult learners. Also part of the kit is a Data Sheet on Student Learning Preferences which contains the Checklist of Preferred Behaviors (60 items) in which the teacher checks his or her own perceptions about the learning preferences of his or her students.

12720
USES Clerical Skills Test. Employment and Training Administration (DOL), Washington, DC 1976
Subtests: Plain Copy Typing; Transcribing Machine Operation; Dictation; Spelling; Statistical Typing; Medical Spelling; Legal Spelling
Descriptors: Adults; *Aptitude Tests; *Clerical Occupations; Job Placement; Occupational Tests; Spelling; Typewriting; Dictation
Identifiers: *Clerical Skills; Legal Spelling; Medical Spelling; Statistical Typewriting; Transcription
Availability: Superintendent of Documents; U.S. Government Printing Office, Washington, D.C. 20402
Target Audience: 18-64

Still used only by U.S. Employment Service office to measure aptitudes of unemployed persons for placement and, rarely, administered to high school students through special arrangement with U.S.E.S. local offices. Norms are based, however, on an experienced population resulting in comparatively low scores for the inexperienced. Typing test measures speed and accuracy. Cassette recordings are used for the transcribing test. The dictation test may also be administered via recording. Earlier versions of this test are still used by the U.S. Employment Service.

12723
Pediatric Early Elementary Examination. Levine, Melvin D. 1983
Subtests: Developmental Attainment; Associated Observations; Neuromaturation; Other Physical Findings; Task Analysis; General Health Assessment

Descriptors: Behavior Development; *Child Development; Child Development Specialists; Cognitive Measurement; Developmental Stages; Developmental Tasks; *Eye Hand Coordination; *Individual Development; Language Processing; *Neurological Impairments; Observation; *Physical Development; *Screening Tests; Tests; *Young Children
Identifiers: PEEX
Availability: Educators Publishing Service; 75 Moulton St., Cambridge, MA 02238-9101
Target Audience: 7-9

The PEEX (Pediatric Early Elementary Examination) is a combined neurodevelopmental, behavioral, and health assessment primarily for children between the ages of 7 and 9. It is designed to provide standardized observation procedures—techniques that can be applied in health care or other settings—to help clinicians characterize children's functional health and its relationship to neurodevelopmental and physical status. It enables clinicians to integrate medical, developmental, and neurological findings while making observations of behavioral adjustment and style. The areas assessed are fine motor, visual-fine motor, visual processing, temporal-sequential organization, linguistic, gross motor, recall, and task analysis. The PEEX does not produce a specific score or diagnosis. Instead, it generates a functional profile—a description of strengths, weaknesses, and stylistic preferences.

12744
The Mensa Test. 1980
Descriptors: Abstract Reasoning; *Adolescents; *Adults; *Cognitive Ability; Cognitive Tests; *Intelligence; *Intelligence Tests; Screening Tests; Spatial Ability
Identifiers: Self Administered Tests; Self Scoring Tests
Availability: Norback, Craig T. Check Yourself Out. New York: Times Books, 1980
Target Audience: 16-64
Notes: Items, 25

Designed to determine individuals who are eligible to join Mensa, an organization for those who score in top 2 percent of population on intelligence tests. An IQ test produced by Mensa is available by writing to: Mensa, Dept. CN, 1701, W. Third St., Brooklyn, NY 11223

12745
The Thinker's Test. Albrecht, Karl 1980
Descriptors: Adults; Cognitive Processes; *Cognitive Tests; Critical Thinking; *Logical Thinking; Problem Solving
Identifiers: Self Administered Tests; Self Scoring Tests
Availability: Norback, Craig T. Check Yourself Out. New York: Times Books, 1980
Target Audience: Adults
Notes: Items, 9

Designed to assess logical powers and problem solving ability. Measures ability to organize ideas into sequence or chains of logic. Instrument originally appeared in *Reader's Digest*, April 1980.

12746
How Resourceful Are You? McGuire, Christine H.; And Others
Descriptors: *Adults; Decision Making Skills; *Persistence; *Personality Measures; *Problem Solving; Simulation
Identifiers: Self Administered Tests; Self Scoring Tests; The Traveler
Availability: Norback, Craig T. Check Yourself Out. New York: Times Books, 1980
Target Audience: Adults

A psychological simulation is presented to assess problem solving and decision making skills. Individual's approach to solving the dilemma yields information about respondent's personality and persistence.

12803
Spanish Culture Fair Intelligence Test: Scale 2. Cattell, Raymond B.; Cattell, A.K.S. 1957
Descriptors: Adolescents; *Adults; Children; Culture Fair Tests; *Elementary School Students; Elementary Secondary Education; Individual Testing; Intelligence; *Intelligence Tests; Nonverbal Tests; *Secondary School Students; *Spanish; *Spanish Speaking; Spatial Ability
Identifiers: Cattell Culture Fair Intelligence Test
Availability: Institute for Personality and Ability Testing; P.O. Box 188, Champaign, IL 61820
Target Audience: 8-64
Notes: Items, 46

A Spanish language translation of the Culture Fair Intelligence Test, Scale 2 (TC001660) which is designed to assess individual intelligence in a manner which reduces the influence of verbal fluency, cultural climate, and educational level. Forms A and B are available for use with children ages 8-14 and adults of average intelligence. Scale 2 is appropriate for majority of subjects.

12804

Spanish Culture Fair Intelligence Test: Scale 3.
Cattell, Raymond B.; Cattell, A.K.S. 1963
Subtests: Series; Classifications; Matrices; Conditions (Topology)
Descriptors: Adults; College Students; *Culture Fair Tests; Higher Education; High Schools; High School Students; Individual Testing; Intelligence; *Intelligence Tests; Nonverbal Tests; *Spanish; *Spanish Speaking; *Spatial Ability; Timed Tests
Identifiers: Cattell Culture Fair Intelligence Test
Availability: Institute for Personality and Ability Testing; P.O. Box 188, Champaign, IL 61820
Target Audience: 15-64
Notes: Time, 13 approx.; Items, 50
A Spanish translation of the Culture Fair Intelligence Test, Scale 3 (TC001661). Test booklets, administration instructions, and answer sheets are in Spanish. Instrument is designed to measure individual intelligence in a manner intended to reduce the influence of verbal fluency, cultural climate, and educational level. Forms A and B are available for Scale 3.

12869

Appraisal of Individual Development Scales, Experimental Edition. Appalachia Educational Laboratory, Charleston, WV 1978
Subtests: Gross Motor; Hand-Eye Coordination; Perception; Independence; Social Maturity; Relating to Adults; Attention-Getting; Self Concept; Emotional Expression; Fantasy or Imagination; Responding to Non-Human Environment; Language; Conceptual Development; Number Concepts; Language Supplement; Self Concept Supplement
Descriptors: Achievement Tests; *Child Development; Cognitive Development; Competency Based Education; Developmental Stages; Eye Hand Coordination; Imagination; Individualized Instruction; Language Acquisition; Observation; Performance Tests; Preschool Education; Psychomotor Skills; *Young Children
Identifiers: AIDS
Availability: Educational Communications, Inc.; 9240 S.W. 124 St., Miami, FL 33176
Target Audience: 3-6
The Appraisal of Individual Development Scales (AIDS) are a developmental assessment tool to help teachers individualize instruction in each of 59 competency areas. The 59 competencies cluster into 14 areas of development. The 14 clusters are gross motor, hand-eye coordination, perception, independence, social maturity, relating to adults, attention-getting, self concept, emotional expression, fantasy or imagination, responding to nonhuman environment, language, conceptual development, and number concepts. There are 2 supplemental sections: language and self concept. The AIDS are to be completed through informal observation of the child's interests, abilities, and behavior patterns. The items should not be administered in a test-like situation but in learning activities or free play situations as much as possible. This is an experimental edition of AIDS, meaning it has not yet undergone a rigid standardization procedure. When the results are in from teachers using this edition, some items will be deleted and others added.

12968

InQ Questionnaire. Harrison, Allen F.; And Others 1980
Subtests: Synthesist; Idealist; Analyst; Realist; Pragmatist
Descriptors: *Administrators; Adults; *Cognitive Style; Decision Making Skills; Management Development; Rating Scales; Self Evaluation (Individuals)
Identifiers: Inquiry Mode Questionnaire; Self Report Measures
Availability: Bramson Parlette Associates; Wells Fargo Bldg., Ste. 1209, 2140 Shattuck Ave., Berkeley, CA 94704
Target Audience: Adults
Notes: Items, 18
Designed to assess individual preferences in thinking styles including question asking, data gathering, problem solving, and decision making. Useful in management development situations. Scores yield a profile of individual's thinking style. Questionnaire, is also available in Computer Decisions; v15 n7 p76-84, Jul, 1983.

12976

Phases of Integrated Problem Solving. Morris, William C.; Sashkin, Marshall 1978
Descriptors: *Adults; *Group Dynamics; *Problem Solving; Rating Scales; Sequential Learning
Identifiers: PIPS; Self Administered Tests; Self Scoring Tests
Availability: University Associates, Inc.; 8517 Production Ave., P.O. Box 26240, San Diego, CA 92126
Target Audience: Adults
Notes: Items, 36

Designed for use during group problem solving as a training aid. The 6 phases of problem solving are Problem Definition; Problem Solution-Generation; Ideas to Action; Solution-Action Planning; Solution-Evaluation Planning; and Evaluation of the Product and the Process. This instrument is available in the 1978 Annual Handbook for Group Facilitators.

13002

Defense Language Aptitude Battery. Defense Language Institute, Monterey, CA 1977
Subtests: Biographical Inventory; Recognition of Stress Patterns; Foreign Language Grammar; Foreign Language Concept Formation
Descriptors: Adults; *Aptitude Tests; Arabic; Armed Forces; Biographical Inventories; Concept Formation; Czech; French; German; Grammar; Korean; *Language Aptitude; Mandarin Chinese; Russian; Screening Tests; *Second Language Learning; Spanish; Thai; Vietnamese
Identifiers: DLAB
Availability: Defense Language Institute; Foreign Language Center, Monterey, CA 93940
Target Audience: 18-64
Notes: Time, 90; Items, 119
Used to screen potential candidates for training in more than 30 foreign languages. Candidates are officers and enlisted personnel from 4 military branches and civilians referred by federal agencies. The test is administered at Armed Forces Entrance and Examination Stations. Has predictive validity for Arabic; Chinese (Mandarin); Czech; French; German; Korean; Russian; Spanish; Thai; Vietnamese. DLAB contains an audio component.

13050

IEA Six-Subject Survey Instruments: Civic Education Tests, Cognition, Population I. International Association for the Evaluation of Education Achievement, Stockholm (Sweden) 1975
Descriptors: *Academic Achievement; *Achievement Tests; *Civics; Cognitive Tests; *Comparative Education; *Cross Cultural Studies; Elementary Education; *Elementary School Students; Foreign Countries; Multiple Choice Tests
Identifiers: International Evaluation Educational Achievement; Sweden
Availability: ERIC Document Reproduction Service; 3900 Wheeler Ave., Alexandria, VA 22304 (ED 102 187, 55 pages)
Target Audience: 10-11
Notes: Time, 35; Items, 41
In 1965 the International Association for the Evaluation of Educational Achievement (IEA) inaugurated a cross-national survey of achievement in 6 subjects: science, reading comprehension, literature, English as a Foreign Language, French as a Foreign Language, and civic education. The overall aim of the project was to use international tests in order to relate student achievement and attitudes to instructional, social, and economical factors, and from the results to establish generalizations of value to policy makers worldwide. This is 1 of 3 civics cognitive tests for Population I which consists of students aged 10 to 11 years. The other tests are for Population II, students 14 to 15 years, and Population IV, students enrolled in the final year of pre-university training.

13051

IEA Six-Subject Survey Instruments: Civic Education Tests, Cognition, Population II. International Association for the Evaluation of Education Achievement, Stockholm (Sweden) 1975
Descriptors: *Academic Achievement; *Achievement Tests; *Civics; Cognitive Tests; *Comparative Education; *Cross Cultural Studies; Foreign Countries; *Junior High School Students; Multiple Choice Tests; Secondary Education
Identifiers: International Evaluation Educational Achievement; Sweden
Availability: ERIC Document Reproduction Service; 3900 Wheeler Ave., Alexandria, VA 22304 (ED102187, 55 pages)
Target Audience: 14-15
Notes: Time, 35; Items, 47
In 1965 the International Association for the Evaluation of Educational Achievement (IEA) inaugurated a cross-national survey of achievement in 6 subjects: science, reading comprehension, literature, English as a Foreign Language, French as a Foreign Language, and civic education. The overall aim of the project was to use international tests in order to relate student achievement and attitudes to instructional, social, and economical factors, and from the results to establish generalizations of value to policy makers worldwide. This is 1 of 3 civics cognitive tests for Population II which consists of students aged 14 to 15 years. The other tests are for Population I, students aged 10 to 11, and Population IV, students enrolled in the final years of pre-university training.

13052

IEA Six-Subject Survey Instruments: Civic Education Tests, Cognition, Population IV. International Association for the Evaluation of Education Achievement, Stockholm (Sweden) 1975
Descriptors: *Academic Achievement; *Achievement Tests; *Civics; Cognitive Tests; College Bound Students; *Comparative Education; *Cross Cultural Studies; Foreign Countries; *Grade 12; High School Students; Multiple Choice Tests; Secondary Education
Identifiers: International Evaluation Educational Achievement; Sweden
Availability: ERIC Document Reproduction Service; 3900 Wheeler Ave., Alexandria, VA 22304 (ED 102 187, 55 pages)
Grade Level: 12
Notes: Time, 35; Items, 48
In 1965 the International Association for the Evaluation of Educational Achievement (IEA) inaugurated a cross-national survey of achievement in 6 subjects: science, reading comprehension, literature, English as a foreign language, French as a foreign language, and civic education. The overall aim of the project was to use international tests in order to relate student achievement and attitudes to instructional, social, and economica factors, and from the results to establish generalizations of value to policy makers worldwide. This is 1 of 3 civics cognitive tests for Population IV which consists of students enrolled in the final year of pre-university training. The other tests are for Population I, students aged 10 to 11, and Population II which consists of students aged 14 to 15 years.

13072

Index Card Work Task Unit: Electromechanical Vocational Assessment. Mississippi State Univ., Rehabilitation Research and Training Ctr. 1983
Descriptors: Adults; *Blindness; Individual Testing; *Memory; *Performance Tests; Psychomotor Skills; *Visual Impairments; *Vocational Evaluation
Identifiers: *Bilateral Dexterity; Electromechanical Vocational Assessment; Finger Dexterity; Frustration; Mississippi State University
Availability: Rehabilitation Research and Training Center; P.O. Box 5365, Mississippi State, MS 39762
Target Audience: Adults
Notes: Time, 50
Designed to provide a flexible system of evaluating a variety of work abilities including bi-manual coordination, finger dexterity, frustration tolerance, and memory for sequence of operations. Purpose is to assist National Industries for the Blind and vocational evaluators to improve assessment of the vocational potential of blind and severely visually impaired persons, particularly multiply handicapped blind persons. Subject is taught the task, then works for a 50 minute period and receives feedback on the rate and accuracy of work. An objective method of comparing visually impaired person's performance with the sighted standard. The Methods-Time Measurement Procedure was used to develop the average sighted standard for this task.

13079

Organizational Problem Solving: Agreement and Difference Management. Rumley, Jacqueline; Lippitt, Gordon 1981
Subtests: The Nature of the Conflict/Difference; The Factors Underlying the Conflict/Differnce; The Stages of Evolution of the Conflict/Difference; The Action Options
Descriptors: *Adults; *Conflict Resolution; Problem Solving; Questionnaires; Self Evaluation (Groups)
Availability: Development Publications; 5605 Lamar Rd., Bethesda, MD 20816-1398
Target Audience: Adults
A problem solving instrument used for creative utilization of differences and agreements between individuals, groups, and organizations.

13122

Teacher's Self-Control Rating Scale. Humphrey, Laura Lynn 1982
Subtests: Behavioral/Interpersonal; Cognitive/Personal-Self Control
Descriptors: Behavior; Cognitive Processes; Intermediate Grades; Rating Scales; *Self Control; Teachers
Identifiers: TSCRS
Availability: Journal of Consulting and Clinical Psychology; v50 n5 p624-33, 1982
Target Audience: Adults
Notes: Items, 15
Items are concerned with a cognitive-personal behavioral conceptualization of self-control. Teacher rates students. Ratings were found to relate to IQ and achievement. A 5 point scale is used. Used along with the Children's Perceived Self-Control Scale (TC013123). Self-control is defined as "goal-directed solitary or social work."

13161
Primary Test of Higher Processes of Thinking. Williams, Winnie 1978
Subtests: Convergent Production; Convergent Analogies; Sequential Relationships; Logic; Deductive Reasoning; Divergent Thinking
Descriptors: *Academically Gifted; *Cognitive Processes; *Cognitive Tests; Convergent Thinking; Deduction; Divergent Thinking; *Elementary School Students; Intermediate Grades; Logic; Primary Education
Identifiers: Analogies; Sequential Relationship; TIM(J)
Availability: Tests in Microfiche; Test Collection, Educational Testing Service, Princeton, NJ 08541
Grade Level: 2-4
Notes: Time, 45; Items, 55

Designed to determine the gifted student's level of cognitive ability in higher-level thinking processes. Items 1-50 are multiple choice. Items 51-55 require a written response in the form of a list of solutions to a problem.

13165
Test of Sales Aptitude, Form A Revised. Bruce, Martin M. 1983
Descriptors: Adults; *Aptitude Tests; Career Guidance; *Job Applicants; Multiple Choice Tests; *Salesmanship; *Sales Occupations; Sales Workers
Identifiers: Self Administered Tests
Availability: Martin M. Bruce, Publishers; 50 Larchwood Rd., P.O. Box 248, Larchmont, NY 10538
Target Audience: Adults
Notes: Time, 30 approx.; Items, 50

Designed to aid in the appraisal of sales aptitude. Provides an objective measure of one important aspect of sales aptitude, namely knowledge and understanding of basic principles of selling. Sales fields include selling to retailers, wholesalers, and consumers. Test can aid in appraising sales ability and potential in selecting sales personnel and for use in vocational guidance. Should be used as an aid only and other important factors must be taken into account.

13166
Early Intervention Developmental Profile, Revised Edition. Rogers, Sally J.; And Others 1981
Subtests: Perceptual/Fine Motor; Cognition; Language; Social Emotional; Self-Care; Gross Motor
Descriptors: Cognitive Development; *Developmental Stages; *Disabilities; Emotional Development; Evaluation Methods; Infant Behavior; Language Processing; Motor Development; Perceptual Development; Profiles; Self Care Skills; Social Development; *Young Children
Identifiers: Developmental Programing Infants and Young Children
Availability: University of Michigan Press; 615 E. University, Ann Arbor, MI 48106
Target Audience: 0-3
Notes: Time, 60 approx.; Items, 299

This infant/preschool assessment instrument is made up of 6 scales which provide developmental milestones in the following areas: perceptual/fine motor, cognition, language, social/emotional, self-care, and gross motor development. The profile contains 274 items and yields information for planning comprehensive developmental programs for children with various handicaps who function below the 36-month developmental level. It is intended to supplement, not replace, standard psychological, motor, and language evaluation data. The profile is not to be used to predict future capabilities or handicaps and should not be used to diagnose handicapping conditions such as mental retardation, emotional disturbance, cerebral palsy, etc. The profile indicates which skills are expected to emerge next in the child's development. Identification of emerging skills enables the teacher/therapist to plan appropriate activities to facilitate the emergence of these skills. There are 5 volumes in the series: Assessment and Application, Early Intervention Development Profile, Stimulation Activities, Preschool Assessment and Application, and Preschool Development Profile.

13230
Similes Test, Recorded Interview Format. Burt, Heather R. 1971
Descriptors: Achievement Tests; Elementary School Students; *Figurative Language; *Intermediate Grades; *Interviews; Language Arts; Language Processing; *Literature Appreciation; *Reading Comprehension; *Reading Skills; Tape Recordings
Identifiers: *Similes; The Research Instruments Project; TRIP
Availability: ERIC Document Reproduction Service; 3900 Wheeler Ave., Alexandria, VA 22304 (ED 091 754, 25 pages)
Grade Level: 4-6
Notes: Items, 10

This test is designed to measure children's understanding of similes found in literature books suitable for grades 4, 5, and 6. The interview is conducted to determine if children have difficulty expressing themselves orally and if the types of responses might be the same as the classifications on the multiple choice test. This document is one of those reviewed in The Research Instruments Projects (TRIP) monograph "Measures for Research and Evaluation in the English Language Arts."

13231
The Developmental Sequence Performance Inventory. University of Washington, Seattle 1980
Subtests: Gross Motor; Fine Motor; Cognitive; Communication; Social Self-Help
Descriptors: Check Lists; Children; *Cognitive Development; Daily Living Skills; Developmental Disabilities; *Developmental Tasks; *Downs Syndrome; *Exceptional Persons; Infants; Language Skills; Mental Retardation; *Motor Development; Performance Tests; *Preschool Education; *Social Development; Student Evaluation
Identifiers: Down Syndrome Performance Inventory; DSPI
Availability: Experimental Education Unit; Child Development Center, University of Washington, Seattle, WA 98165
Target Audience: 0-7

This inventory is based on normal sequential developmental patterns. Skills are arranged linearly from simple to complex assuring the mastery of requisite skills at each level of attainment within the following levels: 0-18 months, 18 months-3 years, 3-4 years, 4-5 years, 5-6 years, 6-9 years. Focus is on sequence of skill development, not age level scores. This instrument is intended primarily as an assessment tool and as a guide for planning specific curriculum objectives for Down's Syndrome children. It is, however, applicable for any developmentally delayed child. The inventory uses a checklist format with a wide sampling of tasks within each skill area to develop a fairly complete profile of skill mastery.

13239
Comprehensive Developmental Evaluation Chart. El Paso Rehabilitation Center, TX 1975
Subtests: Reflexes; Gross Motor; Manipulation; Feeding; Receptive Language; Expressive Language; Cognitive-Social; Vision, Hearing
Descriptors: Cerebral Palsy; Cognitive Development; *Developmental Stages; Expressive Language; Hearing (Physiology); High Risk Persons; *Infant Behavior; Language Acquisition; Motor Development; *Physical Development; Receptive Language; Vision; *Young Children
Identifiers: CDE
Availability: El Paso Rehabilitation Center; 2630 Richmond, El Paso, TX 79930
Target Audience: 0-3

This evaluation chart is specific for young children who are developmentally between the ages of birth to 3 years. The test items of each area are detailed so that the quality of the child's functioning can be adequately assessed. The chart is divided into small time intervals to allow for observations of minute changes in developmental stages. This instrument was designed to fill a gap in the total approach toward the treatment of young children with developmental delays. It was designed to be comprehensive, specific, and consistent. The areas covered are reflexes, gross motor, manipulation, feeding, receptive language, expressive language, cognitive-social, vision, and hearing.

13241
Skills Inventory, Revised Edition. The Oregon Project for Visually Impaired and Blind Preschool Children. Brown, Donnise; And Others 1979
Descriptors: *Blindness; *Child Development; Cognitive Development; Curriculum Design; Developmental Stages; Individual Development; Individual Needs; *Infants; Language Acquisition; Measures (Individuals); Motor Development; Performance; Self Care Skills; Skill Development; Socialization; *Visual Impairments; *Young Children
Identifiers: Oregon (Jackson County)
Availability: OREGON Project; Jackson County Education Service District, 101 N. Grape St., Medford, OR 97501
Target Audience: 0-6
Notes: Items, 700

The Skills Inventory assesses the blind or visually handicapped child's development in the areas of cognition, language, self-help, socialization, fine motor and gross motor. The skills are organized by one-year intervals. A total of 700 skills are assessed. The items which may not be appropriate for a totally blind child and which may be acquired by a totally blind child are marked. The items which are appropriate either for the child who will need orientation and mobility training or will be a braille reader are also marked. The items are presented in behavioral terms and are generally clearly stated. Scoring criteria are not provided, but examples are offered for some of the items. The purpose is not to obtain a precise score, but rather the child's performance level. The Skills Inventory is not a normed assessment instrument but is a curriculum guide and enables educators to find a visually impaired or blind child's performance level, select long- and short-range objectives and record the child's progress. It contains items that are unique to the development of the visually handicapped child.

13255
Gifted and Talented Scale. Dallas Educational Services, Richardson, TX 1983
Subtests: Numerical Reasoning; Vocabulary; Synonyms-Antonyms; Similarities; Analogies
Descriptors: Abstract Reasoning; *Academically Gifted; *Elementary School Students; Intermediate Grades; Logical Thinking; *Screening Tests; *Talent; Talent Identification; Verbal Ability; Vocabulary
Identifiers: Antonyms; Synonyms
Availability: Dallas Educational Services; P.O. Box 831254, Richardson, TX 75083-1254
Grade Level: 4-6
Notes: Items, 50

Designed to identify children with special skills in grades 4, 5, and 6. Limited to identifying those children with talent only in those areas necessary for success in gifted and talented school programs in the classroom environment. A group test and essentially a power test rather than a timed test. The items in all 5 subtests are designed to measure abstract concepts.

13343
Educational Development Series, Revised. Level 10A. Anderhalter, O.F.; And Others 1984
Descriptors: Abstract Reasoning; *Achievement Tests; Basic Skills; *Cognitive Tests; Elementary School Mathematics; *Kindergarten Children; Language Arts; Language Processing; Mathematics Achievement; Primary Education; Reading Achievement
Identifiers: EDSeries; Test Batteries
Availability: Scholastic Testing Service; 480 Meyer Rd., Bensenville, IL 60106
Grade Level: K
Notes: Time, 170

Test battery which comprises ability and achievement tests, as well as reports of school plans, career plans, and interests. Ability measures cover nonverbal and verbal cognitive skills. Achievement tests cover reading, language arts, mathematics, reference skills, science, and social studies. Provides a single report for all areas and permits teacher, counselor, or administrator to examine and evaluate each student from broadest possible perspective, while allowing for comparisons among students. Test results may be analyzed to identify students who may need counseling because of conflicts among achievement, ability, and school/career plans. Several battery formats are available: complete battery, core achievement battery, basic skills battery, or cognitive and basic skills battery. Level 10A test should be administered in 5 sessions over a 1-week period.

13344
Educational Development Series, Revised. Level 11A. Anderhalter, O.F.; And Others 1984
Descriptors: Abstract Reasoning; *Achievement Tests; Basic Skills; *Cognitive Tests; Elementary School Mathematics; *Elementary School Students; *Grade 1; *Grade 2; Language Arts; Language Processing; Mathematics Achievement; Primary Education; Reading Achievement; Sciences; Social Studies; Student Interests; Study Skills
Identifiers: EDSeries; Test Batteries
Availability: Scholastic Testing Service; 480 Meyer Rd., Bensenville, IL 60106
Grade Level: 1-2

Test battery which comprises ability and achievement tests, as well as reports of school plans, career plans, and interests. Ability measures cover nonverbal and verbal cognitive skills. Achievement tests cover reading, language arts, mathematics, reference skills, science, and social studies. Provides a single report for all areas and permits teacher, counselor or administrator to examine and evaluate each student from broadest possible perspective, while allowing for comparisons among students. Test results may be analyzed to identify students who may need counseling because of conflicts among achievement, ability, and school/career plans. Several battery formats are available: complete battery, core achievement battery, basic skills battery, or cognitive and basic skills battery.

13345
Educational Development Series, Revised. Level 12A. Anderhalter, O.F.; And Others 1984
Descriptors: Abstract Reasoning; *Achievement Tests; Basic Skills; *Cognitive Tests; Elementary School Mathematics; *Elementary School Students; *Grade 2; *Grade 3; Language Arts; Language Processing; Mathematics Achievement; Primary Education; Reading Achievement; Sciences; Social Studies; Student Interests; Study Skills

Identifiers: EDSeries; Test Batteries
Availability: Scholastic Testing Service; 480 Meyer Rd., Bensenville, IL 60106
Grade Level: 2-3
Notes: Items, 368

Test battery which comprises ability and achievement tests, as well as reports of school plans, career plans, and interests. Ability measures cover nonverbal and verbal cognitive skills. Achievement tests cover reading, language arts, mathematics, reference skills, science, and social studies. Provides a single report for all areas and permits teacher, counselor or administrator to examine and evaluate each student from broadest possible perspective, while allowing for comparisons among students. Test results may be analyzed to identify students who may need counseling because of conflicts among achievement, ability, and school/career plans. Several battery formats are available: complete battery, core achievement battery, basic skills battery, or cognitive and basic skills battery.

13346
Educational Development Series, Revised. Level 13A. Anderhalter, O.F.; And Others 1984
Descriptors: Abstract Reasoning; *Achievement Tests; Basic Skills; *Cognitive Tests; Elementary Education; Elementary School Mathematics; *Elementary School Students; *Grade 3; *Grade 4; Language Arts; Language Processing; Mathematics Achievement; Reading Achievement; Sciences; Social Studies; Student Interests; Study Skills
Identifiers: EDSeries; Test Batteries
Availability: Scholastic Testing Service; 480 Meyer Rd., Bensenville, IL 60106
Grade Level: 3-4
Notes: Items, 388

Test battery which comprises ability and achievement tests, as well as reports of school plans, career plans, and interests. Ability measures cover nonverbal and verbal cognitive skills. Achievement tests cover reading, language arts, mathematics, reference skills, science, and social studies. Provides a single report for all areas and permits teacher, counselor or administrator to examine and evaluate each student from broadest possible perspective, while allowing for comparisons among students. Test results may be analyzed to identify students who may need counseling because of conflicts among achievement, ability, and school/career plans. Several battery formats are available: complete battery, core achievement battery, basic skills battery, or cognitive and basic skills battery.

13347
Educational Development Series, Revised. Level 14A. Anderhalter, O.F.; And Others 1984
Descriptors: Abstract Reasoning; *Achievement Tests; Basic Skills; *Cognitive Tests; Educational Attainment; Elementary School Mathematics; *Elementary School Students; *Grade 4; *Grade 5; Interest Inventories; Intermediate Grades; Language Arts; Language Processing; Mathematics Achievement; Reading Achievement; Sciences; Social Studies; Student Interests; Study Skills; Vocational Interests
Identifiers: EDSeries; Test Batteries
Availability: Scholastic Testing Service; 480 Meyer Rd., Bensenville, IL 60106
Grade Level: 4-5
Notes: Time, 355; Items, 503

Test battery which comprises ability and achievement tests, as well as reports of school plans, career plans, and interests. Ability measures cover nonverbal and verbal cognitive skills. Achievement tests cover reading, language arts, mathematics, reference skills, science, and social studies. Provides a single report for all areas and permits teacher, counselor or administrator to examine and evaluate each student from broadest possible perspective, while allowing for comparisons among students. Test results may be analyzed to identify students who may need counseling because of conflicts among achievement, ability, and school/career plans. Several battery formats are available: complete battery, core achievement battery, basic skills battery, or cognitive and basic skills battery. Test battery should be administered over 3 sessions.

13348
Educational Development Series, Revised. Level 15A. Anderhalter, O.F.; And Others 1984
Descriptors: Abstract Reasoning; *Achievement Tests; Basic Skills; *Cognitive Tests; Educational Attainment; Elementary School Mathematics; *Elementary School Students; *Grade 5; *Grade 6; Interest Inventories; Intermediate Grades; Language Arts; Language Processing; Mathematics Achievement; Reading Achievement; Sciences; Social Studies; Student Interests; Study Skills; Vocational Interests
Identifiers: EDSeries; Test Batteries
Availability: Scholastic Testing Service; 480 Meyer Rd., Bensenville, IL 60106
Grade Level: 5-6
Notes: Time, 355; Items, 513

Test battery which comprises ability and achievement tests, as well as reports of school plans, career plans, and interests. Ability measures cover nonverbal and verbal cognitive skills. Achievement tests cover reading, language arts, mathematics, reference skills, science, and social studies. Provides a single report for all areas and permits teacher, counselor or administrator to examine and evaluate each student from broadest possible perspective, while allowing for comparisons among students. Test results may be analyzed to identify students who may need counseling because of conflicts among achievement, ability, and school/career plans. Several battery formats are available: complete battery, core achievement battery, basic skills battery, or cognitive and basic skills battery. Test battery should be administered in 3 sessions.

13349
Educational Development Series, Revised. Level 15B. Anderhalter, O.F.; And Others 1984
Descriptors: Abstract Reasoning; *Achievement Tests; Basic Skills; *Cognitive Tests; Educational Attainment; Elementary School Mathematics; *Elementary School Students; *Grade 6; *Grade 7; Interest Inventories; Intermediate Grades; Junior High Schools; Language Arts; Language Processing; Mathematics Achievement; Reading Achievement; Sciences; Secondary School Mathematics; Social Studies; Student Interests; Study Skills; Vocational Interests
Identifiers: EDSeries; Test Batteries
Availability: Scholastic Testing Service; 480 Meyer Rd., Bensenville, IL 60106
Grade Level: 6-7
Notes: Time, 355; Items, 513

Test battery which comprises ability and achievement tests, as well as reports of school plans, career plans, and interests. Ability measures cover nonverbal and verbal cognitive skills. Achievement tests cover reading, language arts, mathematics, reference skills, science, and social studies. Provides a single report for all areas and permits teacher, counselor or administrator to examine and evaluate each student from broadest possible perspective, while allowing for comparisons among students. Test results may be analyzed to identify students who may need counseling because of conflicts among achievement, ability, and school/career plans. Several battery formats are available: complete battery, core achievement battery, basic skills battery, or cognitive and basic skills battery. Test battery should be administrered in 3 sessions.

13350
Educational Development Series, Revised. Level 16A. Anderhalter, O.F.; And Others 1984
Descriptors: Abstract Reasoning; *Achievement Tests; Basic Skills; *Cognitive Tests; Educational Attainment; *Grade 7; *Grade 8; Interest Inventories; Junior High Schools; *Junior High School Students; Language Arts; Language Processing; Mathematics Achievement; Reading Achievement; Sciences; Secondary School Mathematics; Social Studies; Student Interests; Study Skills; Vocational Interests
Identifiers: EDSeries; Test Batteries
Availability: Scholastic Testing Service; 480 Meyer Rd., Bensenville, IL 60106
Grade Level: 7-8
Notes: Items, 513

Test battery which comprises ability and achievement tests, as well as reports of school plans, career plans, and interests. Ability measures cover nonverbal and verbal cognitive skills. Achievement tests cover reading, language arts, mathematics, reference skills, science, and social studies. Provides a single report for all areas and permits teacher, counselor or administrator to examine and evaluate each student from broadest possible perspective, while allowing for comparisons among students. Test results may be analyzed to identify students who may need counseling because of conflicts among achievement, ability, and school/career plans. Several battery formats are available: complete battery, core achievement battery, basic skills battery, or cognitive and basic skills battery.

13351
Educational Development Series, Revised. Level 16B. Anderhalter, O.F.; And Others 1984
Descriptors: Abstract Reasoning; *Achievement Tests; Basic Skills; *Cognitive Tests; Educational Attainment; *Grade 8; *Grade 9; Interest Inventories; Junior High Schools; *Junior High School Students; Language Arts; Language Processing; Mathematics Achievement; Reading Achievement; Sciences; Secondary School Mathematics; Social Studies; Student Interests; Study Skills; Vocational Interests
Identifiers: EDSeries; Test Batteries
Availability: Scholastic Testing Service; 480 Meyer Rd., Bensenville, IL 60106
Grade Level: 8-9
Notes: Items, 513

Test battery which comprises ability and achievement tests, as well as reports of school plans, career plans, and interests. Ability measures cover nonverbal and verbal cognitive skills. Achievement tests cover reading, language arts, mathematics, reference skills, science, and social studies. Provides a single report for all areas and permits teacher, counselor or administrator to examine and evaluate each student from broadest possible perspective, while allowing for comparisons among students. Test results may be analyzed to identify students who may need counseling because of conflicts among achievement, ability, and school/career plans. Several battery formats are available: complete battery, core achievement battery, basic skills battery, or cognitive and basic skills battery.

13352
Educational Development Series, Revised. Level 17A. Anderhalter, O.F.; And Others 1984
Descriptors: Abstract Reasoning; *Achievement Tests; Basic Skills; *Cognitive Tests; Educational Attainment; *Grade 9; High Schools; *High School Students; Interest Inventories; Language Arts; Language Processing; Mathematics Achievement; Reading Achievement; Sciences; Secondary School Mathematics; Social Studies; Student Interests; Study Skills; Vocational Interests
Identifiers: EDSeries; Test Batteries
Availability: Scholastic Testing Service; 480 Meyer Rd., Bensenville, IL 60106
Grade Level: 9
Notes: Items, 523

Test battery which comprises ability and achievement tests, as well as reports of school plans, career plans, and interests. Ability measures cover nonverbal and verbal cognitive skills. Achievement tests cover reading, language arts, mathematics, reference skills, science, and social studies. Provides a single report for all areas and permits teacher, counselor or administrator to examine and evaluate each student from broadest possible perspective, while allowing for comparisons among students. Test results may be analyzed to identify students who may need counseling because of conflicts among achievement, ability, and school/career plans. Several battery formats are available: complete battery, core achievement battery, basic skills battery, or cognitive and basic skills battery.

13353
Educational Development Series, Revised. Level 17B. Anderhalter, O.F.; And Others 1984
Descriptors: Abstract Reasoning; *Achievement Tests; Basic Skills; *Cognitive Tests; Educational Attainment; *Grade 10; High Schools; *High School Students; Interest Inventories; Language Arts; Language Processing; Mathematics Achievement; Reading Achievement; Sciences; Secondary School Mathematics; Social Studies; Student Interests; Study Skills; Vocational Interests
Identifiers: EDSeries; Test Batteries
Availability: Scholastic Testing Service; 480 Meyer Rd., Bensenville, IL 60106
Grade Level: 10
Notes: Items, 523

Test battery which comprises ability and achievement tests, as well as reports of school plans, career plans, and interests. Ability measures cover nonverbal and verbal cognitive skills. Achievement tests cover reading, language arts, mathematics, reference skills, science, and social studies. Provides a single report for all areas and permits teacher, counselor or administrator to examine and evaluate each student from broadest possible perspective, while allowing for comparisons among students. Test results may be analyzed to identify students who may need counseling because of conflicts among achievement, ability, and school/career plans. Several battery formats are available: complete battery, core achievement battery, basic skills battery, or cognitive and basic skills battery.

13354
Educational Development Series, Revised. Level 18A. Anderhalter, O.F.; And Others 1984
Descriptors: Abstract Reasoning; *Achievement Tests; Basic Skills; *Cognitive Tests; Educational Attainment; *Grade 11; High Schools; *High School Students; Interest Inventories; Language Arts; Language Processing; Mathematics Achievement; Reading Achievement; Sciences; Secondary School Mathematics; Social Studies; Student Interests; Study Skills; Vocational Interests
Identifiers: EDSeries; Test Batteries
Availability: Scholastic Testing Service; 480 Meyer Rd., Bensenville, IL 60106
Grade Level: 11
Notes: Time, 360; Items, 523

Test battery which comprises ability and achievement tests, as well as reports of school plans, career plans, and interests. Ability measures cover nonverbal and verbal cognitive skills. Achievement tests cover reading, language arts, mathematics, reference skills, science, and social studies. Provides a single report for all areas and permits teacher, counselor or administrator to examine and evaluate each student from broadest possible perspective, while allowing for comparisons among students. Test results may be analyzed to identify students who may need counseling because of conflicts among achievement, ability, and school/career plans. Several battery formats are available: complete battery, core achievement battery, basic skills battery, or cognitive and basic skills battery. Test battery should be administered over 3 sessions.

13355
Educational Development Series, Revised. Level 18B. Anderhalter, O.F.; And Others 1984
Descriptors: Abstract Reasoning; *Achievement Tests; Basic Skills; *Cognitive Tests; Educational Attainment; *Grade 12; High Schools; *High School Students; Interest Inventories; Language Arts; Language Processing; Mathematics Achievement; Reading Achievement; Sciences; Secondary School Mathematics; Social Studies; Student Interests; Study Skills; Vocational Interests
Identifiers: EDSeries; Test Batteries
Availability: Scholastic Testing Service; 480 Meyer Rd., Bensenville, IL 60106
Grade Level: 12
Notes: Time, 360; Items, 523

Test battery which comprises ability and achievement tests, as well as reports of school plans, career plans, and interests. Ability measures cover nonverbal and verbal cognitive skills. Achievement tests cover reading, language arts, mathematics, reference skills, science, and social studies. Provides a single report for all areas and permits teacher, counselor or administrator to examine and evaluate each student from broadest possible perspective, while allowing for comparisons among students. Test results may be analyzed to identify students who may need counseling because of conflicts among achievement, ability, and school/career plans. Several battery formats are available: complete battery, core achievement battery, basic skills battery, or cognitive and basic skills battery. Test battery should be administered over 3 sessions.

13359
Piaget Infancy Scales. Honig, Alice S. 1970
Subtests: Object Permanence; Means-Ends Scale; Development of Schemas in Relation to Objects; Development of Causality; Developmental Achievement of the Construction of the Object in Space; Development of Vocal and Gestural Imitation; Prehension
Descriptors: Behavior Rating Scales; *Child Development; *Infant Behavior; *Infants
Identifiers: Piaget Battery
Availability: Family Development Research Program; Attn: Alice S. Honig, 201 Slocum Hall, Syracuse University, Syracuse, NY 13210
Target Audience: 0-2
Notes: Time, 120 approx.

Designed to assess the development of infants from ages 6 months to 2 years. Assessments are conducted at 3 month intervals. Used to assess development of children attending the Syracuse University Children's Center.

13361
Slosson Pre-Testing Guide. Slosson, Steven W. 1984
Descriptors: Adolescents; Adults; Behavior Patterns; Check Lists; Children; Cognitive Style; *Individual Characteristics; *Individual Testing; Physical Health; Psychological Patterns; Rating Scales
Identifiers: SPTG
Availability: Slosson Educational Publications; P.O. Box 280, East Aurora, NY 14052
Target Audience: 0-64

Used to provide examiner with more complete background information on an examinee. May be used for any age or grade range. Useful in conjunction with Slosson Intelligence Test or other individually administered tests. Pre-testing guide consists of 3 forms. The Psychological and Medical Profile is designed to summarize client's past medical history and covers 8 areas: adaptive behavior deficits, developmental ability-disability, medication, mobility, seizure disorder, expressive language, receptive language. The Chronic Health Checklist covers physical ailments and problems. The Profile of Behavioral Correlations covers cognitive, affective, and behavioral problem areas and is divided into the following: cognitive, comprehension, receptive language, expressive language, conversational tone, affective area, behavioral area, attentive listening, social interaction.

13367
Computer Aptitude, Literacy, and Interest Profile. Poplin, Mary S.; And Others 1984
Subtests: Estimation (Aptitude); Graphic Patterns (Aptitude); Logical Structures (Aptitude); Series (Aptitude); Interest; Literacy
Descriptors: *Achievement Tests; *Adolescents; *Adults; *Aptitude Tests; Career Counseling; *College Students; *Computer Literacy; *Computers; Higher Education; *Interest Inventories; Knowledge Level; *Programing; Secondary Education; *Secondary School Students
Identifiers: CALIP

Availability: PRO-ED; 8700 Shoal Creek Blvd., Austin, TX 78758
Grade Level: 7-16
Target Audience: 12-60
Notes: Time, 45 approx.; Items, 138

Comprehensive, standardized test battery designed to assess computer-related abilities. Can be administered individually, in groups. Measures aptitudes relevant to computer programing and aptitudes relevant to a wide variety of computer-related uses, e.g., graphics, systems analysis, and repair. Also assesses computer literacy, interest and experience. In addition to use in educational settings, may also be used in business and industry for personnel decisions. Designed to accomplish 4 main purposes: identify talented minorities, women, individuals with reading disabilities, and disadvantaged persons; to broaden range of realistic career options; to provide an empirical basis for administrators, business, managers, and teachers to allocate organizational resources; and to document person's progress as a result of training.

13375
Test of Problem Solving. Zachman, Linda; And Others 1984
Subtests: Explaining Inferences; Determining Causes; Negative Why Questions; Determining Solutions; Avoiding Problems
Descriptors: Children; *Cognitive Tests; Elementary Education; *Elementary School Students; *Expressive Language; Individual Testing; Norm Referenced Tests; Pictorial Stimuli; *Problem Solving
Identifiers: Oral Tests; TOPS
Availability: LinguiSystems; 1630 Fifth Ave., Moline, IL 61265
Target Audience: 6-12
Notes: Time, 20 approx.; Items, 50

Expressive test designed to assess children's thinking and reasoning abilities concerned with events in everyday living. Test stimuli are based on language and situations commonly experienced or witnessed by young children. Test is composed of 5 subtests which examine 5 thinking tasks. There are no basals or ceilings. All responses are elicited by questions from the examiner and refer to 15 illustrations. Questions were designed to be socially and conversationally relevant. Establishes a child's level of problem solving skills which can be compared with his or her peers. Norms have been established on children from 6 years to 11 years, 11 months. May be administered to children older than 12 years, but administering test to children younger than 6 years is not recommended.

13384
Cambridge Kindergarten Screening Test. Shahzade, Ann M.; And Others 1984
Subtests: Articulation; Discrimination; Vocabulary; Association-Categorization; Object-Function; Action-Agent; Color Concepts; Number Concepts; Commands-Spatial Relations; Memory for Commands; Digit Repetition; Diadochokinesis; Story Sequencing-Languaging; Pragmatic Ability
Descriptors: Articulation (Speech); Communication Skills; Culture Fair Tests; Expressive Language; Individual Testing; *Kindergarten Children; *Language Processing; *Language Skills; Pictorial Stimuli; Primary Education; Recall (Psychology); Receptive Language; *Screening Tests; Vocabulary
Identifiers: CKST
Availability: DLM Teaching Resources; 1 DLM Park, P.O. Box 4000, Allen, TX 75002
Grade Level: K
Target Audience: 4-6
Notes: Time, 20 approx.

Comprehensive screening instrument for speech and language. Based on educational premise that one needs to know what child knows, not just what child does not know. Designed to help specialist or teacher determine a child's current level of functioning in areas of speech and language. Uses culture-free items. Designed for screening only; it is not to be used as part of a formal speech and language evaluation.

13400
General Mental Ability Test, Test 1-A; Revised 1983. Hadley, S. Trevor; Stouffer, George A.W., Jr. 1983
Descriptors: Abstract Reasoning; Adults; *Aptitude Tests; *Cognitive Ability; *Cognitive Tests; *Employees; *Job Applicants; Multiple Choice Tests; Vocational Aptitude
Identifiers: ETSA Tests
Availability: Employers' Tests and Services Associates; 341 Garfield St., Chambersburg, PA 17201
Target Audience: Adults
Notes: Time, 45 approx.; Items, 75

Part of the ETSA series of occupational aptitude tests. Test 1-A is designed to assess those mental abilities important in almost any type of learning and thinking. Emphasizes concepts and experiences familiar to examinees,

requires careful reasoning, and the ability to comprehend and draw conclusions. Includes computational and nonverbal items so that examinee with good reasoning ability but poor reading skills or verbal development also receives consideration. Test 1-A is not timed. ETSA tests are a series of aptitude tests and a personality inventory, designed to be administered, scored, and interpreted in one's own business, industry, organization or institution. Tests emphasize power rather than speed. Each test has a time limit long enough to permit examinees to attempt all items. For a complete profile of an applicant, it is recommended that the General Mental Ability Test 1-A (TC013400) and the Personal Adjustment Index Test 8-A (TC013405) be administered with the additional ETSA test designed for the particular job under consideration.

13401
Office Arithmetic Test, Test 2-A, Revised 1984. Hadley, S. Trevor; Stouffer, George A.W., Jr. 1984
Descriptors: Adults; *Aptitude Tests; *Arithmetic; Clerical Workers; *Employees; *Job Applicants; *Mathematical Applications; Occupational Tests; *Office Occupations; Mathematics Tests; Timed Tests; Vocational Aptitude
Identifiers: ETSA Tests
Availability: Employers' Tests and Services Associates; 341 Garfield St., Chambersburg, PA 17201
Target Audience: Adults
Notes: Time, 60; Items, 50

Part of the ETSA series of occupational aptitude tests. Test 2-A measures the ability to use arithmetic in solving numerical problems encountered in most offices. Measures skills with addition, subtraction, multiplication, division, fractions, and percentages. Ability to read, comprehend and extract needed information from tables and graphs is involved. Helps hire, place, and promote qualified person to a job requiring average or better mathematical ability or skills. This test is a timed test. ETSA tests are a series of aptitude tests and a personality inventory, designed to be administered, scored and interpreted in one's own business, industry, organization or institution. Tests emphasize power rather than speed. Each test has a time limit long enough to permit examinees to attempt all items. For a complete profile of an applicant, it is recommended that the General Mental Ability Test 1-A (TC 013 400) and the Personal Adjustment Index Test 8-A (TC 013 405) be administered with the additional ETSA test designed for the particular job under consideration.

13402
General Clerical Ability Test, Test 3-A, Revised 1984. Hadley, S. Trevor; Stouffer, George A.W., Jr. 1984
Descriptors: Adults; *Aptitude Tests; *Clerical Occupations; *Clerical Workers; *Employees; *Job Applicants; Occupational Tests; Office Occupations; Screening Tests; Timed Tests; Vocational Aptitude
Identifiers: *Clerical Aptitude; ETSA Tests
Availability: Employers' Tests and Services Associates; 341 Garfield St., Chambersburg, PA 17201
Target Audience: Adults
Notes: Time, 30; Items, 131

Part of the ETSA series of occupational aptitude tests. Measures the general skills required of clerical personnel in the performance of routine office work. Abilities assessed include skill to alphabetize, match numbers, name check, spell, use office vocabulary. Knowledge of mailing procedures and practices are included. This is a timed test. ETSA tests are a series of aptitude tests and a personality inventory, designed to be administered, scored and interpreted in one's own business, industry, organization or institution. Tests emphasize power rather than speed. Each test has a time limit long enough to permit examinees to attempt all items. For a complete profile of an applicant, it is recommended that the General Mental Ability Test 1-A (TC013400) and the Personal Adjustment Index Test 8-A (TC013405) be administered with the additional ETSA test designed for the particular job under consideration.

13403
Stenographic Skills Test, Test 4-A, Revised 1984. Hadley, S. Trevor; Stouffer, George A.W., Jr. 1984
Descriptors: Adults; *Aptitude Tests; Clerical Occupations; Clerical Workers; *Employees; *Job Applicants; Occupational Tests; Office Occupations; Screening Tests; *Secretaries; *Shorthand; *Typewriting; Vocational Aptitude
Identifiers: ETSA Tests
Availability: Employers' Tests and Services Associates; 341 Garfield St., Chambersburg, PA 17201
Target Audience: Adults
Notes: Time, 45 approx.; Items, 120

Part of the ETSA series of occupational aptitude tests. Measures typing and/or shorthand and general skills required of secretaries and stenographers. Spelling, grammar, filing, and general information needed by secretaries and stenographers are evaluated. Included as a supplement, which is optional, is a prepared letter to be dictated to, and then typed, by the examinee. For the typing test, the examinee is allowed 5 minutes. For taking a letter in shorthand and transcribing it, examinee is allowed a maximum of 18 minutes. ETSA tests are a series of aptitude tests and a personality inventory, designed to be administered, scored and interpreted in one's own business, industry, organization or institution. Tests emphasize power rather than speed. Each test has a time limit long enough to permit examinees to attempt all items. For a complete profile of an applicant, it is recommended that the General Mental Ability Test 1-A (TC013400) and the Personal Adjustment Index Test 8-A (TC013405) be administered with the additional ETSA test designed for the particular job under consideration.

13404
Sales Aptitude Test, Test 7-A, Revised 1983. Hadley, S. Trevor; Stouffer, George A.W., Jr. 1983
Subtests: Sales Judgment; Interest in Selling; Personality Factors; Identification of Self with Selling Occupation; Level of Aspiration; Insight into Human Nature; Awareness of the Sales Approach
Descriptors: Adults; *Aptitude Tests; *Employees; *Job Applicants; Occupational Tests; *Salesmanship; *Sales Occupations; Screening Tests; Vocational Aptitude
Identifiers: ETSA Tests; *Sales Aptitude
Availability: Employers' Tests and Services Associates; 341 Garfield St., Chambersburg, PA 17201
Target Audience: Adults
Notes: Time, 60 approx.; Items, 100
Part of the ETSA series of occupational aptitude tests. Measures abilities and skills required in effective selling. Designed to aid in appraisal of sales aptitude and potential. Attempts to assess knowledge of basic principles of selling. Covers selling to wholesalers, retailers, and consumers and the sale of a wide variety of products. Test samples areas of sales judgment, interest in selling, personality factors involved in selling, identification with sales occupation, level of aspiration, insight into human nature, and awareness of sales approach. ETSA tests are a series of aptitude tests and a personality inventory, designed to be administered, scored, and interpreted in one's own business, industry, organization, or institution. Tests emphasize power rather than speed. Each test has a time limit long enough to permit examinees to attempt all items. For a complete profile of an applicant, it is recommended that the General Mental Ability Test 1-A (TC013400) and the Personal Adjustment Index Test 8-A (TC013405) be administered with the additional ETSA test designed for the particular job under consideration.

13409
CID Preschool Performance Scale. Geers, Ann E.; Lane, Helen S. 1984
Subtests: Manual Planning; Manual Dexterity; Form Perception; Perceptual Motor Skills; Preschool Skills; Part Whole Relationships
Descriptors: Early Childhood Education; *Hearing Impairments; *Intelligence Tests; Kindergarten Children; *Language Handicaps; *Nonverbal Tests; *Predictive Measurement; *Preschool Children; Preschool Tests
Identifiers: Randalls Island Performance Series
Availability: Stoelting Co.; 620 Wheat Ln., Wood Dale, IL 60191
Target Audience: 2-5
An adaptation of the Randall's Island Performance Series (1931) which was used to measure the intelligence of mentally retarded children at Randall's Island, a New York City institution. Test is nonverbal, both in instructions and in response. The CID was revised and standardized. It retains most of the items from the earlier test but the items have been regrouped into 6 subtests with point scores that can be converted into scaled scores and a deviation IQ. The test can now be administered to hearing- and language-impaired children. The subtests are administered individually and take varying amounts of time to complete. Validity and reliability data are reported.

13410
Assessment of a Deaf-Blind Multiply Handicapped Child, Third Edition. Rudolph, James M.; And Others
Subtests: Gross Motor Development; Fine Motor Development; Personal - Self Help Skills; Communication; Auditory Development; Visual Development; Cognition; Social Development; Mobility

Descriptors: Adolescents; Auditory Stimuli; Children; Cognitive Development; Communication Skills; Daily Living Skills; *Deaf Blind; *Educational Assessment; Elementary School Students; Elementary Secondary Education; Employment Potential; Interpersonal Competence; Motor Development; Multiple Disabilities; Performance Tests; Physical Mobility; Rating Scales; Secondary School Students; Self Care Skills; *Severe Disabilities; Sheltered Workshops; Visual Stimuli
Availability: Midwest Regional Center for Services to Deaf-Blind Children; P.O. Box 30008, Lansing, MI 48909
Target Audience: 5-18
This manual is designed to measure a student's progress in individual skill areas that often overlap. It is not intended to be a curriculum guide but is an instrument for measuring the performance of students. It should be used to supplement the total assessment endeavor. The manual is to be used to assess the deaf-blind child and provides an opportunity to alert parents and staff to general developmental directions, to the student's present level of development, and to the focus of training needs. This guide identifies the minimum skills in 5 skill areas required for entrance into most protected work environments. It is an assessment tool, an aid for planning long-range goals and short-term objectives, and a guide to developing activities for the classroom. The guide will indicate the student's present skill level in relationship to the minimum skills necessary for entrance into the sheltered work environment.

13414
Harvard Manager/Supervisor Staff Selector. Harvard Personnel Testing, Montreal, Canada 1984
Subtests: Intelligence/Problem Solving; Supervisory Practices; Business Judgment; Communication Skills; Ability to Work with People; Emotional Stability
Descriptors: *Administrators; Adults; Communication Skills; Emotional Adjustment; Intelligence; Interpersonal Competence; *Occupational Tests; *Personnel Selection; Problem Solving; *Supervisors; Supervisory Methods
Identifiers: Judgment
Availability: Harvard Personnel Testing; P.O. Box 319, Oradell, NJ 07649
Target Audience: Adults
Notes: Time, 45 approx.
Screening test for job applicants. Available in English and French. Provides an overall rating from excellent to unacceptable and a rating of "Likelihood for Success" ranging from "far above" to "far below average." Includes a narrative report and a plot of the applicants' performance against ideal performance in all 6 subtest areas. Normed on a population of supervisory trainees.

13420
Harvard Learning Ability Profile. Harvard Personnel Testing, Oradell, NJ 1984
Descriptors: Adults; *Aptitude Tests; Decision Making Skills; *Occupational Tests; Problem Solving; *Vocational Aptitude
Identifiers: Flexibility (Cognitive); Frustration; *Learning Ability
Availability: Harvard Personnel Testing; P.O. Box 319, Oradell, NJ 07649
Target Audience: 18-64
Notes: Time, 90
Designed to measure the ability to learn a job. Measures ability to learn, flexibility, frustration level, problem solving ability, decisiveness. Norms provided by race, sex, age and education. Said to be compatible with EEO requirements. Hand-scored by administrator. Said to be useful with any position.

13421
Harvard Accounting Staff Selector. Harvard Personnel Testing, Oradell, NJ 1984
Descriptors: *Accountants; Adults; Emotional Adjustment; French; Intelligence; Interpersonal Competence; Mathematics Skills; Memory; *Occupational Tests; Office Practice; *Personnel Selection; Problem Solving; Psychological Needs; Reliability
Identifiers: Initiative; Organizational Skills; Self Sufficiency; Tough Mindedness
Availability: Harvard Personnel Testing; Box 319, Oradell, NJ 07649
Target Audience: 18-64
For use in hiring accounting or financial staff. Designed to predict success on the job. Covers general intelligence, attention to detail, memory, problem solving ability, numerical skills, knowledge of office terms, layout and organization, emotional stability, people contact desired, consistency, self-sufficiency, initiative, tough-mindedness. Available in English or French. A narrative report and graphical summary are prepared by the publisher.

13422
Harvard Sales Staff Selector. Harvard Personnel Testing, Oradell, NJ 1984
Subtests: Intelligence; Communication Skills; People Contact Needed; Emotional Stability; Sales Motivation; Comprehension of Selling Principles
Descriptors: Adults; Communication Skills; Emotional Adjustment; French; Intelligence; Interpersonal Competence; Motivation; *Occupational Tests; *Personnel Selection; Psychological Needs; *Salesmanship; *Sales Workers
Availability: Harvard Personnel Testing; P.O. Box 319, Oradell, NJ 07649
Target Audience: 18-64
Designed for use in predicting performance of sales staff including: sales clerks, technical services and sales representatives, sales engineers, and sales supervisors. Available in English and French. Scored by publisher.

13423
Harvard Secretarial Staff Selector. Harvard Personnel Testing, Oradell, NJ 1984
Subtests: Intelligence/Problem Solving; Facility with Numbers, Files, Codes, Symbols; Attention to Detail, Words and Numbers; Emotional Stability
Descriptors: Adults; *Clerical Workers; Emotional Adjustment; French; Intelligence; Mathematics Skills; *Occupational Tests; *Personnel Selection; Problem Solving; *Secretaries
Availability: Harvard Personnel Testing; Box 319, Oradell, NJ 07649
Target Audience: 18-64
Designed for use in the selection of secretarial staff. Available in English and French. Test is scored by publisher.

13432
IPI Aptitude Series: Junior Clerk. Industrial Psychology, Inc., New York, NY 1981
Subtests: Perception; Numbers
Descriptors: *Adults; *Aptitude Tests; Clerical Occupations; *Clerical Workers; File Clerks; Filing; *Job Applicants; Job Performance; Job Skills; *Occupational Tests; Personality Measures; Profiles
Identifiers: Extraversion; Introversion; Test Batteries
Availability: Industrial Psychology, Inc.; 515 Madison Ave., New York, NY 10022
Target Audience: 18-64
Notes: Time, 25 approx.
This instrument is a battery of tests designed to assess one's aptitude for the position of junior clerk on a lower clerical level. Assignments are minor, simple, routine, unskilled, repetitive, detailed, and require no decision-making. Typical duties include filing, sorting, copying, classifying, compiling, checking, verifying, identifying, routing, distributing, posting, coding, recording, receiving, and shipping. This battery is suitable for use with applicants or employees for the position of checker, coder, mail clerk, shipper, sorter, or stock clerk. This battery consists of Perception, Office Terms, CPF, Numbers and biography-clerical.

13433
IPI Aptitude Series: Numbers Clerk. Industrial Psychology, Inc., New York, NY 1981
Subtests: Numbers; Judgment; Perception; Office Terms; Parts
Descriptors: Accounting; *Adults; *Aptitude Tests; Bookkeeping; Clerical Occupations; *Clerical Workers; Insurance Occupations; *Job Applicants; Job Performance; Job Skills; *Occupational Tests; Personality Measures; Profiles; *Mathematics Tests
Identifiers: Extraversion; Introversion; Test Batteries
Availability: Industrial Psychology, Inc.; 515 Madison Ave., New York, NY 10022
Target Audience: 18-64
Notes: Time, 30 approx.
This instrument is a battery of tests designed to assess one's aptitude for the position of numbers clerk, a field which includes jobs involving systems. Numbers clerks need mathematical-quantitative outlook and attitude, such as involved in accounting, bookkeeping, billing, statistical, and inventory fields. This battery is suitable for evaluating applicants for the position of accounting, billing, insurance, inventory, payroll or statistical clerk. The following tests comprise this battery: numbers, perception, office terms, judgment, biography-clerical, NPF (Neurotic Personality Factor), and CPF (Contact Personality Factor).

13434
IPI Aptitude Series: Office Machine Operator. Industrial Psychology, Inc., New York, NY 1981
Subtests: Perception; Numbers; Judgment; Parts; Memory; Office Terms

Descriptors: Accounting; *Adults; *Aptitude Tests; Clerical Occupations; Clerical Workers; *Job Applicants; Job Performance; Job Skills; *Occupational Tests; *Office Machines; Personality Measures; Profiles; *Spatial Ability; Typewriting
Identifiers: Keypunch Operators; *Manual Dexterity; Test Batteries
Availability: Industrial Psychology, Inc.; 515 Madison Ave., New York, NY 10022
Target Audience: 18-64
Notes: Time, 30 approx.

This instrument is a battery of tests designed to assess one's aptitude for the position of office machine operator. This job field includes jobs involving setting up, operation, and minor adjustment of various types of office machines for such uses as typing, duplicating, recording, calculating, checking, billing, and sorting. Applicant needs manual dexterity and space relations aptitudes for machine operations. This battery is suitable for evaluating applicants for positions of accounting or billing clerk, key punch operator or typist. The battery consists of Dexterity, Parts, Perception, Office Terms, Biography-Clerical, NPF (Neurotic Personality Factor), and CPF (Contact Personality Factor).

13435
IPI Aptitude Series: Contact Clerk. Industrial Psychology, Inc., New York, NY 1981
Subtests: Fluency; Perception; Memory; Judgment; Numbers
Descriptors: *Adults; *Aptitude Tests; Clerical Workers; *Communication Skills; *Job Applicants; Job Performance; Job Skills; Language Fluency; Memory; *Occupational Tests; Personality Measures; Profiles; *Receptionists
Identifiers: Test Batteries
Availability: Industrial Psychology, Inc.; 515 Madison Ave., New York, NY 10022
Target Audience: 18-64
Notes: Time, 30 approx.

This instrument is a battery of tests designed to assess one's aptitude for the position of contact clerk, a job field which includes jobs of contact with the public, along with clerical duties. Contact clerk is in fairly continuous contact with people and needs contact aptitude of memory and fluency, extroverted personality, and good appearance. This battery is useful in evaluation of applicants for positions of receptionist, complaint, information, or reservation clerk. The battery consists of CPF, Memory, Fluency, Perception, Sales Terms, and Biography-Clerical.

13436
IPI Aptitude Series: Senior Clerk. Industrial Psychology, Inc., New York, NY 1981
Subtests: Office Terms; Judgment; Perception; Parts; Numbers; Memory
Descriptors: *Adults; *Aptitude Tests; Bookkeeping; Clerical Occupations; *Clerical Workers; Decision Making Skills; *Job Applicants; Job Performance; Job Skills; Memory; *Occupational Tests; Personality Measures; Profiles
Identifiers: Test Batteries
Availability: Industrial Psychology, Inc.; 515 Madison Ave., New York, NY 10022
Target Audience: 18-64
Notes: Time, 30 approx.

This instrument is a battery of tests designed to assess one's aptitude for the position of senior clerk, a job field which includes higher level clerical jobs. Assignments are fairly complex, difficult, nonroutine, and nonrepetitive. Tasks require good intelligence, and some amount of judgment and decision making. This battery is useful in evaluation of applicants for the position of administrative, correspondence, cost, or production clerks, and bookkeepers. The battery consists of Office Terms, Perception, CPF, Numbers, Judgment, 16 PF, Fluency, and Biography-Clerical.

13437
IPI Aptitude Series: Secretary. Industrial Psychology, Inc., New York, NY 1981
Subtests: Perception; Office Terms; Judgment; Memory; Parts
Descriptors: *Adults; *Aptitude Tests; Clerical Occupations; Clerical Workers; *Job Applicants; Job Performance; Job Skills; Memory; *Occupational Tests; Personality Measures; *Secretaries; Shorthand
Identifiers: Test Batteries
Availability: Industrial Psychology, Inc.; 515 Madison Ave., New York, NY 10022
Target Audience: 18-64
Notes: Time, 30 approx.

This instrument is a battery of tests designed to assess one's aptitude for the position of secretary. Assignments are complex and difficult. Tasks involve public relations, clerical duties, screening appointments, typing, shorthand, handling correspondence, and relieving executive of minor administrative details. Applicants should have an extroverted personality and a good appearance. This battery

consists of Judgment, Parts, Perception, Sales Terms, Fluency, Memory, 16 PF, Biography-Clerical, NPF (Neurotic Personality Factor), CPF (Contact Personality Factor).

13438
IPI Aptitude Series: Unskilled Worker. Industrial Psychology, Inc., New York, NY 1981
Subtests: Motor; Precision; Tools; NPF; Biography-Mechanical
Descriptors: *Adults; *Aptitude Tests; Biographical Inventories; Hand Tools; *Job Applicants; Job Performance; Job Skills; Laborers; Mechanical Skills; *Occupational Tests; Personality Measures; Psychomotor Skills; *Unskilled Workers
Identifiers: Test Batteries
Availability: Industrial Psychology, Inc.; 515 Madison Ave., New York, NY 10022
Target Audience: 18-64
Notes: Time, 30 approx.

This instrument is a battery of tests designed to assess one's aptitude for the position of unskilled worker. The test battery includes motor, precision, tools, NPF (Neurotic Personality Factor), and Biography-Mechanical. The battery is suitable for applicants to positions of janitor, laborer, loader, material handler, packer, and trucker.

13439
IPI Aptitude Series: Semi-Skilled Worker. Industrial Psychology, Inc., New York, NY 1981
Subtests: Precision; Motor; NPF; Blocks; Tools; CPF
Descriptors: *Adults; *Aptitude Tests; Assembly (Manufacturing); Biographical Inventories; Building Trades; Hand Tools; *Job Applicants; Job Performance; Job Skills; Machine Tools; *Mechanical Skills; *Occupational Tests; Personality Measures; Production Technicians; Psychomotor Skills; *Semiskilled Occupations; *Semiskilled Workers
Identifiers: Test Batteries
Availability: Industrial Psychology, Inc.; 515 Madison Ave., New York, NY 10022
Target Audience: 18-64
Notes: Time, 30 approx.

This instrument is a battery of tests designed to assess one's aptitude for the position of semi-skilled worker in mechanical occupations. The test battery includes precision, motor, NPF (Neurotic Personality Factor), Blocks, Tools, CPF (Contact Personality Factor), and Biography-Mechanical. The battery is suitable for evaluating applicants for positions as assembler, helper, production, or construction worker.

13440
IPI Aptitude Series: Factory Machine Operator. Industrial Psychology, Inc., New York, NY 1981
Subtests: Motor; Precision; Tools; NPF; Blocks; CPF; Dexterity
Descriptors: *Adults; *Aptitude Tests; Biographical Inventories; Dental Technicians; *Job Applicants; Job Performance; Job Skills; *Machine Tool Operators; *Machine Tools; Machinists; *Mechanical Skills; *Occupational Tests; Personality Measures; Psychomotor Skills; *Sewing Machine Operators; Welding
Identifiers: *Manual Dexterity; Test Batteries
Availability: Industrial Psychology, Inc.; 515 Madison Ave., New York, NY 10022
Target Audience: 18-64
Notes: Time, 30 approx.

This instrument is a battery of tests designed to assess one's aptitude for the position of factory machine operator. The test battery includes motor, precision, tools, NPF (Neurotic Personality Factor), Blocks, CPF (Contact Personality Factor), Dexterity, and Biographical-Mechanical. The battery is appropriate for evaluation of applicants for positions as cutters, dental lab technicians, lathe operators, sewing machine operators, pressers, or welders.

13441
IPI Aptitude Series: Vehicle Operator. Industrial Psychology, Inc., New York, NY 1981
Subtests: Motor; Dimension; NTF; Precision; CPF; Tools; Dexterity; Biography-Mechanical
Descriptors: *Adults; *Aptitude Tests; Biographical Inventories; *Job Applicants; Job Performance; Job Skills; Mechanical Skills; *Motor Vehicles; *Occupational Tests; Personality Measures; Psychomotor Skills; *Service Vehicles
Identifiers: *Manual Dexterity; Test Batteries
Availability: Industrial Psychology, Inc.; 515 Madison Ave., New York, NY 10022
Target Audience: 18-64
Notes: Time, 30 approx.

This instrument is a battery of tests designed to assess one's aptitude for the position of vehicle operator. The test battery includes motor, dimension, NPF (Neurotic Personality Factor), Precision, CPF (Contact Personality Factor), Tools, Dexterity, and Biographical-Mechanical. The battery is appropriate for evaluation of applicants for positions as crane, elevator, motor, taxi, teamster, tractor, or truck operator.

13442
IPI Aptitude Series: Inspector. Industrial Psychology, Inc., New York, NY 1981
Subtests: Precision; Dimension; CPF; Parts; NPF; Tools; Blocks; Biography-Mechanical
Descriptors: *Adults; *Aptitude Tests; Biographical Inventories; *Classification; Hand Tools; Inspection; *Job Applicants; Job Performance; Job Skills; Machine Tools; *Mechanical Skills; *Occupational Tests; Personality Measures; Psychomotor Skills
Identifiers: *Inspectors; Test Batteries
Availability: Industrial Psychology, Inc.; 515 Madison Ave., New York, NY 10022
Target Audience: 18-64
Notes: Time, 30 approx.

This instrument is a battery of tests designed to assess one's aptitude for the position of inspector. The test battery includes Precision, Dimension, CPF (Contact Personality Factor), Parts, NPF (Neurotic Personality Factor), Tools, Blocks, and Biography-Mechanical. The battery is appropriate for evaluation of applicants for positions as checker, classifier, examiner, grader, pairer, scaler, or sorter.

13443
IPI Aptitude Series: Skilled Worker. Industrial Psychology, Inc., New York, NY 1981
Subtests: Blocks; Factory Terms; NPF; Numbers; Motor
Descriptors: *Adults; *Aptitude Tests; Biographical Inventories; *Job Applicants; Job Performance; Job Skills; Machine Tools; *Machinists; Mechanical Skills; Mechanics (Process); *Occupational Tests; Personality Measures; Psychomotor Skills; *Skilled Workers; *Tool and Die Makers
Identifiers: Test Batteries
Availability: Industrial Psychology, Inc.; 515 Madison Ave., New York, NY 10022
Target Audience: 18-64
Notes: Time, 60 approx.

This instrument is a battery of tests designed to assess one's aptitude for the position of skilled worker. The test battery includes Blocks, Factory Terms, NPF (Neurotic Personality Factor), Numbers, Motor, 16 Personality Factor, Office Terms, Tools, Precision, and Biography-Mechanical. The battery is appropriate for evaluation of applicants for positions as lineman, machinist, maintenance, mechanic, or tool maker.

13444
IPI Aptitude Series: Sales Clerk. Industrial Psychology, Inc., New York, NY 1981
Subtests: CPF; Numbers; Perception; Memory; Sales; Terms; Fluency
Descriptors: *Adults; *Aptitude Tests; *Job Applicants; Job Performance; Job Skills; Language Fluency; Memory; *Occupational Tests; Personality Measures; *Sales Occupations; *Sales Workers
Identifiers: Extraversion; Introversion; Test Batteries
Availability: Industrial Psychology, Inc.; 515 Madison Ave., New York, NY 10022
Target Audience: 18-64
Notes: Time, 30 approx.

This instrument is a battery of tests designed to assess one's aptitude for the position of sales clerk. Tests in battery include CPF (Contact Personality Factor), Numbers, Perception, Memory, Sales Terms, Fluency, and Biography-Clerical. The battery is suitable for use in the evaluation of applicants for positions as department store sales clerk, post office clerk, teller, ticket clerk, waiter or waitress. This test may be purchased by businesses that hire salespersons. Scoring the test is done by the purchaser.

13445
IPI Aptitude Series: Salesman. Industrial Psychology, Inc., New York, NY 1981
Subtests: 16 PF; Numbers; Sales Terms; Fluency; Memory; CPF; Perception; Biography-Sales
Descriptors: *Adults; *Aptitude Tests; Insurance Occupations; *Job Applicants; Job Performance; Job Skills; Language Fluency; Memory; *Occupational Tests; Personality Measures; *Salesmanship; Sales Occupations; *Sales Workers
Identifiers: Extraversion; Introversion; Test Batteries
Availability: Industrial Psychology, Inc.; 515 Madison Ave., New York, NY 10022
Target Audience: 18-64
Notes: Time, 45 approx.

This instrument is a battery of tests designed to assess one's aptitude for the position of salesman/saleswoman. Tests in the battery include 16 PF (16 Personality Factors); Numbers; Sales Terms; Fluency; Memory; CPF (Contact Personality Factor); Perception; and Biography-Sales. The battery is useful in the evaluation of applicants for positions as agent; demonstrator; insurance, retail, route, or wholesale salesperson. This test may be purchased by businesses that hire salespersons. Scoring the test is done by the purchaser.

13446
IPI Aptitude Series: Sales Engineer. Industrial Psychology, Inc., New York, NY 1981
Subtests: 16 PF; Parts; Judgment; Numbers; Fluency; Memory; CPF; NPF; Biography-Sales
Descriptors: *Adults; *Aptitude Tests; *Job Applicants; Job Performance; Job Skills; Language Fluency; Memory; *Occupational Tests; Personality Measures; Salesmanship; *Sales Occupations
Identifiers: Extraversion; Introversion; Test Batteries
Availability: Industrial Psychology, Inc.; 515 Madison Ave., New York, NY 10022
Target Audience: 18-64
This instrument is a battery of tests designed to assess one's aptitude for the position of sales engineer. Tests in the battery include Sales Terms; 16 PF (16 Personality Factors); Parts; Judgment; Numbers; Fluency; Memory; CPF (Contact Personality Factors); NPF (Neurotic Personality Factors); Biography-Sales. This battery may be used in the evaluation of applicants for positions as claims adjuster, purchasing agent, technical salesperson, or underwriter. This test may be purchased by businesses that hire salespersons. Scoring the test is done by the purchaser.

13447
IPI Aptitude Series: Scientist. Industrial Psychology, Inc., New York, NY 1981
Subtests: Judgment; Decision; CPF; NPF; Factory Terms; Precision; Office Terms; 16 PF; Numbers; Dexterity; Biography-Technical
Descriptors: *Abstract Reasoning; *Adults; *Aptitude Tests; *Job Applicants; Job Performance; Job Skills; Logical Thinking; *Occupational Tests; Personality Measures; Professional Occupations; *Scientists; Spatial Ability
Identifiers: Extraversion; Introversion; Manual Dexterity; Test Batteries
Availability: Industrial Psychology, Inc.; 515 Madison Ave., New York, NY 10022
Target Audience: 18-64
Notes: Time, 60 approx.
This instrument is a battery of tests designed to assess one's aptitude for the position of scientist. Tests in the battery include Judgment, Dimension, CPF (Contact Personality Factor), NPF (Neurotic Personality Factor), Factory Terms, Precision, Office Terms, 16 PF (16 Personality Factors), Numbers, Dexterity, and Biography-Technical. This battery may be used in the evaluation of applicants for positions as biologist, chemist, economist, inventor, physicist, or research scientist.

13448
IPI Aptitude Series: Engineer. Industrial Psychology, Inc., New York, NY 1981
Subtests: Factory Terms; Dimension; CPF; NPF; Judgment; Office Terms; Numbers
Descriptors: *Abstract Reasoning; *Adults; *Aptitude Tests; Emotional Adjustment; *Engineers; Hand Tools; *Job Applicants; Job Performance; Job Skills; Logical Thinking; Machine Tools; Mathematical Concepts; *Occupational Tests; Personality Measures; Professional Occupations; *Spatial Ability
Identifiers: Extraversion; Introversion; Test Batteries
Availability: Industrial Psychology, Inc.; 515 Madison Ave., New York, NY 10022
Target Audience: 18-64
Notes: Time, 60 approx.
This instrument is a battery of tests designed to assess one's aptitude for the position of engineer. The tests in the battery include Factory Terms, Dimension, CPF (Contact Personality Factor), NPF (Neurotic Personality Factor), Judgment, Office Terms, Numbers, 16 PF (16 Personality Factors), Precision; Tools; Biography-Technical. The battery is suitable for evaluation of applicants for positions as automotive, chemical, electrical, mechanical, or production engineer.

13449
IPI Aptitude Series: Office Technical. Industrial Psychology, Inc., New York, NY 1981
Subtests: Office Terms; Perception; CPF; NPF; Judgment; Numbers; 16 PF
Descriptors: Abstract Reasoning; *Accountants; *Adults; *Aptitude Tests; Emotional Adjustment; *Job Applicants; Job Performance; Job Skills; *Logical Thinking; Mathematical Concepts; *Memory; *Occupational Tests; Personality Measures; Professional Occupations
Identifiers: Extraversion; Introversion; Test Batteries
Availability: Industrial Psychology, Inc.; 515 Madison Ave., New York, NY 10022
Target Audience: 18-64
Notes: Time, 60 approx.
This instrument is a battery of tests designed to assess one's aptitude for the position of office technical personnel. The battery includes Office Terms, Perception, CPF (Contact Personality Factor), NPF (Neurotic Personality Factor), Judgment, Numbers, 16 PF (16 Personality Factors), Parts, Memory, and Biography-Technical. Battery is suitable for evaluation of applicants to positions as accountant, estimator, methods clerks, statistician, or time study person.

13450
IPI Aptitude Series: Writer. Industrial Psychology, Inc., New York, NY 1981
Subtests: Fluency; Sales Terms; CPN; NPF; Memory; Judgment; 16 PF
Descriptors: Abstract Reasoning; *Adults; Advertising; *Aptitude Tests; *Authors; Emotional Adjustment; *Job Applicants; Job Performance; Job Skills; Journalism; *Language Fluency; Logical Thinking; Memory; *Occupational Tests; Personality Measures; Professional Occupations; Publicity
Identifiers: Test Batteries
Availability: Industrial Psychology, Inc.; 515 Madison Ave., New York, NY 10022
Target Audience: 18-64
Notes: Time, 60 approx.
This instrument is a battery of tests designed to assess one's aptitude for the position of writer. The battery includes Fluency, Sales Terms, CPF (Contact Personality Factor), NPF (Neurotic Personality Factor), Memory, Judgment, 16 PF (16 Personality Factors), Perception, Parts, Biography-Technical. Battery is suitable for the evaluation of applicants in the areas of advertising and publicity, as well as the positions of author, copywriter, critic, editor, or journalist.

13451
IPI Aptitude Series: Designer. Industrial Psychology, Inc., New York, NY 1981
Subtests: Dimension; Precision; NPF; CPF; Blocks; Dexterity; Sales Terms; 16 PF
Descriptors: *Adults; *Aptitude Tests; *Architects; *Artists; *Drafting; Emotional Adjustment; *Job Applicants; Job Performance; Job Skills; *Layout (Publications); Mathematical Concepts; *Occupational Tests; Personality Measures; *Photography; Professional Occupations; *Spatial Ability
Identifiers: Extraversion; Introversion; Manual Dexterity; Test Batteries
Availability: Industrial Psychology, Inc.; 515 Madison Ave., New York, NY 10022
Target Audience: 18-64
Notes: Time, 60 approx.
This instrument is a battery of tests designed to assess one's aptitude for the position of designer. Tests in the battery include Dimension, Precision, NPF (Neurotic Personality Factor), CPF (Contact Personality Factor); Blocks, Dexterity, Sales Terms; 16 PF (16 Personality Factors), Parts, and Biography-Technical. Battery is suitable for the evaluation of applicants for positions as artist, architect, draftsman, layout person, or photographer.

13452
IPI Aptitude Series: Instructor. Industrial Psychology, Inc., New York, NY 1981
Subtests: Fluency; 16 PF; Sales Terms; Parts; Memory; Judgment; CPF; NPF; Perception; Biography-Technical
Descriptors: *Adults; *Aptitude Tests; *Counselors; Emotional Adjustment; *Job Applicants; Job Performance; Job Skills; *Language Fluency; Logical Thinking; Mathematical Concepts; Memory; *Occupational Tests; Personality Measures; Professional Occupations; Spatial Ability; *Teachers
Identifiers: Extraversion; Introversion; Test Batteries
Availability: Industrial Psychology, Inc.; 515 Madison Ave., New York, NY 10022
Target Audience: 18-64
Notes: Time, 60 approx.
This instrument is a battery of tests designed to assess one's aptitude for the position of instructor. Tests in the battery include Fluency, 16 PF (16 Personality Factors), Sales Terms, Parts, Memory, Judgment, CPF (Contact Personality Factor), NPF (Neurotic Personality Factor), Perception, and Biography-Technical. The battery is suitable for the evaluation of applicants for positions as counselors, instructors, safety director, teachers, or training director.

13453
IPI Aptitude Series: Office Supervisor. Industrial Psychology, Inc., New York, NY 1981
Subtests: 16 PF; Judgment Parts; Fluency; Office Terms; Numbers; NPF; CPF; Perception; Memory
Descriptors: *Administrators; *Adults; *Aptitude Tests; Emotional Adjustment; *Job Applicants; Job Performance; Job Skills; *Language Fluency; Managerial Occupations; Mathematical Concepts; Memory; Middle Management; *Occupational Tests; Personality Measures; *Supervisors
Identifiers: Extraversion; Introversion; Test Batteries
Availability: Industrial Psychology, Inc.; 515 Madison Ave., New York, NY 10022
Target Audience: 18-64
Notes: Time, 60 approx.
This instrument is a battery of tests designed to assess one's aptitude for the position of office supervisor. The tests in the battery include 16 PF (16 Personality Factor), Judgment, Parts, Fluency, Office Terms, Numbers, NPF (Neurotic Personality Factor), CPF (Contact Personality Factors), Perception, Memory, and Biography-Supervisor. Battery is suitable for evaluation of applicants to positions as administrator, controller, department head, or vice president.

13454
IPI Aptitude Series: Sales Supervisor. Industrial Psychology, Inc., New York, NY 1981
Subtests: 16 PF; Fluency; Sales Terms; Memory; Judgment; CPF; Parts; Numbers; NPF; Perception; Biography-Supervisory
Descriptors: *Adults; *Aptitude Tests; Emotional Adjustment; *Job Applicants; Job Performance; Job Skills; Language Fluency; Managerial Occupations; *Marketing; Memory; Merchandising; *Occupational Tests; Personality Measures; Professional Occupations; Sales Occupations; *Supervisors
Identifiers: Extraversion; Introversion; Test Batteries
Availability: Industrial Psychology, Inc.; 515 Madison Ave., New York, NY 10022
Target Audience: 18-64
Notes: Time, 60 approx.
This instrument is a battery of tests designed to assess one's aptitude for the position of sales supervisor. Tests in the battery include 16 PF (16 Personality Factors), Fluency, Sales Terms, Memory, Judgment, CPF (Contact Personality Factor), Fluency, Memory, and Biography-Supervisor. The battery is suitable for cvaluation of applicants for the position of advertising, credit, merchandise, service, or store sales supervisor. This test may be purchased by businesses that hire salespersons. Scoring the test is done by the purchaser.

13455
IPI Aptitude Series: Factory Supervisor. Industrial Psychology, Inc., New York, NY 1981
Subtests: 16 PF; Factory Terms; Parts; NPF; Office Terms; Tools; Numbers; Judgment; CPF; Fluency; Memory
Descriptors: *Administrators; *Adults; *Aptitude Tests; Emotional Adjustment; Hand Tools; *Job Applicants; Job Performance; Job Skills; Language Fluency; Logical Thinking; Machine Tools; Mathematical Concepts; Memory; *Occupational Tests; Personality Measures; Spatial Ability; *Superintendents; *Supervisors
Identifiers: Extraversion; Introversion; Test Batteries
Availability: Industrial Psychology, Inc.; 515 Madison Ave., New York, NY 10022
Target Audience: 18-64
Notes: Time, 60 approx.
This instrument is a battery of tests designed to assess one's aptitude for the position of factory supervisor. The tests in the battery include 16 PF (16 Personality Factors), Factory Terms, Parts, NFP (Neurotic Personality Factor); Office Terms, Tools, Numbers, Judgment, CPF (Contact Personality Factor), Fluency, Memory, and Biography-Supervisor. The battery is suitable for the evaluation of applicants for the position of foreman, maintenance, or production supervisor, or superintendent.

13467
Eby Elementary Identification Instrument. Eby, Judy W. 1984
Descriptors: *Ability Identification; *Academically Gifted; Elementary Education; *Elementary School Students; Junior High Schools; *Junior High School Students; *Screening Tests; *Student Placement
Identifiers: EEII
Availability: Slosson Educational Publications; P.O. Box 280, East Aurora, NY 14052
Grade Level: K-8
Developed to provide administrators of gifted programs an easily administered, objective, and comprehensive process to select students for gifted programing on the basis of performance and behavior. Emphasis is on academic talent or gifted behavior. Assessment areas are based on Joseph Renzulli's work. The instrument consists of 3 components: general selection matrix, teacher recommendation form, and unit selection matrix.

13468
Arlin Test of Formal Reasoning. Arlin, Patricia Kennedy 1984
Subtests: Volume; Probability; Correlations; Combinations; Proportions; Momentum; Mechanical Equilibrium; Frames of Reference
Descriptors: *Abstract Reasoning; Adults; Cognitive Development; *Cognitive Tests; Gifted; Individual Testing; Learning Disabilities; *Logical Thinking; *Middle Schools; Multiple Choice Tests; Screening Tests; Secondary Education; *Secondary School Students
Identifiers: ATFR; Inhelder Piaget System; *Reasoning Ability
Availability: Slosson Educational Publications; P.O. Box 280, East Aurora, NY 14052
Grade Level: 6-12
Notes: Time, 60 approx.; Items, 32

Designed for large-group administration to assess students' levels of cognitive development. Also yields specific subtest scores which refer to each of Inhelder and Piaget's 8 formal schemata. May be used diagnostically by teachers in instructional planning. May also be used in conjunction with other instruments to screen students for programs for the gifted and for early admission to special science and mathematics classes. Can also be individually administered to students with reading and other learning disabilities, to probe their logical reasoning skills separately from general achievement and intelligence tests. In addition to testing the instrument on students in grades 6-12, some selected adult samples were also used. The majority of those in the norm sample represents White middle-class students for whom English is a first language. The publisher is planning to provide a wider range of forms for other representative populations in North America.

13471
Automobile Mechanic Assistant Work Sample. Shawsheen Valley Regional Vocational-Technical High School, Billerica, MA 1979
Descriptors: *Aptitude Tests; *Auto Mechanics; *Disabilities; High Schools; High School Students; Job Performance; Job Skills; Occupational Tests; Prevocational Education; Trade and Industrial Education; *Vocational Aptitude; *Vocational Evaluation; Vocational Interests; *Work Sample Tests
Availability: ERIC Document Reproduction Service; 3900 Wheeler Ave., Alexandria, VA 22304 (ED236421, 40 pages)
Grade Level: 9-12

The Automobile Mechanic Assistant Work Sample is intended to assess a handicapped student's interest in and potential to successfully pass a Training Program in Automotive Mechanics or in a similar automotive job. On this Work Sample, the student is to look over and inspect the thermostat housing to intake manifold set-up. The student is to remove the thermostat housing, gasket, and thermostat in order to replace a new thermostat in the intake manifold. The sample involves physical demands and must be done by a 2-armed person standing in front of the work sample. The work sample is timed from the moment the student signifies he/she is ready to begin until the last tool needed is put down and he/she indicates completion.

13472
Automotive Work Sample. Shawsheen Valley Regional Vocational-Technical High School, Billerica, MA 1979
Descriptors: *Aptitude Tests; *Auto Mechanics; *Disabilities; High Schools; *High School Students; Job Performance; Job Skills; Occupational Tests; Prevocational Education; Trade and Industrial Education; *Vocational Aptitude; *Vocational Evaluation; Vocational Interests; *Work Sample Tests
Availability: ERIC Document Reproduction Service; 3900 Wheeler Ave., Alexandria, VA 22304 (ED236422, 34 pages)
Grade Level: 9-12

The Automotive Mechanic Assistant Work Sample II is intended to assess a handicapped student's interest in, and potential to successfully pass, a Training Program in Automotive Mechanics or in a similar automotive job. The work sample is timed from the moment the student signifies that he/she understands the instructions and picks up the first tool or piece of equipment and indicates that he/she is ready to begin the removal phase, until the last tool or piece of equipment needed for the replacement phase is finished and the student indicates completion. This work sample deals with oil filters and the student is to replace the old filter with a new one. The sample involves physical demands and must be done by a 2-armed person standing in front of the work sample.

13473
Bagger Work Sample. Shawsheen Valley Regional Vocational-Technical High School, Billerica, MA 1979
Descriptors: *Aptitude Tests; *Disabilities; *Distributive Education; High School Students; Job Performance; Job Skills; Occupational Tests; Prevocational Education; Service Occupations; *Vocational Aptitude; *Vocational Evaluation; Vocational Interests; *Work Sample Tests
Identifiers: *Baggers
Availability: ERIC Document Reproduction Service; 3900 Wheeler Ave., Alexandria, VA 22304 (ED 236 423, 25 pages)
Grade Level: 9-12

The Bagger Work Sample is intended to assess a handicapped student's interest in and to screen interested students into a training program in Distributive Education I in the Shawsheen Valley Regional Vocational-Technical High School. The course is based upon the entry level of a bagger job. The sample involves medium work, and must be performed by a person with both hands or one who has equivalent manual and finger dexterity from a chair or wheelchair. The work sample is timed from the moment the student signifies he/she understands the instructions and is ready to begin until the student has placed the last grocery bag in the basket and indicates that he/she is finished.

13474
Clerical Machine Operator Work Sample. Shawsheen Valley Regional Vocational-Technical High School, Billerica, MA 1979
Descriptors: *Aptitude Tests; *Clerical Occupations; Clerical Workers; *Disabilities; High Schools; *High School Students; Job Performance; Job Skills; Occupational Tests; *Office Machines; Office Occupations Education; Prevocational Education; *Typewriting; *Vocational Aptitude; *Vocational Evaluation; Vocational Interests; *Work Sample Tests
Availability: ERIC Document Reproduction Service; 3900 Wheeler Ave., Alexandria, VA 22304 (ED 236 424, 42 pages)
Grade Level: 9-12

The Clerical Machine Operator-Typist Work Sample is intended to assess a handicapped student's interest in and potential to successfully pass a clerical business machine course (typing) in a comprehensive or vocational high school. This test can be done by a 2-armed person sitting in a wheel chair. The sample is designed to simulate the functions and methods of a typist in the clerical area as it may exist in a training program or a comprehensive or technical school. The work sample is timed from the moment the student signifies he/she understands the instruction and is ready to begin until the student indicates completion.

13475
Color Discrimination Work Sample. Shawsheen Valley Regional Vocational-Technical High School, Billerica, MA 1979
Descriptors: *Aptitude Tests; *Color; *Disabilities; High Schools; *High School Students; Industrial Arts; Job Performance; Job Skills; Occupational Tests; Painting (Industrial Arts); Prevocational Education; *Visual Perception; *Vocational Aptitude; *Vocational Evaluation; Vocational Interests; *Work Sample Tests
Identifiers: *Color Discrimination
Availability: ERIC Document Reproduction Service; 3900 Wheeler Ave., Alexandria, VA 22304 (ED236425, 21 pages)
Grade Level: 9-12

The Color Discrimination Work Sample is intended to assess a handicapped student's ability to see likenesses or differences in colors or shades, by identifying or matching certain colors and selecting colors which go together. The sample can be done by a 1- or 2-armed person from a chair or wheelchair. The sample is timed from the moment the student signifies that the instructions are understood and begins until the student signifies that the sample is completed.

13476
Drafting Work Sample. Shawsheen Valley Regional Vocational-Technical High School, Billerica, MA 1979
Descriptors: *Aptitude Tests; *Disabilities; *Drafting; Engineering Drawing; High Schools; *High School Students; Industrial Arts; Job Performance; Job Skills; Occupational Tests; Prevocational Education; *Vocational Aptitude; *Vocational Evaluation; Vocational Interests; *Work Sample Tests
Availability: ERIC Document Reproduction Service; 3900 Wheeler Ave., Alexandria, VA 22304 (ED236426, 31 pages)
Grade Level: 9-12

The Drafting Work Sample is intended to assess a handicapped student's interest in and to screen interested students into a training program in basic mechanical drawing. The sample involves sedentary work and must be performed by a person with both hands or one who has equivalent manual and finger dexterity from a chair or wheelchair. This sample is limited to a right-handed student; a left-handed drafting machine must be substituted if the student is left-handed. The work sample is timed from the moment the student signifies he/she understands the instructions until the student indicates that he/she is finished.

13477
Drill Press Work Sample. Shawsheen Valley Regional Vocational-Technical High School, Billerica, MA 1979
Descriptors: *Aptitude Tests; *Disabilities; High Schools; *High School Students; Job Performance; Job Skills; *Machine Tool Operators; *Machine Tools; Machinists; Occupational Tests; Prevocational Education; Trade and Industrial Education; *Vocational Aptitude; *Vocational Evaluation; Vocational Interests; *Work Sample Tests
Availability: ERIC Document Reproduction Service; 3900 Wheeler Ave., Alexandria, VA 22304 (ED236427, 27 pages)
Grade Level: 9-12

The Drill Press Work Sample is intended to assess a student's interest in and screen interested students into a training program in Basic Machine Shop I. The sample involves light work and must be performed by a person with both hands or one who has equivalent manual and finger dexterity from a chair or wheelchair. The sample is timed from the moment the student signifies he or she is ready to begin until the subject indicates that he or she is finished.

13478
Electrical Wiring Work Sample. Shawsheen Valley Regional Vocational-Technical High School, Billerica, MA 1979
Descriptors: *Aptitude Tests; *Disabilities; *Electricians; *Electricity; High Schools; *High School Students; Industrial Arts; Job Performance; Job Skills; Occupational Tests; Prevocational Education; Trade and Industrial Education; *Vocational Aptitude; *Vocational Evaluation; Vocational Interests; *Work Sample Tests
Identifiers: *Electrical Wiring
Availability: ERIC Document Reproduction Service; 3900 Wheeler Ave., Alexandria, VA 22304 (ED236428, 27 pages)
Grade Level: 9-12

The Electrical Work Sample is intended to assess a handicapped student's interest in and to screen interested students into a training program in basic electricity. The work sample involves light work and must be performed by a person with both hands or one who has equivalent manual and finger dexterity from a chair or wheelchair. The work sample is timed from the moment the student is ready to begin until he/she indicates that the sample is completed. The test is to wire an electrical duplex outlet.

13479
Electronics Assembly Work Sample. Shawsheen Valley Regional Vocational-Technical High School, Billerica, MA 1979
Descriptors: *Aptitude Tests; *Assembly (Manufacturing); *Disabilities; *Electronics; High Schools; *High School Students; Industrial Arts; Job Performance; Job Skills; Occupational Tests; Prevocational Education; *Vocational Aptitude; *Vocational Evaluation; Vocational Interests; *Work Sample Tests
Identifiers: *Electronics Assemblers
Availability: ERIC Document Reproduction Service; 3900 Wheeler Ave., Alexandria, VA 22304 (ED 236 429, 26 pages)
Grade Level: 9-12

The Electronics Assembler Work Sample is intended to assess a handicapped student's interest in and potential to enter a training program in electronics assembly or a similar program. The sample involves sedentary work and can be done by a 2-armed person from a chair or wheelchair. Time is not a factor in this work sample.

13480
Finger Dexterity Work Sample. Shawsheen Valley Regional Vocational-Technical High School, Billerica, MA 1979
Descriptors: *Aptitude Tests; *Disabilities; High Schools; *High School Students; Job Performance; Job Skills; *Motor Development; *Object Manipulation; Occupational Tests; Prevocational Education; *Vocational Aptitude; *Vocational Evaluation; Vocational Interests; *Work Sample Tests
Availability: ERIC Document Reproduction Service; 3900 Wheeler Ave., Alexandria, VA 22304 (ED236430, 22 pages)
Grade Level: 9-12

The Finger Dexterity Work Sample is intended to assess a handicapped student's ability to move the fingers and manipulate small objects with fingers, rapidly and accurately. The sample can be done by a 1- or 2-armed person from a chair or wheelchair. The sample is timed from the moment the student signifies readiness to completion of the task.

13481
Manual Dexterity Work Sample. Shawsheen Valley Regional Vocational-Technical High School, Billerica, MA 1979
Descriptors: *Aptitude Tests; *Disabilities; High Schools; *High School Students; Job Performance; Job Skills; *Motor Development; *Object Manipulation; Occupational Tests; Prevocational Education; *Vocational Aptitude; *Vocational Evaluation; Vocational Interests; *Work Sample Tests
Identifiers: *Manual Dexterity
Availability: ERIC Document Reproduction Service; 3900 Wheeler Ave., Alexandria, VA 22304 (ED236431, 21 pages)
Grade Level: 9-12

The Manual Dexterity Work Sample is intended to assess a handicapped student's ability to move the hands easily and skillfully and the ability to move the hands in placing and turning motions. The sample can be done by a 2-armed person from a chair or wheelchair. Time is not a factor in this work sample

13482
Small Parts Assembler Work Sample. Shawsheen Valley Regional Vocational-Technical High School, Billerica, MA 1979
Descriptors: *Aptitude Tests; *Assembly (Manufacturing); *Disabilities; High Schools; *High School Students; Job Performance; Job Skills; Occupational Tests; Prevocational Education; Secondary Education; Secondary School Students; Trade and Industrial Education; *Vocational Aptitude; *Vocational Evaluation; Vocational Interests; *Work Sample Tests
Identifiers: *Assemblers
Availability: ERIC Document Reproduction Service; 3900 Wheeler Ave., Alexandria, VA 22304 (ED236432, 29 pages)
Grade Level: 9-12

The Small Parts Assembler Work Sample is intended to assess a handicapped student's interest in and potential to enter a training program in small parts assembly or in a similar job. The sample involves light to medium work and can be done by a 2-armed person with good eyesight from a chair or wheelchair. Time is not a factor in scoring this work sample but is kept for informational purposes only.

13483
Diagnosis of Language Competency Inventory (DLCI). Blake, Howard E.; Maull, Ethel M. 1977
Subtests: Motor Functions; Memory Functions; Visual Functions; Tactile-Kinesthetic Functions; Vocal Functions; Auditory Functions; Following Instructions; Language Concepts
Descriptors: Elementary School Students; *Expressive Language; *Individual Testing; *Language Acquisition; Language Aptitude; *Language Skills; *Language Tests; Primary Education; *Receptive Language
Identifiers: DLCI; *The Research Instruments Project
Availability: ERIC Document Reproduction Service; 3900 Wheeler Ave., Alexandria, VA 22304 (ED236650, 12 pages)
Grade Level: K-3
Notes: Items, 57

This instrument is designed to measure children's receptive and expressive language competence in 8 language subareas. It is to be administered individually.

13501
Human Information Processing Survey. Torrance, E. Paul; And Others 1984
Descriptors: Adults; *Brain Hemisphere Functions; *Cognitive Style; Decision Making; *Forced Choice Technique; *Labor Force Development; Problem Solving; Training Methods
Identifiers: HIP
Availability: Scholastic Testing Service; 480 Meyer Rd., Bensenville, IL 60106
Target Audience: Adults
Notes: Time, 30 approx.; Items, 40

A training tool for use in the field of human resource development. Individuals are assessed in terms of processing preferences: left, right, integrated, or mixed. The survey provides a description of a person's overall approach as well as specific tactics in problem solving and decision making. A special Research edition has also been prepared, using the same 40 items, for the user who is primarily interested in using the instrument to study human information processing behavior. The research version contains alternatives to the self scoring and feedback features of the professional edition. Deals with the ways in which the left and right hemispheres of the human brain process information.

13504
Word Processor Assessment Battery. Stanard, Steven J. 1984
Subtests: Machine Aptitude; Typing Speed and Accuracy; Machine Transcription
Descriptors: Achievement Tests; Adults; Aptitude Tests; Business Correspondence; Dictation; *Occupational Tests; Personnel Evaluation; Personnel Selection; Typewriting; Vocational Aptitude; *Word Processing; *Work Sample Tests
Identifiers: Transcription; WPAB
Availability: Science Research Associates; 155 N. Wacker Dr., Chicago, IL 60606
Target Audience: Adults
Notes: Time, 55

A test consisting of 3 parts designed to measure specific skills and abilities necessary for success in word processing. Can be used to evaluate experienced and inexperienced persons for promotion, transfer, or hire, regardless of the type of equipment available for use in the evaluation. Part 1 is predictive of training success and job performance for word processors. Part 2 measures a person's ability to type quickly and accurately. Part 3 measures a person's ability to transcribe dictated material accurately and to produce a mailable letter.

13520
A Tentative Criterion-Referenced Test to Measure Thinking Processes, Forms A and B. Oliver, Jo Ellen 1978
Descriptors: Beginning Reading; *Cognitive Processes; Cognitive Tests; *Criterion Referenced Tests; Elementary Education; Elementary School Students; Logical Thinking; *Reading Comprehension; Reading Skills
Identifiers: The Research Instruments Project
Availability: ERIC Document Reproduction Service; 3900 Wheeler Ave., Alexandria, VA 22304 (ED236645, 34 pages)
Target Audience: 7-11
Notes: Time, 30 approx.

This instrument is designed to measure children's abilities to synthesize concepts from several sources and is based on the assumptions that children move from the concrete to the abstract, from specific to generic, and that the ability to synthesize and form new concepts is an important prerequisite to reading comprehension. Each form of the test is divided into 3 parts: the first focuses on letters, the second on words, and the third on stories. The test is written on a primer level of difficulty, is easy to score, and requires about 30 minutes to complete. The test may be administered individually or in groups.

13532
C.U.B.E. Learning Disabilities Empirical Mapping Instrument. Vincennes University, IN 1979
Descriptors: *Adult Basic Education; Adults; Cognitive Mapping; *Cognitive Style; *Diagnostic Tests; Educational Environment; *Individual Testing; Interviews; *Learning Disabilities; Learning Modalities
Identifiers: Continuity and Unity in Basic Education Program; CUBE
Availability: ERIC Document Reproduction Service; 3900 Wheeler Ave., Alexandria, VA 22304 (ED211833, 437 pages)
Target Audience: 18-64
Notes: Items, 38

A simplified cognitive style mapping technique. Consists of an interview type survey, given individually, which results in a pictorial "map" of the adult basic education student's preferred learning style. Covers preferred modality, physical environment, organization of learning materials, and instruction.

13533
C.U.B.E. Learning Disabilities Diagnostic Test. Vincennes University, IN 1979
Subtests: Early's Informal Test of Cognitive Overloads; Copying (Far Point); Copying (Near Point); Writing from Dictation; Spelling (Oral); Spelling (Written); Sentence Formation (Oral); Sentence Formation (Written)
Descriptors: *Adult Basic Education; Adults; Cognitive Processes; *Diagnostic Tests; Instructional Development; *Learning Disabilities; *Learning Processes
Identifiers: Continuity and Unity in Basic Education Program; CUBE
Availability: ERIC Document Reproduction Service; 3900 Wheeler Ave., Alexandria, VA 22304 (ED211833, 437 pages)
Target Audience: 18-64

Series of instruments designed to indicate the presence of learning disabilities in general. Does not identify specific disabilities. Used to gather information that will help the teacher of adult basic education students to understand their learning processes and develop an instructional plan. See also ERIC Documents ED211831 and ED211832 for further information on reading and vocabulary tests.

13537
How a Child Learns. Gnagey, Thomas; Gnagey, Patricia 1970
Descriptors: *Classroom Observation Techniques; Cognitive Style; Elementary Education; *Elementary School Students; *Learning Modalities; Observation
Availability: Facilitation House; P.O. Box 611, Ottawa, IL 61350
Grade Level: K-6

A direct observation method for use by classroom teachers to assess students' learning skills and help the teacher sort out the strengths and weaknesses in a child's learning channels.

13543
Clinton Assessment of Problem Identification Skills of Instructional Supervisors, Forms A and B. Clinton, Barbara Jeanne 1981
Descriptors: *Administrative Problems; Adults; Critical Thinking; *Information Seeking; Supervision; Teachers
Identifiers: CAPIS; TIM(J)
Availability: Tests in Microfiche; Test Collection, Educational Testing Service, Princeton, NJ 08541
Target Audience: Adults
Notes: Time, 30; Items, 3

Three scenarios concerned with problem situations, found in classrooms, school systems, and instructional programs, are presented. The supervisor of instruction or graduate student being evaluated must respond to each scenario by identifying the problems contained in each, but not solving them. Scorers are required to complete practice exercises. Free response is required.

13553
Aston Index, Revised: A Classroom Test for Screening and Diagnosis of Language Difficulties. Newton, Margaret; Thompson, Michael 1982
Subtests: Picture Recognition; Vocabulary Scale; Goodenough Draw-a-Man Test; Copying Geometric Designs; Grapheme/Phoneme Correspondence; Schonell Reading Test; Spelling Test; Visual Discrimination; Child's Laterality; Copying Name; Free Writing; Visual Sequential Memory Picture; Auditory Sequential Memory; Sound Blending; Visual Sequential Memory Symbolic; Sound Discrimination; Graphomotor Test
Descriptors: Academic Aptitude; *Diagnostic Tests; Elementary Education; *Elementary School Students; Individual Testing; Junior High Schools; *Junior High School Students; *Language Handicaps; *Learning Disabilities; *Screening Tests; *Written Language
Availability: United Educational Services; P.O. Box 357, East Aurora, NY 14052
Grade Level: K-8
Target Audience: 5-14

Consists of 17 subtests used to indicate the nature of a child's learning potential for literacy. Used as a screening and diagnostic tool for early recognition of educationally at-risk children. Can be used to indicate the particular learning pattern of a child and to identify specific types of learning patterns. May be used to identify specific written language difficulties, slow learners, culturally different children, neurologically damaged children, language disordered children, specific auditory difficulties, specific visual difficulties, or specific graphic difficulties. The 17 subtests are organized on 2 levels. Level 1 is used as a screening test for children who have been in school approximately 6 months. Level 2 is for use with children over age of 7 years. Some of the tests can be group administered; others must be given individually. Total administration time for Level 1 is 45 minutes and for Level 2, approximately 60 minutes. It is best to give the test over a period of several days.

13574
Johnson O'Connor Research Foundation Aptitude Test. Johnson O'Connor Research Foundation, Chicago, IL 1940
Descriptors: Adults; *Aptitude Tests; Career Guidance; Creative Thinking; Delay of Gratification; Individual Testing; Job Satisfaction; Language Aptitude; Memory; Personality Measures; Spatial Ability; *Vocational Aptitude
Identifiers: Analytical Reasoning; Clerical Aptitude; Deductive Reasoning; Finger Dexterity; Inductive Reasoning; Manual Dexterity; Music Ability; Test Batteries; Tweezer Dexterity
Availability: Johnson O'Connor Research Foundation; Human Engineering Laboratory, 161 E. Erie St., Chicago IL 60611
Target Audience: Adults
Notes: Time, 360

An extensive aptitude battery measuring 18 work-related aptitudes through the performance of tasks such as manipulation of blocks, and paper folding. Some of the subscores are: visualization in 3 dimensions, abstract thinking, working alone, working with others, idea production, clerical aptitudes, immediate versus delayed rewards, inductive reasoning, analytical reasoning, musical aptitude, memory, verbal aptitude, finger, and spatial aptitude. The test is administered by trained personnel at 16 offices nationwide. It cannot be purchased. New forms of tests are developed periodically.

13579
SEVTC Assessment Scales for Community Integration of the Severely/Profoundly Handicapped, Post-Entry Monitoring Instrument, Adolescent-Adult Form. Southeastern Virginia Training Center for the Mentally Retarded, Chesapeake, VA 1977
Subtests: Motor Development; Self-Help; Academic/Cognitive; Language; Socialization
Descriptors: Adolescents; Adults; Behavioral Objectives; Check Lists; Children; Cognitive Development; Daily Living Skills; *Deinstitutionalization (of Disabled); Language Acquisition; Motor Development; Observation; *Severe Disabilities; Social Development
Availability: ERIC Document Reproduction Service; 3900 Wheeler Ave., Alexandria, VA 22304 (ED167565, 52 pages)
Target Audience: 8-64

For use in a program to deinstitutionalize mentally retarded individuals and return them to a less restrictive environment. This instrument measures observed behavioral change and progress through a short rehabilitation period. Each subscale has 5 levels from minimally to independently functioning. Each item appears as a behavioral objective. Scoring depends on whether the behavior was self-initiated, cued, or not performed.

13594
Grassi Basic Cognitive Evaluation. Grassi, Joseph R. 1977
Subtests: Form and Color Discrimination; Concepts; Identification; Directional Orientation; Visualization; Number Concepts; Auditory Discrimination; Kinesthesia; Sequencing; Recall; Vocabulary
Descriptors: *Academic Aptitude; Auditory Discrimination; *Cognitive Development; Cognitive Measurement; Cognitive Tests; Diagnostic Teaching; *Diagnostic Tests; Individual Testing; Kinesthetic Perception; Number Concepts; Recall (Psychology); Visual Discrimination; Vocabulary Development; *Young Children
Availability: Joseph R. Grassi; 3501 Jackson St., No. 110, Hollywood, FL 33021
Target Audience: 4-8

Designed for the identification of developmental deficits, to predict academic success or failure and provide information for prescriptive developmental stimulation programs. Each child is tested individually using a series of black and white and color plates. The child's level of cognitive development, determined by the test, is compared with the child's Binet mental age, or the tests vocabulary score in the absence of a formal intellectual evaluation. The latter comparison is said to be less effective. Norms are reported for an unidentified group of 75 first graders.

13597
IPI Aptitude Series: Dental Office Assistant. Industrial Psychology, Inc., New York, NY 1981
Subtests: Numbers; Perception; CPF; Office Terms; NPF; Judgment
Descriptors: Abstract Reasoning; *Adults; *Aptitude Tests; *Dental Assistants; Emotional Adjustment; *Job Applicants; Job Performance; Job Skills; Mathematical Concepts; Neurosis; *Occupational Tests; Personality Measures; Visual Perception; Vocabulary
Identifiers: Extraversion; Introversion; Test Batteries
Availability: Industrial Psychology, Inc.; 515 Madison Ave., New York, NY 10022
Target Audience: 18-64

This is a battery of tests designed to assess one's aptitude for the position of dental assistant. Duties would include chairside work, light secretarial tasks, and working with patients and the dentist.

13598
IPI Aptitude Series: Dental Technician. Industrial Psychology, Inc., New York, NY 1981
Subtests: Dexterity; Dimension; CPF; NPF
Descriptors: *Adults; *Aptitude Tests; *Dental Technicians; Emotional Adjustment; *Job Applicants; Job Performance; Job Skills; Neurosis; *Occupational Tests; Perceptual Motor Coordination; Personality Measures; Spatial Ability
Identifiers: Extraversion; Introversion; Test Batteries
Availability: Industrial Psychology, Inc.; 515 Madison Ave., New York, NY 10022
Target Audience: 18-64

This is a battery of tests designed to assess one's aptitude for the position of dental technician. Duties would include laboratory work at 4 classification levels: cast metal, denture, crown and bridge, and porcelain and acrylic.

13599
IPI Aptitude Series: Optometric Assistant. Industrial Psychology, Inc., New York, NY 1981
Subtests: Numbers; NPF; CPF; Office Terms; Judgment; Perception; Fluency
Descriptors: Abstract Reasoning; *Adults; *Aptitude Tests; Emotional Adjustment; *Job Applicants; Job Performance; Job Skills; Language Fluency; Mathematical Concepts; Neurosis; *Occupational Tests; *Optometry; *Paraprofessional Personnel; Personality Measures; Visual Perception; Vocabulary
Identifiers: Extraversion; Introversion; Test Batteries
Availability: Industrial Psychology, Inc.; 515 Madison Ave., New York, NY 10022
Target Audience: 18-64

This is a battery of tests designed to assess one's aptitude for the position of optometric assistant. Duties include working as support person for optometrist, working with optometrist and patients, reception duties, and light secretarial work.

13600
IPI Aptitude Series: General Clerk. Industrial Psychology, Inc., New York, NY 1981
Subtests: Perception; Judgment; Numbers; Office Terms; Memory; Parts; Fluency
Descriptors: Abstract Reasoning; *Adults; *Aptitude Tests; *Clerical Occupations; *Clerical Workers; *Job Applicants; Job Performance; Job Skills; Language Fluency; Mathematical Concepts; Memory; *Occupational Tests; Personality Measures; Spatial Ability; Visual Perception; Vocabulary
Identifiers: Test Batteries
Availability: Industrial Psychology, Inc.; 515 Madison Ave., New York, NY 10022
Target Audience: 18-64

This is a battery of tests designed to assess one's aptitude for the position of a general clerk who would perform a number of routine clerical tasks such as typing, filing, billing, coding, verifying, transcribing, writing, sorting, and answering telephones. Battery is suitable to evaluate applicants for an office with a small staff in which employee might perform a number of the functions listed above or in a large office where clerk might circulate among various departments.

13617
Multidimensional Aptitude Battery. Jackson, Douglas N. 1983
Subtests: Information; Comprehension; Arithmetic; Similarities; Vocabulary; Digit Symbol; Picture Completion; Spatial; Picture Arrangement; Object Assembly
Descriptors: Adolescents; Adults; *Aptitude Tests; *Intelligence Quotient; *Intelligence Tests; Reading Comprehension; Screening Tests; Spatial Ability; Transformational Generative Grammar; Transformations (Mathematics)
Identifiers: IQ; MAB
Availability: Research Psychologists Press; P.O. Box 984, Port Huron, MI 48060
Target Audience: 13-64
Notes: Time, 90 min.

The Multidimensional Aptitude Battery (MAB) assesses aptitudes and intelligence, yielding a profile of 10 subtest scores, Verbal IQ, Performance IQ, and Full Scale IQ. It was designed to assess the same factors as the Wechsler family of scales but with greater ceiling and a structured format amenable to group administration and objective hand or computer scoring. Each battery (verbal and performance) contains 5 subtests and each subtest can be group administered using automated instructions and timing with respondents using machine-scorable answer sheets. The time limit for each subtest is 7 minutes. The battery can be used for assessment of adults and adolescents in clinics, counseling offices, referral agencies, schools, and is appropriate for preliminary screening of individuals who might require an individualized intellectual assessment.

13619
The Singer-Loomis Inventory of Personality, Experimental Edition. Singer, June; Loomis, Mary 1984
Subtests: Introverted Thinking; Introverted Feeling; Introverted Sensation; Introverted Intuition; Extraverted Thinking; Extraverted Feeling; Extraverted Sensation; Extraverted Intuition
Descriptors: Adolescents; Adults; *Cognitive Style; College Students; Higher Education; High Schools; High School Students; *Personality Measures; *Personality Traits; *Self Evaluation (Individuals)

Identifiers: Jung (Carl G); Self Report Measures; SLIP
Availability: Consulting Psychologists Press; 577 College Ave., Palo Alto, CA 94306
Notes: Items, 120

Designed to measure the cognitive style of individuals, based on the assumption that there is a relationship between the way people perceive and understand their environments and the way they behave. SLIP is a self-report measure for assessing personality factors which may help an individual toward greater self-understanding and to use skills, talents, and abilities in his/her interactions with the environment. The defining categories of cognitive style used to assess personality are derived from Jung's theory of psychological types. This version is an experimental edition.

13620
IPI Aptitude Series: Computer Programmers. Industrial Psychology, Inc., New York, NY 1984
Subtests: Perception; Parts; Judgment; Numbers; Office Terms
Descriptors: *Adults; *Aptitude Tests; *Job Applicants; Job Performance; Job Skills; *Occupational Tests; *Programers
Identifiers: Test Batteries
Availability: Industrial Psychology, Inc.; 515 Madison Ave., New York, NY 10022
Target Audience: Adults

A battery of tests designed to assist in the screening and selection of those applicants most likely to succeed in the programing area at an entry-level position. May also be used to identify employees in clerical positions who might possess the necessary skills to succeed in computer-related positions and are possible candidates for training programs.

13624
Letter Comparison Test. Cunningham, Walter R. 1975
Descriptors: *Cognitive Measurement; *Older Adults; *Perception Tests
Identifiers: *Perceptual Speed
Availability: Walter C. Cunningham; Psychology Dept., University of Florida, Gainesville, FL 32611
Target Audience: 60-99
Notes: Time, 3

Used in a study to assess correlations between age and factor scores of abilities drawn from the domains of intellectual functioning and information processing tasks. The letter comparison test assessed perceptual speed.

13633
Unicorns Are Real. Vitale, Barbara Meister
Descriptors: Adolescents; Adults; *Brain Hemisphere Functions; Check Lists; *Children; *Learning Modalities; Observation
Availability: Ann Arbor Publishers; P.O. Box 7249, Naples, FL 33941
Target Audience: 6-64

The book *Unicorns are Real* contains right-hemispheric teaching strategies and is a right-brained approach to learning. Also contained in the book are screening checklists that allow parents and teachers to identify individual learning preferences through observing eye and hand dominance, handwriting position, muscle strength, body symmetry, eye movements, and responses to open-ended questions.

13638
Study of Children's Learning Styles. McDermott, Paul A.; Beitman, Barbara S. 1984
Descriptors: *Behavior Rating Scales; Classroom Observation Techniques; *Cognitive Style; *Kindergarten Children; *Learning Strategies; Primary Education
Identifiers: SCLS
Availability: Psychology in the Schools; v21 n1 p5-14, Jan 1984
Grade Level: K
Notes: Items, 16

Designed to study learning styles of preschool level children. Teachers rate kindergarten children on a 3-point scale based on their observation of the child's learning-related behavior.

13639
Learning Style Checklist. Neumann, Karl F.; And Others 1979
Descriptors: Check Lists; Classroom Observation Techniques; *Cognitive Style; Junior High Schools; *Junior High School Students; *Learning Strategies; Student Behavior
Availability: Perceptual and Motor Skills; v48 p723-28, 1979
Grade Level: 8
Notes: Items, 40

Used by teachers to rate their students' learning styles. Checklist is based on Rosenberg's descriptive theory of 4 learning styles: rigid-inhibited, undisciplined, acceptance-anxious, and creative.

13658
Battelle Developmental Inventory. Svinicki, John 1984
Subtests: Personal-Social; Adaptive; Motor; Communication; Cognitive
Descriptors: *Child Development; Cognitive Ability; Communication Skills; *Developmental Tasks; Individualized Education Programs; Individual Testing; Instructional Development; Interpersonal Competence; Psychomotor Skills; *Screening Tests; Self Care Skills; Young Children
Identifiers: BDI
Availability: DLM Teaching Resources; P.O. Box 4000, 1 DLM Park, Allen, TX 75002
Target Audience: 0-8
Notes: Time, 120 approx.; Items, 341
Standardized individually administered assessment battery of key developmental skills in children up to age 8. Primarily for use by infant, preschool, and primary teachers and special education teachers. May also be used by speech pathologists, psychologists, and other clinicians to assess functional abilities in young handicapped and non-handicapped children. BDI is behaviorally based and provides a method to determine in which areas of development a child needs to be comprehensively assessed. Data are collected by structured test format, interviews with parents, caregivers or teachers, and observation of the child in a natural setting. Serves 4 specific purposes: assessment and identification of the handicapped child, assessment of the nonhandicapped child, planning and providing instruction, and evaluation of groups of handicapped children. Within each of the 5 domains assessed, items are grouped by specific skill areas. Useful in developing individualized education programs.

13659
Early Screening Inventory. Meisels, Samuel J.; Wiske, Martha Stone 1983
Subtests: Initial Screening Items; Visual-Motor/Adaptive; Language and Cognition; Gross Motor/Body Awareness
Descriptors: Check Lists; *Child Development; Cognitive Development; *Developmental Tasks; Eye Hand Coordination; Individual Testing; *Intervention; Language Proficiency; Motor Development; *Screening Tests; Visual Discrimination; *Young Children
Identifiers: ESI; Fine Motor Skills; Gross Motor Skills
Availability: Teachers College Press; Harper and Row, Publishers, Keystone Industrial Park, Scranton, PA 18512
Target Audience: 4-6
Notes: Time, 20 approx.
The Early Screening Inventory (ESI) is a brief developmental screening instrument that is individually administered to children 4-6 years of age. It is designed to identify children who may need special educational services in order to perform adequately in school. The ESI represents one phase of a comprehensive screening process. Other elements are a parent questionnaire, a medical examination, and hearing and vision testing. As a developmental screening instrument, the ESI should be used only as an indicator of a learning or handicapped condition that might affect a child's overall potential for success in school. The items primarily sample developmental tasks rather than specific accomplishments that indicate academic readiness. The Visual-Motor/Adaptive section of the test examines fine motor control, eye-hand coordination, the ability to remember visual sequences, the ability to draw visual forms, and the ability to reproduce visual structures. The Language and Cognition items focus on language comprehension and verbal expression, the ability to reason and count, and the ability to remember auditory sequences. The Gross Motor/Body Awareness section examines balance, large motor coordination, and the ability to imitate body positions from visual cues. The EIS includes 2 other items: the Draw a Person task (DAP) and letter writing. The DAP allows the examiner to see how the child organizes a response to a relatively unstructured request and the letter-writing item, which is not scored, offers additional information about fine motor control. Although the 3 sections are designed to investigate a child's ability within a particular area, they are not meant to stand alone in their assessment of that ability. Any conclusions drawn from ESI results are based on the child's overall performance as well as information obtained from parents, teachers, medical professionals, and other informed sources.

13671
VITAS: Vocational Interest, Temperament and Aptitude System. Vocational Research Institute, Philadelphia, PA
Descriptors: Adolescents; *Aptitude Tests; *Disadvantaged Youth; *Mild Mental Retardation; Performance Tests; Personality Traits; *Vocational Aptitude; *Vocational Evaluation; Vocational Interests; *Work Sample Tests; Young Adults
Identifiers: VITAS

Availability: Vocational Research Institute; 1528 Walnut St., Ste. 1502, Philadelphia, PA 19102
Target Audience: 18-30
The Vocational Interest, Temperament and Aptitude System (VITAS) includes 22 different work samples and was developed for use with disadvantaged and educable mentally retarded persons. It requires less than sixth grade level reading ability. In each of the work samples, the individual performs a task which is identical or similar to a job experience. Performance and reaction to work samples form the basis of vocational recommendations. VITAS assesses aptitudes, vocational interests, and work-related temperaments. The work samples are: nuts, bolts and washers assembly, packing matchbooks, tile sorting and weighing, collating material samples, verifying numbers, pressing linens, budget book assembly, nail and screw sorting (2 parts), pipe assembly, filing by letters, lock assembly, circuit board inspection, calculating, message taking, bank teller, proof-reading, payroll computation, census interviewing, spot welding, laboratory assistant, and drafting. It takes about 2 1/2 days to administer VITAS.

13672
VIEWS: Vocational Information and Evaluation Work Samples. Vocational Research Institute, Philadelphia, PA
Descriptors: Adolescents; Adults; *Aptitude Tests; Individualized Education Programs; *Mild Mental Retardation; *Moderate Mental Retardation; Performance Tests; Personality Traits; *Prevocational Education; *Severe Mental Retardation; *Vocational Aptitude; Vocational Evaluation; Vocational Interests; *Work Sample Tests
Identifiers: IEP; Public Law 94 142; VIEWS
Availability: Vocational Research Institute; 1528 Walnut St., Ste. 1502, Philadelphia, PA 19102
Target Audience: 12-64
The Vocational Information and Evaluation Work Samples (VIEWS) instrument is a vocational assessment for mentally retarded individuals. It is a hands-on assessment system which includes 16 work samples to be used in a simulated work environment. VIEWS requires no reading ability and since it was developed specifically for mentally retarded subjects, allows for repeated instruction. Each work sample incorporates a period of training prior to the measurement of time and quality of performance. This instrument meets prevocational and vocational requirements for Individualized Education Programs (IEPs), is suitable for mildly, moderately, and severely retarded individuals, measures rate of learning, quality of work, and productivity and provides industrial time standards (MODAPTS) for each work sample. VIEWS assesses aptitudes, vocational interests, and work-related behaviors. During the 4 to 5 day period of evaluation, the subjects perform a variety of tasks including sorting, cutting, collating, assembling, weighing, typing, measuring, using hand tools, tending a drill press, and electric machine feeding.

13673
APTICOM. Vocational Research Institute, Philadelphia, PA 1984
Descriptors: Adolescents; Adults; *Aptitude Tests; *Career Counseling; *Computer Assisted Testing; Employment Potential; *Interest Inventories; Job Training; Profiles; *Vocational Aptitude; Vocational Education; *Vocational Interests; Vocational Rehabilitation
Identifiers: Department of Labor; OAP
Availability: Vocational Research Institute; 1528 Walnut St., Ste. 1502, Philadelphia, PA 19102
Target Audience: 13-66
Notes: Time, 90
APTICOM, developed by the Vocational Research Institute, is a computerized, desktop console designed specifically for assessing aptitudes and job interests. It is intended for use in the vocational guidance and counseling process and in employment and training selection and placement. The tests were designed to measure aptitude constructs which have been related to occupational success using the Department of Labor's defined aptitudes. They are: Intelligence; General Learning Ability, Verbal Aptitude, Numerical Aptitude, Spatial Aptitude, Form Perception, Clerical Perception, Motor Coordination, Finger Dexterity, Manual Dexterity, and Eye-Hand-Foot Coordination. APTICOM is computerized and is self-scoring and self-timing, portable, and can be administered individually or up to 12 people at one time. The APTICOM Occupational Interest Inventory provides schools, rehabilitation, industry, and job training programs with an interest measure that stimulates examinees' enthusiasm, minimizes time requirements, and is computerized. When both the aptitude and interest inventories are administered, the results are a means of initiating occupational exploration with information refined to the level of the Department of Labor Work Groups. The APTICOM Report gives aptitude scores and Occupational Aptitude Patterns (OAPs) based on these scores. It also gives interest scores and the interest areas related to these scores. The Occupational Interest Inventory Report reveals the degree of interest indicated by the test taker and an individual profile is generated showing the interest in various work tasks as compared to the normative sample. The final portion of

the report lists those areas of employment in which the applicant has shown both the required aptitude and high interest. The accompanying Educational Skills Development Battery measures achieved math and language skills levels.

13674
J.E.V.S. Work Samples. Vocational Research Institute, Philadelphia, PA
Descriptors: Adults; *Aptitude Tests; *Career Guidance; Interest Inventories; *Interpersonal Competence; Job Skills; Occupational Tests; Physical Disabilities; Vocational Aptitude; *Vocational Evaluation; *Vocational Interests; Vocational Rehabilitation; *Work Sample Tests
Availability: Vocational Research Institute; 1528 Walnut St., Ste. 1502, Philadelphia, PA 19102
Target Audience: 18-64
J.E.V.S. Work Samples are hands-on activities to assess aptitudes, vocational interests, and work-related behaviors. It is a complete vocational evaluation program which includes hardware for 28 work samples, recording, report, and evaluation forms, consultation, and training for users. The work samples involve tasks, materials and tools which are identical or similar to those in actual jobs and are administered in a work-like environment over 5-7 days. Reading is necessary only in work samples related to occupational areas where reading is required. This instrument can be used with disadvantaged or unsuccessful students who have no idea what they like or want to do, students with emotional problems who are failing to adjust in school, a physically injured person whose current physical capabilites must be assessed, an emotionally disabled person whose behavior on the job needs analysis, a psychiatric patient re-entering the community after hospitalization, and persons with little or no work history. The evaluation report includes information on: discriminatory abilities, manipulative skills, communication, behavior in interpersonal situations, worker characteristics, learning and comprehension, physical appearance, and interests. Recommendations are made for appropriate areas of employment and/or training and supportive services that may be needed. The work samples are: nut, bolt, and washer assembly, rubber stamping, washer threading, budget book assembly, sign making, tile sorting, nut packing, collating leather samples, grommet assembly, union assembly, belt assembly, ladder assembly, metal square fabrication, hardware assembly, telephone assembly, lock assembly, filing by numbers, proofreading, filing by letters, nail and screw sorting, adding machine, payroll computation, computing postage, resistor reading, pipe assembly, blouse making, vest making, condensing principle.

13675
Bloomer Learning Test. Bloomer, Richard H. 1978
Subtests: Activity; Visual Short Term Memory; Auditory Short Term Memory; Visual Apprehension Span; Serial Learning; Recall and Relearning; Free Association; Paired Associate Learning; Concept Recognition and Concept Production; Problem Solving
Descriptors: *Elementary School Students; Elementary Secondary Education; *Learning Modalities; Learning Problems; *Screening Tests; *Secondary School Students; Teaching Methods
Identifiers: BLT
Availability: Dr. Richard Bloomer; Decker Hill Rd., Willimantic, CT 06226
Grade Level: 1-12
Developed to provide an instrument which would give a profile indicating strengths and weaknesses in a child's learning process. Profile could be used as a guide to appropriate teaching strategies. BLT should be used as a starting point in planning instructional strategies. Standardization population included reading or learning disabled, emotionally disturbed, and gifted, as well as nonhandicapped subjects.

13684
Hester Evaluation System. Human Services Data Center, Chicago, IL
Descriptors: Adults; *Aptitude Tests; Culture Fair Tests; Deafness; Disabilities; Gifted; Illiteracy; Mental Retardation; Non English Speaking; Nonverbal Tests; *Occupational Tests; Perceptual Motor Coordination; *Physical Disabilities; Psychomotor Skills; *Vocational Aptitude
Identifiers: Finger Dexterity; HES; Manual Dexterity; Mechanical Aptitude; Perceptual Motor Skills; Verbal Aptitude
Availability: Lafayette Instrument Co., Inc.; P.O. Box 5729, Sagamore Pwy., Lafayette, IN 47903
Target Audience: Adults
A series of 26 tests measuring factor-pure abilities actually used in a wide range of occupations. Relates to the Dictionary of Occupational Titles. Raw scores can be compared to profiles for 1500 jobs. This test is useful for aptitude testing for gifted, nonhandicapped, physically handicapped, mentally handicapped, deaf, illiterate, and non-English-speaking people.

13703
Denman Neuropsychology Memory Scale. Denman, Sidney B. 1984
Subtests: Presentation and Immediate Recall of a Story; Paired Associate Learning and Immediate Recall; Copying a Complex Figure; Immediate Recall of the Complex Figure; Memory for Digits; Memory for Musical Tones and Memories; Remotely Stored Verbal Information; Memory for Human Faces; Remotely Stored Non-Verbal Information; Delayed Recall of Complex Figures; Delayed Recall of Paired Associates; Delayed Recall of the Story
Descriptors: Adolescents; Adults; Children; *Individual Testing; *Long Term Memory; Older Adults; Psychological Evaluation; Psychological Testing; *Recall (Psychology); *Short Term Memory
Availability: Sidney B. Denman; Clinical Neuropsychology, 1040 Fort Sumter Dr., Charleston, SC 29412
Target Audience: 10-69
Notes: Time, 60 approx.
Designed for use in clinical situations where there is a need of quantitative assessment of immediate recall, short-term memory, and long-term memory in verbal and non-verbal areas. Scale has the capacity to assess a variety of memory functions, and to help in differentiating normal subjects from those with memory dysfunction. It should also be able to help in differentiating memory dysfunction from psychiatric depression. Examiners should be trained in the use of individually administered psychological tests and should follow the specific directions in the manual.

13708
Jansky Diagnostic Battery. Jansky, Jeannette
Descriptors: *Diagnostic Tests; Expressive Language; High Risk Persons; *Individual Testing; *Kindergarten Children; Primary Education; *Reading Diagnosis; *Reading Readiness; *Reading Readiness Tests; Receptive Language
Availability: Jeannette Jansky; 120 E. 89th St., New York, NY 10028
Grade Level: K
Notes: Time, 30 approx.
Assesses reading readiness ability of kindergarten children who have been identified as at-risk by the Jansky Screening Index (TC 008 031). Assesses oral language, pattern matching, pattern memory, visuo-motor organization, receptive language and ability to work alone, persist, and think independently. Instructions for administration and scoring can be found in Preventing Reading Failure by Jansky and Hirsch and published by Harper and Row.

13718
EMI Assessment Scale. University of Virginia School of Medicine, Dept. of Pediatrics, Charlottesville
Subtests: Gross Motor Skills; Fine Motor Skills; Socialization; Cognition; Language
Descriptors: Behavioral Objectives; *Child Development; Cognitive Development; Developmental Stages; *Infants; Intervention; Language Acquisition; Measures (Individuals); *Multiple Disabilities; *Psychomotor Skills; Socialization
Identifiers: Developmental Age
Availability: University of Virginia School of Medicine; Dept. of Pediatrics, Education for Multihandicapped Infants, P.O. Box 232, Medical Center, Charlottesville, VA 22901
Target Audience: 0-2
Notes: Time, 45 approx.; Items, 360
Designed to provide information about levels of functioning in multihandicapped infants to assist in planning intervention activities. Can be used as a checklist of instructional objectives or to obtain a score to compare individuals or assess growth over time. This scale was developed by sequencing items from other, standardized, scales. The EMI is not standardized. It is untimed. Each skill is evaluated with 15 items. A method of ordinal scoring is used to arrive at a developmental age. A series of common items, such as ball and crayons, are required for administration.

13725
An Adaptation of the Wechsler Preschool and Primary Scale of Intelligence for Deaf Children. Ray, Steven; Ulissi, Stephen Mark 1982
Subtests: Animal House; Picture Completion; Mazes; Geometric Design; Block Design
Descriptors: *Deafness; *Hearing Impairments; *Intelligence Tests; *Preschool Children; *Young Children
Identifiers: WPPSI
Availability: Steven Ray Publishing; P.O. Box 751, Sulphur, OK 73086
Target Audience: 4-7
This test was adapted from the Wechsler Preschool and Primary Scale of Intelligence (WPPSI) for use with hearing impaired children in the lower age ranges. It is designed to supplement the regular WPPSI manual and to facilitate the testing of hearing impaired children. No attempt has

been made to change the test items or their scoring procedure. The instructions have been adapted to meet the necessity posed by communication methods other than spoken English.

13726
An Adaptation of the Wechsler Intelligence Scales for Children-Revised-for the Deaf. Ray, Steven 1979
Subtests: Picture Completion; Picture Arrangement; Block Design; Object Assembly; Coding
Descriptors: *Adolescents; *Children; *Deafness; Elementary School Students; *Hearing Impairments; *Intelligence Tests
Identifiers: WISC
Availability: Steven Ray Publishing; P.O. Box 751, Sulphur, OK 73086
Target Audience: 6-17
This test is an adaptation of the "Wechsler Intelligence Scales for Children—Revised" for deaf persons. The psychologist administering this test does not have to be a skilled signer, but the test can be administered by one having limited ability to communicate with deaf children. It was developed so that children possessing only minimal standard language could receive an appropriate assessment. The instrument contains alternate and supplemental materials designed to minimize the adverse effects of handicapping conditions within the testing situation.

13737
Detroit Tests of Learning Aptitude, DTLA-2. Hammill, Donald D. 1985
Subtests: Word Opposites; Sentence Imitation; Oral Directions; Word Sequences; Story Construction; Design Reproduction; Object Sequences; Symbolic Relations; Conceptual Matching; Word Fragments; Letter Sequences
Descriptors: *Academic Aptitude; *Adolescents; *Aptitude Tests; *Children; *Cognitive Ability; Diagnostic Tests; Individual Testing; Intelligence; Learning Disabilities; Long Term Memory; Nonverbal Ability; Psychomotor Skills; Short Term Memory; Verbal Ability
Identifiers: DTLA2; Test Batteries
Availability: Pro-Ed; 5341 Industrial Oaks Blvd., Austin, TX 78735
Target Audience: 6-17
A revision and restandardization of a test battery to assess specific abilities. Used to isolate individual strengths and weaknesses and to identify students deficient in general or specific aptitudes. Useful for diagnosing learning disabilities. Subtests should be administered in same order they were used when tests were standardized. Time required to administer entire battery varies from 50 minutes to 2 hours. Subtests are also used to formulate nine composite scores in 4 domains: linguistic, attention, cognitive, and motor. DTLA-2 has 3 main uses: determine strengths and weaknesses among intellectual abilities, identify children and adolescents significantly below their peers in aptitude, and use in research studies investigating aptitude, intelligence, and cognitive behavior. There are also 3 special use composites for testing blind, deaf, or physically impaired persons.

13739
The Preverbal Assessment-Intervention Profile. Connard, Patricia 1984
Descriptors: Adolescents; Adults; Children; *Communication Skills; Developmental Stages; *Diagnostic Tests; *Individual Testing; *Multiple Disabilities; *Nonverbal Ability; Observation; Perceptual Handicaps; *Perceptual Motor Learning; Physical Disabilities; *Severe Disabilities; Severe Mental Retardation
Identifiers: PAIP; Piagetian Tasks; *Preverbal Communication; Public Law 94 142
Availability: ASIEP Education Co.; 3216 N.E. 27th, Portland, OR 97212
Target Audience: 2-65
Developed as an individualized assessment for severely and multihandicapped preintentional learners. The sensori-motor domains of auditory, visual, vocal/oral, and motor are evaluated and yield an individualized preverbal/ motor assessment profile. Test incorporates Piagetian sensori-motor framework, stages I-III. Test is used to evaluate prelinguistic behavior of subjects on whom the profile was standardized: severely mentally, physically, and sensory handicapped persons.

13758
Haptic Memory Matching Test. McCarron, Lawrence; Dial, Jack G. 1976
Descriptors: Adults; Blindness; Kinesthetic Perception; Mental Retardation; Nonverbal Tests; Perception Tests; Recognition (Psychology); *Sensory Integration; *Short Term Memory; *Tactile Adaptation; *Visual Impairments; *Visualization
Identifiers: HMMT
Availability: McCarron-Dial Systems; Common Market Press, P.O. Box 45628, Dallas, TX 75245

Target Audience: 18-64
Notes: Items, 48
The Haptic Memory Matching Test (HMMT) was designed to assess a person's capacity to function and accommodate to the loss of vision; to assess the tactile-matching skills, short term haptic memory and spatial localization skills. Subjects are asked to manipulate objects which vary in shape, size, texture, and spatial configuration. After they have had an opportunity to feel all of the objects in a set, they will be presented another object which matches one of those they felt. Their task is to return to the previous set and find an identical object. Subjects are instructed to give their best performance since the information is important for determining the rehabilitation program and training strategies. This test has been used with nonhandicapped subjects as well as mentally retarded adults with visual impairments.

13759
The Perceptual Memory Task. McCarron, Lawrence 1984
Subtests: Memory for Spatial Relations; Visual Recognition and Sequential Memory; Auditory Recognition and Sequential Memory; Intermediate Term Memory and Visual Discrimination
Descriptors: Adolescents; Adults; Children; *Cognitive Processes; *Learning Modalities; *Memory; Perception Tests; Recall (Psychology); Serial Ordering; *Short Term Memory; *Spatial Ability; *Visual Discrimination
Identifiers: PMT; *Sequential Memory
Availability: McCarron-Dial Systems; Common Market Press, P.O. Box 45628, Dallas, TX 75245
Target Audience: 4-64
The Perceptual Memory Task (PMT), an assessment of individual learning style, was designed to provide measures of the individual's perception and memory for spatial relationships; visual and auditory sequential memory; intermediate term memory; and discrimination of detail. The components of the PMT include: 1) memory for spatial relations, 2) visual recognition and sequential memory, 3) auditory recognition and sequential memory, 4) intermediate term memory and visual discrimination. Supplementary procedures are available for testing hearing and visually impaired persons.

13769
Educational Administrator Effectiveness Profile. Human Synergistics, Plymouth, MI 1984
Subtests: Setting Goals and Objectives; Planning; Making Decisions and Solving Problems; Managing Business and Fiscal Affairs; Assessing Progress; Delegating Responsibilities; Communicating; Building and Maintaining Relationships; Demonstrating Professional Commitment; Improving Instruction; Developing Staff
Descriptors: *Administrator Evaluation; *Administrator Responsibility; Administrator Role; *Administrators; Decision Making Skills; *Formative Evaluation; Interpersonal Communication; *Management Development; Planning; Problem Solving; *Professional Development; Rating Scales; *School Administration; *Self Evaluation (Individuals)
Identifiers: Danforth Foundation; EAEP
Availability: Human Synergistics; 39819 Plymouth Rd., Plymouth, MI 48170
Target Audience: 18-64
Notes: Time, 30 approx.; Items, 120
The Educational Administrator Effectiveness Profile (EAEP) is a self-diagnostic instrument designed to assist elementary, secondary, and central office public school administrators in assessing 11 key skill/behavior areas which are essential to their effectiveness. The 11 areas are: setting goals and objectives, planning, making decisions and solving problems, managing business and fiscal affairs, assessing progress, delegating responsibilities, communicating, building and maintaining relationships, demonstrating professional commitment, improving instruction, and developing staff. In addition to the questionnaire for the administrator, there are 5 instruments which assess the same skill/behavior areas to be completed by individuals chosen by the administrator who know his/her administrative role. Based on the feedback, a self-improvement program can be designed to strengthen weak areas. A 7-point rating scale is used, ranging from almost never to always. The development of this instrument was sponsored by the Danforth Foundation.

13770
Management Effectiveness Profile System. Human Synergistics, Plymouth, MI 1983
Subtests: Setting Goals and Objectives; Identifying and Solving Problems; Planning Effectively; Organizing; Making Decision; Delegating; Building Teams; Evaluating Performance; Developing Subordinates; Managing Conflict; Using Time Effectively; Handling and Preventing Stress; Demonstrating Commitment; Increasing Trust; Being Results Oriented

Descriptors: *Administrator Evaluation; Administrators; Adults; Business Administration; Conflict Resolution; Decision Making Skills; *Formative Evaluation; *Interpersonal Communication; Problem Solving; Profiles; Questionnaires; Rating Scales; *Self Evaluation (Individuals); Stress Management
Identifiers: Leadership Effectiveness; MEPS
Availability: Human Synergistics; 39819 Plymouth Rd., Plymouth, MI 48170
Target Audience: 18-64
Notes: Items, 95

The Management Effectiveness Profile System (MEPS) is part of a multi-level diagnostic system. The purpose of the battery of instruments is to provide accurate, detailed information about healthy human behavior and to identify possible problem areas. This instrument focuses on managerial behavior and measures 15 management skill areas as reported by the subject and by 4 or 5 people who work with him/her. The self-description portion is done by the manager. There are 95 items; each has 2 different descriptions of how the manager might behave in different situations. The subject chooses on a 7 point scale which is the better answer, from react almost exactly like A to react almost exactly like B. Two sets of scores are produced. The first will be from the items the person filled out about him/herself and the second will be the average scores of the questionnaires other people were asked to fill out by the manager. There must be at least 3 other questionnaires filled out to protect the anonymity of those who did respond.

13799
Language Arts Test of Cognitive Functioning. Brazee, Edward N. 1981
Subtests: Interest and Investigation Style; Reasons for Events; Relationships; Use of a Model as a Theory; Type of Categorization; Depth of Interpretation
Descriptors: *Cognitive Development; Cognitive Processes; Cognitive Tests; Elementary School Students; Elementary Secondary Education; *Language Arts; Secondary School Students; *Self Expression
Identifiers: Cognitive Evaluation; LATCF; Sequencing Continguity
Availability: Edward N. Brazee; 14 Park St., Orono, ME 04473
Grade Level: K-12

This test was developed to determine if such a measure could give specific information about the thinking required for language arts tasks. It consists of 6 anecdotes or tasks which the student must solve/complete. The 6 functions are: interest and investigation style, reasons for events, relationships, use of a model as a theory, type of categorization, and depth of interpretation (of descriptive passages). The anecdotes require students to perform a variety of problem solving activities. A profile for each student was completed after taking the test and was rated as showing evidence of concrete, transitional, or formal level thinking. An alternate source for the test is the Journal of Early Adolescence; v1 n4 p373-84, 1981.

13802
Wolfe Staff Selector Test Kits. Wolfe Personnel Testing Systems, Oradell, NJ 1977
Descriptors: Adults; Cognitive Ability; French; Interpersonal Competence; *Occupational Tests; *Personnel Selection
Identifiers: Test Batteries
Availability: Wolfe Personnel Testing Systems; P.O. Box 319, Oradell, NJ 07649
Target Audience: Adults

Custom-selected test kits to be administered to job candidates to evaluate intellectual abilities and interpersonal skills of candidates for a wider range of positions, including sales representatives, administrators or managers, clerical personnel, procedures and business systems analysts, bookkeepers or accountants, secretaries or word processing personnel, and other positions where client provides a job description. Test kits are available in one of the following formats: comprehensive, screening, or priority response. Available in English or French. Tests are administered in client's office.

13803
Learning Ability Profile. Wolfe Personnel Testing Systems, Oradell, NJ 1975
Descriptors: Adults; Culture Fair Tests; French; *Intelligence; *Intelligence Tests; *Personnel Selection; Spanish
Identifiers: LAP
Availability: Wolfe Personnel Testing Systems; P.O. Box 319, Oradell, NJ 07649
Target Audience: Adults
Notes: Time, 90 approx.

Intelligence test that measures a person's capacity to learn. Measures the following attributes: overall ability to learn, inductive and deductive reasoning, decisiveness, adaptability to new life and learning situations, and level of frustration. Has been designed to be culture fair. Test is administered in client's office. Available in English, French, and Spanish.

13805
Micro W-Apt Programming Aptitude Test. Wolfe Personnel Testing Systems, Oradell, NJ 1984
Descriptors: Adults; *Aptitude Tests; Microcomputers; *Occupational Tests; *Personnel Selection; *Programing; *Vocational Aptitude
Availability: Wolfe Personnel Testing Systems; P.O. Box 319, Oradell, NJ 07649
Target Audience: Adults
Notes: Items, 5

Consists of 5 questions on a microcomputer diskette which candidate works on and solves interactively on a microcomputer. Currently, test can be administered on an IBM-PC or compatibles.

13806
Data Entry Operator Aptitude Test. Wolfe Personnel Testing Systems, Oradell, NJ 1982
Descriptors: Adults; Aptitude Tests; French; Input Output Devices; *Occupational Tests; *Personnel Selection; *Vocational Aptitude
Identifiers: *Data Entry; DEOAT
Availability: Wolfe Personnel Testing Systems; P.O. Box 319, Oradell, NJ 07649
Target Audience: Adults
Notes: Time, 20

An aptitude test used to evaluate job candidate's aptitude as a data entry operator. Is designed to evaluate coding ability, numerical facility, manual dexterity, and clerical accuracy, detail, and editing. Test may be used for following purposes: to hire experienced data entry operators, to determine expertise of existing staff, to determine training needs, to determine training effectiveness, to identify error-prone candidates, and to do a skills inventory analysis. Test is suitable to assess candidates for data entry operator or terminal operator. Available in English and French.

13812
Sequenced Inventory of Communication Development, Revised Edition. Hedrick, Dona Lea; And Others 1984
Subtests: Receptive Scale; Expressive Scale
Descriptors: Autism; *Communication Skills; Diagnostic Tests; Eskimos; *Expressive Language; *Language Acquisition; *Language Handicaps; Language Patterns; Language Processing; Measures (Individuals); Mental Retardation; Nonverbal Communication; Profiles; *Receptive Language; Remedial Programs; Spanish Speaking; Speech Habits; Syntax; *Young Children
Identifiers: SICD(R)
Availability: Slosson Educational Publications; P.O. Box 280, East Aurora, NY 14052
Target Audience: 0-4

The Sequenced Inventory of Communication Development-Revised (SICD-R) is to assist clinicians in remedial programing for the deviant child. It can be used to assign communication ages and in screening broad spectrums of behavior for more intensive study or for initial management goals. The test items are the original ones in the SICD, but have been classified according to semantic-cognitive, syntactic, and pragmatic aspects of communication. The test may be given by one person, but it is easier if there is another to act as a recorder. The Receptive Scale is usually administered first, followed by the Expressive Scale. The complete test is never given to a child, but testing begins where consistent success is anticipated. The testing continues until a ceiling is reached, this is when 3 consecutive items are failed. Behaviors included in the Receptive Scale are: awareness, discrimination, understanding. The behaviors included in the Expressive Scale are: motor response, vocal response, verbal response, imitating behaviors, initiating behaviors, and responding behaviors. The SICD has been modified and standardized for special populations: Yup'ik Eskimo, Autistic and other difficult-to-test children, hearing impaired children. There is a Spanish translation of the instrument also. Useful from 4 months to age 4.

13814
Performance Management Simulation. Hersey, Paul; Natemeyer, Walter E. 1983
Descriptors: Adults; *Conflict Resolution; *Decision Making; Group Dynamics; *Management Games; *Problem Solving; *Simulation
Availability: University Associates; 8517 Production Ave., P.O. Box 26240, San Diego, CA 92126
Target Audience: 18-64

The Performance Management Simulation is an individual/group decision-making exercise. Individuals are given a management problem, a brief biographical sketch of the employees involved and are to do the first part of the exercise; the second part is done in a group decision-making process. Guidelines are given for the group to use in the decision-making process.

13825
SOI Abilities Test: Dental Assistant Test. Meeker, Mary; Meeker, Robert 1975
Descriptors: Adults; *Aptitude Tests; *Dental Assistants; *Personnel Selection
Availability: SOI Systems; P.O Box D, Vida, OR 97488
Target Audience: Adults

Developed in conjunction with practicing dental groups to help screen for dental assistants. Test is self-administering. Includes scores for attention to details, classification skills, perception of objects in space, perception of spatial perspective, following directions, detail judgments, dexterity, and logic and reasoning.

13830
Receptive One-Word Picture Vocabulary Test. Gardner, Morrison F. 1985
Descriptors: *Basic Vocabulary; Bilingual Students; Children; *Cognitive Development; Elementary School Students; Emotional Disturbances; *Individual Testing; *Norm Referenced Tests; Physical Disabilities; Pictorial Stimuli; Preschool Children; *Receptive Language; *Screening Tests; Spanish; Spanish Speaking; Speech Handicaps; Visual Measures
Identifiers: Oral Tests; ROWPVT
Availability: Academic Therapy Publications; 20 Commercial Blvd., Novato, CA 94947-6191
Target Audience: 2-11
Notes: Time, 20 approx.

Individually administered, norm-referenced, untimed test developed to obtain an estimate of a child's one-word hearing vocabulary based on what child has learned from home and formal education. When used alone, provides a means for evaluating receptive vocabulary of those with expressive difficulties, such as bilingual, speech-impaired, immature and withdrawn, and emotionally or physically impaired children. Norms for the Receptive One-Word Picture Vocabulary Test and the Expressive One-Word Picture Vocabulary Test are equivalent. When both tests are used, comparison of results provides information about differences in these language skills that could be due to specific language impairment, language delay, bilingualism, nonstimulating home environment, cultural differences, learning difficulties or other factors to be investigated. Spanish Forms are also available to obtain an estimate of a child's Spanish vocabulary.

13833
Miller-Yoder Language Comprehension Test, Clinical Edition. Miller, Jon F.; Yoder, David E. 1984
Descriptors: Cognitive Processes; *Developmental Disabilities; *Educational Diagnosis; *Language Handicaps; *Language Processing; Language Tests; *Mental Retardation; Standard Spoken Usage; *Visual Measures; *Young Children
Identifiers: *Language Comprehension; MY
Availability: Slosson Educational Publications; P.O. Box 280, East Aurora, NY 14052
Target Audience: 4-8
Notes: Time, 30 approx.; Items, 42

The Miller-Yoder Language Comprehension Test (MY) (Clinical Edition) is a measure of mainstream American-English language comprehension and was designed as a clinical research tool for exploring the grammatical comprehension abilities of mentally retarded persons. The test can also be used with children who are not diagnosed as mentally retarded, but who are suspected to be delayed in their understanding of language. The 84 sentences, forming 42 sentence pairs, represent 10 basic grammatical forms: active, preposition, possessive, negative/affirmative, pronoun, singular/plural, verb inflection, modification, passive, reflexivization. Each sentence is represented by a line drawing. There are 42 different test plates with 4 pictures on each plate. Two of the pictures represent stimulus sentences and 2 are distractors. The distractor pictures represent sentences of the same grammatical form as the experimental sentences but vary in either subject, verb, or object vocabulary from the stimulus sentences. The stimulus sentence is read to the child and the child points to 1 of the 4 pictures as the answer. The time for administration varies, dependent on how much of the test the examiner chooses to present.

13836
Ball Aptitude Battery. Ball Foundation, Glen Ellyn, IL 1983
Subtests: Clerical; Idea Fluency; Tonal Memory; Pitch Discrimination; Inductive Reasoning; Word Association; Writing Speed; Paper Folding; Vocabulary; Ideaphoria; Finger Dexterity; Grip; Shape Assembly; Analytical Reasoning
Descriptors: *Ability Identification; Adults; *Aptitude Tests; *Career Counseling; *Career Guidance; *Cognitive Processes; Employment Opportunities; High Schools; High School Students; Induction; Language Acquisition; Motor Development; *Object Manipulation; Performance Tests; Personnel Selection; *Vocational Aptitude; Vocational Evaluation; *Vocational Interests; Writing Skills
Identifiers: BAB; Pitch (Music); Test Batteries
Availability: The Ball Foundation; 800 Roosevelt Rd., Bldg. C, Ste. 206, Glen Ellyn, IL 60137

Target Audience: 16-64
Notes: Time, 180 approx.

The Ball Aptitude Battery (BAB) is a multiple ability test battery designed to measure various aptitudes needed for successful performance in a variety of jobs. The BAB can be used to help determine the most appropriate occupations for an individual as well as the most appropriate individuals for an occupation. It can be used for individual career decision making and vocational guidance. The battery was developed for the senior high school population and for the general adult population. It can also be used in organizational decision making, specifically for personnel selection and placement.

13838
McDermott Multidimensional Assessment of Children. McDermott, Paul A.; Watkins, Marley W. 1985
Descriptors: *Academic Achievement; *Adjustment (to Environment); Children; *Cognitive Ability; *Computer Software; *Diagnostic Tests; *Emotional Adjustment; *Exceptional Persons; *Individualized Education Programs; Microcomputers; *Student Evaluation
Identifiers: MMAC
Availability: The Psychological Corp.; 555 Academic Ct., San Antonio, TX 78204-0952
Target Audience: 3-12

Comprehensive system of over 100 computer programs that integrates data from psychological evaluations, classifies childhood exceptionality, and designs individualized education programs. The system has 2 major levels. The Classification Level provides a diagnosis of exceptionality along 4 dimensions: general intellectual functioning, academic achievement, adaptive behavior, and social-emotional adjustment. The Program Design Level generates behavioral objectives for individualized educational planning based on skills identified by criterion referenced evaluation in reading, mathematics, general learning style, or adaptive skills. The following classifications are generated: exceptional talent, normal intellectual functioning, borderline intellectual functioning, mental retardation, intellectual retardation, educational retardation, and commensurate achievement.

13850
PSI Basic Skills Tests: Problem Solving. Ruch, William W.; And Others 1981
Descriptors: Adults; *Clerical Occupations; Culture Fair Tests; *Mathematical Applications; *Occupational Tests; *Office Occupations; *Personnel Selection; *Problem Solving
Availability: Psychological Services Inc.; 100 W. Broadway, Ste. 1100, Glendale, CA 91210
Target Audience: Adults
Notes: Time, 10

One of a series of 20 practical, brief personnel selection tests. Designed to aid personnel managers in business, industry, and government in the selection and placement of employees. Test content was constructed to be bias-free. Validated against job performance in a nationwide survey. Measures the ability to solve story problems requiring the application of mathematical operations.

13855
PSI Basic Skills Tests: Reasoning. Ruch, William W.; And Others 1981
Descriptors: *Abstract Reasoning; Adults; *Clerical Occupations; Culture Fair Tests; *Occupational Tests; *Office Occupations; *Personnel Selection
Availability: Psychological Services Inc.; 100 W. Broadway, Ste. 1100, Glendale, CA 91210
Target Audience: Adults
Notes: Time, 5

One of a series of 20 practical, brief personnel selection tests. Designed to aid personnel managers in business, industry, and government in the selection and placement of employees. Test content was constructed to be bias-free. Validated against job performance in a nationwide survey. Measures the ability to analyze facts and to make valid judgments on the basis of the logical implications of such facts.

13861
PSI Basic Skills Tests: Memory. Ruch, William W.; And Others 1981
Descriptors: Adults; *Clerical Occupations; Culture Fair Tests; *Occupational Tests; *Office Occupations; *Personnel Selection; *Short Term Memory
Availability: Psychological Services Inc.; 100 W. Broadway, Ste. 1100, Glendale, CA 91210
Target Audience: Adults
Notes: Time, 10

One of a series of 20 practical, brief personnel selection tests. Designed to aid personnel managers in business, industry, and government in the selection and placement of employees. Test content was constructed to be bias-free. Validated against job performance in a nationwide survey. Measures the ability to recall information after having a chance to study it.

13886
SOI Learning Abilities Test: Arithmetic-Math Form. Meeker, Mary; Meeker, Robert 1975
Subtests: Constancy of Objects in Space; Spatial Conservation; Comprehension of Abstract Relations; Comprehension of Numerical Progressions; Math Concepts; Auditory Attending; Auditory Sequencing; Inferential Memory; Judgment of Arithmetic Similarities; Judgment of Correctness of Numerical Facts; Application of Math Facts; Form Reasoning-Logic
Descriptors: *Cognitive Ability; *Cognitive Tests; Elementary School Students; Intermediate Grades; *Mathematical Concepts; Secondary Education; *Secondary School Students
Identifiers: SOI(LA)
Availability: SOI Systems; P.O. Box D, Vida, OR 97488
Grade Level: 5-12
Notes: Time, 60 approx.

Subset of the Structure of Intellect (SOI) Learning Abilities Test, Form A. Uses those subtests that relate to arithmetic, mathematics, and science. Abilities assessed are considered prerequisites to cognitive skills required for school achievement in mathematics. Especially recommended for students in upper elementary grades who are having difficulty with arithmetic or mathematical concepts. The SOI is a series of test forms designed to assess a wide range of cognitive abilities or factors of intelligence and is based on Guilford's multifactor model of intelligence. There are a total of 26 separate abilities assessed by the SOI comprehensive form. The arithmetic-math form assesses 12 of these.

13889
Classroom Test of Formal Reasoning. Lawson, Anton E. 1978
Descriptors: *Abstract Reasoning; *Cognitive Ability; *Cognitive Tests; *College Students; *Developmental Stages; Higher Education; Secondary Education; *Secondary School Students
Identifiers: Piagetian Tasks
Availability: Journal of Research in Science Teaching; v15 n1 p11-24, 1978
Grade Level: 7-16
Notes: Time, 100 approx.; Items, 15

Development of a 15-item test to measure concrete and formal operational reasoning, defined as those reasoning processes that guide the search for and evaluate evidence to support or reject hypothetical causal propositions. Each item involves a demonstration using some physical materials and/or apparatus. Each demonstration was used to pose a question or call for a prediction. Students wrote 3 answers in test booklets. Test is meant primarily for use by teachers interested in assessing developmental levels of their students.

13964
Severely Handicapped Progress Inventory. Dunlap, William C.; And Others 1983
Subtests: Motor Development; Perceptual; Self Care; Cognition and Language; Social; Individual Living
Descriptors: *Achievement Gains; Adolescents; Adults; Children; Communicative Competence (Languages); Daily Living Skills; *Deaf Blind; Individualized Programs; Interpersonal Competence; Motor Development; Perceptual Development; Questionnaires; Self Care Skills; Severe Disabilities
Identifiers: TIM(K)
Availability: Tests in Microfiche; Test Collection, Educational Testing Service, Princeton, NJ 08541
Target Audience: 0-64
Notes: Time, 30 approx.; Items, 199

Specifically developed for use with deaf-blind persons in order to provide assessment necessary for individual program planning and for measuring progress. Organized into 6 major categories with 19 subsections. Major categories are motor development, perceptual skills, self-care skills, cognition and language, social skills, independent living.

14003
Long Performance Efficiency Test. Long, Thomas Rex 1983
Descriptors: Adults; *Cognitive Ability; Individual Testing; Job Applicants; *Job Performance; Job Placement
Identifiers: Oral Tests; PET
Availability: Stoelting Co.; 620 Wheat Ln., Wood Dale, IL 60191
Target Audience: Adults
Notes: Time, 6 approx.

Measures the ability to use intellectual potential for satisfactory performance in any job situation. Will identify those least likely to succeed in a job. Test does not suggest to subjects what is being measured and therefore is not threatening to them. Requires subject to read color names or identify colors on stimulus cards.

14024
Cognitive Observation Guide. Foley, Gilbert M.; Appel, Marilyn H.
Descriptors: *Cognitive Development; *Criterion Referenced Tests; *Infants; Observation
Identifiers: COG; Piaget (Jean)
Availability: Gilbert M. Foley; Albright College, 13th and Exeter Sts., Reading, PA 19603
Target Audience: 0-2

An informal, criterion-referenced observation guide for assessing cognition. Composed of 24 subskills with behavioral indicators for each, arranged by age level. Indicates child's progress toward developing cognitive skills. Uses Piaget's concepts.

14045
The Body Image of Blind Children. Cratty, Bryant J.; Sams, Theressa A. 1968
Descriptors: Adolescents; *Blindness; *Body Image; Children; Concept Formation; Individual Testing
Identifiers: Lateral Awareness
Availability: The American Foundation for the Blind; 15 W. 16th St., New York, NY 10011
Target Audience: 5-16
Notes: Items, 80

Designed to measure the concept of body image in blind children. The child responds to simple commands concerned with the identification of body planes, body parts, body movements, laterality, and directionality. Data are available from a norming administration to a group of 90 blind children in a school for the blind.

14057
Schubert General Ability Battery, Revised. Schubert, Herman J.P.; Schubert, Daniel S.P. 1979
Subtests: Word Meaning (Vocabulary); Relations (Verbal Analogies); Arithmetic Problems; Logical Answers (Syllogisms)
Descriptors: *Abstract Reasoning; *Adults; *Arithmetic; Clerical Workers; *Cognitive Ability; *Cognitive Tests; *College Students; Females; Graduate Students; Higher Education; High Schools; *High School Students; Males; Occupational Tests; Sales Workers; Skilled Occupations; Supervisors; *Verbal Ability; Vocabulary
Identifiers: GAB; Test Batteries
Availability: Slosson Educational Publications; P.O. Box 280, East Aurora, NY 14052
Grade Level: 9-16
Target Audience: Adults
Notes: Items, 115

A measure of mental ability designed for use in industry with applicants for technical, supervisory, and highly skilled jobs, and also with high school, college, and graduate students. Norms are available for adult males, high school senior boys and girls, college entrants, graduate students in education, factory workers, foremen, industrial executives, retail store managers, wholesale salesmen, and office clerks. Can be used as a selector, placement, and counseling tool in school, talent-search agencies, and industry. The battery assesses verbal, arithmetic, and syllogistic measures of reasoning ability.

14077
Non-Language Learning Test. Bauman, Mary K. 1947
Descriptors: Adults; Aptitude Tests; *Blindness; Clinical Diagnosis; *Learning; Nonverbal Tests; Performance Tests; *Predictive Measurement; Tactual Perception
Availability: Associated Services for the Blind; 919 Walnut St., Philadelphia, PA 19107
Target Audience: Adults
Notes: Time, 5

A formboard said to be useful for observing learning in blind adults in a standard way, rather than a test in the usual sense. It is for clinical use by experienced administrators to supplement a verbal I.Q. Said to be useful in predicting success on jobs involving concrete materials, though no statistical data are given. Abilities observed are: learning with insight, superficial memorization, dealing with complexity, discrimination by touch. Plans for construction of the board by the user are included.

14078
Self-Control Schedule. Rosenbaum, Michael 1980
Descriptors: Adults; Behavior Problems; Emotional Response; Problem Solving; Responses; *Self Control; Self Evaluation (Individuals)
Identifiers: SCS
Availability: Behavior Therapy; v11 p109-21, 1980
Target Audience: Adults
Notes: Items, 36

A self-report designed to assess tendencies to apply self-control techniques in situations where one's behavior could be a problem. The scale items describe use of cognitions and self statements to control emotional and physiological responses, the application of problem-solving strategies, the ability to delay immediate gratification, and perceived self-efficacy.

14081
SOI Learning Abilities Test-Reasoning Readiness. Meeker, Mary; Meeker, Robert 1975
Descriptors: *Abstract Reasoning; Early Childhood Education; Gifted; Individual Testing; Primary Education; *School Readiness Tests
Identifiers: Reasoning Tests
Availability: SOI Systems; P.O. Box D, Vida, OR 97488
Grade Level: K-1

A selection of subtests from the full battery SOI Learning Abilities Test. Some are individually administered. Measures cognition of figural units, cognition of figural relationships, vocabulary, problem solving, visual and auditory memory, identification of identical forms, classification of objects, divergent production.

14082
Color Span Test. Richman, Lynn C. 1978
Subtests: Visual Presentation-Visual Response; Visual Presentation-Verbal Response; Verbal Presentation-Visual Response; Verbal Presentation-Verbal Response
Descriptors: Children; Color; *Hearing Impairments; *Language Handicaps; *Learning Disabilities; *Memory; Verbal Tests
Identifiers: *Sequential Memory; Verbal Memory
Availability: Lynn C. Richman; Dept. of Pediatrics, 2523 JCP, University of Iowa Hospitals, Iowa City, IA
Target Audience: 8-12

Measures a child's verbal memory by requiring the child to remember color names in sequences of increasing length, to minimize the effects of other factors aiding memory. Designed for use with clinical populations such as learning disabled, language disordered, and hearing impaired children.

14133
Mobile Vocational Evaluation. Hester, Edward J.
Subtests: Finger Dexterity; Wrist-Finger Speed; Arm-Hand Steadiness; Manual Dexterity; 2-Arm Coordination; 2-Hand Coordination; Perceptual Accuracy; Spatial Perception; Aiming; Reaction Time; Abstract Reasoning; Verbal Reasoning; Numerical Reasoning; Reading; Arithmetic; Leadership Consideration; Leadership Structure; Sales; Following Directions
Descriptors: *Abstract Reasoning; *Adults; *Aptitude Tests; Arithmetic; Clinics; *College Students; *Disabilities; Eye Hand Coordination; Group Testing; Higher Education; High Schools; *High School Students; Individual Testing; Leadership; Reaction Time; Reading; Rehabilitation Centers; Salesmanship; *Spatial Ability; *Vocational Evaluation
Identifiers: Finger Dexterity; Following Directions; *Manual Dexterity
Availability: Hester Evaluation Systems; 2709 W. 29 St., Topeka, KS 66614
Grade Level: 9-16
Target Audience: Adults
Notes: Time, 240

A measure of vocationally related abilities. Given in a series of group and brief individual tests. The test is portable, weighing less than 30 lbs. All electronic parts are battery powered and it may be administered by nonprofessional staff. The ability factor scores are combined with 17 personal characteristics to identify specific jobs out of a database of 700. For use by colleges, high schools, technical schools, rehabilitation agencies, hospitals and clinics.

14154
SOI Learning Abilities Test: A Screening Form for Atypical Gifted. Meeker, Mary; Meeker, Robert 1975
Subtests: Convergent Production; Evaluation of Figural Classes; Evaluation of Symbolic Classes; Cognition of Symbolic Relations; Memory of Symbolic Units-Auditory; Memory of Symbolic Systems-Auditory; Cognition of Figural Systems; Cognition of Figural Transformations; Convergent Production of Symbolic Transformation; Convergent Production of Symbolic Implications
Descriptors: Abstract Reasoning; *Academic Ability; Adults; *Aptitude Tests; Attention; Convergent Thinking; Decision Making; Elementary Secondary Education; *Gifted Disadvantaged; Language Handicaps; Listening; Memory; Psychomotor Skills; Spatial Ability; Word Recognition
Identifiers: Convergent Production; Guilfords Structure of Intellect; Sequencing Skills; Symbols
Availability: SOI Systems; P.O. Box D, Vida, OR 97488
Grade Level: K-12
Target Audience: Adults
Notes: Time, 60

A version of the SOI Learning Abilities Test (TC 009 264) for use in identifying gifted low-socioeconomic students and those who may be nonlanguage proficient but gifted. The SOI series is based on Guilford's multifactor model of intelligence. Instead of giving a single I.Q., the SOI series of tests provides a profile of learning abilities. Form AG covers psychomotor readiness, judging similarities, understanding abstract relations, auditory attending and sequencing, spatial perceptions, word recognition, reasoning with forms.

14155
SOI Learning Abilities Test: Precursor Abilities for Reading/Language Arts/Social Studies. Meeker, Mary; Meeker, Robert 1975
Subtests: Cognition of Figural Units; Cognition of Figural Classes; Evaluation of Figural Units; Evaluation of Figural Classes; Memory of Symbolic Units-Visual; Memory of Symbolic Systems-Visual; Cognition of Semantic Relations; Cognition of Semantic Systems; Convergent Production of Symbolic Transformations; Cognition of Semantic Units
Descriptors: *Academic Ability; *Aptitude Tests; Attention; Convergent Thinking; Decision Making; Diagnostic Tests; *Elementary School Students; Elementary Secondary Education; Language Arts; Memory; *Reading; *Secondary School Students; Social Studies; Visual Discrimination; Visual Perception; Vocabulary; Word Recognition
Identifiers: Closure; Guilfords Structure of Intellect; Sequencing Skills; Symbols
Availability: SOI Systems; P.O. Box D, Vida, OR 97488
Grade Level: K-12
Notes: Time, 60

A version of the SOI Learning Abilities Test (TC009264) for use in measuring the abilities necessary for functioning in subject matter areas requiring reading. The SOI series is based on Guilford's multifactor model of intelligence. Instead of giving a single IQ, the SOI series provides a profile of the learner's abilities. This test covers visual closure, visual conceptualization, visual discrimination, judging similarities and matching concepts, visual attending and concentration for sequencing, comprehension of verbal relations, and extended verbal information, speed of word recognition, vocabulary.

14157
SOI Learning Abilities Test: Developmental Vision Form. Meeker, Mary; Meeker, Robert 1975
Subtests: Cognition of Figural Units; Cognition of Semantic Units; Memory of Symbolic Systems-Visual; Memory of Symbolic Units-Visual; Convergent Production of Figural Units; Divergent Production of Semantic Units; Evaluation of Figural Units; Convergent Production of Symbolic Transformations; Cognition of Figural Transformations
Descriptors: *Academic Ability; Aptitude Tests; Cognitive Ability; Convergent Thinking; Creative Writing; Creativity; Decision Making; Diagnostic Tests; Divergent Thinking; *Elementary School Students; Elementary Secondary Education; *Learning Disabilities; Memory; Psychomotor Skills; School Readiness; *Screening Tests; *Secondary School Students; Spatial Ability; *Vision; Visual Discrimination; Vocabulary; Word Recognition
Identifiers: Closure; Guilfords Structure of Intellect
Availability: SOI Systems; P.O. Box D, Vida, OR 97488
Grade Level: K-12

A use of the SOI Learning Abilities Test (TC009264) subtests that will screen for vision problems which affect learning. This test is for use by teachers, nurses and health personnel. It covers: visual closure, vocabulary, visual attending, visual concentraion for sequencing, psychomotor readiness, creativity with words and ideas, visual discrimination, speed of word recognition, spatial conservation. A checklist of behaviors that accompany severe subtle vision problems is included.

14158
SOI Abilities Assessment; Career and Vocations Forms. Meeker, Mary; Meeker, Robert 1975
Subtests: Divergent Production of Figural Units; Divergent Production of Semantic Units; Cognition of Figural Units; Cognition of Semantic Units; Cognition of Figural Systems; Cognition of Figural Systems; Cognition of Figural Transformations; Cognition of Semantic Relations; Cognition of Semantic Systems; Divergent Production of Semantic Relations; Cognition of Symbolic Relations; Memory of Symbolic Units-Auditory; Memory of Symbolic Systems-Auditory; Convergent Production of Figural Units; Cognition of Figural Classes; Evaluation of Figural Classes; Evaluation of Symbolic Classes; Cognition of Symbolic Systems; Evaluation of Symbolic Systems; Convergent Production of Symbolic Systems; Convergent Production of Symbolic Transformations; Convergent Production of Symbolic Implications; Memory of Figural Units
Descriptors: Abstract Reasoning; Adults; Aptitude Tests; Attention; Career Choice; *Career Counseling; College Students; Convergent Thinking; Creative Thinking; Creativity; Decision Making; Divergent Thinking; Elementary School Students; Higher Education; Intermediate Grades; Listening; Mathematics; Memory; Psychomotor Skills; Reading Comprehension; Secondary Education; Secondary School Students; Self Evaluation (Individuals); Spatial Ability; Visual Perception; Vocabulary; Vocational Aptitude; Word Recognition
Identifiers: Closure; Guilfords Structure of Intellect; Sequencing Skills; Symbols
Availability: SOI Systems; P.O. Box D, Vida, OR 97488
Grade Level: 4-17
Target Audience: Adults
Notes: Time, 105; Items, 350

A use of the subtests of the SOI Learning Abilities Test (TC009264) for career guidance and vocational decision-making. The aptitude tests are scored via computer and a list of 12 suitable occupations or professions is generated based on the scores. The SOI series was developed from Guilford's multifactor model of intelligence. This test may be purchased by individuals for self-testing. A cassette is available to administer it. Covers: creativity with objects and figures, creativity with words and ideas, vocabulary, constancy of objects in space, spatial conservation, comprehension of verbal relations, comprehension of extended verbal information, creativity with math, abstract relations, auditory attending, auditory sequencing, psychomotor readiness, visual conceptualization, judging similarities and matching concepts, arithmetic similarities, comprehension of numerical progressions, judgment of correctness of numerical facts, application of math facts, speed of word recognition, form reasoning and logic, visual memory for details, and memory of associations.

14159
SOI Abilities Test: Career and Vocations Form, Dental Receptionist. Meeker, Mary; Meeker, Robert 1975
Descriptors: Adults; *Aptitude Tests; *Clerical Workers; *Dentistry; *Personnel Selection
Identifiers: *Dental Receptionists
Availability: SOI Systems; P.O. Box D, Vida, OR 97488
Target Audience: Adults

Developed in conjunction with practicing dental groups to help screen for dental receptionists. Test is self administering. Includes scores for attention to details, vocabulary, verbal reasoning, following directions, management of details, management of numerical information, dexterity, and logic and reasoning.

14160
SOI Learning Abilities Test: Spanish Edition. Meeker, Mary; Meeker, Robert 1975
Subtests: Visual Closure; Visual Conceptualization; Visual Discrimination; Judging Similarities and Matching of Concepts; Visual Attending; Visual Concentration for Sequencing; Vocabulary of Math and Verbal Concepts; Comprehension of Verbal Relations; Ability to Comprehend Extended Verbal Information; Visual Memory for Details; Speed of Word Recognition; Constancy of Objects in Space; Spatial Conservation; Comprehension of Abstract Relations; Comprehension of Numerical Progressions; Auditory Sequencing; Inferential Memory; Judgment of Arithmetic Similarities; Judgment of Correctness of Numerical Facts; Application of Math Facts; Form Reasoning; Creativity with Things; Creativity with Math Facts; Creativity with Words and Ideas
Descriptors: *Academic Ability; Adults; *Cognitive Ability; *Cognitive Tests; Convergent Thinking; Creativity; Decision Making; Diagnostic Tests; Divergent Thinking; Elementary School Students; Elementary Secondary Education; Mathematics; Memory; Psychomotor Skills; Reading; Screening Tests; Secondary School Students; *Spanish; Spanish Speaking; Spatial Ability; Verbal Ability; Visual Discrimination; Vocabulary; Word Recognition
Identifiers: Guilfords Structure of Intellect Closure; SOI LA
Availability: SOI Systems; P.O. Box D, Vida, OR 97488
Grade Level: 2-12
Target Audience: Adults
Notes: Time, 180

This test is a Spanish translation of the SOI Learning Abilities Test (TC009264) based on Guilford's multifactor model of intelligence. Twenty-six subtests assess cognitive abilities or factors of intelligence in children and adults to provide a profile of separate learning abilities. Other forms of the SOI-LA, consisting of combinations of these 26 subtests, focus on abilities in specific learning areas such as reading and math, or screening for the gifted and vocational aptitude. All may be group or individually administered. The subtests concern mental processes (cognition memory, evaluation, convergent production, divergent production) combined with a content area (figural, symbolic, semantic or behavioral) and a product (units, classes, relations, systems, transformations, implications), e.g., Cognition of Figural Units which measures visual closure. All SOI materials are available to anyone interested in their use.

14161
SOI Learning Abilities Test: SOI Process and Diagnostic Screening Test, Spanish Edition. Meeker, Mary; Meeker, Robert 1975
Subtests: Cognition of Figural Units; Cognition of Figural Classes; Cognition of Semantic Units; Memory of Symbolic Units; Convergent Production of Figural Units; Memory of Figural Units; Cognition of Semantic Relations; Cognition of Semantic Systems; Evaluation of Figural Classes; Convergent Production of Symbolic Transformations; Cognition of Symbolic Systems
Descriptors: Academic Ability; Cognitive Ability; *Cognitive Processes; Cognitive Style; Convergent Thinking; Decision Making; *Diagnostic Tests; Disabilities; Elementary School Students; Gifted; Large Type Materials; Memory; *Primary Education; Psychomotor Skills; Reading; Reading Skills; School Readiness Tests; Screening Tests; *Spanish; *Spanish Speaking; Special Education; Student Placement; Translation; Verbal Ability; Visual Discrimination; Visual Perception; Vocabulary; Word Recognition
Identifiers: Closure; Guilfords Structure of Intellect; SOI; Symbols
Availability: SOI Systems; P.O. Box D, Vida, OR 97488
Grade Level: K-3
Notes: Items, 91
A use of the SOI Learning Abilities Test (TC009264) subtests that will assess students' reading skills and cognitive style. Items are in large print for easy reading by young children. Five subtests measure figural abilities, 3 measure symbolic abilities and 3 measure semantic abilities. This is a translation of a test developed for an English-speaking population.

14170
SOI Abilities Test, Career and Vocations Form: Dental Assistant. Meeker, Mary 1975
Subtests: Cognition of Figural Units; Cognition of Figural Classes; Cognition of Figural Systems; Cognition of Figural Transformations; Cognition of Semantic Systems; Evaluation of Figural Units; Convergent Production of Figural Units; Convergent Production of Symbolic Implications
Descriptors: Abstract Reasoning; Adults; Aptitude Tests; Cognitive Ability; Convergent Thinking; *Dental Assistants; Logic; Psychomotor Skills; Self Evaluation (Individuals); Spatial Ability; Verbal Ability; Visual Discrimination; Visual Perception; *Vocational Aptitude
Identifiers: Closure; Guilfords Structure of Intellect; SOI
Availability: SOI Institute; 343 Richmond St., El Segundo, CA 90245
Target Audience: Adults
Notes: Items, 157
A use of the SOI Learning Abilities Test (TC009264) subtests developed in conjunction with practicing dental groups to help screen for dental assistants. The test is self-administering and covers visual closure; visual conceptualization; constancy of objects in space; spatial conservation; comprehension of extended verbal information; visual discrimination; psychomotor readiness; form reasoning and logic.

14171
SOI Learning Abilities Test: SOI Process and Diagnostic Screening Test. Meeker, Mary; Meeker, Robert 1975
Subtests: Cognition of Figural Units; Cognition of Figural Classes; Cognition of Semantic Units; Memory of Symbolic Units; Convergent Production of Figural Units; Memory of Figural Units; Cognition of Semantic Relations; Cognition of Semantic Systems; Evaluation of Figural Classes; Convergent Production of Symbolic Transformations; Cognition of Symbolic Systems

Descriptors: Academic Ability; Cognitive Ability; *Cognitive Processes; Cognitive Style; Convergent Thinking; Decision Making; *Diagnostic Tests; Disabilities; Gifted; Large Type Materials; Memory; Primary Education; Psychomotor Skills; Reading; *Reading Skills; School Readiness Tests; Screening Tests; Special Education; Student Placement; Translation; Verbal Ability; Visual Discrimination; Visual Perception; Vocabulary; Word Recognition
Identifiers: Closure; Guilfords Structure of Intellect; SOI; Symbols
Availability: SOI Systems; P.O. Box D, Vida, OR 97488
Grade Level: K-3
Notes: Items, 91
A use of the SOI Learning Abilities Test (TC009264) subtests that will assess students' reading skills and cognitive style. Items are in large print for easy reading by young children. Five subtests measure figural abilities, 3 measure symbolic abilities and 3 measure semantic abilities.

14230
Manual for the Assessment of a Deaf-Blind Multiply Handicapped, Child, Third Edition. Rudolph, James M.; And Others 1978
Subtests: Gross Motor Development; Fine Motor Development; Personal-Self Help Skills; Communication; Auditory Development; Cognition; Social Development; Mobility
Descriptors: Adolescents; Auditory Perception; *Child Development; Children; Cognitive Ability; *Deaf Blind; Elementary Secondary Education; Interpersonal Communication; Job Skills; *Multiple Disabilities; Physical Fitness; Psychomotor Skills; Self Care Skills; *Sheltered Workshops; Social Development
Identifiers: Fine Motor Skills; Gross Motor Skills
Availability: Midwest Regional Center for Services to Deaf-Blind Children; P.O. Box 30008, Lansing, MI 48909
Target Audience: 6-18
Notes: Items, 1000
A collection of scales for use in measuring a deaf-blind student's development and progress. They are said to possess more accuracy for this population than do scales designed for students without sensory impairments. May be used by parents, houseparents, teacher aides, and other staff. A training guide is included. Used to measure skills necessary for entrance into the protected work environment.

14239
Johnson O'Connor Research Foundation Number Checking Work Sample. Johnson O'Connor Research Foundation, Chicago, IL 1980
Descriptors: Adolescents; Adults; *Aptitude Tests; Children; Clerical Occupations; *Numbers
Identifiers: Clerical Checking; Graphoria; *Number Checking
Availability: Johnson O'Connor Research Foundation; Human Engineering Lab. 161 E. Erie St., Chicago, IL 60611
Target Audience: 12-65
Notes: Time, 6
A measure of the ability to read numbers quickly and accurately. This aptitude is called graphoria. It is useful in a wide variety of clerical and nonclerical occupations such as computer programing, banking and accounting and in coursework in algebra, chemistry and economics. It is part of a large battery of tests administered at various locations nationwide, designed to assist in choosing a career or college major.

14296
Adolescent and Adult Psychoeducational Profile. Mesibov, Gary B.; And Others 1982
Subtests: Direct Observation Scale; School/Work Scale
Descriptors: Adolescents; Adults; *Autism; *Clinical Diagnosis; Cognitive Ability; Communication Skills; *Daily Living Skills; *Educational Diagnosis; Interpersonal Competence; *Job Skills; Mental Retardation; Observation; Perceptual Motor Coordination; Psychoeducational Clinics; *Psychomotor Skills; Verbal Ability
Identifiers: AAPEP
Availability: Orange Industries; 229 W. Tyron St., Hillsborough, NC 27278
Target Audience: 13-65
An adolescent and adult version of the Psychoeducational Profile (TC010778) designed to measure an autistic person's functioning: imitation, perception, fine and gross motor skills, eye-hand integration, cognitive performance, verbal performance, pathology. Also includes observations of skills at home and in the school or work environment. Each scale covers 6 areas: vocational skills, independent functioning, leisure, vocational behavior, functional communication, and interpersonal behavior. Used with au-

tistic persons functioning intellectually within the moderately to severely retarded range, higher functioning autistic persons, and retarded persons.

14320
SRA Survey of Basic Skills, Level 20. Science Research Associates, Chicago, IL 1985
Subtests: Auditory Discrimination; Reading: Letters and Sounds; Reading: Decoding; Listening Comprehension; Mathematics: Concepts/Problem Solving
Descriptors: *Academic Achievement; Academic Aptitude; *Achievement Tests; Aptitude Tests; Auditory Discrimination; *Basic Skills; Decoding (Reading); Elementary School Mathematics; Elementary School Students; *Grade 1; *Kindergarten Children; Knowledge Level; Listening Comprehension; Norm Referenced Tests; *Primary Education; Reading Processes
Identifiers: EAS; Educational Ability Series; SBS; *Test Batteries
Availability: Science Research Associates; 155 N. Wacker Dr., Chicago, IL 60606
Grade Level: K-1
Notes: Time, 100 approx.
A battery of norm-referenced, standardized tests in basic curriculum areas for grades K-12. Designed to survey students' general academic achievement. Contents of tests are based on learner objectives most commonly taught in the United States. Two forms are available, Forms P and Q. An optional test to include with the achievement battery is the Educational Ability Series (EAS) which provides an estimate of general learning ability for students in grades K-12. The EAS assesses those factors most closely associated with overall academic performance, such as verbal, numerical, and reasoning abilities. Test administrators may decide to do out-of-level testing with the Survey of Basic Skills for special groups of students, such as Chapter I, special education, gifted or high-achieving students. Level 20 test is designed for spring testing in kindergarten and fall testing in grade 1 at most schools.

14321
SRA Survey of Basic Skills, Level 21. Science Research Associates, Chicago, IL 1985
Subtests: Letters and Sounds; Listening Comprehension; Vocabulary; Reading Comprehension; Language Arts; Mechanics; Mathematics: Concepts/Problem Solving; Mathematics Computation
Descriptors: *Academic Achievement; Academic Aptitude; *Achievement Tests; Aptitude Tests; *Basic Skills; Elementary School Mathematics; Elementary School Students; *Grade 1; *Grade 2; Knowledge Level; Language Arts; Listening Comprehension; Norm Referenced Tests; *Primary Education; Reading Comprehension; Reading Processes; Vocabulary
Identifiers: EAS; Educational Ability Series; SBS; *Test Batteries
Availability: Science Research Associates; 155 N. Wacker Dr., Chicago, IL 60606
Grade Level: 1-2
Notes: Time, 165 approx.
A battery of norm-referenced, standardized tests in basic curriculum areas for grades K-12. Designed to survey students' general academic achievement. Contents of tests are based on learner objectives most commonly taught in the United States. Two forms are available, Forms P and Q. An optional test to include with the achievement battery is the Educational Ability Series (EAS) which provides an estimate of general learning ability for students in grades K-12. The EAS assesses those factors most closely associated with overall academic performance, such as verbal, numerical, and reasoning abilities. Test administrators may decide to do out-of-level testing with the Survey of Basic Skills for special groups of students, such as Chapter I, special education, gifted or high-achieving students. Level 21 test is designed for spring testing in first grade and fall testing in second grade at most schools.

14322
SRA Survey of Basic Skills, Level 22. Science Research Associates, Chicago, IL 1985
Subtests: Letters and Sounds; Vocabulary; Reading Comprehension; Language Arts: Mechanics; Language Arts: Usage; Spelling; Mathematics: Concepts/Problem Solving; Mathematics Computation
Descriptors: *Academic Achievement; Academic Aptitude; *Achievement Tests; Aptitude Tests; *Basic Skills; Elementary School Mathematics; Elementary School Students; *Grade 2; *Grade 3; Knowledge Level; Language Arts; Norm Referenced Tests; *Primary Education; Reading Comprehension; Reading Processes; Spelling; Vocabulary
Identifiers: EAS; Educational Ability Series; SBS; *Test Batteries
Availability: Science Research Associates; 155 N. Wacker Dr., Chicago, IL 60606
Grade Level: 2-3

Notes: Time, 165 approx.

A battery of norm-referenced, standardized tests in basic curriculum areas for grades K-12. Designed to survey students' general academic achievement. Contents of tests are based on learner objectives most commonly taught in the United States. Two forms are available, Forms P and Q. An optional test to include with the achievement battery is the Educational Ability Series (EAS) which provides an estimate of general learning ability for students in grades K-12. The EAS assesses those factors most closely associated with overall academic performance, such as verbal, numerical, and reasoning abilities. Test administrators may decide to do out-of-level testing with the Survey of Basic Skills for special groups of students, such as Chapter I, special education, gifted or high-achieving students. The level 22 test is designed for spring testing in grade 2 and fall testing in grade 3 at most schools.

14323
SRA Survey of Basic Skills, Level 23. Science Research Associates, Chicago, IL 1985
Subtests: Vocabulary; Reading Comprehension; Language Mechanics; Language Usage; Spelling; Mathematics: Concepts/Problem Solving; Mathematics Computation; Reference Materials
Descriptors: *Academic Achievement; Academic Aptitude; *Achievement Tests; Aptitude Tests; *Basic Skills; *Elementary Education; Elementary School Mathematics; Elementary School Students; *Grade 3; *Grade 4; Knowledge Level; Language Arts; Norm Referenced Tests; Reading Comprehension; Reference Materials; Spelling; Vocabulary
Identifiers: EAS; Educational Ability Series; SBS; *Test Batteries
Availability: Science Research Associates; 155 N. Wacker Dr., Chicago, IL 60606
Grade Level: 3-4
Notes: Time, 215 approx.

A battery of norm-referenced, standardized tests in basic curriculum areas for grades K-12. Designed to survey students' general academic achievement. Contents of tests are based on learner objectives most commonly taught in the United States. Two forms are available, Forms P and Q. An optional test to include with the achievement battery is the Educational Ability Series (EAS) which provides an estimate of general learning ability for students in grades K-12. The EAS assesses those factors most closely associated with overall academic performance, such as verbal, numerical, and reasoning abilities. Test administrators may decide to do out-of-level testing with the Survey of Basic Skills for special groups of students, such as Chapter I, special education, gifted or high-achieving students. Level 23 test is designed for spring testing in grade 3 and fall testing in grade 4 in most schools. The reference materials subtest is optional.

14324
SRA Survey of Basic Skills, Level 34. Science Research Associates, Chicago, IL 1985
Subtests: Vocabulary; Reading Comprehension; Language Mechanics; Language Usage; Spelling; Mathematics Computation; Mathematics Concepts; Mathematics Problem Solving; Reference Materials; Social Studies; Science
Descriptors: *Academic Achievement; Academic Aptitude; *Achievement Tests; Aptitude Tests; *Basic Skills; Elementary School Mathematics; Elementary School Science; *Elementary School Students; *Intermediate Grades; Knowledge Level; Language Arts; Norm Referenced Tests; Reading Comprehension; Reference Materials; Social Studies; Spelling; Vocabulary
Identifiers: EAS; Educational Ability Series; SBS; *Test Batteries
Availability: Science Research Associates; 155 N. Wacker Dr., Chicago, IL 60606
Grade Level: 4-6
Notes: Time, 280 approx.

A battery of norm-referenced, standardized tests in basic curriculum areas for grades K-12. Designed to survey students' general academic achievement. Contents of tests are based on learner objectives most commonly taught in the United States. Two forms are available, Forms P and Q. An optional test to include with the achievement battery is the Educational Ability Series (EAS) which provides an estimate of general learning ability for students in grades K-12. The EAS assesses those factors most closely associated with overall academic performance, such as verbal, numerical, and reasoning abilities. Test administrators may decide to do out-of-level testing with the Survey of Basic Skills for special groups of students, such as Chapter I, special education, gifted or high-achieving students. Levels 34 through 37 are multilevel tests designed for use from the spring of grade 4 through high school. The reference materials, social studies, and science subtests are optional.

14325
SRA Survey of Basic Skills, Level 35. Science Research Associates, Chicago, IL 1985
Subtests: Vocabulary; Reading Comprehension; Language Mechanics; Language Usage; Spelling; Mathematics Computation; Mathematics Concepts; Mathematics Problem Solving; Reference Materials; Social Studies; Science
Descriptors: *Academic Achievement; Academic Aptitude; *Achievement Tests; Aptitude Tests; *Basic Skills; Elementary School Mathematics; Elementary School Science; *Grade 6; Intermediate Grades; Junior High Schools; Junior High School Students; Knowledge Level; Language Arts; Norm Referenced Tests; Reading Comprehension; Reference Materials; Secondary School Mathematics; Secondary School Science; Social Studies; Vocabulary
Identifiers: EAS; Educational Ability Series; SBS; *Test Batteries
Availability: Science Research Associates; 155 N. Wacker Dr., Chicago, IL 60606
Grade Level: 6-8
Notes: Time, 280 approx.

A battery of norm-referenced, standardized tests in basic curriculum areas for grades K-12. Designed to survey students' general academic achievement. Contents of tests are based on learner objectives most commonly taught in the United States. Two forms are available, Forms P and Q. An optional test to include with the achievement battery is the Educational Ability Series (EAS) which provides an estimate of general learning ability for students in grades K-12. The EAS assesses those factors most closely associated with overall academic performance, such as verbal, numerical, and reasoning abilities. Test administrators may decide to do out-of-level testing with the Survey of Basic Skills for special groups of students, such as Chapter I, special education, gifted or high-achieving students. Levels 34 through 37 are multilevel tests designed for use from the spring of grade 4 through high school. The reference materials, social studies, and science subtests are optional.

14326
SRA Survey of Basic Skills, Level 36. Science Research Associates, Chicago, IL 1985
Subtests: Vocabulary; Reading Comprehension; Language Mechanics; Language Usage; Spelling; Mathematics Computation; Mathematics Concepts; Mathematics Problem Solving; Reference Materials; Social Studies; Science
Descriptors: *Academic Achievement; Academic Aptitude; *Achievement Tests; Aptitude Tests; *Basic Skills; Knowledge Level; Language Arts; Norm Referenced Tests; Reading Comprehension; Reference Materials; Secondary Education; Secondary School Mathematics; Secondary School Science; *Secondary School Students; Social Studies; Spelling; Vocabulary
Identifiers: EAS; Educational Ability Series; SBS; *Test Batteries
Availability: Science Research Associates; 155 N. Wacker Dr., Chicago, IL 60606
Grade Level: 8-10
Notes: Time, 280 approx.

A battery of norm-referenced, standardized tests in basic curriculum areas for grades K-12. Designed to survey students' general academic achievement. Contents of tests are based on learner objectives most commonly taught in the United States. Two forms are available, Forms P and Q. An optional test to include with the achievement battery is the Educational Ability Series (EAS) which provides an estimate of general learning ability for students in grades K-12. The EAS assesses those factors most closely associated with overall academic performance, such as verbal, numerical, and reasoning abilities. Test administrators may decide to do out-of-level testing with the Survey of Basic Skills for special groups of students, such as Chapter I, special education, gifted or high-achieving students. Levels 34 through 37 are multilevel tests designed for use from the spring of grade 4 through high school. The reference materials, social studies, and science subtests are optional.

14327
SRA Survey of Basic Skills, Level 37. Science Research Associates, Chicago, IL 1985
Subtests: Vocabulary; Reading Comprehension; Language Mechanics; Language Usage; Spelling; Mathematics Computation; Mathematics Concepts; Mathematics Problem Solving; Reference Materials; Social Studies; Science
Descriptors: *Academic Achievement; Academic Aptitude; *Achievement Tests; Aptitude Tests; *Basic Skills; High Schools; *High School Students; Knowledge Level; Language Arts; Norm Referenced Tests; Reading Comprehension; Reference Materials; Secondary School Mathematics; Secondary School Science; Social Studies; Spelling; Vocabulary
Identifiers: EAS; Educational Ability Series; SBS; *Test Batteries
Availability: Science Research Associates; 155 N. Wacker Dr., Chicago, IL 60606
Grade Level: 9-12
Notes: Time, 280 approx.

A battery of norm-referenced, standardized tests in basic curriculum areas for grades K-12. Designed to survey students' general academic achievement. Contents of tests are based on learner objectives most commonly taught in the United States. Two forms are available, Forms P and Q. An optional test to include with the achievement battery is the Educational Ability Series (EAS) which provides an estimate of general learning ability for students in grades K-12. The EAS assesses those factors most closely associated with overall academic performance, such as verbal, numerical, and reasoning abilities. Test administrators may decide to do out-of-level testing with the Survey of Basic Skills for special groups of students, such as Chapter I, special education, gifted or high-achieving students. Levels 34 through 37 are multilevel tests designed for use from the spring of grade 4 through high school. The reference materials, social studies, and science subtests are optional.

14335
School Readiness Screening Test. Gesell Institute of Child Development 1978
Subtests: Visuals 1 and 3; Animals and Interests; Incomplete Man; Copying; Cube Test; Initial Interview; Interview
Descriptors: Age Grade Placement; Attention Span; Child Development; Eye Hand Coordination; Grade 1; Kindergarten; Psychomotor Skills; School Readiness; *School Readiness Tests; Verbal Development; Visual Perception; *Young Children
Availability: Programs for Education; 1200 Broadway, New York, NY 10001
Target Audience: 4-5
Notes: Time, 20

Designed for use as a measure of school readiness based on developmental not chronological age. Norms are included for preschool children for accuracy in diagnosing 5-year-olds responding at a younger than 5-year level. Tests include: figure copying, completing a figure, visual matching of figures, recalling names of animals. They measure: eye-hand coordination, attention span, level of functioning in a structured motor task, visual perception, and verbal ability.

14340
Detroit Tests of Learning Aptitude—Primary. Hammill, Donald D.; Bryant, Brian R. 1986
Subtests: Verbal Aptitude; Nonverbal Aptitude; Conceptual Aptitude; Structural Aptitude; Attention-Enhanced Aptitude; Attention-Reduced Aptitude; Motor Enhanced Aptitude; Motor-Reduced Aptitude
Descriptors: *Academic Aptitude; *Aptitude Tests; *Cognitive Ability; Individual Testing; Intelligence; Learning Problems; Long Term Memory; Nonverbal Ability; Psychomotor Skills; Screening Tests; Short Term Memory; Verbal Ability; *Young Children
Identifiers: DTLA(P)
Availability: PRO-ED; 8700 Shoal Creek Blvd., Austin, TX 78758
Target Audience: 3-9
Notes: Time, 45 approx.; Items, 130

Designed to measure intellectual abilities of children ages 3-9. Measures the same basic theoretical domains as the Detroit Tests of Learning Aptitude, Revised (TC013737); linguistics, cognition, attention, and motor. Items are arranged in developmental order from easiest to most difficult. Particularly useful with low-functioning school-aged children. Can be used to isolate special individual strengths and weaknesses and to identify children deficient in general and specific aptitudes. May also be used in research studies investigating aptitude, intelligence, and cognitive behavior.

14364
Preschool Preposition Test. Aaronson, May 1980
Descriptors: *Cognitive Development; Developmental Disabilities; Mental Retardation; *Preschool Children; *Receptive Language; *Screening Tests
Availability: May R. Aaronson; National Institute of Mental Health, 5600 Fishers Ln., Rockville, MD 20857
Target Audience: 3-5
Notes: Time, 5; Items, 23

A quick screening method for determining delay in cognitive development. Uses receptive language. Can be used with mentally retarded, autistic, emotionally disturbed and physically handicapped children. A test board and a magnetized ball are required for administration. These are loaned by the author upon request. The test taker places a ball into position on a board in compliance with a direction containing a preposition.

14365
Pre-Vocational Readiness Battery. Valpar International Corp., Tucson, AZ
Subtests: Developmental Assessment; Workshop Evaluation; Vocational Interest Screening; Interpersonal Social Skills; Independent Living Skills

Descriptors: Adolescents; Adults; Aptitude Tests; Daily Living Skills; Interpersonal Competence; Job Skills; *Mental Retardation; Occupational Tests; Personnel Evaluation; Vocational Interests; *Vocational Rehabilitation; *Work Sample Tests
Availability: Valpar International Corp.; 3801 E. 34th St., Tucson, AZ 85713
Target Audience: 13-65

Designed to assess the trainable retarded person's ability to function in a vocational or independent living setting. Uses hands-on work samples that require little or no language or reading skills. Identifies the subject's barriers to competitive employment. Performance is compared to 9 norm groups: independent living, competitive employment, special learning disabilities, high school special needs, rehabilitation workshop, sheltered workshop, activity center, homebound employment, institutionalized work, institutionalized nonworking. Uses kit materials, photos, and manipulative devices.

14368
Bi/Polar Inventory of Core Strengths. Thomas, J.W.; Mayo, Clyde C. 1983
Descriptors: Adults; *Creativity; Individual Development; Interpersonal Communication; Marital Satisfaction; Organizational Development; *Personality Measures; Personality Traits; Rating Scales; Salesmanship; Teacher Effectiveness
Availability: Bi/Polar, Inc.; P.O. Box 160220, Austin, TX 78716-0220
Target Audience: Adults

Bi/Polar philosophy assumes that every individual has a creative core at the center of his or her personality. Core is made up of 3 pairs of polar opposite strengths which interact with each other. The 2 basic strengths which constitute the first pair of core strengths are thinking and risking. The second pair emanates from the basic thinking strength and are practical thinking and theoretical thinking. The third pair derives from the basic risking strength and are dependent risking and independent risking. The inventories are designed to help individuals identify their lead strengths in each pair. They are not meant to measure how strong the strengths are. Individuals must be certified by Bi/Polar, Inc. to administer and interpret the inventories. Inventories may be used in the areas of personal development; management development, sales training, teacher effectiveness, marriage enrichment and with other groups whose focus is on strengthening relationships and communications between the professional and his or her clients.

14371
Steps Up Developmental Screening Program for Children Birth to Three. Carr, Diane; And Others 1977
Descriptors: *Child Development; Cognitive Ability; Developmental Disabilities; Hearing (Physiology); *Infants; Interpersonal Competence; Language Skills; Physical Development; Physical Disabilities; Psychomotor Skills; *Screening Tests; *Toddlers; Vision; Young Children
Identifiers: SUDS
Availability: El Paso Rehabilitation Center; 2630 Richmond, El Paso, TX 79930
Target Audience: 0-3
Notes: Time, 5

Designed for use as a brief screening tool to identify children who need further evaluation, for wholesale screening in the community, in clinics, doctors' offices, by social workers, day care staff, and others not experienced with developmental problems. There are 33 test cards with different cards for each 2-week age category for children under 1 year and for 3-month categories for children between ages 1 and 3. Each card contains items covering: gross and fine motor skills, language skill, cognitive-social skills, vision, hearing, head circumference, dislocated hip, and convulsions.

14395
Valpar Component Work Sample 5 (Clerical Comprehension and Aptitude). Valpar International Corp., Tucson, AZ
Descriptors: Adults; Aptitude Tests; Bookkeeping; *Clerical Occupations; Deafness; Disabilities; Occupational Tests; Personnel Evaluation; Sign Language; Spatial Ability; Typewriting; *Work Sample Tests
Identifiers: Finger Dexterity; Manual Dexterity
Availability: Valpar International Corp.; 3801 E. 34th St., Tucson, AZ 85713
Target Audience: Adults

Measures a person's ability to learn and perform a variety of clerical tasks. Measures verbal and numerical ability, spatial and form perception, finger and manual dexterity. Three sections measure general clerical skills, bookkeeping skills, and typing skills. The kit includes a modified typewriter and requires the use of an adding machine. Can also be used with disabled persons. Signed, videotaped instructions are available for use with deaf persons.

14396
Valpar Component Work Sample 6 (Independent Problem Solving). Valpar International Corp., Tucson, AZ
Descriptors: Adults; Color; Deafness; Disabilities; Occupational Tests; Perceptual Motor Coordination; Personnel Evaluation; *Problem Solving; Sign Language; Spatial Ability; Visual Discrimination; *Work Sample Tests
Identifiers: Finger Dexterity; Manual Dexterity
Availability: Valpar International Corp.; 3801 E. 34th St., Tucson, AZ 85713
Target Audience: Adults

Measures a person's ability to perform work tasks requiring the visual comparison and proper selection of a series of abstract designs. The purpose of the work sample is to determine a person's basic independent problem solving ability. Also measures verbal and numerical skills, spatial and form perception, motor coordination, finger and manual dexterity, and color discrimination. May be used with disabled persons. Evaluee must be sighted.

14400
Valpar Component Work Sample 10 (Tri-Level Measurement). Valpar International Corp., Tucson, AZ
Descriptors: Adults; Aptitude Tests; Blindness; Deafness; Decision Making; Disabilities; *Inspection; Job Skills; *Measurement; Occupational Tests; Perceptual Motor Coordination; Personnel Evaluation; Sign Language; Visual Impairments; *Work Sample Tests
Identifiers: Finger Dexterity; Manual Dexterity
Availability: Valpar International Corp.; 3801 E. 34th St., Tucson, AZ 85713
Target Audience: Adults

Measures a person's ability to perform very simple to very precise inspection and measurement tasks. The evaluee makes increasingly difficult decisions as to whether machined parts fall within specific tolerances. Skills needed are reasoning, clerical aptitude, finger and manual dexterity and motor coordination. Can be administered to disabled or nondisabled persons. A special kit is available for blind subjects. Signed, videotaped instructions are available for deaf persons.

14401
Valpar Component Work Sample 11 (Eye-Hand-Foot Coordination). Valpar International Corp., Tucson, AZ
Descriptors: Adults; Deafness; Disabilities; Occupational Tests; *Perceptual Motor Coordination; Personnel Evaluation; Physical Mobility; Sign Language; *Spatial Ability; *Work Sample Tests
Identifiers: Manual Dexterity
Availability: Valpar International Corp.; 3801 E. 34th St., Tucson, AZ 85713
Target Audience: Adults

Measures the ability of a person to use eyes, hands, and feet simultaneously and with coordination. Abilities measured are spatial perception, and finger and manual dexterity. May be used with disabled and nondisabled persons, but they must be sighted. Signed, videotaped instructions for deaf persons are also available.

14402
Valpar Component Work Sample 12 (Soldering and Inspection Electronic). Valpar International Corp., Tucson, AZ
Descriptors: Adults; Deafness; Disabilities; *Electronics; Evaluative Thinking; Inspection; Occupational Tests; Personnel Evaluation; Sign Language; Spatial Ability; Visual Perception; *Work Sample Tests
Identifiers: *Soldering
Availability: Valpar International Corp.; 3801 E. 34th St., Tucson, AZ 85713
Target Audience: Adults

Measures a person's ability to acquire and apply the basic skills necessary to perform soldering tasks that vary in difficulty. Also concerns evaluee's ability to follow instructions, visual acuity, frustration tolerance, attentiveness, judgment, reasoning ability, and spatial and form perception. Can be used with disabled and nondisabled persons, but they must have a reasonable level of sight and coordination. Signed, videotaped instructions for deaf persons are available.

14404
Valpar Component Work Sample 14 (Integrated Peer Performance). Valpar International Corp., Tucson, AZ
Descriptors: Adults; Assembly (Manufacturing); Color; Disabilities; *Interpersonal Competence; Occupational Tests; *Peer Relationship; Perceptual Motor Coordination; Personnel Evaluation; Spatial Ability; *Visual Impairments; *Work Sample Tests
Identifiers: Finger Dexterity; Manual Dexterity
Availability: Valpar International Corp.; 3801 E. 34th St., Tucson, AZ 85713
Target Audience: Adults

Designed to encourage observable interaction of 3 to 5 evaluees working together, during completion of actual assembly tasks. Also measures reasoning skills, spatial and form perception, finger and manual dexterity, motor coordination, and color discrimination. Can be used with sighted disabled and nondisabled persons.

14405
Valpar Component Work Sample 15 (Electrical Circuitry and Print Reading). Valpar International Corp., Tucson, AZ
Descriptors: Adults; Blueprints; Deafness; Disabilities; *Electrical Systems; Engineering Drawing; Occupational Tests; Perceptual Motor Coordination; Personnel Evaluation; Sign Language; Spatial Ability; *Work Sample Tests
Identifiers: Finger Dexterity; Manual Dexterity
Availability: Valpar International Corp.; 3801 E. 34th St., Tucson, AZ 85713
Target Audience: Adults

Measures a person's ability to understand and apply principles of electrical circuits and to use pictorial materials such as blueprints, drawings, and schematics. Also concerns reasoning, spatial and form perception, finger and manual dexterity, and motor coordination. Not recommended for those with severe visual or coordination problems. Signed, videotaped instructions are available for deaf persons.

14406
Valpar Component Work Sample 16 (Drafting). Valpar International Corp., Tucson, AZ
Descriptors: Adults; *Blueprints; Deafness; Disabilities; *Drafting; Occupational Tests; Perceptual Motor Coordination; Personnel Evaluation; Sign Language; Spatial Ability; *Work Sample Tests
Identifiers: Finger Dexterity; Manual Dexterity
Availability: Valpar International Corp.; 3801 E. 34th St., Tucson, AZ 85713
Target Audience: Adults

Measures a person's potential for jobs involving drafting and blueprint reading, from minimal needs to high-level performance. Also covers reasoning, spatial and form perception, finger and manual dexterity, and motor coordination. May be used with disabled or nondisabled persons. Signed, videotaped instructions are available for deaf persons. Disabled persons must be sighted.

14437
Paced Auditory Serial Addition Task (PASAT). NeuroTech, Galveston, TX
Descriptors: Adults; *Cognitive Processes; Injuries; Minimal Brain Dysfunction; *Neurological Impairments; Timed Tests
Identifiers: PASAT
Availability: NeuroTech; 10 Quintana Dr., Galveston, TX 77551
Target Audience: Adults
Notes: Items, 124

A method of assessing the recovery of information processing speed after a head injury. Subject listens to a tape recording of numbers and pauses and adds spoken number to the previously spoken number. Norms are available for persons age 21-56 with 12-20 years of education (mean 15.7). Four series of numbers are presented.

14449
Human Figures Drawing Test. Gonzales, Eloy 1986
Descriptors: Children; *Cognitive Tests; *Concept Formation; *Freehand Drawing; *Human Body; Individual Testing; *Nonverbal Tests
Identifiers: HFDT
Availability: PRO-ED; 8700 Shoal Creek Blvd., Austin, TX 78758
Target Audience: 5-10
Notes: Time, 15 approx.

Developed to address concerns about presently available drawing tests. Provides a valid and reliable nonverbal measure of the cognitive maturation of children from ages 5 through 10. May be used in individual or group administration and can be integrated into any battery of tests designed for screening, determining current level of functioning, or identifying deficits. Test is recommended as a screening device for teachers, diagnosticians, psychologists, speech therapists. Since it requires no speech, it is also useful with non-English speakers or others suspected of having verbal problems.

14459
Schaie-Thurstone Adult Mental Abilities Test, Forms A and OA. Schaie, K. Warner 1985
Subtests: Recognition Vocabulary; Figure Rotation; Letter Series; Number Addition; Word Fluency; Object Rotation (Form OA); Word Series (Form OA)
Descriptors: Abstract Reasoning; Addition; Adults; *Cognitive Ability; Cognitive Processes; *Cognitive Tests; Older Adults; Spatial Ability; Vocabulary

Identifiers: *Primary Mental Abilities Test; STAMAT; Thurstone Seales
Availability: Consulting Psychologists Press; 577 College Ave., Palo Alto, CA 94306
Target Audience: 22-84
Notes: Time, 30 approx.

Research and assessment tool for measuring mental abilities of adults. Represents an extension of the seminal work of L.L. and T.G. Thurstone on measurement of primary mental abilities. There are 2 forms: Form A for adults and Form OA for older adults. Form A is essentially the Thurstone Primary Mental Abilities Test Form 11-17 with new adult norms. Form OA has 2 additional scales designed specifically for use with persons over age 55 and has new norms for older adults. STAMAT has so far been used primarily for research purposes to investigate patterns of stability and decline in intellectual processes. May have use in counseling returning adult students, assessing skills necessary for independent living, counseling adults for second careers, making diagnostic judgments about individual competence in disability examinations.

14473
ASSETS: A Survey of Students' Educational Talents and Skills—Later Elementary. Grand Rapids Public Schools, MI 1978
Descriptors: *Elementary School Students; *Enrichment Activities; Gifted; Intermediate Grades; Needs Assessment; Parent Attitudes; Rating Scales; Student Attitudes; *Student Interests; *Talent Identification; Teacher Attitudes
Availability: Learning Publications; P.O. Box 1326, Holmes Beach, FL 33509
Grade Level: 4-6

Helps in identification of children's gifts and talents and in planning enrichment activities and experiences for these students. Provides a means of surveying individual student interests and creative abilities as well as academic strengths and talents. Can serve a variety of purposes such as selecting students for special programs, individualizing curricula in the classroom, enhancing curriculum planning, discovering knowledge and skills students bring to the classroom, and helping parents and teachers to discuss student's needs. There are separate forms for parents, students, and teachers to fill out. Information from all 3 sources is combined in a single profile and can be viewed together to obtain a thorough and balanced assessment of each student's educational talents and skills, including academic aptitude, motivational characteristics, creative thinking ability, and visual and performing arts aptitude/talent.

14474
ASSETS: A Survey of Students' Educational Talents and Skills—Early Elementary. Grand Rapids Public Schools, MI 1979
Descriptors: Elementary School Students; *Enrichment Activities; Gifted; Needs Assessment; Parent Attitudes; *Primary Education; Rating Scales; Student Attitudes; *Student Interests; *Talent Identification; Teacher Attitudes
Availability: Learning Publications; P.O. Box 1326, Holmes Beach, FL 33509
Grade Level: K-3

Helps in identification of children's gifts and talents and in planning enrichment activities and experiences for these students. Provides a means of surveying individual student interests and creative abilities as well as academic strengths and talents. Can serve a variety of purposes such as selecting students for special programs, individualizing curricula in the classroom, enhancing curriculum planning, discovering knowledge and skills students bring to the classroom, and helping parents and teachers to discuss student's needs. There are separate forms for parents, students, and teachers to fill out. Information from all 3 sources is combined in a single profile and can be viewed together to obtain a thorough and balanced assessment of each student's educational talents and skills, including academic aptitude, motivational characteristics, creative thinking ability, and visual and performing arts aptitude/talent.

14483
Conceptual Understanding through Blind Evaluation. Valpar International Corp., Tucson, AZ
Descriptors: Adults; Blindness; Disabilities; Occupational Tests; *Perceptual Motor Coordination; Physical Mobility; Spatial Ability; *Visual Impairments; *Work Sample Tests
Identifiers: CUBE
Availability: Valpar International Corp.; 3801 E. 34th St., Tucson, AZ 85713
Target Audience: Adults

Designed to measure the perceptive abilities that help compensate for visual handicaps. It is a performance test that assesses the perceptual skills necessary to meet basic needs, including judgment, mobility, orientation, discrimination and balance.

14509
La Serie de Pruebas de Aptitud Hay. Hay, Edward N. 1984
Subtests: Warm-Up; Number Perception Test; Name Finding Test; Number Series Completion Test
Descriptors: Adults; *Aptitude Tests; *Clerical Occupations; *Occupational Tests; *Spanish; *Vocational Aptitude
Identifiers: *Clerical Skills; Hay Aptitude Test Battery; *Numerical Ability; Test Batteries
Availability: E.F. Wonderlic Personnel Test, Inc.; 820 Frontage Rd., Northfield, IL 60093
Target Audience: Adults
Notes: Time, 13

Spanish version of the Hay Aptitude Test Battery. Battery originally developed to use in selecting applicants for clerical workers. Has proved effective in selecting employees in banks, utility firms, and insurance companies. Also proven valid for plant jobs and operating positions. Battery consists of 4 tests: a warm-up test, number perception test, name finding test, and number series completion test.

14511
Cosmetology Student Admissions Evaluation. Colletti, Anthony B. 1977
Descriptors: Adults; *Aptitude Tests; *Cosmetology; *Vocational Aptitude; Work Sample Tests
Identifiers: Manual Dexterity
Availability: Keystone Publications; 1657 Broadway, New York, NY 10019
Target Audience: Adults
Notes: Time, 30 approx.; Items, 50

Developed to be used for predicting the successful training of an applicant in the field of cosmetology. It is not to be used as a device to reject applicants. Used to assess certain components of aptitude for the practice of cosmetology. Parts I, II, and III are written tests and consist of an interest inventory, word analogy items, and a comprehension and reasoning test. Part IV is a performance measure that assesses hand, finger, and fingertip dexterity.

14523
Matrix Analogies Test, Expanded Form. Naglieri, Jack A. 1985
Descriptors: *Abstract Reasoning; *Adolescents; *Children; *Cognitive Tests; Disabilities; *Individual Testing; Limited English Speaking; *Nonverbal Ability; *Spatial Ability
Identifiers: MAT
Availability: The Psychological Corp.; 555 Academic Ct., San Antonio, TX 78204-0952
Target Audience: 5-17
Notes: Time, 30 approx.; Items, 64

Designed as an individually administered measure of nonverbal ability. Allows individuals to either point or say aloud the number of their answers. Uses 64 abstract designs of the standard progressive matrix type. Test format reduces the effects of such variables as motor coordination, verbal skills, time pressure, and primary language. Can be used with individuals with limited English language skills, or those with a handicap, such as deafness, cerebral palsy, or communication disorders. May also be useful with exceptional populations, such as hearing impaired or mentally retarded persons. Items are organized in 4 item groups: pattern completion, reasoning by analogy, serial reasoning, and spatial visualization. Designed to be used as part of a comprehensive testing battery.

14529
Test of Cognitive Style in Mathematics. Bath, John B.; And Others 1986
Subtests: Mental Computation; Arithmetic; Geometry/Visual; Algebra
Descriptors: Adolescents; Adults; *Cognitive Processes; *Cognitive Tests; College Students; Elementary Education; Elementary School Students; Higher Education; *Individual Testing; *Mathematics Skills; *Problem Solving; Secondary Education; Secondary School Students
Identifiers: TCSM
Availability: Slosson Educational Publications; P.O. Box 280, East Aurora, NY 14052
Grade Level: 6-16
Target Audience: 12-64
Notes: Time, 20 approx.; Items, 20

Designed to identify the cognitive-perceptual style of the subject's mathematics problem solving skills. Gives information on how subject solves mathematics in 4 areas: mental computation, arithmetic, geometry/visual, and algebra. Test is a power test and is therefore untimed. It is individually administered. Assesses individual's problem solving style on a continuum from the intuitive Gestalt thinker to one who solves problems in a logical sequential manner and is stimulus bound.

14562
Language Processing Test. Richard, Gail; Hanner, Mary Anne 1985
Subtests: Associations; Categorization; Similarities; Differences; Multiple Meanings; Attributes
Descriptors: Children; *Diagnostic Tests; *Individual Testing; Language Handicaps; *Language Processing; Remedial Instruction
Identifiers: LPT
Availability: Linguisystems; 716 17th St., Moline, IL 61265
Target Audience: 5-12
Notes: Time, 30 approx.

Used to identify childrens' language processing strengths and weaknesses in a hierarchical framework so that professionals can determine special program placement, remedial placement, the point at which children's language processing breaks down, and which behaviors contribute to the processing disorders. These disorders may be caused by word retrieval difficulties, inappropriate word substitutions, nonspecific word usage, inability to correct recognized errors, avoidance of responding, rehearsal of responses, or unusual responses. Hierarchy of tasks used in test was based on A.R. Luria's model of brain organization.

14570
Prueba para El Diagnostico del Lenguaje Pre-Escolar. Blank, Marion; And Others 1983
Descriptors: Abstract Reasoning; Classroom Communication; *Individual Testing; *Language Skills; Learning Readiness; Perceptual Development; Pictorial Stimuli; *Preschool Children; *Preschool Tests; *Screening Tests; *Spanish; *Spanish Speaking; Young Children
Identifiers: PDLP; Preschool Language Assessment Instrument
Availability: Grune and Stratton; 111 Fifth Ave., New York, NY 10003
Target Audience: 3-6
Notes: Time, 20 approx.; Items, 60

Individually administered test designed to assess young children's skills in coping with the language demands of the teaching situation. In cases where children's language skills are questionable, the test may be administered to children up to 10 years of age. Test was developed to meet 2 major objectives: to offer a picture of a child's language skills so that teaching can be matched to the child's level of functioning and to allow for the early identification of children who may encounter severe difficulties in school. Based on a model of classroom discourse where teacher is seen as placing demands on the child that require varying levels of abstraction which can be viewed as being on a continuum: matching perception, selective analysis of perception; reordering perception, and reasoning about perception. This test has been adapted for Spanish-speaking children from the English version, The Preschool Language Assessment Instrument.

14573
Boehm Test of Basic Concepts, Revised. Boehm, Ann E. 1986
Descriptors: Abstract Reasoning; Achievement Tests; *Concept Formation; Elementary School Students; *Primary Education; *School Readiness; *Screening Tests; *Verbal Communication; Visual Measures
Availability: The Psychological Corp.; 555 Academic Ct., San Antonio, TX 78204-0952
Grade Level: K-2
Notes: Time, 40 approx.; Items, 50

Designed to assess children's mastery of basic concepts that are fundamental to understanding verbal instruction and necessary for early school achievement. Test is read aloud by the classroom teacher. Results of test may be used to identify children with basic concept deficiencies and to identify concept areas that should be targeted for further instruction. Basic concepts measured are relational concepts, a subset of concepts children use to make relational decisions about persons, objects, and situations. Concepts targeted in test also involve judgments that can be made across the contexts of space, quantity, and time, at increasingly complex levels of abstraction. There is also an Applications booklet consisting of 26 items of basic concepts frequently used in combination with easier concepts, with each other, or with other concepts familiar to the child.

14587
Problem Management Survey, Revised. Kolb, David A.; Baker, Richard J. 1984
Descriptors: *Administrator Evaluation; Adults; Organizational Objectives; Participative Decision Making; Problem Solving; Rating Scales; Self Evaluation (Individuals); *Supervisory Methods
Identifiers: PMS
Availability: McBer and Co.; 137 Newbury St., Boston, MA 02116
Target Audience: Adults
Notes: Items, 48

Measures manager's self-perception and coworkers' perceptions of how the administrator manages the problems and opportunities that arise in his/her job. Survey focuses primarily on 2 complementary modes of effective management: analytic management and intuitive/participative management. Also assesses manager's skills and priorities in 4 stages of the problem-management process: situation analysis, problem analysis, solution analysis, and implementation analysis.

14588
Learning Style Inventory, Revised. Kolb, David A. 1985
Descriptors: Adults; *Cognitive Style; Experiential Learning; Questionnaires; *Self Evaluation (Individuals); Training Methods
Identifiers: LSI
Availability: McBer and Co.; 137 Newbury St., Boston, MA 02116
Target Audience: 18-60
Notes: Time, 10 approx.; Items, 12

Self-descriptive instrument designed to assess an individual's preferred learning style. Helps learners identify their learning style: how they absorb and deal with new information. Gives learners information about their strengths and weaknesses in accomplishing tasks, solving problems, relating to and managing others, and indicates preferences leading to career choices. For each item, individual selects 1 sentence ending that corresponds to 1 of 4 learning orientations: concrete experience, abstract conceptualization, active experimentation, or reflective observation. Can be used by classroom teachers or management trainers.

14608
Southern California Ordinal Scales of Development: Scale of Communication. California State Dept. of Education 1977
Descriptors: Behavior Rating Scales; Children; *Communication Skills; *Criterion Referenced Tests; Culture Fair Tests; *Developmental Disabilities; *Developmental Tasks; *Expressive Language; *Learning Disabilities; *Multiple Disabilities; *Receptive Language
Identifiers: Piaget (Jean); *Piagetian Tests; SCOSD
Availability: Foreworks; P.O. Box 9747, N. Hollywood, CA 91609
Target Audience: 2-12

Developed by the Diagnostic School for Neurologically Handicapped Children, Southern California, State Department of Education as a complete Piagetian system that combines classroom and clinical assessment. The series consists of 6 cross-referenced Piagetian developmental scales. Each scale assesses all levels of development from sensorimotor through formal operations. Useful for comparative assessments, ability grouping, research, and individualized education program (IEP) development. Designed especially for use with multiply handicapped, developmentally delayed, and learning disordered persons, but may be used with all other children. Scales are considered to be culture-free and nonsexist. Administration of the scale consists of informal observation of the child within the environment. This scale is designed to assess the full range of oral and gestural expression and comprehension within a framework of Piaget's model of development. Scale is divided into receptive and expressive behavior, and within each area, the development strands assessed include awareness of self and environment, imitation, communicative mediation, and symbolization.

14609
Southern California Ordinal Scales of Development: Scale of Cognition. California State Dept. of Education 1977
Descriptors: Behavior Rating Scales; Children; *Cognitive Ability; *Criterion Referenced Tests; Culture Fair Tests; *Developmental Disabilities; *Developmental Tasks; *Learning Disabilities; *Multiple Disabilities
Identifiers: Piaget (Jean); *Piagetian Tests; SCOSD
Availability: Foreworks; P.O. Box 9747, N. Hollywood, CA 91609
Target Audience: 2-12

Developed by the Diagnostic School for Neurologically Handicapped Children, Southern California, State Department of Education as a complete Piagetian system that combines classroom and clinical assessment. The series consists of 6 cross-referenced Piagetian developmental scales. Each scale assesses all levels of development from sensorimotor through formal operations. Useful for comparative assessments, ability grouping, research, and individualized education program (IEP) development. Designed especially for use with multiply handicapped, developmentally delayed, and learning disordered persons, but may be used with all other children. Scales are considered to be culture-free and nonsexist. Administration of the scale consists of informal observation of the child within the environment. This scale relies on Piaget's model of intellectual development to determine child's level of cognitive functioning and to assess quality of sensory and information processing at that level. Areas assessed are development of means, object, concept, and imitation.

14637
Helsinki Test. Bruhn, Karl 1984
Descriptors: Adolescents; Adults; Children; Foreign Countries; *Intelligence Tests; Older Adults; *Personality Assessment; *Projective Measures; Psychological Testing
Identifiers: Finland

Availability: ERIC Document Reproduction Service; 3900 Wheeler Ave., Alexandria, VA 22304 (ED256734, 60 pages)
Target Audience: 7-65

This simplified Rorschach-type inkblot test is designed to render scoring possible by mathematical procedures, rather than subjective interpretation, through the assignment of point values for each of the more common responses to the plates. Responses are scored to describe IQ and personality factors, such as impulsiveness. For use by school psychologists and teachers as it does not require special training prior to administration.

14648
Keystone Adaptive Behavior Profile. Keystone Area Education, Elkader, IA 1983
Subtests: School Coping Behaviors; Social Skills; Emotional Development; Language Skills; Self Care Skills; Applied Cognitive Skills; Academic Development
Descriptors: Academic Aptitude; *Adaptive Behavior (of Disabled); Cognitive Processes; Coping; *Elementary School Students; Elementary Secondary Education; Emotional Development; Family Environment; Interpersonal Competence; Language Skills; Rating Scales; *Secondary School Students; Self Care Skills; *Special Education
Availability: ERIC Document Reproduction Service; 3900 Wheeler Ave., Alexandria, VA 22304 (ED250867, 59 pages)
Grade Level: K-12

Designed to measure adaptive behavior of special education students in Northeastern Iowa. A school-related scale and a home-related scale are included. The school scale emphasizes the child's behavior in the school setting. The home scale was devised to describe the child's adaptation to home and community. Both scales assess the same domains for comparison. The Home Scale has 2 additional subtests; the community and the family. The family scale covers relationships, participation, responsibility and self-concept. The Home Scale has not been normed. It is completed by either parent.

14655
Aphasia Screening Test for Adults and Older Children. Reitan, Ralph M. 1984
Descriptors: Adolescents; Adults; *Aphasia; Children; Expressive Language; *Individual Testing; Language Handicaps; *Neurological Impairments; Receptive Language; *Screening Tests; Spatial Ability; Speech Communication
Availability: Neuropsychology Press; 1338 E. Edison St., Tucson, AZ 85719
Target Audience: 9-64

An adaptation of the Halstead-Wepman Aphasia Screening Test used to evaluate deficits in the ability to use aspects of language for communication purposes in brain injured persons. It covers areas of language and verbal expression including: oral speech; letter recognition; number recognition; simple arithmetic, reading, spelling, and writing; receptive and expressive language, right-left orientation, spatial abilities. The test is individually administered via flashcards. A version for young children is available (See TC014656).

14656
Aphasia Screening Test for Young Children. Reitan, Ralph M. 1984
Descriptors: *Aphasia; Expressive Language; *Individual Testing; Language Handicaps; *Neurological Impairments; Receptive Language; *Screening Tests; Spatial Ability; Speech Communication; *Young Children
Availability: Neuropsychology Press; 1338 E. Edison St., Tucson, AZ 85719
Target Audience: 5-8

An adaptation of the Halstead Wepman Aphasia Screening Test used to evaluate deficits in the ability to use language for communication purposes in brain-damaged or learning-disabled children whose dysphasia does not have a demonstrated neurological basis. Covers oral speech, letter or number recognition, simple arithmetic, reading, perception of communication (both expressive and receptive), right-left orientation, and spatial abilities. The test is individually administered.

14659
ACT Career Planning Program, Level 1, Third Edition, Form J. American College Testing Program, Iowa City, IA 1983
Descriptors: *Career Planning; Clerical Occupations; High Schools; Junior High Schools; Language Usage; Mathematics; Mechanical Skills; Questionnaires; Reading Comprehension; Secondary Education; Spatial Ability; *Vocational Aptitude; *Vocational Interests; *Work Experience
Identifiers: CPP
Availability: ACT Career Planning Services; Operations Div., P.O. Box 168, Iowa City, IA 52243

This career-oriented assessment and feedback system is designed to assist students in assessing interests, abilities and work-related experiences for career exploration and planning. It consists of questions concerning: previous experiences; self-ratings of career-related abilities; reading skills; language usage; clerical speed; spatial relations; numerical skills; and mechanical reasoning. This instrument uses the Unisex edition of the ACT Interest Inventory. A second level for grades 11, 12 and adults is available. Levels are similar in content for use with mixed groups. Level 1 is lower in difficulty level in some areas and helps prepare students for selection of high school courses. For a description of Level 2, see TC014660.

14660
ACT Career Planning Program, Level 2, Third Edition, Form J. American College Testing Program, Iowa City, IA 1983
Descriptors: Adults; *Career Planning; Clerical Occupations; High Schools; *High School Students; Language Usage; Mathematics; Mechanical Skills; Postsecondary Education; Reading Comprehension; Spatial Ability; *Vocational Aptitude; *Vocational Interests; *Work Experience
Availability: ACT Career Planning Services; Operations Div., P.O. Box 168, Iowa City, IA 52243
Grade Level: 11-12
Target Audience: Adults

This career-oriented assessment and feedback system is designed to assist students in assessing interests, abilities and work-related experiences. A second level for grades 8-10 is available. Levels are similar in content for use with mixed groups. Level 2 has greater difficulty in some areas and emphasizes concepts and information related to employment, educational options and decisions to be faced in the transition out of high school. Questions concern: previous experiences; self-ratings of career-related abilities; reading skills; language usage; clerical speed; spatial relations; numerical skills; and mechanical reasoning. Uses the Unisex edition of the ACT Interest Inventory. For a description of Level 1, see TC014659. No separate adult norms are provided.

14661
Learning Accomplishment Profile, Revised Edition. Sanford, Anne R.; Zelman, Janet G. 1981
Descriptors: *Child Development; Cognitive Ability; *Criterion Referenced Tests; Disabilities; Early Childhood Education; Interpersonal Competence; Language Skills; Preschool Education; Primary Education; Profiles; Psychomotor Skills; *Spanish; Student Behavior; Writing Skills; *Young Children
Identifiers: Fine Motor Skills; Gross Motor Skills
Availability: Kaplan School Supply Corp.; 1310 Lewisville-Clemmons Rd., Lewisville, NC 27023
Target Audience: 3-6

A criterion-referenced assessment of a young nonhandicapped or handicapped child's skills. Designed for use in identifying developmentally appropriate learning objectives for each child. Measures child's progress in 7 developmental areas: gross motor skills, fine motor skills, personal skills, social skills, self-help, pre-writing, cognitive and language skills. The difference between this revised edition and the earlier one is the translation of general descriptors of developmental milestones into behavioral objectives. Another edition is available for ages 0-36 months. See the Early Learning Accomplishments Profile (TC012159). A Spanish edition is available.

14662
Evaluating Children's Progress: A Rating Scale for Children in Day Care. Southeastern Day Care Project
Descriptors: *Child Development; Cognitive Ability; Daily Living Skills; *Day Care Centers; Emotional Adjustment; Hygiene; *Infants; Interpersonal Competence; Psychomotor Skills; Rating Scales; Self Care Skills; *Young Children
Availability: Kaplan School Supply Corp.; 1310 Lewisville-Clemmons Rd., Lewisville, NC 27023
Target Audience: 0-5

A series of rating scales constructed from items standardized for children from birth through age 5. These can be administered by day care staff and provide immediate feedback. Children are rated at program entrance and at 6-month intervals. Covers: cognitive, social-emotional, motor skills, hygiene and self-help skills.

14665
Visual Selective Attention Test. Avolio, Bruce J. 1981
Descriptors: Adults; *Cognitive Style; *Computer Assisted Testing; Research Tools; Visual Measures; *Visual Perception
Identifiers: VSAT
Availability: Applied Psychological Measurement; v5 n1 p29-42 Win 1981
Target Audience: Adults
Notes: Items, 24

This test is designed to determine individual differences in information processing. It was constructed to approximate a visual counterpart of the Auditory Selective Attention

Test which consists of 24 spoken messages. It is presented on a computer screen as pairs of letters, words and numbers. Information processing, as used here, refers to perceptual style.

14666
Career Survey. American Testronics, Iowa City, IA 1984
Descriptors: Adults; Career Guidance; *Cognitive Ability; *Interest Inventories; Nonverbal Ability; Secondary Education; *Secondary School Students; Verbal Ability; *Vocational Interests
Availability: American Testronics; P.O. Box 2270, Iowa City, IA 52244
Grade Level: 7-12
Target Audience: Adults
Notes: Time, 45 approx.
Consists of 2 major parts: an interest survey called The Ohio Career Interest Survey and an abilities survey called The Career Ability Survey. The Ohio Career Interest Survey has 12 scales: accommodating/entertaining, humanitarian/caretaking, plant/animal/caretaking, mechanical, business detail, sales, numerical, communications/promotion, science/technology, artistic expression, educational/social, and medical. The ability survey consists of 2 subtests: verbal reasoning (verbal analogies) and nonverbal reasoning (number series and concept relationships). The interest scales were developed by The Ohio State Department of Education and consists of 132 items. The ability sale has 40 items.

14670
Screening Assessment for Gifted Elementary Students. Johnsen, Susan K.; Corn, Anne L. 1987
Subtests: Reading; School-Acquired Information; Divergent Production
Descriptors: *Academic Achievement; *Academic Aptitude; *Children; Creative Thinking; *Divergent Thinking; Elementary Education; *Elementary School Students; *Gifted; Individual Testing; Norm Referenced Tests; Screening Tests; *Student Placement
Identifiers: SAGES
Availability: PRO-ED; 8700 Shoal Creek Blvd., Austin, TX 78758
Target Audience: 7-12
Notes: Time, 90 approx.
Developed to address certain needs in identifying gifted, elementary-school children and to examine those areas most commonly found in gifted and talented programs: aptitude, achievement, and creativity. Test focuses on 3 areas of giftedness: reasoning, school-acquired information, and divergent production. These areas correspond to the 3 areas of giftedness as defined by the United States Office of Education (USOE). Test may be either individually or group administered. It takes longer to administer the test to groups than to individuals. One major purpose to administer the test is to obtain information helpful in identifying children for gifted classes. The test is not meant to identify children for classes that emphasize talent in leadership, visual or performing arts and/or psychomotor areas. Test may also be used as a screening device, clinically to examine a child's relative strengths and weaknesses in constructs incorporated into the test, or as a research tool. Samples of both nongifted and gifted children were used to norm the instrument.

14702
Cognitive Abilities Test, Form 4, Level 1. Thorndike, Robert L.; Hagen, Elizabeth 1986
Subtests: Oral Vocabulary; Verbal Classification; Quantitative Concepts; Relational Concepts; Figure Matrices; Figure Classification
Descriptors: *Academic Aptitude; *Cognitive Ability; *Cognitive Tests; *Grade 1; *Kindergarten Children; Mathematical Concepts; Nonverbal Ability; *Primary Education; Verbal Ability
Identifiers: Basic Skills Assessment Program; CogAT; Test Batteries
Availability: Riverside Publishing Co.; 8420 Bryn Mawr Ave., Chicago, IL 60631
Grade Level: K-1
Notes: Time, 90; Items, 140
One of 3 test batteries that comprise the Basic Skills Assessment Program, a comprehensive, standardized testing program designed to assess student achievement and abilities. The Cognitive Abilities Test (CogAT) was developed to assess the development of cognitive abilities related to verbal, quantitative, and nonverbal reasoning and problem solving. In Levels 1 and 2, there are 6 subtests that are (1) based on content that children in the appropriate age group are likely to have experienced; (2) require students to use familiar content in a new way; (3) yield reliable assessments of cognitive development for children at different stages of development; (4) emphasize cognitive skills related to school tasks students are expected to master; and (5) are of interest to students with various backgrounds. At Levels 1 and 2, CogAT is a power test, not a speed test. The test administrator reads each item to the students, allowing them enough time to try each item. In Levels A-H, there are 3 subtests each for the verbal, quantitative, and nonverbal sections. Each of the 3 subtests in each section uses only 1 type of symbol: verbal,

quantitative, or geometric. CogAT measures developed abilities, not innate abilities. The cognitive skills measured reflect cognitive strategies and general cognitive control processes developed experientially which allow the individual to learn new tasks or solve problems when instruction is absent or incomplete. The Iowa Tests of Basic Skills, the Cognitive Abilities Test, and the Tests of Achievement and Proficiency were normed concurrently.

14703
Cognitive Abilities Test, Form 4, Level 2. Thorndike, Robert L.; Hagen, Elizabeth 1986
Subtests: Oral Vocabulary; Verbal Classification; Quantitative Concepts; Relational Concepts; Figure Matrices; Figure Classification
Descriptors: *Academic Aptitude; *Cognitive Ability; *Cognitive Tests; *Grade 2; *Grade 3; Mathematical Concepts; Nonverbal Ability; *Primary Education; Verbal Ability
Identifiers: Basic Skills Assessment Program; CogAT; Test Batteries
Availability: Riverside Publishing Co.; 8420 Bryn Mawr Ave., Chicago, IL 60631
Grade Level: 2-3
Notes: Time, 90; Items, 165
One of three test batteries that comprise the Basic Skills Assessment Program, a comprehensive, standardized testing program designed to assess student achievement and abilities. The Cognitive Abilities Test (CogAT) was developed to assess the development of cognitive abilities related to verbal, quantitative, and nonverbal reasoning and problem solving. In levels 1 and 2, there are 6 subtests that are (1) based on content that children in the appropriate age group are likely to have experienced; (2) require students to use familiar content in a new way; (3) yield reliable assessments of cognitive development for children at different stages of development; (4) emphasize cognitive skills related to school tasks students are expected to master; and (5) are of interest to students with various backgrounds. At levels 1 and 2, CogAT is a power test, not a speed test. The test administrator reads each item to the students, allowing them enough time to try each item. In levels A-H, there are 3 subtests each for the verbal, quantitative, and nonverbal sections. Each of the 3 subtests in each section uses only one type of symbol: verbal, quantitative, or geometric. CogAT measures developed abilities, not innate abilities. The cognitive skills measured reflect cognitive strategies and general cognitive control processes developed experientially which allow the individual to learn new tasks or solve problems when instruction is absent or incomplete. The Iowa Tests of Basic Skills, the Cognitive Abilities Test, and the Tests of Achievement and Proficiency were normed concurrently.

14704
Cognitive Abilities Test, Form 4, Level A. Thorndike, Robert L.; Hagen, Elizabeth 1986
Subtests: Verbal Classification; Sentence Completion; Verbal Analogies; Quantitative Relations; Number Series; Equation Building; Figure Classification; Figure Analogies; Figure Analysis
Descriptors: *Academic Aptitude; *Cognitive Ability; *Cognitive Tests; Elementary Education; *Elementary School Students; *Grade 3; Grade 4; Mathematical Concepts; Nonverbal Ability; Verbal Ability
Identifiers: Basic Skills Assessment Program; CogAT; Test Batteries
Availability: Riverside Publishing Co.; 8420 Bryn Mawr Ave., Chicago, IL 60631
Grade Level: 3-4
Notes: Time, 90; Items, 200
One of 3 test batteries that comprise the Basic Skills Assessment Program, a comprehensive, standardized testing program designed to assess student achievement and abilities. The Cognitive Abilities Test (CogAT) was developed to assess the development of cognitive abilities related to verbal, quantitative, and nonverbal reasoning and problem solving. In levels 1 and 2, there are 6 subtests that are (1) based on content that children in the appropriate age group are likely to have experienced; (2) require students to use familiar content in a new way; (3) yield reliable assessments of cognitive development for children at different stages of development; (4) emphasize cognitive skills related to school tasks students are expected to master; and (5) are of interest to students with various backgrounds. At Levels 1 and 2, CogAT is a power test, not a speed test. The test administrator reads each item to the students, allowing them enough time to try each item. In Levels A-H, there are 3 subtests each for the verbal, quantitative, and nonverbal sections. Each of the 3 subtests in each section uses only 1 type of symbol: verbal, quantitative, or geometric. CogAT measures developed abilities, not innate abilities. The cognitive skills measured reflect cognitive strategies and general cognitive control processes developed experientially which allow the individual to learn new tasks or solve problems when instruction is absent or incomplete. The Iowa Tests of Basic Skills, the Cognitive Abilities Test, and the Tests of Achievement and Proficiency were normed concurrently.

14705
Cognitive Abilities Test, Form 4, Level B. Thorndike, Robert L.; Hagen, Elizabeth 1986

Subtests: Verbal Classification; Sentence Completion; Verbal Analogies; Quantitative Relations; Number Series; Equation Building; Figure Classification; Figure Analogies; Figure Analysis
Descriptors: *Academic Aptitude; *Cognitive Ability; *Cognitive Tests; *Grade 4; *Grade 5; *Intermediate Grades; Mathematical Concepts; Nonverbal Ability; Verbal Ability
Identifiers: Basic Skills Assessment Program; CogAT; Test Batteries
Availability: Riverside Publishing Co.; 8420 Bryn Mawr Ave., Chicago, IL 60631
Grade Level: 4-5
Notes: Time, 90; Items, 200
One of 3 test batteries that comprise the Basic Skills Assessment Program, a comprehensive, standardized testing program designed to assess student achievement and abilities. The Cognitive Abilities Test (CogAT) was developed to assess the development of cognitive abilities related to verbal, quantitative, and nonverbal reasoning and problem solving. In Levels 1 and 2, there are 6 subtests that are (1) based on content that children in the appropriate age group are likely to have experienced; (2) require students to use familiar content in a new way; (3) yield reliable assessments of cognitive development for children at different stages of development; (4) emphasize cognitive skills related to school tasks students are expected to master; and (5) are of interest to students with various backgrounds. At Levels 1 and 2, CogAT is a power test, not a speed test. The test administrator reads each item to the students, allowing them enough time to try each item. In Levels A-H, there are 3 subtests each for the verbal, quantitative, and nonverbal sections. Each of the 3 subtests in each section uses only 1 type of symbol: verbal, quantitative, or geometric. CogAT measures developed abilities, not innate abilities. The cognitive skills measured reflect cognitive strategies and general cognitive control processes developed experientially which allow the individual to learn new tasks or solve problems when instruction is absent or incomplete. The Iowa Tests of Basic Skills, the Cognitive Abilities Test, and the Tests of Achievement and Proficiency were normed concurrently.

14706
Cognitive Abilities Test, Form 4, Level C. Thorndike, Robert L.; Hagen, Elizabeth 1986
Subtests: Verbal Classification; Sentence Completion; Verbal Analogies; Quantitative Relations; Number Series; Equation Building; Figure Classification; Figure Analogies; Figure Analysis
Descriptors: *Academic Aptitude; *Cognitive Ability; *Cognitive Tests; *Grade 5; *Grade 6; *Intermediate Grades; Mathematical Concepts; Nonverbal Ability; Verbal Ability
Identifiers: Basic Skills Assessment Program; CogAT; Test Batteries
Availability: Riverside Publishing Co.; 8420 Bryn Mawr Ave., Chicago, IL 60631
Grade Level: 5-6
Notes: Time, 90; Items, 200
One of 3 test batteries that comprise the Basic Skills Assessment Program, a comprehensive, standardized testing program designed to assess student achievement and abilities. The Cognitive Abilities Test (CogAT) was developed to assess the development of cognitive abilities related to verbal, quantitative, and nonverbal reasoning and problem solving. In Levels 1 and 2, there are 6 subtests that are (1) based on content that children in the appropriate age group are likely to have experienced; (2) require students to use familiar content in a new way; (3) yield reliable assessments of cognitive development for children at different stages of development; (4) emphasize cognitive skills related to school tasks students are expected to master; and (5) are of interest to students with various backgrounds. At Levels 1 and 2, CogAT is a power test, not a speed test. The test administrator reads each item to the students, allowing them enough time to try each item. In Levels A-H, there are 3 subtests each for the verbal, quantitative, and nonverbal sections. Each of the 3 subtests in each section uses only 1 type of symbol: verbal, quantitative, or geometric. CogAT measures developed abilities, not innate abilities. The cognitive skills measured reflect cognitive strategies and general cognitive control processes developed experientially which allow the individual to learn new tasks or solve problems when instruction is absent or incomplete. The Iowa Tests of Basic Skills, the Cognitive Abilities Test, and the Tests of Achievement and Proficiency were normed concurrently.

14707
Cognitive Abilities Test, Form 4, Level D. Thorndike, Robert L.; Hagen, Elizabeth 1986
Subtests: Verbal Classification; Sentence Completion; Verbal Analogies; Quantitative Relations; Number Series; Equation Building; Figure Classification; Figure Analogies; Figure Analysis
Descriptors: *Academic Aptitude; *Cognitive Ability; *Cognitive Tests; *Grade 6; *Grade 7; *Intermediate Grades; *Junior High Schools; Mathematical Concepts; Nonverbal Ability; Verbal Ability
Identifiers: Basic Skills Assessment Program; CogAT; Test Batteries

Availability: Riverside Publishing Co.; 8420 Bryn Mawr Ave., Chicago, IL 60631
Grade Level: 6-7
Notes: Time, 90; Items, 200

One of 3 test batteries that comprise the Basic Skills Assessment Program, a comprehensive, standardized testing program designed to assess student achievement and abilities. The Cognitive Abilities Test (CogAT) was developed to assess the development of cognitive abilities related to verbal, quantitative, and nonverbal reasoning and problem solving. In Levels 1 and 2, there are 6 subtests that are (1) based on content that children in the appropriate age group are likely to have experienced; (2) require students to use familiar content in a new way; (3) yield reliable assessments of cognitive development for children at different stages of development; (4) emphasize cognitive skills related to school tasks students are expected to master; and (5) are of interest to students with various backgrounds. At Levels 1 and 2, CogAT is a power test, not a speed test. The test administrator reads each item to the students, allowing them enough time to try each item. In Levels A-H, there are 3 subtests each for the verbal, quantitative, and nonverbal sections. Each of the 3 subtests in each section uses only 1 type of symbol: verbal, quantitative, or geometric. CogAT measures developed abilities, not innate abilities. The cognitive skills measured reflect cognitive strategies and general cognitive control processes developed experientially which allow the individual to learn new tasks or solve problems when instruction is absent or incomplete. The Iowa Tests of Basic Skills, the Cognitive Abilities Test, and the Tests of Achievement and Proficiency were normed concurrently.

14708
Cognitive Abilities Test, Form 4, Level E. Thorndike, Robert L.; Hagen, Elizabeth 1986
Subtests: Verbal Classification; Sentence Completion; Verbal Analogies; Quantitative Relations; Number Series; Equation Building; Figure Classification; Figure Analogies; Figure Analysis
Descriptors: *Academic Aptitude; *Cognitive Ability; *Cognitive Tests; *Grade 7; *Grade 8; *Junior High Schools; Junior High School Students; Mathematical Concepts; Nonverbal Ability; Verbal Ability
Identifiers: Basic Skills Assessment Program; CogAT; Test Batteries
Availability: Riverside Publishing Co.; 8420 Bryn Mawr Ave., Chicago, IL 60631
Grade Level: 7-8
Notes: Time, 90; Items, 200

One of 3 test batteries that comprise the Basic Skills Assessment Program, a comprehensive, standardized testing program designed to assess student achievement and abilities. The Cognitive Abilities Test (CogAT) was developed to assess the development of cognitive abilities related to verbal, quantitative, and nonverbal reasoning and problem solving. In Levels 1 and 2, there are 6 subtests that are (1) based on content that children in the appropriate age group are likely to have experienced; (2) require students to use familiar content in a new way; (3) yield reliable assessments of cognitive development for children at different stages of development; (4) emphasize cognitive skills related to school tasks students are expected to master; and (5) are of interest to students with various backgrounds. At Levels 1 and 2, CogAT is a power test, not a speed test. The test administrator reads each item to the students, allowing them enough time to try each item. In Levels A-H, there are 3 subtests each for the verbal, quantitative, and nonverbal sections. Each of the 3 subtests in each section uses only 1 type of symbol: verbal, quantitative, or geometric. CogAT measures developed abilities, not innate abilities. The cognitive skills measured reflect cognitive strategies and general cognitive control processes developed experientially which allow the individual to learn new tasks or solve problems when instruction is absent or incomplete. The Iowa Tests of Basic Skills, the Cognitive Abilities Test, and the Tests of Achievement and Proficiency were normed concurrently.

14709
Cognitive Abilities Test, Form 4, Level F. Thorndike, Robert L.; Hagen, Elizabeth 1986
Subtests: Verbal Classification; Sentence Completion; Verbal Analogies; Quantitative Relations; Number Series; Equation Building; Figure Classification; Figure Analogies; Figure Analysis
Descriptors: *Academic Aptitude; *Cognitive Ability; *Cognitive Tests; Mathematical Concepts; Nonverbal Ability; *Secondary Education; *Secondary School Students; Verbal Ability
Identifiers: Basic Skills Assessment Program; CogAT; Test Batteries
Availability: Riverside Publishing Co.; 8420 Bryn Mawr Ave., Chicago, IL 60631
Grade Level: 8-10
Notes: Time, 90; Items, 200

One of 3 test batteries that comprise the Basic Skills Assessment Program, a comprehensive, standardized testing program designed to assess student achievement and abilities. The Cognitive Abilities Test (CogAT) was developed to assess the development of cognitive abilities related to verbal, quantitative, and nonverbal reasoning and problem solving. In Levels 1 and 2, there are 6 subtests that are (1) based on content that children in the appropriate age group are likely to have experienced; (2) require students to use familiar content in a new way; (3) yield reliable assessments of cognitive development for children at different stages of development; (4) emphasize cognitive skills related to school tasks students are expected to master; and (5) are of interest to students with various backgrounds. At Levels 1 and 2, CogAT is a power test, not a speed test. The test administrator reads each item to the students, allowing them enough time to try each item. In Levels A-H, there are 3 subtests each for the verbal, quantitative, and nonverbal sections. Each of the 3 subtests in each section uses only 1 type of symbol: verbal, quantitative, or geometric. CogAT measures developed abilities, not innate abilities. The cognitive skills measured reflect cognitive strategies and general cognitive control processes developed experientially which allow the individual to learn new tasks or solve problems when instruction is absent or incomplete. The Iowa Tests of Basic Skills, the Cognitive Abilities Test, and the Tests of Achievement and Proficiency were normed concurrently.

14710
Cognitive Abilities Test, Form 4, Level G. Thorndike, Robert L.; Hagen, Elizabeth 1986
Subtests: Verbal Classification; Sentence Completion; Verbal Analogies; Quantitative Relations; Number Series; Equation Building; Figure Classification; Figure Analogies; Figure Analysis
Descriptors: *Academic Aptitude; *Cognitive Ability; *Cognitive Tests; *High Schools; *High School Students; Mathematical Concepts; Nonverbal Ability; Verbal Ability
Identifiers: Basic Skills Assessment Program; CogAT; Test Batteries
Availability: Riverside Publishing Co.; 8420 Bryn Mawr Ave., Chicago, IL 60631
Grade Level: 10-12
Notes: Time, 90; Items, 200

One of 3 test batteries that comprise the Basic Skills Assessment Program, a comprehensive, standardized testing program designed to assess student achievement and abilities. The Cognitive Abilities Test (CogAT) was developed to assess the development of cognitive abilities related to verbal, quantitative, and nonverbal reasoning and problem solving. In Levels 1 and 2, there are 6 subtests that are (1) based on content that children in the appropriate age group are likely to have experienced; (2) require students to use familiar content in a new way; (3) yield reliable assessments of cognitive development for children at different stages of development; (4) emphasize cognitive skills related to school tasks students are expected to master; and (5) are of interest to students with various backgrounds. At Levels 1 and 2, CogAT is a power test, not a speed test. The test administrator reads each item to the students, allowing them enough time to try each item. In Levels A-H, there are 3 subtests each for the verbal, quantitative, and nonverbal sections. Each of the 3 subtests in each section uses only 1 type of symbol: verbal, quantitative, or geometric. CogAT measures developed abilities, not innate abilities. The cognitive skills measured reflect cognitive strategies and general cognitive control processes developed experientially which allow the individual to learn new tasks or solve problems when instruction is absent or incomplete. The Iowa Tests of Basic Skills, the Cognitive Abilities Test, and the Tests of Achievement and Proficiency were normed concurrently.

14711
Cognitive Abilities Test, Form 4, Level H. Thorndike, Robert L.; Hagen, Elizabeth 1986
Subtests: Verbal Classification; Sentence Completion; Verbal Analogies; Quantitative Relations; Number Series; Equation Building; Figure Classification; Figure Analogies; Figure Analysis
Descriptors: *Academic Aptitude; *Cognitive Ability; *Cognitive Tests; High Schools; *High School Seniors; Mathematical Concepts; Nonverbal Ability; Verbal Ability
Identifiers: Basic Skills Assessment Program; CogAT; Test Batteries
Availability: Riverside Publishing Co.; 8420 Bryn Mawr Ave., Chicago, IL 60631
Grade Level: 12
Notes: Time, 90; Items, 200

One of 3 test batteries that comprise the Basic Skills Assessment Program, a comprehensive, standardized testing program designed to assess student achievement and abilities. The Cognitive Abilities Test (CogAT) was developed to assess the development of cognitive abilities related to verbal, quantitative, and nonverbal reasoning and problem solving. In Levels 1 and 2, there are 6 subtests that are (1) based on content that children in the appropriate age group are likely to have experienced; (2) require students to use familiar content in a new way; (3) yield reliable assessments of cognitive development for children at different stages of development; (4) emphasize cognitive skills related to school tasks students are expected to master; and (5) are of interest to students with various backgrounds. At Levels 1 and 2, CogAT is a power test, not a speed test. The test administrator reads each item to the students, allowing them enough time to try each item. In Levels A-H, there are 3 subtests each for the verbal, quantitative, and nonverbal sections. Each of the 3 subtests in each section uses only 1 type of symbol: verbal, quantitative, or geometric. CogAT measures developed abilities, not innate abilities. The cognitive skills measured reflect cognitive strategies and general cognitive control processes developed experientially which allow the individual to learn new tasks or solve problems when instruction is absent or incomplete. The Iowa Tests of Basic Skills, the Cognitive Abilities Test, and the Tests of Achievement and Proficiency were normed concurrently.

14712
Cognitive Abilities Test, Form 4, Multilevel Edition, Levels A-H. Thorndike, Robert L.; Hagen, Elizabeth P. 1986
Subtests: Verbal Classification; Sentence Completion; Verbal Analogies; Quantitative Relations; Number Series; Equation Building; Figure Classification; Figure Analogies; Figure Analysis
Descriptors: *Academic Aptitude; *Cognitive Ability; *Cognitive Tests; *Elementary School Students; Elementary Secondary Education; Mathematical Concepts; Nonverbal Ability; *Secondary School Students; Verbal Ability
Identifiers: Basic Skills Assessment Program; CogAT; Test Batteries
Availability: Riverside Publishing Co.; 8420 Bryn Mawr Ave., Chicago, IL 60631
Grade Level: 3-12
Notes: Time, 90; Items, 200

One of 3 test batteries that comprise the Basic Skills Assessment Program, a comprehensive, standardized testing program designed to assess student achievement and abilities. The Cognitive Abilities Test (CogAT) was developed to assess the development of cognitive abilities related to verbal, quantitative, and nonverbal reasoning and problem solving. In Levels 1 and 2, there are 6 subtests that are (1) based on content that children in the appropriate age group are likely to have experienced; (2) require students to use familiar content in a new way; (3) yield reliable assessments of cognitive development for children at different stages of development; (4) emphasize cognitive skills related to school tasks students are expected to master; and (5) are of interest to students with various backgrounds. At Levels 1 and 2, CogAT is a power test, not a speed test. The test administrator reads each item to the students, allowing them enough time to try each item. In Levels A-H, there are 3 subtests each for the verbal, quantitative, and nonverbal sections. Each of the 3 subtests in each section uses only 1 type of symbol: verbal, quantitative, or geometric. CogAT measures developed abilities, not innate abilities. The cognitive skills measured reflect cognitive strategies and general cognitive control processes developed experientially which allow the individual to learn new tasks or solve problems when instruction is absent or incomplete. The Iowa Tests of Basic Skills, the Cognitive Abilities Test, and the Tests of Achievement and Proficiency were normed concurrently.

14728
SAGE Vocational Assessment System. Train-east Corp Pleasantville, NY 1985
Subtests: Vocational Interest Inventory; Cognitive and Conceptual Abilities; Vocational Aptitude Battery; Assessment of Attitudes; Temperament Factor Assessment
Descriptors: Adults; Aptitude Tests; Attitude Measures; *Cognitive Ability; *Employee Attitudes; Hearing Impairments; Interest Inventories; Interpersonal Relationship; Personality Measures; *Personality Traits; Reading Difficulties; Visual Impairments; *Vocational Aptitude; *Vocational Evaluation; *Vocational Interests
Availability: KeySystems; 2055 Long Ridge Rd., Stamford, CT 06903
Target Audience: Adults

A system that matches the aptitudes, interests, educational levels, attitudes, and temperaments of people to jobs and training. May be used with handicapped populations and may be group or individually administered. The system consists of 5 units. The Vocational Interest Inventory assesses areas of interest related to the 12 interest areas of the Guide for Occupational Exploration. May be used with hearing impaired or visually impaired persons, or nonreaders. The Cognitive and Conceptual Abilities unit measures the 3 General Educational Development (GED) factors of reasoning, mathematics, and language. The Vocational Aptitude Battery has been validated against the General Aptitudes Test Battery (GATB) and assesses 11 aptitudes by means of the following individual job-related tests: general, verbal, numerical, spatial, form perception, clerical perception, motor coordination, finger dexterity, manual dexterity, eye-hand-foot coordination, and color discrimination. The Assessment of Attitudes presents real-life situations in which the individual must evaluate on-the-job social situations, such as dealing with coworkers, supervisors, or employers. The Temperament Factor Assessment provides an objective measure of an individual's temperament.

14763
MINDEX: Your Thinking Style Profile. Albrecht, Karl 1983

Subtests: Kinesthetic; Visual Auditory; Time Orientation; Detail Orientation; Technical Orientation; Goal Orientation; Tolerance for Ambiguity; Opinion Flexibility; Semantic Flexibility; Positive Orientation; Sense of Humor; Investigative Orientation; Resistance to Enculturation; Idea Fluency; Logical Fluency
Descriptors: Adults; *Cognitive Processes; Cognitive Tests; Individual Testing; Rating Scales; *Self Evaluation (Individuals); *Sensory Experience
Availability: Shamrock Press; 1277 Garnet Ave., San Diego, CA 92109
Target Audience: Adults
Notes: Items, 100

A self assessment test of thinking style. Offers 20 scores in the general areas of thinking mode preference, sensory mode preference, structure preference, mental flexibility, and thinking fluency. Thinking mode preference scores are plotted on a matrix consisting of abstract concepts and concrete experience on the x-axis and left-brained and right-brained thinking process in the x-axis. Sensory mode preference covers kinesthetic, visual, and auditory perceptions. Structure preference covers time orientation, detail orientation and goal orientation. Mental flexibility covers tolerance for ambiguity, opinion flexibility, positive orientation, sense of humor, investigative orientation, and resistance to enculturation. Thinking fluency covers idea fluency. By helping people to understand themselves and one another, the test can lead to improvement in interpersonal communication, personal relationships, counseling, sales, management, team building and job placement.

14769
Matrix Analogies Test, Short Form. Naglieri, Jack A. 1985
Subtests: Pattern Completion; Reasoning by Analogy; Serial Reasoning; Spatial Visualization
Descriptors: Abstract Reasoning; Adolescents; Children; *Cognitive Ability; Culture Fair Tests; Deafness; Disabilities; Elementary Secondary Education; Group Testing; Learning Disabilities; Limited English Speaking; Mental Retardation; *Nonverbal Tests; Norm Referenced Tests; Pattern Recognition; *Screening Tests; Spatial Ability; Underachievement
Availability: The Psychological Corp.; 555 Academic Ct., Austin, TX 78204-0952
Grade Level: K-12
Notes: Items, 34

Designed to provide a measure of nonverbal reasoning that could be administered as a screening test in a group setting. Uses abstract designs of the standard progressive matrix type and brief directions. It was based on factors identified for the Raven's Progressive Matrices (TC810027). Said to be especially useful for those with limited English skills, a handicap or other cause for lack of verbal ability. It is norm referenced and standardized on a national sample of children living in the United States. May be used in screening for learning problems in the case of an ability/achievement discrepancy. Some training in group testing is required for administration. Because of its nonverbal nature, the test is said to be culture reduced. It may be used with deaf and mentally retarded individuals as well. Percentile ranks, stanines and age equivalent scores can be computed.

14791
PACE. Barclay, Lisa K.; Barclay, James R. 1986
Subtests: Motor Coordination; Visual Perception; Recognizing Rhythm Patterns; Listening; Visual Matching; Tactile Skills; Motor Behavior Memory; Verbal Memory; Attending; Social Development
Descriptors: Attention Span; *Behavior Rating Scales; *Computer Assisted Testing; *Learning Disabilities; Listening Skills; Memory; Parents; Perceptual Motor Coordination; *Preschool Education; Psychomotor Skills; *Screening Tests; Social Development; *Student Placement; Tactual Perception; Verbal Ability; Visual Perception
Identifiers: Rhythm
Availability: Institute for Personality and Ability Testing; P.O. Box 188, Champaign, IL 61822
Target Audience: 3-5

A behavior rating designed to identify deficits in learning skills of preschool children for screening, educational placement, and remediation. Uses parent observation and classroom findings to generate a developmental report. Currently runs on Apple IIe and 2 drives and 64kb RAM or IBM-PC and compatibles.

14793
Multiple Assessment Programs and Services of the College Board. Educational Testing Service, Princeton, NJ

Subtests: English; Mathematics; Reading; Written English Expression; Computation; Applied Arithmetic; Elementary Algebra; Intermediate Algebra; Test of Standard Written English; Scholastic Aptitude Test; American History and Social Studies; Biology; Chemistry; English Composition; French Reading; German Reading; Mathematics Level 1; Physics; Spanish Reading; European History and World Cultures; French Listening-Reading; Literature; Mathematics Level 2; German Listening Comprehension; German Listening-Reading; Spanish Listening Comprehension; Spanish Listening Reading; Hebrew; Greek; Russian Reading; Russian Listening-Reading; Italian Reading; Italian Listening-Reading; Conventions of Written English; Critical Reasoning
Descriptors: Academic Aptitude; Achievement Tests; Algebra; Arithmetic; Biology; Chemistry; *College Admission; *College Students; Computation; *Counseling; Diagnostic Tests; *Educational Diagnosis; English; Equivalency Tests; European History; Foreign Culture; French; German; Greek; Hebrew; Higher Education; Listening Comprehension; Mathematics; Physics; Reading; Second Language Learning; Social Studies; Spanish; *Student Placement; Tests; United States History; Writing (Composition); Writing Skills
Identifiers: MAPS; Self Scoring Tests; Writing Sample
Availability: Multiple Assessment Program and Services of the College Board; P.O. Box 2869, Princeton, NJ 08541
Grade Level: 13-14

This series of tests is for use by colleges, for admissions, placement of students, remedial or developmental studies, exemption, guidance and counseling. Some of the tests are drawn from the national Admissions Testing Program, including the Test of Standard Written English, Scholastic Aptitude Test and Achievement Tests. Some are self-scoring (English, Mathematics). See also TC013001 Assessment and Placement Services for Community Colleges and TC015421 comparative Guidance and Placement Program.

14797
The Creatrix Inventory. Byrd, Richard E. 1986
Descriptors: Adults; *Creativity; *Occupational Tests; Personnel Evaluation; Rating Scales; *Risk; *Self Evaluation (Individuals)
Identifiers: C and RT
Availability: University Associates; 8517 Production Ave., San Diego, CA 92121
Target Audience: Adults
Notes: Items, 56

This inventory is designed to help people identify their levels of creativity, defined as the degree to which they can produce unconventional ideas, and their orientation toward risk (high, medium, low). Uses a 5-point Likert-type agree/disagree scale. The test taker scores into 1 of 8 categories: reproducer, modifier, challenger, practicalizer, innovator, synthesizer, dreamer, or planner. The test taker scores the inventory and interprets it.

14811
Test de Vocabulario en Imagenes Peabody: Adaptacion Hispanomerica. Dunn, Lloyd M.; And Others 1986
Descriptors: *Academic Aptitude; *Achievement Tests; Adolescents; Bilingual Students; Children; Individual Testing; Mexicans; Nonverbal Tests; Pictorial Stimuli; Puerto Ricans; *Screening Tests; Second Languages; *Spanish; *Spanish Speaking; *Vocabulary
Identifiers: Oral Tests; Peabody Picture Vocabulary Test; PPVT, TVIP
Availability: American Guidance Service; Publishers' Bldg., Circle Pines, MN 55014
Target Audience: 2-18
Notes: Time, 15; Items, 125

This measure of Spanish hearing vocabulary is a version of the Peabody Picture Vocabulary Test developed for use with Spanish speaking children and adolescents. It was standardized in Puerto Rico and Mexico. The manual is available in both Spanish and English. When it is used as an achievement test, it may be used to show student progress when Spanish is the language of instruction or when assessing proficiency in Spanish as a second language. It may be used as a screening test of scholastic aptitude when Spanish is the language of the home and community and when Spanish is the language of instruction. It is individually administered and does not require reading, verbal or written responses. Also said to be useful for screening at the kindergarten and first grade level for follow-up assessment, to determine language of instruction for bilingual children. The examinee points to one of a series of plates in response to an oral stimulus. Norms for Hispanic children and youth on the U.S. mainland will be developed if examiners volunteer to test a group of these students.

14814
Student Profile and Assessment Record. Miller, Theodore K.; Winston, Roger B., Jr. 1985
Subtests: General Information; Academic Information; Career; Test Scores; High School Record; Health and Wellness; Activities and Organizations; Special Concerns
Descriptors: Background; Career Planning; Cognitive Style; *College Students; *Educational Background; Grades (Scholastic); Health Activities; *Higher Education; Learning Problems; *Records (Forms); Social Problems
Availability: Student Development Associates; 110 Crestwood Dr., Athens, GA 30605
Grade Level: 13-16

This form for recording data on students entering college also includes sections assessing their perceived learning style, learning problems, career plans, health habits and social and personal areas in which the students anticipate difficulty and need some help.

14819
Battelle Developmental Inventory Screening Test. Svinicki, John 1984
Subtests: Personal-Social; Adaptive; Gross Motor; Fine Motor; Motor; Receptive; Expressive; Communication; Cognitive
Descriptors: Adjustment (to Environment); *Child Development; Children; Cognitive Development; Communication Skills; *Developmental Tasks; Disabilities; Expressive Language; Individual Testing; Infants; Language Acquisition; Motor Development; Receptive Language; *Screening Tests; Social Development
Availability: DLM Teaching Resources; 1 DLM Park, Allen, TX 75002
Target Audience: 0-8
Notes: Time, 20; Items, 96

This inventory is standardized and individually administered to assess developmental skills. It is for use primarily with nonhandicapped children. Some tasks are added for use with a handicapped population. Used as a general screening tool, to monitor student progress, and to identify developmentally delayed children.

14820
Birth to 3 Assessment and Intervention System: Screening Test of Language and Learning Development. Bangs, Tina E. 1986
Descriptors: *Child Development; *Cognitive Development; Developmental Disabilities; Disabilities; Expressive Language; *Language Acquisition; Motor Development; *Norm Referenced Tests; Problem Solving; Receptive Language; *Screening Tests; Social Development; *Young Children
Availability: DLM Teaching Resources; 1 DLM Park, Allen, TX 75002
Target Audience: 0-3
Notes: Items, 68

This norm-referenced test is designed for use by teachers to identify behaviors exhibited by a child that show the child as being at high risk for delay. Areas covered are: oral language (comprehension and expression); problem solving, social/personal skills, and motor skills. It is accompanied by a Criterion-Referenced Checklist of Language and Learning Behavior (TC014831).

14822
Personal Resource Intelligence Test. Palmer Testing Service, Andover, MA 1985
Descriptors: Adults; Aptitude Tests; Individual Testing; *Intelligence Tests; Vocabulary
Availability: Palmer Testing Service; 93 Main St., Andover, MA 01810
Target Audience: Adults
Notes: Time, 20; Items, 100

This test was designed to measure verbal intelligence (IQ) and 5 aptitudes: mathematics, vocabulary, practical reasoning, abstract thinking and general knowledge. It is scored by the source cited above and a report is provided. No validity or reliability information is included.

14823
Stanford-Binet Intelligence Scale: Fourth Edition. Thorndike, Robert L.; And Others 1986
Subtests: Vocabulary; Comprehension; Verbal Absurdities; Pattern Analysis; Matrices; Paper Folding and Cutting; Copying; Quantitative; Number Series; Equation Building; Memory for Sentences; Memory for Digits; Memory for Objects; Bead Memory
Descriptors: Abstract Reasoning; *Adolescents; *Adults; *Children; Culture Fair Tests; *Individual Testing; *Intelligence Tests; Mathematics Tests; Oral Language; Short Term Memory; Verbal Ability; Vocabulary
Identifiers: Verbal Reasoning; Visual Reasoning
Availability: Riverside Publishing Co.; 8420 Bryn Mawr Ave., Chicago, IL 60631
Target Audience: 2-23

Notes: Time, 90

This revision of the 1972 edition is individually administered to children from below age 2 through superior adults. Tests cover 4 major areas: verbal reasoning, quantitative reasoning, abstract/visual reasoning, and short-term memory. Scores include raw scores and scaled scores for each of the 15 subtests, scaled scores and percentile ranks for a composite of the 4 area scores, a composite of any combination of the 4 area scores and a profile of all 15 subtests, based on scaled scores. Separate norms are provided for each score. A pretest is administered to identify the level at which to begin testing. The test is said to have minimal sex or ethnic bias. The examiner must be professionally trained and certified. Adult norms are for the age 18-23 group. Other norms are available for demographic groups based on parental education, occupation, community size, gender, racial/ethnic groups. Scores corresponding to IQ's are called "standard age scores."

14831
Birth to 3 Assessment and Intervention System: Checklist of Language, and Learning Behavior. Bangs, Tina E. 1986
Descriptors: *Check Lists; *Child Development; Cognitive Development; *Criterion Referenced Tests; Disabilities; Expressive Language; Language Acquisition; Motor Development; Problem Solving; Receptive Language; Social Development; *Young Children
Availability: DLM Teaching Resources; 1 DLM Park, Allen, TX 75002
Target Audience: 0-3
Notes: Items, 240

This program was designed for use by parents and teachers to evaluate children's developmental skills. Includes another component, the Screening Test of Language and Learning Development (TC014820). The Checklist is a criterion-referenced measure that organizes 240 behaviors into 5 categories so that they may be observed and scored in the young child. Categories are: language comprehension, language expression, problem solving, social personal behavior, and motor behaviors.

14841
National Association of Secondary School Principals Learning Style Profile. Keefe, James W.; Monk, John S. 1986
Subtests: Analytic Skill; Spatial Skill; Discrimination Skill; Categorizing Skill; Sequential Processing Skill; Memory Skill; Perceptual Response-Auditory; Perceptual Response-Visual; Perceptual Response-Emotive; Persistence Orientation; Verbal Risk Orientation; Verbal Spatial Preference; Manipulative Preference; Study Time Preference: Late Morning, Early Morning, Afternoon; Evening; Grouping Preference; Posture Preference; Mobility Preference; Sound Preference; Lighting Preference; Temperature Preference
Descriptors: *Cognitive Style; Educational Environment; *Elementary School Students; Elementary Secondary Education; Learning Processes; Memory; Persistence; *Psychomotor Skills; Questionnaires; *Secondary School Students; Spatial Ability; *Study Habits; Verbal Ability
Identifiers: *Learning Style
Availability: National Association of Secondary School Principals; 1904 Association Dr., Reston, VA 22091
Grade Level: 6-12
Notes: Items, 126

This inventory measures learning style defined as characteristic cognitive, affective, and psychological factors that are indicators of how a learner sees, interacts with and responds to the environment for learning. It consists of 23 independent scales representing 4 factors: cognitive skills, perceptual responses, study preferences, and instructional preferences. The reading level of the test is grade 5-6. Useful as a first diagnostic tool. Some subscale scores are based on 5 or fewer items. Questionable results should be examined by further testing. Can be machine or hand scored. Norms are available. The Learning Style Profile and examiner's manual are also available in microfiche as ERIC documents ED275769 and ED275770.

14844
Personal Resource Assessment Battery. Aposhyan, Joseph 1985
Descriptors: Adults; Antisocial Behavior; *Career Planning; Cognitive Ability; *Intelligence Tests; Personality Traits; Reading Comprehension; Self Evaluation (Individuals); Values; Visual Perception
Availability: Palmer Testing Service; 93 Main St., Andover, MA 01810
Target Audience: 18-65
Notes: Time, 20

This untimed scale is designed to measure mental ability, perceptual ability, reading comprehension, occupational interest, personality traits and deviances, moral attitudes or values. It is said to correlate with the Wonderlic Personnel Test and the Wechsler Adult Intelligence Scale for I.Q. A technical manual is not offered. The test is mailed to individuals free of charge. The test is then returned to the publisher for scoring. Separate fees are charged for scoring for I.Q. and for the other factors. Said to be useful for career planning.

14853
Prevocational Assessment Screen. Piney Mountain Press, Cleveland, GA 1984
Subtests: Alphabetizing; Etch-a-Sketch Maze; Calculating Numbers; Small Parts; Pipe Assembly; O-Rings; Block Design; Color Sort
Descriptors: Adolescents; Adults; Aptitude Tests; Clerical Occupations; Color; *Disabilities; *Job Placement; Job Skills; Psychomotor Skills; *Screening Tests; Spatial Ability; *Vocational Education; Vocational Training Centers
Identifiers: Finger Dexterity; Manual Dexterity; Numerical Aptitude; PAS
Availability: Piney Mountain Press, Inc.; P.O. Box 333, Cleveland, GA 30528
Target Audience: 14-64
Notes: Time, 50

Designed to provide a method of screening individuals for training and job placement. It is said to be useful for assessing large numbers of students in a short period of time in informal settings. No training is required for administration. PAS is normed on handicapped students, average vocational students, and employed workers. The subtests measure verbal clerical perception, motor coordination, numerical clerical perception, finger dexterity, manual dexterity, form perception, spatial perception, and color perception.

14854
Everyday Spatial Activities Test. Lunneborg, Patricia W.; Lunneborg, Clifford E. 1986
Subtests: Handtools; Science Courses; Arranging Objects; Mechanical Drawing
Descriptors: Academic Achievement; Career Choice; *College Students; Higher Education; Job Performance; Norm Referenced Tests; Rating Scales; Self Evaluation (Individuals); *Sex Differences; *Spatial Ability
Identifiers: ESAT; Likert Scale
Availability: Journal of Vocational Behavior; v28 n2 p135-41, Apr 1986
Grade Level: 13-16
Target Audience: Adults
Notes: Items, 20

Norm-referenced test used to measure sex-related differences in the spatial abilities of college students. Answers were self-reported using a 5-point Likert scale. The precollege variables of high school English grade point average, high school mathematics grade point average, vocabulary composite scores, Quantitative composite scores, Spatial Ability scores, Mechanical Reasoning scores, and all-college first year predicted grade point average were correlated with this test to establish preliminary validity. Test is intended for further use as a research instrument to study how differential spatial activities contribute to vocational performance and educational achievement.

14870
Preschool Interpersonal Problem Solving Test. Shure, Myrna B.; Spivack, George 1974
Descriptors: *Cognitive Ability; Individual Testing; *Interpersonal Relationship; Pictorial Stimuli; *Preschool Children; Problem Solving; *Social Adjustment
Identifiers: PIPS
Availability: George Spivack; Hahnemann Medical College and Hospital, Dept. of Mental Health Sciences, Community Mental Health/Mental Retardation Center, Philadelphia, PA 19102
Target Audience: 4-5

An individually administered test which measures preschool children's cognitive ability to solve interpersonal problems. Various pictures of people with or without toys are shown to the child while the test administrator tells the child the problem the character is having. The child then verbalizes solutions to the problem or tells what the character should do next. Test may be used as a criterion measure of social adjustment, a measure of evaluation for programs which aim to enhance interpersonal thinking skills or as a research tool. Information on validity and reliability included.

14871
Dental Hygiene Candidate Admission Test. Psychological Corp., San Antonio, TX
Descriptors: Academic Ability; *Admission Criteria; *College Entrance Examinations; *Dental Hygienists; Multiple Choice Tests; *Postsecondary Education; Scientific Concepts
Identifiers: DHCAT
Availability: The Psychological Corp.; 555 Academic Ct., San Antonio, TX 78204-0952
Target Audience: Adults
Notes: Time, 240 approx.

A multiple choice test designed to measure general academic ability and scientific knowledge for use by applicants seeking admission to dental hygiene programs. The extent to which test results are used as admission criteria varies from school to school but, in general, test results are combined with other information such as school records, references, and the results of personal interviews.

14874
Skills Assessment Module. Rosinek, Michele 1985
Subtests: Revised Beta Examination; Learning Styles Inventory; Personnel Test for Industry; Mail Sort; Alphabetizing Cards; Etch a Sketch Maze; Payroll Computation; Patient Information Memo; Small Parts; Ruler Reading; Pipe Assembly; O-Rings; Block Design; Color Sort; Circuit Board
Descriptors: Aptitude Tests; Arithmetic; Behavior Patterns; Clerical Occupations; Cognitive Ability; Disabilities; Disadvantaged; High Schools; *High School Students; Job Skills; Mechanical Skills; Occupational Tests; Spatial Ability; *Student Placement; *Vocational Education; Work Attitudes; Work Sample Tests
Identifiers: Clerical Aptitude; Learning Style; Manual Dexterity
Availability: Piney Mountain Press, Inc.; P.O. Box 333, Cleveland, GA 30528
Grade Level: 9-12
Notes: Time, 120

Designed to assess a student's affective, cognitive and manipulative strengths and weaknesses prior to placing students in vocational training programs within school systems. Norms are available for average students, students with disabilities, disadvantaged students and employed workers. Both paper and pencil tests and hands-on skills modules are included. Work behaviors such as appearance, endurance, communication skills, safety consciousness can be rated during performance.

14875
Test on Appraising Observations. Norris, Stephen P.; King, Ruth 1984
Descriptors: Cognitive Processes; *Critical Thinking; *Data Interpretation; Foreign Countries; High Schools; High School Students; Observation
Identifiers: Canada
Availability: Institute for Educational Research and Development, Memorial University of Newfoundland, St. John's Newfoundland, Canada A1B 3X8
Grade Level: 9-12
Notes: Time, 40

This test is designed to measure one aspect of critical thinking ability, the ability to correctly appraise observed data. It is intended for use with high school students but may be used at other levels such as undergraduates. It deals with factors that affect the accuracy of observation and the reporting of data observed. A situation is presented in the form of a story and the respondent indicates which of a pair of statements, about an observed happening, is more believable. The test is contained in "Studies in Critical Thinking, Research Report 1."

14894
Kindergarten Screening Inventory. Milone, Michael N.; Lucas, Virginia H. 1980
Subtests: Naming and Matching Familiar Objects; Naming and Matching Money; Naming and Matching Basic Colors; Naming and Matching Shapes; Naming and Matching Sets; Naming and Matching Numerals; Naming and Matching Letters; Naming and Matching Words; Sequence Words and Ordinal Numbers; Sequencing Counting; Child Writes Own Name; Tracing Basic Strokes; Copying Basic Strokes; Tracing, Letters and Numerals; Copying Letter and Numerals
Descriptors: Cognitive Development; *Criterion Referenced Tests; *Curriculum Development; *Individual Development; Individual Testing; *Kindergarten Children; Learning Readiness; *Preschool Tests; Primary Education; Reading Readiness; *School Readiness Tests; Writing Readiness
Identifiers: KSI
Availability: Zaner-Bloser; 1459 King Ave., Columbus, OH 43212
Grade Level: K
Target Audience: 5-6

The KSI is a curriculum planning for the kindergarten teacher. It is an individually administered criterion-referenced instrument designed to identify educationally relevant differences in children beginning kindergarten. The KSI comprises skills that appear in the Zaner-Bloser Kindergarten Program, but it can serve as a prelude to almost any kindergarten program. The 23 skills that are assessed are those important to pre-reading, pre-writing and prearithmetic. Some examples include naming and matching objects, sequencing, counting, copying, and tracing. Scoring for each skill is based on a 6-point scale and yields a Pupil Skill Profile.

14897
Fullerton Language Test for Adolescents, Revised Edition. Thorum, Arden R. 1986
Subtests: Auditory Synthesis; Morphology Competency; Oral Commands; Convergent Production; Divergent Production; Syllabication; Grammatic Competency; Idioms
Descriptors: *Adolescents; *Expressive Language; Grammar; Idioms; Individual Testing; Language Handicaps; Language Processing; Language Proficiency; *Language Tests; Morphemes; Norm Referenced Tests; Phonemes; *Preadolescents; *Receptive Language; Screening Tests; Syllables
Availability: Consulting Psychologists Press; 577 College Ave., Palo Alto, CA 94306
Target Audience: 11-18
Notes: Time, 45 approx.; Items, 142

Developed as a valid language assessment instrument to differentiate nonlanguage-impaired adolescents from language-impaired subjects. Consists of 8 subtests, each assessing a specific function important to the acquisition and use of language skills. Two of the subtests, oral commands and syllabication, assess receptive processing skills. The other 6 subtests assess expressive language production skills. The subtests do not have to be administered in any order and the test does not have to be given in 1 administration.

14898
Cognitive Abilities Scale. Bradley-Johnson, Sharon 1987
Subtests: Language; Reading; Mathematics; Handwriting; Enabling Behaviors
Descriptors: *Academic Aptitude; *Cognitive Ability; *Cognitive Tests; Handwriting; Imitation; Mathematical Concepts; Memory; Norm Referenced Tests; Oral Language; Reading Skills; Writing Readiness; *Young Children
Identifiers: CAS
Availability: PRO-ED; 8700 Shoal Creek Blvd., Austin, TX 78758
Target Audience: 2-3
Notes: Items, 88

Designed to provide norm-referenced assessment of cognitive skills of children ages 2 and 3. Also meant to provide detailed, educationally useful information on performance in 5 areas related to later success in school. Also provides specific information for planning educational programs in the areas tested. Also useful for researchers who study the cognitive development of young children. The language subtest assesses the ability to understand and use oral language. The reading subtest assesses early reading skills including book handling ability, skills related to comprehension, naming letters, and giving sounds for letters. The mathematics subtest covers seriation, knowledge of selected mathematical concepts, recognition of numbers, meaningful counting, matching numbers with quantities, and matching sets. The handwriting subtest measures skills directly related to manuscript writing. The enabling behaviors subtest assesses abilities important for efficient learning, including ability to remember auditory information, and the ability to initiate vocal and nonvocal behaviors. Also test allows for obtaining results for performance on nonverbal items.

14902
Scales of Creativity and Learning Environment. Slosson, Steven W. 1986
Subtests: Scale of Divergent/Convergent Thinking; Scale of Gifted Students
Descriptors: Classroom Environment; *Classroom Observation Techniques; Cognitive Style; Creativity; *Divergent Thinking; *Elementary School Students; Elementary Secondary Education; *Gifted; *Secondary School Students; Self Concept
Identifiers: SCALES
Availability: Slosson Educational Publications; P.O. Box 280, East Aurora, NY 14052
Grade Level: K-12

Two descriptive, 5-point Likert-type rating scales designed to assist school personnel to recognize students' gifted characteristics and the traits of creative, divergent thinkers. Both scales are based on Bloom's theory of taxonomy. Ratings are based on teacher's observations of student behavior over the previous month. The Scale of Gifted Students is designed to aid in the recognition of gifted characteristics in exceptionally talented students. The form is divided into the following areas: cognitive, comprehension, language, affective, problem solving, hobbies, and play. The Scale of Divergent/Convergent Thinking is used to assist in recognizing attributes of the divergent versus convergent thinker. It covers knowledge, ability, creativity, task commitment, synthesis, and evaluation. The manual also includes self-evaluation questionnaires for teachers to assess their teaching environment, and students to assess their learning style and their self image.

14997
Luria-Nebraska Neuropsychological Battery: Children's Revision. Golden, Charles J. 1987
Subtests: Motor Functions; Rhythm; Tactile Functions; Visual Functions; Receptive Speech; Expressive Speech; Writing; Reading; Arithmetic; Memory; Intellectual Processes; Spelling-Optional; Motor Writing-Optional; Pathognomonic; Left Sensorimotor; Right Sensorimotor; Academic Achievement; Integrative Functions; Spatial-Based Movement; Motor Speed and Accuracy; Drawing Quality; Drawing Speed; Rhythm Perception and Production; Tactile Sensations; Receptive Language; Expressive Language; Word and Phrase Repetition
Descriptors: Abstract Reasoning; Academic Achievement; Arithmetic; *Children; *Diagnostic Tests; Expressive Language; Freehand Drawing; *Individual Testing; Memory; *Neurological Impairments; Oral Reading; Patients; Psychiatry; Psychomotor Skills; Reading Skills; Receptive Language; *Screening Tests; Spatial Ability; Spelling; Tactual Perception; Visual Perception; Writing Skills
Identifiers: Neuropsychology; Reasoning Tests
Availability: Western Psychological Services; 12031 Wilshire Blvd., Los Angeles, CA 90025
Target Audience: 8-12
Notes: Time, 150; Items, 149

This individually administered battery was designed to assess a broad range of neurological functions including screening and diagnosing general and specific cognitive deficits such as lateralization and localization of focal brain impairments, and diagnosing brain damage in children with psychiatric disorders. It is not useful with children whose verbal ability is low. It can be used in planning and evaluation of rehabilitation programs. Clinical scales assess sensorimotor, perceptual, and cognitive abilities. Summary scales concern discrimination between brain injured and normal children. Factor scales assess specific neuropsychological functions.

15005
COACH-Cayuga-Onondago Assessment for Children with Handicaps, Second Edition. Giangreco, Michael F. 1986
Descriptors: *Cognitive Processes; Criterion Referenced Tests; *Curriculum; *Disabilities; Educational Needs; *Elementary School Students; Elementary Secondary Education; *Environmental Influences; Integrated Curriculum; Secondary School Students; Special Education; Student Evaluation
Identifiers: COACH; *Function Based Curriculum
Availability: National Clearinghouse of Rehabilitation Training Materials; 115 Old USDA Bldg., Oklahoma State University, Stillwater, OK 74078
Grade Level: 1-12
Notes: Time, 60 Approx.

Designed for use with school-aged learners having moderate, severe or profound handicapping conditions. Designed to assist in educational planning and evaluation process. A curriculum-based criterion-referenced assessment tool generated from a functional curriculum model which combines environmental and cognitive curriculum components. Functional curriculum refers to teaching activities which have practical applications in daily life within the context of Domestic, School, Community and Vocational settings for use in the learner's current and future environment. Cognitive curriculum is geared toward teaching concepts in communication and math via functional activities. Blends the environmental and cognitive curricula to maximize general learning and simultaneously teach relevant skills to the learner. To be administered by special education professionals in conjunction with the families of the learner.

15008
Bay Area Functional Performance Inventory. Williams, Susan Lang; Bloomer, Judith 1987
Subtests: Memory for Written and Verbal Instructions; Organization of Time and Materials; Attention Span; Evidence of Thought Disorder; Ability to Abstract; Task Completion; Errors; Efficiency; Motivation and Compliance; Frustration Tolerance; Self Confidence; General Affective and Behavioral Impression; Verbal Communication; Psychomotor Behavior; Socially Appropriate Behavior; Response to Authority Figures; Independence/Dependence; Work with Others; Group Participation

Descriptors: Abstract Reasoning; Adolescents; Adults; Affective Behavior; Attention Span; Cognitive Processes; Compliance (Psychology); *Daily Living Skills; Disabilities; Efficiency; Interpersonal Competence; Memory; Mental Disorders; Mental Retardation; Motivation; Neurological Impairments; Observation; Older Adults; *Patients; Performance Tests; Planning; Power Structure; *Psychiatry; Psychomotor Skills; Self Esteem; *Social Adjustment; Social Attitudes; Time Management; Verbal Communication
Identifiers: Bafpe; Closure; Dependence; Frustration; Independence; SIS; Social Interaction Scale; Task Completion; Task Orientation; Task Oriented Assessment; TOA
Availability: Consulting Psychologists Press; 577 College Ave., Palo Alto, CA 94306
Target Audience: 17-70
Notes: Time, 45

This standardized instrument is designed to measure skills and abilities necessary for functioning in everyday living activities, performing goal-directed and task-oriented activities as well as maintaining social relations with others. For use in occupational therapy or other rehabilitation and treatment programs. The TOA covers cognitive, affective, and performance areas of functioning evaluated in the context of completing 5 specific tasks. The Social Interaction Scale (SIS) evaluates 7 parameters of social behavior observed in 5 social settings: 1-to-1, mealtime, instructional group, structured task, or structured verbal group. Norms are available for males and females as patients in a psychiatric hospital. May be used with psychiatric patients, neurological patients, and mentally retarded adults. Norms are not included for these groups at this time.

15011
Learning Model Instrument. Murrell, Kenneth L. 1987
Descriptors: Administrators; Adults; Affective Behavior; *Cognitive Style; *Managerial Occupations; *Occupational Tests; Supervisory Methods
Identifiers: Learning Style
Availability: University Associates; 8517 Production Ave., San Diego, CA 92121
Target Audience: Adults
Notes: Items, 20

This forced-choice inventory is designed to assist individual managers in determining their preferred learning style. They indicate their preference for cognitive or affective learning and for concrete or abstract experiences. The manager is described as a thinking planner, feeling planner, task implementer, participative implementer. This scale is available in "The 1987 Annual: Developing Human Resources."

15019
Metropolitan Readiness Tests, Level 1, Fifth Edition. Nurss, Joanne R.; McGauvran, Mary E. 1986
Subtests: Auditory Memory; Beginning Consonants; Letter Recognition; Visual Matching; School Language and Listening; Quantitative Language; Copying
Descriptors: Auditory Perception; Cognitive Development; Language Skills; *Learning Readiness; Listening Skills; *Preschool Education; Preschool Tests; *Reading Readiness; Reading Readiness Tests; *School Readiness; *School Readiness Tests
Identifiers: Metropolitan Readiness Assessment Program; MRT
Availability: Psychological Corp.; 555 Academic Ct., San Antonio, TX 78204-0952
Target Audience: 4-5
Notes: Time, 90 approx.; Items, 77

Metropolitan Readiness Test (MRT) provides a skill-based assessment of the enabling skills that are important for early school learning, particularly, reading, mathematics, and language development. Specifically designed to determine the child's level of cognitive development as it relates to beginning reading and mathematics instruction. Identifies instructional needs of each child, allowing the teacher to group children according to their needs. Provides content-referenced information that helps instructional planning, facilitates small-group instruction and determines a pupil's strengths and weaknesses. Test content is based on current theories related to early childhood education and is drawn from the auditory, visual, language and quantitative concept areas. Two levels provide flexibility in assessing the diverse range of pre-reading skills present in pre-kindergarten, kindergarten and beginning grade 1 students. Content of each level is different because of the different stages of development between 4 and 5 and 6 year olds. Level 1 is designed for use at the end of pre-kindergarten and at the beginning and middle of kindergarten. Level 1 concentrates on the more basic reading skills.

15020
Metropolitan Readiness Tests, Level 2, Fifth Edition. Nurss, Joanne R.; McGauvran, Mary E. 1986
Subtests: Beginning Consonants; Sound-Letter Correspondence; Visual Matching; Finding Patterns; School Language Listening; Quantitative Concepts; Quantitative Operations; Copying
Descriptors: Auditory Perception; *Beginning Reading; Cognitive Development; Elementary School Mathematics; *Grade 1; *Kindergarten Children; Language Skills; *Learning Readiness; Listening Skills; Primary Education; Reading Readiness; Reading Readiness Tests; *School Readiness; *School Readiness Tests
Identifiers: Metropolitan Readiness Assessment Program; MRT
Availability: Psychological Corp.; 555 Academic Ct., San Antonio, TX 78204-0952
Grade Level: K-1
Target Audience: 5-6
Notes: Time, 90 approx.; Items, 97

Metropolitan Readiness Test (MRT) provides a skill-based assessment of the enabling skills that are important for early school learning, particularly, reading, mathematics, and language development. Specifically designed to determine the child's level of cognitive development as it relates to beginning reading and mathematics instruction. Identifies instructional needs of each child, allowing the teacher to group children according to their needs. Provides content-referenced information that helps instructional planning, facilitates small-group instruction and determines a pupil's strengths and weaknesses. Test content is based on current theories related to early childhood education and is drawn from the auditory, visual, language and quantitative concept areas. Two levels provide flexibility in assessing the diverse range of pre-reading skills present in pre-kindergarten, kindergarten and beginning grade 1 students. Content of each level is different because of the different stages of development between 4 and 5 and 6 year olds. Level 2 is designed for use at the middle and end of kindergarten and at the beginning of grade 1. Level 2 focuses on the more advanced skills that are important in beginning reading and mathematics.

15026
Early School Inventory—Developmental. Nurss, Joanne R.; McGauvran, Mary E. 1986
Subtests: Physical Development; Language Development; Cognitive Development; Social-Emotional Development
Descriptors: Check Lists; *Child Development; Cognitive Development; Emotional Development; *Grade 1; *Kindergarten Children; Language Acquisition; Measures (Individuals); Physical Development; *Preschool Education
Identifiers: ESID
Availability: Psychological Corp.; 555 Academic Ct., San Antonio, TX 78204-0952
Grade Level: K-1
Target Audience: 4-6
Notes: Items, 80

Designed to supplement information provided by the Metropolitan Readiness Tests. A checklist for recording physical, language, social-emotional, and cognitive development. Helps teacher gain a better understanding of child and helps determine the most effective instructional planning. To be used with children in pre-kindergarten and with those entering school for the first time in kindergarten or first grade.

15027
Early School Inventory—Preliteracy. Nurss, Joanne R.; McGauvran, Mary E. 1986
Subtests: Print Concepts; Writing Concepts; Story Structure
Descriptors: Individual Testing; Language Skills; *Literacy; Measures (Individuals); *Preschool Education; Preschool Tests; *Reading Readiness; *Writing Readiness
Identifiers: ESI(P)
Availability: Psychological Corp.; 555 Academic Ct., San Antonio, TX 78204-0952
Target Audience: 4-5
Notes: Time, 20 approx.

Designed to assist in the interpretation of the child's performance on the Metropolitan Readiness Tests. Provides information about child's preliteracy concepts. An inventory which assesses a child's concept of print, writing and story. Provides teacher with information for planning reading and writing instruction. Is individually administered.

15029
Boehm Test of Basic Concepts—Preschool Version. Boehm, Ann E. 1986
Descriptors: *Cognitive Development; *Individual Testing; Language Acquisition; Language Skills; Learning Disabilities; *Preschool Children; Preschool Education; *Preschool Tests; *School Readiness Tests; Standardized Tests
Identifiers: BOEHM (Preschool)

Availability: Psychological Corp.; 555 Academic Ct., San Antonio, TX 78204-0952
Target Audience: 3-5
Notes: Time, 15 approx.; Items, 52

An individually administered instrument designed to measure a child's knowledge of 26 relational concepts considered necessary for achievement in the first years of school. These concepts include characteristics of size, direction, position in space, quantity, and time. Can be used by a preschool teacher as an indicator of school readiness and as a guide for planning language instruction, but should not be used as the sole determinant of school readiness. Also appropriate for older children who have special educational needs. Yields norm-referenced scores for children at 5 age levels between 3 and 5.

15059
Wonderlic Personnel Test: Scholastic Level Exam. E.F. Wonderlic and Associates, Northfield, IL 1984
Descriptors: *Academic Aptitude; Adolescents; Adults; Aptitude Tests; Problem Solving; Schools
Identifiers: SLE
Availability: Publishers Test Service; 2500 Garden Rd., Monterey, CA 93940
Target Audience: 15-65
Notes: Time, 12; Items, 50

Wonderlic Personnel Test provides a highly accurate estimate of individual adult intelligence. A test of problem solving ability for people 15 to 65 years. Measures how easily people may be trained to perform job tasks, how well they can adjust and solve problems on the job, and how well-satisfied they are likely to be with the demands of the job. The Scholastic Level Exam (SLE) comprises 2 alternate forms, T-51 and T-71. Restricted to the use of educational institutions evaluating the academic potential of students. SLE forms have been constructed using the same methodology as Personnel Test forms and therefore result in the same measurement.

15066
Family Crisis Oriented Personal Evaluation Scales. McCubbin, Hamilton I.; And Others 1983
Descriptors: Adjustment (to Environment); Adults; Children; *Coping; *Family Problems; Family Relationship; Parents; *Problem Solving; Stress Variables
Identifiers: FCOPES
Availability: McCubbin, Hamilton; Thompson, Anne I. Family Inventories for Research and Practice. Madison: University of Wisconsin, 1987
Target Audience: Adults
Notes: Items, 30

Designed to identify problem-solving and behavioral strategies used by families in difficult or problematic situations. This instrument contains coping behavior items which focus on the ways a family handles difficulties between its members internally and the ways a family handles problems that emerge outside its boundaries but affect the family unit and its members.

15101
mCircle Instrument. Brain Technologies Corp., Ft. Collins, CO 1986
Descriptors: Adults; Behavior Patterns; *Decision Making; Decision Making Skills; Organizations (Groups); Personality; Problem Solving
Availability: Brain Technologies Corp.; 414 Buckeye St., Ft. Collins, CO 80524
Target Audience: Adults
Notes: Items, 20

Designed to identify the typical way an individual responds to others when confronted with a choice between 2 difficult alternatives, the kind of circumstance found in high-stress, rapid change business or organizational environments. Said to be different from other conflict resolution measures in that it uses mental "reframing" abilities to turn problems into opportunities. Explores the use of 5 strategies: Get Out; Give In; Take Over; Trade Off; Breakthrough.

15113
Stress Processing Report. Human Synergistics, Plymouth, MI 1984
Subtests: Time Use; Time Orientation; Cooperation; Synergy; Receptiveness; Trust; Intimacy; Interpersonal-Relaxed; Inclusion; Approval; Internal Control; Positive Past View; Self Image; Effectiveness; Growth; Optimistic Future View; Achievable Expectations; Goal Directedness; Satisfaction
Descriptors: *Administrators; Adults; Behavior Patterns; Cognitive Processes; Occupational Tests; Self Esteem; Social Behavior; *Stress Variables; Time Management
Availability: Human Synergistics; 39819 Plymouth Rd., Plymouth, MI 48170
Target Audience: Adults
Notes: Items, 160

This inventory identifies factors that contribute to psychological stress. It is a self-report and self-evaluation designed to help improve thought patterns related to stress-producing behavior. The respondent answers questions that reveal 19 different thinking styles said to be related to stress, strain and medical problems. Responses are plotted on a circular graph. Items are concerned with self-perceptions, belief systems, goal directedness, relationships with others, and effectiveness. Suggestions are given for causes and improvement of stress-producing thinking styles.

15123
Test Your Intuitive Powers. Agor, Weston H. 1985
Descriptors: Adults; Cognitive Style; Decision Making; *Intuition; Occupational Tests; Surveys
Identifiers: AIM Survey
Availability: Organization Design and Development; 2002 Renaissance Blvd., Ste. 100, King of Prussia, PA 19406
Target Audience: Adults
Notes: Items, 10

This survey is a measure of underlying or potential intuitive ability and whether or not intuitive powers are actually being used to help guide decision-making in situations where uncertainty is high; there is little precedent; variables are less scientifically predictable; facts are limited; there are several plausible solutions with good arguments; time is limited; and there is pressure to be right.

15132
Post-Wechsler Memory Scale. Cooper, Shawn 1980
Subtests: Verbal; Performance; Type
Descriptors: *Elementary School Students; Elementary Secondary Education; Individual Testing; *Memory; *Secondary School Students
Identifiers: Wechsler Intelligence Scale for Children (Revised)
Availability: Shawn Cooper; 170 Waterman St., Providence, RI 02906
Target Audience: 6-16
Notes: Items, 40

Provides an estimate of incidental and intermediate term memory for the verbal and visuospatial information contained in the Wechsler Intelligence Scale for Children—Revised (TC007461). Administered immediately after the Wechsler Scale, the examiner asks the child to recall details of the just-completed instrument and to answer questions either verbally or by drawing. The subject's memory performance can be categorized according to whether the child correctly answered more verbal items or more drawing items, and whether the child recalled information in general or more specific details.

15136
Creative Constructs Inventory. Smith, August William 1986
Descriptors: *Administrators; Adults; *Creativity; *Managerial Occupations; Rating Scales
Identifiers: C2I; *Management Style; TIM(M)
Availability: Tests in Microfiche; Test Collection, Educational Testing Service, Princeton, NJ 08541
Target Audience: Adults
Notes: Items, 60

Used to assess the way individuals relate to various dimensions and approaches to management. Combines concerns for ideas and imagination with the level of intensity to carry out creative ideas.

15145
Screening Test for the Luria-Nebraska Neuropsychological Battery: Adult and Children's Forms. Golden, Charles J. 1987
Descriptors: Adolescents; Adults; Children; *Cognitive Measurement; *Cognitive Psychology; *Neurological Impairments; Older Adults; *Screening Tests
Identifiers: ST(LNNB)C; ST(LUNNB)A
Availability: Western Psychological Services; 12031 Wilshire Blvd., Los Angeles, CA 90025
Target Audience: 8-99
Notes: Time, 20 approx.; Items, 15

The adult and children's versions of this instrument are each made up of 15 items taken from the Luria-Nebraska Neuropsychological Battery: Form II (TC010673) and the Luria-Nebraksa Neuropsychological Battery: Children's Revision (TC014997), respectively. The purpose of the screening test is to predict overall performance on the respective full-length battery, which diagnoses general and specific cognitive deficits.

15153
Inventory of Ghosts. Laus, Michael; Champagne, David W. 1986
Descriptors: Adults; Behavior Patterns; *Cognitive Style; Learning Strategies; Management Development; Occupational Tests; Self Evaluation (Individuals)
Identifiers: Learning Style

Availability: Organization Design and Development; 2002 Renaissance Blvd., Ste. 100, King of Prussia, PA 19406
Target Audience: Adults
Notes: Time, 20; Items, 50

Designed to identify behaviors, styles and needs that have become internalized from prior learning situations and which may adversely affect learning in management development situations or facilitate learning. Scores are developed in: ghosts of classroom history, work history, time/life demands, and personal needs. It is self-scored and an interpretive guide is included.

15157
Phases of Integrated Problem Solving, Revised Edition. Morris, William C.; Sashkin, Marshall 1985
Descriptors: Adults; Behavior Patterns; *Group Behavior; Occupational Tests; *Problem Solving; Rating Scales
Identifiers: PIPS
Availability: Organization Design and Development; 2002 Renaissance Blvd., Ste. 100, King of Prussia, PA 19406
Target Audience: Adults
Notes: Items, 36

Designed for use during a group problem-solving discussion. Six problem-solving phases are identified: problem definition, problem solution generation, ideas to actions, solution-action planning, solution-evaluation planning, evaluation of the product and process. The group evaluates its behavior in each phase via a 36 5-point scale rating the problem-solving behaviors they exhibited.

15173
Problem Solving Efficiency Questionnaire. Littlepage, Glenn E.
Descriptors: Adults; Conflict; Emotional Problems; Family Problems; *Males; *Military Personnel; *Problem Solving; Questionnaires
Identifiers: *Absent Without Leave; *AWOL; Problem Events
Availability: Glenn E. Littlepage; Psychology Dept., Middle Tennessee State University, Murfreesboro, TN 37132
Target Audience: Adults
Notes: Items, 48

Questionnaire which examines the problem solving efficiency of male military personnel. Used to compare AWOL (absent without leave) offenders with non-AWOL offenders in terms of their problem solving ability. Subject is presented with a problem and is asked to respond in a short written description to 6 questions pertaining to the problem. Subject is asked to list ways to solve the problem, relate what he would do in such a situation, and provide several alternative courses of action. Based on the theory that men with poor problem solving skills are most likely to go AWOL.

15181
Holbrook Screening Battery and Parent Questionnaire, Revised. Holbrook Public Schools, Holbrook, MA 1986
Subtests: Information; Sentences; Similarities; Language Sample; Colors; Letters; Shapes; Arithmetic; Visual Matching; Name Writing; Copy Forms; Pencil Grasp; Draw-a-Person; Cutting; Gross Motor
Descriptors: *Child Development; *Kindergarten; *Language Skills; *Preschool Children; Primary Education; *Psychomotor Skills; *School Readiness; School Readiness Tests; *Screening Tests
Identifiers: Fine Motor Skills; Gross Motor Skills; HSB; *Test Batteries; TIM(M)
Availability: Tests in Microfiche; Test Collection, Educational Testing Service, Princeton, NJ 08541
Grade Level: K
Target Audience: 4-5

Screening battery used by the Holbrook Public Schools in Massachusetts each spring to evaluate children about to enter kindergarten and who will be 5 years old by the end of the calendar year. Children are individually tested by each member of a team of 5 examiners. The battery consists of 15 subtests divided into 4 major groups: language, readiness, fine motor skills, and gross motor skills. Some of the subtests used are part of the Wechsler Preschool and Primary Scale of Intelligence (1963) (TC001424). There is also a developmental questionnaire to be filled out by the parents.

15189
Howell Prekindergarten Screening Test. Howell Township Public Schools, Howell, NJ 1984
Subtests: Shapes; Listening Comprehension; Auditory Memory; Color Words; Vocabulary; Classification; Letter Identification; Rhyming; Letter Writing; Directionality and Spatial Relation; Consonant Sounds; Visual Motor; Visual Discrimination; Name; Number Identification; Number Writing; Counting Sets; Math Concepts; Addition and Subtraction; Copying
Descriptors: Kindergarten; *Kindergarten Children; *School Readiness; *School Readiness Tests; *Screening Tests
Availability: Book-Lab; 500 74th St., N. Bergen, NJ 07047
Grade Level: K
Notes: Time, 120 approx.; Items, 73

A pencil and paper screening instrument which identifies students in need of appropriate supportive instructional programs. Students are classified into 3 general categories: those who may need special assistance, those with appropriate skills, and those with unusually well developed skills. The abilities that are assessed represent a sampling of verbal, quantitative, perceptual, and general cognitive skills that are commonly recognized as necessary for adequate participation in kindergarten-level activities. Does not specifically test gross motor activities. Suggested that the test be administered in 4 sittings over a 2-day period.

15190
Help for Special Preschoolers: Assessment Checklist, Ages 3-6. Santa Cruz County Office of Education, CA 1987
Descriptors: Check Lists; *Child Development; Cognitive Development; Communication Skills; Developmental Disabilities; *Developmental Tasks; *Disabilities; Motor Development; Observation; *Preschool Children; *Preschool Tests; *Screening Tests; Self Care Skills
Availability: VORT Corp.; P.O. Box 60132, Palo Alto, CA 94306
Target Audience: 3-6
Notes: Time, 120 approx.; Items, 625

An assessment of the developmental skills of disabled and non-disabled preschool children. Covers 625 skills in 28 separate Goal Areas which are clustered into 5 major developmental areas of Self Help, Motor, Communication, Social, and Cognitive Skills. Intended to be used as a practical tool for identifying needs, setting objectives, and tracking and commenting on individual progress. The skills covered are developmentally sequenced and the age ranges represent "normal" developmental milestones. The majority of the skills can be assessed through observation, unobtrusive play interaction, and parent interviews.

15199
Conceptual Systems Test. Harvey, O.J.; Hoffmeister, James K. 1971
Subtests: Divine Fate Control; Need for Structure-Order; General Pessimism; Need to Help People; Need for People; Interpersonal Aggression
Descriptors: Abstract Reasoning; Adults; Aggression; Altruism; *Beliefs; *Concept Formation; *Interpersonal Relationship; Rating Scales; *Self Evaluation (Individuals)
Identifiers: Concrete Operations; CST; Pessimism
Availability: Test Analysis and Development Corp.; 855 Inca Pwy., Boulder, CO 80303
Target Audience: Adults
Notes: Items, 48

Instrument used to measure subjects' levels of conceptual functioning. On a 5-point scale, subjects rate the extent to which they agree or disagree with statements concerning their beliefs, interactions with others, and need for order in their life. The Divine Fate Control section of the instrument may be used to determine if the person is functioning on an abstract or concrete level.

15200
Comprehensive Identification Process, Spanish Language Edition. Zehrbach, R. Reid 1985
Subtests: Cognitive-Verbal; Fine Motor; Gross Motor; Speech and Expressive Language; Hearing; Vision; Socio-affective Behavior; Medical History
Descriptors: Affective Measures; Auditory Tests; *Cognitive Development; Cognitive Measurement; Language Tests; Motor Development; *Preschool Children; *Preschool Tests; *Screening Tests; Social Development; Spanish; *Spanish Speaking; Speech Tests; Verbal Tests; Vision Tests
Identifiers: CIP
Availability: Scholastic Testing Service; 480 Meyer Rd., Bensenville, IL 60106
Target Audience: 3-5

A total process of locating, screening, and evaluating preschool children. Provides data that will quickly screen these children and help identify those who appear to warrant further testing to determine eligibility for special programs. It accomplishes this task in such a manner that there is no labeling of children or arousal of anxiety in parents before all necessary information is available. Most test materials available in both Spanish and English language.

15211
Reading Style Inventory. Carbo, Marie 1982
Descriptors: *Cognitive Style; *Diagnostic Tests; *Elementary School Students; Elementary Secondary Education; Reading Habits; *Reading Instruction; *Secondary School Students
Identifiers: RSI
Availability: Learning Research Associates; P.O. Box 39, Dept. 8, Roslyn Heights, NY 11577
Grade Level: 1-12
Notes: Time, 35 approx.; Items, 52

A diagnosis of how a student learns best, allowing educators to select the most appropriate reading method(s) and materials for each student. Based on the model of learning styles developed by Rita and Kenneth Dunn, this instrument groups learning characteristics into 4 major categories: Environmental Stimuli; Emotional Stimuli; Sociological Stimuli and Physical Stimuli. These 4 categories are further broken down into 30 elements of style. Also available as a software program for the Apple, TRS-80 and Commodore computers.

15234
Wolfe Microcomputer User Aptitude Test—W-Micro. Wolfe Personnel Testing and Training Systems, Oradell, NJ
Descriptors: *Adults; *Aptitude Tests; French; *Microcomputers; *Occupational Tests; Personnel Evaluation; *Personnel Selection
Identifiers: WMICRO
Availability: Wolfe Personnel Testing and Training Systems; P.O. Box 319, Oradell, NJ 07649
Target Audience: Adults
Notes: Time, 75

Evaluates a candidate's practical and analytical skills required for effective use of the microcomputer. (Does not include programing skills.) Traits measured include understanding supplier manuals; problem solving skills; ability to understand and use common spreadsheet and database packages; ability to work accurately and rapidly; and ability to sustain concentration and solve in-depth problems. Also available in French. Test scoring done by Wolfe.

15235
Programmer Analyst Aptitude Test. Wolfe Personnel Testing and Training Systems, Oradell, NJ 1984
Descriptors: Adults; *Aptitude Tests; Computers; *Occupational Tests; *Personnel Selection; *Programers; *Programing
Identifiers: PAAT
Availability: Wolfe Personnel Testing and Training Systems; P.O. Box 319, Oradell, NJ 07649
Target Audience: Adults
Notes: Time, 90; Items, 6

Used to pre-screen applicants and in-house personnel for their computer programing aptitude and business analysis potential. Consists of 6 problems which evaluate logical ability, skill in interpretation of business specifications, and potential for translating business problems into symbolic logic. Tests can be scored by Wolfe or by client.

15236
Wolfe Sales Staff Selector. Wolfe Personnel Testing and Training Systems, Oradell, NJ 1977
Subtests: Numerical Facility; Problem Solving Skills; Verbal Fluency; Sales Comprehension; Sales Motivation; Emotional Stability; People Contact Desired
Descriptors: Adults; *Aptitude Tests; French; *Occupational Tests; *Personnel Selection; Salesmanship; *Sales Occupations; *Sales Workers
Availability: Wolfe Personnel Testing and Training Systems; P.O. Box 319, Oradell, NJ 07649
Target Audience: Adults
Notes: Time, 75 approx.

Evaluates the suitability of candidates of all levels of experience for sales positions. Measures the following job criteria: numerical skills; problem solving and logical ability; verbal fluency and communication skills; comprehension of selling principles; sales motivation; emotional stability; and people contact desired. Tests can be scored either by Wolfe or the client.

15237
Wolfe Clerical Staff Selector. Wolfe Personnel Testing and Training Systems, Oradell, NJ 1977
Subtests: Problem Solving; Numerical Skills; Attention to Detail; Emotional Stability
Descriptors: Adults; *Aptitude Tests; *Clerical Occupations; *Clerical Workers; French; *Occupational Tests; *Personnel Selection
Availability: Wolfe Personnel Testing and Training Systems; P.O. Box 319, Oradell, NJ 07649
Target Audience: Adults
Notes: Time, 30 approx.

Evaluates the suitability of candidates of all levels of experience for clerical positions. Job criteria measured include problem solving and logical ability, numerical skills, attention to detail, and emotional stability. Scoring can be done by the client or by Wolfe. Also available in French.

15238
Wolfe Manager/Supervisor Staff Selector. Wolfe Personnel Testing and Training Systems, Oradell, NJ 1977

Subtests: Logic, Problem Solving Ability, Planning and Conceptualization; Numerical Skills and Reasoning; Verbal Fluency-Communication Skills; Business Judgment-Ability to Deal with Peers; Supervisory Practices-Practical Leadership; Emotional Stability; People Contact Required
Descriptors: Adults; *Aptitude Tests; French; *Managerial Occupations; *Occupational Tests; *Personnel Selection; Supervisors
Availability: Wolfe Personnel Testing and Training Systems; P.O. Box 319, Oradell, NJ 07649
Target Audience: Adults
Notes: Time, 75 approx.

Measures important intellectual and personality characteristics needed for the successful Manager/Supervisor. Measures the following job criteria: logic, problem solving ability, planning and conceptualizing; numerical skills and reasoning; communication skills; business judgment; supervisory practices; emotional stability; and people contact required. Scoring can be done by the client or by Wolfe. Also available in French.

15239
Wolfe Secretarial Staff Selector. Wolfe Personnel Testing and Training Systems, Oradell, NJ 1977
Subtests: Numerical Facility; Problem Solving; Attention to Detail; Manual Dexterity; Alphabetizing and Filing; Grammar and Punctuation; Spelling and Vocabulary; People Contact Desired; Emotional Stability
Descriptors: Adults; *Aptitude Tests; French; *Occupational Tests; *Personnel Selection; *Secretaries; Word Processing
Availability: Wolfe Personnel Testing and Training Systems; P.O. Box 319, Oradell, NJ 07649
Target Audience: Adults
Notes: Time, 75

Evaluates the suitability of candidates of all levels of experience for secretarial positions. Measures the following job criteria: attention to detail, alphabetizing and filing, grammar and punctuation, spelling and vocabulary, people contact desired, manual dexterity, emotional stability, logical and problem solving ability, and numerical skills. Can be scored either by client or Wolfe. Also available in French.

15273
Berger Tests of Programming Proficiency: B-Word Aptitude. Psychometrics, Inc., Sherman Oaks, CA 1986
Subtests: Proofreading; B-WORD Word Processor
Descriptors: Adults; *Aptitude Tests; Clerical Occupations; Computer Assisted Testing; Data Processing Occupations; *Occupational Tests; *Personnel Selection; *Word Processing; Proofreading
Availability: Psychometrics, Inc.; 13245 Riverside Dr., Ste. 360, Sherman Oaks, CA 91423
Target Audience: Adults
Notes: Time, 105

Designed to select word processor trainees who have a high potential for operating any word processing system. No prior experience or training is required. The test consists of 2 parts. Proofreading takes 15 minutes and requires correction of 40 errors. The word processor subtest requires 75 minutes to answer 25 multiple-choice questions. Examinees are expected to correct errors in spelling, punctuation and formatting consistency in the proofreading section and then read about and apply information about word processors. A paper and pencil version and an on-line version are available. Scored by publisher.

15297
Test of Relational Concepts. Edmonston, Nellie K.; Thane, Nancy Litchfield 1988
Descriptors: Cognitive Development; Communication Skills; *Concept Formation; *Preschool Children; Preschool Education; Primary Education; *Relationship; *Screening Tests; *Young Children
Identifiers: *Relational Concepts; TRC
Availability: PRO-ED; 8700 Shoal Creek Blvd., Austin, TX 78758
Target Audience: 3-7
Notes: Time, 15 approx.; Items, 56

An individual screening device for young children designed to measure the comprehension of relational terms, including dimensional adjectives, quantitative words, and spatial and temporal concepts. The test is normed for the age range 3 to 7, and consists of 56 line drawings each of which requires only a pointing response from the child. Quickly and easily identifies deficits in the comprehension of relational concepts, a process important both to communication development and to school success.

15299
Five P's: Parent Professional Preschool Performance Profile. Variety Preschoolers Workshop, Syosset, NY 1987
Subtests: Classroom Adjustment; Communicative Competence; Toileting and Hygiene; Mealtime Behaviors; Dressing; Receptive Language; Expressive Language; Emerging Self-Relationships to Adults; Relationships to Children; Gross Motor/Balance/Coordination Skills; Perceptual/Fine Motor Skills; Cognitive Development Scale
Descriptors: Adjustment (to Environment); *Behavior Problems; *Child Development; *Children; Classroom Environment; Cognitive Development; Communication Skills; Expressive Language; Family Environment; Hebrew; *Infants; Interpersonal Competence; Language Acquisition; Language Handicaps; *Learning Problems; Observation; Perceptual Development; *Preschool Children; Psychomotor Skills; Rating Scales; Receptive Language; Self Care Skills; Spanish
Identifiers: Fine Motor Skills; Gross Motor Skills
Availability: Variety Preschoolers Workshop; 47 Humphrey Dr., Syosset, NY 11791
Target Audience: 0-5

An assessment instrument for use with children who have learning, language and behavior problems, who function between the ages of 6 to 60 months and for whom standardized testing is not adequate. Both parent and teacher rate the child according to observations in home and school. Five P's can be used to gather information for the preparation of individualized education programs (IEPs). The 13 scales are composed of 458 skills. Both developmental skills and behaviors that interfere with these skills are evaluated. Evaluation is done in fall and spring, at home and in school. Spanish and Hebrew versions are available.

15311
Intermediate Measures of Music Audiation. Gordon, Edwin E. 1986
Subtests: Tonal; Rhythm
Descriptors: *Aptitude Tests; Elementary Education; *Elementary School Students; Magnetic Tape Cassettes; *Music; *Music Education
Identifiers: *Audiation; IMMA
Availability: G.I.A. Publications; 7404 S. Mason Ave., Chicago, IL 60638
Grade Level: 1-4
Notes: Time, 45 approx.; Items, 80

Recorded group tests of short, musical phrases. Includes 2 tests: Tonal and Rhythm. Each test is recorded on a separate cassette. Aids a child in making best use of his or her music aptitudes. Purpose is to evaluate tonal and rhythm aptitudes of each child, identify young children who can profit from study and instruction and evaluate tonal and rhythm aptitudes of each child as compared to similar children. For children in grades 1 through 4.

15419
Job Effectiveness Prediction System. Life Office Management Association, Atlanta, GA 1981
Descriptors: Adults; *Aptitude Tests; *Entry Workers; *Insurance Companies; Job Applicants; *Personnel Selection
Identifiers: JEPS
Availability: Life Office Management Association; 5770 Powers Ferry Rd., Atlanta, GA 30327
Target Audience: Adults

A series of tests used to assess skills required for entry-level positions in life and casualty-property insurance companies. The tests are used to assess numerical ability, mathematical skills, spelling, language usage, reading comprehension, verbal comprehension, filing, coding and converting, comparing and checking. Tests are used for job applicants for clerical, technical, and professional positions.

15421
Comparative Guidance and Placement Program. Educational Testing Service, Princeton, NJ
Descriptors: Achievement Tests; Biographical Inventories; Cognitive Tests; *College Students; *Educational Counseling; Higher Education; *Postsecondary Education; Student Interests; *Student Placement; *Undergraduate Students; Two Year College Students
Identifiers: CGP; MAPS; Multiple Assessment Programs and Services
Availability: Educational Testing Service; Comparative Guidance and Placement Program/MAPS, Princeton, NJ 08541
Grade Level: 13-16

Comprehensive information gathering and interpretation system to meet counseling and placement needs of community colleges, vocational-technical institutes, and 4-year institutions. Program consists of several components. The Biographical Inventory provides information on students' background, attitudes, plans, needs, and aspirations in personal and academic areas. The Comparative Interest Index asks students to indicate their degree of interest in numerous academic and related fields. It may be self administered by the student. The English and Mathematics Achievement/Placement Tests are useful for determining students who are adequately prepared for regular placement and those who may need developmental work. There are achievement/placement tests in reading and written English expression and 3 levels of mathematics tests, depending on the student's background in high school algebra. The achievement/placement tests are also available in self-scoring format. In addition, there are 3 special abilities tests which are less dependent than others on knowledge obtained in a formal setting: Year 2000 Test, Mosaic Comparisons Test, and Letter Groups Test. To meet the varying needs of users, CGP offers 3 options: full CGP program, modified CGP program, or English and Mathematics Achievement/Placement Test in self-scoring form.

15429
Combined Cognitive Preference Inventory. Tamir, Pinchas 1985
Descriptors: Cognitive Processes; *Cognitive Style; High Schools; *High School Students; Questionnaires; *Sciences
Availability: Pinchas Tamir; Israel Science Teaching Center, University of Gavat Ram, Jerusalem, Israel
Grade Level: 9-12
Notes: Items, 20

Designed to measure a student's perception of science information. Student selects which of 4 correct responses to a statement about a scientific concept is most appealing. Other responses are ordered according to their appeal. Responses are concerned with purely factual information; a further question that stimulates wondering; a statement suggesting an actual use of the concept; a statement that enlarges on the complete question.

15435
Mega Test. Hoeflin, Ronald K. 1988
Subtests: Verbal Analogies; Spatial Problems; Numerical Problems
Descriptors: Adults; *Gifted; Individual Testing; *Intelligence Tests; Self Evaluation (Individuals)
Availability: Ronald K. Hoeflin; P.O. Box 7430, New York, NY 10116
Target Audience: Adults
Notes: Items, 48

An untimed, unsupervised, self-administered intelligence test for the gifted adults. Serves as an admission test for the following high-IQ societies: Triple Nine, ISPE, Prometheus, Titan, and Mega. Scored by the publisher. Consists of 3 parts: verbal analogies, spatial problems, numerical problems.

15437
Microcomputer Evaluation and Screening Assessment. Valpar International Corp., Tucson, AZ 1986
Subtests: Hardware Exercise; Independent Perceptual Screening; Talking-Persuasive Screening; Physical Capacity and Mobility; Vocational Interest and Awareness; Access Profile
Descriptors: Academic Ability; Adolescents; Adults; Career Awareness; *Career Exploration; *Computer Assisted Testing; Eye Hand Coordination; *Job Placement; *Job Training; Language Skills; Physical Fitness; Problem Solving; *Screening Tests; Spatial Ability; Tactual Perception; Vision Tests; Vocational Interests
Identifiers: Manual Dexterity; MESA
Availability: Valpar International Corp.; P.O. Box 5767, Tucson, AZ 85703-5767
Target Audience: 13-65
Notes: Time, 270 approx.

Assesses individual's job-related knowledge, skills, and aptitudes for use in career exploration and job or training placement. It is a comprehensive, computerized screening instrument that gathers large quantities of information in short periods of time. Although it is meant to interface with other assessment programs, it can also stand alone. The subject's performance is measured against the Worker Qualifications Profile of the Dictionary of Occupational Titles. During the computer exercises, a large number of factors are measured in approximately 30 minutes. These factors include shape discrimination, problem solving, and academics. Subjects begin with a brief vision screening test and a hand-eye coordination component. Other components include a hardware exercise which assesses tool use, assembly skills, dexterity, manipulation, and ability to follow instructions; independent perceptual screening to measure tactile sensitivity and spatial aptitude; talking/persuasive screening related to language development; physical capacity and mobility to provide nonmedical screening before training or job placement; and vocational interests and awareness used to analyze vocational interests and to assess subject's basic understanding of the world of work; and an access profile which allows comparison of evaluee's performance to specific requirements for success in a job, training, or classroom setting. Available for use on IBM PC or XT or Apple IIe.

15438
Microcomputer Evaluation and Screening Assessment—Short Form 2. Valpar International Corp., Tucson, AZ 1986

Descriptors: Academic Ability; Adolescents; Adults; *Career Exploration; *Computer Assisted Testing; *Job Placement; *Job Training; Memory; Problem Solving; Psychomotor Skills; *Screening Tests; Visual Perception
Identifiers: MESA SF2
Availability: Valpar International Corporation; P.O. Box 5767, Tucson, AZ 85703-5767
Target Audience: 13-65
Notes: Time, 75 approx.

Computerized screening instrument used to assess an individual's job-related knowledge, skills, and aptitudes for use in career exploration, and job training or placement. Uses game-like exercises to measure motor coordination, academics, problem solving, size and shape discrimination, and memory. Computer exercises are self administered and automatically scored. There is also a paper-pencil survey which is self-administered. This is a shorter version of the Microcomputer Evaluation and Screening Assessment (TC015437). Available for use on IBM PC or XT or Apple IIe.

15470
Continuous Visual Memory Test. Trahan, Donald E.; Larrabee, Glenn J. 1988
Subtests: Aquisition Task; Delayed Recognition Task; Visual Discrimination Task
Descriptors: Adults; Individual Testing; Long Term Memory; *Memory; Older Adults; Short Term Memory; Visual Discrimination; *Visual Measures
Identifiers: CUMT
Availability: Psychological Assessment Resources; P.O. Box 998, Odessa, FL 33556
Target Audience: 18-70
Notes: Time, 45 approx.; Items, 126

A continuous visual recognition memory test. Uses complex nonverbal stimuli to assess memory functions in adults. Consists of 3 tasks. The Acquisition Task tests recognition memory. The Delayed Recognition Task measures retrieval from long-term storage. The Visual Discrimination Task distinguishes visual discrimination deficits from visual memory problems.

15492
Cognitive Control Battery. Santostefano, Sebastiano 1988
Subtests: Scattered Scanning Test; Fruit Distraction Test; Level-Sharpening House Test
Descriptors: *Cognitive Development; *Cognitive Tests; Learning Disabilities; *Preadolescents; Visual Measures; *Young Children
Identifiers: CCB; FDT; LSHT; SST
Availability: Western Psychological Services; 12031 Wilshire Blvd., Los Angeles, CA 90025
Target Audience: 4-12
Notes: Time, 28 approx.

Developed for children 4 to 12 years old. Consists of 3 tests: Scattered Scanning Test (SST), Fruit Distraction Test (FDT) and Level-Sharpening House Test (LSHT). Can be used as an assessment battery as well as individually. Main purpose of each test is to assess the developmental status of one aspect of a child's cognitive control functioning, namely visual scanning (SST), selective attention (FDT), or comparing memory images of information with present perceptions (LSHT). Results in a cognitive control profile. Used to predict learning disabilities; diagnose existing learning disabilities, diagnose the role of cognitive dysfunctions in a child's school and adjustment problems; and assess cognition in studies of the relations between personality and cognition in development and adaptation.

15497
Wechsler Intelligence Scale for Children—Revised. Abbreviated Version. Kennedy, L. Patricia; Elder, S. Thomas 1982
Descriptors: Adolescents; Children; *Elementary School Students; Elementary Secondary Education; *Emotional Disturbances; Individual Testing; *Intelligence; Intelligence Quotient; *Intelligence Tests; *Learning Problems; Performance Tests; *Secondary School Students; *Slow Learners
Availability: Journal of Clinical Psychology; v38 n1 p174-78, Jan 1982
Target Audience: 6-16

Extracts five subscales from the Wechsler Intelligence Scale for Children-Revised (WISC-R) (TC007461): Information, Block Design, Comprehension, Picture Assembly, and Coding. Scale may be used with learning disabled children or emotionally disturbed children. Should be used for re-evaluation purposes only. The WISC-R should be administered during initial clinical diagnosis. The equation to be used when scoring the abbreviated form of the scale is presented.

15509
Einstein Assessment of School-Related Skills, Level K. Gottesman, Ruth L.; Cerullo, Frances M. 1988

Subtests: Language/Cognition; Letter Recognition; Auditory Memory; Arithmetic; Visual-Motor Integration
Descriptors: Arithmetic; *High Risk Students; *Individual Testing; Kindergarten; *Kindergarten Children; Language Tests; *Learning Disabilities; *Learning Problems; Mathematics Tests; Perceptual Motor Coordination; *Primary Education; *Screening Tests; Short Term Memory
Availability: Modern Curriculum Press; 13900 Prospect Rd., Cleveland, OH 44136
Grade Level: K
Target Audience: 5
Notes: Time, 10 approx.; Items, 17

An individually administered screening instrument that measures the major skill areas underlying school achievement. Designed to identify kindergarten children who are at risk for, or are experiencing, learning difficulties, and who therefore should be referred for a comprehensive evaluation. Easily administered without special training. There are 5 additional test levels to be used with grades 1-5 (see TC015510-TC015514).

15510
Einstein Assessment of School-Related Skills, Level 1. Gottesman, Ruth L.; Cerullo, Frances M. 1988
Subtests: Language/Cognition; Word Recognition; Oral Reading; Reading Comprehension; Auditory Memory; Arithmetic; Visual-Motor Integration
Descriptors: Arithmetic; *Elementary School Students; *Grade 1; *High Risk Students; *Individual Testing; Language Tests; *Learning Disabilities; *Learning Problems; Mathematics Tests; Oral Reading; Perceptual Motor Coordination; Primary Education; Reading Comprehension; Reading Tests; *Screening Tests; Short Term Memory; Word Recognition
Availability: Modern Curriculum Press; 13900 Prospect Rd., Cleveland, OH 44136
Grade Level: 1
Notes: Time, 10 approx.; Items, 24

An individually administered screening instrument that measures the major skill areas underlying school achievement. Designed to identify first grade children who are at risk for, or are experiencing, learning difficulties, and who therefore should be referred for a comprehensive evaluation. Easily administered without special training. There are 5 additional test levels to be used with grades Kindergarten and 2-5 (See TC 015509, TC015511-TC015514).

15511
Einstein Assessment of School-Related Skills, Level 2. Gottesman, Ruth L.; Cerullo, Frances M. 1988
Subtests: Language/Cognition; Word Recognition; Oral Reading; Reading Comprehension; Auditory Memory; Arithmetic; Visual-Motor Integration
Descriptors: Arithmetic; *Elementary School Students; *Grade 2; *High Risk Students; *Individual Testing; Language Tests; *Learning Disabilities; *Learning Problems; Mathematics Tests; Oral Reading; Perceptual Motor Coordination; Primary Education; Reading Comprehension; Reading Tests; *Screening Tests; Short Term Memory; Word Recognition
Availability: Modern Curriculum Press; 13900 Prospect Rd., Cleveland, OH 44136
Grade Level: 2
Notes: Time, 10 approx.; Items, 25

An individually administered screening instrument that measures the major skill areas underlying school achievement. Designed to identify second grade children who are at risk for, or are experiencing learning difficulties, and who therefore should be referred for a comprehensive evaluation. Easily administered without special training. There are five additional test levels to be used with grades kindergarten-1, and 3-5 (see TC 015509-TC 015510, TC 015513-TC 015514).

15512
Einstein Assessment of School-Related Skills, Level 3. Gottesman, Ruth L.; Cerullo, Frances M. 1988
Subtests: Language/Cognition; Word Recognition; Oral Reading; Reading Comprehension; Auditory Memory; Arithmetic; Visual Motor Integration
Descriptors: Arithmetic; Elementary School Students; *Grade 3; *High Risk Students; *Individual Testing; Language Tests; *Learning Disabilities; *Learning Problems; Mathematics Tests; Oral Reading; Perceptual Motor Coordination; *Primary Education; Reading Comprehension; Reading Tests; *Screening Tests; Short Term Memory; Word Recognition
Availability: Modern Curriculum Press; 13900 Prospect Rd., Cleveland, OH 44136

Grade Level: 3
Notes: Time, 10 approx.; Items, 21

An individually administered screening instrument that measures the major skill areas underlying school achievement. Designed to identify third grade children who are at risk for, or are experiencing, learning difficulties, and who therefore should be referred for a comprehensive evaluation. Easily administered without special training. There are 5 additional test levels to be used with grades kindergarten-2, 4-5 (see TC 015509-TC015511, TC015513-TC105514).

15513
Einstein Assessment of School-Related Skills, Level 4. Gottesman, Ruth L.; Cerullo, Frances M. 1988
Subtests: Language/Cognition; Word Recognition; Oral Reading; Reading Comprehension; Auditory Memory; Arithmetic; Visual-Motor Integration
Descriptors: Arithmetic; Elementary Education; *Elementary School Students; *Grade 4; *High Risk Students; *Individual Testing; Language Tests; *Learning Disabilities; *Learning Problems; Mathematics Tests; Oral Reading; Perceptual Motor Coordination; Reading Comprehension; Reading Tests; *Screening Tests; Short Term Memory; Word Recognition
Availability: Modern Curriculum Press; 13900 Prospect Rd., Cleveland, OH 44136
Grade Level: 4
Notes: Time, 10 approx.; Items, 23

An individually administered screening instrument that measures the major skill areas underlying school achievement. Designed to identify fifth grade children who are at risk for, or are experiencing, learning difficulties, and who should therefore be referred for a comprehensive evaluation. Easily administered without special training. There are 5 additional test levels to be used with grades K-3 and 5 (see TC015509-015512, TC015514).

15514
Einstein Assessment of School-Related Skills, Level 5. Gottesman, Ruth L.; Cerullo, Frances M. 1988
Subtests: Language/Cognition; Word Recognition; Oral Reading; Reading Comprehension; Auditory Memory; Arithmetic; Visual-Motor Integration
Descriptors: Arithmetic; Elementary Education; *Elementary School Students; *Grade 5; *High Risk Students; *Individual Testing; Language Tests; *Learning Disabilities; *Learning Problems; Mathematics Tests; Oral Reading; Perceptual Motor Coordination; Reading Comprehension; Reading Tests; *Screening Tests; Short Term Memory; Word Recognition
Availability: Modern Curriculum Press; 13900 Prospect Rd., Cleveland, OH 44136
Grade Level: 5
Notes: Time, 10 approx.; Items, 25

An individually administered screening instrument that measures the major skill areas underlying school achievement. Designed to identify fifth grade children who are at risk for, or are experiencing, learning difficulties, and who therefore should be referred for a comprehensive evaluation. Easily administered without special training. There are 5 additional test levels to be used with grades kindergarten-4, (see TC015509-TC015513).

15517
Clymer-Barrett Readiness Test, Revised Edition, Forms A and B. Clymer, Theodore; Barrett, Thomas C. 1983
Subtests: Recognizing Letters; Matching Words; Beginning Sounds; Ending Sounds; Completing Shapes; Copy A Sentence
Descriptors: Auditory Discrimination; Early Childhood Education; Eye Hand Coordination; Perceptual Motor Coordination; Pretests Posttests; *Primary Education; *Reading Readiness; *Reading Readiness Tests; Reading Tests; Visual Discrimination
Availability: Chapman, Brook and Kent; 27775 Hwy. 189, Arrowhead, CA 92352
Grade Level: K-1
Notes: Time, 90; Items, 110

A readiness for reading measure that considers visual and auditory discrimination and visual-motor coordination. Used at end of kindergarten to determine success of readiness program, and at beginning of first grade to group students and determine which skills need emphasis. Two forms are available as pre- and posttest. To create a short form, the first test of each discrimination subarea can be used as a quick readiness survey (Recognizing Letters; Beginning Sounds). Each section of the test is given in one separate half-hour sitting.

15526
Randt Memory Test. Randt, C.T.; Brown, E.R. 1984

Subtests: General Information; Five Items; Repeating Numbers; Paired Words; Short Story; Picture Recognition; Incidental Learning
Descriptors: Adults; *Individual Testing; *Memory; *Neurological Impairments; Older Adults; *Visual Measures
Identifiers: Memory Deficits
Availability: Life Science Associates; 1 Fenimore Rd., Bayport, NY 11705
Target Audience: 20-90

Measures memory processes in neurologically impaired adult populations, including elderly persons. Evaluates primary, rote, associative, discourse and incidental memory functions as well as visual recall and recognition. Does not assist in the locating of brain lesions or functions nor is it intended for detailed research investigations into specific facets of normal human memory. Useful for the early detection of significant memory deficits in older populations and in repeated applications in the longitudinal testing of memory over time.

15567
Wechsler Memory Scale, Revised. Wechsler, David 1987
Subtests: Information and Orientation Questions; Mental Control; Figural Memory; Logical Memory I; Visual Paired Associates I; Verbal Paired Associates I; Visual Reproduction; Digit Span; Visual Memory Span; Logical Memory II; Visual Paired Associates II; Verbal Paired Associates II; Visual Reproduction
Descriptors: Adolescents; Adults; *Diagnostic Tests; *Individual Testing; *Memory; Older Adults; *Screening Tests
Identifiers: WMS R
Availability: The Psychological Corp.; 555 Academic Ct., San Antonio, TX 78204-0952
Target Audience: 16-74
Notes: Time, 45 Approx.

The Wechsler Memory Scale-Revised (WMS-R) is an individually administered, clinical instrument for appraising major dimensions of memory functions in adolescents and adults. Intended as a diagnostic and screening device for use as part of a general neuropsychological examination or any other clinical examination requiring the assessment of memory functions. Comprised of a series of brief subtests. The functions assessed include memory for verbal and figural stimuli, meaningful and abstract material, and delayed as well as immediate recall. WMS-R represents an extensive revision of the original Wechsler Memory Scale. Changes include norms stratified at 9 age levels, replacement of a single global summary score with 5 composite scores, addition of new subtests measuring figural and spatial memory, addition of measures of delayed recall, revision of the scoring procedures for several subtests to improve scoring accuracy. A brief version of the scale can be administered which excludes the 4 delayed-recall trials.

15578
WICAT Early Childhood Profile. WICAT Systems, Orem, UT 1987
Subtests: Alphabet Recognition; Number Recognition; Counting; Listening Comprehension; Concept Relations; Classification Skills; Sound/Symbol Identification
Descriptors: *Academic Ability; *Computer Assisted Testing; Concept Formation; Curriculum Development; *Early Childhood Education; Learning Readiness; Listening Comprehension; Multiple Choice Tests; Numbers; Preschool Education; Pretests Posttests; Reading Readiness; *School Readiness; Young Children
Availability: WICAT Systems; 1875 S.State St., Orem, UT 84058
Target Audience: 3-6
Notes: Time, 30; Items, 24

Consists of 2 levels of a computer-administered test designed to assess the academic abilities of young children. Level 1 is for ages 3.5 to 4.5 and Level 2 is for ages 4.5 to 6.0. Items are read to the child who selects the answer from a multiple-choice format. Can be used to determine readiness for preschool or kindergarten, for curriculum planning and as a pretest/posttest measure of student progress. WICAT supplies the computer systems that run this software. Also runs on IBM-PC and Apple IIe.

15581
WICAT Learner Profile. WICAT Systems, Orem, UT 1987
Descriptors: Abstract Reasoning; *Academic Ability; *Adaptive Testing; Adolescents; Adults; Aptitude Tests; Children; *Cognitive Ability; Cognitive Style; *Computer Assisted Testing; Computer Software; Learning Strategies; Mathematics; Memory; School Attitudes; Spatial Ability; Verbal Ability
Availability: WICAT Systems; 1875 S.State St., Orem, UT 84058
Target Audience: 8-65
Notes: Items, 20

This series of computerized adaptive tests profiles students' cognitive strengths and weaknesses, learning styles and attitudes. Thirty individual tests are available covering key learning skills, verbal ability, visual/spatial ability, quantitative ability, reasoning ability, memory ability, preferences related to learning. May be used to identify those with gifts or deficiencies in cognitive skills. Profiles of all students' cognitive skills are produced. The computer selects the difficulty level of the student's next question based on the previous response during testing. WICAT software is used with WICAT systems hardware. Also runs on IBM-PC and Apple IIe.

15591
Kindergarten Readiness Test. Larson, Sue L.; Vitali, Gary J. 1988
Descriptors: Developmental Tasks; *Kindergarten Children; Norm Referenced Tests; *School Readiness Tests; *Screening Tests
Identifiers: KRT
Availability: Slosson Educational Publications; P.O. Box 280, East Aurora, NY 14052
Grade Level: K
Target Audience: 4-6
Notes: Time, 20 approx.

Developed to assess a child's functioning on various developmental tasks. Intended for use by early education teachers and other professionals to assess levels of maturity and development of typical 4.5- to 6-year olds who are entering Kindergarten. Is meant to be used in combination with other factors to provide additional information to help parents determine if their children are developmentally ready to enter Kindergarten. It is designed so that the majority of children will successfully complete between 78 and 90 percent of the measured tasks. Handicapped children and non-English speaking children may have difficulties with some items. Although the test was intended to remove as many ethnic and socioeconomic biases as possible, consideration should be given to the child's social, family, and cultural environments if a significantly low score is obtained. The general assessed skill areas include understanding, awareness, and interaction with one's environment; judgment and reasoning in problem solving; numerical awareness; visual and fine-motor coordination; and auditory attention span and concentration.

15605
Primary Measures of Music Audiation. Gordon, Edwin E. 1986
Subtests: Tonal; Rhythm
Descriptors: *Aptitude Tests; Elementary School Students; Magnetic Tape Cassettes; *Music Education; *Primary Education
Identifiers: *Audiation; PMMA
Availability: G.I.A. Publications; 7404 S. Mason Ave., Chicago, IL 60638
Grade Level: K-3
Notes: Time, 45 approx.; Items, 80

Group test of short musical phrases designed to act as objective aids for teachers and parents to help children make best use of their musical aptitudes by providing them with appropriate opportunities and instruction. Includes 2 tests: tonal and rhythm. Serves 3 purposes: evaluate comparative tonal and rhythm aptitudes of each child; identify young children who can profit from additional study and private instruction; and to evaluate tonal and rhythm aptitudes of each child compared to other children of similar age on a periodic basis.

15620
College Admissions Practice Test for the Scholastic Aptitude Test. Psychological Corp., San Antonio, TX 1987
Subtests: Verbal Ability; Mathematical Ability
Descriptors: *Aptitude Tests; *College Entrance Examinations; High Schools; *High School Students; Junior High Schools; *Junior High School Students; Mathematical Concepts; Verbal Ability
Identifiers: CAPT; *Practice Tests; SAT; Scholastic Aptitude Test
Availability: The Psychological Corp.; 555 Academic Ct., San Antonio, TX 78204-0952
Grade Level: 8-12
Notes: Time, 70 approx.; Items, 80

Group-administered test designed to resemble the content and format of typical college admissions tests. Consists of a verbal ability section and a mathematical ability section. Provides students with experience in answering items typical of general college admissions tests and scholastic aptitude tests which measure verbal and mathematical reasoning abilities. Can be used by guidance counselors and teachers of college-bound students to assist them in preparing for college admissions tests, to advise students of areas of strengths and weaknesses, and to help reduce test anxiety or pressure by providing a nonthreatening practice situation. Was developed from extensive analysis of the Scholastic Aptitude Test (SAT), and items were written to parallel the content and style of the SAT.

15645
Problem Solving Rehabilitation I and II. Sbordone, Robert J. 1984

Descriptors: Adolescents; Adults; *Computer Assisted Testing; *Neurological Impairments; *Problem Solving; *Rehabilitation
Availability: Robert J. Sbordone; Orange County Neuropsychology Group, 8840 Warner Ave., Ste. 301, Fountain Valley, CA 92708
Target Audience: 13-65

Problem Solving I trains cognitively impaired patients to improve their problem-solving skills and ability to tolerate frustration. Computer-administered program in which patient is visually presented with a series of 10 tasks of increasing complexity requiring the use of a joystick. Problem Solving II is similar to Program Solving I in developing problem-solving skills and learning to anticipate the consequences of his/her actions. Problem Solving II should be used after the patient has reached Level 7 or 8. Requires the patient to consider multiple variables while evaluating a problem from several different perspectives. Computer administered.

15646
Digit-Digit Test II. Sbordone, Robert J. 1984
Descriptors: Adolescents; Adults; *Attention Control; Children; *Computer Assisted Testing; *Neurological Impairments; *Rehabilitation
Availability: Robert J. Sbordone; Orange County Neuropsychology Group, 8840 Warner Ave., Ste. 301, Fountain Valley, CA 92708
Target Audience: 5-65

Assesses and trains complex attentional skills in normal, brain-injured, and cognitively impaired patients. Patient's motor and cognitive processing speed can be separately assessed and compared using a numerical coding task. Computer administered.

15647
Sbordone-Hall Memory Battery. Sbordone, Robert J. 1984
Subtests: Free Recall of Alpha Numeric Stimuli; Recognition of Alpha-Numeric Stimuli; Immediate Recognition of Familiar Words; Delayed Recognition of Pictures Test; Recognition of Single Geometric Figures; Delayed Recognition of Familiar Words; Recognition of Multiple Geometric Figures
Descriptors: Adults; *Computer Assisted Testing; *Memory; Recall (Psychology); Recognition (Psychology); *Rehabilitation
Identifiers: SHMB
Availability: Robert J. Sbordone; Orange County Neuropsychology Group, 8840 Warner Ave., Ste. 301, Fountain Valley, CA 92708
Target Audience: Adults
Notes: Time, 60 approx.

Provides serial testing of memory functioning using randomly generated test stimuli. Administered and scored by microcomputer. Provides short (1-1/2 pages) or full (12 pages) analysis of a patient's performance. Test instructions are clear. No direct supervision required during administration of battery. Includes personalized interaction with the patient, positive reinforcement to the patient, automatic response cueing and brief rest periods during testing to reduce the effect of fatigue. Can be taken by normal, brain-injured, and cognitively impaired adults. Used for clinical assessment, cognitive rehabilitation or research. Computer administered.

15692
Cognitive Speed Battery. Carver, Ronald P. 1987
Descriptors: *College Students; *Conceptual Tempo; *Elementary School Students; Elementary Secondary Education; Higher Education; *Reaction Time; *Reading Rate; *Secondary School Students
Identifiers: SDT; STT
Availability: Revrac Publications; 207 W. 116th St., Kansas City, MO 64114
Grade Level: 2-16
Target Audience: Adults

Consists of 2 tests, the Speed of Thinking Test (STT) and Speed of Deciding Test (SDT). The STT was designed to measure cognitive speed or thinking rate, which has been theorized to limit or influence reading rate. Is a 2-minute timed test that measures how fast individuals can determine answers to simple mental problems. The SDT is a 1-minute test given to control for simple reaction time and the psychomotor speed of marking. Measures how fast students can mark empty boxes configured exactly the same as on the STT. The Cognitive Speed Battery was developed so that influence of cognitive speed upon reading rate can be investigated.

15700
Short Category Test, Booklet Format. Wetzel, Linda C.; Boll, Thomas J. 1987
Subtests: Number of Figures in a Linear Array; Original Position of the Atypical Figure in a Linear Array; Identify the Atypical Quadrant; Number of Quadrants Joined by Solid Lines

Descriptors: *Abstract Reasoning; Adolescents; Adults; *Cognitive Tests; *Concept Formation; Individual Testing; *Neurological Impairments; Older Adults; Visual Stimuli
Identifiers: Brain Functions; SCT
Availability: Western Psychological Services; 12031 Wilshire Blvd., Los Angeles, CA 90025
Target Audience: 15-80
Notes: Items, 100

Shortens the length and complexity of the Category Test. Measures an individual's ability to solve problems requiring abstract concept formations. Most commonly used as part of a comprehensive test battery to assess overall brain functioning. Short, transportable, can be administered at bedside and does not require expensive equipment. Intended for adolescents and adults aged 15 and older. Consists of 5 booklets with 20 cards per subtest. Useful in detecting subtle effects of closed-head injuries, organic components of psychiatric illness, early states of dementia and effects of renal failure and diabetes.

15701
Kindergarten Diagnostic Instrument. Robinson, Robert W.; Miller, Daniel C. 1986
Subtests: Auditory Memory; Body Awareness; Concept Mastery; Form Perception; General Information; Gross Motor; Number Skills; Verbal Associations; Verbal Opposites; Visual Discrimination; Visual Memory; Visual-Motor Integration; Vocabulary
Descriptors: Academically Gifted; Diagnostic Tests; Enrichment; Individual Testing; *Kindergarten; *Kindergarten Children; Primary Education; School Readiness; *School Readiness Tests; Screening Tests; Student Placement
Identifiers: KDI
Availability: Kindergarten Interventions and Diagnostic Services; P.O. Box 26631, Columbus, OH 43226
Grade Level: K
Notes: Time, 45 approx.

Screens children for kindergarten readiness skills. Can be used diagnostically for program placement for alternative kindergarten programs, Chapter 1 reading programs, and for enrichment/gifted programs and/or prescriptively to aid in educational programing. Can be administered individually but is designed to be used primarily in a screening team approach. Identifies children's kindergarten readiness skills from below average to above average. Consists of 13 subtests. Short form of the test, consisting of 9 subtests, takes approximately 25 minutes. Long form, consisting of all 13 subtests, takes approximately 45 minutes.

15728
Creative Styles Inventory. McBer and Co., Boston, MA 1986
Descriptors: Adults; *Cognitive Processes; *Creative Thinking; *Intuition; *Logical Thinking; Rating Scales; Self Evaluation (Individuals)
Identifiers: CSI
Availability: McBer and Co.; 137 Newbury St., Boston, MA 02116
Target Audience: Adults
Notes: Items, 32

Brief self-scoring inventory that distinguishes 2 modes of individuals' information processing. These modes are important because they affect ways individuals learn, make decisions, and solve problems. The 2 modes are logical/analytical and intuitive.

15741
Auditory Discrimination Test, Second Edition. Reynolds, William M. 1987
Descriptors: *Auditory Discrimination; *Auditory Tests; Norm Referenced Tests; *Preschool Children; *Screening Tests; *Young Children
Identifiers: ADT
Availability: Western Psychological Services; 12031 Wilshire Blvd., Los Angeles, CA 90025
Target Audience: 4-8
Notes: Items, 40

Developed as a brief, easy-to-administer procedure to assess children's ability to discriminate between commonly used phonemes in English. The ADT measures the ability to hear spoken language accurately. This ability is a precursor to formal classroom learning and represents an important perceptual skill in children. It is developmental in nature. In this test, word pairs are presented and the child indicates whether the words are different or the same. There are 2 alternate forms which allows for retesting children within a short period of time. In this revision, the word pairs remain the same as in previous editions; however, the manual has been revised and updated by expanding the age range for which the test may be used.

15750
Screening Test for Educational Prerequisite Skills, IBM Computer Format. Smith, Frances 1987

Descriptors: Attention Span; *Child Development; Children; Computers; Grade 1; Motivation; Parent Attitudes; Persistence; Psychomotor Skills; *School Readiness; *Screening Tests; Speech Skills; Young Children
Identifiers: Fine Motor Skills; Gross Motor Skills; STEPS
Availability: Western Psychological Services; 12031 Wilshire Blvd., Los Angeles, CA 90025
Target Audience: 5-6
Notes: Time, 10

Designed for use with children eligible to enter first grade, within 1 year of the test date, to identify those who need structured help in preparing for first grade. Can be administered by volunteers and paraprofessionals. Evaluates first-grade competency skills that are expected at the time of testing. A 20-item scale that allows for parent evaluation is also included which measures general behavioral competence and motivation for school entry. Covers task persistence, attentional set, motivation, and developmental readiness in terms of fine motor skills, gross motor skills, speech skills and cognitive readiness. Computer program scores and produces a parent report.

15799
Berkeley Paired-Associate Learning Test. Lambert, Nadine, M.; And Others 1974
Descriptors: *Early Childhood Education; *Individual Testing; Learning Processes; *Paired Associate Learning; Recall (Psychology); *Visual Measures; Young Children
Availability: Lambert, Nadine, and Others. The Educationally Retarded Child. New York: Grune & Stratton, Inc., 1974
Target Audience: 4-7
Notes: Items, 52

Assesses the ability of 4 to 7-year-old students to learn new material through the use of a paired associate learning test. Test is administered to students individually. In succession, the student is presented with 20 cards with pictures of 2 objects on each. The student is then shown a picture of 1 of the pair and must try to remember what the other member of the pair was. May provide useful information for classroom presentation of material to be learned.

15840
Murphy-Durrell Reading Readiness Screen. Murphy, Helen A.; Durrell, Donald D. 1988
Subtests: Lowercase Letter Names; Letter-Name Sounds in Spoken Words; Writing Letters from Dictation; Syntax Matching; Identifying Phonemes in Spoken Words
Descriptors: *Grade 1; *Kindergarten Children; *Phonics; Primary Education; *Reading Readiness; *Screening Tests
Availability: Curriculum Associates; 5 Esquire Rd., N. Billerica, MA 01862-2589
Grade Level: K-1
Notes: Time, 125 approx.; Items, 109

Screening instrument that provides information about children's phonics abilities before entering a formal reading program. Consists of 5 inventories administered in 5 sittings, usually over a 3-day period. Each sitting requires from 15 to 25 minutes. May be individually or group administered. The 5 inventories relate clusters of sounds in speech to clusters of letters in print. Intended for use with children in kindergarten or grade 1 who are being considered for placement in a formal reading program. Identifies those children who will be successful in a formal reading program and at-risk children, noting their reading readiness deficiencies.

15911
Iowa Tests of Basic Skills, Forms G and H, Levels 9-11, Writing Supplement. Hieronymus, A.N.; Hoover, H.D. 1987
Subtests: Narrative; Explanation; Description; Informative Report; Persuasive Essay
Descriptors: *Achievement Tests; Elementary Education; *Elementary School Students; *Essay Tests; Holistic Evaluation; Writing (Composition); *Writing Evaluation; *Writing Skills
Identifiers: Basic Skills Assessment Program; ITBS
Availability: Riverside Publishing Co.; 8420 Bryn Mawr Ave., Chicago, IL 60631
Grade Level: 3-5
Notes: Time, 35

Measures the productive writing skills of students. Assesses the students' ability to generate, to organize, and to express their ideas in a variety of written forms. Designed to complement the language tests in the regular battery of the Iowa Tests of Basic Skills. Measures the students' technical knowledge of written English and their ability to apply that knowledge to a specific writing situation. An essay topic was developed in each of 5 modes: narrative, explanation, description, informative report, and persuasive essay. Each essay requires 35 minutes of working time. Scored on a 4 point, focused holistic score scale. Level 9-11 is intended for use in grades 3 through 5.

15912
Iowa Tests of Basic Skills, Forms G and H, Levels 12-14, Writing Supplement. Hieronymus, A.N.; Hoover, H.D. 1987
Subtests: Narrative; Explanation; Description; Informative Report; Persuasive Essay
Descriptors: *Achievement Tests; Elementary Education; *Elementary School Students; *Essay Tests; Holistic Evaluation; Writing (Composition); *Writing Evaluation; *Writing Skills
Identifiers: Basic Skills Assessment Program; ITBS
Availability: Riverside Publishing Co.; 8420 Bryn Mawr Ave., Chicago, IL 60631
Grade Level: 6-8
Notes: Time, 35

Measures the productive writing skills of students. Assesses the students' ability to generate, to organize, and to express their ideas in a variety of written forms. Designed to complement the language tests in the regular battery of the Iowa Tests of Basic Skills. Measures the students' technical knowledge of written English and their ability to apply that knowledge to a specific writing situation. An essay topic was developed in each of 5 modes: narrative, explanation, description, informative report, and persuasive essay. Each essay requires 35 minutes of working time. Scored on a 4 point, focused holistic score scale. Level 12-14 is intended for use in grades 6 through 8.

800004
ACER Advanced Test N. Australian Council for Educational Research, Hawthorn 1961
Descriptors: *Academic Aptitude; *Adolescents; Adults; Career Choice; Foreign Countries; *Intelligence; *Intelligence Tests; *Mental Age; Multiple Choice Tests; *Predictive Measurement; Secondary School Students; Student Evaluation; Timed Tests
Identifiers: Australia
Availability: Australian Council for Educational Research; P.O. Box 210, Hawthorn, Victoria, Australia, 3122
Target Audience: 15-64
Notes: Time, 50; Items, 76

A general ability test consisting of both verbal and nonverbal questions used to measure the verbal, numerical and abstracting reasoning abilities of Australians age 15 and older. Purposes include 1) comparison of students' grades with their general ability; 2) classification of students; 3) career choice and choice of school courses.

800010
ACER Junior Test A. Australian Council for Educational Research, Hawthorn 1946
Descriptors: Children; *Elementary School Students; Foreign Countries; *Intelligence; *Intelligence Tests; *Mental Age; Multiple Choice Tests; Student Evaluation; Timed Tests
Identifiers: ACER General Test T; Australia; Junior Test A
Availability: Australian Council for Educational Research; P.O. Box 210, Hawthorn, Victoria, Australia 3122
Target Audience: 8-11
Notes: Time, 30; Items, 75

First designed in 1946 under the title General Test T, the test measures the mental age and intelligence of children ages 8-11. Type of questions include relationships, verbal reasoning, arithmetical reasoning, etc. The test itself is timed for 30 minutes; additional time is required for instructions and practice questions. Answers include multiple choice types, computational and short answer.

800033
ACER Junior Non-Verbal Test. Australian Council for Educational Research, Hawthorn 1949
Subtests: Pictorial Classification; Geometrical or Spatial Relations; Pictorial Analogies; Time Sequence
Descriptors: Children; *Cognitive Ability; Cognitive Processes; *Elementary School Students; Foreign Countries; Individual Testing; *Intelligence; *Intelligence Tests; Mental Age; Multiple Choice Tests; Nonverbal Ability; *Nonverbal Tests; Student Evaluation; Timed Tests; Visual Stimuli
Identifiers: Australia; Junior Non Verbal Test; Oral Tests
Availability: Australian Council for Educational Research; P.O. Box 210, Hawthorn, Victoria, Australia 3122
Target Audience: 8-11
Notes: Time, 34; Items, 60

To assess the general ability of Australian children ages 8-11. Consists of pictorial or diagramatic items. Each subtest contains 15 items. It takes 60 minutes to administer the entire test; 34 minutes for the actual test. The authors feel that the instrument is useful in assessing students who are handicapped by poor ability in reading; in confirming the diagnosis for backwardness of children who have taken verbal tests, and in evaluating migrant children whose English is poor.

800063
ACER Speed and Accuracy Test (Form A). Australian Council for Educational Research, Hawthorn 1965
Subtests: Number Checking; Name Checking
Descriptors: Adolescents; Adults; *Employment Potential; Foreign Countries; *Job Skills; *Occupational Tests; *Predictive Measurement; Timed Tests; *Vocational Aptitude
Identifiers: Australia; *Perceptual Speed
Availability: Australian Council for Educational Research; P.O. Box 210, Hawthorn, Victoria, Australia 3122
Target Audience: 13-64
Notes: Time, 12; Items, 320

Designed to measure ability to perceive, retain, and check relatively familiar material consisting of printed letters and names while working under a time limit. The authors feel that this test is useful in predicting the performance on the job in such occupations as clerical work, printing trades, some engineering types of jobs and other technical positions. The respondent is asked to determine whether the words or names in one column are identical to those in the second column.

800086
Kindergarten Behavioral Index: A Screening Technique for Reading Readiness. Banks, Enid M. 1972
Descriptors: Behavior Patterns; Foreign Countries; *Grade 1; Handicap Identification; *Kindergarten Children; Learning Disabilities; Perceptual Development; Primary Education; *Reading Readiness; School Readiness; *School Readiness Tests; Screening Tests
Identifiers: Australia
Availability: Australian Council for Educational Research; P.O. Box 210, Hawthorn Victoria, Australia 3122
Grade Level: K-1
Notes: Items, 37

Designed for use at the end of a child's first year in school when he or she is at least 5-1/2 years of age. Developed for use in assessing academic readiness and identification of children with potential learning disabilities.

800124
ACER Tests of Learning Ability. Australian Council for Educational Research, Hawthorn 1974
Subtests: Verbal Comprehension; General Reasoning (Problem Solving); Syllogistic Reasoning (Verbal Analysis)
Descriptors: *Aptitude Tests; Cognitive Tests; *Deduction; *Elementary School Students; Foreign Countries; Intellectual Development; Intermediate Grades; Logical Thinking; Multiple Choice Tests; *Problem Solving; Timed Tests; *Verbal Ability; Verbal Tests
Identifiers: Australia; *Reasoning Ability; TOLA 4; TOLA 6
Availability: Australian Council for Educational Research; P.O. Box 210, Hawthorn, Victoria, Australia 3122
Grade Level: 4-6
Notes: Time, 33; Items, 83

To measure general intellectual ability, especially broad language and reasoning abilities at the end of the fourth or sixth year of schooling. Limited to English speaking children. Used to assess current status and to assist in predicting future scholastic achievement. Not intended as a measure of innate academic intelligence or capability. Each subtest is timed separately. The test for year 4 has 71 questions and the year 6 has 83.

800125
Weber Advanced Spatial Perception Test. Weber, P.G. 1976
Subtests: Form Recognition; Pattern Recognition; Shape Analysis; Reflected Figures
Descriptors: Adolescents; Cognitive Tests; Foreign Countries; Secondary Education; *Secondary School Students; *Spatial Ability; Visual Perception
Identifiers: Australia; WASP
Availability: Australian Council for Educational Research, Ltd.; Frederick St., Hawthorn E.2, Victoria, Australia 3122
Target Audience: 13-17
Notes: Time, 45 approx.; Items, 136

Designed to measure spatial ability. Subtests include Form Recognition consisting of 30 items to be completed in 4 minutes; Pattern Perception is an 8 minute test of 43 items; Shape Analysis is an 8 minute test of 38 items; and Reflected Figures is a 4 minute test of 25 items.

800137
ACER Tests of Reasoning in Mathematics. Australian Council for Educational Research, Hawthorn 1971

Descriptors: *Aptitude Tests; *Associative Learning; Cognitive Measurement; *Cognitive Processes; Foreign Countries; *Mathematical Concepts; Multiple Choice Tests; Problem Solving; *Mathematics Tests; Secondary Education; *Secondary School Students; Timed Tests
Identifiers: Australia; *Reasoning Ability; TRIM
Availability: Australian Council for Educational Research; P.O. Box 210, Hawthorn, Victoria, Australia 3122
Grade Level: 8-11
Notes: Time, 60; Items, 30

To determine a student's ability to work with mathematical concepts and to sample the kind of thinking and problem-solving activities that are broadly considered mathematical. Skills required are the ability to: 1) understand and interpret mathematical material; 2) translate between verbal, symbolic, tabular and diagramatic material; 3) apply previously acquired mathematical skills to the solution of problems presented in new situations; and 4) analyse mathematical problems and to determine the ways their parts relate to each other. The authors feel that the tests are useful in 1) determining the composition of math classes and 2) identifying differences between achievement and aptitude. Consists of 4 tests, Level 1, 2, 3 and 4; Levels 2-4 have 30 questions each and Level 1 has 29. 60 minutes is allowed for each Level; this time does not include the preliminary instructions, etc. The authors suggest administering 2 of the tests with a 2-week interval in order to increase reliability. This is not designed to test student's mathematical knowledge. Called an experimental edition.

800176
Test of Enquiry Skills. Fraser, Barry J. 1979
Subtests: Library Usage; Index and Table of Contents; Reading Scales; Averages, Percentages and Proportions; Charts and Tables; Graphs; Comprehension of Science Reading; Design of Experimental Procedures; Conclusions and Generalizations
Descriptors: *Achievement Tests; Cognitive Tests; Experiments; Foreign Countries; *Inquiry; Learning Processes; *Library Skills; Logical Thinking; Reference Materials; Secondary Education; *Secondary School Science; *Secondary School Students; Study Skills; Visual Learning; *Visual Literacy
Identifiers: Australia; TOES
Availability: Australian Council for Educational Research; P.O. Box 210, Hawthorn, Victoria, Australia 3122
Grade Level: 7-10
Notes: Time, 180 approx.; Items, 87

Based upon those teaching approaches which emphasize enquiry and individualization, this untimed series of tests measures subject-content-free enquiry skills relevant for science, social sciences, history and geography. Skills are 1) use of reference materials; 2) interpretation and processing of information; and 3) critical thinking in science. Administered in two or more sessions depending upon the grade level.

800193
ACER Early School Series. Rowe, Helga A.H. 1981
Subtests: Auditory Discrimination; Recognition of Initial Consonant Sounds; Number; Figure Formation; Prepositions; Verb Tense; Pronouns; Negation; Comprehension; Word Knowledge
Descriptors: Adults; Auditory Discrimination; Basic Vocabulary; *Cognitive Development; *Cognitive Measurement; Concept Formation; Consonants; Diagnostic Tests; Disabilities; *Elementary School Students; Foreign Countries; Individual Testing; Numbers; Primary Education; Remedial Instruction; *Screening Tests; Syntax
Identifiers: Australia; Power Tests
Availability: Australian Council for Educational Research; Frederick St., Hawthorn 3122, Victoria, Australia
Grade Level: K-3
Notes: Time, 200 approx.; Items, 150

Designed to provide a series of estimates of a child's cognitive development and maturity. In addition to identifying particular strengths and weaknesses of individual school beginners, tests may also be useful as counseling and guidance tools in lower grades of primary schools and with certain groups of handicapped adults. Also useful with children who cannot read and for remedial students as reading is not required with this series. All tests are power tests. Suitable for administration with small groups but more valid results obtained when individually administered.

800197
ACER Intermediate Test G. de Lemos, Marion M. 1980

Descriptors: Abstract Reasoning; *Adolescents; Career Guidance; *Cognitive Ability; *Cognitive Measurement; Educational Counseling; Foreign Countries; *Intelligence Tests; Intermediate Grades; Junior High Schools; Number Concepts; *Youth
Identifiers: Australia; *Numerical Reasoning; *Reasoning Ability; *Verbal Reasoning
Availability: Australian Council for Educational Research; P.O. Box 210, Hawthorn, Victoria, Australia 3122
Target Audience: 10-15
Notes: Time, 30; Items, 76

Group test designed to assess general reasoning ability of students between the ages of 10 and 15 years. Based on a revision of the ACER Intermediate Tests A and D. Test is based on the traditional model of group general ability or intelligence tests and comprises items assessing verbal and numerical reasoning abilities. Tests are intended primarily for use in educational and vocational guidance but may also be used in other appropriate situations such as selection and screening of students for various programs or in research or evaluation studies. Should not be used as the sole basis for making important decisions about an individual student.

800198
ACER Higher Test ML-MQ (Second Edition) and Test PL-PQ. Australian Council for Educational Research, Hawthorn 1982
Subtests: Linguistic; Quantitative
Descriptors: Abstract Reasoning; Academic Ability; *Adolescents; Adults; Career Guidance; Cognitive Ability; *Cognitive Measurement; Foreign Countries; Higher Education; *Intelligence; *Intelligence Tests; Predictive Measurement; Problem Solving; Secondary Education; Vocational Aptitude
Identifiers: Australia
Availability: Australian Council for Educational Research; P.O. Box 210, Hawthorn, Victoria, Australia 3122
Target Audience: 15-65
Notes: Time, 35; Items, 68

Parallel forms of a group test designed to measure general intellectual ability. Intended for use with secondary level students, young people who have left school, and with adults. Tests are intended to measure intelligence as demonstrated by the ability to see relationships and to solve problems. Items are restricted to verbal and number questions since test is primarily intended as a measure of general scholastic ability in predicting school achievement and in vocational counseling and other areas where ability to think clearly with words and numbers is necessary. May also be used for selection of occupations which involve reasoning ability. Tests are inappropriate for use with individuals whose cultural or linguistic backgrounds are such as to be considered disadvantaged in taking this test. Although separate scores are available for 2 subtests, they should be regarded as substantially measures of the same general ability.

800204
ACER Advanced Test B40. Australian Council for Educational Research, Hawthorn 1982
Descriptors: Abstract Reasoning; *Adults; *Cognitive Ability; Foreign Countries; High Schools; *High School Students; *Intelligence; Intelligence Tests; Timed Tests; Verbal Ability
Identifiers: Australia; *Reasoning Ability
Availability: Australian Council for Educational Research; Frederick St., Hawthorn, Victoria, Australia 3122
Target Audience: 13-50
Notes: Time, 55; Items, 77

A test of general ability which assesses verbal and arithmetical reasoning.

800221
Jenkins Non-Verbal Test, 1981 Edition. Jenkins, J.W. 1981
Descriptors: Classification; Elementary School Students; Foreign Countries; *Intelligence; *Intelligence Tests; Intermediate Grades; Junior High Schools; Junior High School Students; Nonverbal Tests; Serial Ordering
Identifiers: Analogies; Australia
Availability: Australian Council for Educational Research; Frederick St., Hawthorn E 2, Victoria, Australia 3122
Target Audience: 10-14
Notes: Time, 24 approx.; Items, 80

An Australian adaptation of the Scale of Non-Verbal Mental Ability originally published in Great Britain. Instrument consists of nonverbal items of a diagramatic type which are separated into 5 subtests. The items within each subtest are arranged in ascending order of difficulty. Two subtests are based on the principle of classification, 2 are on the identification of serial order, and 1 on the solution of diagramatic analogies. Actual working time for the test is 24 minutes.

800222
ACER Higher Test WL-WQ. Australian Council for Educational Research, Hawthorn 1982
Subtests: Linguistic; Quantitative
Descriptors: Abstract Reasoning; Academic Ability; Adolescents; *Adults; *Career Guidance; Cognitive Ability; Cognitive Measurement; *College Students; Foreign Countries; Higher Education; Intelligence; *Intelligence Tests; Secondary Education; *Secondary School Students; Vocational Aptitude
Identifiers: Australia
Availability: Australian Council for Educational Research; Frederick St.; Hawthorn E 2, Victoria, Australia 3122
Target Audience: 13-64
Notes: Time, 60 approx.; Items, 72
Designed to measure general intellectual ability for use in vocational guidance of adolescents and adults. The linguistic section consists of items such as analogies, classifications, proverbs, and logical reasoning. The quantitative section consists of items concerning number series, number matrices, and arithmetical reasoning questions. Form W was produced as a parallel form of Form M (TC800198).

800224
Wechsler Adult Intelligence Scale-Revised. Australian Adaptation. Wechsler, David 1981
Subtests: Information; Digit Span; Vocabulary; Arithmetic; Comprehension; Similarities; Picture Completion; Picture Arrangement; Block Design; Object Assembly; Digit Symbol
Descriptors: *Adolescents; *Adults; Foreign Countries; Individual Testing; *Intelligence; *Intelligence Tests; *Older Adults
Identifiers: Australia
Availability: Australian Council for Educational Research; P.O. Box 210 Hawthorn, Victoria, Australia 3122
Target Audience: 16-74
Notes: Time, 60 approx.
This instrument is a modified version of the WAIS-R (TC011190) adapted for use in Australia. The WAIS-R Australian supplement and inserts to the WAIS-R manual are inserted into the WAIS-R kits when they arrive in Australia. There is no additional charge for these materials. The Australian record forms are then purchased as required. The publisher's distribution agreement does not allow them to sell these forms outside Australia. If one wanted to purchase the record forms, the publisher would have to apply to the Psychological Corporation for permission to supply them. Ten of the original 29 items in the Information test were modified. Minor changes were made to the other tests in the battery. These involved terminology or rewording. This instrument has been developed as a measure of verbal and nonverbal intelligence. The verbal, performance, and full-scale scores may be converted to intelligence quotients. Marion M. de Lemos prepared the WAIS-R Australian Supplement.

800242
ACER Advanced Tests AL-AQ (2nd Edition) and BL-BQ. Australian Council for Educational Research, Hawthorn 1978
Subtests: Linguistic; Quantitative
Descriptors: Academic Ability; Adults; Foreign Countries; High Schools; *High School Students; Intelligence; *Intelligence Tests; Timed Tests; Verbal Ability
Identifiers: Arithmetic Reasoning; Australia; Verbal Reasoning
Availability: Australian Council for Educational Research Ltd.; P.O. Box 210, Hawthorn, Victoria, Australia 3122
Target Audience: 15-64
Notes: Time, 60 approx.; Items, 58
Designed to measure general intellectual ability of secondary school students in years 11 and 12, first year students at colleges of advanced education (CAEs) and technical and further education colleges (TAFE), as well as superior adults. General intelligence is measured by the ability to see relationships and solve problems. Parallel forms AL-AQ and BL-BQ are available. Section L contains 29 items to be completed in 15 minutes. Section Q contains 29 items to be completed in 20 minutes.

800243
ACER Test of Cognitive Ability. Australian Council for Educational Research, Hawthorn 1978
Descriptors: Abstract Reasoning; Academic Aptitude; Adolescents; Adults; Career Planning; *Cognitive Ability; *Cognitive Tests; Foreign Countries; Group Testing; *Intelligence; Number Concepts; *Predictive Measurement; Problem Solving; Standardized Tests; Verbal Ability; Vocational Aptitude
Identifiers: Australia
Availability: Australian Council for Education Research; P.O. Box 210, Hawthorn, Victoria, Australia 3122
Target Audience: 15-64

Notes: Items, 75
Group test to measure general intellectual ability. Intended for use with students in grade 9 or above, with adolescents who have left school and with the general adult population. Norms are provided for secondary school students aged 15 and for first-year students in colleges of advanced education. Test is intended to measure general intelligence as demonstrated by the ability to see relationships and to solve problems. Uses verbal and quantitative materials. Test is primarily intended as a measure of general academic ability in prediction of school achievement, in counseling in relationship to training and for other purposes where the ability to think clearly with words and numbers is necessary, and for selection of occupations which involve a high level of reasoning ability. Test is inappropriate for use with those whose linguistic or cultural backgrounds could qualify them as disadvantaged in taking tests of this type.

800246
ACER Mechanical Reasoning Test, Revised Edition. Australian Council for Educational Research, Hawthorn 1979
Descriptors: Adults; *Aptitude Tests; Career Counseling; Foreign Countries; High Schools; *High School Students; Personnel Selection; *Vocational Aptitude
Identifiers: Australia; *Mechanical Aptitude
Availability: Australian Council for Educational Research; P.O. Box 210, Hawthorn, Victoria, Australia 3122
Target Audience: 15-64
Notes: Time, 20; Items, 24
Designed to assess an individual's aptitude for solving problems requiring the understanding of mechanical ideas. Appropriate for use in vocational counseling and selection of personnel for apprenticeships or jobs of a mechanical nature.

800247
ACER Intermediate Test F. deLemos, Marion M. 1980
Descriptors: Abstract Reasoning; *Adolescents; Career Guidance; *Cognitive Ability; *Cognitive Measurement; Educational Counseling; Foreign Countries; *Intelligence Tests; Intermediate Grades; Junior High Schools; Number Concepts; *Youth
Identifiers: Australia; *Numerical Reasoning; *Reasoning Ability; *Verbal Reasoning
Availability: Australian Council for Educational Research; Radford House, 9 Frederick St., Hawthorn, Victoria, Australia 3122
Target Audience: 10-15
Notes: Time, 30; Items, 76
Group test to assess general reasoning ability of students between the ages of 10 and 15 years. Based on a revision of ACER Intermediate Tests A and D. Developed to provide a more up-to-date measure to assess general ability at the upper primary and lower secondary levels. Based on the traditional model for group general ability or intelligence type tests. Items assess verbal and numerical reasoning abilities. Intended for use mainly in educational and vocational counseling, but may also be used in research or evaluation studies and for selection and screening purposes for particular programs or to screen for further assessment or treatment. Should not be used as the sole basis for making important decisions about an individual student.

800249
Otis-Lennon School Ability Test, Intermediate. Form R. Australian Adaptation. Otis, Arthur S.; Lennon, Roger T. 1982
Descriptors: Abstract Reasoning; *Academic Aptitude; *Aptitude Tests; Cognitive Ability; *Elementary School Students; Foreign Countries; Intermediate Grades; Junior High Schools; *Junior High School Students; Timed Tests; Verbal Development
Identifiers: Australia; OLSAT
Availability: Australian Council for Educational Research; Radford House, 9 Frederick St., Hawthorn, Victoria, Australia 3122
Grade Level: 5-9
Target Audience: 10-15
Notes: Time, 45; Items, 80
An Australian adaptation of the OLSAT: Intermediate Form R (TC010144). Designed to assess a student's scholastic aptitude. Results yield a deviation intelligence quotient (DIQ).

800260
Harding Skyscraper, Form B-C. Harding, Chris 1973
Descriptors: Adults; Foreign Countries; Gifted; *Intelligence Tests
Identifiers: Australia
Availability: Harding Tests; P.O. Box 5271, Rockhampton Mail Center, Queensland, Australia 4702
Target Audience: Adults

Notes: Items, 40
A difficult test purporting to discriminate at highest intelligence levels. Uses analogies, word problems, and number series with a British flavor. Must be scored by publisher.

800262
General Clerical Test, Australian Edition. Psychological Corp., San Antonio, TX 1969
Subtests: Clerical; Numerical; Verbal
Descriptors: Adults; *Aptitude Tests; Arithmetic; *Clerical Workers; *Job Applicants; *Occupational Tests; Office Practice; Verbal Ability
Identifiers: *Clerical Skills; GCT
Availability: Australian Council for Educational Research; Radford House, Frederick St., Hawthorn, Victoria, Australia, 3122
Target Audience: Adults
Notes: Time, 46
Australian adaptation of the General Clerical Test which measures aptitudes important in all kinds of clerical work. Test is published in 2 editions. Regular edition consists of a single 12-page booklet and includes all nine parts. The other edition consists of 2 partial booklets. Booklet A contains the 5 parts which make up the clerical and numerical subscores. Booklet B includes the 4 parts for the verbal subscore. Clerical subscore covers checking and alphabetizing and is based on speed and accuracy in routine clerical tasks. Numerical subscore covers arithmetic computation, error location, and arithmetic reasoning. Verbal subscore covers spelling, reading comprehension, vocabulary, and grammar.

800273
Non-Verbal Ability Tests. Rowe, Helga A.H. 1986
Subtests: Matching Shapes; Matching Direction; Categorization; Picture Completion; Embedded Figures; Figure Formation; Mazes; Sequencing; Picture Arrangement; Visual Search; Simple Key Test; Complex Key Test; Code Tracking I; Code Tracking II; Visual Recognition; Auditory Recognition; Auditory Recall; Visual Recall
Descriptors: Abstract Reasoning; Adults; *Aptitude Tests; Cognitive Style; Concept Formation; *Culture Fair Tests; Foreign Countries; Memory; *Nonverbal Ability; *Nonverbal Tests; Perceptual Motor Coordination; Psychomotor Skills; Spatial Ability; Visual Perception
Identifiers: Australia; NAT
Availability: Australian Council for Educational Research, Ltd.; P.O. Box 210, Hawthorn, Victoria Australia, 3122
Target Audience: 18-65
The NAT is a domain-referenced battery of nonverbal tests for the assessment of general and specific abilities. It is group administered. An ability profile is produced in addition to an overall score. Tests in the battery deal with perceptual speed and accuracy, classification and concept formation, pattern analysis, reasoning, synthesis, visual-spatial scanning ability, motor sequencing skills, visual-motor coordination, memory, attention and concentration, recall and recognition. Said to be useful in testing culturally different persons.

800290
Personnel Selection Testing Program. Australian Council for Educational Research, Victoria, Australia 1987
Descriptors: Adults; Apprenticeships; *Aptitude Tests; *Clerical Occupations; Foreign Countries; *Personnel Selection; *Semiskilled Occupations; *Vocational Aptitude
Identifiers: Australia; GATB; General Aptitude Test Battery; PSTP; Test Batteries
Availability: Australian Council for Educational Research; P.O. Box 210, Hawthorn, Victoria, Australia, 3122
Target Audience: Adults
Secure testing program offered by the Australian Council for Educational Research. Australian adaptation of the paper-and-pencil tests from the U.S. Department of Labor's General Aptitude Test Battery (GATB). There are 4 tests used for the selection of clerical personnel: vocabulary, arithmetic, arithmetic reasoning, and name comparison. The following 5 tests are a battery used to select trade apprentices: 3-dimensional space, figure matching, shape matching, mark making, and ACER Mathematics Test E (which is a non-GATB test and is being revised). This testing program is still in the developmental stages and will be subject to continuing revision.

810013
Group Test 90A (NIIP). National Institute of Industrial Psychology, London, England
Subtests: Same and Opposite; Analogies; Jumbled Sentences; Completing Sentences
Descriptors: Adults; Foreign Countries; Intelligence; *Intelligence Tests; *Job Applicants; Personnel Selection; *Skilled Workers; *Supervisors
Identifiers: Great Britain; NIIP

Availability: NFER Nelson Publishing Co., Ltd.; Darville House, 2 Oxford Rd. E., Windsor, Berkshire shire SL4 1DF, England
Target Audience: 18-64
Notes: Time, 30 approx.; Items, 137

Designed to measure intelligence and verbal aptitude. Useful in selection of personnel for management, supervisory, clerical, and skilled positions. Form 90B is an alternative though not precisely parallel form. Instrument is part of Engineering Apprentice Selection Battery.

810014
Group Test 36 (NIIP). National Institute of Industrial Psychology, London, England
Subtests: Verbal Reasoning; Word which Doesn't Belong; Verbal Analogies; Jumbled Sentence Word Order; Same or Opposite
Descriptors: Adolescents; Adults; *Apprenticeships; Children; Clerical Occupations; *Cognitive Processes; Cognitive Tests; Foreign Countries; *Job Applicants; *Personnel Selection; Semiskilled Occupations
Identifiers: Great Britain; NIIP; *Reasoning Ability
Availability: NFER Nelson Publishing Co., Ltd.; Darville House, 2 Oxford Rd. E., Windsor, Berkshire shire SL4 1DF, England
Target Audience: 10-64
Notes: Time, 35 approx.; Items, 195

Designed to assess applicants for some types of semiskilled jobs, craft apprenticeships and lower grade clerical jobs. Measures verbal reasoning ability.

810015
Group Test 33. National Institute of Industrial Psychology, London, England
Subtests: Opposites; Analogies; Mixed Sentences; Completing Sentences; Reasoning
Descriptors: Adolescents; Adults; Clerical Occupations; Cognitive Tests; Foreign Countries; *Intelligence; *Job Applicants; Personnel Selection; Supervisors; *Verbal Ability
Identifiers: Great Britain; NIIP; Reasoning
Availability: NFER Nelson Publishing Co., Ltd.; Darville House, 2 Oxford Rd. E., Windsor, Berkshire shire SL4 1DF, England
Target Audience: 15-64
Notes: Time, 50 approx.; Items, 143

Designed to measure general intelligence and verbal ability. Useful in selection of applicants for supervisory posts, clerical and skilled work.

810025
Mill Hill Vocabulary Scale. Raven, J.C. 1943
Descriptors: *Adolescents; *Adults; *Cognitive Ability; *Cognitive Style; Cognitive Tests; *Definitions; Foreign Countries; *Long Term Memory; Verbal Ability
Identifiers: *Synonyms; United Kingdom
Availability: Australian Council for Educational Research; P.O. Box 210, Hawthorn, Victoria, Australia 3122
Target Audience: 14-64
Notes: Time, 60 approx.; Items, 68

Measures the degree to which the respondent's present recall of acquired information and verbal ability agrees with his or her present capacity for intellectual activity and rational judgment. Only form still available is the Senior Form 2. In Set A a synonym is selected from a group of words; Set B requires the respondent to write out a brief definition of the given word. Designed to complement Raven's Progressive Matrices test.

810026
The Crichton Vocabulary Scale. Raven, J.C. 1950
Descriptors: Elementary Education; *Elementary School Students; Foreign Countries; *Preschool Children; Preschool Education; *Verbal Ability; Verbal Development; Verbal Tests; *Vocabulary
Identifiers: England
Availability: H.K. Lewis and Co., Ltd.; P.O. Box 66, 136 Gower St., London W. C. 1, England
Grade Level: K-6
Target Audience: 4-11
Notes: Items, 80

Designed to assess vocabulary and verbal ability. Child is asked to explain the meaning of each word. Developed for use with the Coloured Progressive Matrices Sets, A, Ab, and B (TC820028).

810027
Progressive Matrices, Standard. Raven, J.C. 1960
Descriptors: Adolescents; Adults; *Cognitive Ability; *Culture Fair Tests; Foreign Countries; Multiple Choice Tests; *Nonverbal Tests
Identifiers: Great Britain; SPM
Availability: The Psychological Corp.; 555 Academic Ct., San Antonio, TX 78204-0952
Target Audience: 13-64
Notes: Time, 45; Items, 60

A nonverbal test designed to assess mental ability via problems concerning abstract figures and designs. Norms are available for English children and adults. Purported to be culture fair.

810028
Progressive Matrices, Coloured. Raven, J.C. 1965
Descriptors: Adults; Children; *Cognitive Ability; *Culture Fair Tests; Foreign Countries; *Moderate Mental Retardation; Multiple Choice Tests; *Nonverbal Tests
Identifiers: CPM; England; Great Britain
Availability: The Psychological Corp.; 555 Academic Ct., San Antonio, TX 78204-0952
Target Audience: 5-11
Notes: Items, 36

A nonverbal test designed to assess mental ability via problems concerning colored abstract figures and designs. Also useful with mentally handicapped adults. Individual or small group administration is necessary. Norms are available for several English groups. Purported to be culture fair.

810044
Compound Series Test. Morrisby, J.R. 1955
Descriptors: *Adults; *College Students; *Comprehension; *Culture Fair Tests; Elementary Education; *Elementary School Students; Foreign Countries; Higher Education; *Intelligence; Intelligence Tests; Personnel Selection; *Pictorial Stimuli; Secondary Education; *Secondary School Students
Identifiers: CST; DTB; Great Britain; Morrisby Differential Test Battery; Test Batteries
Availability: Educational and Industrial Test Services Ltd.; 83, High St., Hemel Hempstead, Hertfordshire, HP1 3AH, England
Target Audience: 6-64
Notes: Time, 30 approx.; Items, 60

The Morrisby Differential Test Battery is a comprehensive battery of tests which objectively assesses a person's intellectual structure and basic personality characteristics. The DTB is supplied only to "Registered Approved Users." Registration as an approved user can be obtained by successfully completing a 5-day training course specifically on the DTB. Test distribution is restricted. Compound Series Test measures a fundamental ability, the capacity to learn by understanding. Test items are of the same type, but they increase in difficulty and complexity. CST has been designed for use with educationally and socially deprived persons, illiterate, physically handicapped, color blind subjects, as well as the general population from the average 6 year old to the intellectually superior adult. Test time for total DTB is 3 1/4 hours.

810045
General Ability Test—Verbal. Morrisby, J.R. 1955
Subtests: Synonyms and Antonyms; Word Classification; Analogies
Descriptors: Academic Achievement; *Adults; *Career Guidance; Cognitive Tests; *College Students; Foreign Countries; Higher Education; *Intelligence; Predictive Measurement; Secondary Education; *Secondary School Students; *Verbal Ability; Vocabulary
Identifiers: DTB; GAT Verbal; Great Britain; Morrisby Differential Test Battery; Test Batteries
Availability: Educational and Industrial Test Services Ltd.; 83, High St., Hemel Hempstead, Hertfordshire, HP1 3AH, England
Target Audience: 11-64
Notes: Time, 16 approx.; Items, 130

The Morrisby Differential Test Battery is a comprehensive battery of tests which objectively assesses a person's intellectual structure and basic personality characteristics. The DTB is supplied only to "Registered Approved Users." Registration as an approved user can be obtained by successfully completing a 5-day training course specifically on the DTB. Designed for individual or group administration to measure verbal intelligence. Useful in vocational guidance especially where good communicating skill is required or emphasis is on written work. May be used in educational guidance as a predictor of academic success. Administration time for complete DTB is three and one quarter hours.

810046
General Ability Test—Numerical. Morrisby, J.R. 1955
Subtests: Computation; Numerical Relationships; Matrix Completion
Descriptors: Academic Achievement; *Adults; *Career Guidance; Cognitive Tests; *College Students; *Computation; Foreign Countries; Higher Education; *Intelligence; *Mathematical Concepts; Predictive Measurement; *Mathematics Tests; Secondary Education; *Secondary School Students

Identifiers: DTB; GAT Numerical; Great Britain; Morrisby Differential Test Battery; Test Batteries
Availability: Educational and Industrial Test Services Ltd.; 83, High St., Hemel Hempstead, Hertfordshire, HP1 3AH, England
Target Audience: 11-64
Notes: Time, 35 approx.; Items, 139

The Morrisby Differential Test Battery is a comprehensive battery of tests which objectively assesses a person's intellectual structure and basic personality characteristics. The DTB is supplied only to "Registered Approved Users." Registration as an approved user can be obtained by successfully completing a 5-day training course specifically on the DTB. GAT-Numerical is useful in career guidance for occupations involving numerical concepts and where good quantitative ability is required. Useful in educational guidance as a predictor of academic success. Administration time for complete DTB is 3 hours and 15 minutes.

810047
General Ability Test—Perceptual. Morrisby, J.R. 1955
Subtests: Same or Different; Classification; Analogous Figures
Descriptors: *Adults; *Career Guidance; Cognitive Tests; *College Students; Foreign Countries; Higher Education; Intelligence; *Nonverbal Ability; Perception Tests; Secondary Education; *Secondary School Students; *Spatial Ability
Identifiers: DTB; GAT Perceptual; Great Britain; Morrisby Differential Test Battery; Test Batteries
Availability: Educational and Industrial Test Services Ltd.; 83, High St., Hemel Hempstead, Hertfordshire, HP1 3AH, England
Target Audience: 11-64
Notes: Time, 27 approx.; Items, 74

The Morrisby Differential Test Battery is a comprehensive battery of tests which objectively assesses a person's intellectual structure and basic personality characteristics. The DTB is supplied only to "Registered Approved Users." Registration as an approved user can be obtained by successfully completing a 5-day training course specifically on the DTB. Designed to measure nonverbal or perceptual intelligence. Useful for career guidance in occupations which deal with real objects rather than verbal or numerical concepts. Item type in subtests 2 and 3 are same as GAT verbal but words are replaced by perceptual figures. Administration time for complete DTB is 3 hours and 15 minutes.

810048
Shapes Test. Morrisby, J.R. 1955
Descriptors: Ability Identification; *Adolescents; *Adults; *Career Guidance; Foreign Countries; Job Applicants; Perception Tests; *Secondary School Students; *Spatial Ability
Identifiers: DTB; Great Britain; Morrisby Differential Test Battery; Test Batteries
Availability: Educational and Industrial Test Services Ltd.; 83, High St., Hemel Hempstead, Hertfordshire, HP1 3AH, England
Target Audience: 13-64
Notes: Time, 13 approx.; Items, 60

The Morrisby Differential Test Battery is a comprehensive battery of tests which objectively assesses a person's intellectual structure and basic personality characteristics. The DTB is supplied only to "Registered Approved Users." Registration as an approved user can be obtained by successfully completing a 5-day training course specifically on the DTB. Designed to assess individual's level of practicality, and whether subject tends to analyze problems in a discreet, step-by-step manner or whether he or she has an overall view.

810049
Mechanical Ability Test. Morrisby, J.R. 1955
Descriptors: *Adults; *Aptitude Tests; *Career Guidance; Engineers; Foreign Countries; Personnel Selection; Predictive Measurement; Secondary Education; *Secondary School Students
Identifiers: DTB; Great Britain; *Mechanical Aptitude; Morrisby Differential Test Battery; Test Batteries
Availability: Educational and Industrial Test Services Ltd.; 83, High St., Hemel Hempstead, Hertfordshire, HP1 3AH, England
Target Audience: 13-64
Notes: Time, 17 approx.; Items, 35

The Morrisby Differential Test Battery is a comprehensive battery of tests which objectively assesses a person's intellectual structure and basic personality characteristics. The DTB is supplied only to "Registered Approved Users." Registration as an approved user can be obtained by successfully completing a 5-day training course specifically on the DTB. Designed to measure natural, rather than learned, mechanical ability. Useful as a predictor for engineering potential. Items consist of an illustrated mechanical principle and a multiple choice question. Administration time for total DTB is 3 hours and 15 minutes.

810055
Non-Verbal Test DH. Calvert, B. 1958
Descriptors: *Abstract Reasoning; Cognitive Ability; Cognitive Mapping; Elementary School Students; Elementary Secondary Education; Foreign Countries; *Nonverbal Tests; Perception; Secondary School Students; Spatial Ability; Visualization; Visual Measures
Identifiers: England; NFER
Availability: NFER—Nelson Publishing Co.; Darville House, 2 Oxford Rd. E., Windsor, Berks SL4 1DF, England
Target Audience: 10-15
Notes: Time, 50; Items, 96

This test is used to assess nonverbal skills in children, ages 10-15. The material was prepared at the National Foundation for Education Research (NFER) and was originally constructed in 1951 when it was called Non-Verbal Test 3. The instrument was intended for children about 11 years of age, but has been found to give satisfactory results with children up to the age of 15 years. A shortened version can be given to younger children, 64 items administered in 35 minutes. The items are drawings in squares with 1 piece missing. The student is to select from the 5 answers which piece would give the best fit.

810057
Non-Verbal Test BD. Pidgeon, D.A. 1965
Subtests: Cypher; Similarities; Analogies; Series
Descriptors: *Abstract Reasoning; Cognitive Ability; Elementary Education; Elementary School Students; Foreign Countries; *Nonverbal Tests; *Perception; *Spatial Ability; Visualization; Visual Measures
Identifiers: England; NFER
Availability: NFER—Nelson Publishing Co.; Darville House, 2 Oxford Rd. E., Windsor, Berks SL4 1DF, England
Target Audience: 8-11
Notes: Time, 40; Items, 100

This instrument is the revised edition of the Non-Verbal Test 5, 1953. It has been designed to measure the nonverbal ability of children in the age range 8-11. There are practice items before each of the sub-tests so that all children will be familiar with the type of item in the test and poor readers will not be handicapped. In each of the 4 area subtests—cypher, similarities, analogies, and series—the student is shown a series of pictures and must choose the answer from another set of pictures. In the age range, there was a significant difference between boys and girls and it is recommended that the sexes be considered separately.

810061
Picture Test 1. Stuart, Joan E. 1971
Descriptors: Cognitive Ability; Elementary Education; Elementary School Students; Foreign Countries; *Intelligence Tests; *Nonverbal Tests; Perception; Visualization
Identifiers: England; NFER
Availability: NFER—Nelson Publishing Co.; Darville House, 2 Oxford Rd. E., Windsor, Berks SL4 1DF, England
Target Audience: 7-8
Notes: Time, 45; Items, 60

This Picture Test was formerly titled Picture Intelligence Test 1. It was developed in England for children 7 and 8 years of age. It is used as an intelligence test and the scores are similar to intelligence quotients in their numerical distribution, but they differ in that they are not arrived at through consideration of mental age. Each child is assessed by comparing him or her with a representative sample of children of exactly the same age.

810100
Progressive Matrices, Advanced Sets I and II. Raven, John C. 1965
Descriptors: *Academically Gifted; Adolescents; Adults; *Cognitive Measurement; *Cognitive Processes; Foreign Countries; *Intellectual Development; Nonverbal Tests
Identifiers: APM I; APM II; England; Great Britain
Availability: The Psychological Corp.; 555 Academic Ct., San Antonio, TX 78204-0952
Target Audience: 12-64
Notes: Time, 40 approx.; Items, 48

A nonverbal test designed for use as an aid in assessing mental ability. Requires the examinee to solve problems presented in abstract figures and designs. Scores are said to correlate well with comprehensive intelligence tests. This form is designed for use with persons having above-average intellectual ability. Norms are estimated for a British population at ages 11 1/2, 14, 20, 30, and 40. Said to be culture fair. Set I covers all intellectual processes covered by the Standard Progressive Matrices Sets. Set II provides a means of assessing all the analytical and integral operations involved in the higher thought processes and differentiates between people of superior intellectual ability.

810122
Group Test of General Intelligence AH4. Heim, A.W. 1973
Subtests: Verbal and Numerical; Diagrammatic
Descriptors: *Adolescents; *Adults; *Children; *Deduction; Foreign Countries; *Intelligence; *Intelligence Tests; *Mental Retardation; Multiple Choice Tests; Timed Tests; Visual Measures
Identifiers: England; Great Britain
Availability: NFER-Nelson Publishing Co. Ltd.; Darville House, 2 Oxford Rd. E., Windsor, Berks, SL4 1DF, England
Target Audience: 10-64
Notes: Time, 20; Items, 130

Developed in England in order to measure general intelligence of the adult population, some groups with below average intelligence, and for all children over 10 years of age. The qualities tested are ability to reason, to obey simple instructions, to understand the meaning of everyday words and to observe details accurately. The emphasis is mainly upon deductive reasoning. The author recommends one administrator for groups of up to 25 and an assistant for each additional 5 to 20 people. The distribution is restricted, available only to recognized professional institutions and qualified psychologists.

810155
Number Test DE. Barnard, E.L. 1978
Descriptors: *Aptitude Tests; *Arithmetic; Children; Computation; Elementary School Mathematics; *Elementary School Students; Foreign Countries; Mathematical Applications; *Mathematics Achievement; *Number Concepts; *Number Systems; *Mathematics Tests
Identifiers: England; Number Test 1
Availability: NFER-Nelson Publishing Co., Ltd.; Darville House, 2 Oxford Rd. E., Windsor, Berks, S14 1DF, England
Target Audience: 10-12
Notes: Time, 50 approx.; Items, 50

Untimed instrument designed to measure a student's understanding of the four number processes. Based upon the theory that a student who understands these processes would be able to utilize them in solving new types of problems and as a basis from which to generalize and draw inferences. This instrument was originally titled Number Test 1 and was restandardized in 1978.

810251
Spatial Test EG. Smith, I. MacFarlane 1959
Subtests: Fitting Shapes; Form Recognition; Pattern Recognition; Shape Recognition; Comparisons; Form Reflections
Descriptors: *Aptitude Tests; Engineering; Engineering Drawing; Foreign Countries; Intermediate Grades; Metal Working; Secondary Education; *Spatial Ability; *Student Placement; *Technical Education; Woodworking
Identifiers: Great Britain; *Spatial Tests
Availability: NFER-Nelson Publishing Co.; Darville House, 2 Oxford Rd. E.. Windsor, Berks, SL4 1DF, England
Target Audience: 11-14
Notes: Time, 60 approx.; Items, 100

This test is designed to measure spatial aptitude in association with general ability and is intended for use in the allocation of pupils to technical courses. When the test was standardized and the validity data collected, the results indicated that the test was a better predictor of performance in engineering, drawing, metalwork and woodwork than were tests of verbal reasoning, arithmetic and English.

810369
Symbolic Play Test: Experimental Edition. Lowe, Marianne; Costello, Anthony J. 1976
Descriptors: *Concept Formation; *Diagnostic Tests; Foreign Countries; Nonverbal Tests; *Speech Handicaps; *Young Children
Identifiers: England; Great Britain; *Symbolic Play; Symbolic Thinking
Availability: NFER-Nelson Publishing Co.; Darville House, 2 Oxford Rd. E., Windsor, SL41DF, Berkshire shire, England
Target Audience: 1-3
Notes: Time, 15; Items, 24

Diagnostic measure using children's spontaneous nonverbal play activities in a structured situation to identify the level of a child's symbolic thinking and early concept formation. To be used with children who have failed to develop receptive or expressive language. Unlike performance tests in that it measures semantic rather than spatial relationships and ability to deal with symbols in their simplest form, main function is to identify children whose failure to communicate is due to an environmental cause, not a lack in the area of symbolization, or a developmental delay.

810398
AH1, Forms X and Y. Heim, A.W.; And Others 1977

Subtests: Series; Likes; Analogies; Differents
Descriptors: *Children; Cognitive Processes; Foreign Countries; *Logical Thinking; Multiple Choice Tests; Nonverbal Tests; *Pattern Recognition; Pictorial Stimuli; *Serial Ordering; Visual Perception
Identifiers: *Analogies; Great Britain
Availability: NFER-Nelson Publishing Co., Ltd.; Darville House, 2 Oxford Rd. E., Windsor, Berks SL4 1DF, England
Target Audience: 5-10
Notes: Time, 45 approx.; Items, 48

AH1, X and Y, are parallel group tests of perceptual reasoning. They differ only in content. Both tests comprise 4 subtests of 12 questions each—Series (S), Likes (L), Analogies (A), Differents (D)—and are always given in the same order, SLAD. In each set, half the items are diagrammatic and half are pictorial and are presented alternately. The diagrams are abstract shapes and the pictures represent objects found in the physical world. All items are multiple-choice with 6 responses from which to choose. The tests are nonverbal in that the subject needs no words to express the answer and a slow reader or non-reader is not penalized—provided he/she fully understood the preliminary examples. The tests are intended for children between the ages of 5 and 10, but it is strongly recommended that, for ordinary classroom purposes, the tests be used only for 7 to 10 years. They are available to psychologists testing children in the 5 to 6 age group for research or clinical purposes; this is because group testing of very young children is difficult.

810416
Group Tests of High-Level Intelligence AH6. Heim, A.W.; And Others 1970
Subtests: Verbal; Numerical; Diagrammatic
Descriptors: *Adolescents; *Adults; College Students; Foreign Countries; *Gifted; High School Students; *Intelligence; *Intelligence Differences; *Intelligence Tests; Multiple Choice Tests; Professional Personnel; Timed Tests; Visual Measures; Vocational Schools
Identifiers: England; Great Britain
Availability: NFER-Nelson Publishing Co., Ltd.; Darville House, 2 Oxford Rd. E., Windsor, Berkshire shire, SL4 1DF, England
Target Audience: 14-64
Notes: Time, 40; Items, 72

Developed in England to effect discrimination among the highly intelligent students and potential students at universities and colleges, potential entrants to professions and senior students at Grammar, Public, and Technical schools. Two forms exist: AG and SEM. SEM is for potential or qualified scientists, engineers, and mathematicians; has 72 questions and is timed for 40 minutes. AG (Arts and General) is for everyone else; has 60 questions and is timed for 35 minutes. Subjects may answer the questions in any order that they choose as the aim is to allow the subject to work at his/her own natural tempo on those questions which appeal most to him/her and to determine which chosen questions he/she can correctly answer. The author recommends 1 administrator for groups up to 25 and an assistant for each additional 5 to 20 people.

810435
Group Tests of General Reasoning AH 2. Heim, A.W.; And Others 1975
Subtests: Verbal; Numerical; Perceptual
Descriptors: *Abstract Reasoning; Adolescents; Adults; Children; *Cognitive Ability; Foreign Countries; *Intelligence Tests; *Verbal Ability
Identifiers: England; Group Test of General Ability; *Numerical Ability
Availability: NFER-Nelson Publishing Co. Ltd.; Darville House, 2 Oxford Rd. E., Windsor Berks SL4 1DF, England
Target Audience: 9-64
Notes: Time, 42 approx.; Items, 120

Group timed test of general reasoning ability for bright 9 year olds through adults. Two parallel forms of the test are available. There are 2 sets of time limits for groups of low, or unknown, ability and subjects of at least average intelligence. The short time limit totals 28 minutes; the long time total is 42 minutes.

810436
Group Tests of General Reasoning AH 3. Heim, A.W.; And Others 1975
Subtests: Verbal; Numerical; Perceptual
Descriptors: *Abstract Reasoning; Adolescents; Adults; Children; Cognitive Ability; Foreign Countries; *Intelligence Tests; *Verbal Ability
Identifiers: England; Group Test of General Ability; *Numerical Ability
Availability: NFER-Nelson Publishing Co. Ltd.; Darville House, 2 Oxford Rd. E., Windsor Berks SL4 1DF, England
Target Audience: 9-64
Notes: Time, 42 approx.; Items, 120

Group timed test of general reasoning ability for bright nine year olds through adults. Two parallel forms of the test are available. There are two sets of time limits for subjects of low, or unknown, ability and subjects of at least average intelligence. The short time limit totals 28 minutes; the long time total is 42 minutes.

810467
Thackray Reading Readiness Profiles. Thackray, Derek; Thackray, Lucy 1974
Subtests: Vocabulary and Concept Development; Auditory Discrimination; Visual Discrimination; General Ability
Descriptors: *Auditory Discrimination; Diagnostic Teaching; Diagnostic Tests; *Elementary School Students; Foreign Countries; *Grade 1; Primary Education; *Reading Readiness; *Reading Readiness Tests; Reading Skills; Visual Discrimination; *Vocabulary
Identifiers: England
Availability: Hodder & Stoughton Educational; P.O. Box 6, Mill Rd., Dunton Green, Sevenoaks, Kent TN13 2XX, England
Grade Level: 1
Notes: Time, 70 approx.; Items, 67

The first original British reading readiness tests to be published are a measure of 4 important reading readiness indicators. Each of 4 subtests should be administrered separately. Children should be given an opportunity to rest between sessions. Total administration may be completed in 2 days. Designed for use with children at the beginning of grade 1. May also be used diagnostically with older nonreaders.

810474
The British Ability Scales, Revised. Elliott, Colin D.; And Others 1983
Subtests: Speed of Information Processing; Formal Operational Thinking; Matrices; Similarities; Social Reasoning; Block Design Level; Block Design Power; Rotation of Letter Line Forms; Visualization of Cubes; Copying; Matching Letter Like Forms; Verbal Tactile Matching; Immediate Visual Recall; Delayed Visual Recall; Recall of Designs; Recall of Digits; Visual Recognition; Basic Number Skills; Naming Vocabulary; Verbal Comprehension; Verbal Fluency; Word Definitions; Word Reading
Descriptors: Abstract Reasoning; *Adolescents; *Children; *Cognitive Ability; *Cognitive Tests; Foreign Countries; Individual Testing; Intelligence Quotient; Intelligence Tests; Knowledge Level; Number Concepts; Perceptual Development; Reading Ability; Short Term Memory; Spatial Ability; Verbal Ability; Vocabulary
Identifiers: BAS; England; Great Britain; Rasch Model; Test Batteries
Availability: NFER-Nelson Publishing Co.; Darville House, 2 Oxford Rd. E., Windsor, SL41DF, Berkshire shire, England
Target Audience: 2-17
Notes: Items, 540

Consists of 23 scales measuring a wide range of cognitive abilities. The 23 scales cover 6 major areas of cognitive development: speed of information processing, reasoning, spatial imagery, perceptual matching, short term memory, and retrieval and application of knowledge. Each scale may be administered separately or in combination with any other scales in the battery. Uses the Rasch model as the basis for the construction of unidimensional scales and as the basis for a number of technical features. Primary purpose of the scale is to diagnose and analyse children's learning difficulties. May also be used to assess change over a period of time or for more traditional functions of identifying, selecting, and classifying children with various learning difficulties. Any scale may be administered completely or in a short form. Standardized on an age range of 2.5 years to 17 years old.

810476
National Adult Reading Test. Nelson, Hazel E. 1982
Descriptors: Adults; Alcoholism; Drug Use; Foreign Countries; Individual Testing; *Intelligence; *Mental Disorders; Older Adults; *Pronunciation; *Reading Tests; *Word Recognition
Identifiers: *Dementia; England; Great Britain; NART; *Premorbid Intelligence
Availability: NFER-Nelson Publishing Co.; Darville House, 2 Oxford Rd. E., Windsor, Berkshire shire SL4 1DF, England
Target Audience: 20-70
Notes: Items, 50

Represents a new technique for estimating premorbid intelligence in the assessment of elements. Consists of 50 words in which the correct pronunciation is based on word recognition. This measure is stable despite deterioration of other intellectual functions. From subject's score, IQ can be predicted which closely approximates premorbid IQ level. Will also be useful in measuring effects of alcohol, drugs or illness on intellectual functioning of 20-70 year olds.

810482
NIIP Group Test 72. National Institute of Industrial Psychology, London, England 1974
Descriptors: *Abstract Reasoning; Adolescents; *Adults; Apprenticeships; Foreign Countries; Intelligence; *Intelligence Tests; Personnel Selection; Semiskilled Workers
Identifiers: England
Availability: NFER-Nelson Publishing Co.; Darville House, 2 Oxford Rd. E., Windsor, SL41DF, Berkshire shire, England
Target Audience: 15-64
Notes: Time, 15 approx.; Items, 48

Paper and pencil tests of intelligence in which problems are presented by means of diagrams using domino designs. Two parallel forms are available. Tests measure general intelligence or reasoning ability and are suitable for use as part of a selection procedure for applicants for operative positions, semiskilled work and for some types of draft apprenticeships. May also be used in selection of applicants for lower-grade clerical positions. Not suitable for use with groups of high educational attainment. Tests should only be used as part of a selection procedure and not as the sole criterion for selection.

810483
NIIP Verbal Test 91. National Institute of Industrial Psychology, London, England 1968
Descriptors: *Abstract Reasoning; Adolescents; Adults; *Aptitude Tests; *Cognitive Ability; Cognitive Tests; Dropouts; *Employees; Foreign Countries; *Job Applicants; *Occupational Tests; Problem Solving; Timed Tests; Verbal Ability; *Verbal Tests; Vocational Aptitude
Identifiers: England; Great Britain; Group Test 91; *Reasoning Ability
Availability: NFER-Nelson Publishing Co.; Darville House, 2 Oxford Rd. E., Windsor, Berkshire shire SL4 1DF, England
Target Audience: 15-64
Notes: Time, 15; Items, 110

Measures verbal general intelligence. Used with employees and job applicants for positions requiring verbal reasoning and usually with subjects who are high school dropouts or have a lower level of educational attainment. Distribution limited to persons who are registered with NIIP as qualified to use it.

810489
NIIP Group Test 82. National Institute of Industrial Psychology, London, England
Descriptors: Employment Potential; *Engineering Technicians; Foreign Countries; *Occupational Tests; *Perception Tests; *Spatial Ability; *Visual Measures; *Visual Perception; Visual Stimuli; *Vocational Education
Identifiers: Engineering Selection Test Battery; Group Test 82; NIIP Engineering Selection Test Battery; United Kingdom
Availability: NFER-Nelson Publishing Co.; Darville House, 2 Oxford Rd. E., Windsor, Berkshire shire SL4 1DF, England
Target Audience: 15-64
Notes: Time, 24; Items, 68

Measures one's spatial perception. Involves the ability to rotate and turn over 2-dimensional shapes in one's mind. Used as selection aid for engineering apprenticeships or engineering training courses. Part of the NIIP Engineering Selection Test Battery (TC810481). Timed. Restricted distribution.

810491
Form Relations Test. National Institute of Industrial Psychology, London, England
Descriptors: Adolescents; Adults; *Apprenticeships; *Engineering; Foreign Countries; Job Placement; *Perception Tests; *Personnel Selection; *Spatial Ability; *Student Placement; Visual Measures; Vocational Aptitude
Identifiers: England
Availability: NFER-Nelson Publishing Co.; Darville House, 2 Oxford Rd. E., Windsor, Berks SL4 1DF, England
Target Audience: 15-64
Notes: Time, 30; Items, 40

Eight part test which measures understanding of spatial relationships. Test takers must decide which of a group of similar geometric shapes fits into diagrams at top of page. Questions are presented in form of 2- and 3-dimensional drawings. Used for selection of applicants for courses, apprenticeships and jobs involving engineering and industrial design.

810492
NIIP Vincent Mechanical Diagrams Test, 1979 Revision. National Institute of Industrial Psychology, London, England 1979
Descriptors: Adolescents; Adults; *Apprenticeships; *Aptitude Tests; *Engineering; Foreign Countries; *Mechanics (Physics); Student Placement
Identifiers: England; VMD
Availability: NFER-Nelson Publishing Co.; Darville House, 2 Oxford Rd. E., Windsor, Berks SL4 1DF, England
Target Audience: 15-64
Notes: Time, 25; Items, 80

Designed to assess mechanical ability. Contains 4 subtests to assess individual's ability to understand the concepts of cog, pulley, and lever systems. Used to evaluate applicants for engineering apprenticeships or other categories of technical trainees. The original version of the test is also available and contains 8 subtests (TC810112).

810511
Programmer Aptitude Series. Saville, Peter; And Others 1980
Subtests: Diagramming; Number Series; Verbal Concepts; Basic Checking; Spatial Recognition; Verbal Critical Reasoning; Diagrammatic Reasoning; Spatial Reasoning; Numerical Critical Reasoning
Descriptors: Adults; *Aptitude Tests; Computer Software; Critical Thinking; *Data Processing; Flow Charts; Program Design; *Programers; Mathematics Tests; Spatial Ability; Verbal Ability
Identifiers: Checking Tests; Coding (Data Processing); Debugging; PAS; Reasoning Ability
Availability: Saville and Holdsworth, Ltd.; N. Lodge, 4 Esher Park Ave., Esher, Surrey KT10 9NP, England
Target Audience: 18-65
Notes: Time, 95; Items, 390

Designed to measure the verbal, numerical, clerical, diagrammatic and spatial abilities required for learning basic programing functions, and intermediate, and higher levels of data processing operations. Three levels with varying subscales are provided. Measures abilities in flow-charting, debugging, maintenance, program design, coding, checking, documentation.

810512
Advanced Test Battery. Holdsworth, Roger; And Others 1980
Subtests: Verbal Concepts; Number Series; Diagramming; Verbal Critical Reasoning; Numerical Critical Reasoning
Descriptors: Adults; *Aptitude Tests; Foreign Countries; *Logical Thinking; *Management Development; *Mathematical Concepts; Personnel Evaluation; Personnel Selection; *Professional Personnel; Timed Tests; *Verbal Ability
Identifiers: ATB; Great Britain; SHL Advanced Test Battery; Test Batteries
Availability: Saville and Holdsworth, Ltd.; N. Lodge, 4 Esher Park Ave., Esher Surrey, KT10 9NP England
Target Audience: Adults
Notes: Time, 115 approx.; Items, 220

This battery of tests is designed to discriminate at the very top range of ability. It should be administered and interpreted only by individuals specifically trained in its application. The battery of 5 tests is designed for managerial assessment and selection of higher-level managers. The subtests may be administered individually, or in any combination deemed appropriate to the position. Level 1 includes 3 aptitude tests. The verbal concepts test consists of 40 items and requires 15 minutes to administer. The number series test consists of 30 items and requires 15 minutes. The diagraming test consists of 50 items and requires 20 minutes. Level 2 includes 2 skills in context tests. The verbal critical reasoning test consists of 60 items requiring 30 minutes. The numerical critical reasoning test consists of 40 items and requires 35 minutes. Two subtests from the Technical Test Battery (TC810515) may be used with the Advanced Test Battery as they have been designed to measure abilities at the higher end of the ability range. These tests are spatial reasoning which consists of 40 items and requires 20 minutes, and diagrammatic reasoning which consists of 40 items and required 15 minutes.

810525
Behavior Assessment Battery. Second Edition. Kiernan, Chris; Jones, Malcolm C. 1982
Subtests: Reinforcement and Experience; Inspection; Tracking; Visuo-Motor; Auditory; Postural Control; Exploratory Control; Constructive Play; Search Strategies; Perceptual Problem Solving; Social, Communication; Self Help Skills
Descriptors: Adolescents; Adults; Behavior Rating Scales; Children; *Cognitive Ability; *Communication Skills; Foreign Countries; Individual Testing; Interviews; *Self Care Skills; *Severe Mental Retardation; *Training Methods
Identifiers: BAB; England; Great Britain; Test Batteries

Availability: NFER-Nelson Publishing Co.; Darville House, 2 Oxford Rd. E., Windsor SL4 1DF, Berkshire shire, England
Target Audience: 2-64
Notes: Time, 260 approx.

Developed for use by psychologists, teachers, doctors, and others who have experience with severely mentally handicapped individuals. Battery is based on premise that children should achieve certain target or criterion behaviors to function adequately in their environment. Battery is not meant to replace other methods of assessing profoundly retarded but to complement other techniques by providing additional or unique details. Each section consists of items and a lattice, which is a visual representation of the sequencing of items. Designed to provide a basis for macro-assessment of profoundly handicapped persons. Battery is teaching or training oriented so that purpose is to aid in setting up training programs. Battery consists of 2 types of items: interview items for use with teacher and parent or guardian of child and behavioral items to assess child's general behavior. Sections of the battery may be administered in the order indicated or in another order. Evaluates cognitive, communicative, and self-help skills. During development of the BAB, 174 children ranging in age from 2 years to 17 years were tested.

810526
Personnel Test Battery. Holdsworth, Roger; And Others 1980
Subtests: Verbal Usage (Level 1); Numerical Computation (Level 1); Checking (Level 1); Classification (Level 2); Verbal Meaning (Level 2); Numerical Reasoning (Level 2); Basic Checking (Optional); Audio Checking (Optional)
Descriptors: Adults; *Aptitude Tests; Career Counseling; Career Development; Food Service; Foreign Countries; Job Placement; *Office Occupations; *Personnel Selection; Sales Workers
Identifiers: England; Great Britain; Proofreaders; PTB; Test Batteries
Availability: Saville and Holdsworth, Ltd.; N. Lodge, 4 Esher Park Ave., Esher, Surrey KT10 9NP, England
Target Audience: Adults

A series of 6 aptitude tests designed to sample abilities relating to many jobs that involve a degree of paperwork. Can be used to select and place employees in areas including office work, stores and warehousing, and retail and wholesale sales occupations. Tests are suitable for school dropouts and those with work experience who are entering jobs that require the quick and accurate routine use of numbers, words, and symbols. Examples of appropriate occupations include clerks, bookkeepers, telephone operators, sales assistants, restaurant and kitchen workers, and proofreaders. Skills measured include language proficiency, numerical computation and reasoning, checking and classifying. Level 1 tests measure basic skills and comprehension. Level 2 tests measure higher-order reasoning skills.

810527
Technical Test Battery. Hawkey, David; And Others 1979
Subtests: Verbal Comprehension (Level 1); Numerical Computation (Level 1); Visual Estimation (Level 1); Mechanical Comprehension (Level 1); Verbal Reasoning (Level 2); Numerical Reasoning (Level 2); Spatial Reasoning (Level 2); Diagrammatic Reasoning (Level 2); Spatial Recognition (Optional)
Descriptors: *Abstract Reasoning; Adults; Apprenticeships; *Aptitude Tests; *Comprehension; Craft Workers; Foreign Countries; Paraprofessional Personnel; Personnel Evaluation; *Personnel Selection; *Semiskilled Occupations; Supervisors; *Technical Occupations; Timed Tests
Identifiers: England; Great Britain; Test Batteries; TTB
Availability: Saville and Holdsworth, Ltd.; N. Lodge, 4 Esher Park Ave., Esher, Surrey, KT10 9NP, England
Target Audience: Adults

Sequential series of 8 aptitude tests designed for selection and development designed for a wide range of apprentice, technical, and technologist categories. The battery is arranged in 2 levels, each consisting of 4 scales. Level 1 is intended primarily for craft apprentice, foreman and similar occupations and is designed to measure comprehension skills. Level 1 consists of 160 items and takes 45 minutes to complete. Level 2 overlaps level 1 but extends it and is more difficult than Level 1. Level 2 is suitable for technicians, supervisors, technologists, technical sales and degree level candidates. The scales measure higher order reasoning skills. Level 2 scales consist of 145 items and takes 55 minutes to complete. An optional scale is one for spatial recognition, and consists of 40 items which can be completed in 15 minutes. Tests in the battery may be given singly or in combination.

810530
Critical Reasoning Test Battery. Nyfield, Gill; And Others 1983

Subtests: Verbal Evaluation; Interpreting Data; Diagrammatic Series
Descriptors: *Abstract Reasoning; Administrator Selection; Adolescents; Adults; Career Choice; *Cognitive Tests; Foreign Countries; *Logical Thinking; *Problem Solving; Student Evaluation; Student Placement
Identifiers: CRTB; England; Great Britain; Test Batteries
Availability: Saville and Holdsworths, Ltd.; N. Lodge, 4 Esher Park Ave., Esher, Surrey KT10 9NP, England
Target Audience: 15-64
Notes: Time, 80; Items, 140

Contains reasoning tests which may be used in education, commerce and industry, and development of students and employees over the age of 15. Appropriate for use with a range of subjects from school dropouts to academic students to junior managers or supervisors in industry. May be used to help students decide on courses of study, to assist them in reaching career decisions, or for employee selection in companies where higher reasoning skills are necessary for certain jobs. May also be used for assessment and guidance within a company. The verbal evaluation section measures the ability to understand and evaluate the logic of various kinds of arguments. The interpreting data section measures the ability to make correct decisions or inferences from numerical or statistical data presented as tables or diagrams. The diagrammatic series assesses reasoning with diagrams and requires subject to discover logical rules governing sequences occurring in rows of symbols and diagrams. Each subtest may be administered alone or the entire test may be given.

810533
Linguistic Awareness in Reading Readiness Test. Downing, John; And Others 1983
Subtests: Recognizing Literacy Behavior; Understanding Literacy Functions; Technical Language of Literacy
Descriptors: Foreign Countries; *Grade 1; *Kindergarten Children; Language Processing; Linguistic Performance; Primary Education; *Reading Readiness Tests
Identifiers: England; Great Britain; LARR
Availability: NFER-Nelson Publishing Co.; Darville House, 2 Oxford Rd. E., Windsor, Berkshire SL4 1DF, England
Grade Level: K-1
Notes: Time, 60 approx.; Items, 75

Series of group tests useful in determining strengths and weaknesses of both individual pupils and the class with regard to their understanding of the linguistic concepts needed for reasoning about the tasks of reading instruction. Each of the 3 subtests has 2 alternate forms, equal in conceptual content and level of difficulty. Based on recent research which shows reading readiness is closely related to linguistic awareness and related concepts of functions and features of written language. Test has its foundations in the work of Jean Piaget and Lev Vygotsky. Principle underlying test is that learner must understand purpose of the skill to be acquired and the concepts used for talking and thinking about how to perform the skill. The subtest recognizing literacy behavior measures extent to which child recognizes kinds of activities involved in skills of reading and writing. The understanding literacy functions subtest deals with the concept of the varied purposes of reading and writing. The technical language of literacy subtest measures child's knowledge of technical terms used in describing features of written language.

810542
Snijders-Oomen Non-Verbal Intelligence Scale. Snijders, J. Th.; Snijders-Oomen, N. 1976
Subtests: Sorting; Mosaic; Combination; Memory; Copying
Descriptors: *Deafness; Foreign Countries; Hearing Impairments; *Intelligence Tests; *Nonverbal Tests; Preschool Children; *Young Children
Identifiers: Netherlands; SON
Availability: NFER-Nelson Publishing Co.; Darville House, 2 Oxford Rd. E., Windsor, Berks, SL4 1DF, England
Target Audience: 2-7
Notes: Items, 50

An intelligence test intended chiefly for use by practicing psychologists. This is a revised and newly standardized version of the original test. Test was standardized on both a hearing sample and a deaf sample.

810545
Information System Skills. Morrisby, Malcolm 1983
Subtests: Reasoning; Form Recognition; Clerical Speed and Accuracy; Manual Speed
Descriptors: Abstract Reasoning; *Adults; *Aptitude Tests; Clerical Occupations; Data Processing; *Data Processing Occupations; Foreign Countries; Occupational Tests; Predictive Measurement; Spatial Ability; Timed Tests; Word Processing

Identifiers: Clerical Aptitude; England; ISS; Speededness (Tests)
Availability: Educational and Industrial Test Services, Ltd.; 83 High St., Hemel, Hempstead HP1 3AH, England
Target Audience: Adults
Notes: Time, 45 approx.

Designed to be a predictive measurement of an individual's success in operating terminal-based information systems. Measures verbal and numerical reasoning ability, perceptual ability, speed and accuracy in checking, and manual speed involving a small amount of manual skill. Assesses abilities important in operating computer-based information and office systems, such as word processing, online data inquiries, stock control, and data entry. Also assesses general aptitude for clerical work.

810547
Educational Abilities Scale. Stillman, Andy; Whetton, Chris 1982
Subtests: Clerical Aptitude; Mechanical Comprehension; Symbolic Reasoning; Spatial Reasoning; Science Reasoning
Descriptors: Abstract Reasoning; *Academic Aptitude; Adolescents; *Aptitude Tests; *Cognitive Ability; *Educational Counseling; Foreign Countries; Logical Thinking; Scientific Concepts; Secondary Education; *Secondary School Students; Spatial Ability
Identifiers: Clerical Aptitude; EAS; England; Great Britain; Mechanical Comprehension
Availability: NFER-Nelson Publishing Co.; Darville House, 2 Oxford Rd. E., Windsor, Berks SL4 1DF, England
Grade Level: 7-9
Target Audience: 13-14
Notes: Time, 150 approx.

Used in Great Britain in the middle years of secondary school education to aid in the selection of courses of study and to provide information across a wide range of abilities. Used in conjunction with achievement test results and knowledge of individual students, EAS can give insight into students' skills and potential and provide information to assist with course selection in England's final 2 years of compulsory schooling. One new feature of the EAS is the answer-until-correct method in 4 out of the 5 scales. This uses a latent-image printing technique and requires students to persevere with each question until they obtain the correct answer. The EAS is a measure of ability and not of attainment or academic achievement. The entire battery should be administered in 2 sessions with a break between sessions. Is a group-administered test.

810553
NIIP Verbal Test 90A/90B. National Institute of Industrial Psychology, London, England 1982
Subtests: Same and Opposite; Analogies; Jumbled Sentences; Completing Sentences
Descriptors: Administrators; Adolescents; Adults; Clerical Workers; *Cognitive Tests; *Intelligence; *Personnel Selection; Skilled Workers; *Verbal Ability
Identifiers: Engineering Selection Test Battery
Availability: NFER-Nelson Publishing Co.; Darville House, 2 Oxford Rd. E., Windsor, Berks SL4 1DF, England
Target Audience: 15-64
Notes: Time, 30 approx.

Paper and pencil tests of intelligence and verbal aptitude. Two forms are alternative tests and are not parallel forms. Not suitable for administration to subjects with lower educational attainment. Form 90A is suitable for use in personnel selection and assessment and in educational institutions and research organizations. Form 90B is only for use in personnel selection and assessment. Used for personnel selection for job applications in management and supervision, clerical positions, and other skilled work. Part of the Engineering Apprentice Selection Test Battery.

810558
Children's Abilities Scales. Childs, Roy 1984
Subtests: Word Pairs; Word Overlap; Flags; Dice; Symbols; Shapes
Descriptors: *Abstract Reasoning; *Aptitude Tests; *Cognitive Tests; Elementary Education; *Elementary School Students; Foreign Countries; Nonverbal Ability; Spatial Ability; Student Placement; Verbal Ability
Identifiers: CAS; England; Great Britain
Availability: NFER-Nelson Publishing Co.; Darville House, 2 Oxford Rd. E., Windsor, Berks SL4 1DF, England
Grade Level: 5-6
Target Audience: 11-12
Notes: Time, 140 approx.

Main purpose is to provide information on students transferring to a secondary school in Great Britain. Scales were standardized during the first term of the school year. These tests are not related to a specific set of learning circumstances but reflect pupils' cognitive development and reasoning ability in verbal, nonverbal, and spatial skills. The inventory consists of 6 tests which can be combined in pairs to form 3 scales: Verbal Scale, Spatial Scale, and Nonverbal Scale. All 6 tests do not have to be administered. The selection of the particular tests to be used can be made by the teacher. Tests may be used to make placement decisions about students.

810559
Bennett Mechanical Comprehension Test, Forms S and T, British Manual. Bennett, George K. 1969
Descriptors: Adolescents; Adults; *Aptitude Tests; Employment Qualifications; Foreign Countries; Higher Education; High Schools; Job Applicants; *Mechanical Skills; *Mechanics (Physics); Personnel Selection; Trade and Industrial Education; *Vocational Aptitude
Identifiers: BMCT; England; Great Britain
Availability: NFER-Nelson Publishing Co.; Darville House, 2 Oxford Rd. E., Windsor, Berks SL4 1D7, England
Target Audience: 15-65
Notes: Time, 30; Items, 68

Measures the ability to perceive and understand the relationship of physical forces and mechanical elements in practical situations. Suitable for applicants for industrial jobs, employees in mechanical jobs, candidates for engineering schools and other groups of comparable ability and education. Forms S and T are alternate forms of the same test. Replaces earlier forms AA, BB and W. Has a wider range of difficulty, equal or better reliability, up-to-date illustrations and simplified scoring. British manual is meant to accompany, not replace, the American manual. British manual geared to educational and industrial groupings of Great Britain.

810567
Shapes Analysis Test. Heim, A.W.; And Others 1972
Descriptors: Adults; Foreign Countries; *Geometric Constructions; *Spatial Ability; *Visual Measures; Vocational Aptitude
Identifiers: England; Geometric Forms; *Shapes
Availability: The Test Agency; Cournswood House, N. Dean, High Wycombe HP14 4NW, England
Target Audience: Adults
Notes: Time, 45 approx.; Items, 36

A test of spatial perception. Assesses the ability to manipulate mentally different shapes and sizes, to visualize how 2-dimensional and 3-dimensional geometric figures will appear if turned over or around to estimate area and to assess spatial relations. Provides predictive value for proficiency in work which demands accurate visual imagery and indicates a general practical ability.

810568
Group Tests of High Level Intelligence, AH6:AG. Heim, A.W.; And Others 1983
Subtests: Verbal; Numerical and Diagrammatic
Descriptors: *Abstract Reasoning; *Academically Gifted; Adolescents; *Cognitive Ability; College Students; Foreign Countries; High School Students; *Intelligence Differences; *Intelligence Tests; Liberal Arts; Professional Personnel; Young Adults
Identifiers: England; Great Britain
Availability: NFER-Nelson Publishing Co., Ltd.; Darville House, 2 Oxford Rd. E., Windsor, Berks SL4 1DF, England
Target Audience: 16-25
Notes: Time, 35 approx.; Items, 60

Test of general reasoning designed for use with selected, highly intelligent subjects such as candidates for or students at university and colleges of education, potential entrants to the professions and senior students at schools and colleges. Form AG is intended for those in liberal arts and social sciences, such as historians, linguists, economists, philosophers, and teachers. Test is meant to discriminate among the intelligent population. Half of the questions in form AG (arts and general subjects) are verbal, one-quarter are numerical and one-quarter are diagrammatic. Tests may be group administered.

810575
Recognition Memory Test. Warrington, Elizabeth 1984
Descriptors: Adults; Foreign Countries; *Neurological Impairments; Older Adults; Screening Tests; *Short Term Memory; Verbal Stimuli; Visual Stimuli
Identifiers: England; Great Britain; RMT
Availability: NFER-Nelson Publishing Co.; Darville House, 2 Oxford Rd. E., Windsor, Berks SL4 1DF, England
Target Audience: 18-70
Notes: Time, 15 approx.; Items, 100

Developed to detect minor visual and verbal memory deficits which may indicate organic neurological disease. Two subtests assess verbal and visual recognition and enable clinicians to distinguish between right and left hemisphere damage.

810578
Group Tests of High Level Intelligence, AH6: SEM. Heim, A.W.; And Others 1983
Subtests: Verbal; Numerical; Diagrammatic
Descriptors: *Abstract Reasoning; *Academically Gifted; Adolescents; *Cognitive Ability; College Students; Foreign Countries; High School Students; *Intelligence Differences; *Intelligence Tests; Professional Personnel; *Scientific Personnel; Young Adults
Identifiers: England; Great Britain
Availability: NFER-Nelson Publishing Co., Ltd.; Darville House, 2 Oxford Rd. E., Windsor, Berks SL4 1DF, England
Target Audience: 16-25
Notes: Time, 40; Items, 72

Test of general reasoning ability designed to discriminate among selected, highly intelligent subjects such as candidates for and students at universities and colleges of education, potential entrants to the professions, and senior students at schools and colleges. SEM is intended for use with scientists, engineers, and mathematicians. On form SEM, questions are divided among verbal, numerical, and diagrammatic. Tests may be group administered.

810585
Graduate and Managerial Assessment. Hatfield Polytechnic, England. Psychometric Research Unit. 1985
Descriptors: Adults; *Aptitude Tests; Foreign Countries; *Managerial Occupations; Multiple Choice Tests; *Personnel Selection; *Professional Personnel; *Promotion (Occupational)
Identifiers: England; GMA; Great Britain
Availability: NFER-Nelson Publishing Co.; Darville House, 2 Oxford Rd. E., Windsor, Berks SL4 1DF, England
Target Audience: 18-64

Intended for use in the recruitment, selection and assessment of college graduates; the identification of management and promotion potential; and the recruitment of individuals who may be capable of entering higher education. There are three test areas: numerical, verbal, and abstract. Each of the tests has been designed on the basis of a separate set of specific objectives. The numerical section can be used to assess graduates in general disciplines for finance-related occupations. The verbal section is applicable in selecting and assessing candidates for occupations which involve the critical appraisal of verbal material. The abstract section was designed to deemphasize educational attainment and to assess skills such as fluid intelligence, divergent thinking, induction, and other cognitive skills. The tests come in 2 forms.

810586
Measures of Musical Abilities. Bentley, Arnold 1966
Subtests: Pitch Discrimination; Tonal Memory; Chord Analysis; Rhythmic Memory
Descriptors: *Ability Identification; Adolescents; Aptitude Tests; Children; *Elementary School Students; Foreign Countries; Individual Testing; Magnetic Tape Cassettes; *Music; Music Activities; *Music Techniques
Identifiers: England; Great Britain; *Music Ability
Availability: NFER-Nelson Publishing Co.; Darville House, 2 Oxford Rd. E., Windsor, Berks SL4 1DF, England
Target Audience: 7-14
Notes: Time, 21; Items, 60

Battery of 4 tests which measure, positively, a child's ability to make the kind of basic judgments that are essential in music making. Four tests are pitch discrimination, tonal memory, chord analysis, and rhythmic memory. Tests are presented on a cassette tape. Tests are self-administering and no musical performance is required of the child. Aids in selection of children, ages 7 to 14 with more than normal ability for special musical activities such as orchestras and instrumental assemblies. Tests do not gauge intelligence, determination, industry, or musical ability as a whole. Tests are influenced only slightly by previous musical training and reveal wide ranges of ability

810587
Kendrick Cognitive Tests for the Elderly. Kendrick, Donald 1985
Subtests: Object Learning; Digit Copying
Descriptors: *Depression (Psychology); Diagnostic Tests; Foreign Countries; *Older Adults; *Patients; Reaction Time; *Schizophrenia; *Screening Tests; Short Term Memory
Identifiers: England; Great Britain; KDCT; Test Batteries
Availability: NFER-Nelson Publishing Co.; Darville House, 2 Oxford Rd. E., Windsor, Berks SL4 1DF, England
Target Audience: 56-99
Notes: Time, 15 approx.

Battery of 2 tests to detect early dementia and depressive psychosis among patients over 55 years old. Two subtests detect early dementia and depressive psychosis by assess-

ing those cognitive abilities which seem most sensitive to age changes: short-term memory and speed of processing and recording information. Administered to patients upon admission and 6 weeks later. Is a revision of the Kendrick Battery for the Detection of Dementia in the Elderly (TC810441).

810595
Check Up Tests in Workskills. Brandling, Redvers 1981
Descriptors: *Achievement Tests; Basic Skills; *Cognitive Development; *Daily Living Skills; *Elementary School Students; Foreign Countries; Intermediate Grades; *Knowledge Level; Language Skills; Preadolescents
Identifiers: England
Availability: Macmillan Education Ltd.; Houndmill, Basingstoke, Hampshire RG21 2XS, England
Target Audience: 10-11

Aim of these tests is to present information to children in a variety of ways and test their ability to use general skills as well as their own experience to answer the questions. There are 22 tests, each one testing a range of skills, and each about 40 minutes in length. The areas of work covered include reference skills, comprehension skills involving assimilating information so that instructions can be followed; interpreting data and presenting answers in visual form and reference skills. Constructed for students 10 to 11 years old.

810625
MD5 Mental Ability Test. Davey, D. Mackenzie 1972
Descriptors: Adults; Career Counseling; *Cognitive Ability; Foreign Countries; *Intelligence Tests; *Job Placement; *Managerial Occupations; *Personnel Selection; Supervisors
Identifiers: England; Great Britain; MD5
Availability: The Test Agency; Cournswood House, N. Dean, High Wycombe, Bucks HP14 4NW, England
Target Audience: Adults
Notes: Time, 15; Items, 57

Test of mental ability that can be used over a wide range of educational and ability levels. Useful for staff selection and placement at managerial and supervisory levels. Provides input for counseling and guidance work especially in the occupational context. Quick and easy to use. Requires both verbal/vocabulary and arithmetical skills so individuals' results will relate to their educational levels. Prime concern is with the abilities to deduce relationships and to apply the rules governing them.

810631
Test of Productive Thinking. Saville and Holdsworth, Surrey, England 1987
Descriptors: *Administrators; *Adults; *Creative Thinking; Foreign Countries; Managerial Occupations; *Occupational Tests; Problem Solving; *Productive Thinking; Professional Occupations
Identifiers: England; Great Britain
Availability: Saville and Holdsworth; The Old Post House, 81 High St., Esher, Surrey, England KT109QA
Target Audience: Adults
Notes: Time, 32; Items, 8

An assessment of the fluency, breadth and originality of a manager or potential manager's problem-solving ability. The 8 items are open-ended, requiring the candidate to either give as many explanations as possible as to why the problem has occurred or to suggest as many solutions as possible to the problem that has been set. Suitable for use with a large number of different groups from entry-level employees to senior management. Also appropriate for a wide range of occupational fields since the instrument is nonindustry specific.

810651
Work Skills Series, Production. Saville and Holdsworth, Surrey, England 1987
Subtests: Understanding Instructions; Working with Numbers
Descriptors: Adults; *Aptitude Tests; Arithmetic; Foreign Countries; Industrial Personnel; Machine Tool Operators; Mathematics; *Occupational Tests; *Personnel Selection; *Production Technicians; Reading
Identifiers: England; Great Britain; WSS
Availability: Saville and Holdsworth; 81 High St., Esher, Surrey, England KT10 9QA
Target Audience: Adults
Notes: Time, 22; Items, 75

An ability or aptitude measure designed for use in selecting employees for jobs in a production or shop environment. Basic verbal and numerical abilities are measured in the context of a subtest on understanding instructions and another on working with numbers. Both subtests use items directly related to production jobs including such examples as instructions to a machine operator, arithmetic calculations related to stocks of items, and reading delivery notices. Information on validity studies will be available from the publisher in subsequent manual supplements.

810661
Group Tests of Musical Ability. Mills, Janet 1988
Subtests: Pitch Test; Pulse Test
Descriptors: *Aptitude Tests; Audiotape Cassettes; Elementary Education; *Elementary School Students; Foreign Countries; Group Testing; *Music; *Music Education
Identifiers: England; Great Britain
Availability: NFER-Nelson Publishing Co.; Darville House, 2 Oxford Rd. E., Windsor, Berks, England SL4 1DF
Target Audience: 7-14
Notes: Time, 20 approx.; Items, 24

Designed to help general class teachers and music teachers monitor children's musical development, discover children with hidden musical abilities, draw up the musical component of a child's cross-curricular profile. The tests measure an individual's ability level at a particular stage of development. Consists of 2 tests on a cassette. The Pitch Test is concerned with the ability to discern small differences in pitch. The Pulse Test is concerned with the ability to maintain a steady beat. Intended for children 7 to 14 years old.

830309
Canadian Cognitive Abilities Test—Primary Battery 1 and 2. Thorndike, Robert L.; And Others 1970
Subtests: Oral Vocabulary; Relational Concepts; Multi-Mental Concepts; Quantitative Concepts
Descriptors: Achievement Tests; *Cognitive Ability; *Cognitive Tests; *Elementary School Students; Foreign Countries; *Kindergarten Children; Primary Education; Visual Measures
Identifiers: Canada; CCAT; Oral Testing
Availability: Thomas Nelson and Sons (Canada) Ltd.; 81 Curlew Dr., Don Mills, Ontario, Canada M3A 2R1
Grade Level: K-3
Notes: Time, 64 approx.

Designed to assess development of cognitive abilities. Primary I is for use in the last half of kindergarten and grade 1. Primary II is for use in grades 2 and 3. Examiner reads test items aloud one at a time, allowing sufficient time for children to try each item. Oral directions eliminate influence of reading skills on test performance. This is a power test. Battery should be administered in at least 2 sessions.

830310
Canadian Cognitive Abilities Tests—Multi-Level Edition, Levels A-F. Thorndike, Robert L.; Hagen, Elizabeth 1974
Subtests: Vocabulary, Sentence Completion; Verbal Classification; Verbal Analogies; Quantitative Relations; Number Series, Equation Building; Figure Analogies; Figure Classification; Figure Synthesis
Descriptors: *Abstract Reasoning; Achievement Tests; Cognitive Ability; *Cognitive Tests; Elementary Education; *Elementary School Students; Foreign Countries; Junior High Schools; *Junior High School Students; *Mathematics Tests; *Verbal Ability
Identifiers: Canada; CCAT; Test Batteries
Availability: Thomas Nelson and Sons (Canada) Ltd.; 81 Curlew Dr., Don Mills, Ontario, Canada M3A 2R1
Grade Level: 3-9
Notes: Time, 312 approx.

Measures individual's ability to use and manipulate abstract and symbolic relationships. Three batteries—verbal, quantitative and nonverbal—assess competence in working with each type of symbol. There are symbols representing words, quantities and spatial geometric or figural patterns. Each battery should be presented at a separate session.

830383
Canadian Cognitive Abilities Test, Primary Battery, Levels 1 and 2, Form 3. Thorndike, Robert L.; Hagen, Elizabeth 1981
Subtests: Relational Concepts; Multimental; Quantitative Concepts; Oral Vocabulary
Descriptors: *Abstract Reasoning; *Academic Aptitude; *Aptitude Tests; *Cognitive Ability; *Elementary School Students; Foreign Countries; *Kindergarten Children; Number Concepts; Primary Education; Problem Solving; Spatial Ability; Vocabulary
Identifiers: Canada; CCAT; Oral Testing; Power Tests; Quantitative Aptitude; Test Batteries
Availability: Nelson Canada Ltd.; 1120 Birchmount Rd., Scarborough, Ontario M1K 5G4, Canada
Grade Level: K-3
Notes: Time, 60 approx.

Part of an integrated test series to assess the development of cognitive abilities related to verbal, quantitative, and nonverbal reasoning, and problem solving skills important in learning activities. Organized in 2 levels: Level 1 for kindergarten and grade 1, and level 2 for grades 2 and 3. It is a power test rather than a speed test. Scores reflect the extent to which children have developed the following skills and competencies: comprehending oral English; following directions; short-term memory; possessing effective strategies for scanning pictorial and figural stimuli to obtain either general or specific information; possessing general information and verbal concepts; comparing stimuli and detecting similarities and differences in relative size, position, quantity, shape and time; classifying, categorizing, or ordering familiar objects; using quantitative and spatial relationships and concepts. Level 1 has 84 items; Level 2 has 98 items.

830384
Canadian Cognitive Abilities Test, Multilevel Edition, Levels A-H, Form 3. Thorndike, Robert L.; Hagen, Elizabeth 1981
Subtests: Vocabulary; Sentence Completion; Verbal Classification; Verbal Analogies; Quantitative Relations; Number Series; Equation Building; Figure Classification; Figure Analysis; Figure Synthesis
Descriptors: *Abstract Reasoning; *Academic Aptitude; *Aptitude Tests; *Cognitive Ability; *Elementary School Students; Elementary Secondary Education; Foreign Countries; Number Concepts; *Secondary School Students; Spatial Ability; Verbal Ability
Identifiers: Canada; CCAT; Quantitative Aptitude; Test Batteries
Availability: Nelson-Canada, Ltd.; 1120 Birchmount Rd., Scarborough, Ontario M1K 5G4, Canada
Grade Level: 3-12
Notes: Time, 98; Items, 240

Measures scholastic aptitude and abstract reasoning ability in verbal, quantitative, and nonverbal situation. Evolved from experience with Canadian Lorge-Thorndike Intelligence Tests and Canadian Cognitive Abilities Test, Form 1. Was normed jointly with the Canadian Tests of Basic Skills (grades 3-8). Based on theories of cognitive development and research on children's and adult's thinking which shows there are 3 major types of symbols involved in abtract reasoning: verbal symbols, quantitative or numerical symbols, and spatial or geometrical symbols.

830448
Printing Performance School Readiness Test. Simner, Marvin L. 1985
Descriptors: Foreign Countries; High Risk Students; Individual Testing; *Kindergarten Children; *Manuscript Writing (Handlettering); *Preschool Children; *School Readiness Tests; Screening Tests
Identifiers: Canada; PPSRT
Availability: Guidance Centre; Faculty of Education, University of Toronto, 10 Alcorn Ave., Toronto, Ontario M4V 2Z8, Canada
Target Audience: 4-5
Notes: Time, 15 approx.; Items, 41

Designed to identify those preschool children who exhibit an excessive number of form errors when they begin to print. Based on research by the author which shows that an excessive number of form errors in a child's printing can be important warning sign of later school failure. Individually administered test in which child is required to print a series of letters and numbers from pictures presented one at a time on cards in a spiral binder. Child's reproductions are scored for presence of form errors.

865011
Concept Development Test V2. Freyberg, P.S.
Descriptors: Children; *Concept Formation; Elementary Education; *Elementary School Students; Foreign Countries; Mathematics Tests
Identifiers: New Zealand; Oral Testing; Piagetian Tests; TIM(D)
Availability: Tests in Microfiche; Test Collection, Educational Testing Service, Princeton, NJ 08541
Target Audience: 6-10
Notes: Items, 75

Designed to examine Piaget's contention that certain kinds of concepts develop contemporaneously. Concepts measured are: numerical correspondence, conservation (continuous quantity), conservation (discontinuous quantity), numerical equivalence, numerical associativity, class concepts (visual), class concepts (nonvisual), conservation (mass), additive composition (money-visual), additive composition (money-nonvisual), conservation (weight), positional relationships, speed concepts, transitive relationships, causal relationships, age concepts, kinship relationships, and ordination.

865016
Test of Scholastic Abilities. Reid, Neil; And Others 1981

Descriptors: *Academic Ability; Adolescents; Children; *Cognitive Measurement; Foreign Countries; Intermediate Grades; Primary Education; Secondary Education; Test Bias; *Verbal Ability
Identifiers: *New Zealand; Numerical Ability; *Reasoning Ability
Availability: New Zealand Council for Educational Research; Box 3237, Education House, 178-182 Willis St., Wellington, I, New Zealand
Target Audience: 9-14
Notes: Time, 30; Items, 70

Used to measure verbal and numerical reasoning abilities necessary for academic success. Items measure conceptualization and convergent reasoning (classification and operational) and consist of word, sentence, and number problems.

865024
ACER Advanced Test BL-BQ; New Zealand Revision. Australian Council for Educational Research, Hawthorn 1986
Descriptors: Abstract Reasoning; *Cognitive Ability; College Students; Foreign Countries; Higher Education
Identifiers: Analogies; New Zealand
Availability: New Zealand Council for Educational Research; Education House, 178-182 Willis St., P.O. Box 3237, Wellington 1, New Zealand
Grade Level: 13-16

This test measures general intellectual ability in senior secondary schools, teacher's colleges and university level students in New Zealand. It is also used to measure general intellectual ability in the employment context. Items consist of verbal analogies and reasoning problems. Norms are available for the above groups.

865025
ACER Higher Test PL-PQ: New Zealand Revision. Australian Council for Educational Research, Hawthorn 1986
Descriptors: Adolescents; Adults; *Cognitive Ability; Foreign Countries
Identifiers: New Zealand
Availability: New Zealand Council for Educational Research; Education House, 178-182 Willis St., P.O. Box 3237, Wellington 1, New Zealand
Target Audience: 15-65

This test measures general intellectual ability in senior secondary schools in a New Zealand population. It is also used to measure general intellectual ability in the employment context. Items consist of number series and brief word problems. Norms are available for ages 15-17.

885030
Escala de Inteligencia Para Adultos de Wechsler. Wechsler, David 1970
Subtests: Informacion; Comprension; Aritmetica; Semejanzas; Digitos; Vocabulario; Clave de Numeros; Figuras Incompletas; Cubos; Historietas; Rompecabezas
Descriptors: Adolescents; Adults; Foreign Countries; Individual Testing; *Intelligence; *Intelligence Tests; Older Adults; *Spanish
Identifiers: Spain; WAIS; Wechsler Adult Intelligence Scale
Availability: Tecnicos Especialistas Asociados, S.A.; Fray Bernardino de Sahagun 24, Madrid, 16, Spain
Target Audience: 15-74
Notes: Time, 120 approx.

This instrument is a Spanish translation of the Wechsler Adult Intelligence Scale. It is composed of 6 verbal and 5 nonverbal subtests.

885035
Tests de Figuras Enmascaradas. Witkin, Herman A.; And Others 1982
Descriptors: Adults; *Cognitive Measurement; *Cognitive Processes; *Cognitive Style; Foreign Countries; *Spanish Speaking
Identifiers: EFT; Embedded Figures Test; Field Dependence; Field Independence; Gottschalk Hidden Figures Test; Spain
Availability: TEA Ediciones S.A.; Fray Bernardino de Sahagun 24, Madrid, 16, Spain
Target Audience: Adults
Notes: Items, 12

Spanish version of the embedded figures test originally designed for use in research on cognitive functioning and cognitive styles. Subjects locate simple geometric figures in complex designs. Fifteen seconds is allowed for the completion of each item.

904001
Test de Habilidades Mentales Primarias. Thurstone, L.L.; Thurstone, Thelma Gwinn 1963
Subtests: Comprension Verbal; Comprension Espacial; Raciocinio; Manejo de Numeros; Fluidez Verbal

Descriptors: Cognitive Ability; *Elementary School
Students; *Intelligence; Intelligence Quotient;
*Intelligence Tests; Intermediate Grades; Math-
ematical Concepts; *Spanish; Spatial Ability;
Verbal Ability
Identifiers: Perceptual Speed; Primary Mental
Abilities Test; Reasoning Ability
Availability: Manual Moderno; Av Sonora 206,
Col. Hipodromo, 06100, Mexico D.F., Mexico
Grade Level: 4-6
Notes: Time, 75 approx.

A Spanish version of the Primary Mental Abilities Test
(TC002212). Designed to provide multifactored and general measures of intelligence. A profile of 5 mental abilities yields scores for verbal meaning, number facility,
reasoning, perceptual speed, and spatial relations.

904003
Test No-Verbal de la Universidad de Purdue.
Tiffin, Joseph; And Others 1957
Descriptors: Abstract Reasoning; *Adolescents;
*Adults; Cognitive Ability; *Cognitive Tests;
Foreign Countries; Nonverbal Tests; *Spanish;
*Spatial Ability
Identifiers: Mexico; Purdue Non Language Per-
sonnel Test
Availability: Manul Moderno; Av. Sonora 206,
Col. Hipodromo, 06100 Mexico D. F., Mexico
Target Audience: 16-64
Notes: Time, 25 approx.; Items, 48

A Spanish translation of the Purdue Non-Language Personnel Test (TC005003). Instrument was designed to measure cognitive ability and spatial aptitude.

SUBJECT INDEX

Architects

Arithmetic

Armed Forces

Art

Art Activities

Art Appreciation

Artists

Asocial Attitudes

Assemblers

Assembly (Manufacturing)

Association Measures

Association (Psychology)

Associational Fluency

Associative Learning

Associative Memory

Attention Control

Attention Span

Audiation

Audiodisks

Audiotape Recorders

Auditory Discrimination

Auditory Perception

Cognitive Development

Cognitive Evaluation

Cognitive Measurement

Cognitive Processes

Cognitive Psychology

Cognitive Style

Cognitive Tests

College Admission

College Applicants

126 / Grade 1 SUBJECT INDEX

Grade 1
Academic Readiness Scale 7012
Cognitive Abilities Test, Form 4, Level 1 14702
The Contemporary School Readiness Test 5488
CTBS Readiness Test, Form S, Level A 8434
Early Identification Screening Program First-Grade Screening 11139
Early School Inventory—Developmental 15026
Educational Development Series, Revised. Level 11A 13344
Einstein Assessment of School-Related Skills, Level 1 15510
The First Grade Readiness Checklist 11498
Henmon-Nelson Tests of Mental Ability: Primary Battery 7588
IEP Educational Diagnostic Inventories: Pre-Reading Screening I and II 12535
Inter-American Series: Test of General Ability, Level 1, Primary 858
Inventory of Readiness Skills. Revised. Third Edition 11360
Kindergarten Behavioral Index: A Screening Technique for Reading Readiness 800086
Kuhlmann-Anderson Tests, Level A. Eighth Edition 11872
Linguistic Awareness in Reading Readiness Test 810533
Meeting Street School Screening Test 6927
Metropolitan Readiness Tests, Level 2, Fifth Edition 15020
Murphy-Durrell Reading Readiness Screen 15840
Otis-Lennon Mental Ability Test, Level II, Primary 2586
Otis-Lennon School Ability Test, Primary I. Forms R and S 10141
PMA Readiness Level 1759
Rhode Island Profile of Early Learning Behavior 11791
School Readiness Test 1810
SOI Learning Abilities Test: Special Edition, K-1 9265
SRA Achievement Series, Forms 1 and 2, 1978 Edition: Level A 9202
SRA Achievement Series, Forms 1 and 2, 1978 Edition: Level B 9203
SRA Survey of Basic Skills, Level 20 14320
SRA Survey of Basic Skills, Level 21 14321
Thackray Reading Readiness Profiles 810467
Wechsler Preschool and Primary Scale of Intelligence 1424
WPPSI Profile Form 9150

Grade 10
Educational Development Series, Revised. Level 17B 13353

Grade 11
Educational Development Series, Revised. Level 18A 13354
Quick Word Test: Level II 4043

Grade 12
Educational Development Series, Revised. Level 18B 13355
IEA Six-Subject Survey Instruments: Civic Education Tests, Cognition, Population IV 13052
Quick Word Test: Level II 4043

Grade 2
Cognitive Abilities Test, Form 4, Level 2 14703
Developing Cognitive Abilities Test. Level 2 11164
Educational Development Series, Revised. Level 11A 13344
Educational Development Series, Revised. Level 12A 13345
Einstein Assessment of School-Related Skills, Level 2 15511
Henmon-Nelson Tests of Mental Ability: Primary Battery 7588
Inter-American Series: Test of General Ability, Level 2, Primary 859
Kuhlmann-Anderson Tests, Level BC. Eighth Edition 11873
Otis-Lennon School Ability Test, Primary II. Forms R and S 10142
Quickscreen. Second Grade 11217
Rhode Island Profile of Early Learning Behavior 11791
SRA Achievement Series, Forms 1 and 2, 1978 Edition: Level B 9203
SRA Survey of Basic Skills, Level 21 14321
SRA Survey of Basic Skills, Level 22 14322

Grade 3
Cognitive Abilities Test, Form 4, Level 2 14703
Cognitive Abilities Test, Form 4, Level A 14704
Developing Cognitive Abilities Test. Level 3 11165
Educational Development Series, Revised. Level 12A 13345
Educational Development Series, Revised. Level 13A 13346
Einstein Assessment of School-Related Skills, Level 3 15512
Inter-American Series: Test of General Ability, Level 2, Primary 859
Kuhlmann-Anderson Tests, Level BC. Eighth Edition 11873
Kuhlmann-Anderson Tests, Level CD. Eighth Edition 11874
Otis-Lennon School Ability Test, Primary II. Forms R and S 10142
SRA Survey of Basic Skills, Level 22 14322
SRA Survey of Basic Skills, Level 23 14323

Grade 4
Cognitive Abilities Test, Form 4, Level B 14705
Developing Cognitive Abilities Test. Level 4 11166
Educational Development Series, Revised. Level 13A 13346
Educational Development Series, Revised. Level 14A 13347
Einstein Assessment of School-Related Skills, Level 4 15513
Kuhlmann-Anderson Tests, Level CD. Eighth Edition 11874
Mathematical Problem Solving Test 8911
Otis-Lennon School Ability Test, Elementary. Forms R and S 10143
SRA Survey of Basic Skills, Level 23 14323

Grade 5
Cognitive Abilities Test, Form 4, Level B 14705
Cognitive Abilities Test, Form 4, Level C 14706
Developing Cognitive Abilities Test. Form 5/6 11167
Educational Development Series, Revised. Level 14A 13347
Educational Development Series, Revised. Level 15A 13348
Einstein Assessment of School-Related Skills, Level 5 15514
Fantasy Measure 9822
Instruments for Assessing Creativity 9818
Kuhlmann-Anderson Tests, Level EF. Eighth Edition 11875
Measures of Breadth of Categorization 9820
Measures of Conceptual Style 9821
Measures of Physiognomic Sensitivity 9823
Otis-Lennon School Ability Test, Elementary. Forms R and S 10143
Test of Verbal Absurdities 10918
Wallach-Kogan Creativity Tests 11965

Grade 6
Addition and Subtraction Correction: N-4 8231
Addition Test: N-1 8228
Arithmetic Aptitude Test: RG-1 8235
Arranging Words: FE-2 8203
Auditory Letter Span Test: MS-3 8224
Auditory Number Span Test: MS-1 8222
Building Memory: MV-2 8226
Cognitive Abilities Test, Form 4, Level C 14706
Cognitive Abilities Test, Form 4, Level D 14707
Concealed Words Test: CS-2 8194
Controlled Associations Test: FA-1 8199
Copying Test: CF-3 8192
The Denny-Ives Creativity Test 794
Developing Cognitive Abilities Test. Form 5/6 11167
Different Uses: XU-4 8261
Division Test: N-2 8229
Educational Development Series, Revised. Level 15A 13348
Educational Development Series, Revised. Level 15B 13349
Elaboration Test: FF-2 8206
Finding A's Test: P-1 8232
First and Last Names Test: MA-3 8221
Gestalt Completion Test: CS-1 8193
Hidden Patterns Test: CF-2 (Revised) 8191
Identical Pictures Test: P-3 8234
Interpretation of Data Test 8797
Kuhlmann-Anderson Tests, Level EF. Eighth Edition 11875
Making Sentences: FE-1 8202
Map Memory: MV-3 8227
Map Planning Test: SS-3 8246
Maze Tracing Speed Test: SS-1 8244
Necessity Arithmetic Operations: RG-3 8237
Number Comparison Test: P-2 8233
Object Number Test: MA-2 8220
Opposites Test: FA-2 8200
Ornamentation Test: FF-1 8205
Otis-Lennon School Ability Test, Intermediate. Forms R and S 10144
Picture Number Test: MA-1 8219
Pimsleur Language Aptitude Battery 152
Rewriting: FE-3 8204
School and College Ability Tests: Series II, Level 3 6797
School and College Ability Tests: Series III, Intermediate Level 9451
The Selected Creativity Tasks 8833
Shape Memory Test: MV-1 8225
Snowy Pictures: CS-3 8195
SRA Survey of Basic Skills, Level 35 14325
Subtraction and Multiplication Test: N-3 8230
Test of Ability to Explain 8796
Visual Number Span Test: MS-2 8223
Word Beginnings and Endings Test: FW-3 8213
Word Beginnings Test: FW-2 8212
Word Endings Test: FW-1 8211

Grade 7
Cognitive Abilities Test, Form 4, Level D 14707
Cognitive Abilities Test, Form 4, Level E 14708
Educational Development Series, Revised. Level 15B 13349
Educational Development Series, Revised. Level 16A 13350
Test of Cognitive Skills, Level 3 11528

Grade 8
Cognitive Abilities Test, Form 4, Level E 14708
Educational Development Series, Revised. Level 16A 13350
Educational Development Series, Revised. Level 16B 13351

Grade 9
Educational Development Series, Revised. Level 16B 13351
Educational Development Series, Revised. Level 17A 13352

Grade Repetition
Light's Retention Scale: Revised Edition 11117

Graduate Students
Graduate Management Admission Test 11943
Law School Admission Test 11972
Miller Analogies Test 2078
Minnesota Engineering Analogies Test 2079
Prueba de Admision para Estudios Graduados 11944
Torrance Tests of Creative Thinking, Revised Edition 11802

Graduate Study
Doppelt Mathematical Reasoning Test 2077

Graphs
A Test of Graphicacy 11748

Group Behavior
Phases of Integrated Problem Solving, Revised Edition 15157

Group Dynamics
Phases of Integrated Problem Solving 12976

Group Testing
The Group Embedded Figures Test 6464

Grouping (Instructional Purposes)
STS High School Placement Test 1841

Guilfords Structure of Intellect
FSM SOI Group Memory Test 9537

Halstead Category Test
The Booklet Category Test 11201

Halstead Reitan Neuropsychological Tests
The Booklet Category Test 11201
Halstead Category Test for Adults 11300
Halstead Category Test for Older Children 11299
Halstead Category Test for Young Children 11203
Halstead-Reitan Neuropsychological Test Battery: Spanish Version. Manual 11202

Handicap Identification
Academic Readiness Scale 7012
Bannatyne System: Early Screening and Diagnostic Tests—Phase I 6162
Checklist for Early Recognition of Problems in Classrooms 10024
Comprehensive Identification Process 7904
The Magic Kingdom: A Preschool Screening Program 8538
McCarthy Scales of Children's Abilities 6903
Quickscreen. Second Grade 11217
Test of Perceptual Organization 4206

Handwriting
Brigance Diagnostic Inventory of Basic Skills 10487

Hearing Impairments
An Adaptation of the Wechsler Intelligence Scales for Children-Revised-for the Deaf 13726
An Adaptation of the Wechsler Preschool and Primary Scale of Intelligence for Deaf Children 13725
CID Preschool Performance Scale 13409
Color Span Test 14082
Hiskey Nebraska Test of Learning Aptitude 4135
WISC-R Performance Scale for Deaf Children 12205

Hemispheric Dominance
Your Style of Learning and Thinking, Adult Form 12175
Your Style of Learning and Thinking, Children's Form 12176

High Achievement
The Hoeflin Intelligence Test. Form H. 10963

High Risk Students
Bannatyne System: Early Screening and Diagnostic Tests—Phase II 8030
Einstein Assessment of School-Related Skills, Level 1 15510
Einstein Assessment of School-Related Skills, Level 2 15511
Einstein Assessment of School-Related Skills, Level 3 15512
Einstein Assessment of School-Related Skills, Level 4 15513
Einstein Assessment of School-Related Skills, Level 5 15514
Einstein Assessment of School-Related Skills, Level K 15509
Learning Accomplishment Profile: Diagnostic Screening Edition 11924

Kindergarten Children

The ABC Inventory	11599
Academic Readiness Scale	7012
Adelphi Parent Administered Readiness Test	11794
Cambridge Kindergarten Screening Test	13384
Canadian Cognitive Abilities Test—Primary Battery 1 and 2	830309
Canadian Cognitive Abilities Test, Primary Battery, Levels 1 and 2, Form 3	830383
Checklist for Kindergarten	8868
Classroom Behavior Inventory. 42 Item Research Version	12434
Cognitive Abilities Test, Form 4, Level 1	14702
Cognitive Skills Assessment Battery. Second Edition.	11093
The Contemporary School Readiness Test	5488
CTBS Readiness Test, Form S, Level A	8434
Developmental Patterns in Elemental Reading Skills	8012
Early Identification Screening Program. Kindergarten Screening	11112
Early School Inventory—Developmental	15026
Educational Development Series, Revised. Level 10A	13343
Einstein Assessment of School-Related Skills, Level K	15509
Florida Kindergarten Screening Battery	11955
General Inventory for Kindergarten	11146
Henmon-Nelson Tests of Mental Ability: Primary Battery	7588
Howell Prekindergarten Screening Test	15189
IEP Educational Diagnostic Inventories: Pre-Reading Screening I and II	12535
Inter-American Series: Test of General Ability, Level 1, Primary	858
Inventory of Readiness Skills. Revised. Third Edition	11360
Jansky Diagnostic Battery	13708
Kindergarten Behavioral Index: A Screening Technique for Reading Readiness	800086
Kindergarten Diagnostic Instrument	15701
Kindergarten Readiness Test	15591
Kindergarten Screening Instrument	9135
Kindergarten Screening Inventory	14894
Kuhlmann-Anderson Tests, Level K. Eighth Edition	11871
Learning Accomplishment Profile: Diagnostic Screening Edition	11924
Linguistic Awareness in Reading Readiness Test	810533
The Lollipop Test: A Diagnostic Screening Test of School Readiness	11601
The Magic Kingdom: A Preschool Screening Program	8538
Manual for Administering the Analysis of Developmental Learning Skills. Revised 1977	10601
Meeting Street School Screening Test	6927
Metropolitan Readiness Tests, Level 2, Fifth Edition	15020
Murphy-Durrell Reading Readiness Screen	15840
Otis-Lennon Mental Ability Test, Level I, Primary	2585
Parent Readiness Evaluation of Preschoolers	4156
PMA Readiness Level	1759
Prereading Skills Test for Kindergarten	11141
PRIDE: Preschool and Kindergarten Interest Descriptor	12612
Printing Performance School Readiness Test	830448
R-B Number Readiness Test	8312
Rhode Island Profile of Early Learning Behavior	11791
Schenectady Kindergarten Rating Scales	8372
The School Readiness Checklist	3424
School Readiness Test	1810
SOI Learning Abilities Test: Special Edition, K-1	9265
SRA Achievement Series, Forms 1 and 2, 1978 Edition: Level A	9202
SRA Survey of Basic Skills, Level 20	14320
Study of Children's Learning Styles	13638
Torrance Tests of Creative Thinking, Revised Edition	11802
Vane Kindergarten Test	4245
Wechsler Preschool and Primary Scale of Intelligence	1424
Zaner-Bloser Kindergarten Screening Inventory	11795

Knowledge Level

Check Up Tests in Workskills	810595
General Information Survey	3515

Labor Force Development

Human Information Processing Survey	13501

Language Acquisition

Birth to 3 Assessment and Intervention System: Screening Test of Language and Learning Development	14820
Comprehensive Language Program	11274
Diagnosis of Language Competency Inventory (DLCI)	13483
Gesell Developmental Schedules	2067
Language Development Inventory for Kindergarten or Preschool	6355
Mehrabian Picture Vocabulary Test	5602
Modes of Learning a Second Language	10177
Muma Assessment Program	11025
Picture Story Language Test	88
Prepositions Inventory/Linguistic Concepts	6147
Schenectady Kindergarten Rating Scales	8372
Sentence Imitation Screening Tests	11781

Sequenced Inventory of Communication Development, Revised Edition	13812

Language Aptitude

Defense Language Aptitude Battery	13002
Guilford-Zimmerman Aptitude Survey: Verbal Comprehension	5927
Modern Language Aptitude Test	259

Language Arts

Brigance Diagnostic Inventory of Basic Skills	10487
Comprehensive Testing Program II, Levels 3, 4, and 5	11507
Language Arts Test of Cognitive Functioning	13799
SRA Achievement Series, Forms 1 and 2, 1978 Edition: Level C	9204
SRA Achievement Series, Forms 1 and 2, 1978 Edition: Level D	9205

Language Comprehension

Miller-Yoder Language Comprehension Test, Clinical Edition	13833

Language Fluency

IPI Aptitude Series: Instructor	13452
IPI Aptitude Series: Office Supervisor	13453
IPI Aptitude Series: Writer	13450

Language Handicaps

Aston Index, Revised: A Classroom Test for Screening and Diagnosis of Language Difficulties	13553
CID Preschool Performance Scale	13409
Color Span Test	14082
Comprehensive Language Program	11274
Hiskey Nebraska Test of Learning Aptitude	4135
Miller-Yoder Language Comprehension Test, Clinical Edition	13833
Porteus Mazes: Extension	2083
Porteus Mazes: Supplement	2084
Porteus Mazes: Vineland Revision	2082
Screening Test of Adolescent Language	11579
Sequenced Inventory of Communication Development, Revised Edition	13812

Language Processing

Cambridge Kindergarten Screening Test	13384
Clinical Language Intervention Program	11612
Language Processing Test	14562
Miller-Yoder Language Comprehension Test, Clinical Edition	13833
Preschool Language Assessment Instrument	10351
Uniform Performance Assessment System	10530

Language Proficiency

Clinical Language Intervention Program	11612
The Three-R's Test. Levels 13-14, Forms A and B. Achievement Edition	11504
The Three-R's Test. Levels 15-18, Forms A and B. Achievement Edition	11505
The Three-R's Test. Levels 9-12, Forms A and B. Achievement Edition	11503
Word Fluency Test	2754

Language Skills

Cambridge Kindergarten Screening Test	13384
Communicative Evaluation Chart from Infancy to Five Years	6822
Diagnosis of Language Competency Inventory (DLCI)	13483
Holbrook Screening Battery and Parent Questionnaire, Revised	15181
Individual Assessment	10909
Pre-Kindergarten Goal Card: 1968 Revision	5719
Preschool Language Assessment Instrument	10351
Prueba para El Diagnostico del Lenguaje Pre-Escolar	14570
Washington Pre-College Test	10737
Wide Range Intelligence and Personality Test	11162

Language Tests

Diagnosis of Language Competency Inventory (DLCI)	13483
Expressive One-Word Picture Vocabulary Test-Upper Extension	12388
Fullerton Language Test for Adolescents, Revised Edition	14897
Modes of Learning a Second Language	10177
Picture Story Language Test	88
Preschool Language Scale. Revised Edition	11039

Language Usage

The Three-R's Test. Levels 13-14, Forms A and B. Achievement Edition	11504
The Three-R's Test. Levels 15-18, Forms A and B. Achievement Edition	11505
The Three-R's Test. Levels 9-12, Forms A and B. Achievement Edition	11503

Lateral Dominance

Index of Perceptual-Motor Laterality	7198

Law Schools

Law School Admission Test	11972

Layout (Publications)

IPI Aptitude Series: Designer	13451

Leadership Qualities

General Information Survey	3515

Learning

Fuld Object Memory Evaluation	11602
Non-Language Learning Test	14077
Western Personnel Test	712
Western Personnel Test: Spanish	4192

Learning Ability

Harvard Learning Ability Profile	13420
SRA Nonverbal Form	12123

Learning Disabilities

Analytic Learning Disability Assessment	12035
Aston Index, Revised: A Classroom Test for Screening and Diagnosis of Language Difficulties	13553
Auditory Pointing Test	7675
Bannatyne System: Early Screening and Diagnostic Tests—Phase I	6162
Bannatyne System: Early Screening and Diagnostic Tests—Phase II	8030
Basic Educational Skills Test	10334
Color Span Test	14082
C.U.B.E. Learning Disabilities Diagnostic Test	13533
C.U.B.E. Learning Disabilities Empirical Mapping Instrument	13532
DIAL	1793
DIAL-R	12396
Einstein Assessment of School-Related Skills, Level 1	15510
Einstein Assessment of School-Related Skills, Level 2	15511
Einstein Assessment of School-Related Skills, Level 3	15512
Einstein Assessment of School-Related Skills, Level 4	15513
Einstein Assessment of School-Related Skills, Level 5	15514
Einstein Assessment of School-Related Skills, Level K	15509
Learning Disability Rating Procedure	10976
The Magic Kingdom: A Preschool Screening Program	8538
PACE	14791
The Pupil Rating Scale Revised. Screening for Learning Disabilities	11212
Quickscreen. Second Grade	11217
SOI Learning Abilities Test: Developmental Vision Form	14157
Southern California Ordinal Scales of Development: Scale of Cognition	14609
Southern California Ordinal Scales of Development: Scale of Communication	14608
Stellern-Show Informal Learning Inventory	11891
Vocabulary Comprehension Scale	7827
Wachs Analysis of Cognitive Structures	9050

Learning Modalities

Bloomer Learning Test	13675
Early Identification Screening Program First-Grade Screening	11139
Early Identification Screening Program. Kindergarten Screening	11112
How a Child Learns	13537
IEP Educational Diagnostic Inventories: Modality Inventory	12548
Neuro-Developmental Observation	5123
The Perceptual Memory Task	13759
Psychological Stimulus Response Test	11787
Swassing-Barbe Modality Index	11930
Unicorns Are Real	13633

Learning Problems

Auditory Pointing Test	7675
Cutrona Child Study Profile of Psycho-Educational Abilities	5156
Early Detection Inventory	3103
Early Identification Screening Program First-Grade Screening	11139
Early Identification Screening Program. Kindergarten Screening	11112
Einstein Assessment of School-Related Skills, Level 1	15510
Einstein Assessment of School-Related Skills, Level 2	15511
Einstein Assessment of School-Related Skills, Level 3	15512
Einstein Assessment of School-Related Skills, Level 4	15513
Einstein Assessment of School-Related Skills, Level 5	15514
Einstein Assessment of School-Related Skills, Level K	15509
Five P's: Parent Professional Preschool Performance Profile	15299
Neuro-Developmental Observation	5123
Pre-School Screening Instrument	10390
Psycho-Educational Battery	8367
Quickscreen. Second Grade	11217
Rhode Island Profile of Early Learning Behavior	11791
Wechsler Intelligence Scale for Children—Revised. Abbreviated Version.	15497
Zeitlin Early Identification Screening	6244

Learning Processes

Auditory Sequential Memory Test	7284
C.U.B.E. Learning Disabilities Diagnostic Test	13533
Inventory for Measuring Individual Differences in Learning Processes	10949
Learning Potential Assessment Device	10777

AUTHOR INDEX

TITLE INDEX